PENGUIN BOOKS

QUEEN CAMILLA

Sue Townsend is one of Britain's bestselling authors. Her hugely success-ful novels include seven Adrian Mole books, *The Queen & I* and *Number Ten*. She is also a well-known playwright. She lives in Leicester.

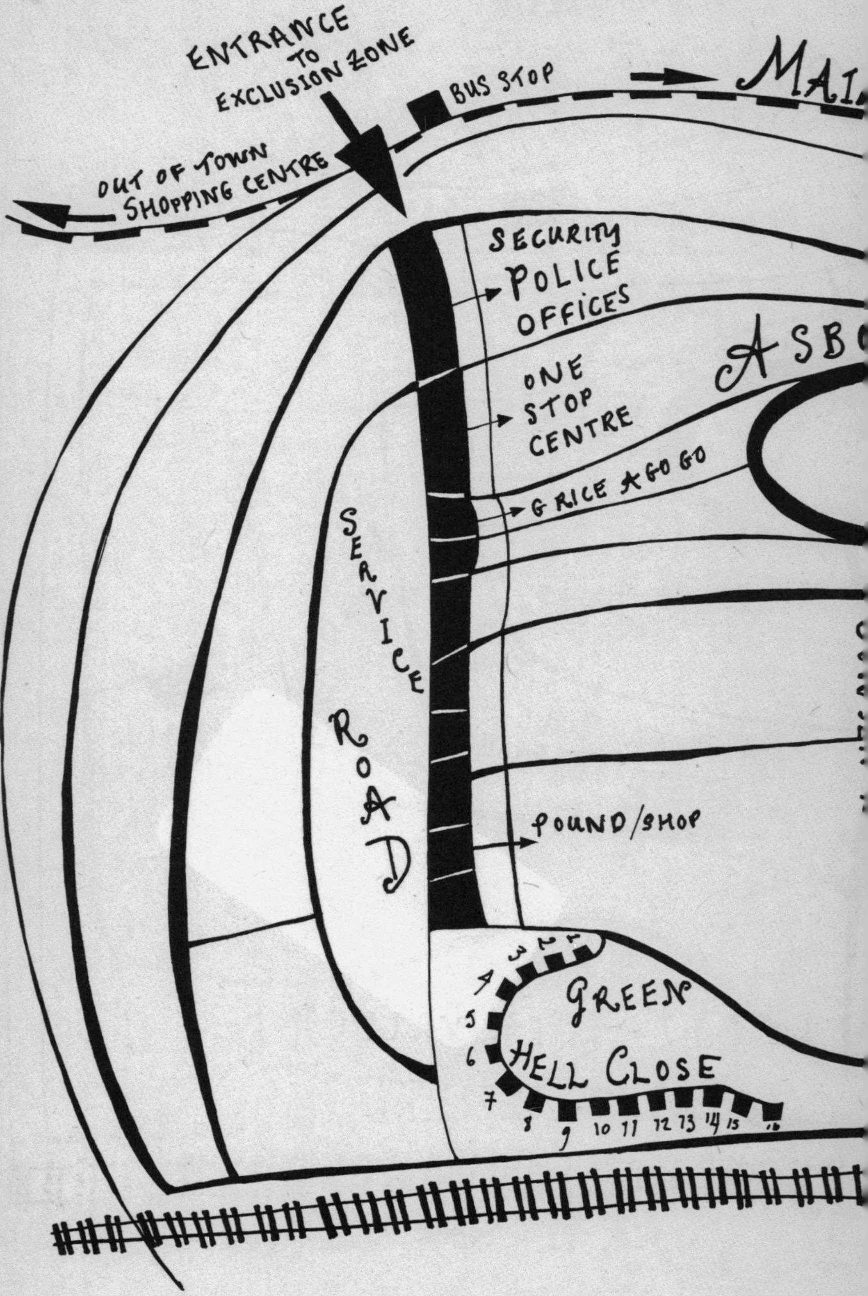
ENTRANCE TO EXCLUSION ZONE
BUS STOP
MAI
OUT OF TOWN SHOPPING CENTRE
SECURITY POLICE OFFICES
ASB
ONE STOP CENTRE
GRICE A GO GO
SERVICE ROAD
POUND/SHOP
GREEN HELL CLOSE
1
2
3
4
5
6
7
8
9
10
11
12
13
14
15
16

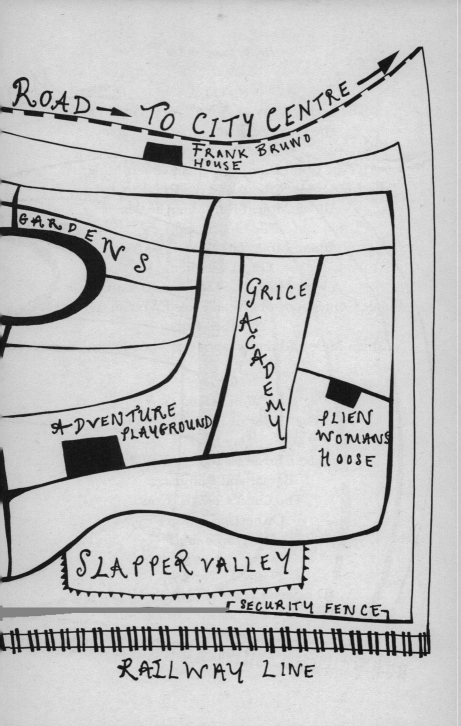

Queen Camilla

SUE TOWNSEND

PENGUIN BOOKS

PENGUIN BOOKS

Published by the Penguin Group
Penguin Books Ltd, 80 Strand, London WC2R ORL, England
Penguin Group (USA) Inc., 375 Hudson Street, New York, New York 10014, USA
Penguin Group (Canada), 90 Eglinton Avenue East, Suite 700, Toronto, Ontario, Canada M4P 2Y3
(a division of Pearson Penguin Canada Inc.)
Penguin Ireland, 25 St Stephen's Green, Dublin 2, Ireland
(a division of Penguin Books Ltd)
Penguin Group (Australia), 250 Camberwell Road, Camberwell, Victoria 3124, Australia
(a division of Pearson Australia Group Pty Ltd)
Penguin Books India Pvt Ltd, 11 Community Centre, Panchsheel Park, New Delhi – 110 017, India
Penguin Group (NZ), 67 Apollo Drive, Mairangi Bay, Auckland 1310, New Zealand
(a division of Pearson New Zealand Ltd)
Penguin Books (South Africa) (Pty) Ltd, 24 Sturdee Avenue, Rosebank, Johannesburg 2196, South Africa

Penguin Books Ltd, Registered Offices: 80 Strand, London WC2R ORL, England

www.penguin.com

First published by Michael Joseph 2006
Published in Penguin Books 2007

1

Typeset by Rowland Phototypesetting Ltd, Bury St Edmunds, Suffolk
Printed in England by Clays Ltd, St Ives plc

ISBN: 978-0-141-02445-5

To Colin Broadway, with my love

And also

To Brian Hall of Parliament Square

There is no scientific evidence that dogs can understand human speech or that they can communicate with other dogs.

Dog owners who insist that their dogs 'can understand every word I say' are misguided.

However, as an old Irish setter said to me recently, 'Dogs understand human speech only too well and find most of what we have to say to them banal, tedious and patronizing.'

(Camilla to Charles)

'Darling, do you think a dog knows it's a dog?' asked Camilla.

'It depends what you mean by know,' said Charles.

Freddie snapped, 'Of course I know I'm a bloody dog. I eat from a bowl on the floor, I shit in the street . . .'

'If you throw live frogs into a pan of boiling water, they will sensibly jump out and save themselves. If you put them in a pan of cold water and gently apply heat until the water boils, they will lie in the pan and boil to death.'

Shami Chakrabarti, Liberty

I

Camilla, the Duchess of Cornwall, stood smoking a cheap cigarette on the back doorstep of Number Sixteen Hell Close. It was a cold afternoon in late summer. Occasionally she turned to watch her husband, Charles, the Prince of Wales, clattering the luncheon pots in the red washing-up bowl he'd bought on impulse that morning from the 'Everything A Pound' shop. He had borne the bowl home and presented it to her as though it were a precious religious artefact plundered from a sacked city.

As she watched him scrubbing at a Doulton gravy boat, she thought, how little it takes to make him happy, and said, 'Happy, darling?' Her voice was husky from years of cigarette smoking and also from sitting up half the night laughing and talking with the next-door neighbours, Beverley and Vince Threadgold.

Vince, a 55-year-old Elvis lookalike, had entertained Camilla and Charles with his terribly amusing stories about Wormwood Scrubs. Charles had said, 'Prison sounds rather agreeable compared to Gordonstoun School, where I often woke in the night to find my narrow iron bed and rough blankets covered in a light sprinkling of snow from the open dormitory windows.'

Beverley, a big boned woman with hair the colour and texture of straw, had said, 'You were bleedin' lucky to 'ave a blanket. I slept under me dad's army greatcoat.'

Charles had looked so mournful that the laughter had died down, until Camilla had said, 'Lighten up, darling, and pour us another glass of your delicious turnip wine.'

After a few more glasses, Charles had recovered his spirits and had slipped into his party piece, an extended Goon routine in which he became Fred and forced Camilla into being Gladys. The Threadgolds watched their guests' improvised performance with stony faces, and were glad when their royal neighbours had staggered next door to their bed.

Camilla asked, 'How's the bowl performing, darling?'

'The bowl is performing absolutely splendidly,' said Charles.

'Clever old you for spotting it.'

'It was on the pavement with a stack of others. One was dazzled by the choice of colours.'

'You did well, my darling. Red is terribly jolly.'

'Yes, that's what I thought. One hovered over the green.'

'Mmm, green is good, but terribly *worthy* and a bit reminiscent of Jonathon Porritt, one imagines *he* has a green washing-up bowl, bought in some dreadful National Trust shop in the Cotswolds.' Her laugh quickly turned into a cough.

Had she been any other person Charles would have defended his old friend Jonathon Porritt, the National Trust and the Cotswolds, but Camilla was licensed to say exactly what she thought.

She was still coughing; Charles turned worried eyes on her, 'Are you all right, darling?'

She nodded that she was.

Somehow, the fact that he had chosen a red washing-up bowl felt significant to him. Perhaps, as Laurens Van der Post had urged, he was finally getting in touch with the 'pagan inside'. He and the long-dead guru had trekked across the Kalahari and sat by a campfire under a vast star-filled sky and talked of what a man needed in order to feel complete in himself. A man must have a passion, they had concluded. Charles remembered the crimson ball of the sun as it sank behind the dunes. Perhaps this metaphysical experience had influenced his choice of washing-up bowl.

Camilla asked, 'How much was your lovely red bowl, darling?'

Charles said a little tetchily, 'I *did* say, I bought it from the "Everything A Pound" shop, darling.' He blushed, remembering the scene when he had asked the morbidly obese shopowner, Mr Anwar, the same question.

Mr Anwar, irritable after a row with his wife about the Kit Kat wrappers she had found under his bed, said in his public school accent, 'Tell me, sir. What is the name of my shop?'

Charles had taken a step back on the pavement and read aloud the shop sign displayed in foot-high letters. 'Everything A Pound.'

Mr Anwar had said, 'You do not need a degree in semiotics to interpret the signage, Mr Saxe-Coburg-Gotha. Everything in my shop costs exactly, precisely, *incontrovertibly*, a pound. I repeat, *a*, that is, *one* pound.'

Charles, stung by Anwar's sarcasm and his use of his German family name, had handed him a pound coin and hurried out of the shop.

Charles's dog, Leo, a Frankenstein-like mixture of many canine breeds, sloped out from beneath the kitchen table and stood by the sink whining and lifting his big wolf's head towards his master. The dog seemed to get taller every day, thought Charles: it was already, at fourteen weeks, up to his knees. Spiggy, Princess Anne's husband, the 'breeder', had assured Charles that Leo would be, 'One of them ankle-snappers, what's good for rattin'.'

Leo whined, 'I'm hungry.'

Charles said, 'I know you're ready to eat, Leo, but can't you see I'm busy?'

The doorbell rang. Charles, still with his hands in the water, said, 'Answer that, will you, darling?'

Camilla said, 'I'm smoking, darling.'

Charles replied with a fixed grin, 'I'm perfectly aware that you're *smoking*, darling, since the smoke is drifting into the kitchen and insinuating itself down to my lungs.'

He gave a little cough and flapped a hand dripping in suds at the pall of tobacco smoke hanging over his head.

Camilla said, raising her voice over the persistent ringing of the doorbell, 'It's against the law of the land to carry a lit cigarette through a building, including one's home, so perhaps *you* will answer the door.' She turned her head away before adding, 'Darling.'

Charles threw a little Spode milk jug into the suds

and said, through clenched teeth, 'I have a washing-up *system* and I need to *concentrate*. Why can you not *grind* out that filthy bloody thing you're sucking on and answer the door? Darling.'

The doorbell rang again.

Camilla said, a little tearfully, 'Charlie, my fag time is terrifically important to me. You did agree before we married that I could smoke five fags a day and that I would not be disturbed whilst doing so.'

Charles scrubbed furiously at the perfectly clean Spode jug with the washing-up brush and said, 'We also agreed to share the housework, but you've driven a coach and horses through that agreement.' He saw the hurt on her face and said in a conciliatory tone, 'You're terribly lazy, darling.'

Camilla walked away down the crazy-paving path to the hen coop at the bottom of the narrow, heavily cultivated garden. She stared through the chicken wire at the hens, Eccles and Moriarty, who were pecking at each other in the casually cruel manner of siblings squashed together in the back seat of the family car.

Camilla was not fond of the hens. She disliked their wattled necks and Goon names, their cold eyes, sharp beaks and prehensile claws. She resented the time and money that Charles spent on their upkeep. In her opinion they were ungrateful feathered bastards. She was sick of having to coax Charles out of his dispro-portionate sense of failure every morning after he returned from the coop, with the egg-collecting basket he insisted on using completely empty.

Her own dogs, Freddie and Tosca, who had produced

two litters together, ran out of the house on their little Jack Russell legs. They joined their mistress at the hen coop.

She said to the hens, 'You're so bloody ungrateful. He simply lavishes attention on you and yet you refuse to give him one measly egg. It's terribly unfair, we're desperately poor.'

Camilla took a last drag on her cigarette and distractedly poked the still-burning stub through the chicken wire. Eccles ran forwards, picked up the burning stub in her beak and then, with a flurry of feathers, leapt on to the roof of the hen house. Camilla laughed when Eccles allowed the cigarette to dangle in the manner of an avian Lauren Bacall.

In the kitchen Charles heard her laughter and smiled with relief. Camilla didn't bear a grudge – unlike his first wife, who had kept a sulk going for . . . *well, years.* He hurried down the path, wiping his hands dry on a tea towel. He had been too hard on her; she'd had servants until very recently, whereas he'd been doing for himself for the last thirteen years, while in exile.

Camilla thought, in the few seconds before Charles saw his precious bird apparently enjoying an imported Chinese copy of a Silk Cut Ultra Low after her dinner, this will make a terribly funny anecdote one day, but the immediate repercussions will be ghastly for poor old me. Charles reached out and spun Camilla round to take her in his arms, and then saw with incredulity that Eccles appeared to be smoking a cigarette and that a fox was sitting behind a row of winter cabbages, staring at him with bold insolence.

Freddie and Tosca crept behind the legs of their mistress; Camilla had never seen a fox at such close quarters, at least not a live one. She'd seen plenty of pieces of dead foxes. She thought to herself, he's terribly beautiful. The fox stood up, gave a lopsided grin then coolly turned his back, strolled to the corner of the garden and disappeared.

Still on the doorstep, though quickly running out of patience, was the Queen. She was suffering from toothache and wondered if Charles had some oil of cloves in his homeopathic medicine box. She had two dogs with her, both Dorgies (a cross between a Corgi and a Dachshund). One was Susan whom she had inherited from her mother, the other Harris, her own dog, was the son of Harris I, who had accompanied her in the furniture van that had brought her to Hell Close thirteen years before.

'This is infuriating,' said the Queen to Harris. 'Why won't they answer the door? We know they're in, don't we, old boy? We can hear them shouting, can't we?'

Harris said nothing to the Queen, but he growled. 'I knew it wouldn't last.'

Susan yapped, 'All married couples quarrel. We do!'

'We quarrel because I'm tired of you,' said Harris.

'You're so cruel,' whimpered Susan, and ran for comfort to the Queen's side.

The Queen bent down and stroked Susan's back, saying, 'What is it, old girl? What is it?'

Beverley Threadgold, still in her dressing gown at two o'clock in the afternoon, stuck her head out of her bedroom window and shouted down, 'They're in the back garden, Liz. They're having a big row about Camilla's smoking. Do you want me to tell 'em it's you at the door?'

Beverley loved a drama, however small. She habitually turned a drama into a crisis, and a crisis into an incident necessitating the attendance of the police, and once the police helicopter.

The Queen said, 'No, please don't bother,' and hurried away down the path.

Beverley shouted after the departing figure of the Queen, 'We all got pissed last night on Charlie's parsnip wine. Charlie was tellin' us about his unhappy childhood. 'Ow 'e 'ad snow on 'is bed at school.'

The Queen said to Harris and Susan, 'I really wish Charles would stop whining about his childhood to all and sundry. He's a man of nearly sixty.'

As the Queen passed Beverley's house, King, a cross Alsatian, leapt up at the front gate and began to bark furiously at the Queen's dogs. He was a troublemaker, like his mistress.

The Queen's early training had taught her to blank out unpleasantness so as she walked along Hell Close she didn't see the obscenities scrawled on the walls or smell the stench of the uncollected rubbish bags on the pavement. The sounds of screaming and domestic arguments did not reach her ears. She could not afford to fully admit to herself that she was living in such dreadful circumstances.

When she was a little princess, her nanny, the beloved Crawfie, had instructed her to whistle a merry tune inside her head when faced with difficult situations.

When she got to Number Twelve, the Queen heard the amplified sound of somebody, a singer she presumed, shouting not lyrics, but threats and exhortations to commit violence. She could not understand Prince Harry's taste for what he had told her was called 'gangsta rap'. True, his royal ancestors had been the gangsters of their day. Was it in the genes? As the Queen stood looking up at the house she could feel the vibrations of the music under her feet. The curtains were drawn and the windows appeared to have been attacked recently with eggs. She said to Harris, 'I told Charles that it was inadvisable to allow the boys to live without supervision. Just look at the place, it looks like a New York tenement.'

The front door opened, releasing a blast of music, and a teenage girl, Chanel Toby, a large-breasted fifteen-year-old with a foghorn voice and artificially coloured and straightened white hair, ran down the front path weeping, closely followed by Prince Harry's dog, Carling, a red-haired mongrel with lanky legs and a small head. Chanel ran past the Queen and into her grandmother's at Number Ten. Carling bounced around the Queen's legs. He was such a harmless fool that Susan and Harris allowed him to continue.

Harris growled, 'If this was a village, Carling would be the idiot.'

The Queen took Carling by the scruff of the neck and dragged him up the path and pushed him through the open door. It was dark inside, all the Queen could see were several hooded figures and a heavy cloud of strong-smelling tobacco. She slammed the front door shut; it had been a thoroughly unsatisfactory afternoon so far.

As she was letting herself into Number Nine, William drove by in a white pick-up truck on the side of which was emblazoned 'Arthur Grice, Scaffolding'. She could hear Wagner's 'The Ride of the Valkyries' pouring out of the open windows. He papped the hooter and pulled up.

'How did it go?' she asked.

William had been given permission to leave the estate and work on a contract erecting scaffolding, in preparation for converting a Norman church into a casino in Swindon.

'It was OK,' said William. 'We stayed in a Travelodge, the other chaps were terribly nice to me. I took a bit of stick at first because my hands were so soft.'

The Queen said, 'Was it horribly hard work?'

'Yes, horribly,' said William. He held out his hands to show the Queen. They were now cut and calloused, but the Queen could see that he was proud of having completed a week of manual work.

She said nothing to him, but she was proud of the boy. He had lived most of his life on the estate, surrounded by some dreadful people, but had managed somehow to remain law-abiding and utterly charming.

2

England was an unhappy land. The people were fearful, believing that life itself was composed of danger, and unknown and unknowable threats to their safety. Old people did not leave their homes after dark, children were not allowed to play outside even in the daylight hours and were escorted everywhere by anxious adults. To make themselves feel better the people spent their money on things that diverted and amused them. There was always something they thought they must have to make them happy. But when they had bought the object of their desire, they found, to their profound disappointment, that the object was no longer desirable, and that far from making them happy, they felt nothing but remorse and the sadness of loss.

To help alleviate the pensions crisis, the laws on euthanasia were liberalized and pensioners contemplating suicide were encouraged by a government information leaflet entitled 'Make Way for the Young'.

In a desperate attempt to be seen to be 'doing something' about crime and social disorder, the Government's Department of Liveability embarked on a bold programme to convert the satellite council estates into Exclusion Zones, where the criminal, the antisocial, the inadequate, the feckless, the agitators, the disgraced professionals, the stupid, the drug-addicted and the morbidly obese lived cheek by jowl.

The Royal Family, those who had not fled abroad, were living in the Flowers Exclusion Zone (known locally as the Fez) one hundred and nineteen miles from Buckingham Palace, in the East Midlands Region. Arthur Grice, a scaffolding magnate and multi-millionaire, owned and managed the estate; he considered it to be his personal fiefdom. The Royals lived in Hell Close, a cul-de-sac of sixteen small semi-detached ex-council houses. The houses had small front gardens, fenced to waist height. A few of the gardens were lovingly kept. Prince Charles regularly won the Grice Best Kept Garden Award, whereas his neighbours', the Thread-golds', garden was an eyesore of old mattresses, vicious brambles and festering rubbish bags.

When Charles offered to clear up and cultivate the Threadgolds' disgraceful garden, Vince Threadgold said, 'You ain't confiscatin' *my* land. This ain't the Middle Ages, an' you ain't got no royal prerogative no more.'

Beverley Threadgold had shouted, 'Anyroad up, there's field mice nesting in them old mattresses. I thought you was *for* wildlife!'

A twenty-foot-high metal fence topped with razor wire and CCTV cameras formed the boundary between the back gardens of Hell Close and the outside world. At the only entrance to the Fez, on a triangular piece of muddy ground, squatted a series of interconnected Portakabins, housing the Grice Security Police. The residents of the zone were required to wear an ankle tag and carry an identity card at all times. Their movements were followed by the security police on a bank of CCTV screens, installed in one of the Portakabins.

When Camilla's tag had been fitted, immediately after her wedding on the estate, she had said, with her usual cheerful pragmatism, 'I think it flatters my ankle beautifully.' By contrast, Princess Anne had wrestled two security police to the floor before a third officer had finally managed to attach her tag.

There were many prohibitions and restrictions imposed on the residents of the Fez. A strict curfew had to be adhered to; residents must be inside their homes from 10 p.m. until 7 a.m. at weekends. During the week they must be inside their houses from 9.30 p.m. Residents were not allowed to leave the estate. All correspondence, both in and out of the Exclusion Zone, was read and censored as appropriate. The telephone system did not extend to the outside world. There were only two free-to-view television channels, the Advertising Channel, which showed a few programmes now and then, and the Government News Channel, which, unsurprisingly, had a perceptible bias in favour of the Government.

The Fez heaved with dogs. They were everywhere, running in the streets, gathering on pavements, fighting on the few areas of scrubby grass and guarding their unlovely territory. There was not a single minute, night or day, when a dog was not barking. After a while the human residents no longer heard the noise: it became as much part of them as the sound of their own breathing. It was a continuing mystery as to how some owners managed to acquire their pedigree dogs, which often cost many hundreds of pounds, since all residents received the same weekly allowance of £71.32.

Jack Barker, leader of the Cromwell Party, Prime Minister and architect of the Exclusion Zones, could not get out of bed. It was ten thirty in the morning and he had already missed three appointments. He lay under the duvet in his bedroom at Number Ten Downing Street, listening to Big Ben striking the minutes and hours of his life away.

He was tired, he lived in a permanent state of déjà vu: he felt that everything he said, he had said before. Everything he did had already been done. Most of his trusted colleagues, those who had been elected with him thirteen years before, on a heady mix of idealism and principle, were dead or had resigned. Jack's wife of twenty-four years, Pat, his childhood sweetheart and political ally, had confronted him one night and accused him of fraternizing with the Devil after he had spent a convivial evening dining with Sir Nicholas Soames at a gentlemen's club in St James's. She had screamed, 'You're the leader of the Republican Party, for Christ's sake! You called the fucking cat Tom Paine!'

Soon after Jack's second election victory, the Republican Party had changed its name. A team of brand management consultants had deliberated for months, at an estimated cost of three million pounds, on the wisdom or otherwise of giving the party a new name. A 402-page report was produced, which almost nobody read in full, but instead turned to the executive summary, which said that, yes, a new name was called for due to constant confusion with the American Republican Government, underlined when Jonathan Ross called the Prime Minister 'Mr Pwesident' on Ross's Friday-night chat show. Another firm of fantastically clever consultants was contracted to think up a new name and logo. This team retired to a country house hotel where they brainstormed for five consecutive days and nights before coming up with the Cromwell Party.

Jack was now married to Caroline, who had fine bones and was the eldest daughter of a baronet, but Caroline found politics 'tiresome' and had recently started to criticize the way he held his fork. Jack was slightly afraid of Caroline, her vowels intimidated him and her pillow talk was formidably intellectual. Last night she had thrown Voltaire's *Dictionnaire Philosophique* across the bedroom, shouting, 'Lightweight!'

Jack had looked up from a report on phone tapping (161 Members of Parliament were currently having extramarital affairs), and said, 'Who's a lightweight? Me?'

'No, fucking Voltaire,' she had said. 'Enlightenment, my arse!'

Jack had looked at her lovely profile, at her angry, heaving breasts, and felt a twinge of desire, but the last time they had made love, Caroline had said, after they had peeled away from each other, 'Jack, you make love like a laboratory rat; your body's there, but your brain is elsewhere!'

If Caroline had a weakness it was her inability to pass a handbag shop. She currently had her name on a waiting list for a black Italian handbag, costing £2,000. When Jack grumbled that she already had eleven black handbags, she screamed, 'I can't be seen with last season's handbag. I'm the wife of the Prime Minister.'

Jack's mother had used the same navy-blue handbag for forty years. When the handles had become frayed she had taken the bag to a cobbler, who had repaired the handles for one and sixpence. When he told Caroline this, she said, 'I've seen photographs of your mother. She made Worzel Gummidge look positively elegant!'

Caroline had a pale beauty that mesmerized the picture editors of the English newspapers. She appeared on the front pages of most of them on a daily basis, often on the flimsiest of pretexts: 'CAZ BREAKS NAIL!' had been one recent headline.

Big Ben struck eleven times. A statement was issued to the press that the Prime Minister was 'indisposed'. The pound fell against the dollar.

Jack's Government was sometimes accused of being totalitarian, which made him laugh. He was far from being a Stalin or a Mao; it wasn't his fault there were no viable opposition parties. He had been forced to detain some of his potential opponents, but only because they had been stirring up trouble. He could not take chances with the security of the country, could he? He was hardly responsible for the political apathy that hung over England like a fog, was he?

A little crowd of agitators, Republican purists, had stirred themselves enough to hold an unlawful protest outside the Palace of Westminster, accusing the Government of revisionism. They had been dealt with but Jack could not help feeling that the tide was about to turn and cut him off from the shore. Perhaps he should not have put Stephen Fry under house arrest. It hadn't done any good: Fry had continued to mock the Government on the Internet, from his Norfolk home. He should have sent Fry to Turkey to have his cuticles seen to by one of their security forces' crack manicurists. That would have wiped the smile off Fry's satirical face. Jack laughed briefly under the duvet, but soon resumed his gloomy thoughts.

His workload was unremitting, remorseless. Just lately, Jack had begun to fantasize about walking away from his desk and never going back. Let some other poor bastard make the decisions, chair the meetings, deal with the arseholes and fools he was surrounded by. Had nobody noticed he was going mad? Were they unaware that he had developed a tick in his right eyelid? That he was forgetting the simplest of words? Didn't the strain show in the way that he occasionally found himself weeping real tears in public? What did they think he was doing when they saw him mopping his eyes?

He was not a quitter; he couldn't give the job up of his own volition. His mother's last words had been, 'Jack, get rid of the monarchy.' Though this was disputed by others round her deathbed, who thought she had said, 'Jack, give Sid me front-door key.' It was hard to be sure because of her oxygen mask.

He knew the Chancellor was after his job. Jack wished Fletcher would make his move and stick a metaphorical dagger in his back; he couldn't do it to himself. He couldn't let his mother down. He pulled the duvet over his head and reviewed the past thirteen years. He'd failed to win England's independence from America; he was spending billions on an asymmetrical intractable war in the Middle East. The roads and motorways were almost at a standstill. He was still subsidizing British farmers for doing fuck all. The rich were vastly richer, and the poor seemed to be morphing into a deviant subculture. The one thing he could be proud of though, Jack thought, was the removal from British life of hereditary titles. He had, with the stroke of a pen, destroyed the monarchy, forever.

3

Inspector Clive Lancer, the senior officer in Arthur Grice's private police force, was giving new recruit Dwayne Lockhart an induction to the Flowers Exclusion Zone. Dwayne was uncomfortable, not only because his uniform was slightly too small for his lanky body but also because he knew most of the people in the Fez and from now on he was expected to order them about and report them for various misdemeanours. As the two men walked around the almost deserted streets, a little plane circled overhead.

'Spotter plane,' said Inspector Lancer, throwing back his huge head. 'He's doing aerial photography, looking for illegal sheds.'

'Is it against the law to have a shed now?' asked Dwayne.

'It is if they've not got planning permission and they're evading council tax. A shed counts as a home improvement,' said the inspector. Sensing Dwayne's disapproval, Lancer said, 'We've got to keep on top of the scum, lad. Give 'em an inch an' they'll thieve the sodding ruler.'

Dwayne thought, yesterday I was one of 'the scum', the only difference between then and now is that I've took this job and had my tag took off official. I can go where I want now.

He couldn't wait to visit the lending library in the town. He had heard that there were thousands of books on the shelves.

They walked down Bluebell Lane; known locally as Slapper Alley because of the preponderance of teenage mothers living there.

'We're on slapper territory now, lad,' said Inspector Lancer. 'Some of these slappers can intoxicate a man and make him lose his head. You're replacing Taffy Jones, who was lured on to the metaphorical rocks by a slapper called Shyanne Grubbett.

'Taffy told me at the disciplinary hearing that he took one look at her white tracksuit, stilettos and hooped earrings and he was already halfway to losing his job. When she unzipped her tracksuit top and he saw her knockers spilling out of her skimpy Nike vest, he said he was lost.

'So keep your guard up, lad. The Jezebels are always waiting for fresh meat.'

Dwayne was extremely well read, but as was so often the case, he was relatively sexually inexperienced. There had been a few fumblings with an older girl at school, but he was still technically a virgin.

Inspector Lancer said, 'We'll stop here and wait for a slapper to come along. I want to demonstrate stop and search procedure.'

They leaned against a wall covered in obscene and possibly libellous graffiti about a woman called Jodie and her relationship with her dog. It wasn't long before a sweet-faced girl pushing a fat baby in a buggy came towards them.

Lancer sprang to attention and said, 'Right, I'll demonstrate a female stop and search.' He held his arm out and the girl sighed and stopped. Lancer said, 'First, ascertain the name and tag registration number of the suspect.'

The girl said, automatically, 'Paris Butterworth, B9176593,' and produced her ID card. She pointed at the baby, who was chewing at the corner of an unopened packet of Monster Munch crisps. ''E's Fifty-cents Butterworth. 'E ain't been tagged yet, 'e ain't old enough.'

Lancer said, 'Ask to see the baby's ID, Dwayne. You can't believe what these slappers tell you.'

Dwayne said, 'Would you mind if I had a look at Fifty-cents' ID, Miss Butterworth?'

She unzipped the baby's mini-anorak, delved beneath his sweatshirt and pulled out an ID card hanging from a blue ribbon. Two of the card's corners had obviously been chewed.

Lancer examined the card closely and said, 'Note the damage to this card, Dwayne.' Then he said to Paris, 'That is damage to government property. I could give you an on-the-spot fine for that.'

Paris said indignantly, ''E's teethin', 'e's chewin' owt 'e gets 'is 'ands on.'

Lancer said quickly, 'We'll let it go this time, Miss Butterworth. Right, having ascertained the identity of the suspects, we proceed to the search. In the absence of a female officer we must proceed carefully, Dwayne. So, avoiding the obvious erogenous zones, give Butterworth a quick pat down.'

Dwayne and Paris exchanged a glance. Dwayne thought, she's got lovely eyes.

'You're looking for drugs, stolen goods, concealed weapons and bomb-making materials,' said Lancer.

Paris said, 'As if! I wouldn't know a bomb-making material if it come up an' smacked me in the gob.'

Lancer said, 'Al Qaeda are known to have infiltrated slapper society in the past, Dwayne. So we take no chances.'

Lancer took his truncheon out and pointed with it at various parts of Paris's slim body, before saying, 'Now you pat her down, Dwayne.'

Dwayne tentatively ran his hands around her waist and shoulders, down her back and around her shins. He could feel her trembling and said, 'Sorry.'

Lancer continued, 'Then, once you are satisfied that the suspect is not concealing anything on her person, we search the baby.'

Dwayne bent down and said, 'Hello, Fifty-cents. Can I tickle your tummy, eh?'

Fifty-cents stared back warily. He wasn't keen on men. Men shouted and made his mother cry. Dwayne quickly ran his hands around the squashy body of the stern-faced baby, finding nothing unusual apart from a chewed-up plastic giraffe, which had fallen inside his vest. Dwayne held the model giraffe out to Paris; she took the animal from him and said, ''E's mad 'bout giraffes.'

Inspector Lancer searched the bag that was hanging from the handles of the buggy and pulled out a letter addressed to Mohammed Yousaf at Wakefield Prison.

He handed the letter to Dwayne and said, 'Why am I going to confiscate this letter, Dwayne?'

Dwayne tried to remember the half an hour that had been devoted to correspondence in his week's training. He said, 'Residents of an Exclusion Zone are prohibited from corresponding with serving prisoners.'

Lancer said, 'You're a naughty girl.'

Paris's face crumpled, and she began to weep. Nothing in Dwayne's training had prepared him for this situation. He stood awkwardly, not knowing what to do.

Paris sobbed. 'It's Mohammed's birthday next week.'

'Well, I'm sure we'll all wish him many happy returns,' said Lancer. 'Be on your way.'

Dwayne wanted to apologize to Paris. He hoped that she could see from his expression when he looked at her, that he would not have confiscated her letter. He didn't know how long he could stand this job if today was anything to go by. Paris zipped up the baby's coat, gave him the giraffe and walked away in the direction of the shops.

As Dwayne and Lancer were crossing the patch of grass in front of the One-Stop Centre, Camilla approached them, followed by Freddie, Tosca and Leo. She said to Lancer, 'Inspector, could you tell me the time, please? My watch has packed in.'

Lancer said, 'Before I tell you the time, madam, I should warn you that there is now a charge for this service.'

Camilla said, 'How extraordinary. All I'm asking of you is that you glance at your watch and tell me the time.'

Dwayne sneaked a look at his own watch. It was 11.14 a.m.

Lancer said, 'We are a public–private partnership and if we want to stay in business we have to charge for our services.'

Camilla said, 'So how much are you going to charge for telling me the time?'

Lancer answered, 'There is now a standard charge of one pound an enquiry.'

'A pound!' said Camilla. 'That's outrageous.'

Lancer said, 'So you no longer want to know the time?'

'No,' said Camilla. 'I can see from the position of the sun that it's almost midday.'

Dwayne pulled the cuff back from his right wrist, exposing his watch. Then pretended to shield his eyes from the wintry sun.

Camilla said, 'Ah, I see it's eleven fifteen. Thank you, Constable.'

Leo lolloped over to Dwayne and dropped a stick he'd been carrying in his mouth at Dwayne's feet. Dwayne picked up the slimy stick and hurled it as far as he could. The three dogs raced towards the stick, which had come to rest in a patch of mud.

Camilla said to Dwayne, 'I hope you're not going to charge me for throwing that stick.'

'No,' said Dwayne. 'There will be no charge.'

When Leo brought the stick back and dropped it again at Dwayne's feet, Lancer said, 'Leave the stick where it is, lad. We've work to do.'

Walking on, they came to a district that was separated from the rest of the Flowers Estate by a high wall.

'This,' said Lancer, as he turned a key in a door in the wall, 'keeps the kiddie fiddlers penned up and out of harm's way.'

He opened the door and they walked through. Dwayne had expected to see furtive-looking men in greasy overcoats maundering around the streets, but to his surprise the men here looked as ordinary as the men on the rest of the estate.

When he remarked on this to Lancer, he was further surprised when Lancer said, 'Most of the poor sods are as innocent as a lamb in springtime, lad.'

Dwayne said, 'What are they doing in here then, sir?'

'Malicious ankle-snappers have borne false witness against these poor blokes, boy. The evil little tykes have led 'em on and once they've eaten their sweeties they've gone squawking to ChildLine.'

Dwayne said nothing, but he wanted to defend abused children. His swimming teacher had often fumbled inside Dwayne's Speedos, claiming he was checking for genital abnormalities. After a quick tour of the area housing the struck-off professionals (where Lancer and Dwayne were abused by a human rights lawyer who shouted, 'You're the puppets of a police state!'), they arrived back at the Control Centre. Inspector Lancer scanned Paris's letter into a computer, showing Dwayne how to do it. The letter said:

Hi Mohammed,

I have wrote you a poem for your birthday, don't laugh. I writ it last night when Fifty-cents was asleep. It took me a long time, I had to keep checking the spelling in that dictionary I nicked from school.

> *How do I love thee?*
> *Let me count the ways.*
> *I love thee to the . . .*

Dwayne realized from the second line that she had attributed the authorship of Elizabeth Barrett Browning's famous poem to herself. He was bitterly disappointed in Paris.

Lancer said, 'That's not a bad poem. I wonder where she went to school?'

He keyed in Paris's name and registration number and the screen came up with Paris's life history:

Name: Paris Butterworth (19).

Father: Lee Butterworth (47), recidivist, prescribed methadone, currently unemployed.

Mother: Lorna Butterworth (51), currently employed at Grice-A-Go-Go as cloakroom attendant, many convictions for petty theft.

Sister: Chelsey Butterworth (19), pole dancer.

Sister: Tropez Butterworth (12), Arthur Grice Academy.

Brother: Dallas Butterworth (4), special needs nursery.

Paris Butterworth: 5' 1", 8 stone 3 lbs.

Medical record: Bronchitis every winter, otherwise healthy.

Menstrual cycle: First week of every month, complains of severe pain.

History: Unsettled at nursery school, constantly cried for mother. At four years could not handle eating implements. Vocabulary v. poor, when showed a picture of a cow could not name it.

Poor standard of hygiene, frequently wore dirty clothes and inadequate shoes for bad weather. Placed on at-risk register after mother could not satisfactorily explain large areas of bruising on buttocks and lower back.

Age eleven: Failed government targets for reading and writing. Skills: Showed some aptitude for maths and art.

Arthur Grice Academy: Paris caught up with her peers under the tutorage of her English teacher. Her project on Elizabeth Barrett Browning's dog, Flush, earned her a pass in English Literature. However, she failed four other subjects and was permanently excluded from the academy when seven months pregnant.

Present circumstances: Lives alone with ten-month-old male child, Fifty-cents Lee Butterworth.

Father of the child: Unknown.

Current boyfriend: Mohammed Yousaf, currently in high-security wing of Wakefield Prison serving an indefinite sentence for potential terrorist activities – unusually large quantity of fertilizer found in outhouse of parents' home. Father claimed fertilizer was for tomatoes. Attending officer reported unusually large quantity of tomatoes growing in greenhouse. Mohammed Yousaf arrested because had funny look in eye, had beard and was verbally abusive. Yousaf resisted arrest and anti-terrorist squad were called to attend before he was restrained.

Butterworth's income: Standard single mother's allowance £84.50 weekly. Butterworth now spends her time looking after the baby and watching property programmes on television. Non-smoker.

Sexual status: Heterosexual. No sexual activity since birth of son.

Dwayne was pleased to find out that Paris had been chaste for such a long period. He scrolled on and was amazed to find that records of all Paris's purchases had been listed. She seemed to buy an inordinate amount of Monster Munch crisps.

When he expressed his amazement at the extent of the information kept, Lancer said, 'Vulcan knows everything about us, lad. It's like a lovely warm duvet on a cold night.'

'Vulcan is the god of fire and metalwork,' said Dwayne, who had not yet realized that imparting such facts would not endear him to his superiors.

Lancer said, 'Vulcan is a policeman's best friend.'

Dwayne said, 'Isn't it a bit . . . well . . . intrusive?'

'I'll tell you what *is* intrusive, Lockhart, and that's a bleeding terrorist bomb!' said Lancer. 'What you've got to take on board, lad, is that we're living in tomorrow's world, today. We *are* science fiction. The Yanks have got satellites that can guide a thread through a fuckin' needle!'

Dwayne glanced out of the window at the grey clouds hanging over the Fez.

Another new recruit, Peter Penny, asked anxiously, 'Can the spy satellite see through curtains, sir?' He was remembering last night's humiliation when he had persuaded his wife of three years to try a daring new sexual position.

'Curtains?' asked Inspector Lancer scornfully.

'Yes,' said Peter Penny, 'thick, velvet curtains with a lining.'

Lancer shook his head. Was this rookie an idiot? 'The new satellites can see inside a fucking mountain! They can pick up a whisper. They're listening to us now.'

'Who is?' asked Dwayne.

Lancer activated the camera at the bottom of Prince Charles's garden and watched Charles pleading with his hens to give him an occasional egg. He said, 'The Yanks. The Chinese. The Russians. The French. The Arabs. The World.'

'And are we listening to them?'

'Of course we are,' said Lancer.

Dwayne wouldn't let it go. 'So everybody knows everything?' he asked.

Lancer watched Charles walk discontentedly up the garden path and go into his kitchen and said, 'We have to work on that premise, lad, yes.'

'So what's the point?'

'Ah, now that I can't tell you, Dwayne. As an employee of a public–private partnership I'm subject to commercial confidentiality.'

Dwayne Lockhart was a local man who had made good. Unable to read at the age of eleven, he had transferred to the Arthur Grice Academy and been taught the basics of reading and writing by Mr Nutting, a shambolic eccentric English teacher who made the children laugh and kept order in the classroom by raising an eyebrow. To Dwayne's distress, Mr Nutting was sacked for 'failing to adhere to the national curriculum'. Before he left he told his classes that they must read at least one book a week. 'Books should be as vital to you as food, water and oxygen,' he said.

He had given them all a sheet of paper on which was written a list of the books he wanted them to read.

Dwayne still kept the paper inside his wallet. He had read all of the books on the list, but he kept the paper because Mr Nutting had scrawled on the bottom of his booklist: 'Dwayne, nobody can choose the family they are born into. Both of my parents were alcoholics. You are an intelligent lad. Don't waste your life. Yours, Simon Nutting.'

Dwayne had told nobody else in the class that Mr Nutting's parents were alkies or that Mr Nutting had put it down in writing that he, Dwayne Lockhart, was intelligent, but he read the words to himself when his own parents were drunk and fighting in the street, when they called him a fucking gay boff because he was always reading.

When Dwayne and Peter Penny were alone in front of a bank of cameras in the surveillance room, Peter said, 'What are we looking for?'

Remembering Inspector Lancer's mini-lecture on surveillance, Dwayne said, 'Unusual or suspicious behaviour.'

Peter said, 'But everybody on the screen looks suspicious.'

Dwayne agreed, he was looking at the on-screen image of Charles and Camilla's living room. Charles was writing at a small bureau. Camilla was talking to one tall and two small dogs as if they were not only human beings but had valid opinions. 'So you think I should have my highlights done, do you, Leo?'

Dwayne could not resist zooming in on the journal Charles was writing.

Still no eggs. I am at my wits' end. What more can I do? I have provided the hens with a decent diet and a splendid coop. I lavish attention on them, but nothing back – they barely acknowledge my existence. I am utterly crushed by their ingratitude.

Camilla and I had an extremely distressing row earlier. I was left trembling and near to tears. God knows, I am the most tolerant of men, but I am finding her inability to stop smoking increasingly irritating. The sight of Eccles, one of God's innocent creatures, with a cigarette hanging from her beak caused me intolerable pain.

Camilla and I are now reconciled, although I notice it was not me she consulted about the advisability of highlights, but Leo – who is ill-qualified to give advice on hair. His own coat is permanently bedraggled however much I brush it.

Dwayne wondered if somebody, somewhere had watched him struggling to write poetry in his bedroom or playing air guitar in front of the mirrored wardrobe door. He blushed at the thought of what else they might have seen.

4

Violet Toby, the Queen's next-door neighbour, best friend and confidante, had dropped in to complain to the Queen that Prince Harry had called her granddaughter Chanel a 'minging spag' and if he ever got to be king, he would lock her in the Tower of London and order her 'minging head to be chopped off'.

The Queen said, 'That's highly unlikely to happen, Violet, since we live in a republic. And anyway, Harry will be king only over my dead body.'

Violet the pedant lifted her swollen feet on to a tapestry-covered footstool and adjusted the skirt of her navy and white polka-dot dress. The Queen noticed that there was a strip of white showing at the roots of Violet's otherwise red hair.

Violet said, 'Charles will be king over your dead body. And if Charles fell under a bus?'

The Queen said, 'Then of course William would be king.'

'And if William fell off some scaffolding . . .' said Violet '. . . and broke his neck and died?'

The Queen said bleakly, 'Given those unlikely circumstances, then Harry *would* be king. Unless, of course, William has married by then and had children.'

Violet said, 'Well that ain't likely, is it? 'E's not even courtin'.'

The Queen gave a deep sigh, imagining Harry and his hoody friends on the balcony of Buckingham Palace swigging from cans of lager and giving the crowd below the V sign. She said to Violet, 'We must find a wife for William.'

The conversation turned to the Queen's toothache and then to teeth in general.

'I 'ad a set of false teeth for my twenty-first birthday,' said Violet. 'Mam and Dad bought the top set and the rest of the family clubbed together an' bought the bottom.'

Violet gnashed her porcelain teeth at the Queen. 'The dentist didn't want to take me teeth out. He said they were perfect, but me dad said, "No. I want all 'er teeth took out, an' false 'uns put in. It'll save her trouble later in life."'

The Queen was horrified. She said, 'What a beastly thing to do.'

Violet bridled, 'No, Dad were right. I've 'ad a lot of trouble in my life, with money, men an' our Barry, but I've never lost a day's work, or a night's sleep, with toothache.'

The Queen momentarily felt a little jealous of Violet's teeth. She had spent a very unpleasant night wishing that Mr Barwell, by royal appointment, dental surgeon to the Queen, was still on call. At the slightest twinge, Barwell would be flown in the royal jet to wherever she was staying. Now, thought the Queen bitterly, she had no dentist at all. Mr Patel, the National Health Service dentist, had recently escaped from the Fez and nobody had taken his place.

Violet said, 'I know a woman what takes her own teeth out with a pair of pliers, do you want me to have a word with 'er?'

'Goodness, no, it sounds terribly dangerous.'

'No, it's dead safe, she sterilizes the pliers first, in a pan of boiling water.'

They were sitting in the Queen's tiny front room on matching Louis XVI armchairs next to the gas fire. They were waiting for *Emmerdale* to come on the television. It was going to be a double episode. This one-off special had been trailed all week. The whole population of Emmerdale Village were to go on a coach outing to an agricultural show in a fictional county. The trails had shown the villagers having a jolly singsong, then cut to the coach braking to avoid a stray sheepdog. There had been close shots of various actors/villagers screaming as the coach slid down an embankment on to a railway line below. The Queen and Violet were avid to find out which of their favourite characters would survive the accident.

Harris and Susan were also waiting; they were curious to find out what was to happen to the dog. Violet's dog, Micky, a gruff-faced, ginger mongrel with a tail that curled on to his back, was not allowed inside the Queen's house; Micky was emotionally unstable, and given to sudden irrational outbursts of aggression. He sat on the Queen's doorstep patiently waiting for Violet to come out.

To change the subject from teeth, the Queen asked how Barry was, Violet's delinquent forty-five-year-old son.

Violet sighed. 'He's got a psychiatric social worker now, a woman. And according to Barry, this woman says Barry's problems are all *my* fault. She says, locking him in the understairs cupboard when he was a little kid has made him want to destroy authority, and has gave him a syndrome.'

The Queen said, 'Charles blames me and his father for most of the problems he's had in his life. He claims he was *neglected*, which is terribly unfair. We saw him at least once a day when we were in the country, and his nanny adored him.'

Violet said, 'I think Barry should be locked up. I'm 'aving to hide all my lighters and matches again.'

The Queen nodded sympathetically. Charles was troubled, but as far as she knew he was not an arsonist. The Queen qualified many of her observations about people by saying, 'As far as one knows.' Even members of her own family seemed to have so many secrets. She had a few herself.

A burst of dramatic, urgent-sounding music caught the two women's attention immediately. A news band at the bottom of the screen said in fat red letters 'Breaking News'.

Violet said, 'Now what?' She was sick of having her programmes interrupted by real life. She never watched the news out of choice. Who wanted to know about wars and disasters? She couldn't do anything to stop them, could she? So why worry herself, she was already on three blood pressure tablets a day.

The leader of the Conservative Party, a grey man in a grey suit, had resigned in order to spend more time with his latest family, and a new leader, a fresh-faced youngish man with a shock of luxuriant black hair, had taken his place. He was 'Boy' English.

'Good gracious,' said the Queen. 'It's Boy. His father ran a stud at Newmarket, his grandmother was one of my ladies-of-the-bedchamber.'

Boy was being interviewed by the BBC's senior political correspondent. 'And what is at the top of your political agenda, Mr English?' asked the bespectacled reporter.

'I want to restore the monarchy,' said Boy. 'I want to see Her Majesty, Queen Elizabeth, back on the throne, and I want to see Jack Barker and the Cromwellians consigned to the dustbin of history.'

When the Queen didn't say anything, Violet said, 'Well, I ain't voting for 'im. I'd sooner casserole me own arm than vote Tory, an' anyway, I don't want to lose you, Liz.'

Half an hour later, the villagers from Emmerdale lay trapped inside the wreckage of their coach as an express train hurtled towards them. The Queen was still thinking about Boy's loyal statement. Even the melodramatic death of the village idiot, played by an actor she had never liked, could not engage her full attention.

Camilla was at the bottom of the garden, in the dark, poking at a smouldering bonfire of wet leaves with a long stick. She had always loved the autumn. She was glad to put away her summer clothes and throw on a baggy sweater, jeans and wellingtons. In the old days, when her affair with Charles was still a secret from the public, she had lived for fox-hunting days. She would rise early to begin the ritual of dressing: in the tight jodhpurs, the white high-necked shirt, the fitted red coat with the brass buttons. And last, but best of all, the tight, black knee-high riding boots.

She knew she looked good in the saddle and was regarded by her fellow huntsmen as a fearless rider. When she strode from the house towards the stables, whip in hand, her breath visible in the frosty air, she felt contained and powerful, and if she was honest with herself, there was the tiniest frisson of sexual excitement. With a horse between her legs and the open countryside in front of her, surrounded by friends she could trust with her life, she experienced a sort of ecstasy; and how wonderful it was to return to a warm house at twilight, to lie in a hot bath with a drink and a fag and, occasionally, Charles.

She heard a noise and looked up from the fire to see a pair of black and gold eyes staring into her own. The fox was back. She waved the blackened end of the stick towards it and shouted, 'Bugger off.' Then she saw that it had a companion.

Beverley Threadgold shouted from her back door, 'Camilla, we're all coughin' our bleedin' lungs up in 'ere.'

The foxes turned their backs and disappeared into the night.

When Camilla went indoors, after dousing the bonfire, Charles was sitting in the front room, composing a letter at the small writing bureau. She could see from the wastepaper basket next to him that he had already gone through several drafts.

She decided not to mention the foxes; he was

obviously in a state of anxiety. Instead, she asked, 'Who are you writing to, darling?'

'The milkman,' said Charles. 'I've been through several drafts, I've written and rewritten the damn thing so many times, and don't know how to end it.'

Camilla picked up the last draft and read:

Dear Milkman,

Awfully sorry to inconvenience you, but would it be at all possible to change our order for today (Thursday) and have two bottles of semi-skimmed instead of our usual one?

If this addition to our usual order leaves you in the ghastly position of being overstretched as far as your stock is concerned, then please do not worry. I would be simply devastated if my request gave you a moment's anxiety or inconvenienced you in the slightest.

May I just add that your cheery whistle in the morning, and in all weathers, somehow exemplifies the very essence of the indomitable British character.

When she finished reading, Charles said, 'Do I sign it "Sincerely, Charles", or "With best wishes", or "Yours respectfully", because I do respect him, or what?'

Camilla tore a strip of paper off the bottom of the letter and quickly scrawled, 'One extra pint please.' She rolled the scrap of paper up, pushed it in the neck of an empty Grice's milk bottle and took the bottle out and put it on the doorstep.

The telephone rang. It was William, telling his father that he was back from Swindon.

Charles said, 'Darling boy, was it horrid putting those scaffold thingies together?'

William said, 'No, it was kind of, satisfying. How's Leo?'

'He's simply enormous,' said Prince Charles. He looked down at the dogs at his feet, he was a little disappointed that William had asked after the dog and hadn't mentioned Camilla. Charles furrowed his brow: was this significant?

William went on, 'Pa, what do you think about the Tories' promise to bring us back if they get elected?'

This came as a surprise to Charles. He had been in the garden reinforcing the fence when the news broke and he hadn't got what he called an 'idiot box', believing that television was nearly one hundred per cent responsible for the nation's moral decline.

William explained that Boy English, the new leader of the Conservative Party, was an ardent monarchist and had promised to reinstate the Royal Family if he was elected. 'Just think, Pa,' he said, 'we could be spending Christmas at Sandringham.'

Hearing this, Freddie barked to Tosca, 'Hear that, *Liebling*? Christmas at Sandringham!'

Tosca rolled on to her back and displayed her hind quarters to Leo. She growled, 'Leo, you'll love the pinewoods and the log fires.'

Freddie yapped, 'Your oversized mongrel friend won't be going with us, Tosca, he'll stay behind here with the other proles.'

Charles shouted, 'Quiet, you little beasts, I'm trying to speak on the telephone!' He said into the mouthpiece,

'I don't think Freddie is getting on frightfully well with Leo, Wills.'

'Too right!' barked Freddie. 'He's a lump of *Kot*.'

'What am I a lump of?' Leo whined to Tosca.

'Literal translation, excrement,' Tosca barked.

Leo didn't like to ask what excrement was, all he knew was that it didn't sound very nice.

5

The Prime Minister and the Deputy Prime Minister, Bill Brazier, were having a pre-cabinet meeting in Jack's sitting room at Number Ten Downing Street. Brazier had requested the meeting, telling Jack's Private Secretary that he needed to see the Prime Minister urgently. Brazier was a corpulent man whose tailor had told him recently that the price of his bespoke suits would have to 'be adjusted due to the extra volume of cloth required'. He sat on the sofa, panting from the stairs, while the Prime Minister prowled round the room fidgeting with various objects as he passed.

'So, what's so urgent?' Jack asked, touching the gilt frame of a painting of Oliver Cromwell, which hung over the fireplace.

'Boy English,' said Brazier.

'I know almost nothing about him,' said Jack.

Brazier said, 'That's because you take no bloody interest in anything much lately.'

'I'm tired,' said Jack. 'Thirteen years is a long time.'

Brazier scowled and said, 'Well, unless you get your bloody finger out, Boy English'll be moving his dainty arse on to this bloody sofa before Christmas.'

'What do we know about him?' asked Jack.

'He's a toff lite,' said Bill Brazier. 'Eton, Oxford, his

dad owns half of Devon, and his wife knows her way round an artichoke.'

Jack said, 'Hardly toff lite.'

Brazier said, 'Yeah, but him and his missus have both had their belly buttons pierced and are in the darts team at their local pub.'

'How is he on fox-hunting?'

'Abstained.'

'National Health Service?'

'Clued up, worked as a porter for three months, donated his wages to bloody Amnesty International!'

Jack laughed. 'And he's still a Tory boy?'

Brazier said, 'Since yesterday, he's the leader of the New Conservatives, says he wants less government, thinks people should be allowed to smoke themselves into an early grave if they want to. Says it will save the National Health Service money in the long run. Wants to ditch the Human Rights Act.'

'What's he like on the monarchy?'

'He wants to bring them back.'

'All of 'em? Princes and all?'

'Immediate family. Queen, the Duke, kids, Charles, Camilla, William, Harry.'

'He's on a loser, Bill. The people will never stand for that. It'd be like voting to bring back boy chimney sweeps or the poll tax, they belong to another age.'

Bill said, 'My own wife would be made up if the Royals came back. She's partial to a bit of pomp and ceremony.'

'You should take her out more,' said Jack. 'How's the Stepladder Bill doing?'

Bill Brazier took great satisfaction in saying, 'Badly,

Jack, I doubt if it'll get past the committee stage. Folk like their stepladders, they don't want to call in a qualified operator every time they paint a ceiling or change a bleedin' light bulb.'

'No,' said Jack, bitterly. 'They want to fall off their bloody ladders and break their bloody necks, and arms, and legs, and collar bones, and give themselves concussion, then demand an ambulance and a bloody hospital bed, and sick pay, and physiotherapy.'

Bill Brazier said, 'You can't legislate for every eventuality, Jack. People must be allowed to fall off stepladders. You'd legislate against death if you could . . .'

'I would,' said Jack, who since a boy had been afraid of the nothingness, the black abyss that death represented. Men were supposed to think about sex every ten seconds, weren't they? Well, he thought about death. 'So, do you reckon that Boy English is a serious contender, Bill?'

'I reckon he is,' answered Bill. 'He's just agreed to pay fifteen thousand quid to have his teeth seen to, and according to my wife – who's a connoisseur of these things – he's got lovely hair, and kind eyes and he relaxes by watching the soaps *while he's ironing*.'

'Ironing?' Jack didn't understand at first. Was it some kind of medieval sport?

'Ironing!' said Bill. 'As in, ironing clothes.'

'Oh, *ironing*,' said Jack. 'The sad bastard.'

Jack, whose hair was falling out at an alarming rate and whose eyes were red through lack of sleep, said, 'We'll see how pretty he looks after he's been in office a few years.'

Bill said, 'You're talking as if he's already beat us.'

Jack asked, 'Have we got anything on him?'

'Nothing much,' said Bill. 'He got cautioned for nicking a traffic cone when he was at Oxford, and a ticket in 1987 for speeding on the M1.'

'How fast was he going?' Jack asked.

'Seventy-five.'

Jack said dreamily, 'Seventy-five . . . it was a golden age. You're lucky to get up to fifty nowadays, it'll soon be quicker to walk to the bloody North.'

Bill said, 'Yeah. Disgusting, isn't it? I blame the Government.'

Jack appeared to join in Bill's laughter, that is, he opened his mouth in a sort of grin and made a laughing noise. But he could just as well have burst into tears.

Bill said, 'I'll ask 'em to dig a bit deeper, shall I?'

Bill lumbered towards the door when Jack stopped him, saying, 'Do you want us to win the next election, Bill? Wouldn't it be nice to have a turn at opposition? Sit on the subs benches for a few years?'

Bill said, 'And let the New Cons in to undo everything we've achieved?'

Jack said, 'Just testing.'

He should have spent the next hour reading briefing papers and consulting by telephone with the Leader of the House in a bid to set a date to talk about setting a date to talk about Peace, but he pushed the papers away, disconnected the telephone and switched the television on. He watched Anna and the King of Siam dancing a polka in a Siamese ballroom. And despite several entreaties from his Private Secretary and the knowledge that the Cabinet had assembled downstairs, Jack kept them waiting until Anna had sung a sad farewell to Yul and the titles were rolling.

6

When Mr Anwar saw on the news that novelty slippers would soon become unlawful, he waited for the price to drop and then ordered an articulated lorry load of them. Bundles of novelty slippers filled the shop. There were lions, tigers, giraffes, cats, dogs, elephants and other more difficult to determine animals. Then there were slippers whose design was based on the human form, iconic politicians or film stars. There were modes of transport: cars, planes, lorries, boats, Thomas the Tank Engine, and the Apollo spacecraft.

Unruly queues of eager purchasers formed outside, waiting for the door to open at 10 a.m. Mr and Mrs Anwar could be seen inside, frantically cutting open cardboard boxes, removing the lurid slippers from their plastic bags and handing them to their podgy daughters who arranged them on racks in order of size, small, medium and large, rather than category or gender suitability.

Mr Anwar said to his wife, 'All of Allah's creatures are here.'

She said, taking out a pair of George Bush slippers, 'And also the Devil's.'

There was outrage when the first few customers emerged with their outsized slippers saying that Mr Anwar was selling the slippers for one pound *each* or two pounds a pair. The only person to think that this was fair was Prince Andrew's neighbour Feroza Amiz, who had lost a leg in mysterious circumstances in Kurdistan. Charles and Camilla joined the queue too late to buy the most popular slippers. The Simpsons, the Teletubbies and the dogs with their squeaking noses had all gone, as had the wiry-whiskered cats. Charles dithered over a pair of elephant slippers, which had uplifted foam trunks and rubber tusks. He tried them on and shuffled across the shop floor to Camilla who was trying to decide between Stalin and King Kong, which were the only slippers remaining in her size.

'What do you think of these, darling?' said Charles. 'Are they *too* ridiculous?'

Camilla said, lowering her voice, 'Aren't the trunks a little, well, phallic, darling?'

Charles blushed and quickly pulled the spongy slippers off his feet.

Mrs Anwar said, 'I have just the thing for you, Mr Saxa-Cobury-Gatha, and for your lady wife also.' She rummaged around inside a carton and said, 'I will sell them to you at cost price, fifty pence a pair, to make room for more popular lines.'

The hard-to-sell slippers were gross caricatures of Charles and Camilla. Charles's prominent ears had been painted red and his brow was deeply furrowed. Camilla's caricature was equally unflattering.

Mr Anwar said, 'They are very amusing, perhaps I will keep a pair for myself.'

Charles said, angrily, 'I will buy your entire stock of

Charles and Camilla slippers. I will not have my wife's face trampled underfoot by some ghastly oik.'

Some of the ghastly oiks in the shop looked over at the sound of raised voices and Maddo Clarke squashed over in his foam-filled Fred Flintstone slippers to involve himself in the argument.

Mr Anwar shouted, 'You didn't object to Lady Di's blessed face appearing on a cloth to dry dishes.'

Charles said, 'I had no control of the merchandising, including the tea towels.'

Mr Anwar said emotionally, 'Every day I think about her, the beautiful Princess of Hearts. If she were still with us there would be world peace.'

'No kids would 'ave to go to bed 'ungry,' added Maddo Clarke. 'Not if Di was still alive.' A resident of Hell Close, Maddo, though in his early forties, still wore the uniform of his hero, Sid Vicious.

Mr Anwar addressed the growing crowd in the shop. 'Remind yourselves who she perished with. Was he a Christian? A Catholic? A Jew? No, he was a Muslim! And for that she was killed.'

Somebody in the crowd shouted, 'Murdered, more like.'

Camilla said, with as much dignity as a person wearing King Kong slippers could summon, 'We'll leave these people to their shopping, Charles.'

Mr Anwar shouted as Charles and Camilla left the shop, 'You will never be Queen Camilla. The people don't want you.'

Camilla untied the dogs from the railings, saying, 'You love us, don't you, darlings?'

As they walked home, the dogs were unusually obedient, conscious that their master and mistress had been humiliated and deeply wounded.

Tosca whimpered, 'It's at times like this that I wish I could *say* something to them.'

Freddie growled, 'Don't feel too sorry for them, Tosca. Remember, we dogs live in a permanent state of subjugation. They're constantly ordering us about.'

Leo extended his tongue and licked Charles's hand. It was meant to be a gesture of comfort and support, but Charles grumbled, 'For God's sake, Leo! Keep your bloody slobber to yourself.'

7

The Cabinet had been in crisis session for over six hours. Sustained only by mineral water and Rich Tea biscuits, they had been discussing the balance of payments, again. The Government had been in power for thirteen long years, having won three general elections, the last by a small majority. Introducing the Exclusion Zones had won them short-term popularity, but water rationing, hospital closures and monumental mistakes by Vulcan – 13,000 paediatricians had been erroneously placed on the paedophile register – had resulted in the pound faltering and falling like a novice ice skater.

The Chancellor was saying to his exhausted, and in some cases tearful, colleagues, 'I warned you that losing the cigarette duty would leave a big financial hole. We have to find another source of revenue.'

Jack Barker, who had been kept awake half the night listening to the Chancellor's dog, Mitzie, yapping through the party wall, said, 'There's plenty of disposable income out there. If the taxpayer can afford bloody aromatherapy candles and grooming products for men, they can afford another tax. I reckon we ought to bring dog licences back.'

There was general laughter. Even the Chancellor smiled.

Jack waited for the laughter to die down, then said,

'There are too many dogs in this country. Did you know there's six million one hundred thousand of them? Or that people spend over three billion quid on feeding the spoilt bastards? And four hundred million a year on buying the yapping flea-bitten hairy-faced ball-lickers Christmas presents? *Four hundred million!*'

The Chancellor looked down and shuffled his papers. Last Christmas he had bought Mitzie a pink latex bone, and a hairbrush and comb set. He'd had them gift-wrapped, at Harrods.

Jack continued, 'And did you know that their combined turds, if laid end to end, would go to the moon and back *twice*?'

Jack had made this last statistic up, but he had no conscience about the fabrication. After years in politics he knew that statistics were statistically unreliable.

Neville Moon, Home Secretary and owner of two excitable chocolate Labradors, said, 'Prime Minister, you can't touch dogs, not in this country. Not in England!'

Jack said, 'I propose we charge three hundred quid a dog.' Looking at Moon he said, 'No, make that five hundred.'

The Deputy Prime Minister growled, 'It's political suicide, Jack. You might just as well jump off the top of the fucking Gherkin.'

Mary Bush, Health Minister and owner of a trembling greyhound, said tentatively, 'It has been shown in various studies that dogs have a beneficial effect on the old and the lonely.'

Jack said, looking directly at Mary, 'Do you know how many kiddies go blind every year because of the

Toxocara canis worm found in dog shit?' After waiting a few seconds, he answered his own question. 'Three,' said Jack, dramatically holding up three fingers.

Bill Brazier said, 'Three? Is that all?'

'Bill, that's three little kids who will never see their mother's face. Never see the wonder of spring blossom on a . . .' Jack's mind went blank, he couldn't remember the name of a single tree. So he went for the generic, '. . . tree,' he finished.

Neville Moon said, 'All the same, three's not many, Jack, not in the scheme of things.'

Jack said, 'I want reports on my desk this time to-morrow. Costs to the National Health Service of dog bites and kids going blind, etc. Costs to the police of dog-related incidents, costs to the fire service of dog rescues. The bleedin' things are always falling down wells and old mine shafts. I want to know how many tonnes of carbon monoxide emissions are caused by transporting dog food around the bloody country. I want television campaigns, I want billboards, I want dog owners to be the next lepers. We did it with smokers, we can do it with bloody dogs.'

Outside, in the corridor after the meeting, Jack felt a twinge of pain in his left arm. His fingers felt numb. This is it, he thought. He took the lift upstairs, not wanting to die on the staircase under the gaze of the portraits of previous prime ministers. He would have liked to have gone to bed, but he was hosting a dinner to introduce his first wife, Pat, to his second wife, Caroline. Sonia, the youngest daughter from his first marriage, was getting married in the morning. Pat had always refused to meet Caroline, saying, 'She's an anorexic bitch.' So no pressure, thought Jack, as he waited for the pain to hit his heart.

However, he had survived the dinner with his wives. The two women had bonded alarmingly well and had moved chairs so that they could converse more easily. Jack had not liked the tone of their laughter.

Later, he was persuaded into telling Annabel, his seven-year-old granddaughter, a bedtime story. She was to be a bridesmaid in the morning. The ceremony would be held at Westminster Abbey. Jack had argued against this venue, but Sonia had insisted, saying that it was the only place big enough to seat their celebrity friends.

'Once upon a time,' Jack said, in his flat Midlands accent, 'there was such a thing called the Royal Family. There was a queen, princes and princesses, and they lived in big castles and had lots of money and cars and servants and jewels and stuff.'

Annabel said in her, to Jack, disconcertingly posh voice, '*I'm* going to be a princess when I grow up.'

Jack laughed and said, 'No, Annabel, you won't be a princess, you'll be something useful to society: an engineer perhaps, or a scientist.'

'No,' she said. 'I'm going to be a princess and wear a sparkly dress and a crown and live in a castle.' She sat up in bed and folded her arms.

Jack said, 'You can't be a princess, because Granddad's got rid of them. He's sent them all away to live like ordinary people. I've sent them into exile.'

'Can I go to exile to see them?' asked Annabel.

'No, you can only go to exile if you're a very bad person,' said Jack.

Jack and Annabel were in one of the guest bedrooms at Number Ten. Jack could hear Mitzie, that bloody King Charles spaniel, yapping through the party wall again. He felt his pulse racing, he was sick of complaining about that bloody dog. Mitzie had been a cause of contention since the Chancellor, Stephen Fletcher, had, with a great deal of press coverage, walked Mitzie from Battersea Dogs Home to Downing Street. Fletcher's approval rating had risen by fifteen per cent in the next YouGov opinion poll. Jack's team of advisers had urged him to be photographed in the back garden of Number Ten with Tommy, his ex-wife's big black cat. But Tommy, unaccustomed to being held by the Prime Minister and frightened by the unruly crowd of press photographers, had resisted and clawed Jack's face in his struggle to be free. A headline in *The Daily Telegraph* the next day had stated: 'BARKER HOLDS ON TO POWER BY A WHISKER.'

Jack said to Annabel, 'Lie down again, pet, and I'll tell you a different story, shall I? About a lady engineer.'

Annabel said, 'No, thank you.' She lay down and turned her back on Jack.

As soon as he got to his office, Jack telephoned the Chancellor on Number Eleven's private line. 'Steve,' he said, when the Chancellor answered. 'Shut that bloody dog up, will you? Our Annabel can't get to sleep. She's got a big day tomorrow.'

8

Graham Cracknall was sitting at his dining-room table in a detached, 1970s pebble-dashed bungalow in Ruislip writing a letter in his neatest handwriting. He could type at a rate of sixty words a minute but he was aware that history was being made and he thought that an historical document, one that would be placed in an archive to be studied by scholars, deserved to be personalized.

He was a tall thin man with jug ears and a prominent Adam's apple. He had been on the books of a dating agency for eighteen months, but the only women to show any interest in him had been on the books even longer. A few thought he had kind eyes and a lovely deep voice on his two-minute video CV.

Graham wrote:

Dear Mr and Mrs Windsor,

I expect this letter will come as a bit of a surprise, not to mention shock!

My mother and father died 62 days ago in an unfortunate lawnmower accident. I do not wish to go into detail at this point in time. Perhaps when we get to know each other better I will tell you the whole tragic story. I comfort myself with the thought that at least they died in the garden, a place they loved.

The artificial waterfall they so lovingly built is cascading as I write. I will get to the nub of this letter without more ado.

It came as an awful shock to me to find out that the 'parents' I had always called 'Mum and Dad' were, in fact, my adoptive parents.

When their wills were read to me there was a codicil letter from my mother (signed by two witnesses) to say that I am the result of a love affair between Prince Charles and Mrs Camilla Parker Bowles.

As you must know, I was born on 21st July 1965 in Zurich, Switzerland, in a private nursing home. How my parents came to adopt me is still a bit of a mystery. All I know is that my 'mother' was desperate to have a baby and that my 'father' was an importer of cuckoo clocks.

As you cannot fail to see, I have enclosed the codicil letter. I await your reply with interest.

All best wishes from your son,

Graham Cracknall aka Windsor-Parker-Bowles

THE CODICIL

Only to be opened on the demise of both John Peter Cracknall and Maria Shirley Cracknall.

Dear Son,

Do not be too downcast because we are both dead. As Mr Fellows, our solicitor, will explain, we have left you the bunga-low, the car and enough money to 'spoil' yourself with now and again.

All we ask is that you take care of Gin and Tonic for the rest of their lives. We know you and Tonic do not always see eye to eye, Graham, but that is because of his diabetes, it makes him snappy and irritable when his blood sugar is low.

He has his insulin injection at eight o'clock every morning. It might be easier if he wears a muzzle until he gets used to you, but you must be firm with him, Graham. Don't let him play you up, he can be a little tinker if he thinks he has got the better of you.

Gin, of course, is a sweetheart. He is used to having a few choc drops at around four o'clock in the afternoon. Please give them to him when Tonic is not looking.

I had better get to the important bit of this letter. Graham, me and your dad are not your real parents. We adopted you a few weeks after you were born on 21st July 1965 in Zurich, Switzerland.

The thing is, Graham, you have got royal blood in you. Your real father is the Prince of Wales and your real mother is Camilla Parker Bowles. So, Graham, you are the rightful second in line to the throne of England. That is the reason we have brought you up knowing about heraldry, British history and royal protocol.

It is up to you, Graham, as to what you do with this knowledge. You may want to remain a private citizen. On the other hand, you might well feel that you need to fulfil your destiny.

You have always been a good son to us and, apart from the incident at scout camp, have given us no trouble. Goodbye, son, and God bless.

Mum and Dad

As the little wooden cuckoo flew out of the clock above his head twelve times, signalling midday, Graham put the two pieces of paper inside an envelope and stuck on a stamp bearing Oliver Cromwell's warty head. After checking that all the doors and windows were locked, that there was nothing boiling on the stove, that the burglar alarm was in operation and that Gin and Tonic were asleep in their respective baskets, Graham slipped a can of pepper spray into his jacket pocket and walked the fifty yards to the postbox on the corner. Within five minutes he was back home and bolting the front door.

Meanwhile, in a locked ward in a hospital for the criminally insane, a patient, Lawrence Krill, was also writing to the future King of England.

Sire,

I beg your indulgence, my liege, to have recognizance of my advice to thee. I have it in my gift to grant you possession of a most wondrous particular: The Lost Crown of England. May my vitals be torn from my living belly if this be not true.

Write to me, do not tarry, my liege. All I ask as a reward is that you touch my scrofulous and most foul body to cure me of the King's Evil. 'Tis this unholy affliction that doth condemn me to endure such cruel incarceration in this most cursed place: The Asylum of Rampton.

May the Almighty anoint thee with blessings.

I am, sire, but a humble and unworthy petitioner,

Lawrence Krill

9

At eight thirty the next morning, the Queen, almost weeping with the pain of toothache, went next door and, without knocking, entered Violet Toby's kitchen, leaving Harris and Susan protesting outside. For a moment, the Queen wondered who the old woman with the mad hair and pale face was, sitting at Violet's little Formica table eating toast with HP sauce. She then realized it was Violet, who had not yet attended to her toilette.

A man with an accent similar to the Queen's was saying on Violet's greasy portable radio, 'The monarchy in this country is dead, defunct. The Royal Family are the woolly mammoths of evolution.'

The Queen said, talking over the radio, 'Violet, I had a dreadful night with toothache. At three o'clock this morning I would have gladly paid somebody to have cut *orf* my head. This pliers woman friend of yours, do you think she could help me?'

Violet turned the radio down and said, ''Ave you took some painkillers?'

The Queen nodded.

'Only I've got some good 'uns that the doctor gave me for my back. I had to cut down on 'em, they turned me into a zombie.'

'At the moment,' said the Queen, 'I find the thought

of being a zombie rather attractive, but I need my wits about me today.'

Violet reached for the telephone and pressed the speed-dial button for her granddaughter, Chantelle, who was at work at the Frank Bruno House nursing home. 'Chan? It's Grandma. You know that woman what takes teeth out . . . ? You do know somebody what takes teeth out. She's married to . . . works at Walkers Crisps. The one with the funny leg . . . you do know him. His sister always sings the *Titanic* song on karaoke night at the One-Stop Centre. Yes, Sheila. Right, you know Sheila's daughter, don't you? . . . Can you ring her and ask her for her aunty's number, the one what takes the teeth out? . . . Good girl. I'm here with the Queen.'

On the radio, a woman with a high-pitched voice was saying that she intended to vote Conservative for the first time in her life, because she wanted to see the Queen back on the throne. The Queen sighed, and clapped her hand over her jaw. Her tongue seemed to have a life of its own. Despite the pain, it kept finding and prodding the wobbly tooth. She wished it would stop.

After Chantelle had rung back, Violet went upstairs to get ready. The Queen fed Micky a few sauce-smeared crusts that Violet had left on her plate. Micky was in a benign mood and allowed the Queen to stroke his coarse ginger hair. The Queen said, 'Have you ever had toothache, Micky? Have you, boy? It's frightful.'

Micky growled, 'I've had toothache for the past three years. Why do you think I keep losing my temper?'

The Queen looked into the dog's eyes and saw that Micky was entirely sympathetic to her plight. Harris and Susan started barking in the street, and Micky ran through the house and hurled himself at the front door. From upstairs, Violet screamed at him to be quiet, and Barry Toby's heavy tread was heard on the stairs. Barry's solicitor habitually described him to the courts as a 'gentle giant' with a 'heart of gold'. Neither of these statements was true. He was tall, and he did have a ladylike demeanour, but his heart was a violent, suspicious organ that had lost him wives, children and jobs.

'Shut the fuck up!' roared Barry, to the furiously barking Micky. Barry then nodded to the Queen and said, 'All right?'

Barry was not much of a conversationalist. The Queen was glad when Violet tottered down the stairs in high heels, with her hair brushed and her face painted. After ordering Barry to behave himself, the Queen and Violet left the house.

Dwayne stood at the entrance to Hell Close. It was the first day he'd been allowed out on patrol without a senior officer. He'd been ordered to carry out spot checks to ensure that the residents were carrying their identity cards. It was impossible to check everyone, so he worked out a system: this morning he'd stop men with beards, anybody with black hair, and old ladies.

After working the last three days in the operations centre, he knew that every move he made was being captured on a screen, so he couldn't let anybody off if they didn't have their ID card with them. When he saw the Queen and Violet Toby approaching, followed by Harris, Susan and Micky, his legs went weak; he was in awe of the Queen.

'Good morning,' he said. 'Could I trouble you ladies for a perusal of your ID cards?'

Why was he talking like an old fart? he thought. How could the wearing of a uniform affect the way he spoke?

Violet said, 'This is the third bleedin' time I've been stopped this week. Why am I being victimized?' She took her card out of her coat pocket and flashed it in front of Dwayne.

The Queen was searching frantically in the compartments of her bag. 'I don't seem to have it with me,' she said with panic in her voice.

Dwayne said, 'I'm sorry, madam, but I have to see it.'

He glanced around at the CCTV cameras perched on top of tall metal poles and wondered if his colleagues at the station were watching and mocking him. Seeing that the Queen was uncharacteristically nervous, Violet had taken charge of looking for the card and was now methodically searching through the Queen's coat, cardigan and trouser pockets.

The Queen said, 'Oh, Harris, where did I put the wretched card?'

Harris growled. '*I haven't had it*, don't look at me.'

Susan yapped at the Queen, 'I know where it is, it's down the back of the sofa.'

Harris began pulling on the bottom of the Queen's trousers; maddened by toothache and anxiety, she smacked him away.

Dwayne said, 'I'll give you twenty-four hours to produce it at the station.' He took out his electronic notebook and, sticking to procedure, he said, 'Name?'

'You know 'oo she is,' said Violet witheringly. 'And I know 'oo you are an' all. You're Dwayne Lockhart. I remember you when you were a rag-arsed kid. Is your mam and dad still alive, or have they finally killed each other?'

Dwayne said, 'Me dad's dead, but Mam's still going strong.' Then, because he was an honest man, he added, 'Well, as strong as a woman with heart disease, cirrhosis of the liver and bipolar disorder can be.

'So, what name do you go by nowadays?' said Dwayne to the Queen. He knew from the history books that the Royal Family changed their names and religion to suit their circumstances.

'My name is Elizabeth Windsor,' said the Queen. 'My registration number is 195311, my tag number is 19531187.' She lifted her trouser leg to the knee and exposed the metal tag.

Dwayne sent them on their way by saying, 'You may resume your perambulations, ladies.'

This caused hilarity back at the station. Inspector Lancer said, 'I shall have to remember that, "You may resume your perambulations, ladies."'

Constable Peter Penny said, 'I'd of just told 'em to fuck off.'

Inspector Lancer said, 'It's all them bleedin' books he reads. He knows too many words.'

As they got nearer Hawthorn Street, where the pliers woman lived, the Queen grew more anxious. Harris and Susan fell silent and pricked up their ears, trying to work out the exact location of Magic, the Dobermann pinscher whose territory they were entering.

Standing in the unkempt front garden of the pliers woman's house was a bitch of such rackety beauty that Harris, an infamous philanderer and connoisseur of bitch loveliness, stopped to gape. She was Britney; she had inherited her father's long legs and blonde coat and her mother's exquisite face and dark long-lashed eyes.

Susan ran up to Britney and sniffed her bum. When she ran back to Harris, Susan reported, 'She's a slag, Harris. Keep away from her.'

But Harris was mesmerized. 'How do you do?' he growled. 'I'm Harris, the Queen's dog.'

Britney lay down, displaying her elegant limbs to their best advantage. 'Am I bovvered?' she said, tossing her blonde head. 'Do I look like I'm bovvered?' she yawned.

Susan yapped, 'Harris! She's had more dogs inside her than the show ring at Crufts!'

But it was too late. Harris lay down beside Britney and began his seduction routine.

A mildly obese teenage girl showed the Queen and Violet into a front room, where to their surprise they joined other people who were sitting around the edges of the room on white plastic garden chairs. Piles of ancient celebrity magazines were stacked on a coffee table. The television in the corner was showing the wedding of the Prime Minister's daughter. The cameras swept around the flower-filled interior of Westminister Abbey, picking out famous faces in the seated congregation. 'Jimmy Savile,' said Violet. 'I thought he was dead.'

'If he's not, he deserves to be,' said the Queen irritably. She had not expected that she would have to wait. After all, it was not as if the pliers woman had a qualification in dentistry. When screams were heard from the next room, the teenage girl came in and turned the volume up on the television. The deep vibrato of the Westminster Abbey organ rattled the pliers woman's sash windows.

Violet Toby said, 'Look, Liz, the Prime Minister's scraping his foot on the steps. He looks like 'e's stepped in dog muck.'

After an hour of agonized waiting for the Queen, the teenage girl came to collect her, saying, 'Mam'll see you now.'

The Queen was shown into the steamy kitchen where a pan was boiling on the stove, watched by a plump woman dressed in Lycra leggings and a white tee shirt, on which was printed the slogan 'NO PAIN, NO GAIN' across the front.

'Won't be a minute,' said the pliers woman. 'Only I 'ave to sterilize between patients, I'm dead careful like that.'

A cigarette burned in an ashtray on the draining board. Every now and then the pliers woman picked up the cigarette and sucked on it as though she was drawing nourishment from it. 'Sit down and take the weight off your legs,' she said, dropping cigarette ash into the pan. The Queen hesitated. It was not too late to apologize for wasting the pliers woman's time, and leave before her consultation began, but she simply could not face another sleepless night. So she sat at the kitchen table and looked at the row of small metal implements laid out on a clean white towel. She recognized some of them: a crochet hook, eyebrow tweezers and a darning needle. A bottle of vodka stood on a tray with a glass next to it.

'I know your daughter-in-law, Camilla,' said the pliers woman, who believed in putting her patients at ease with small talk.

'Oh, really,' said the Queen, who was possibly the world's leading expert on inconsequential chat.

'Yeah. She goes down the One-Stop Centre on Thursdays, karaoke night. She's a mate of that big gob, Beverley Threadgold. Camilla's all right, though.'

'Does Camilla sing?' asked the Queen, who knew very little about nightlife on the estate.

'Yeah, she does. Gloria Gayner, "I Will Survive". She ain't bad, but it don't sound the same in a posh voice. Right, let's get started.'

She put on a pair of Marigold gloves and, using barbecue tongs, grabbed the pliers out of the boiling water. While they cooled she examined the Queen's mouth.

'Yeah, you got a nasty back molar there. I'll soon 'ave that out, it's as wobbly as Pavarotti's arse.'

After asking the Queen 'to keep dead still', she yanked on the tooth with the pliers. The Queen felt a violent pain, which subsided almost immediately.

The pliers woman dropped the tooth into a paper tissue and said, 'That bleeder's better out than in.'

After swilling her mouth out with vodka and spitting into the sink, the Queen said, 'How much do I owe you?'

The pliers woman said, 'Just give us a couple of quid towards the vodka.'

Before she left the kitchen the Queen said, 'I'm terribly grateful.'

The pliers woman said, 'Perhaps you'll remember me when you're back in the palace.'

The Queen could not imagine the extraordinary circumstances that would compel her to call on the services of the pliers woman again, but she said, 'I most certainly will.' Thinking to herself, if the honours system is restored I will recommend the pliers woman gets an OBE, for services to the community.

It should have been the wedding of the year. The guest list was an impressive mix of British society. There was Sir David Frost, Jordan, Cliff Richard, Nancy del'Olio, Frank Bruno, Simon Cowell, Elton John, Peter Mandelson, Sharon and Ozzy Osbourne, Chris Evans, Charlotte Church, Kate Moss, Steve Redgrave, Ben Elton, Carol Thatcher and numerous foreign dignitaries and heads of state. Jeremy Paxman had declined, claiming he had an important fishing match to attend.

Sonia was marrying a public relations executive. There were gratifyingly large crowds outside the Abbey when Jack arrived with her in the open-topped golden coach that Prince Charles and Diana, Princess of Wales, had used many years before. There were some in the crowd of onlookers who thought that this was rather excessive for a proclaimed Republican, and a few brave souls protested. There were shouts of 'You've sold out, Barker' and a madwoman shouted 'Golden coaches for cockroaches!' But the police moved in and dragged the dissidents away, citing the new Disrespect to Those in Public Office Law.

The day was suffused with autumnal sunshine and Sonia looked spectacularly beautiful in her white, strapless, satin dress with the long shimmering train. When Jack stepped out of the carriage, he trod straight into a mound of dog muck that had just been deposited by a sniffer dog with an upset stomach. The dog was Mercury from the Metropolitan Police Bomb Squad. His handler was Sergeant Andrew Crane. (An investigation by the *News of the World* later found that Sergeant Crane had been transferred to the Falkland Islands. Despite an intensive search, Mercury was never traced. Now and again, on a 'slow news day' one of the tabloids will raise the question: What happened to Mercury?)

Jack managed to push Sonia away from the mess on the otherwise immaculately clean red carpet, but his own right shoe was covered in the stinking muck. There was a gasp from the crowd, then a ripple of laughter.

From inside the Abbey came the sound of the organ playing the 'Arrival of the Queen of Sheba'. Jack had no other option but to walk on, up the steps. He hoped there would be an opportunity to clean his shoes before he escorted Sonia down the aisle. But no such opportunity arose.

The smell intensified under the television lights, as Jack and Sonia processed down the aisle. When they passed Cliff Richard, Jack saw the singer wrinkle his nose in disgust. He glanced behind and saw that he had trailed dog muck up the red carpet and that the bridesmaids holding Sonia's train were inadvertently spreading more of the nightmare substance on their white-ribboned ballet shoes.

When they reached the altar, the groom and the best man covered their noses. Jack watched the Archbishop of Canterbury as he struggled with ecclesiastical duty versus human revulsion. Nothing showed on the cleric's face, but when Jack looked down he saw that the Archbishop was wearing open-toed sandals and that he was curling his toes back in an effort to protect them from the pollution. He heard his first wife crying behind him.

At that moment, having ruined his daughter's wedding day and humiliated himself in front of the world, Jack vowed to rid England of dogs.

When the Queen emerged from the pliers woman's
house, holding a clean white handkerchief against her
jaw, she saw, with some disgust, that Harris and Britney
were mating in the middle of the road, and were holding
up the traffic.

Susan ran up to the Queen and howled, 'He's gone
too far this time. He's humiliated me for the last time.'

The Queen made several futile attempts to separate
the conjoined dogs, but nothing would disconnect
them. A van driver at the head of the queue of traffic
sounded his horn and shouted, 'If that was 'umans
doing it in the middle of the road, they'd be arrested.'

Seeing the Queen's distress, Violet went into the
house and came out moments later with a bucket of
water, which she threw over the two trysting dogs. They
flew apart immediately and the Queen angrily clipped
the lead on Harris's collar and dragged him back to Hell
Close.

Several people had stopped her on the way to say
that they would be sorry to see her leaving the Fez.
Maddo Clarke, skunk dealer and single father of seven
unruly boys, said, 'We seen it on the news, 'ow you
might be going home to Buckingham Palace like. I said
to one of my customers, 'ow you brung a bit of class
to the neighbourhood like.'

Violet said, after Maddo had lurched away, 'I know it's not the done thing to talk about why we're all in the Exclusion Zone, but do you know why Maddo got sent here?'

The Queen bent her head to hear Violet's story.

Everyone in Hell Close had at least one dog, except for Maddo Clarke, who had been forbidden by a magistrates court after the five dogs he'd owned at the time had destroyed the council house he rented and made it unfit for human habitation. The Society for the Prevention of Cruelty to Animals had brought a prosecution, claiming that Maddo's dogs were emaciated and covered in sores caused by untreated flea bites. Maddo had defended himself in court, maintaining that a thin dog was a fit dog and that fleas were nature's natural parasites. When the five dogs had been rounded up and taken away, Maddo was bereft; he started drinking heavily and then stumbled into the brotherhood of the drug-dependent.

Finally, when to his great disappointment, his wife Hazel gave birth to a seventh boy, Maddo cracked, and under the influence of drugs and drink tried to snatch a baby girl from a maternity-ward nursery and substitute his newborn son for the day-old child. He was caught trying to remove the kidnapped child's plastic identity bracelet with his teeth, earning him the sobriquet of 'Wolf Man' after a headline in the popular press: 'WOLF MAN GNAWS ON BABY'S ARM.'

For some reason, Maddo had always blamed his five-year prison sentence and subsequent banishment to an Exclusion Zone on dogs.

As Violet and the Queen turned into Hell Close, the Queen saw Camilla in her front garden planting bulbs. Camilla looked up and said, 'Beverley Threadgold told me you were having a tooth pulled by the pliers woman. Was it wretched?'

The Queen prodded the gap where the molar had been with the tip of her tongue and said, 'Not as wretched as watching one's dog copulate in public.'

Later, after a rest on the sofa, the Queen was cleaning her front-room windows when she saw Arthur Grice's yellow Rolls-Royce draw up outside her house. Grice's Dobermann, Rocky, could be seen snarling on the back seat. The Queen ducked out of sight and hoped that Grice was not about to call on her; she was not dressed for company. She was wearing an apron and slippers and had two plastic rollers in the front of her hair.

To her great annoyance, she heard an aggressive knock on the front door. Harris and Susan ran into the hallway and barked their usual hysterical warning. The Queen tore her apron off, snatched the rollers out of her hair and stuffed them into a drawer of the Chippendale bureau in the hall. As she reluctantly opened the door, Arthur Grice removed his custom-made baseball cap and swept it in front of his bulky body with a theatrical gesture, reminiscent of a bad actor in a Restoration drama. He then gave a deep bow and waited for the Queen to speak first.

Arthur had ordered Sandra, his wife, to download and print out a few pages on royal etiquette from the Web. The pages had told him he must not address the Queen first, but must wait until she had spoken to him.

He must not touch her on any part of her body. He must call her 'Your Majesty' the first time he spoke to her, and thereafter call her 'Ma'am'.

After a brief silence, the Queen said, 'Mr Grice, how do you do?'

Grice lifted his head and gave the Queen one of his rarely seen smiles. 'I'm all right, Your Majesty,' he said. 'In fact, I'm champion.'

The Queen led him into the front room; it was the closest she had ever been to Grice. His face and scalp showed the evidence of a life lived in violent confrontation; knives, knuckles and broken bottles had embedded themselves in Grice as he had battled and cheated his way to riches. The Queen did not ask him to sit down and they stood facing each other, Grice's bulk towering over the Queen's slight frame.

The Queen said, 'How may I help you, Mr Grice?'

Grice said, 'It's not so much me I've come about, Ma'am. It's my wife, Sandra.'

The Queen nodded.

Grice rumbled on. 'I don't know if you are aware, Ma'am, but Sandra runs herself ragged for 'er charities.'

'And what are your wife's charities?' asked the Queen.

Grice said, 'She's the one what started VOICE.'

'Voice?' queried the Queen.

Grice said, slowly and carefully, 'Victims Of Incompetent Silicone Enhancement.' He then added, 'She 'ad a boob job what went wrong. One of 'er boobs is twice the size of the other. She's lopsided for life.'

Grice dropped his head and stared gloomily at the floor.

The Queen murmured, 'How very unfortunate.'

Grice said, 'An' she does a lot of work with teenage boys.'

'Very admirable,' said the Queen, who had often seen Mrs Grice driving around the estate playing pounding music in her cabriolet with various louts in the front passenger seat. Mrs Grice had been cosmetically enhanced to such a degree that she looked like a suntanned trainee astronaut undergoing G-force training.

The Queen said, 'And your point is, Mr Grice?'

Grice said, 'You wun't believe the grief she gets from some people. They're jealous of course, she's a beautiful woman an' she ain't ashamed to show her body off. Some people put it about that she's a slag. I had 'em dealt with, but if she was Lady Grice she'd feel a bit better about herself.'

The Queen muttered, 'No doubt.'

Grice said, 'So if you could see yourself honouring her like.'

The Queen played for time, saying, 'Perhaps, in the future . . .'

Grice said, 'Couldn't you give me a knighthood, now, while I'm here. I've gotta sword in the boot of the Rolls.'

The Queen said, 'I'm afraid not, Mr Grice. There is a procedure to be followed . . . advisory committees.'

Grice said, 'But you'll be the Queen again soon. If you wanted to honour a local philanthropist what's overcome all the odds to run the biggest scaffolding business in the Midlands an' who owns an Exclusion Zone, who could stop you?'

The Queen looked up into Grice's scarred face and said, 'I'm afraid my answer is no, Mr Grice.'

'No?' said Grice, who rarely heard the word. 'But I'm the biggest employer on this estate. I break my back for charity. It was me what funded the academy.'

The Queen said, 'We live in an age when every citizen is of equal worth, Mr Grice. I no longer have the power or, quite frankly, the inclination to grant your wish.'

Grice said, 'But I set your grandson on as a scaffolder.'

The Queen said, 'I'm sure William is an excellent scaffolder. He's a very conscientious boy.'

Grice said, more to himself than to the Queen, 'She's ordered new address cards with Sir Arthur and Lady Grice and a coat of arms on 'em. Three scaffolding poles in a triangular configuration with a rampant lion and a panda bear in the centre; she loves pandas.'

The Queen said, 'It was somewhat premature of your wife to have ordered new stationery, Mr Grice.'

'She's an impulsive woman,' said Grice.

He was not looking forward to going home to his restored watermill and telling his wife that he had failed to secure her an honour. She was high maintenance, he thought. He'd spent two hundred and fifty grand on doing the Old Mill up, and his wife was already banging on that the sound of the water got on her nerves.

'Well, perhaps when you leave 'ere, you'll visit me and my wife at home, Your Majesty. We've got a glass floor in the living room so you can watch the water

75

going by. We're both nature lovers,' he said, 'like yourself.'

The Queen gave him one of her frosty smiles but he did not respond. She walked to the front door and opened it, giving Grice no option but to leave the house. Harris and Susan stood on the doorstep barking at the Dobermann on the back seat.

'*Heil*, Rocky, we hope you fall through the glass floor and drown!' barked Harris. Rocky threw himself against the car window in a frenzy of frustrated anger.

Grice shouted, 'Get down, you stupid bleeder!' Once inside the car he added, 'Another do like that, Rocky, and I'll have your balls cut off and fried up for me tea.'

Rocky lay down on the back seat and calmed himself. Grice didn't make idle threats.

The Queen realized she could no longer ignore the possibility that she would have to once again take up her royal duties, and decided that the Royal Family should have a meeting to discuss the possibility of their return to public life. But first she would visit her husband and ask him for advice.

HRH Prince Philip, the Duke of Edinburgh, had been confined to bed for two years after suffering a stroke that snatched away his vision, memory and mobility. He was a long-stay resident in the Frank Bruno House nursing home at the far end of Arthur Road, which ran through the centre of the Fez, a fifteen-minute walk from Hell Close. He languished in a dark back room that he shared with a garrulous former trade union official – the wheelchair-bound Harold Bunion, aka 'Bolshie' Bunion. Bolshie talked in his sleep with the same aggrieved tone he used in the day, when he was fully, aggressively, awake.

The Duke of Edinburgh was confined to his bed and considered himself a prisoner of Bolshie's. He constantly complained to the staff that he had been moved from Heaven, the royal palaces, into Hell, the Fez, and was now living in Purgatory.

Dogs were not allowed inside Frank Bruno House, so the Queen tied Harris and Susan by their leads to a wooden bench bearing a little bronze plaque, on which was written 'This seat is dedicated to the memory of Wilf Toby: 1922–1997'. Until recently, residents of Frank Bruno House had been allowed, even encouraged, to sit on the bench. Others had sat nearby in their wheelchairs, to take the air and watch life on the estate pass by. However, the new manager, Mrs Cynthia Hedge, had stopped this practice. She was a firm-jawed woman who maintained that she was introducing a 'locked-door policy', to protect the residents from a possible terrorist attack.

The Queen pressed the intercom at the side of the door and waited in the cold wind for it to be answered. Eventually a voice crackled something incomprehensible. The Queen shouted, 'It's Elizabeth Windsor,' into the intercom.

Several long minutes passed, during which an old lady in a nightgown, with hair like a dandelion gone to seed, made obscene gestures at the Queen through the plate-glass door. Eventually, Mrs Hedge herself, not often to be seen in contact with the residents, led the old lady away, then returned and opened the door to the Queen.

Mrs Hedge said brusquely, 'Identity card, please.'

The Queen said, 'I'm terribly sorry but I have temporarily mislaid my card.'

'Then I can't let you in,' said Mrs Hedge. 'Now you'll have to excuse me, we are short-staffed. Three of the Somalis have not turned up for work.'

The Queen laughed. She said, 'But you know who I am, Mrs Hedge.' She laughed again and tried to pass through the door.

Mrs Hedge barred her way, saying, 'I'm sorry you have such a light-hearted attitude towards security and the war against terror, Mrs Windsor.'

The Queen said, 'Mrs Hedge, I do not think that Frank Bruno House is a likely target for Hamas or Al Qaeda.'

Mrs Hedge said, 'If I were to let you in without a valid ID card, it would invalidate our insurance.'

Harris jumped up at the Queen and barked, 'Your card is down the back of the sofa! How many more times, woman!'

Susan joined in, barking, 'Take us home and we'll find it for you!'

The Queen shouted, 'Quiet! Quiet! You silly dogs.'

They stopped barking and fell into a sulk. Harris said, 'You try to help them out and what do you get? Abuse.'

Mrs Hedge closed the door. The Queen untied the dogs and dragged them home.

When they arrived at the house Harris and Susan ran

into the sitting room and began to drag the cushions off the sofa. Harris forgot for a moment that he was burrowing into soft upholstery and imagined himself feral, out in the field, digging for a small warm-blooded creature that he could savage, kill and then eat.

The Queen was appalled at Harris and Susan's behaviour. 'You horrid little dogs,' she shouted. 'Look what you've done to my sofa.'

She smacked the dogs away from the torn upholstery. A few goose feathers had escaped from the tapestry cushions and were floating, like tiny feathered gliders, in the air.

Harris growled to Susan, 'Shall I risk another slap and go for it?'

Susan growled, 'If you find her the card there'll be something in it for us. There's a box of mint-flavoured Bonios on the top shelf.'

Before the Queen could replace the cushions, Harris leapt on to the sofa and stuck his muzzle down the back. Ignoring the blows the Queen was raining on him, he pulled out a black Mont Blanc pen, a handkerchief and the mislaid identity card.

The Queen was delighted and said, 'Clever boy, Harris, clever boy!'

Harris and Susan ran into the kitchen and looked up at the top shelf in the small pantry where the Queen kept the dog treats.

'There,' she said, giving each dog a greenish bone-shaped biscuit. 'Eat these and go to your baskets.'

The Queen herself would have liked to rest for a while, she was feeling every one of her eighty years, and her jaw was throbbing, but she had not visited her husband for two consecutive days and she knew that he would be fretting for her. So, after placing her ID card carefully in her handbag, she left the house again, and leaving the dogs to sleep, retraced her steps to Frank Bruno House.

The light was fading when Chantelle Toby, trainee care assistant and sister of Chanel, opened the door to the Queen.

Chantelle said, 'I'm glad you've come, Liz. We've 'ad a right do with 'im. He says 'e's got to go to the trooping of the colour – whatever that is. 'E's asking us to saddle 'is 'orse an' polish the buttons on his uniform.'

The Queen was struck again by Chantelle's beauty; she really does have an exquisite face, thought the Queen. Some genetic malfunction had given her sculpted bones and long limbs, unlike the rest of the Toby clan, who were stumpy and coarse-featured.

The Queen asked, 'For how long has my husband been agitated?'

'I dunno, I've only just come back on duty. I've been off for three days with stress,' Chantelle said.

They passed through the residents' lounge where elderly people with dead eyes were watching Teletubbies cavorting on a flickering television. The smell of urine and cheap disinfectant was overwhelming.

'Why are you stressed?' asked the Queen as they jerked slowly to the second floor, inside a lift only just big enough to take a coffin and two undertakers.

Chantelle sighed and said, 'Sometimes I think I'll never leave the Flowers. I don't think it's fair that I've got to live 'ere just 'cause my family's a nightmare. I ain't done nothing wrong.'

The Queen said, 'I agree, it is terribly unfair.'

'An' this job is the pits,' said Chantelle, lowering her voice as they neared the second floor. 'There ain't enough of us to look after the old people properly, an' Mrs Hedge is a right cow.'

They came out of the lift and passed the open door of Mrs Hedge's office, where she could be heard on the phone giving the weekly food order, '. . . and don't send custard creams again. I'm not made of money.'

Chantelle said, 'This was a lovely place when Grand-dad was 'ere. 'E 'ad a budgie in 'is room and 'e could stay up an' watch the late film.'

The Queen had visited Wilf, Violet's husband, after a stroke had paralysed him and taken his speech. A kinder regime had prevailed then. Wilf's dog, Micky, had been a frequent visitor.

The Queen had been hoping that Harold Bunion would be out; a member of staff occasionally wheeled him to the One-Stop Centre where he borrowed talking books from the small visual impairment section. But Bunion was sitting in his wheelchair in his usual place, by the window. He was dressed in a heavy overcoat, a green woolly hat and a matching scarf. He was listening to an actor reading *Stalin*. When he saw the Queen and Chantelle, he sighed and pressed the pause button on his tape recorder.

The Queen said, 'Are you about to go out, Mr Bunion?'

'No,' said the old man. 'I'm dressed like this because it's as cold as an Eskimo's dick in here.'

'You shouldn't use words like that,' said Chantelle.

'I'm sure the Queen has heard the word "dick" before,' said Bunion.

'No,' Chantelle said. 'You shouldn't use words like "Eskimo", it's against the law. You have to say "Inuit people".'

'Oh, I'm sorry,' said Bunion savagely. 'I meant, of course, to say that it's as cold as an Inuit person's dick in here.'

The Queen sat next to her husband's bed and watched him sleeping. She recalled a visit to Baffin Island, part of northern Canada, when Prince Philip had recited part of 'Eskimo Nell' after an official dinner. He had caused a diplomatic incident and British imports to Canada had dropped by five per cent.

His duvet cover was printed with: 'Property of FBH. Not to be removed from the premises.' As if anybody would want to steal the horrid thing, thought the Queen, smoothing the worn grey cotton.

Prince Philip opened his eyes. 'He's been torturing me with Stalin's biography, Lilibet,' he groaned.

Bunion shouted. 'By talking when I'm trying to listen 'e's infringing my 'uman rights. I'll take it to the European Parliament if 'e don't stop.'

'Oh, my dearest darling,' whispered the Queen, looking at her husband's gaunt face and skeletal fingers. 'Have you been eating?'

'Can't eat,' he said hoarsely.

'He can't hold a knife or fork an' 'e struggles with a spoon,' said Bunion.

There was a tray on Prince Philip's bedside table. The

Queen lifted the metal cover from a plate of food. In the middle of the plate were a few spoonfuls of congealed grey mince, and two scoops of off-white potato. A few soggy diced vegetables were scattered around the edge of the plate. The Queen shuddered and replaced the metal cover. She took her husband's cold hands between her own and examined him closely. He hadn't been shaved and he was still wearing the pyjamas he'd been in three days before, when she had last seen him.

Bunion said, 'I tried to get some water down him last night, but I can't get near enough in my wheelchair.'

'Did you ring the bell?' asked the Queen, alarmed at the implications behind Bunion's statement.

Bunion said, 'I rang the bell, but nobody came. Nobody ever comes.'

Chantelle looked up from making Bunion's bed and said, 'The night staff are lazy bleeders.'

The Queen peeled back the sheets and blankets and saw at once that her husband's pyjamas were wet. She tried to soothe his agitation by saying, 'I'm going to change your pyjamas, darling. You seem to have spilt water in your bed.'

In the narrow wardrobe allocated to him she found a collection of mismatched pyjama tops and bottoms. None of them belonged to him. When she and Chantelle removed his wet pyjamas, both of them were shocked by the angry-looking bedsores that had developed on the pressure points of his body. His heels, buttocks and elbows were fiery red.

Bunion said, 'This is a care home, Mrs Windsor. But nobody cares.'

Chantelle said, 'That ain't fair, Harold. I fetched you that Stalin tape from the library, didn't I?'

Bunion shouted back, 'I asked for a biography of Marx.'

Chantelle said, 'The woman in the library said they was both Commies and that you wouldn't mind.'

The Queen said, 'Please ask Mrs Hedge to come here, would you, Chantelle? And bring some clean bed linen back with you.'

As the Queen washed and creamed her husband's emaciated body, Bunion said, 'We live in harsh times, Mrs Windsor. Do you remember the fifties?' Without waiting for an answer, he continued. 'The summers were hot, the winters were cold. We children had free milk and orange juice. The National Health Service looked after us from the cradle to the grave. There was plenty of work for your dad and your mam. There were songs on the radio that you could dance to. There was no such thing as bloody teenagers. We'd never heard of stress. If you were a clever-clogs you could go to university and it wouldn't cost your mam and dad a penny. They scrapped national service, and if you went into hospital the matron would make bloody certain that none of her patients got bed-sores.'

Mrs Hedge stood half in and half out of the doorway as though matters of great importance and urgency would not allow her to fully enter the room. She said, 'You wanted to see me?'

The Queen said, 'My husband's condition has deteriorated, Mrs Hedge.'

'How?' she asked.

Bunion said, 'If this was the fifties, you'd have been out on your arse, Mrs Hedge.'

Chantelle came into the room holding freshly laundered white linen.

When Mrs Hedge looked at Prince Philip's bedsores, she said, 'I'm not responsible for nursing care. I'll ask our duty doctor, Dr Goodman, to call in.'

The Queen said, 'As you must know, Mrs Hedge, Dr Goodman was struck off for gross incompetence. I saw him only a few days ago, sitting on the doorstep of Grice's Off-Licence, drinking from a bottle of Burgundy.'

Chantelle put her arm around the Queen and said, 'I'll look after Prince Philip. I'll make sure he gets fed an' I'll put cream on 'is bum an' that.'

Mrs Hedge said, 'I shall record in the incident book that your husband was offered medical assistance but you declined on his behalf.'

When Mrs Hedge left the room, the Queen and Chantelle dressed Prince Philip in clean pyjamas, and stripped and remade his bed.

The Queen said, 'I would love to take him home, Chantelle, but as you can see, it took two of us to lift him. He's a tall man, and I'm a short woman.'

Chantelle turned the thermostat up on the radiator and wheeled Bunion out of the room, saying, 'Come and sit in the lounge until the room warms up.'

When they were alone, the Queen said to her husband, 'Darling, I need your advice. Would you mind terribly if I were to abdicate?'

Prince Philip moved his head slightly. It was not a definitive no, but then neither was it a definite yes.

The Queen waited until he had gone to sleep before she felt able to go home.

Boy English had been holed up in a conference room at New Con headquarters for most of the morning, with a team of advisers hammering out the script of his first party political broadcast. The room was low-ceilinged and brightly lit. The windows were sealed shut and the air conditioning was too cold for comfort. Sandwiches had been sent for, and to Boy's disgust each one had been contaminated with mayonnaise. Eventually, at twelve thirty, the script had been printed out and copies were handed around for a final edit.

PARTY POLITICAL BROADCAST

The film opens with Boy and his wife in their IKEA bed romping with their young children.

Voice-over Boy: I care deeply about the future of this wonderful country. I care even more about my family.

Cut to Boy bathing the children.

Voice-over Boy: I'm a hands-on kinda dad. I cut the umbilical cords for both my kids.

Close shot: Boy has bubbles on nose.

Voice-over Boy: My children bring me down to earth.

Close shot: kid laughing in the bath.

Voice-over Boy: They keep me in touch with what really matters.

Cut to Boy taking wife a cup of tea in bed.

Voice-over Boy: I believe that women have had a rough deal over the years.

Cut to Boy walking a dog in an urban street and stopping to talk to a pensioner.

Voice-over Boy: My constituency is also my community. Walking the dog keeps me in touch. I'm always willing to talk to my constituents.

Cut to Boy riding his bike while listening to rock music on his iPod.

Voice-over Boy: The bike keeps me fit, it gets me to work, and I can listen to some of my music at the same time.

Cut to Boy laughing with a black policeman at the House of Commons.

Voice-over Boy: I love this place, it truly is the Mother of all Parliaments.

Cut to Boy in his office at Westminster with his secretary in a wheelchair.

Voice-over Boy: My staff are more than my employees, they've become friends I can trust. Trust is everything.

Cut to a recording of Boy at Prime Minister's Questions, asking the PM why the Government is banning novelty slippers, confirming that his wife bought him novelty reindeer slippers for Christmas.

Boy: Mr Speaker, why, when the country is facing unprecedented economic challenges is the Government fiddling around with legislation to ban stepladders and novelty slippers? My wife bought me a pair of reindeer slippers for Christmas and I'm rather fond of them.

Cut to laughter of New Cons and shot of Speaker laughing – calling for order. Then cut to Boy on a football pitch coaching multi-ethnics, both boys and girls (background sound).

Voice-over Boy: Football is a major passion of mine; my team is Tower Hamlets Juniors.

Cut to Boy and his wife entering a pub with a dog. They go into the public bar.

Voice-over Boy: Once a week my wife and I leave our children in the capable hands of my mother-in-law and we have a night out together. We've made some good mates in our local pub.

Close shot: Boy drinking a pint with an Asian man in a turban.

Voice-over Boy: I want to live in a society . . .

Close shot: Boy's wife and Asian women in saris playing darts.

Voice-over Boy: . . . that embraces multi-ethnicity . . .

Cut to Boy walking in a gay and lesbian parade with a gay Chelsea Pensioner who is carrying a placard reading 'Gay and Proud'.

Voice-over Boy: . . . and sexual tolerance.

*Cut to footage of the Royal Family on the balcony at
Buckingham Palace.*

Voice-over Boy: Above all, I love our Royal Family.

Fade in soundtrack of 'Land of Hope and Glory'.
Fade out music and dissolve into Boy addressing the viewer.

Boy: I give you this promise. If you vote New Con, we will bring
our Royal Family back from their cruel exile and place them
where they belong, at the head and heart of our country.

*Bring music back up. Closing shot of Boy wiping tears from
his eyes.*

When Boy finished reading, he looked around at his
advisers and said, 'I love all that stuff about my dog.
The problem is, I haven't got a fucking dog.'

'Even better,' said an excited media adviser. 'We'll
film you saving one from a rescue centre.'

'Not Battersea,' said another adviser, 'the Chancellor
has already done that, the opportunistic bastard.'

'I'll get one from my constituency,' said Boy. 'All
politics is local.'

The script was adjusted accordingly and a visit to
Norfolk was hastily arranged for later that afternoon.

As they were shuffling their papers together and closing their laptops, Boy said, 'I don't have to keep this
fucking dog, do I? I can't stand the bloody things.'

'No,' said a press adviser. 'It can go missing. We
could spin it out for weeks.' The adviser began to fore-

see the press campaign, saying, 'I can see it now, Boy tramping the streets looking for his lost dog. You could give one of your "blinking back tears" interviews, Boy.'

Boy said, 'Good work, team. Win, win, eh?'

Dwayne was sitting with five other trainees including Peter Penny in an improvised classroom at the Control Centre. Inspector Lancer was giving a lecture on 'patriotic protection'. A stun gun was being passed from hand to hand around the small room.

Lancer was saying, 'A stun gun is a most effective non-lethal weapon. If you're attacked by Exclusion Zoners, or threatened by one of their mad dogs, don't panic or cry for your mother. You only need to touch your attacker with one of these stun guns for three or, in the case of fat bastards, five seconds. The high-voltage shock will immobilize them for a few minutes: long enough to get a few hard kicks in, eh lads?'

Dwayne handed the stun gun back to the inspector. He could think of no circumstances in which he would use the horrible thing. Inspector Lancer patted the stun gun fondly, as though it were a household pet.

Lancer continued, 'Life in the Exclusion Zones is full of danger; your average street is chock-a-block with ruthless criminals, terrorists and the like, and because lily-livered poofs like Prince Charles cry into their lentils at the very mention of arming the police with AK47s, we have to settle for the next best thing. So, now I turn to the Grice taser gun, which happens to be a particular favourite of mine. If you've been attacked by an assailant before you'll know how important it is to have a powerful weapon.' He took the little taser gun from the holster around his waist and said, 'Come up here, Dwayne.'

Dwayne got up from his chair reluctantly, keeping his eyes on the small black gun; Lancer waved him to the end of the room. Dwayne stood with his back against the wall.

Lancer said, 'Just point and shoot the taser at your assailant. The taser will fire wires up to a range of fifteen feet and attach themselves by little hooks to the assailant's clothing, thereby sending powerful "T" waves through the wires into their scumbag bodies. This will jam the criminal's nervous system. The sudden deadlock will cause total incapacitation.'

Lancer pulled the trigger of the gun and two wires shot out and attached themselves to Dwayne's jacket. Dwayne screamed in agony, dropped to the floor, curled into a foetal position and lay there, motionless. Peter Penny rose to his feet, then sat down again.

Lancer carried on addressing the rest of the group, 'This will give you time to leave the location or call for reinforcements. The Grice taser gun does not cause long-term damage, you'll be pleased to know, Dwayne, and it's more effective and faster than poncy chemical sprays. So that's your common or garden taser. Any questions?'

'How much do they cost, sir?' asked Peter Penny when it became obvious that no one else was going to speak.

'They'll cost you about five hundred quid a go.'

'They'll cost *us*?' checked Peter Penny.

Inspector Lancer gave Dwayne a gentle kick to check that he was still alive. 'Yes,' he said. 'Mr Grice has generously offered to accept four easy payments of one hundred and twenty-five pounds to be docked out of your wages over the coming months.'

After fifteen minutes Dwayne had recovered enough to be able to sit up and accept a glass of water from Peter Penny. When Lancer came over to him to take his order for the taser, Dwayne said, 'I think I'll pass on it, sir.'

Lancer said, 'Think again, lad. From today a taser is considered to be essential equipment, and you can't work for Grice Security without one.'

'And they're not provided free?' checked Dwayne.

'No,' said Lancer. 'Mr Grice is not made of money.'

Boy had represented the Great Clutterbuck constituency in Norfolk for five years. He had won the seat with a majority of over five thousand when the incumbent Member of Parliament had been discovered pocketing some of the funds of a children's hospice. Boy hardly ever visited Great Clutterbuck. It was difficult to get there by car, the trains were infrequent and overcrowded and the local airport closed down at 5 p.m. Few of his constituents noticed his absence. He kept the elderly women activists happy by attending the Christmas Fayre, the Easter Bonnet Competition, the Summer Fête and the annual Bonfire Party held in the grounds of nearby Sandringham House on November the fifth.

His constituency agent, a retired butcher, Derek Proudfoot MBE, dealt with the usual tedious constituency problems: complaints about damp housing, demands for zebra crossings and the constant drip of grievances against Vulcan, the government computer which, when it was not erroneously paying pensioners a million pounds a week, was expecting single parents to live on one pound ten pence for the same period. Boy loathed the flat vastness of the horizon that surrounded Great Clutterbuck. He found the local accent incomprehensible and his wife complained that it was impossible to find focaccia in the village shop.

It was sunny when a convoy of 4 x 4s swept along Great Clutterbuck High Street on its way to the 'Fossdyke Rescue Centre', where a madwoman, Ms Fossdyke, harboured stray dogs from the Greater Norfolk Area. Ms Fossdyke patrolled the byways in a converted ambulance on a constant lookout for down-and-out dogs. When Boy's press officer had rung her to ask if she would object to being filmed helping Boy choose a dog, she had hesitated. When an 'incon-venience fee' of three hundred and fifty pounds was mentioned, she agreed.

It was grisly filming. Boy had to trudge in his wellingtons up and down the narrow cinder path in front of the cages of rescued dogs, trying to look inter-ested. Nothing went right. The dogs seemed to take an instant dislike to him.

The director said to Ms Fossdyke, 'Isn't there a sweet little puppy with, you know . . . big eyes?'

'There's Tommy,' Ms Fossdyke croaked. 'He's got a thyroid complaint.'

The director had already decided that Ms Fossdyke would be edited out of the footage. She was alarmingly eccentric. Boy thought, if I was told by somebody that Ms Fossdyke had been suckled by wolves, I'd believe them.

In a break from filming caused by a series of low-flying jets, a car drew up in the lane at the end of the drive to the kennels. A door opened then slammed shut. The car sped away, with a melodramatic squeal of its brakes. Ms Fossdyke excused herself, saying, 'Another poor wretch.' She lurched away down the drive.

She came back holding a potato sack tied at the top with many knots. The sack was moving, something was whimpering inside. The cameraman shouted, 'Wait,' as Ms Fossdyke began to undo the knots.

The director shouted, 'Boy, I want you in shot. Ms Fossdyke, fuck off and let Boy open the sack.'

Boy said, 'I'm not up to date with my tetanus shots. Let her open the sack.'

Ms Fossdyke's knobbly fingers picked at the few final knots and a little black-haired puppy blinked in the daylight. There was a collective, 'Aah.' Boy put his hand out and the little dog licked his fingers. Once again the crowd of onlookers said, 'Aah.'

Boy picked the dog out of the sack and cradled it in his arms, saying into the camera, with a wavering voice that was not entirely bogus, 'I've found my dog.'

The director shouted, 'Cut! Make-up, our little friend in the sack looks a bit too healthy for a puppy that's just been dumped. Break it down a bit, will you? Give it a bit of wear and tear.'

Boy was overwhelmed by the immediate love he felt for this little nameless dog. He had witnessed his eldest child, Dora, being born, but when the midwife had passed the baby to Boy, his main emotion had been relief that his wife, Cordelia, had stopped screaming, and he was glad when the midwife took the child away to be cleaned and weighed. But now he held on to the little dog and would not allow the make-up artist or anybody else to take it from him.

To break the long drive back to London, Boy and his entourage called on Stephen Fry. They knew he would be at home in his old mellow-bricked rectory because he was under house arrest. He'd been found guilty at Norwich Crown Court of 'inappropriate and deliberate mockery of the authorities'.

Boy had previously met Fry at the opening of a new pig-slaughtering house in Watton. Until very recently, Fry had been a National Treasure and Boy's most famous constituent. His trial had been seen as a watershed: many comedians had fled the country and were living, for some inexplicable reason, in Belgium.

As they drove down the country lanes that led to Fry's house, Boy sat with the dog on his lap, addressing it directly, talking gibberish. His advisers debated among themselves about what the dog should be called.

'The name needs to be politically expedient,' said one.

'It needs to appeal to a wide demographic,' said another.

Boy said, 'Fuck all that, his name is Billy.'

Fry came to the door, accompanied by a lolloping chestnut-coloured dog with sad eyes and long drooping ears.

'This is Chaucer,' said Fry. 'He won't hurt you, though he has a vicious tongue.'

Chaucer looked up at Billy, who was still in Boy's arms, and asked, 'How old are you?'

Billy said, 'Three months.'

'Three months!' said Chaucer. 'I'm a very old dog. Is he your first owner?'

'No,' said Billy. 'My first owner didn't like me peeing in his shoes. He threw me into a black bag and dumped me on the side of the road.'

Chaucer appraised Boy, who was talking and laughing with Stephen Fry on the doorstep.

Chaucer said, 'A word of advice, young fellow. Whatever your opinions, keep them to yourself. Our masters like us to have spirit, but not independence. Fry is a good master, I can't fault him — apart from a tendency he has to open his heart to me. He tells me things that frankly, Billy, I don't want to hear. He's not as confident as he looks. Bless him.'

Boy asked Fry how he was finding house arrest.

Fry said, 'I'm having a splendid time. I read, I fart about in the house; I drop to my knees every day in thanks to Jack Barker. He's given me a lovely, albeit enforced, holiday.'

Boy asked, 'Are you doing any work at all?'

Fry drawled, 'I scribble a few words now and then, when the fancy takes me.'

Boy took this to mean that Fry was writing another book. He said, 'I wondered if I could count on your support, Stephen?'

Fry said, enigmatically, 'I wonder. Pray, do tell me how your policies differ from those of your rivals.'

Boy said, 'There's no point in pretending that we'd manage the economy any better: the western world is on the same fiscal treadmill, but the Cromwellians are against the monarchy and dogs, and we New Cons are very much for them.'

Fry said, 'The paucity of your ambitions will, I expect, be matched by the parochialism of their execution.'

Boy was unsure if he had been insulted or not. He

said, 'If you vote for me, and I win, Stephen, you'll be released immediately from house arrest.'

Fry said, 'Oh dear, and I was so enjoying my sojourn in the country.'

Boy said, 'Can we use a photograph of you and Chaucer in our election campaign?'

Fry said, 'If I did that, Boy, I'd risk being sent to the Cromer Exclusion Zone. Which truly would be a fate worse than death.'

As Boy turned to leave, Chaucer barked to Billy, 'Good luck, and remember to use your eyes. They can't resist our eyes.'

13

Arthur Grice was staring gloomily through the glass in his living-room floor to the fast-running mill stream below. The branch of a tree had wedged itself in the narrow channel and had gathered around itself an old Coke can, several plastic bags and, to Grice's disgust, a condom which, full of water, mocked Grice's male appendage. Grice was trying to work out how to clear the rubbish. He had invited several VIPs to a cocktail party that evening, and he had wanted to impress them with the Old Mill's outstanding feature. He had rehearsed in his mind the moment when, having gathered his guests in a circle around the glass floor, he would use the remote control to switch on the lights that illuminated the millstream. He anticipated the gasps of amazement and the cries of, 'Wow!'

Sandra, his wife, had told the snooty estate agent, employed to find them a character property, that the house must have 'the wow factor'. Arthur wondered if, in the hour before the guests were due to arrive, he could borrow a small child from somewhere and get the kid to jump in the stream and free the branch and the rubbish.

Sandra called to him from the hot tub on the veranda outside the living room. He slid open the glass doors and removed his terry-towelling robe. As he climbed

into the tub Sandra closed her eyes against his naked-
ness. Her new breasts bobbed above the bubbling water
like two huge pink ping-pong balls. Arthur was dying
to get his hands on them but Sandra had told him
that her breasts must not be touched or fondled for
at least eighteen months. Arthur preferred his wife's
old, original breasts. They were less intimidating, and
friendlier, he thought.

Sandra said, 'How did you get on with the Queen,
then?'

Arthur sighed, 'I done everything right, din't lay a
finger on her, I called her by the right names, but she
din't seem keen on giving us a title, Sandra.'

Sandra said, 'We work our fingers to the bone, Arthur,
and what do we get for it? A slap in the fucking face.'

They talked for a while about the various Grice
businesses. Sandra said, 'We've got so much money in
the bank, I'm running out of ways to spend it, but do
you know what we 'aven't got?'

Arthur didn't know. As far as he was concerned
they'd got it all: electric curtains, gigantic plasma tellies
on the wall of every room, white carpets throughout,
an Italian coffee-making machine, a French stove, an
American fridge, four cars in the garage. 'What ain't we
got?' he asked, genuinely wanting to know.

'Respect,' she said, examining her red-painted nail
extensions. 'People think we're common. I want to be
respectable, Arthur. I want to mingle with people with
class, and a bit of refinement.'

Arthur took her hand. She was asking for the one
thing he could not give her.

She cried, 'I'm fucking sick of havin' friends called Mad Mick or Brutal Bob, even your mam's called Knuckles Nora!'

Arthur took umbrage and said, 'You're going too far now, Sandra. It's years since me mam 'ad a fistfight.'

Arthur's mother, Nora, was downstairs preparing food for the cocktail party. She lived in the granny annexe that had been converted from a building where sacks of grain were once stored. Arthur worshipped his mother, and she worshipped him. In Nora's eyes Arthur had thrown himself away on Sandra, who she considered to be 'as spoilt as a sailor's arse'.

'You could go on a "Find Your Inner Princess" course,' said Arthur. 'The Queen's butler is running one at Cavendish Manor. We done a scaffolding job there. You could learn to talk better and how to lay a table and 'ow to geddout of a car without showing your fanny.'

Sandra said unenthusiastically, 'I went on a course once and I ended up on probation.'

Arthur said, placatingly, 'Yeah, but that yoga wanker was asking to be duffed up. This course is a different barrel of monkeys, it's five grand a week, and you'd be mixing with near aristocracy.'

Nora Grice slid open the glass doors and shouted, 'I've done the cheese an' pineapple, and the chipolatas are in the oven. I'll get off now, I've got to change the bandages on me legs.'

Arthur said, 'Thanks, Mam.'

Sandra said, 'Nora, if you're thinking of joining us later, have a shave first, will you?'

Nora stomped away on her ulcerated legs.

Arthur said, 'I'll ring that butler bloke tomorrow and get you a place.'

Sandra said, despondently, 'Don't bother, Arthur. You can't teach an old dog new tricks.'

'But you can!' said Arthur. He called Rocky upstairs and tried to get the puzzled dog to sit upright on his hind legs.

When Rocky repeatedly fell over, Grice lost his temper and kicked Rocky across the decking, saying, 'You're neither use nor ornament.'

Rocky growled, 'Kick me again and I'll rip your throat out,' then turned and ran downstairs.

Later that evening, as Arthur and Sandra were chatting to their guests, most of whom were drawn from the professional criminal classes, Arthur mentioned with apparent nonchalance that he had been talking to the Queen earlier in the day, in her own home. 'A very nice lady,' said Arthur, 'very regal. I'd lay my life down for 'er.'

There was loud assent from the criminals, their wives and girlfriends, all of whom considered themselves to be true patriots.

Later, one of the criminals sidled up to Arthur and, putting his mouth close to Arthur's ear, said, 'There's a story doing the rounds, that the Queen has got the Imperial State Crown 'idden somewhere in her 'ouse. It's said by them in the know, that the crown is priceless, Arthur, and we all know how much that is, don't we?'

Arthur said, 'Anybody what even *thinks* of 'avin' that crown away is already dead: 'is legs is in concrete buckets. 'E's 'anging from a meat hook. 'E's falling from an 'igh building. In fact, I'm startin' to feel very sorry for that bloke.'

After their guests had departed and Nora was washing up downstairs, Arthur said, 'I think that went well, don't you?'

Sandra yawned, 'Apart from your mother's shaving cuts. She might have wiped the blood off before she went round with the chipolatas.'

14

Camilla was having her hair coloured in Beverley Threadgold's spectacularly untidy kitchen, where a small television was balanced precariously on a cluttered work surface. Camilla was slightly alarmed at the eye-watering strength of the peroxide solution that Beverley was sloshing on to her hair. She said, 'Bev, are you an experienced colourist?'

Beverley bridled and said, 'I've only ever had one client whose hair fell out.'

In her youth Beverley had been briefly apprenticed to a unisex salon in the town. She was still at the shampooing and sweeping-up stage when she had been dismissed for 'gross insubordination' after her malicious gossip caused two clients, the wife and the mistress of a third client, to fight among the washbasins in the salon. The subsequent car chase had escalated into tragedy: an attempted murder charge, a hospital admission and a botched suicide.

Camilla had been reluctant to entrust her hair to Beverley, but she couldn't bring herself to go to Grice's salon, Pauper's, again. Not after the last time, when a sixteen-year-old boy stylist had minced up and told her that her hairstyle, the one she had kept for over thirty years, made her look like 'one of them old women what models thermal underwear on the back pages of pensioner magazines'.

Camilla was always careful what she said in front of Beverley, who had a gift for wheedling things out of one. Only yesterday Beverley had caused trouble on the estate by claiming she had seen Mr Anwar, the highly prudish owner of the 'Everything A Pound' shop, sneaking into the entrance of Grice-A-Go-Go, the pole-dancing club in the shopping parade. The gentleman in question had not been Mr Anwar, but a similar-looking, morbidly obese, middle-aged Hindu, an environmental health inspector, making a professional visit. Mrs Anwar had still not returned from her brother's house, where she had fled to avoid the scandal.

Beverley had once auditioned to work in Grice-A-Go-Go, but Arthur Grice had laughed at her performance on the pole and told her to come back when she had lost four stone. Beverley had gone home and told Vince she'd got the job but couldn't take it because she'd been allergic to the pole. 'I forgot, I can only wear precious metal,' she had lied.

Beverley stuffed Camilla's dripping hair into a plastic shower cap and said, 'Maddo Clarke told me he saw Princess Michael taking her Louis Vuitton luggage down from her attic.'

'How would Maddo know?' asked Camilla, who was certain that Maddo Clarke had never set foot inside Princess Michael's house.

'He's a peeping Tom,' said Beverley, matter-of-factly.

Camilla said, 'What's the significance of the luggage?'

Beverley said, 'She's planning to go back to London, after the election.'

Camilla said, 'The New Cons don't stand a chance of being elected.'

'I dunno,' said Beverley, looking at the television where Boy English was shown in flattering profile being interviewed on *Politics F'da Yoot*.

'I wun't climb over 'im to make a cup of cocoa,' said Beverley.

Camilla said, 'He's terribly nice. I knew his mother, in the old days.'

Beverley said, 'Do you miss your old life, Camilla?'

Camilla said, 'Oh, I *ache* for it sometimes. But what else could I do? I was terribly in love with Charles.'

Beverley sighed and said, 'An' you gave it all up for love, like me. I'd have been a famous actress by now if I hadn't bumped into Vince's dodgem car an' broke 'is nose.'

Beverley locked the door and drew the kitchen curtains against the snooping cameras, and they lit cigarettes.

Camilla said, 'I hope Boy doesn't get elected, Bev. I couldn't bear to be the wife of the King of England.'

Beverley's eyes widened, she pounced on to this titbit like a tiger leaping on to a soft-eyed antelope and said, 'Charlie can't be the King until the Queen is dead.' She gasped. 'Don't tell me the Queen is dying! Oh, my God! What's she got? A bad heart? Cancer? TB? How long's she got to live?'

Camilla's scalp felt as though it was on fire. She said,

'Bev, I'm terribly sorry, but there's something dreadfully wrong with my scalp.'

Beverley pulled up the shower cap and inspected Camilla's scalp. 'Fuckin' 'ell,' she said. 'Get your head under that cold tap, quick.'

When Camilla's hair had been towelled dry and the fire in her scalp had almost subsided, they watched the remainder of the Boy English interview.

As a concession to the young viewing audience Boy had left off his tie and was wearing jeans and an open-necked pink shirt. Together with his stylist he had agonized about trainers. Should he buy some, and if so, which brand? He had tried a few pairs on in the privacy of his office, but he decided that he looked ridiculous in them, and anyway, they made him feel as though he had bloody mattresses for feet. He much preferred to feel the hard ground when he walked.

The interviewer was a black girl called Nadine, who spoke in a form of 'Yoof' speak he could barely understand. He got through by doing a lot of quick summations but really, he thought, this is worse than doing bloody *Beowulf* at Oxford. He had just finished talking about his passion for Bob Marley and Puff Daddy when Nadine hit him below the belt by saying in very clear English indeed, 'Boy, do you still have a serious cigarette habit?'

Boy had a split second in which to think. If he admitted he was a smoker, he was jeopardizing his chances of winning the next election. If he said he was a non-smoker, he might be exposed as a liar. Perhaps somebody had evidence; but he didn't know how. He only ever smoked in his own house these days, when his wife was out, with the blinds drawn and an extractor fan going. In the recent past he had visited Gasper's, one of the private smoking clubs that had sprung up in Soho, but he could no longer take the risk, not now his face was so well known.

Boy put on his 'I'm going to make a brave statement now' expression and said, 'Nadine, I'm going to be absolutely straight with you. In my youth I experimented with cigarettes, most people did. I was anxious to fit in with my peers.' He ducked his head and gave a shy smile, 'I was not a confident youngster, I thought that cigarettes would make me look cool. I got drawn into it when I was seventeen, in my last year at school.'

Beverley, watching at home, said, 'What took him so long? I were on twenty a day by the time I was fourteen.'

In the studio, Boy was saying, 'I bought an expensive lighter. Soon there were ashtrays in every room, then, before I knew it, I was up to ten a day.'

Beverley snarled, 'Amateur.'

Boy lowered his eyes. His lashes, enhanced by a touch of midnight-black Maybelline, fluttered against his pale skin. This single gesture won him hundreds of thousands of votes from a particular demographic: women, ex-smokers.

'What about the Exclusion Zones, will you keep them?'

Boy said carefully, 'We are currently reviewing the situation. Exclusion Zones have undoubtedly had a part to play in making the streets safer for hard-working, taxpaying families.'

Nadine said, 'OK. Now I'm gonna ask you to do our quick quiz. Which jeans, Levi's or Wrangler?'

Boy answered, 'Levi's.'

Nadine asked, 'Who's your favourite slapper, Jordan or Jodie?'

Boy hesitated; he didn't want to antagonize either slapper's supporters.

'Pass,' he laughed.

Nadine's next question was easier to answer, 'Queen Elizabeth or Queen Camilla?'

'Oh, I think Queen Camilla,' he said, without hesitation.

Camilla could not help feeling pleased, though the thought of actually being the Queen of England horrified her.

Vince Threadgold almost fell through the kitchen door. King followed him in.

'You've bin drinkin',' accused Beverley.

'It's our lad's birthday,' slurred Vince.

'I know *that*,' said Beverley savagely.

'King's birthday?' asked Camilla, stretching her hand out to stroke the old Alsatian. 'How old is he?'

There was an uncharacteristic silence from the Threadgolds, as both waited for the other to speak. Eventually Vince said, 'We 'ad a lad, Aaron. He were born thirty years ago.'

''E was took off us by social services,' said Beverley, lighting another cigarette even though the first was still smouldering in the ashtray.

''E kept breakin' 'is bones,' said Vince.

'An' they thought me an' Vince was doin' it,' said Beverley.

'I knew *I* weren't,' said Vince, 'so I thought Bev must 'ave been.'

'An' I knew *I* weren't,' said Beverley, 'so . . .'

'So how *did* he break his bones?' asked Camilla.

''E 'ad brittle bone disease,' said Beverley with a ghastly smile, 'but by the time social services found out, 'e'd bin adopted, an 'e didn't know us.'

Beverley's face crumpled, 'An' now 'e won't want to know us, will 'e? Not living in an Exclusion Zone.'

Vince patted Beverley's shoulder.

Camilla said, 'Children always want to know their blood parents, Bev. He'll come looking for you, one day.' She left as soon as decency allowed.

By six o'clock in the evening, a story had spread around the estate that the Queen had six months/two weeks/ days to live, because she was suffering from heart disease/leukaemia/tuberculosis. It took only a few hours for the rumour about the Queen's imminent death to reach Prince Charles; Maddo Clarke told him at the frozen-food cabinet in Grice's Food-Is-U.

'Sorry to 'ear 'bout your mam,' said Maddo. 'I only seen her today, an' I thought she looked a bit green round the gills.'

Charles took a step back from Maddo's beery breath and said, 'Yes, she's been in dreadful pain, but she'll be perfectly all right soon.'

'Yeah,' said Maddo, 'it'll be a merciful release.'

Charles frowned and thought, Mummy's toothache can't be pleasant but it hardly warrants the tears in Maddo's eyes.

'It must be 'ard for you,' said Maddo. 'Seeing as 'ow close you are to your mam.'

'Well, I'll certainly be glad when it's all over,' said Charles, as he searched fruitlessly through the cabinet for a frozen organic chicken.

'Can't bear to see 'er suffer, eh?' Maddo put a tattooed hand on Charles's shoulder.

Charles gave up looking for an organic chicken, and the cooking instructions on the battery chickens appeared to be written in Chinese anyway. He moved on down the aisle to the greengrocery section.

Maddo followed him, saying, 'I never got over my mam's passin'. When she took bad they 'ad to get the fire service to lift her out of the bedroom.'

'Whatever for?' asked Charles.

'She were quite a *big* lady,' said Maddo. 'She were forty-two stone at the end.'

'How appalling,' said Charles.

'It weren't 'er fault!' said Maddo angrily. 'Nobody can 'elp their glands, can they?'

'Indeed not,' said Charles. 'I meant, how appalling for you.'

'I worshipped that woman,' Maddo said, openly crying. 'When we buried her, a pizza box blew into the grave. It were a sign from Mam that she were all right.'

Charles put his wire basket down and his arms around Maddo, who was now distraught and attracting attention from the other shoppers.

'She loved her pizza. She'd get through three a night,' Maddo sobbed. He recited like a litany his mother's favourites. 'Hawaiian, five cheeses, and pepperoni with extra onions. Every night, regular as clockwork, at nine o'clock, the pizza van would arrive. I've been drunk ever since.' He was mopping his eyes now, with Charles's handkerchief. 'So look after your mam, and if there's owt I can do to make sure your mam's last few days or weeks are 'appy, then let me know.'

Charles was baffled. It was hard for him to take in. Why hadn't his mother told him she was terminally ill? He'd believed her when she'd told him that she was suffering from toothache. Outside the shop, with the money allocated for groceries still in his pocket, he bumped into his brother, Andrew, who was arm-in-arm with a thin red-haired woman in city shorts and high heels.

Before Charles could get a word in about their mother, Andrew said, 'Charlie, this is Marcia Boycott, or as *The News of the Screws* called her, Marcia Boy Cock.' He nudged Charles and laughed, 'D'you geddit?'

'So unfair,' said Marcia, assuming that Charles was aware of her notoriety. 'The boy was gagging for it.' She pushed her red mane back with a slim white hand. 'He lied his fifteen-year-old head off in court. I got no credit for getting him through his French GCSE.'

'Marcia's just moved into Pedo Street,' said Andrew.

'You make it sound as though I had a choice,' said Marcia bitterly. She turned her intense gaze on to Charles and, addressing him directly, asked, 'Do *you* think it's fair that I've lost my job, that I'm on a list of known paedophiles, that I'm barred from going anywhere near a school or playground? I've been demonized for teaching a clumsy provincial schoolboy the art of love.'

Charles stammered, 'It does seem a little harsh.' He was longing to get away but Marcia continued.

'None of the other boys I slept with complained.'

'Quite,' said Charles.

Andrew said, 'The sneaky little bastard went to the police when Marcia refused to cough up for an iPod.'

'I have my principles,' said Marcia. 'I will not pay for sex.'

Charles judged that this was not the moment to tell his brother that their mother was terminally ill. He could see that Andrew was eager to get Marcia somewhere he could give her a good seeing-to. As Charles hurried home to share the news with Camilla, he comforted himself with the thought that at least he wouldn't have to be king. He thanked God that he now lived in a republic and the monarchy would never be restored. The New Cons would never win an election; Boy English had too many skeletons in his cupboard, and Charles was sure that one day they would come out dancing.

Mr Anwar told Violet Toby that the Queen was dying when Violet was in his shop looking for a butter dish. 'It is most sad, she is a very gracious lady, only last week she was in the shop buying clothes pegs.'

Violet had been forced to sit down; she had lived next to the Queen for the past thirteen years and she'd taught her how to cook and clean and look after herself.

'When I first met her,' said Violet, 'she couldn't mash

a spud, and didn't know you 'ad to shake a bottle of HP to get the sauce to come out.'

Anwar said, 'She will be a great loss to our community. Most of the people here are the dregs of society.' He looked out of the shop window to where two struck-off solicitors were arguing over a can of Kestrel lager.

'I 'ope you're not callin' me a dreg,' said Violet. 'I'm only 'ere because of our Barry. If it weren't for 'im I could live anywhere I pleased.'

Mr Anwar said, 'I am also punished for my son's behaviour. He rang the police and told them that Osama bin Laden was living in our attic. The boy was thirteen, he'd been reading *The Diary of Anne Frank*, he'd fallen under the book's influence. It was foolish, yes, but why punish the whole family?'

'Didn't they find some guns in the attic, though?' asked Violet.

'A few Kalashnikovs,' said Mr Anwar. 'Souvenirs from Afghanistan.'

'Never mind,' said Violet, comfortingly. 'You'd 'ave been put in 'ere anyway, because of your weight, wouldn't you? What are you now, thirty stone?'

When Violet got home, she dumped her shopping on the kitchen table and went straight round to the Queen's house. She was disappointed to find that the lights were out and the front door was locked. She would have to wait until the morning before hearing the clinical details of the Queen's terminal illness.

Charles had also called at his mother's house and, finding her out, had knocked on Violet's door. Violet had obviously been crying, thought Charles. Mascara had run down her cheeks, leaving dark trails as if a spider had gone for a jog after falling into black paint.

'I 'eard about your mam,' said Violet. 'I don't know what I'll do without her.'

'I can't understand why Mummy didn't tell me,' said Charles.

'She wun't want to worry you,' said Violet, who wished that Barry would stop telling her about the alarming thoughts that went through his head. 'Do your brothers and sister know?' she asked.

'Not yet,' said Charles. He was dreading breaking the news to them.

Before Charles had the chance to speak to his siblings, the Queen rang him.

'Charles,' she said, 'I've something terribly important to tell the family.'

'Oh, Mummy, I can't bear it,' said Charles.

Both of them were conscious that all telephone conversations were listened to by the security police. It made them more circumspect than usual.

The Queen said, 'Can you and Camilla come to Anne's at eight tonight?'

'Of course,' said Charles. 'But are you well enough?'

The Queen said, 'The pain has been dreadful, but it's out now.'

'Yes,' said Charles. 'Maddo Clarke told me. I do wish you'd told me yourself, Mummy.'

The Queen said, 'I can't be bothering you with every detail of my life.'

Charles thought, or death. He said, 'You are *magnificently* brave, Mummy. When my turn comes I hope I shall be able to display such courage.'

The Queen said, 'The worst bit is the waiting.'

Charles said, 'I can imagine. It must be agony.'

'But there's television to watch, and magazines,' said the Queen.

After he replaced the receiver, Charles thought, I doubt if there are televisions or magazines in Heaven, but if his mother was comforted by that belief, then who was he to disabuse her? When Charles thought about Heaven, he imagined it to be an English pastoral landscape with farmers in moleskin trousers driving horse-drawn ploughs, but he couldn't quite decide where he fitted into this heavenly Utopia. Would there be a roped-off enclosure for VIPs or would the dead have equal rights?

15

The Queen had asked for the meeting to take place in the Princess Royal's house because it was the largest private venue available. Anne's husband, Spiggy, had knocked their living room, hall and kitchen into one large space. He'd demolished the walls one night after returning home from a karaoke night at the One-Stop Centre, where he'd bought a lump hammer from a glue sniffer desperate for a couple of quid.

When he'd finished the demolition, he'd said, looking through the thick dust at the large space he'd created, 'Now the dog can see the bleedin' rabbit.' He'd had to prop the ceiling up with the odd bit of scaffolding, it was still there three years later, but Anne didn't seem to mind.

When Spiggy let the Queen into the living room, he issued the usual warning, 'Watch the poles, Liz.'

The room was haphazardly furnished with a mixture of garish antiques and the junk that Spiggy seemed to accumulate every time he left the house. The Queen chose to sit in a high-backed armchair, rejecting Spiggy's offer of a footstool. She was always a little nervous with Spiggy, so she bent her head and talked to Harris and Susan, telling them to stop running in and out of the poles.

Spiggy muttered, 'Anne'll be down in a minute, she's trimming her nose hairs.'

A commotion at the front door told them that Charles and Camilla had arrived and had brought their three dogs to the meeting. When Spike, Princess Anne's Staffordshire bull terrier, thundered down the stairs to join them, there were six dogs in the room.

Leo let the smaller dogs do all the barking and was rewarded when Charles said to him, 'Leo, you are a very good boy.' Charles stood in front of the log-effect gas fire with its regulated blue flames and said to his mother, 'How are you, Mummy?'

The Queen said, 'I'm extremely tired, it's been a horrid day.'

Charles searched his mother's face for clues as to how she truly felt about her imminent death. He had not expected her to go to pieces, but surely she would at last, under such circumstances, show some human frailty. He longed to give her some comfort, to put his arms around her, to reassure her that he would be there at her side when the end finally came. He tried to think of some way to broach the subject, but before he could formulate the perfect sentence, Camilla had taken his mother's hand and said, 'Your Majesty, Charles and I are both *devastated* to hear about your illness. How long have the doctors given you?'

The Queen said, 'I haven't seen a doctor for three years. I'm perfectly well.'

Charles thought, poor Mummy, she's in denial.

The Queen laughed. 'Violet came to see me in floods of tears. Mr Anwar told her that I'd got only days to live!'

'Maddo Clarke told me,' said Charles.

Camilla said, 'So we're not gathering to hear bad news?'

The Queen said, guardedly, 'Shall we wait for the others?'

While they waited, Spiggy tried to entertain them. 'I 'ad a right shock this mornin',' he laughed. 'I woke up. About seven, it were. An' I were feeling a bit randy, like, so I stretched me hand out and stroked Annie's belly. I still had me eyes closed, an' I said, "Are you up for it, Annie? I'm up for it." She didn't say owt but I could hear her breathing heavy, so I took me boxers off and I were just getting ready for a nice bit of lovey-dovey when I 'eard Annie downstairs talking to the milkman. I opened me eyes an' saw Spike lying next to me. I shot outa bed as if I'd got a firework up me arse. Don't get me wrong, I don't mind a dog *on* the bed, but I draw the line at 'aving it *in* the bed, with its 'ead on the bleedin' pillow. I ain't been able to look the bloody dog in the eye since.'

The Queen gave a tight smile.

Later that night, Camilla said to Charles, 'Your sister must have an extremely hairy belly.'

The next to arrive was Prince Andrew, who said he hoped the meeting wouldn't last long because he'd left Marcia Boycott at home 'cooking up a storm'.

'She's enormous fun, Mummy,' said Andrew. 'You'd like her. She's a bit of an intellectual, very deep, like Charlie here. I don't know what she sees in me, as you know I'm a . . . oh, what is it? A something, an animal of some kind, of very little brain.'

'A bear,' supplied Charles. 'You're a bear of very little brain, from *Winnie-the-Pooh*.'

'Never liked Winnie-the-Pooh,' said Andrew. 'Thought he was a bit of a wimp, to tell you the truth. And as for that Christopher Robin, he was definitely a poofter in the making.'

Charles said earnestly, 'But don't you see, Andrew? All the animals in the wood represent human archetypes.' Seeing the bafflement on Andrew's face, he continued, 'They, er . . . represent us humans.'

'So which are you?' asked Andrew.

While Charles was thinking, Anne came into the room and said, 'I think Eeyore, the neurotic donkey, don't you, Charles?'

Charles forced himself to laugh with the others.

Prince Edward and Sophie, the Countess of Wessex, arrived next. They had the misfortune to live next door to Maddo Clarke and his seven rampaging sons.

Sophie said, 'We are totally exhausted. The Clarke rabble were up all night doing kung fu on the stairs.'

Edward said, 'A spell in the army would do them all good.'

Anne said, 'It didn't do you any good, Eddy. You had a bloody nervous breakdown.'

Sophie said, 'Edward doesn't like to talk about his time in the Marines.'

Anne said, 'His *brief* time.'

Edward said, 'All your military titles were honorary, Anne. You were not woken up at midnight by a screaming sergeant major, made to run thirty miles in the rain wearing heavy boots, in full kit, with a seventy-pound pack on your back, having to wade through ice-cold water holding your rifle above your head. Then, on your return to camp, being ordered to pick up two handfuls of mud, which you had to throw at the walls, the floor, your bed and your dress uniform. Then, weeping with exhaustion, being told that everything in the room must be cleaned, washed and pressed before inspection later in the morning. Add to that the merciless bullying I received from all and sundry.'

Andrew said, 'Oh, for Christ's sake, get over it, Eddy.'

But Edward continued, 'If I'd been allowed to go into the theatre after leaving school . . .' His voice trailed away.

Charles said, 'I was horribly bullied at prep school. It didn't help that the headmaster addressed me – a little boy, eight years old – as "sir".'

In an attempt to lighten the tense atmosphere (even Camilla was biting her nails), Spiggy started to tell the company about a fight he'd witnessed outside Grice-A-Go-Go between a pole dancer and Mrs Anwar. Thankfully his vivid narration was interrupted by the arrival of Prince William and Prince Harry and their respective dogs, Althorp, a lurcher, and Carling. Spike growled a warning, saying, 'This is my territory.'

Charles said to William, 'A good day at work, darling?'

William sighed and said, 'If you count climbing a rickety ladder while carrying freezing-cold scaffolding poles in an east wind at a height of forty feet as being a good day, then yes, I suppose I did have a good day at work, Dad.'

Harry said, 'I had a good day. I stayed in bed and watched my Puff Daddy videos.'

Spiggy was acutely aware that he was the only commoner in the room. Even the dogs had a superior air about them, he thought. He sat slightly on the edge of the family group, jiggling one crossed leg over the other. Being in the presence of the Queen always made him nervous.

Anne had, somewhat ungraciously, made them all tea, and had opened a tin of assorted biscuits. Spiggy was pleased that she was using the hostess trolley he'd given her for Christmas.

He'd had thirteen years to get used to the fact that he was related by marriage to the Royal Family, but sometimes, when they were all together, like this, he felt that he was in a dream and that one day he'd wake up relieved that it was over. He'd given up a lot to marry Anne. He was used to roaming the country doing a bit of this and a bit of that, bit of asphalting, buying and selling a few horses, arranging the odd dogfight, trading cars for vans, and vans for lorries. He never used to leave the house without at least a thousand quid in a roll in his back pocket. He'd given it all up for love. Me and Annie are soulmates, he mused, as he watched his wife steer the hostess trolley around the feet of his in-laws, avoiding the dogs and the scaffolding poles.

What a woman Anne was, he thought. There was nothing that woman couldn't do. She was the perfect wife: she could weld with an oxyacetylene torch, pull a horse out of a ditch, intervene in a dogfight and mend a burst pipe, and she never minded if his boots were filthy. And look at her, look at those thighs and that hair – hair she would let down and allow him to bury his face in. You could have a laugh with Anne, and she always called a spade a spade.

She was good at reading and writing, and best of all she loved *him*, little fat Spiggy who didn't go to school and, until he met Anne, thought horses and dogs were better than people. So what if she hated cooking? Grice's Chinese Chip Shop was only round the corner. He could eat chips and battered sausage every day of his life, and almost did. It was rubbish about needing to eat fruit and veg. His grandma had lived solely on mashed spuds and treacle pudding. She could only manage soft stuff due to all her teeth being knocked out when a lorry jack slipped while she was changing a wheel. Spiggy cleared his throat; it always choked him up when he thought about his grandma in her coffin wearing a cloth cap and big boots.

He looked at his in-laws. His mother-in-law, the Queen, was all right, she didn't bother them much, she kept herself to herself. He struggled with his brother-in-law Charles a bit. Charlie sometimes talked like a bender, hark at him now. He watched as Charles tried to decide which biscuit to select from the compartmentalized tin.

'*So* hard to choose, *impossible* to decide between a custard cream and a bourbon. A custard cream is so fondanty, a little like having sunshine in one's mouth, whereas a bourbon has a certain French earthiness about it.'

Spiggy thought, if he talked like that in my grandma's house she'd have smacked his head. He watched and listened approvingly as Anne said, 'Oh, for Christ's sake, Charles, choose a bloody biscuit.'

Andrew grabbed a chocolate digestive and crammed it into his big-jawed mouth.

Edward looked at his wife, Sophie. She said, 'Have the wafer.' He obediently took a pink wafer and nibbled at its edge. Sophie held the flat of her hand up and turned her head as Anne proffered her the tin.

Anne said, 'What the fuck does that mean?'

Sophie replied, 'It means that I do not want one of your biscuits, Anne. The last time I had one of your biscuits, it was covered in dog hair and I was ill for a week.'

When the tin was held out to Harry, he said, 'I'm cool.'

Anne said, 'We all know you're cool, Harry, but do you want a bloody biscuit?'

Harry gave a contemptuous laugh, as though the eating of biscuits was only undertaken by geeks and dorks.

William said, 'Would anybody mind if I took the last chocolate one?' Only when everyone had reassured him did he take it.

There was a commotion at the front door, a high-pitched yapping and a woman's voice shouting, 'I'm here, I'm here. Masses of apologies.'

Spike, asleep on the hearthrug, opened one eye, twitched an ear and went back to sleep. Princess Michael of Kent, wearing a fur jacket against the autumn night, strode into the living room with Zsa-Zsa, a beribboned Russian toy terrier in a matching fur jacket, under her arm. Spike smelled Zsa-Zsa's intoxicating perfume and stirred on the rug.

'Am I the last?' trumpeted Princess Michael. 'Oh, I

can't bear it, do forgive me, but Prince Michael rang to say that he had heard on the World Service about our imminent return. He said to tell you all that he's thrilled, absolutely thrilled.'

Anne said, 'I'd like to know why you are allowed to speak to people outside the bloody Exclusion Zone, and we're not?'

Princess Michael said, 'Are you accusing me of collaborating with the enemy in return for favours?'

Anne said, 'It wouldn't be the first time your family was on the wrong side in a war.'

Princess Michael said icily, 'You forget perhaps, Anne, that Prince Philip's sisters were married to officers in the Luftwaffe.'

The Queen said hurriedly, 'From where was Prince Michael ringing this time?'

'A desert somewhere, I forget which one,' said Princess Michael.

Anne said to her, 'Has it ever crossed your mind that he's left you?'

Princess Michael said, 'He has not left me. He chose to escape rather than be exiled to this place of Hell.'

Anne said, 'But my point is, he didn't take you with him, did he?'

When the biscuit tin got to her, Camilla said, 'No, thanks Annie, darling, I'll have a fag instead.' As she passed Zsa-Zsa, she put out her hand to stroke the tiny dog's head, saying, 'And how are *you*, you funny little scrap?'

In return, Zsa-Zsa sank her needle-sharp teeth into Camilla's index finger.

Princess Michael said angrily to Camilla, 'Please don't approach her without warning, she is very easily frightened.'

Charles said, 'Are you terribly injured, darling?'

Camilla sucked on her bleeding finger and said, 'No, I hardly felt a thing.' Then said to her little fat brother-in-law, 'Can I bum a fag, Spiggy, darling?'

Spiggy got up and went to a battered wall unit, opened a cupboard, and took out a carton of two hundred cigarettes. Spiggy said, 'You can have a packet. I know a bloke what's just come back from Spain.'

They moved further down the room and leaned against the cooker. Spiggy turned on the extractor fan; they lit their cigarettes and watched the smoke being sucked up inside the greasy hood.

The Queen raised her voice slightly and said, 'I am conscious that time is passing and that we are under the midweek curfew of nine thirty, so if we could start.' When she had the full attention of the family she said, 'I think we are all aware of the strong possibility that the New Conservatives will win the next election. Should they do so, Boy has promised to reinstate the monarchy – us. I would be expected to take my place once again as, and I will give the condensed description of my title, "Elizabeth the Second, by the Grace of God, of the United Kingdom of Great Britain and Northern Ireland and of my other Realms and Territories Queen, Head of the Commonwealth, Defender of the Faith".'

Princess Michael struggled out of the deep leather-look sofa Spiggy had recently swapped for a chainsaw and said, 'Thank God! It's been a hideous ordeal living among the little people in their little houses. Allow me to be the first to congratulate you on your return, Your Majesty.' She gave a deep curtsey.

The Queen pursed her lips. She found Princess Michael irritating at the best of times, now she had interrupted the Queen at an important historical moment.

Andrew said, 'I think it would be superb. Christ, I've missed the good life. I can't wait to get back to civilization. Kensington,' he added.

Sophie said, 'Edward and I are desperate to get Louise into a decent girls' school.'

Edward said, 'She'll need intensive elocution lessons before she's allowed into any decent school, she's got the most frightful local accent.'

The Queen said, 'If you will allow me to continue.' She fiddled with an earring and then touched her brooch. Finally she said, 'After a great deal of thought, I have decided to abdicate.'

Camilla said to Spiggy, 'Oh, shit.'

Charles said, 'But, Mummy, the people would want you to be Queen.'

The Queen continued, 'Charles, I am eighty years of age and I simply cannot face . . .' She hesitated.

Anne said, 'Another bloody Royal Variety Performance?'

There was laughter. Camilla looked over at Charles and saw that he was not laughing. He had lost his customary ruddy complexion and looked pale and frightened. Camilla threw her cigarette into the sink then crossed the room, stepping over dogs and feet.

'Oh, darling,' he murmured when she sat down next to him.

She knew how he felt. They had often talked about the possibility that one day he would be king. They had never been happy conversations.

Spiggy said, 'How do you abdicate, Liz? Is there, like, a ceremony, or is it paperwork 'n' stuff?'

The Queen said, 'Since I am, under the present regime, a private citizen, I can do as I damn well please.'

Andrew said, 'Whoa, Ma! Less of the damns, you'll be effing and blinding next.'

Anne said, 'I'm with you, Ma. I didn't bloody ask to be born royal and I'm not prepared to go back to opening hospitals and bloody bridges. Let some other poor bugger get the curtsey and the bouquet. Me and Spiggy will be happy with a bit of land and a few horses.'

Spiggy shouted across the room, 'In sickness an' in 'ealth, for richer or poorer, eh Annie?'

The Queen said to Charles, 'What do you think, Charles?'

Charles clutched Camilla's hand and said, 'Would Camilla be my queen?'

'No,' said the Queen. 'Camilla would be your consort.'

Charles thought about the morning he had discovered that one day he would be king. His nanny had explained to him that he must never, ever, appear outside the nursery without first checking that his shoes were highly polished, his socks pulled up to the knee, his shorts smartly pressed, his face and hands scrubbed clean and his hair carefully parted and brushed. He must be polite at all times, stand with his hands behind his back, and must not be heard shouting or laughing, because one day he would be the ruler of millions of people. Later that night he had wept silently in his bed in the nursery; he knew that he was not good enough or clever enough to be the King of England and the Commonwealth. He knew that he was an ordinary boy.

Charles said, 'I'm terribly sorry, Mummy, but I will not be crowned the King of England unless my wife, the woman I love, is crowned Queen.'

The Queen said, falling back on arcane language, 'I advise you to seek counsel.'

Camilla said, 'Charles, darling, I'm not at all bothered about not being a queen.'

'I am,' said Charles with a surge of anger. 'Unless you are Queen, I will not be King!'

Anne said, 'Don't lose your bloody rag.'

Charles shouted, 'If I had been allowed to marry Camilla when we were young and first in love, there would have been no question about her status in this family. But I was not allowed to marry her because, er . . . well . . . she was not without carnal knowledge, that is, she had lain with a man. She was not exactly virgo intacta.'

Camilla disengaged her hand from Charles's and said, 'It was the sixties.'

The Queen bent down and picked up Harris, and buried her embarrassment in his grizzled neck.

Princess Michael said, 'If I may defend your mother, it would not have been fitting for the heir to the throne to have married a woman who had been around the block a bit. Or in Camilla's case, around several blocks.'

Andrew said, 'Steady on, Pushy. You'd been round a few blocks yourself before you married Prince Michael.'

Anne muttered, 'Including the Eastern bloc.'

Charles said, 'Mummy, we will be King Charles and Queen Camilla, or nothing.'

William said, his voice shaking with emotion, 'Grandmama, if my father refuses to carry out his duty then as his eldest son and heir I offer myself.'

William brushed the biscuit crumbs from his trousers and knelt before the Queen. The Queen did not know what to do or say. She thought, he has a taste for melodrama, obviously inherited from his mother. She patted him on the shoulder and said what mothers and grandmothers all over the world say at times of indecision, 'We'll see.'

Harris struggled off the Queen's lap, waddled round the side of William and began to lick the future king's boots.

16

Walking home from the family meeting, Harry said, 'You was well out of order, kneeling an' sayin' you was gonna be king.'

William said, 'It's what Mum would have wanted, Harry.'

Harry pulled up his sweatshirt hood so that it partly obscured his face. They rarely talked about their mother, both of them were aware of the pain her absence caused the other.

Harry said, 'Mum would have been a well top Queen.'

The police helicopter suddenly clattered over Hell Close and descended to such a height that William and Harry ducked, fearing decapitation. The powerful beam of the helicopter searchlight rolled over William and Harry many times, then an amplified voice boomed out. 'This is an official police announcement: three minutes to curfew. Will residents please return to their homes and stay there.'

William and Harry quickened their pace. They were almost home, when a happy slappy gang turned the corner and came towards them. It wasn't long before the taunting began. One of Maddo's sons, Lee, shouted, 'Hey, Ginger, is your knob hair red an' all?'

William said, 'Let's not run this time, Harry.'

William and Harry stood their ground and the happy

slappies passed them with only a few pushes and shoves.

William said, 'When I'm king, I'll solve the problem of violent gangs.'

Harry said, 'Cool. How will you do it?'

William answered, 'I'll have them all rounded up and then I'll have them dispatched.'

'What, like kill them?' said Harry.

'No,' said William. 'I shall be a kind and fair king and my subjects will love me and there will be much hysteria when I die. Women will throw themselves on my coffin.'

Harry said, 'When you die, I'll be king. Wicked.'

William thought to himself that he owed it to the nation to produce an heir to the throne, soon.

At the other end of the close, Camilla and Charles were hurrying down the road to their front gate. Camilla said, 'Darling, I don't care in the least about being queen; the most important thing to me is that I'm your wife.'

She put her arm around his waist and turned her face to be kissed, but he was too angry with himself, his mother and the world to be placated.

He said, 'At the age of nearly fifty-eight I'm still being treated like a boy.'

When they arrived indoors, Charles immediately went to his writing desk and began to scrawl a letter to his best friend.

My dearest Nick,

Why have you stopped replying to my letters? I am tremendously upset by your baffling failure to reply. This has hurt me deeply, I had thought that we would be friends for life.

I am simply desperate for inside news of the current political situation. Do you think Boy will pull it off? It would be absolutely marvellous if he did.

Mummy has abdicated and expects me to be king, however she does not approve of Camilla being my queen. I have said, in no uncertain terms, that Camilla and I reign as a couple, or we do not reign at all.

Nick, I am seeking your counsel. Will the people accept Camilla? Does the present constitution allow her to be queen? If not, could you put your not inconsiderable weight behind a constitutional change?

Please forgive the lined notepaper. I send you, as always, my love.

Charles

PS: Please reply care of Dwayne Lockhart, at the attached address.

By nine thirty the streets of the Flowers Exclusion Zone were deserted, save for a few policemen and the entire dog population.

Dwayne found himself patrolling Slapper Alley; he walked past Paris Butterworth's house four times. He could hear Fifty-cents crying in an upstairs bedroom. He wanted to knock on the door and ask if the baby was all right, but ever conscious that his movements were being watched back at the Control Centre, he walked on.

He had wanted to give Paris a book he had just finished

reading, *Nineteen Eighty-Four*. It was very far-fetched, because it was set in the future when a totalitarian government controlled the population using a television screen. But at the heart of the book was a romance between the hero, Winston Smith, and a girl called Julia.

Dwayne would have liked to discuss the book with Paris, whose sweet face he could not forget.

The Queen had been escorted to her front door by Spiggy, who had said, 'I don't want you bumping into them happy slappies, Liz.'

Now she sat by the gas fire in her favourite Louis XVI armchair, brought with her from Buckingham Palace thirteen years before. Like everything else in the tiny sitting room, it was showing signs of wear. The Aubusson carpet had lost its glow thanks to heavy-duty wear by Harris and Susan, and the weighty brocade curtains at the sash windows had come unfastened in a few places from the hooks that held them on to the filigreed curtain pole, giving a slovenly appearance that offended the Queen's sense of order.

The Queen was writing her journal, a habit she had developed in childhood. Her nanny Marion Crawford, 'Crawfie', had said, 'Elizabeth, you are going to meet many interesting people and visit exciting and exotic countries. It behoves you to keep a note of your thoughts and feelings.'

The young Elizabeth, barely able to write her own name, had asked Crawfie what 'feelings' were. Crawfie had said, 'A good feeling is how happy you are when Mama comes into the nursery to kiss you goodnight.'

'And a bad feeling is when Mama doesn't come?' asked Elizabeth.

'You mustn't have a bad feeling when Mama doesn't come. She is a very busy woman; she's the wife of the King of England's brother.'

'Papa is the King's brother?'

'He most certainly is,' said Crawfie.

'Why?'

'Because he has the blue blood. You have it too.'

But the next day Elizabeth had fallen on gravel and scraped her knee, and the blood that seeped out was unmistakably red. She had to keep quiet about her injury; nobody must find out that she had red blood.

The Queen closed her eyes for a moment, savouring the peace, the warmth from the fire and the glorious realization that once she had written in her journal about the day's events, she had absolutely nothing to do. She opened her journal and wrote:

A busy day. Had tooth pulled out by pliers woman, visited Philip, had row with manager of Frank Bruno House, called family meeting. Abdicated.

Charles making ridiculous fuss about Camilla being queen. William offered himself but he is too young and I thought him a little too eager.

A rumour circulated around the estate, apparently started by Beverley Threadgold, that I was dying. Well, in a sense Queen Elizabeth is dead, long live Elizabeth Windsor!

The weather is autumnal, as one would expect in late summer.

She closed her journal and switched on the television, where she watched the daughter of an ex-prime minister eating a kangaroo's testicle in an equatorial jungle in Australia.

As she waited for the milk to boil for cocoa she thought, never again will I have to be presented to the ghastly line-ups of obsequious actors, singers and comedians at charity events. My God, she thought, I've certainly done my porridge! She shuddered when she reflected on the sheer bloody embarrassment of having to read the Queen's Speech. Turning the pages while wearing white gloves was bad enough, then there was the vacuous content of the speech itself . . .

As she sat sipping her cocoa with her feet resting on the sleeping Susan, she said to Harris, 'Where shall we live when we leave this place, boy? I understand that most of the palaces have been turned into places of public entertainment. Poor boy, you've never known anything but the Flowers Estate, have you? You've never ridden in a Rolls-Royce, have you? You don't know what it's like to fly in a private aeroplane or to be surrounded at all times by lovely things, do you? You're my bit of rough, aren't you, lad?'

Harris growled, 'Aye, I'm as rough as a whore's dirty laugh, but I'm nae stupid.'

Before she went to bed, the Queen thumped three times on the party wall, and Violet Toby thumped back. It was an arrangement they had; it signified that all was well.

*

Marcia Boycott was a woman who could not live in disorder. Unkind friends and colleagues had described her as 'the control freak's control freak'.

When Prince Andrew arrived home, he hardly recognized the place. Marcia had filled four black bin bags with rubbish and had transformed the rooms downstairs beyond recognition. A delicious smell was seeping from the kitchen, a smell so aromatic that it made his mouth water. Marcia had arranged his CDs in alphabetical order, cleaned the food stains off the sofa, swept and mopped the floors and bleached all the surfaces in the kitchen.

'Crikey,' Andrew said, 'you've been busy, Marcia.'

She said, 'The mince and onion pie will need another ten minutes in the oven. Why don't I fix us a drink and you can tell me all about the meeting.'

Andrew took his shoes off and sprawled across the sofa, from where he could see Marcia constructing cocktails in two highball glasses. She was a bit on the scrawny side, he thought. He usually liked a woman to have a bit more meat on her, but she had been amazing in bed that afternoon. Abso-bloody-lutely amazing.

Marcia handed him a pinkish drink and said, 'So, how did it go?'

Andrew said, 'It was dullsville. Mummy abdicated, Charlie got into a strop, and Princess Michael's dog bit Camilla's finger.'

Marcia, an ardent monarchist, whose parents ran a dry-cleaning business and never raised their voices, was enthralled. She said, 'Andy, more detail, please. Start from when you arrived at your sister's house.'

*

When Edward and Sophie arrived home, they found their daughter, Louise, asleep in front of the television. Their babysitter, Chanel Toby, was watching *I'm a Celebrity, Get Me Out of Here.*

Chanel said, 'Some woman 'as just ate a kangaroo's ball. I've gave a few blow jobs in my life, but I wouldn't eat a animal's ball. That's disgustin'.'

After she had been paid, and had hurried home to beat the curfew, they put Louise to bed. As they were tucking her in, the little girl woke and said, 'Ay oop, our Mam. Ay oop, our Dad.'

Sophie said, 'Louise, we may be leaving this house soon and going to live in a place called London, some-where with a beautiful garden.'

'I don't want to leave 'ere, Mam,' said Louise. 'We've gotta nice 'ouse 'ere in 'Ell Close. I don't wanna nice garden. I like playin' in the street wi' Courtney Toby.'

Sophie felt her throat tightening at the mention of Courtney, a seven-year-old harpy in mini-slapper gear with a precocious foul mouth, whose imaginative play included drive-by shootings and domestic violence involving the intervention of social workers.

After they had crept out of Louise's bedroom, Sophie said, 'If we don't get away from here soon, she'll be stuck with that accent for life, Ed.'

17

The transcript of the Royal Family's meeting was emailed to Boy English at his breakfast table the next morning. Boy read it on his laptop. With a mouth full of toast he said to Cordelia, 'Christ! The Queen's going to abdicate.'

Cordelia said, 'Boy, you're spitting crumbs all over the fucking table.'

Boy said, 'Fuck the crumbs! My whole monarchy thingy is centred around the bloody Queen. I need her, that indomitable little figurehead that everybody respects, doing her bloody duty, keeping her gob shut and her upper lip stiff.'

Cordelia said, 'But it isn't as though the Queen ever did anything remarkable or said anything particularly memorable when she was on the throne.'

Boy said, 'She doesn't have to do or say anything, she just has to *be* there.'

Cordelia said, 'But mobs haven't taken to the streets demanding her return. Have they, sweetness?'

Boy said, 'Not yet. But the monarchy is the same as any other commodity, we must create a demand.'

Cordelia laughed. 'Can't you buy a cheap queen from China?'

Boy didn't laugh; he dipped the butter knife into a

jar of coarse-cut Oxford marmalade and smeared the orange jelly across his toast.

Cordelia said, 'How many times do I have to ask you not to do that? Your habits are truly disgusting.'

'I can't help it,' said Boy. 'I went to Eton, I lived among savages.'

'So you can't play your Queen card, then?' said Cordelia.

'No,' said Boy, slurping his coffee. 'I'm left with the fucking Joker, Prince Charles.'

'And isn't Charles popular?' asked Cordelia.

'Is he popular with you and your set?' asked Boy sarcastically.

'No, my set think he's a bit of a bed-wetter,' drawled Cordelia.

'And Camilla?'

'Oh, Camilla's all right, but the proles would sooner see Jordan on the throne showing her pants than Camilla in the full queen regalia.'

'The public will learn to love her,' said Boy.

Cordelia said, 'And perhaps one day you'll learn to love your brats.'

Boy said, 'I wish now I hadn't told you how I feel about the children. I do love them in the abstract, it's just their physical presence I can't cope with.' He put his hand out to his wife. 'Come on, Cordelia, admit you find their conversation repetitive and childish.'

Cordelia said dully, 'Hugo is three and Dora is five. They're not going to chat to you about Keynesian economics, are they?'

From upstairs, in the nursery, came the sound of little feet stamping out an angry tattoo.

Cordelia said, 'They'll have to be sent away to school. There's a place in Surrey that will take boarders at three and a half. It would be for their own good, Boy. We're awful parents.'

Boy said, 'After the election, honeybun. I'm Mr Family Man, heterosexual and potent.'

'But most importantly,' said Cordelia, 'you've got a lovely head of hair.'

Boy said, 'I could be a fucking model for Head and Shoulders and it wouldn't do me any good unless I can get the great electorate to learn to love Camilla.'

Boy's mobile phone played 'Land of Hope and Glory', a voice said, 'I'm outside, Mr English, on double yellows.'

Boy said, 'One minute.' He kissed the top of Cordelia's head and said, 'I must go, that bloody dentist charges sixty quid for every minute you're late for an appointment.'

The letters from Graham Cracknall and Lawrence Krill arrived in the same post as one from Sir Nicholas Soames at the Flowers Control Centre, and were being read with some amusement by WPC Virginia Birch, a youngish woman who in her spare time attended *Star Trek* conventions dressed as Admiral Kathryn Janeway. She put Cracknall's and Krill's letters in a wire 'In' tray marked 'Nutters correspondence' and opened the Soames letter. It read:

Dearest Charles,

How are you, sir? I am exceedingly well. I dined with the Prime Minister at the club recently, what an oik he is. My blood boils when I think that he represents our great country. The fellow holds his fork as though he were pitching hay — as, no doubt, his ancestors did.

I fabricated a reason for the meeting, saying, when asked by his Private Secretary, that I wished to talk to him, post foot and mouth, in my capacity as Vice Deputy Chairman of the Sussex Cattle Society.

But my true agenda was to discuss with him the possibility of allowing you and your family to draw stumps and leave your present vile locale and relocate, perhaps to Windsor, which has yet to be turned into a People's Palace.

Incidentally, one of the Ruthermere girls went to Buckingham Palace the other day to see The History of the Working Class Exhibition. She reported back that everything fine and of beauty had gone and had been replaced by grim depictions of labour — women down mines, boys up chimneys, etc. She said it was terribly distressing to see the Throne Room transformed into a Lancashire Cotton Mill with barefoot children in rags asleep under the looms.

There's an almighty row going on about Windsor Castle. Hilton Hotels welshed on their deal to turn it into a country house hotel and golf course when they realized that it lay under a direct flight path to Heathrow.

Now the Department of Health is after it to house the alarming number of madmen and madwomen who are at present roaming the streets making life thoroughly unpleasant for the rest of us. (Apparently the Exclusion Zones are full to overflowing.) Another possible use for Windsor is as HQ for the Scientologist Movement.

So, over the meat course (lark and pigeon pie) I suggested that Windsor could be utilized as a living history exhibit, saying that the Royal Family could live there and the public would be allowed in to gawp three times a week.

Barker said, 'Fatty, your attempts to inveigle the Royal Family back into public life are pathetically obvious.'

I think you would have been proud of my reaction, Charles. I stood up and said, 'Firstly, sir, only my friends call me Fatty. Secondly, sir, I do not know what I find more deplorable, your table manners or your politics.'

His security people hustled me away from the table before I could finish my pudding, a rather scrumptious spotted dick.

Not much else to report here. The traffic is foul, four and a half hours from Gloucestershire to town. Scandalous!

My housekeeper tells me she has failed to find an English replacement for Baines, my old butler. A new chap starts next week, a Chinese chap called Keith Woo. As you know, Charles, I'm not a racialist and I will give this Woo chap a fair crack of the whip, but I can't help feeling that it's a bad day at Bad Man's Gulch when we can't even manufacture our own butlers but have to import them from China.

By the way, my dear old friend, it would be delightful to hear from you. I sometimes wonder if you are getting these letters.

Yours truly,

Nick

PS. I don't suppose you get to see The Daily Telegraph, so I am enclosing a clipping from last Monday's edition.

WPC Birch unfolded the clipping and saw a photograph of Princess Michael of Kent, posed dramatically against a backdrop of the graffiti-sprayed house front of Maddo Clarke. A wheel-less wrecked car standing on bricks was in the background, flanked by four of Maddo's seven sons, who were all pulling gruesome faces for the camera.

Birch read:

Ex-Princess Michael (61), the wife of Prince Michael of Kent (64), who is believed to be living in Dubai, spoke out yesterday against what she called her 'cruel and inhuman exile' in the Flowers Exclusion Zone.

In her first interview in thirteen years she told our undercover reporter, Tom Cuttlefish (posing as a British Telecom engineer), of her missing years living on state benefits, surrounded by hostile neighbours.

'The shops are appalling,' she said. 'They do not stock asparagus or Helena Rubinstein lipstick, for instance – things that other people take for granted.'

Looking drawn and older than her years, she wept, 'I urge the country to vote New Con and release me from my living hell.'

Soames had written in the margin, in a bold hand, 'Christ! Pass the sick bag, Mabel!'

WPC Birch tore Soames's letter in half and passed it through a shredder. She then took the letters out of the tray and gave them to Peter Penny, saying, 'More letters from nutters to the future King of England. See that they get delivered, will you?'

Zachary Stein was a celebrity dentist. His waiting room was full of modish Italian furniture. Some of the chairs were so stylish that patients could not work out how to sit on them. On the walls were signed photographs of major and minor celebrities from the worlds of show business, politics and the seriously rich. The one thing these disparate people had in common was their dazzling, perfect teeth. Ken Dodd's photograph hung over the fireplace. Across his famous buck teeth, Dodd had scrawled in marker pen, 'To Zach, who saved my career.'

Zachary considered himself to be an artiste. He was a temperamental and acerbic practitioner. In a recent *Sunday Times* profile, he had admitted to being totally obsessed with teeth. He told the interviewer, 'I visited the Grand Canyon recently and my first thought was: My God! It would take a shitload of dental cement to fill *that* gap.'

Boy was three minutes late for his appointment; Duncan, his driver, a bull-necked morose man with childcare problems, had taken them on a circuitous route from Kennington to Harley Street in an attempt to beat the traffic. On the way Duncan had received several phone calls from distraught-sounding women. Boy, feeling the need to comment, had said, 'Women, eh?'

Duncan had unleashed a torrent of misogynistic vitriol that had alarmed Boy and made him think that it would be no bad thing if Duncan were to be kept away from women, preferably behind a locked cell door. When they finally arrived, a nervous receptionist told Boy that a fine of one hundred and eighty pounds would be added to his bill. With pretended nonchalance Boy said, 'No matter.'

From behind the door of the surgery, Boy heard the sound of a drill and a man shouting, 'Wider! Wider!'

'He's with a patient at the moment,' said the receptionist.

'If you'd like to take a seat in the waiting room.'

Boy was yawning his way through an article in *The Economist* about EU farming subsidies when an actress he vaguely recognized from a TV series he could not name gushed into the waiting room.

'It's *official*, we now live in a police state! I was stopped *twice* on my way here, by absolute *fascists*! Each time I showed my ID, and the bloody card would not *register* due to some ludicrous cock-up! I told them I had an appointment with Stein, but they affected never to have heard of him.' She looked closer at Boy and said, 'Omigod, you're Boy whatsisname.'

Boy gave her a modest closed-mouth smile and said, 'I loved you in that thing . . .'

'Oh, please,' she said. 'My best scenes were cut.'

'But you were jolly good in those remaining,' said Boy.

'Is Stein in a good mood?' she asked anxiously. 'He

was absolute hell at my last appointment – he's a complete *diva*!'

Boy began to feel a little anxious himself.

After he'd been shown into the surgery, Boy held out his hand towards the masked dentist.

'No time for that,' said Stein brusquely. 'Get in the chair, lie back and open your mouth.'

He pressed a foot pedal and the chair turned into a bed.

Stein shouted at the dental nurse hovering nearby and said, 'For Christ's sake! Stop *breathing*, Angela, you're distracting me!'

Boy opened his mouth. Stein shouted, 'Wider,' and began to examine Boy's teeth. 'Christ, it's like the ruins of an ancient city in here,' he said. 'Have you been to Pompeii?'

Boy shook his head.

'Keep still,' yelled Stein. Then, 'It's how I'd like to see all Eyeties: encased in volcanic rock.'

Boy stared up at the ceiling, where tropical fish swam in a huge suspended aquarium. As he watched, a big purple fish ate an orange tiddler. Stein stamped on the foot pedal and Boy jerked back upright in the chair.

Boy said, 'So, is much work needed?'

'Did London need work after the Blitz?' said Stein, whose own teeth, Boy noticed, were yellowish and unremarkable.

'Smile,' ordered Stein. 'Give me your politician's "I've just kissed a baby" smile.'

Boy drew his mouth back.

'Yeah, I thought so,' said Stein. 'You're wolf boy in pinstripe. Those incisors look like they've just torn a small animal apart.'

'So what do you suggest?' asked Boy, weakly.

'Angela, you're breathing again,' yelled Stein. 'I'm trying to fucking *think* here.'

Angela said, 'I'm sorry, Mr Stein, but I . . . need to breathe.'

'But do I have to hear it?' said Stein.

'I'll try not to . . .'

Stein said to Boy, 'Watch and listen.' He shoved his face up to Angela's and said, 'What's the population of Reykjavik?'

Angela said, 'I don't know.'

'The circumference of the moon?'

Again Angela answered, 'I don't know.'

'The hibernation period of the American brown bear?'

Once more she answered, 'I don't know.'

Zachary turned triumphantly to Boy and said, 'See! See! This girl has spent eleven years in British Education and she knows *nothing*.'

Angela said falteringly, 'I've got three "A" levels, Mr Stein.'

'"A" levels,' scoffed Stein. 'A fucking wardrobe can get "A" levels nowadays.'

Boy slumped uncomfortably in the chair. He had been a signatory to a parliamentary anti-bullying campaign recently, but he was too afraid of Zachary Stein to come to Angela's defence. Instead, he said, 'A New Con Government will revolutionize education. Every child leaving school will, er . . . know the population of Reykjavik.'

Stein bellowed, 'You're breathing again!'

Angela said, 'I'm sorry, Mr Stein, but I . . .' She left the room on the verge of tears.

'None of them stay for long,' said Stein. 'I blame the Government. Did you know that teeth are not on the national curriculum? So when these girls come to me, they are dentally ignorant. Perhaps when you're running things, you'll do something about it.'

'Can we get back to my teeth?'

'Thirty grand,' said Zachary.

'Did you say thirty *grand*, as in thirty thousand pounds?' asked Boy.

'I dare say you could go to another Harley Street dentist and they'd do a moderately good job, but you wouldn't have Zachary Stein teeth, unlike the Prime Minister.'

'You do Jack Barker's teeth?' asked Boy.

Stein said, 'I remodelled his mouth. Before he came to me he was living on soup and slops, his gums were rotting, he was in constant pain. I gave him a smile, made him human and got him elected for two further terms.'

Boy said, 'So, you're taking the credit for Jack Barker's electoral success, are you?'

Stein said, modestly, 'Only the last two terms.'

'Won't there be a conflict of interests?' asked Boy.

'No,' said Stein, 'I have no interests outside dentistry.'

'But thirty thousand pounds,' said Boy.

'Legitimate election expenses,' said Stein, who was

growing impatient. 'Do you want Zachary Stein teeth or not?'

Boy imagined himself smiling on the election posters, baring his teeth to Jeremy Paxman, grinning for the cameras as he entered the front door of Number Ten as prime minister. 'When can you start?' he said.

18

Dwayne was in Hell Close knocking on doors and doing spot checks to make sure that the residents had valid ID cards and had not tampered with, or even removed, their tags. It was deeply embarrassing work, and on days like this he wished he were employed elsewhere: digging out a cesspit or taming grizzly bears. He had known from his first day on duty that he was not cut out to police other people. He remembered the time, not so long ago, when he'd had to submit to having the despised metal tag on his own ankle inspected by a condescending official.

When he knocked on the door of Number Sixteen, it was Camilla who answered. It seemed to Dwayne that the narrow hallway was filled with barking dogs, though when they had settled down a bit he could see that there were only three of them.

'Good morning,' said Dwayne. 'Tag and ID check. Do you mind?'

Camilla led Dwayne into the sitting room and said, 'Please sit down. I'll call my husband, he's in the garden.'

When she had left the room, Dwayne went to the bookcase and quickly ran his fingers over the mostly leather-bound books: Shakespeare, Dickens, Homer, Robert Louis Stevenson, Nikolaus Pevsner, Churchill, Jilly Cooper, Laurens Van der Post . . .

When Camilla returned with Charles, Dwayne said, 'Sorry about this.'

Charles said, 'Please don't apologize, officer. Camilla, darling, where are our ID cards?'

She said, 'Aren't they in the usual place, in the jug on the kitchen dresser?'

Charles went to see, then shouted, 'No, they're not here.'

Camilla said, 'We're dreadfully absent-minded lately. Charles blames Grice's horrid food. He says it's packed full of toxins that rot the brain.'

As he watched Charles and Camilla search for their cards, Dwayne said, 'I left my card at home yesterday. They wouldn't give me any books at the library, I had to go home empty-handed.'

'You must borrow some of our books,' said Charles, gesturing towards the bookcases.

'If you want a jolly good laugh, take a Jilly Cooper,' said Camilla. 'She's terribly wicked, but awfully good fun.'

But Charles could see that Dwayne was not looking for fun in his reading matter. He said, 'Darling, let the officer choose something for himself, while we look for those wretched cards.'

Dwayne took down Laurens Van der Post's *The Lost World of the Kalahari* and saw that written on the title page was: 'The dogs bark and the caravan moves on. LVdP.'

Looking over Dwayne's shoulder, Charles said, 'I take great comfort from that inscription.'

When Camilla came in with the ID cards, having

found them in a cardigan pocket in the washing machine, Dwayne gave them a cursory glance. Much more interesting was the conversation he was having with Charles about the meaning of life. Charles, who considered himself the Flowers Estate's foremost intellectual, was delighted to have Dwayne hanging on his every word.

Eventually, conscious that they might be watching him on CCTV back at the Control Centre, Dwayne said, 'It would be lovely to stay talking but . . . if I could see your tags?'

Charles rolled his right trouser leg up and pulled his sock down, and Dwayne gave the exposed metal tag a quick inspection, saying, 'Thank you, sir.'

Camilla sat down and extended her left leg towards Dwayne. As he inspected the tag, to ease his obvious embarrassment, she said, 'I used to loathe the beastly thing, but now I think I'd miss it, were it not there.'

Dwayne was offered and accepted a cup of tea; it was served by Charles in delicate china cups decorated with roses.

When Charles had gone out of the room to look for biscuits, Camilla said, 'Charlie must like you, Dwayne. Not everybody gets a china cup.'

Charles said, returning with Grice's Chinese short-cake biscuits, 'Dwayne is a chap with fine sensibilities, Camilla. I'm going to lend him my copy of *The Heart of the Hunter*.'

'No,' said Dwayne, 'I couldn't.'

'No! No! I absolutely *insist*,' said Charles, pressing the book into Dwayne's hands.

So, when Camilla whispered to Dwayne, 'We're experiencing a few difficulties with our correspondence lately,' and slipped Dwayne the envelope addressed to Mr Nicholas Soames, Dwayne could not possibly refuse to post it, avoiding the censorship that all mail received, both in and out of the Flowers Exclusion Zone. He pushed the letter deep into his trouser pocket.

Camilla said to him, 'This is so sweet of you, Dwayne. Why don't you call round tomorrow, perhaps we could give you lunch?'

At the Arthur Grice Academy, fifteen-year-old Chanel Toby was being taught about the English kings by a nervous supply teacher called Gordon Wall. It was halfway through the lesson and so far all Chanel had written in her rough book was, 'King Alfred was a minger with a beer'd who cun't even watch a cake in the oven.'

As Wall droned on, Chanel had lost concentration and had allowed her thoughts to meander along familiar byways. Who should she give her virginity to? There were a few contenders; Prince William, who was nice an' that, but he wouldn't do it until she was sixteen; Prince Harry, who were a right laugh but were a proper ginga. Chanel didn't mind the ethnicity of a person, or their size or shape. She was a big girl herself. She'd messed about with boys with acne and those with aggressive and delinquent personalities, but she drew the line at gingas. To be a natural redhead was to be a social pariah, a target for the happy slappy gangs who patrolled the streets.

Chantelle, Chanel's older sister, had swapped her virginity for hair straighteners and a Grice's food voucher, but Chanel was a romantic girl who wanted the rupturing of her hymen to take place in lovely surroundings. The loveliest place she'd ever seen was the island flower bed in the school drive that spelt out 'Grice's Scaffolding' in red, white and blue flowers. Chantelle had lost her virginity in the back of a transit van parked behind Grice's Chinese Chip Shop. She had complained that her lover had stopped halfway through her ordeal and said, 'I really fancy a battered sausage, do you?'

Chantelle had said, 'Oh, I thought that's what I was getting.'

Chanel didn't want that; she had aspirations. She was going to get five GCSEs, which would mean automatic release from the tag around her ankle. She would then be free to study floristry at the college in the town.

When she looked up, Gordon Wall was talking about a king she'd never heard of. In January 956, Edwyn the Fair was crowned King of the English at Kingston-upon-Thames. On the day of the coronation, Edwyn left the celebration banquet and was later discovered by St Dunston (later the Archbishop of Canterbury) sandwiched between two women: 'His mistress and her mother; wallowing between the two of them in evil fashion, as if in a vile sty!'

As instructed by Gordon Wall, Chanel wrote a summation of this in her rough book.

Towards the end of the lesson, when shafts of sunlight had reached Chanel's desk and had almost lulled her to sleep, the classroom door opened and Arthur Grice came in with a school inspector, Ms Abigail Pike. The class rose at once to their feet and droned, 'Good afternoon, Mr Grice.'

Grice boomed, 'Ms Pike 'ere is 'aving a good look round to make sure we're up to scratch, so just carry on.'

Gordon Wall's throat tightened, he managed to stammer out that they were doing the English kings.

Ms Pike addressed the class. 'So, what have you learnt about the English kings this afternoon?'

A few hands flew up, but it was Ms Pike's policy to ignore the eager beavers. It was more the reluctant students in the back row she was interested in. She looked around the class and noticed Chanel playing with her hair, a look of studied indifference on her face.

She walked to Chanel's side and said, 'May I have a look at your work?'

Chanel closed the page of her rough book.

Grice said, 'This is Chanel Toby. We've had our difficulties, 'aven't we, Chanel? But she's kept 'er nose clean lately, 'aven't you?'

Chanel muttered, 'Yes, sir.'

Ms Pike picked up Chanel's book and read: 'Edwyn the Fair was a filthy bastard who was found by a vicar being the meat in a fuck sandwich. The bread was his mistress and her mam. I wonder what the papers said about that in January 956!!!'

Chanel was suspended and ordered to leave the school immediately. Some say that blinded by tears she inadvertently trampled over the floral island in the school's drive. Others say that she went out of her way to flatten as many flowers as she could before being restrained by Arthur Grice.

Later, in Grice's office at the school, Ms Pike asked, 'How many students have been suspended this term, Mr Grice? Would you look the figure up for me?'

Grice said, 'No need to look owt up, Ms Pike. I keep it all up 'ere in me 'ead.' He tapped the side of his head. It made a hollow sound. 'This term, we've 'ad to expel sixteen students. Twenty-seven 'ave been suspended, nine of them for a week or longer.'

Ms Pike murmured, 'But if you carry on shedding students at this rate, you'll be down to single figures, Mr Grice.'

Grice gestured towards the window that looked out over the Flowers Exclusion Zone. 'It's the catchment area,' he said. 'Our students are taken from the shallow end of the gene pool. Some of 'em arrive 'ere at the age of eleven, not knowing 'ow to tie a shoelace; they're totally reliant on Velcro.'

'You don't appear to have a head teacher, Mr Grice.'

Grice frowned. The furrows in his brow resembled a freshly ploughed field. 'We 'ave trouble 'anging on to an 'ead teacher,' he confided. 'So I've took it on myself to fill in, like.'

'But you have no teaching qualifications, Mr Grice,' said Ms Pike.

'I teach basic and advanced scaffolding Tuesdays and Thursdays,' he said.

'But not any academic subjects?' asked Ms Pike.

'Listen,' said Grice, menacingly, 'it ain't airy-fairy, let's-talk-about-civilization-in-Latin bollocks what this country needs, it's more scaffolders. Where would your cathedrals be without scaffolding? Nowhere. 'Ow do you think the Seven Wonders of the World was built? With scaffolding!

'If it weren't for scaffolding, you wouldn't 'ave no civilization. We'd still be savages living in the bleedin' caves.'

Ms Pike stood up and gathered her bag and coat together. 'What will happen to Chanel Toby now?' she asked.

Grice reached for the school registration book, turned to the letter T in the index, found Toby and drew a line through Chanel Toby's name.

'She's gone,' he said to Ms Pike. 'She's dead meat.'

As Chanel ran home to Hell Close, she passed her grandmother and the Queen walking back from the shops.

Violet said, 'What you doing out of school, Chanel?'

Chanel sobbed, 'I've been suspended for writing the truth about that dirty bleeder Edwyn the Fair.' She looked at the Queen accusingly. 'One of your relatives,' she said. 'That ponce, Grice, has said I can't do my GCSEs. Now I'll never be a florist.'

Violet said, 'We'll see about that,' and turned round and began to march towards the Grice Academy.

The Queen called, 'Shall I come with you, Violet?'

Violet shouted over her shoulder, 'No, Liz, I'm going to use language. And I know you don't like language. Walk 'ome with our Chanel.'

19

The Queen was holding the loft ladder steady as William climbed up the last few rungs and clambered into the attic. He stretched out an arm and the Queen handed him a Maglite torch and said, 'Somewhere up there is a large cardboard box marked "Glassware this way up", next to your grandfather's box of ceremonial swords.'

After a few moments, during which the beam of the torch flickered across the opening, William shouted, 'Found it!'

The Queen said, 'Splendid. Bring it down, will you?'

With some difficulty William scrambled down the ladder, carrying the heavy box. When the ladder had been retracted, the Queen and William went downstairs carrying the box between them. William had come straight from work and was still wearing his working clothes: boots with steel toecaps, ragged jeans, a plaid shirt and an orange fluorescent waistcoat. His hands and face were not entirely clean, the Queen noticed. William was impatient to find out what was inside the box. All the Queen had said to him had been, 'There's something in the attic I'd rather like you to see.'

The Queen took the bread knife from out of a drawer and began to cut through the parcel tape that sealed the lid. She opened the cardboard flaps and took out an object wrapped in a black plastic bin liner. She pulled away the plastic and revealed a large dark-blue velvet casket. She said tactfully, 'I think, perhaps, before we go any further, we should both wash our hands.' They washed their hands at the kitchen sink. The Queen said, 'Dry them thoroughly,' and handed William a clean tea towel.

When she had washed and dried her own hands, the Queen lifted the lid of the casket. Inside, standing on a base of white satin was the Imperial State Crown; its jewelled magnificence made William gasp. There was only a single light bulb hanging from the ceiling, but it seemed to find every facet of every precious gemstone that covered the surface of the crown.

The Queen said, 'This is the Imperial State Crown. I hope that you will wear it one day.'

She used the corner of her apron to polish a glowing ruby. William had often watched the black and white film of his grandmother's coronation; he and Harry had laughed at the sight of their four-year-old father in white satin knickerbockers and girly shoes. However many times William watched the film, he still felt nervous at the moment the Archbishop of Canterbury placed the crown on his grandmother's young head. The crown looked heavy and his grandmother's fragile neck looked as though it would snap under the weight.

'It looks heavy,' said William.

'I hardly slept the week before,' said the Queen. 'I was terrified it would fall off, and so was the Archbishop. Would you like to try it on?'

William sat down on a kitchen chair. The Queen braced herself and hoisted the crown free of its sumptuous packing. She held it against herself for a moment, remembering the triumphant peal of the bells and the shouts of 'Long live the Queen' that celebrated her crowning. As she placed the crown on William's head, a presenter on the television in the next room said, 'It was the first time our vet had performed a Caesarean on a mongoose.' The crown was a little too small for William's head; he sat very still, not daring to move.

The Queen stepped back and said, 'It suits you. How does it feel?'

'It feels brilliant, actually,' said William.

The Queen said, 'Sit very still and I'll bring you a looking glass.' When she had left the room, William raised his arms to imaginary cheers and patriotic shouts of, 'Long live the King. Long live King William.'

The Queen returned with a looking glass she'd taken from a wall in the hallway. When she lifted it, and he saw his reflection, he had a pang of longing for his mother, and it was only by using rigid self-control that he was able to hide his emotions.

The Queen said, 'I think you will be a very good king, William.'

William said, 'Yes, but it will be a sad day for me. It will mean that Dad is dead.'

'Not necessarily,' murmured the Queen. 'Your father could renounce his succession and pass it on to you. Are you prepared for that eventuality?'

William stiffened his back, as though he were on the parade ground at Sandhurst, and said, 'I am, Your Majesty, I *have* to be the King. I promised Mum I'd do it. It was what she wanted.'

'And you?' asked the Queen.

'I promised her,' William replied.

'I repeat, and you?' the Queen asked again.

'She brought me up to be a new kind of king. "King Lite", she called it,' said William.

'"King Lite"?' asked the Queen.

'Y'know, like Coke Lite,' said William.

'Ah! The drink?' asked the Queen.

'Yeah. She thought I could, sort of, mix with the people more. Visit the homeless at their, well, not *homes*, obviously, but their doorways and hostels and things,' said William.

'Very noble,' said the Queen. 'But to what purpose?'

'To find out about their problems,' said William, who was getting a little exasperated with his grandmother. Why was she questioning such a noble act of charity?

'And when you ascertain what the problems of the destitute are, what will you do?' asked the Queen.

William said, 'I'll try to help them, like my mum did.'

'Will you throw open the doors of Buckingham Palace, then?' the Queen asked.

William said, 'Well, not all the doors.'

The Queen said, 'You're a very kind boy and I'm extremely fond of you. Please think carefully before you sacrifice your life to an institution that is increasingly irrelevant. I think it's time we thought less of the Royal and more of the Family.'

20

Charles was reading aloud to Camilla from *Macbeth*. He was characterizing the speeches and reading the stage directions in his own voice. His only piece of costume was a Hermès silk scarf, which he used ingeniously to denote character. He had tried to interest his first wife in Shakespeare by performing *Richard III* to her, but she had ruined his concentration by flipping through *Cosmopolitan* and yawning.

Camilla, on the other hand, was giving every appearance of being thrilled by *Macbeth* and his performance; commenting occasionally on the action, saying, 'How horrid!' when Macduff's children were killed and, 'Mad cow!' when Lady Macbeth/Charles was screeching during the hand-washing scene. At one point Charles's performance grew to Donald Sinden-like proportions, causing Vince Threadgold to thump on the party wall and shout, 'Keep the bleedin' noise down!'

Camilla was trying to love Shakespeare as Charles did, but she simply could not make sense of the old-fashioned language. Why didn't the people in his plays simply say what they meant, instead of beating around the bush? And honestly, did Shakespeare think his audiences were stupid or something? She had been to see *A Midsummer Night's Dream* at Stratford as a child and the costumes were lovely, but it was terribly far-fetched.

How did Shakespeare expect his audiences to believe that a sleeping girl would wake up and fall in love with a donkey? I mean, she adored her pony, but not *romantically*. That was bestiality, wasn't it? Similar to what Prince Philip had told her that the Welsh did with sheep.

Charles swirled the silk scarf and began the final scene. Camilla was longing for *Macbeth* to come to an end, but she sat as though enraptured, as she had done so many times at cocktail parties when trapped by some dreadful bore droning on about a third party she did not know. She heard letters drop through the letterbox and said to Charles, who was halfway through a long speech, 'I'll pick the letters up before the dogs get to them.'

As it was, she was only just in time. Freddie and Tosca were playing at tug of war with one letter and Leo had slobbered over the other. Charles had draped the silk scarf over his head as one of the witches and was eagerly awaiting her return. She resumed her seat on the sofa and the performance continued. At the end she applauded until her hands smarted. Charles took several bows and allowed himself to laugh with pleasure. Perhaps the demons associated with Gordonstoun School's production of *Macbeth* would finally leave him.

When he was a boy he had played Macduff and had been directed to fall to the floor and wriggle around the stage in his death agonies. There had been a deathly silence in the school auditorium, apart from the sound of one person laughing very loudly. That person was his father, The Duke of Edinburgh. In the dressing room later, the English teacher who had directed the play congratulated the other boys on their performances but said to Charles, 'Well, Wales, I'm glad your father found your portrayal in our tragedy so amusing. Perhaps we should forget Shakespeare and do *Charlie's Aunt* next time.' Charles had taken this to be not only a rebuke to himself but also a reference to his louche aunt, Princess Margaret. His cheeks had burned with shame.

His mother had been kind, saying, 'I think you did awfully well to have learnt all those lines. However did you do it?'

His father had cuffed him on the side of the head, in what was probably meant to be an affectionate gesture, and said, 'Why didn't you play Macbeth, eh? Not good enough?'

Charles opened Lawrence Krill's letter first, then threw it over to Camilla saying, 'Another poor devil with mental health problems.'

Charles then opened Graham's letter, scanned it quickly and said, 'Extraordinary the lengths that some of these poor lunatics will go to. This one claims to be our love child.' He laughed. 'Graham from Ruislip.'

Camilla reached for her cigarettes, then remembered she was forbidden to light up in the house. Nevertheless, she took one out of the packet and held it in her right hand. 'What else does he say?' she asked quietly.

Charles was looking through the three enclosures he'd pulled out of the envelope with the Ruislip postmark.

'It all looks terribly authentic,' said Charles. 'He's been to enormous trouble: there's a DNA certificate, a codicil letter and a copy of a birth certificate. It seems that Graham was born in Zurich. You were at finishing school in Zurich, weren't you, darling?'

'Yes, in 1965,' she said.

'Graham was born in 1965, on July 21st,' said Charles.

There was a long pause. Charles felt like a character in a Pinter play.

'Yes,' said Camilla. 'It was awfully hot that July, all the windows were open in the delivery room, but it was still stifling. I could hear the cowbells ringing outside.'

Charles said, 'Delivery room? Were you on a school visit? Was it part of your conversational French course?'

'No,' said Camilla. 'I was definitely screaming in English.' She began to weep. '*I* didn't call him Graham, I called him Rory. Rory George Windsor.'

Charles looked at the letter and the papers in his hand and said, 'So are you telling me, darling, that this *Graham* is our *son?*'

Camilla nodded.

Charles asked, 'How did it happen?'

Camilla said, 'You remember, darling. We got carried away after that food fight at Nicky's place.'

'No!' said Charles, irritably. 'What I mean is, why didn't you have the, er . . . operation? The, er . . . procedure. You must have been desperate to get rid of the, er . . . er . . . foetus . . . Why didn't you?'

'I didn't get round to it in time,' she replied.

'You are a dreadful procrastinator, darling,' he said. 'But you really should have told me.'

'Once I was back in England it sort of slipped my mind,' she said. She put her arms around his neck and said, 'Are you frightfully angry with me, my little prince?'

Charles thought, I'm a character in Shakespeare. Charles said, 'Allow me to read the letter again in the sure knowledge that my son be the scribe and not some gibbering fool whose jest it be to claim false kinship.'

Camilla absented herself. She hated it when Charles slipped into what she called his pompous language. She went outside and sat on the back doorstep and lit the cigarette she'd been longing for. It was not that Camilla had completely forgotten about the baby she had given birth to in Zurich. She certainly remembered the event; it was just that she wasn't a woman who dwelt on things that could not be changed. What was the point of crying on the unknown child's birthday? She occasionally thought about the boy, wondered about him, but when she did so, she imagined him happy, strong, living in Ruislip where she understood his adoptive parents had a socially prominent position. She had not enquired any further. She wasn't the only girl at her finishing school to 'fall from grace', as the nuns in the nursing home called it. But she was the least neurotic about it. Camilla simply couldn't understand why people beat themselves up about the beastly things that happened in life.

When she went back to the sitting room, Charles said, 'Graham wants to come and see us.'

'Oh, does he?' said Camilla unenthusiastically.

'We must see him, darling,' said Charles. 'He is *our*

son, our only child. And he's older than William, which makes him second in line to the throne.'

'But bastards don't count, they can't inherit,' said Camilla.

'Those old laws were thrown out with the Dissolution of the Monarchy Act,' said Charles.

Freddie and Tosca were pretending to be asleep on the rag rug that Charles had made out of old cardigans using a clothes peg and an old sack for the base. They had heard the conversation between their mistress and master.

Freddie growled to Tosca, 'As if *Macbeth* wasn't bad enough, now we're into melodrama.'

Leo came into the room panting, after running away from Spike. 'What you laughing at?' he barked.

Freddie growled, 'It's a private pedigree joke.'

'Right,' yapped Leo, who never questioned the implicit suggestion that he was in every respect inferior to Freddie and Tosca. He always allowed them to feed first and get nearer to the fire.

When Charles had finished writing to Graham he read the letter aloud:

My dear Graham,

First allow me to commiserate with you on the loss of Mr and Mrs Cracknall, your adoptive parents. You must be simply devastated by their deaths. Then to discover that you were not their flesh and blood must have caused you enormous anguish.

Camilla, your mother, and I would terribly like to see you.

'Terribly like to see you?' queried Camilla.

'Well, I *would* terribly like to see my son,' said Charles with a flash of anger.

Camilla said tearfully, 'I'm not questioning your sentiment, darling, just your way of expressing it. "Terribly" sounds wrong, couldn't you drop the "terribly"?'

Charles said, 'You're quibbling over syntax because you're trying to deflect me from the beastly fact that you kept Graham's existence a secret for forty-one years. Forty-one years of deceit!'

Leo crept up to Camilla and laid his big head across her knees. Camilla automatically started to check Leo's thick coat for fleas.

'Carry on with the letter,' she said. 'I promise not to interrupt.'

But Charles was still angry. 'I love you desperately,' he said, 'but I will not take lessons in the use of the English language from somebody who managed to pass only one "O" level.'

'It's more than your first wife got,' she shouted. 'The most *she* managed at school was a prize for Best Kept Guinea Pig.'

Vince Threadgold shouted through the wall, 'Guinea pigs are filthy little bleeders, it takes a lot to keep 'em clean.'

Charles and Camilla continued the row with lowered voices. 'I was at *Cambridge*,' said Charles. 'I got a *degree*.'

Camilla blew her nose on a piece of kitchen towel and said, 'You're writing to *our* son. I ought to have an input.'

'What do you want to say?' asked Charles with his pen poised over a new piece of writing paper.

'Dear Graham,' Camilla dictated. 'We were terribly sorry to hear about the loss of your adoptive parents. It would be lovely to see you at your convenience.'

'At your *convenience*,' scoffed Charles. 'You make him sound like a bloody lavatory attendant.'

'He could be, for all we know about him,' said Camilla, who was still smarting from the 'O' level jibe earlier. She thought, if I'd put my mind to it I could easily have gone to university. But hanging out with a bunch of boffo students was not her style. As far as she knew, neither Oxford nor Cambridge hunted or had stabling facilities.

'Oh, just write to him and tell him to apply for a visiting order,' said Camilla. 'I'm going to bed. Come, Tosca; come, Freddie.'

She went out of the room without kissing Charles, but he caught up with her and the dogs on the stairs and said, 'We mustn't quarrel, darling. We mustn't let Graham come between us.' Charles followed Camilla into the bedroom and they began to walk down the well-worn path of forgiveness and reconciliation.

When their strenuous lovemaking was over and Camilla and Charles were lying in a post-coital daze, the dogs crept out from under the bed.

Freddie growled, 'I thought he was never going to stop.'

Tosca yelped, 'It's so *embarrassing*.'

Freddie growled, 'Er . . . talking about sex, er . . .

Zsa-Zsa is coming on heat soon. Would you mind if I . . .'

'No,' snapped Tosca. 'Mount the bitch, see if I care.'

Freddie said, 'I'm not a one-bitch dog, Tosca. At least I'm being honest.'

Tosca turned her back on him and scratched at the bedroom door. Camilla disentangled herself from Charles and got out of bed to open the door. Tosca ran down the stairs and went to lie alongside Leo under the kitchen table. 'I've left him,' she whimpered.

Leo licked her face. 'Are you sure, babe? We're all a bit jumpy with this Graham doodah.'

Tosca said, 'No, I'm sure, Leo. Freddie's rubbing his philandering nose in my face a little too often now.'

Leo pressed his nose against hers, and panted, 'Don't you mind that I'm a mongrel?'

Tosca thought, Ugh! He's got dreadful dog breath; we'll have to do something about that. Their relationship was less than a minute old and she was already trying to change him.

In the morning Camilla was surprised to find Tosca and Leo entwined on the kitchen floor. Stepping over them, she said, 'How long have you two been such good pals?'

Leo barked, 'We're not pals, we're lovers.'

When Freddie came downstairs for breakfast, he saw the two dogs together and went for Leo's throat, snarling, 'She's my bitch, you flea-bitten mongrel!'

When Charles came down to find the cause of the uproar, he took Leo's side in the argument and called Camilla's beloved Freddie, 'A beastly little dog.'

Camilla had shouted, 'Poor Freddie has been given the cold shoulder. He's terribly upset.'

King, the Threadgolds' Alsatian, barked through the wall, 'Good luck to you, Leo. Give her one for me.'

21

Before leaving the Control Centre, Dwayne tampered with the surveillance cameras trained on Charles and Camilla's house. He wanted to be able to talk to Charles about *The Heart of the Hunter*, without having his colleagues sniggering and calling him a fucking boff.

As he walked through the estate, he viewed the inhabitants with a Kalahari Bushman's eye. Some of them were savage, capable of pouncing on a man and pulling him down to the desert floor, others were merely pariah dogs that slunk away as they saw him approaching. Once again, he found himself outside Paris Butterworth's house. He could see her through the living-room window, watching *Balamory* with Fifty-cents.

She was surprised to see him at the door. She said, 'Has owt 'appened to me mam?'

Dwayne said, more gruffly than he intended, 'I dunno. I've come to check your tag.'

'It's still on. What more do you want to know?' she asked.

He wanted to kiss her sulky mouth and unfasten her piled-up black hair. His forearms were thicker than her thighs, he noticed.

'I need to check it's not been tampered with,' he said.

She said, 'Come in, but you'll 'ave to take your shoes off. I've got a pale carpet.'

She was wearing disconcertingly realistic-looking cat's head slippers. The glass eyes sparkled and the whiskers vibrated as she padded across an expanse of pale carpet in the hallway and living room. He left his boots on the doorstep and followed her in.

Fifty-cents was sitting strapped in his baby buggy, watching the television with a glazed expression as PC Plum cycled up a hill. The room was clean and uncomfortably tidy; Fifty-cents' toys were stored in their original boxes, on a shelf in one of the alcoves. Paris and Dwayne sat on the sofa and faced each other.

Paris said, 'You're not supposed to be alone with me, not in Slapper Alley.'

'I'm not alone,' said Dwayne. 'He's here, aren't you, Fifty-cents?'

Fifty-cents didn't respond to his name; he kept his gaze on the television screen.

'He likes his telly,' said Dwayne.

'He does,' said Paris, adding proudly, 'he knows all the adverts.'

'He's the same colour as me,' said Dwayne. 'Is his dad black?'

'Yes, his dad is Carlton Williams. Do you know him?'

'No,' said Dwayne.

'No!' exclaimed Paris. 'You must know him.'

'Just 'cause I'm black,' said Dwayne, 'it don't mean I know everybody in the town who's black.'

They looked at each other, and then looked quickly away. Dwayne thought he now knew what a heart-shaped face was like. She could have modelled for Valentine's Day cards. He said, 'That poem you wrote.'

Paris looked away. 'Yeah.'

'Elizabeth Barrett Browning wrote it, didn't she?'

''Ow did you know that?' she asked in amazement.

'I'm a policeman,' said Dwayne. 'I know everything. Can I have a look at your tag, then?'

She pulled off a cat's head and extended her thin white leg. Dwayne took the weight of her bare foot, holding it by the heel. He stared at the blue veins, which crossed the foot like a faded road map. She had painted her toenails a pearlized pink. He gently turned the metal tag on her ankle.

She said, 'I have wrote some poems. But they're crap.'

'I bet they're not,' he said.

'They are,' she said. 'Trouble is, I don't get no time. I've got 'im to look after, an' he's a mardy-arse when he wants to be. It was all right for Elizabeth Barrett Browning, all she had to do was lie around on a settee all day, being ill an' playing with 'er dog.'

Dwayne said, 'You did her for a project at school, didn't you?'

'No,' said Paris. 'I did her dog, Flush.'

Dwayne took out the battered Penguin edition of *Nineteen Eighty-Four* and put it on the coffee table, saying, 'Will you read this, please, Julia?'

'Who's Julia?' asked Paris.

Camilla said, 'What do policemen eat for lunch, Charles?'

Charles said, in one of his Goon-like voices, 'I don't know, what do policemen eat for lunch?'

Camilla said, 'No, I'm not telling you a joke, Charles. I'm asking you what policemen eat for lunch, because I have invited a policeman to lunch.'

Charles thought hard before saying, 'Don't they eat bangers and mashy-type stuff? Sardines, perhaps.'

Camilla loved entertaining, but in the past there had always been other people to do the hard work: the invitations, the shopping, the cooking, the table-setting and the washing-up.

Charles said, as she hoped he would, 'Don't worry, darling. I'll see that your policeman is fed and watered.'

He opened a tin of sardines and arranged them in a criss-cross pattern on a small white plate, then went into the garden and picked a trug full of distorted root and salad vegetables that he had grown according to organic principles. A blackbird flew on to the razor wire surmounting the metal boundary fence and serenaded Charles as he knocked clods of mud off a bunch of twisted carrots. Camilla sat on an upturned flowerpot, smoking her second cigarette of the day.

'Oh, darling,' said Charles, looking around the garden. 'Isn't it *heavenly* here, doesn't your heart swell with happiness to hear the song of a blackbird?'

Camilla said, guardedly, looking at the razor wire, the CCTV cameras and the Threadgolds' broken bedroom window, smashed during a midnight altercation, 'It's sort of heavenly, but sometimes I long for the proper countryside.'

Charles pulled up a leek that was covered in tiny scurrying creatures and said, 'But we have built our own paradise here, haven't we?'

Camilla thought about the outside world and imagined herself walking through woodland and alongside a river. She envisaged hills in the distance and shafts of burnished sunlight glowing through a vast cloud-dotted sky. She began to cry. She tried desperately to stop, knowing that tears and a contorted face did not flatter a woman of late middle age.

Charles threw the leek into the trug and knelt beside her. 'Please, darling,' he said. 'Please, don't cry. I simply cannot bear it.'

'Sorry, darling, but I can't bear this place either.'

The doorbell rang. Camilla blew her nose, and wiped her eyes with the hem of her flowered skirt. 'That's our policeman,' she said. 'Do I look hag-like?'

'No,' said Charles. 'To me, you will always be beautiful.'

His qualifying phrase, 'To me,' was not lost on Camilla.

Camilla and Dwayne were sitting at the kitchen table. Charles was washing up at the sink. Camilla stifled a yawn. Charles and Dwayne had been talking almost non-stop about a wretched book she'd never read, written by a man she'd never met.

Charles said to Dwayne, 'When Laurens and I were in the Kalahari, we washed our cooking pots, plates and utensils in sand.'

'Sand!' said Dwayne politely.

'Yes,' said Charles. 'It's nature's Fairy Liquid.'

Camilla said, 'And you'd never run out. Of sand,

I mean. There's a *huge* amount of sand in the desert.'

Even Dwayne was beginning to weary of the Kala-hari. He felt as though he'd been staggering across it in the midday sun without a hat. Charles's intensity had drained him. He had quite enjoyed his lunch of sardines and strange-looking vegetables, but he was ready to leave now. He stood up and scraped his chair back, and said, 'Well, thank you very much for everything, but duty calls.'

'Yes, you must go,' said Prince Charles. 'I know about duty.'

Camilla whispered, 'I wonder if you'd mind posting this?' She handed him a letter with a Ruislip address.

He thought, I can hardly say no, can I? and put it in his pocket.

Camilla walked with him to the garden gate and said, 'Is it terribly difficult to remove one's tag? I mean, do people do it?'

'Oh yes,' said Dwayne. 'There's people been on holi-day before now.'

'Really,' said Camilla. 'Do they use a special sort of tool?'

Dwayne said, 'Mrs Windsor, you're better off here in the Fez.' He hesitated. How could he break it to her that she was not that popular in the outside world? Eventually he said, 'Everybody knows your face, you'd soon be spotted.'

When Dwayne got back to the Lilliputian studio flat he rented in the town, he steamed open the letter and read the contents.

16 Hellebore Close
Flowers Exclusion Zone
East Midlands Region
EZ 951

Dear Graham,

One wonders how to reply to one's long-lost son, a son whose existence one was unaware of until yesterday, when we received your letter. Your mother confirmed that she did in fact give birth to you in Zurich, on 21st July 1965.

We both send our condolences on your recent double bereavement. To lose one parent is a misfortune; to lose two is a catastrophe.

Naturally, we are both absolutely longing to see you. However, we are confined at present to the Exclusion Zone and, sadly, we are not allowed visitors from outside, though I understand that visiting orders can be issued to certain government officials, so a meeting may not be possible in the immediate future. But we must not lose contact.

It was quite extraordinary to discover that your mother and I have a forty-one-year-old son together. I wonder, do you resemble either of us physically in any way? When you next write, would you please enclose a photograph?

As I write, I feel the hand of history on my shoulder.

Adieu, my son.

I send you the warmest of wishes.

Your father,

Charles

P.S. Your mother and I would be terribly grateful if you would
keep our relationship confidential, for the moment.

Please reply
c/o PC Dwayne Lockhart
Flat 31, The Old Abattoir
Leicester
East Midlands Region

Dwayne's first thought was, What a cheek! They might have asked me first. He was ashamed of his second thought, which was, I'm holding an historical document here. I wonder how much it would fetch on eBay?

He took the letter with him when he went to the library and photocopied it on the ancient machine that seemed to be used only by mad people copying their epic poems. On his way home, he posted the original letter in a postbox, pausing for a few seconds before he allowed the letter to drop from his hand.

Freddie was in the kitchen having his overlong claws clipped. It was taking the combined strength of Charles and Camilla to hold the little dog down. He had been barking, 'Help! Help!' throughout the procedure. Freddie remembered the time Camilla had cut into his pad and made him bleed.

Charles said, 'Oh, Freddie, do cooperate. Your claws are terribly long, you must be awfully uncomfortable.'

Camilla said, 'If you were human, Freddie, you'd be Edward Scissorhands.'

Upstairs on the small landing, taking advantage of Freddie's absence, were Leo and Tosca. Leo was telling

Tosca about the miserable time he'd had as a puppy before being saved by Spiggy and then adopted by Prince Charles.

'There were nine of us in the litter an' I was the runt. I could hardly get near my mum's teats. I could've starved to death.'

'Who were your parents?' yapped Tosca, who could trace her pedigree back nineteen generations.

'I dunno who my dad was,' said Leo mournfully. 'My mum was a total *dog* when she came on heat, she had half the bleedin' estate after 'er! She'd take on anything with four legs an' a tail.'

'Is she still alive?' barked Tosca.

'No, she went under a Grice delivery lorry,' whimpered Leo. 'She's buried in Lee Butterworth's back garden. She was a *pig* of a mother. Before she'd finished whelping, she was out every night. I used to cry my bleedin' eyes out for 'er.'

'What happened to your brothers and sisters?' asked Tosca.

Leo whimpered, 'All I know is that Lee Butterworth put 'em all in a sack an' told 'is kids that the pups was goin' to live on a farm in Wales. As if.'

'Perhaps they did,' said Tosca.

Leo barked, 'No. Butterworth was back in 'alf an hour. I don't know where Wales is, but it ain't around the corner, is it?'

Tosca barked, 'Why weren't you put in the sack?'

Leo whimpered, 'I were upstairs being dressed up in dolls' clothes by one of Maddo's kids. My life was 'ell in that 'ouse.'

Tosca was growing weary of Leo's self-pity. 'You were obviously saved for a purpose, Leo. The hand of destiny intervened to bring you to this house, to live with the future King of England.'

Leo looked at Tosca with new eyes. She wasn't bad looking and she had a lovely glossy coat. He could overlook her short legs; what did it matter that she was half his size? They were equals when they were lying down. Leo edged near to Tosca and sniffed her hind quarters. Instead of snapping at him, like she usually did, Tosca allowed him to take his time.

When Freddie came bounding up the stairs to find Tosca, he was less than pleased to find Leo with his nose up her bum.

Freddie snarled, 'Get away from my bitch, you low-life mongrel.' He launched himself at Leo, expecting the bigger dog to slink away and hide as usual.

But Leo snarled, 'Back off, short-arse,' and bared his large yellow teeth.

Freddie yelped, 'Who do you think you are?'

'I'm somethink special,' growled Leo. 'I'm the future King of England's best friend.'

When it was Tosca's turn for a pedicure she submitted to the procedure with uncharacteristic good grace.

Camilla said, 'Tosca's not herself at all, Charles. Do you think she's unwell?'

Charles answered, 'Perhaps she needs worming.'

Tosca barked, 'I haven't got worms. You're obsessed with worms. If I did have worms I'd be scooting my bum along the ground, wouldn't I?'

Charles said, 'I'll put a worm tablet in their food tonight. It's better to be safe than sorry.'

'No,' snarled Tosca, 'it's better to be sorry than safe. There's nothing wrong with me, I've never been happier.'

To divert Charles and Camilla from any more worming talk she held out her paw, offering it up to be clipped.

Camilla said, 'She's adorable. Isn't she adorable, darling?'

22

It didn't take long for Camilla to remove her tag: a few minutes of torsion with a pair of secateurs in the bathroom and she was free. She waited until Charles had gone to his Resistible Materials class at the One-Stop Centre, where he was halfway through building an elaborate bird-feeding table. All three dogs were waiting for her outside the bathroom door.

She said, 'I'm going to get into frightful trouble, darlings. But I don't bloody care.'

The dogs gathered around her as she put on her waxed coat and tied her headscarf round her head. When she went out of the front door, slamming it behind her and leaving the dogs in the hall, they barked in protest.

Camilla dawdled through the estate, enjoying the warm autumn sunshine and the knowledge that she was not tagged and had no ID card. She thought, I could be anybody and nobody. When she approached the Control Centre, she quickened her pace and without looking right or left walked straight through. No alarms sounded, nobody shouted after her and Dwayne Lock-hart, who had seen her approaching through the window, excused himself to Inspector Lancer and went into the lavatory until he judged that Camilla would be out of sight.

Camilla ambled down the road leading into the town, marvelling at the goods in the shop windows, wishing she had money to spend. But it was the countryside she had wanted to see. She asked an elderly woman with a walking frame, who was standing at a bus stop, where the countryside was.

'The countryside?' the woman repeated. 'What, fields and trees and things like that?'

'Yes,' said Camilla. 'Is there a bus that will take me there?'

'You want a forty-seven,' the woman said. She was staring at Camilla as if she knew her, taking in the waxed coat, the sensible shoes and the Hermès headscarf printed with horseshoes.

'Is there something wrong?' asked Camilla.

'No,' said the woman. 'You put me in mind of somebody, that's all. Prince Charles's wife.'

'Camilla?' supplied Camilla.

'Yes, that's 'er,' said the woman darkly. 'She dragged the Royal Family through the mud, that one. She lives back there you know, in the Flowers Exclusion Zone.'

Camilla nodded and began to move away.

The woman said, 'By all accounts she's a total alcoholic. Drinks a bottle of vodka with each meal. Lies in a filthy bed all day, only gets up to feed 'er dogs. Fifteen dogs she's got, none of 'em house-trained. It's no wonder Prince Charles gives her a clout round the head now and then, is it?'

Camilla asked, 'How do you know all this?'

The woman said, 'It's common knowledge. I've got a friend who's related by marriage to Prince Charles's next-door neighbour.'

'Beverley Threadgold,' said Camilla.

'Yes,' said the woman. 'Poor Beverley has to put up with 'earing Prince Charles and Camilla screaming at each other all through the night. Furniture smashed, dogs barking. When they're not trying to kill each other, they're in the garden burning leaves and smoking the place out.'

Camilla was relieved when the woman staggered on to a number 49 bus. As she stood and waited, she noticed a few drivers looking at her curiously as they passed by. She wished now that she'd dressed less conspicuously and worn a pastel-coloured tracksuit and white trainers, like most women of her generation wore round here.

On the opposite side of the road, a man was standing on the top rung of a ladder, pasting a large poster on to a billboard. It was hard to see what the poster was advertising at first, but when the man had finished and removed himself and his ladder, Camilla saw that the poster was of a hugely enlarged black Labrador retriever's head. The dog's eyes were mad and its jaws were open, showing vicious teeth. There were no words. Camilla thought, but Labrador retrievers are Britain's favourites. They are national treasures; the Alan Bennetts of the dog world. Why would anybody want to put up such a vicious poster?

The driver of the number 47 bus was baffled when Camilla asked how much it was to be taken to the countryside.

He said, 'The nearest I go to the countryside is the out-of-town retail park. The Orchards.'

She climbed the stairs to the upper deck and sat at the front, holding on to the rail as she had been told to do when she was a child on her regular trips to their London house.

She would quarrel with her brother and sister about which was best, the town or the country. The problem was, when she was in the country she loved the country best, but when she was in the town she was seduced by its excitement and glamour. Her childhood had been one long sunny afternoon with ponies in the paddock, theatre in the town, and Mummy and Daddy and Mark and Sarah, always there. Always laughter and treats and holidays, when nobody minded if she hadn't brushed her hair or ran around barefoot.

The bus passed over a road bridge. Below the bridge was a river and a small wood. Camilla ran down the stairs of the moving bus and asked the driver to stop.

He said, 'I'm not a bleedin' taxi service,' and drove on to the next bus stop.

She ran back to the bridge and saw that a path of sorts had been made down the embankment. There were a few brambles in the way, with some rotting blackberries still hanging from the branches, but she pushed through them in her waxed coat and was soon standing on the riverbank. After a few minutes walking, she was out of earshot of the road. When it was no longer possible to walk alongside the river due to the thick tangle of vegetation, she sat down in the long grass and smoked a cigarette.

The loveliness of the birdsong overwhelmed her. She had never been good with birds, she could just about identify a sparrow or a blackbird, and of course robins were easy. But now she understood what people like Charles were talking about when they lamented the slow demise of the English songbird. It was glorious, simply glorious, to think that nobody, not even Charlie, knew where she was. She lay back in the long grass and watched the clouds passing in the astonishingly blue sky.

On the return journey the bus was crowded with shoppers, and her preferred seat at the front of the top deck was occupied. She glanced quickly down the bus; there were only three vacant seats. She chose to sit next to an innocuous-looking middle-aged woman who was marooned by a sea of Marks and Spencer's bags.

Camilla said, 'May I?'

The woman moved a few of the bags so that Camilla could sit down. 'I only went in for a loaf of bread,' said the woman.

Camilla laughed and said, 'My husband does that. He went out for a loaf and came back with a washing-up bowl.'

The woman looked at Camilla curiously. They were silent for a few moments, each woman assessing the other for class, status and level of attractiveness. Having decided that further conversation was possible, the woman with the bags said, 'It's lovely on the top of a bus, isn't it?'

'Yes,' said Camilla. 'One can see into people's gardens and backyards.'

The woman said, 'The buses are quite civilized since those dreadful hoodies and yobs were rounded up and tagged. The Government will certainly get my vote at the next election.'

Camilla said, 'Oh, if I had a vote I'd give it to Boy English. He's a real sweetie.'

The woman said, 'Do you not have a vote?'

Camilla was not a good liar. She stammered unconvincingly, 'My husband doesn't allow me to vote.'

The woman's eyes widened. She took in Camilla's headscarf and asked, 'Who are you married to, a Muslim fundamentalist?'

'No, though my husband is interested in Eastern religions,' said Camilla and lowered her voice. 'Do you remember Prince Charles?'

The woman said, 'Of course. And he's another reason why I'll vote for the Government. I certainly don't want the New Cons to win, not if it means bringing back those dreadful Windsors. I suppose at a pinch I could just about accept the Queen, but the thought of Prince Charles and that hideous woman, Camilla, reigning over me makes my blood run cold.'

An inspector clumped up the stairs and shouted, 'Tickets and registration cards, please. Have them ready for inspection.'

There was an audible groan from the passengers and an anxious search through bags and purses. Wallets were taken out, pockets were patted and bumbags were unzipped.

The inspector started at the back of the bus. Camilla could hear him saying, 'Thank you, sir; thank you, madam,' as he moved inexorably towards her.

The bag woman next to her kept her ID card in a

burgundy leather wallet. As she held it out towards the inspector, Camilla saw a photograph of a balding man with his arms around a large smiling dog. After he had checked the woman's documents, the inspector stood looking down expectantly at Camilla. She showed him her ticket.

He glanced at it and said, 'ID card, please.'

Camilla said, 'Sorry, I seem to have left it at home.'

The inspector sighed and said, 'I'm going to have to give you an on-the-spot fine.'

Camilla said, 'I haven't any money.'

He took out a book of forms and said, 'Name?'

The other passengers on the bus had fallen silent.

Camilla said, 'I would rather not give my name.'

The inspector said, 'I would rather you did.'

Camilla said, 'Can't I just get off the bus? I'll walk the rest of the way.'

She half rose to her feet; the woman next to her was now looking studiedly out of the window, detaching herself from the scene.

The inspector said, 'You're not going anywhere, madam, until you give me your name.'

Camilla said, 'I'm sorry, but I can't.'

The inspector took out a small radio and spoke into it. 'Driver, stop the bus. I've got a UP up here.'

The bus came to a jerky stop.

A voice from the back shouted, 'How long we going to be? I've got kids to pick up from school.'

The bag woman said, 'I've got a dog to let out. He's been in the house since nine o'clock this morning. He'll burst his bladder if I'm late.'

An old man across the aisle said, 'I know who she is. She's Camilla Parker Bowles, as was.'

'She lives in an Exclusion Zone,' said the inspector. 'It can't be her. She's on the tag.'

'I remember his first wife,' said the old man. 'Beautiful, she was. A saint. They say she could cure cancer.'

A sarcastic voice behind Camilla said, 'Yeah! An' she turned the bleedin' water into wine.'

The inspector said, 'I'm going to ask you again, madam, to give me your name and your full address.'

Camilla said, 'I'm terribly sorry, but I can't.'

'Then you give me no alternative but to inform the security police.'

When Prince Charles arrived home he was exhausted, having carried the bird-feeding table almost a mile. He wished now that he hadn't constructed such an elaborate edifice. It was multi-levelled, each level having its own thatched roof. There were indents for bowls of water and little troughs for seeds. He lugged it through the house and out into the back garden, shouting, 'Darling, I'm home. I've finished it.'

The dogs danced around him as he searched every room, looking for Camilla.

'She can't have gone out,' he said to them. 'She's left her ID card in the little jug on the dresser.'

Leo led him into the bathroom where, to Charles's great alarm, he found the secateurs and his wife's ankle tag.

23

Camilla's interrogation had been conducted with the utmost civility by Deputy Chief Constable Peter Manning, in his austere office in the huge, recently built Regional Police Headquarters. After a strip-search by two silent policewomen, Camilla had been taken for forensic investigation. No trace of explosives was found on her, only an unusual quantity of dog hair.

Manning would not usually have bothered himself with the questioning of terrorist suspects; he had specialist teams for that, who, by various methods, were able to extract information. But he could not resist questioning Camilla. It would be an engrossing chapter in the book he was writing about modern policing, he thought.

M: Why did you leave the Exclusion Zone?

C: I wanted to go to the countryside.

M: You were meeting somebody there?

C: No, I just wanted, you know, to *see* it.

M: You're a member of BOMB, aren't you?

C: BOMB? I don't know what that is.

M: They, as you well know, are terrorists dedicated to bringing the monarchy back. BOMB, Bring Our Monarchy Back. You arranged to meet them yesterday.

C: No, I've never heard of them. They don't sound like my kind of people. I'm not a political animal.

M: So, you maintain, do you, that you removed your tag . . . incidentally, how did you do it?

C: Secateurs.

[Manning nodded, he was a gardener himself.]

M: Not a cheap pair, obviously.

C: No, I don't think one should economize on secateurs. A good strong pair will last a lifetime.

M: So, you removed your tag and left your ID card at home?

C: Yes.

M: That's two offences.

C: Yes. I suppose it is.

M: How did you pass the control point? Did you have an accomplice?

C: No, I just sort of walked by. Nobody stopped me, so I carried on walking.

M: You arranged to meet somebody on the riverbank, didn't you, Mrs Windsor? You waited for thirteen minutes, during which time you smoked a Silk Cut cigarette. But the person or persons you had arranged to meet didn't come, did they? So you retraced your steps and were arrested on the forty-seven bus.

Camilla closed her eyes. It was as though Manning had snatched a precious crystal from her and had smashed it to smithereens. She had expected to keep those thirteen minutes of tranquillity and freedom to herself. She had planned to withdraw memories as needed, like she used to withdraw money from the bank. She would not have been extravagant with her memories. She would have remembered the flash of the sun on the river perhaps, or the angle of the reeds as they bent forwards in the breeze like a crowd sharing a secret. But she would not have recalled the glorious singing of the birds in the woodland next to the river.

That loveliness would have been too terrible to bear.

C: I wanted to be free for a while, to be out of sight.

M: You're a romantic, Mrs Windsor. I understand; I'm a bit that way myself. A golf course in the early morning can bring tears to my eyes.

C: What will happen to me?

M: You have broken seven laws in all, Mrs Windsor. Eight, if we prosecute you for reckless smoking. You were surrounded by dried grasses, you could have started an inferno.

C: I'm to be prosecuted, am I?

M: You've committed serious offences, Mrs Windsor. [Manning smiled.] By committing such offences you have forfeited your right to go to court.

C: I see.

But she didn't *truly* see. On the other hand, Manning seemed to be a thoroughly decent chap. Not the type to muck about with civil liberties. All the same, Camilla had taken it for granted that if you broke the law you were entitled to be tried in a court of law. Wasn't that the English way?

C: So who punishes me?

M: Ultimately, God will punish you, Mrs Windsor, but for now, con-tractually, I have to turn you over to Arthur Grice Security.

C: Can I telephone my husband, Inspector? He'll be frantic with worry.

M: I'm sorry, Mrs Windsor, that privilege does not extend to terrorist suspects. Incidentally, the secateurs, which brand?

C: Wilkinson's.

An investigation was being conducted at the Flowers Control Centre into how Camilla had managed to walk past them into the outside world. Inspector Lancer was showing CCTV footage of Camilla as she strolled past the Control Centre with her hands in her pockets.

Lancer said, 'Note the time on the film. She passed us at precisely eleven thirty-five a.m.' He held up the duty roster. 'Those on duty at eleven thirty-five were police constables Julie Cutherwaite, Dwayne Lockhart and Lee Clegg, and police dogs Emperor and Judge. So, what I want to know is, what the fuck went wrong?'

Dwayne held up his hand and said, 'Excuse me, sir. You've forgotten one other person.'

'And who would that be?' snarled Lancer.

'Yourself,' said Dwayne.

Lancer said, 'I was busy working out the duty rosters, Lockhart. Surveillance is below my pay scale. So, somebody's head has got to roll. Headquarters want blood.' He turned to Julie Cutherwaite and said, 'You're a moody cow and you've got no tits to speak of. So, you'll write to Mr Grice and offer your resignation, and take full responsibility for this morning's breach of security.'

Julie said, angrily, 'That's sexism. You wouldn't sack Dwayne for having a small cock.'

Dwayne was tempted to defend himself against the

charge, but he kept quiet, judging it wise in the circumstances.

The forty-six residents of Hell Close were evacuated from their homes at midnight by the security police and were gathered together in the main hall of the One-Stop Centre. Groups of sleepy people sat about on spindly-legged plastic chairs, yawning and complaining. Camilla was notably absent. Charles was sick with worry; he went from group to group asking if anybody knew the whereabouts of his wife. Since he had already knocked at every door in Hell Close that afternoon without result, it was a futile exercise.

The ex-Royal Family sat together at the back of the hall, speculating in low voices on the reason for Camilla's disappearance. Harry was of the view that a police death squad was in operation.

The Queen said, 'This is England, Harry, not Guatemala.'

Andrew speculated that there had been a coup, and that the Government had been overthrown by ardent monarchists.

Anne said angrily, 'It's obviously something to do with Camilla. As if she hasn't brought enough trouble to this family.'

Princess Michael said, 'In my opinion, she's left Charles for another man. I knew their marriage would never last.'

Edward and Sophie turned from watching anxiously as Louise ran wild with Maddo Clarke's boys.

Sophie said, 'I can't stop thinking about the Romanovs.

They were rounded up in the middle of the night, weren't they?'

Edward took Sophie's hand and said, 'Try to stay calm. Take one of your pills, darling.'

William yawned, 'It's all right for the rest of you, but I have to get up for work in the morning.'

When Charles returned to his family group he said, 'Nobody knows anything about Camilla's whereabouts.'

Beverley Threadgold, in a grubby pink dressing gown and Elvis Presley slippers, sat nearby telling Maddo Clarke that she wouldn't be surprised if Camilla had been murdered. She looked across the room at Prince Charles and said, ''E was diggin' in 'is garden, after dark last night.'

Dwayne Lockhart, armed with a taser gun that he had no intention of using, was guarding the exit doors. He wanted to confide in Charles that he had seen Camilla leaving the Exclusion Zone earlier in the day. But how could he, without losing his job and his flat in town? He shifted the taser carefully from one hand to the other, aware that a single pull on the trigger could send a 50,000-volt shock through the human body. He hoped fervently that he wouldn't be forced to use the thing.

Violet Toby was reminiscing with the Queen about the last time Hell Close had been evacuated.

'It was before you come here, Liz. A crack 'ead in Number Sixteen held his social worker hostage with a starting pistol. It were lovely. We 'ad cups of tea and sandwiches from the WRVS, and a good singsong.' She sighed. 'Happy days.'

The Queen asked, 'What was the outcome? Did all end well?'

'Oh, yes,' said Violet. 'The crack 'ead shot 'iself an' the social worker 'ad a breakdown.'

The Queen yawned and covered her mouth; she was longing to return to her bed. She had been in a deep sleep when an announcement from the police helicopter hovering over Hell Close had startled her awake and ordered her to leave the house immediately. Once outside, a phalanx of security police had corralled the residents and marched them to the One-Stop Centre. There had been no WRVS and, thought the Queen, it was unlikely there would be a singsong.

At half past three in the morning, when even Maddo Clarke's boys were flagging, the double doors burst open and Camilla was led in, surrounded by a cordon of security police. She blinked in the harsh fluorescent light and looked around the gaping crowd for Charles. When she saw him pushing through the crowd, she raised her handcuffs above her head, like a triumphant boxer, but there was no joy in the gesture, only recognition that she accepted her capture, punishment and humiliation. Arthur Grice followed with a face like a dark cloud.

Charles shouted, 'Camilla, darling,' and tried to take her hand, but his way was blocked by PC Peter Penny, and he was pushed back into the crowd.

'I'm sorry, darling,' Camilla shouted.

A policeman in a beribboned uniform addressed the exhausted residents. He said, 'I am Deputy Chief Constable Manning. Yesterday, this woman . . .' he indicated Camilla.

Charles shouted, 'How dare you call my wife a woman!'

Manning continued, 'Yesterday, this lady removed her tag and left the Exclusion Zone. As a consequence of her actions she will be placed under house arrest for ten days, and you, her friends and neighbours, will be restricted to the environs of Hellebore Close for a seven-day period.'

'*Pour encourager les autres*,' murmured the Queen.

Camilla bowed her head. There was a low rumble of anger from the crowd, like the soundtrack in a cowboy film of buffalo running across distant plains. All eyes turned to her.

Princess Michael rushed forwards and said, 'But there is not a food shop in Hell Close. Do you intend to starve us to death? Or perhaps turn us into cannibals!'

Deputy Chief Constable Manning turned to Arthur Grice, seeking elucidation.

Princess Michael continued, her voice reaching a hysterical note. 'Yes! Now I see your plan. You want us to eat each other, to destroy the monarchy ourselves. Very clever, Kommandant.'

Many eyes examined Princess Michael with close attention, noting where the fleshy bits were.

'I wouldn't mind a slice of her arse,' shouted Maddo Clarke. He looked around, grinning. But people were in no mood to laugh.

Spiggy leapt from his chair and barged through the crowd, grabbing Maddo by the front of his shirt. He roared, 'You insult a member of my family, and you insult me!'

Anne shouted, 'Leave it, Spiggy, leave it! He's not worth it!'

Spiggy pushed Maddo like he thought they did in the films, and walked back with as much dignity as a little fat man, dressed in paisley pyjama trousers and a Meat Loaf tee shirt, could muster.

Charles said, 'I presume, Deputy Chief Constable, that you will be providing us with the necessities of life.'

Arthur Grice said savagely, 'If it was up to me, you'd be on bread and water, but Deputy Chief Constable Manning 'ere is a 'umanitarian, so you'll be provided with a Grice grocery box.'

Sophie said, 'I'm on a low-potassium diet, Mr Grice, I can't eat tomatoes, mushrooms or bananas.'

'You'll eat what you bleedin' well get,' shouted Grice. I ain't a fookin' diet gnu.'

'Guru,' corrected the Deputy Chief Constable irritably. He was furious with Grice and his privatized security police. He had warned HQ that minimum wage policing was a non-starter.

Vince Threadgold said, 'You said we'd 'ave the necessities of life. Does that include fags an' booze?'

'No,' said Grice, tapping the ash from his cigar on to the floor. 'Now would be a good time to give 'em up.'

The Queen said, 'Deputy Chief Constable, my husband is a resident of Frank Bruno House. He depends on my visits . . .'

Manning waved the Queen's implied request away with a black-gloved hand. He was anxious to get away from the fusty smell of unhealthy bodies packed into an unventilated room.

When William asked Grice if he was expected to turn up for work in the morning, and other people made enquiries about doctor's appointments and school attendance, Grice lost his patience. He roared, 'You 'eard what Mr Manning said, you're not allowed to leave 'Ell Close for seven days and seven nights. Don't blame me, blame 'er.' He glared at Camilla, remembering the angry confrontation he'd had the previous evening when Manning had warned him that future contracts to police the Flowers Exclusion Zone would have to be reviewed. He then ordered Dwayne Lockhart to escort Charles and Camilla to their house, and told him that if they gave him any trouble to 'let 'em 'ave it with the taser'.

When Charles and Camilla were allowed out into the cold early-morning air they found their dogs waiting for them. Freddie and Tosca jumped up to Camilla with such wild enthusiasm that they almost knocked her off her feet. 'Are you pleased to see me, darlings?' she said.

Leo pressed his head against Charles's thigh and rasped, 'I'm glad she's back.'

Charles said, 'You're glad to see her back, aren't you, Leo? You're glad to see her back, aren't you, boy?'

Leo growled, 'I've already *said* I'm glad to see her back. Do you have to repeat *everything*?'

Charles said to Dwayne, 'Would it be possible to remove my wife's handcuffs?'

Dwayne said, 'Sorry, Mr Windsor, but she'll have to keep 'em on until she's inside the house.'

Camilla said, 'I quite understand why I'm being

punished, but why does everyone else in Hell Close have to suffer?'

Charles said, 'It's collective punishment, darling. Didn't you come across it at school?'

Camilla thought back to her schooldays. What a laugh they had been: the teachers had been absolute sweethearts, so understanding if one forgot the wretched capitals of South America.

As they passed Mr Anwar's shop, Camilla pointed out that the 'Everything A Pound' shop sign had been replaced with one that said 'Grice's Everything A Fiver Shop'.

Charles grumbled, 'Somebody should report ghastly Grice to the Monopolies Commission.'

'Funny thing about the Monopolies Commission,' said Dwayne. 'It's got a monopoly on monopolies commissions, hasn't it?'

'He'll be erecting a statue of himself next,' said Charles.

'In gold, on the recreation ground,' laughed Camilla.

'Parties of schoolchildren will be brought to his effigy to sing his praises and wave their little Grice flags. Sometimes . . . I think . . . well . . . we are, er . . . sleepwalking into a dictatorship,' said Charles.

'Be careful what you say,' whispered Dwayne. He caught Charles's eye and gestured with a slight indication of his head and the lift of an eyebrow towards the trees they were passing.

Tosca yelped to Leo, 'I wondered why a BT engineer was pruning trees. Now I know.'

Leo sniffed Tosca's bum and said, 'I love you, Tosca. You're so clever.'

Tosca ran around the back of Leo and stood up on her back paws and sniffed Leo's bum. Freddie pretended not to notice the other two dogs' public display of affection, but he burned with jealousy inside. If he hadn't been so exhausted, he thought, he would have torn Leo's throat out. He'd thought he could cope with having three dogs in the marriage, but he was wrong. He vowed to get rid of Leo, who, after all, was only a mongrel, whereas he, Freddie, could trace his bloodline back through the centuries.

As soon as Dwayne had left them alone, Charles and Camilla threw themselves into each other's arms. Then, to Freddie's disgust, they went upstairs to the bedroom and made love.

Freddie lay outside the bedroom door, listening to the cries of passion and the shouted endearments. When he judged that the couple were reaching their climax, he threw himself against the door in a frenzy of barking and didn't stop until the door was flung open and Camilla, naked and flushed, gave him a swift kick that sent him flying across the landing. When he was on his feet again, he bared his teeth at her.

Camilla shouted, 'What *is* wrong with you, Freddie?'

Freddie gave a deep growl from the back of his throat and said, 'You'll be sorry for that one day, woman.'

24

The anti-dog campaign had started slowly with bus shelter posters depicting a blown-up photograph of a slathering Rottweiler with froth hanging from its jaws. A government public service film showed a pack of feral dogs running amok on a deserted suburban estate. Menacing music played and a spectral voice said: 'They kill. They maim. They spread disease. The dogs are taking over.'

The Prime Minister chose to announce the date of the general election at Great Ormond Street Hospital, from the bedside of a seven-year-old called Sophie Littlejohn. A Rottweiler had bitten the little girl on her forearm two days before on Hampstead Heath. Sophie was in a hospital bed because she had developed an allergic reaction to the tetanus injection she had been given in Outpatients. The iciest of hearts would have melted at the pathetic sight of the little girl: the golden curls, the bandages and the intravenous drip.

When Jack first saw Sophie, he was concerned that there didn't appear to be 'enough bandages on the kid'. He said so to his media advisers, who in turn suggested to the ward manager that Sophie might be more 'comfortable with a bit more padding'. More bandages and a sling had been applied. A media adviser removed the pillows so that Sophie was forced to lie flat on her back, but the camera operative had complained that he wasn't bloody Houdini; he needed her sitting up. Once the lights and microphones had been arranged, a make-up girl had applied a little pale foundation to Sophie's pink cheeks. When Sophie's mother objected, she was asked to leave the ward by one of Jack's entourage. When she refused, security officers were sent for and she was led away for an ID check.

Jack and his media advisers waited impatiently for Sophie to stop crying for her mother. It was not that they were unsympathetic, but the kid didn't realize that the Prime Minister was working to a tight schedule and they were anxious for the election announcement to make the lunchtime news. A giant teddy bear had been ordered from Hamleys. Its arrival caused a heated discussion among the advisers. Should the giant bear be present throughout the announcement, or should the Prime Minister be filmed presenting it to Sophie? Eventually, it was decided that the bear would be in shot throughout the announcement, wearing a Cromwell Party rosette.

Immediately before the filming began, the director instructed Sophie to close her eyes and not to open them again until she was told to do so. The bear was placed on the bed sitting between the apparently unconscious child and the Prime Minister. But the camera operative said, 'That bloody bear is filling the shot.'

The bear was repositioned to everyone's satisfaction, but as Jack was making his announcement, saying, 'I am sitting at the bedside of a very poorly little girl called Sophie. She was savaged by a dog yesterday on

Hampstead Heath,' the bear lurched to the left, falling across the intravenous line and toppling on to the terrified child. When the bear had been lifted off her and her sobs had abated it was repositioned yet again, this time by standing it upright, on the floor, between Jack's chair and the hospital bed.

Jack stared down at Sophie, lying with her eyes tightly shut. His voice trembled as he looked back into the camera and continued. 'The dog that savaged this little girl was a Rottweiler, a foreign dog that should never have been allowed into this country in the first place. To stop such incidents recurring I am proposing to bring in legislation that will severely curtail the freedom of dogs to threaten and maim our children. For such a revolutionary piece of legislation the Government requires a mandate, from you, the people. To this end I am calling a general election. Polling will take place six weeks from this Thursday, that's Thursday November the eleventh.

'English men and English women must decide. Are you on the side of kiddies like Sophie who ought to be able to play safely in our public parks? Or will you choose to support mad dogs who pollute our public areas and savage our precious children?'

Jack had moved himself to tears and the camera focused on his eyes as he turned to look down at Sophie. The little girl opened her eyes because the man had stopped speaking. She looked up and saw the glassy eyes of the giant bear staring down at her, and she started to cry for her mother.

As Jack and his media advisers were going down

from the ward in the lift, Jack said, 'I hope they got the tears.'

After two days of getting in everybody's way the giant bear was taken by two porters down to the hospital basement where it was stuffed into a room with many other giant bears donated to the hospital by generous, but unthinking, well-wishers.

Beverley and Vince Threadgold had watched the lunch-time news with tears in their eyes. When the camera had shown the close-up of Sophie, lying as though unconscious with her blonde curls spread over her pillow, Beverley had said, 'Oh, Vince, you'll have to turn it off, I'm far too sensitive to watch owt upsetting about kiddies.'

Vince looked angrily at King, who was sleeping innocently in a corner of the sofa, and said, 'If our King ever attacked a kiddie, I'd tear his fucking 'ead from his shoulders.'

King woke up when he heard his name and wondered why Vince was glaring at him with such hatred.

Beverley said, 'When I 'ad my tonsils out, our dad bought me a big bear like that, but it gorrin' the nurses' way an' me dad 'ad to take it 'ome, on the bus. 'E got in a fight with some lads who were takin' the piss.'

Vince said, looking at the Prime Minster, ''E looks fuckin' old lately, don't 'e?'

Beverley said, ''As the digital gone funny, or 'as 'e gotta twitch?'

A picture of the Rottweiler that had bitten Sophie was shown with its owner, a tall man in a pinstriped suit and flamboyant tie.

An announcer said, 'The Rottweiler at the centre of the Sophie Littlejohn tragedy has been identified as belonging to a leading politician, the Party Chairman of the New Conservatives, Tarquin Forbes-Hamilton. In a statement released today, he said, "My dog, Lucy, adores children. Perhaps the little girl was teasing her. Lucy has been under the weather lately after giving birth to eight puppies. I see no reason why such an affectionate and loyal dog should be put down."'

When the picture went back to the studio, a woman in a pink suit with carefully coiffed hair and immaculate make-up said, 'What do you, the viewer, think? Should Lucy be destroyed? For "Yes", press the red button on your remote, for "No", press green.'

Vince picked up the remote control, and said to Beverley, 'It's worth spendin' a quid to put that kiddie killer down,' and pressed the red button.

That evening, the first anti-dog advertisements were shown on all the major television channels. Old films of rabid dogs were shown to a soundtrack that had been strongly influenced by horror films. All over England, dog owners looked at their pets with unease for the future. After a phone call from Boy English, it was announced on the six o'clock news that Lucy was dead and that Tarquin Forbes-Hamilton had resigned his chairmanship of the New Con Party. At nine o'clock, in time for the news, Boy was filmed sitting by Sophie Littlejohn's bed, silently holding her hand.

25

Camilla stood on the front doorstep, looking towards the entrance to Hell Close where a temporary barrier had been constructed from portable crowd-control fences. Grice's security police were on duty, turning away cars and inquisitive pedestrians, assisted by police dogs, Emperor and Judge. A gang of dogs were running excitedly through the spindly trees on the little patch of ground in the middle of Hell Close. Micky, Tosca, King, Althorp and Carling were trying to catch Leo, but by weaving from side to side with constant changes of direction, Leo was evading capture.

Freddie pushed past Camilla and, after watching the chasing dogs for a few moments, growled, 'Look at the fools, have they nothing better to do?'

Camilla patted the top of his head and said, 'Go on, boy. Go and play.'

Charles was in their front garden digging a hole in the lawn for his bird table. When he finished he said, 'Darling, could you help me put it in place?'

Camilla said, 'No, darling. I can't leave the house, can I?' She thought, there are *some* advantages to being under house arrest.

Charles said, 'Sorry, darling. It's absolutely absurd, banning you from your own garden.'

He hefted the bird table into the hole and replaced

the turf around the base, then stepped back to look at the effect it made. He said, with a frown, 'You don't think it's too ... er ... *dominant*, do you? It does *loom* somewhat.'

'It's certainly imposing,' said Camilla, looking at the seven-foot-high construction with its multi-ledges, tables and roosting boxes. 'But I'm sure the birds will be terribly appreciative.' She watched him fondly as he attached a piece of coconut on a string and hung it from a nail, then placed nuts and seeds on to the various surfaces. She said, 'Look at our lovely bird table, Freddie. Isn't Charles clever?'

Freddie waddled over to the bird table, cocked his leg and urinated over the base.

Charles shouted, 'You horrid little beast!'

Freddie scrambled through a hole in the low privet hedge and ran out into the close and down to the barrier, where he barked, 'Let me through, I've got an appointment in Slapper Alley.'

Judge barked back, 'Try to leave this close, you short-arsed fleabag, and I'll rip your bleedin' throat out.'

The gang of dogs stopped their chasing game and lay flat on the ground, panting and watching the altercation at the barrier.

Emperor barked, 'And that goes for all you Hell Close low-life scum. You're all forbidden to leave the close.'

Princess Anne was looking out of her front-room window. She said, 'Spig, what's that tower thing Charles has just put up in his front garden?'

Spiggy looked out of the window and said glumly, 'Christ knows. Give me a clue.' Spiggy was in a bad mood, he had people to see and things to do on the estate today, and now, because of his sister-in-law, he couldn't do anything. He said, 'I'll go stir-crazy stuck in the bleedin' 'ouse.'

Anne said, 'You can do something about those bloody scaffolding poles. I've been living with them for ten years and I'm sick of manoeuvring round them, it's like the bloody slalom course at Klosters.'

It didn't suit Spiggy to be confined; it was like living in an open prison, and he knew what that was like. He'd spent seven months at North Sea Camp for a tarmacking scam. He had, for three of those months, worked in the prison kitchens with Jeffrey Archer, who had encouraged Spiggy to tell him his life story. The great man had subsequently published his prison diaries and Spiggy had featured in them, under the alias of a Russian mafia hit man.

Spiggy said, 'There ain't no point in doing the house up, is there? We could be out of 'ere in six weeks if the New Cons win the election.' He threw himself down on the mock-leather sofa and propped his head in his hands.

Anne said, 'You don't sound delighted at the prospect. What's wrong, Spig?' She cuffed him round the head playfully.

Spiggy said, gloomily, 'You're not goin' to want me if you go back into the outside world, are you?'

Anne said, 'So, who will I want?'

'Some bloody posho with no chin,' said Spiggy.

Anne said, 'I've had two of those, and neither of them was half the man you are, Spig.'

But Spiggy was wallowing in his misery. 'I'll 'ave to wear a suit,' he said, 'an' eat artichokes.'

Anne laughed and said, 'Come on, Spig. What's really up with you?'

Spiggy said, 'I've run out of fags and I can't go to the bleedin' shops to buy some because your brother's wife fancied a stroll outside.'

Anne said, 'If you help me with the housework, I'll ask Camilla if she's got a few fags to spare.'

Spiggy could turn his hand to anything, but the mysterious arts of cooking, laundering and cleaning continued to keep their secrets from him. He had never used a lavatory brush in his life, and he felt nothing but contempt for any man that would.

Spiggy said, 'No, don't bother, Maddo Clarke owes me a few favours.'

Harris and Susan were lying on the end of the Queen's bed, watching her sleep. Harris said, 'She's never slept this late before. It's nearly midday.'

Susan whimpered, 'I'm dying for a pee. We'll have to wake her soon.'

Harris tramped along the silk coverlet and began to lick the Queen's face. The Queen woke and said, 'Hello, boy.' She glanced at the little carriage clock on the bedside table; it was 11.54 a.m.

Susan ran to the bedroom door and barked, 'I'm hungry and thirsty and I want a pee.'

The Queen said, sleepily, 'Yes, I hear you.'

Violet Toby shouted from downstairs, 'Where are you, Liz?'

The Queen shouted back, 'I'm upstairs. Come up.'

She heard Violet wheezing on the stairs, then the bedroom door opened, and Violet said, 'Are you poorly?'

Violet had been in the Queen's bedroom on only a few occasions. Each time she had been almost overwhelmed by the loveliness of the furniture and accoutrements. The room was like the inside of the Fabergé egg that the Queen kept on her dressing table. It was lustrous and mirrored; objects seemed to shimmer above the surfaces on which they were placed. The room reminded Violet that her friend and neighbour had once been the Queen of England and the Commonwealth, and had been fabulously wealthy.

The Queen sat up and put her glasses on. 'No,' she said, 'I'm perfectly well. I've been lying in bed listening to the radio. Did you hear the Prime Minister's announcement?'

Violet said, 'I seen it on the telly. That poor little kiddie.'

'Yes, dreadful,' said the Queen.

'If the Government don't get back in,' said Violet, 'you'll be leaving 'ere.'

'If the New Cons keep their promise,' said the Queen.

Violet said, straightening the silken coverlet, 'I won't know what to do with myself if you leave here and go back to your palace.'

The Queen picked at a loose thread on the monogrammed sheet and said, 'I'll miss you, Violet. Would you consider coming with me?'

Violet said, 'I'd love to, but I couldn't leave our Barry.'

The Queen was tempted to say that Barry would be welcome to live in one of the royal palaces, but instead she said, 'Yes, family comes first.'

Violet said, 'I've come round to borrow a tin of dog food. My poor Micky will be chewing his own leg off if he don't get fed soon.'

Harris and Susan barked in protest. Harris growled, 'Away with you, woman. Let the mangy moron eat his own leg. He's nae having my food.'

The Queen started to get out of bed.

Violet said, 'Stay there, I'll make you a cup of tea, and let the dogs out, shall I?'

When Violet and the dogs had gone downstairs, the Queen lay back on her pillows, remembering how agreeable it had been in the old days to have people helping her with the bothersome necessities of everyday life. There was the sound of a dogfight in the back garden. She heard Freddie, Susan and Micky snarling and snapping, then Violet's voice screaming, 'Leave our Micky alone, you nasty little bleeders.'

The Queen got out of bed and looked out of the window and saw Violet laying into the dogs with a sweeping brush. When the dogs had gone their separate ways and run out of the garden, the Queen got back into bed. She felt a little guilty, but she thought, I am eighty years old, and I have been up most of the night.

Violet stomped up the stairs again; this time she carried a tray of tea and hot buttered toast.

Violet said, 'You must be right pissed off with Camilla.'

The Queen sipped at her tea and said, 'Yes, I am rather. I'm absolutely furious with her, putting us all to a great deal of trouble. I won't be able to visit Philip.'

Violet said, 'And I'm running out of my blood pressure pills. If I have a stroke, it'll be Camilla what killed me.'

The Queen said, 'She really should have thought about the consequences before she went AWOL.'

'She's a bit of a loose cannon, though, ain't she?' said Violet. 'I mean, tell me if I'm speaking out of order, but I'm not sure she's queen material.'

The Queen said, 'My own sentiments entirely, Violet. She's been well enough brought up, but she hasn't had the training. I had the spontaneity knocked out of me at an early age. The only impulsive thing I ever did in my whole life was to fall in love with Philip at first sight. He'll be pining for me.'

Violet said, 'I can't tell our Chantelle to look out for 'im either. She tried to go to work this morning, but the police turned 'er back. So I've got 'er and Chanel moping round the 'ouse, an' Barry talkin' to 'imself in 'is bedroom. They're as wound up as a milkman's alarm clock.'

The Queen said, 'Stay here, Violet. We'll have some lunch and watch the afternoon film.'

Violet said, 'With a bit of luck, it'll be in black and white.'

Both women believed that films had deteriorated since colour was introduced.

26

Panic broke out among the residents when the Grice grocery van pulled into Hell Close. Earlier that morning a rumour had swept from house to house that there would not be enough food to go round. Beverley Threadgold claimed she had heard on the grapevine that the residents were to be given British army rations earmarked for Afghanistan. She had told Maddo Clarke, who had in turn passed it on to Chantelle Toby, that they were expected to live on dehydration salts and dry biscuits.

Grice security police, in riot gear, had bellowed at the residents to form a queue. But panicked by the thought of going hungry, several people, including Prince Andrew, pushed to the front and were beaten back with batons. Camilla watched from the doorstep as Charles was pushed further and further back until he was at the very end of the agitated queue.

When Princess Anne walked by with a cardboard box full of groceries, she said, 'Camilla, if I were you I'd go inside and close the door. People are blaming you for this and things could turn nasty.'

Camilla took Anne's advice.

The Hell Close dogs were also in a state of agitation; examination of the first food box carried away by Barry

Toby revealed that there was no dog food among the tins, packets and bottles.

Micky said to Leo, 'It's gonna be dog eat dog,' as he followed Barry back to the house.

When Charles finally arrived home, he and Camilla unpacked the groceries on to the kitchen table. They were far from being army rations, which are meticulously assembled for nutritional and calorific value. These foods were devoid of minerals, vitamins, fibre, goodness and taste. Most of them had been processed from dubious ingredients in eastern European industrial units.

Camilla said, 'We've run out of loo roll and there's none here.'

Grice's groceries included a tin of pink sausages in brine, two 'Mexican-style' pot noodles, a box of economy tea bags, a chicken and mushroom pie (three days past its sell-by date), a tin of spam, a tin of grey mince, two tired leeks, a bag of defrosted oven chips, a block of margarine and one of lard, a white sliced loaf, a pot of Slovenian jam, a two-pound bag of granulated sugar, and surprisingly, in the bottom of the box, under a packet of Vesta chow mein, an envelope bearing the House of Commons portcullis.

Dwayne Lockhart had lifted the visor on his helmet as he handed Charles his provisions, and whispered, 'There's a bit of a treat for you in the bottom of the box.'

Charles opened the envelope and read:

To His Royal Highness, The Prince of Wales
c/o PC Dwayne Lockhart
Flat 31, The Old Abattoir
Leicester
East Midlands Region

My Dearest Charles,

How could you think that I would desert you in your hour of need? I confess myself hurt that you think me capable of such calumny.

I was knocked sideways when my man brought your letter to me in bed this morning. I recognized your distinctive hand and almost choked on my Cumberland sausage.

I am somewhat baffled myself as to why you have not received my numerous letters. I curse myself now for not having made copies; mes belles lettres would have transmogrified into a decent little book, 'Letters to a Prince in Exile'. What do you think, eh?

I managed to get some shooting in at Buffy Haight-Fernemore's place in Northampton — a couple of dozen brace of partridge and, as a special request from Buffy's Mallorcan cook, a dozen larks for a pie.

Did you see the television footage of our illustrious Prime Minister, Mr Barker, stepping into the dog poo? It was priceless. Goofy Guggenheim, who was there at the Abbey in an aisle seat, said the smell was so foul that he almost retched into his top hat.

Buffy tells me that Boy English is so confident of winning

*the election that he has already contracted Colefax and Fowler
to do up Number Ten. He also advised me to put money on it.
Apparently the odds are extremely favourable on him winning.
It will be simply marvellous to have you back in London.*

*I consulted the top chap at Burke's Peerage and there is no
sound constitutional reason why Camilla cannot be your queen.
The public are a little lukewarm, but they could, I think, be
made to learn to love Camilla as you and I do. Anyway, that's
far into the future, as your mama will undoubtedly live to be a
hundred!!!*

*Must dash, I'm speaking against the Stepladder Bill in twenty
minutes but I wanted to get back to you asap.*

Love to Camilla and your mother, Her Majesty, of course.

Yours, as always

Nick

Charles passed the letter to Camilla and said, 'Fatty
seems to think we could be back in London in only six
weeks. It's terribly exciting, isn't it, darling?'

Camilla said, faintly, 'Yes, terribly,' and turned away
from him as she began to put the groceries away.

Charles asked, 'Is anything wrong, darling? You seem
a little, er . . . distracted.'

Camilla said, 'It's nothing. I'm worried about the loo
paper. How will I blow my nose?'

Charles said, 'It's not like you to let a small problem,
such as a lack of loo paper, get you down. What is it,
darling?'

'The people hate me,' she burst out. 'I don't want to
be queen.'

Charles said, 'How could anybody hate you? You're utterly adorable.'

Camilla said, sadly, 'There are three people in our marriage, Charlie. She's still around in people's memories. They loved her because she was beautiful.'

Charles said, comfortingly, 'At a certain angle, in a flattering light, with professional make-up and an expert hairdresser, I admit she could sometimes look beautiful.'

Camilla shouted. 'What do they expect? I'm fifteen years older than her.'

'But, *I* think you're beautiful,' said Charles.

Camilla shouted back, 'Have you any idea how insulting that is?' She opened the back door and was about to run down the garden when she remembered that she was under house arrest.

Beverley Threadgold shouted through the party wall, 'Ay oop, Camilla, I'll swap you a toilet roll for a bag of sugar. And don't beat yourself up about 'is first wife, she would only have got 'ard-faced, running around wi' them Eurotrash gangsters.'

Later that evening, Charles went out to talk to the hens. He explained to them that food was in short supply and that he would be awfully grateful if they could manage to produce a few eggs. The creatures did not seemingly pay any attention to his entreaties; they continued to cluck and scratch at the earth inside their wire compound. At the bottom of the garden the fox had scrambled through the narrow gap it had burrowed under the wire fence and stood quite brazenly watching

Charles. It was some time before Charles saw the pair of glittering eyes that appeared to be assessing him.

The fox said, 'We have a family connection, Your Royal Highness. You, together with your wife and friends, hunted down and tore apart my great-great-great-grandmother in a copse in Leicestershire. Family legend has it that the hounds followed her scent for miles across the Vale of Belvoir.

'At dusk, exhausted and terrified, she ran from the fields into a private garden to seek sanctuary from a sympathetic householder. The hounds maddened and encouraged by the humans following on horseback, jumped over the garden fence and corralled my ancestor, forcing her through the open door of a greenhouse. A witness reported that my great-great-great-grandmother begged the hounds for mercy, telling them that she had cubs at home that needed her milk. She cried that if the hounds killed her, they would also kill her cubs, who would die slowly and painfully of starvation.

'She appealed to them, saying, "You and I are the same species, we owe allegiance to each other, not to humankind." But the hounds were baying with blood-lust and few heard her appeal. Before the first dog could sink his teeth into her fur and flesh, her heart burst. Again, legend has it that in the few moments remaining of her life, my great-great-great-grandmother cursed you and your kind, and predicted that there would be great tragedy in your life. I am here now to witness events as you and your family tear yourselves apart.'

As Charles and the fox stared into each other's eyes,

Charles had a terrible sense of foreboding and shouted, 'Be away with you.' But the fox stood his ground. Charles picked up a terracotta flowerpot and threw it at the fox, but before it landed the fox had disappeared.

Camilla was waiting to listen to *The Archers* – there had been another suicide in Ambridge due to an organic sausage business failure – but before the familiar music played, she shouted from the back doorstep, 'I've just heard the seven o'clock news. Avian flu has been found along the M1 corridor; we have to bring the poultry indoors.'

'Indoors?' queried Charles. 'Are you sure, darling?'

'Quite sure,' she said. 'The minister from the Department of the Environment, Food and Rural Affairs said quite explicitly that all poultry are to be brought indoors.'

It seemed to take forever to capture the two hens. Eccles escaped from Charles's hands and flew on to the Threadgolds' fence, causing Vince Threadgold to shout from his back door that, 'If me or Bev gets avian flu, I'll torch your house and destroy your family, fair enough?'

Charles said, 'Certainly, fair enough.' Eventually he managed to grab both of the hens and throw them into the kitchen.

With dogs and hens milling around their feet, Camilla said, 'They're going to make a dreadful mess.'

Charles said, 'Darling, it's a peasant tradition to share one's living quarters with animals.'

Camilla said, with more vehemence than she'd

intended, 'But we are *not* peasants, Charles. You're *certainly* not; you listen to the Reith Lectures and own a pair of black velvet evening slippers.' She went into the sitting room, closing the kitchen door firmly behind her.

Charles began to clean the floor of hen droppings. Freddie stood by the pantry door, assessing the contents, and thought, by my estimation the dog food will run out by tomorrow evening. He growled and snapped at the hens, who were already pecking at the few remaining crumbs of biscuits in the three dog-feeding bowls. The hens fluttered up to the draining board, giving Freddie the opportunity to inspect them more carefully. He reckoned that, of the two, Moriarty would provide the better meal.

Later that night, after listening more carefully to the news, a shamefaced Charles rounded up the hens and took them back to their coop and locked them inside their nesting shed. On his return, he said to Camilla, 'They're going to miss their freedom dreadfully.'

Camilla said, 'I know exactly how they feel.'

Dwayne kept his eye on Paris Butterworth by watching her on CCTV. He was delighted when she finally picked up *Nineteen Eighty-Four*. He didn't mind that she moved her lips when she read; it proved to him that she was a diligent reader. He was immensely proud of her when, only a few days later, she reached the notoriously difficult middle section of the book, where Orwell lectures the reader about the nature of totalitarianism. Dwayne had skipped a few of the more impenetrable passages, but Paris had ploughed on through the scholarly text, stopping only to look up a few words in the dictionary she had borrowed from school and never taken back. Sometimes, when Fifty-cents was fretful and tired of the television, Paris turned his pushchair around to face her and read aloud to him from the book. Fifty-cents seemed to be entertained by *Nineteen Eighty-Four*, though Dwayne suspected that it was his mother's attention he really enjoyed.

Dwayne couldn't wait to see Paris again and have a literary discussion. The last time he had talked about books to his colleagues, it had resulted in them calling him Dorky Dwayne. Afterwards, Inspector Lancer had taken him aside and confided in him that he, himself, had read several books in the fifteen years since leaving school and had 'quite enjoyed them'. Dwayne was pre-occupied with how he could visit Paris without it being noticed. It was not only that he wanted to talk about *Nineteen Eighty-Four*. He suspected that the strange ache he had around his heart might be caused by love. He was too young for it to be angina.

27

There was an atmosphere of barely controlled hysteria in the chamber of the House of Commons as the elected members waited for the entrance of the Prime Minister. Boy English, flanked by a handsome black woman, the Member for Grimsby North, and the famously flamboyant gay Member for Shropshire South, was looking happy and relaxed in his 'man of the people' Marks and Spencer's dark-blue 'Italian' suit, white shirt and pink tie.

The colour of the tie had been the subject of an acrimonious row between Boy's media adviser and his team of stylists. Baby blue had been rejected by some because it 'lacked gravitas', olive green because it was 'militaristic'; red was 'bolshie', maroon 'old fart', silver 'bride's father'; brown could signify 'depression'; yellow indicated 'cowardice'; lilac, purple and lime green were considered by some as 'opportunistic'; royal blue was rejected as being 'a bit Harold Macmillanish'. Eventually, as the clock ticked remorselessly towards noon, the choice came down to baby pink – non-threatening, women love pink, pink is optimistic and fun – or pistachio green, a colour that many people painted their walls. With five minutes to go, Boy chose the pink and, pausing only to allow a stylist to tease a curly lock of hair over his forehead, he left his office.

When the Prime Minister entered and took his place on the Government Front Bench, there were cries and laughter from the New Cons opposite: 'Poo, poo, poo, what's that on your shoe?'

This jibe reduced some Opposition MPs to tears of laughter. The Prime Minister allowed himself a wintry smile. Jack had not enjoyed his schooldays. Whenever his name had been called out in registration it was inevitably followed by some wag muttering 'woof-woof'. Sometimes, if the teacher was unable to keep discipline, the whole class would bark in unison. Jack would grin at his classmates to show that he didn't care, but when he was thirteen he had looked up 'deed poll' in the dictionary and considered changing his name.

The first few questions were more or less a formality, asked by tame MPs who had to pretend that they were interested in the Prime Minister's appointments for the day. Then Boy English stood up and congratulated the Prime Minister on his daughter's marriage. Once again, there were cries of, 'Poo, poo, poo, what's that on your shoe?'

Hysteria broke out again, which was mostly halted by the Speaker shouting, 'Order! Order!' A few MPs remained convulsed.

Boy rose and said, 'Prime Minister, can you confirm that according to figures released today by the Home Office, there are now six million, five hundred thousand and eighty-two persons currently living in Exclusion Zones?'

Jack stood up and said, 'The honourable gentleman

is correct: six million, five hundred thousand plus anti-social criminals, suspected terrorists, drug addicts and social incompetents have been taken off the streets and are now living in restricted areas, enabling stakeholders and decent hard-working families to get on with their lives in peace.' There were loud Government cheers as Jack sat down.

Boy stood up again, 'Prime Minister, these figures are rising at an alarming rate. How long will it be before there are more people *inside* the Exclusion Zones than there are *outside*?' There was loud laughter, during which the Speaker called for order.

The Prime Minister rose and jabbed his finger at Boy across the Dispatch Box. 'The courts decide who is excluded from our society. Does the honourable gentleman question the probity of our legal system?'

Boy stood up and said, 'I do question the impartiality of our present system of justice, yes! Since all magistrates and judges are now appointed by your Government, I ask you this: Are you aware that a constituent of mine, a Mrs Lucinda Haddock, was sentenced by a Guildford magistrates court to three years in an Exclusion Zone for the heinous crime of posting a letter without a stamp?'

There were shouts of, 'Disgraceful! Shame!' A few Government backbenchers shifted uncomfortably in their seats.

Jack rose and read from the folder in front of him, 'Post Office fraud is a very serious crime, one that this Government takes *very* seriously. Such fraud deprives the Post Office of hundreds of millions of pounds each year. Revenue that could go towards life-saving equipment for cancer patients.'

There were some half-hearted cheers and a few muted 'hear, hear's.

Boy fingered his pink tie and licked his lips, relishing his next question, 'Prime Minister, are you aware that Mrs Haddock is suffering from a virulent form of cancer herself, and that the prognosis for her survival is poor?'

The House fell quiet. Jack glanced at the folder, but there was no help there, and it was some time before his instinctive political acumen took over. 'I deplore the honourable gentleman's naked opportunism in seeking to exploit Mrs Haddock's tragic medical condition. I wish Mrs Haddock and her family well and would seek to reassure them that excellent palliative care is available to all English citizens, whatever their circumstances.'

Government backbenchers released their tension with prolonged cheering until quietened by the Speaker. A Government backbencher stood and asked, 'Does the Prime Minister agree with me that this is the finest Government of all time?'

Jack agreed.

A New Con backbencher, the member for Windsor Central, asked, 'Does the Government have any plans to release the Royal Family from exile, bearing in mind that a recent opinion poll concluded that seventy per cent of the English public supported the reinstatement of the monarchy?'

There was long and sustained cheering from the Opposition benches.

Jack shouted, 'The survey the honourable gentleman

is quoting has been discredited by all political analysts. The questions in this specious questionnaire were, and I quote,' Jack put on the horn-rimmed glasses that he only ever wore at Prime Minister's Questions, and read, 'who would you rather see as head of state? a) Sir Elton John, b) Dame Judi Dench, or c) the Queen?' To loud Government laughter, he went on, 'Fifteen per cent voted for Sir Elton John, fifteen per cent for Dame Judi, seventy per cent for the Queen, but ... *but* fifty per cent of those polled did not understand the meaning of the word "prefer".'

Tom Bass, the Minister for Education, frowned. If it were true that half of those surveyed did not understand the meaning of the word 'prefer', it reflected badly on him and his department. He scribbled a note in his diary to have the words, prefer, preferred, preferring and preferment added to the National Curriculum.

A few mundane questions followed: the Member of Parliament for the Isle of Wight West asked if the Prime Minister would join him in congratulating the Needles Academy for their achievement in gaining several bronze medals in the Isle of Wight non-competitive sports challenge.

Jack did.

Another, the Member for Chelsea, asked, 'Is the Prime Minister aware that three of my constituents have fallen from stepladders during the last financial year, at a cost of one hundred and fifty thousand pounds to the National Health Service, and can he confirm that the Stepladder Bill will be made law before the dissolution of this parliament?'

Jack confirmed that it would.

Then, in the final few minutes, a New Con MP, the Member for Cheltenham East, Marjorie Coddington, rose to her sensibly shod feet and said, 'Is it true that the Government is proposing to rush through new legislation reintroducing dog licences, and is planning to charge dog owners five hundred pounds a year . . . ?'

There were cries of dismay from both sides of the House. The Chancellor stared down at his pinstriped trousers and removed several of Mitzie's hairs. He had brushed her coat earlier that morning.

After the Speaker had intervened, Mrs Coddington continued, saying, '. . . and will the Prime Minister confirm that only one dog is to be allowed per household?'

Jack glanced quickly along the row of Cabinet Ministers. Some bastard has been talking, he thought. The details of the proposed dog legislation were meant to be a secret. The Queen, watching at home with Harris and Susan, waited anxiously for the Prime Minister's reply. Harris and Susan nuzzled closer to their mistress.

Jack thought, in the seconds before he answered Mrs Coddington's question, thank God, I'll soon be out of here, out of office and out of politics. 'Yes,' he said.

The Queen looked from Harris to Susan and back. How could she possibly choose between them?

Harris whimpered, 'She'll keep me, I'm her favourite.'

Susan said, 'I'm her mother's dog, she promised to look after me.'

The Queen looked away from the dogs and stared down at her hands resting on her lap. She was unable to look either dog in the eye.

28

Graham found Prince Charles's letter on the coconut-fibre doormat when he arrived home from his work as a health and safety officer. Gin and Tonic, having very little to do all day, had been speculating since the post had been delivered that morning about the contents of the letter.

'The envelope is cheap,' said Tonic.

'But the pen used is a Mont Blanc,' said Gin. 'And if I'm not mistaken, the ink is Quink, India black.'

'The handwriting belongs to somebody confident and of high status,' said Tonic. 'Although the down strokes indicate that the confidence is only skin-deep.'

The dogs waited impatiently for Graham to put his umbrella in the stand by the back door, take off his anorak and hang it on a coat hanger in the cloakroom.

Gin said, 'Let's fetch his slippers.'

Tonic said, 'Sod him, let him fetch his own slippers. He leaves us here all day with bugger all to do. Not even a squeaky toy to lighten our futile existence.'

Gin said, 'I can't talk to you when you're in one of your nihilistic moods.'

Graham was pleasantly surprised when Gin waddled into the living room dragging one of the huge Bart Simpson novelty slippers that Graham had bought for himself as a recent birthday present. 'Good boy, Gin,' he said. He would have died of embarrassment if anybody had come to the door while he was wearing the slippers, but as nobody ever did come to the door, he felt fairly safe. When Gin dragged the second slipper up to him, he said, 'You're my best dog, Gin. Yes you are, yes you are. You're my friend, aren't you? My bestest friend.'

From the doorway, Tonic barked, 'Bestest friend? If I had fingers I'd be sticking them down my throat. Why don't you have human friends, Graham? Could it be because you're a social pariah?'

Graham took off a Bart Simpson slipper and hurled it at Tonic's head, shouting, 'Shut the fuck up!'

Tonic slunk off to the kitchen to avoid being hit by the other slipper. As he passed Gin, he growled, 'I'll get the bastard back for that.'

Graham opened the envelope and took out the letter from his parents, Charles and Camilla. He read it with growing excitement, and at the end he said to the little dog at his feet, 'I'm the heir to the throne, Gin, and that means that one day, you'll be top dog.'

He went to the cupboard and pulled out a photograph album, saying to Gin, 'They want a photograph of me. Which one should I send?' As Graham turned the pages, he said, 'How about the one that was on the front page of the *Ruislip Trumpet*, recording my third successive victory in the Ruislip Tiddlywinks Championship, captioned "The Tiddlywink King"?'

Gin looked at the photograph and remembered that even Graham's adoring adoptive mother had said, 'My God, Graham, I can't put this in a frame.' His less adoring father had looked at the newspaper and laughed.

But he did have a short video of himself filmed at the Hardtopleeze Dating Agency offices earlier in the year. In Graham's opinion it gave an absorbing and fascinating portrait of his life and character. After editing out a few glitches (at one point Graham had nervously blurted out, 'I usually eat serial killers for breakfast,' when, of course, what he meant to say was 'cereal') he had shown the film to his parents and asked them for their opinion.

'Be honest,' he'd said.

His father had lowered *The Daily Telegraph* and watched the video without changing his expression, only saying at the end, 'You shouldn't have asked for somebody "bubbly". In my experience, women who start out bubbly end up crying in public and wearing red shoes.'

Graham's mother had said, 'You can't have it all, Graham. Your dream woman can't be financially secure *and* like board games. The two are incompatible.'

At the end of the video, Gin muttered to Tonic, 'So that's a mystery solved.'

Gin and Tonic had often speculated about the precise nature of Graham's sexuality. Graham had never brought a girl home, but Gin didn't think he was gay. Gin was sometimes allowed into Graham's bedroom and he had seen Graham leafing through copies of *Playboy*, cutting out the photographs of women and pasting them into a scrapbook that he kept on the top shelf of his wardrobe, underneath a pile of winter-weight sweaters.

Tonic said, 'So what? I'm gay, but I'm still attracted to bitches.'

Gin and Tonic had been gay lovers ever since they came to sexual maturity, at the age of eighteen months. Gin was the submissive partner; Tonic sometimes complained about that, saying, 'You're too bloody lazy to get up off your front legs. You just *stand* there and let me do all the work.'

Graham had ignored the advice of his parents and posted the video on the Net. He received two hits almost immediately, one from a lady-boy in Bangkok and the other from an 89-year-old Mantovani fan, Clarice Witherspoon of Rugby. Mrs Witherspoon had sent an attachment back to Graham at grahamcracknall@ hotmail.co.uk with a photograph of herself in corsets, wearing a red fez. 'I'm a bit of a character,' wrote Mrs Witherspoon. 'I'm young at heart and own my own house, love *OFAH* and think David Jason is a dish! You tick most of my boxes. Do I tick yours?'

Over the next few months, Graham checked his email many times a day, hoping for the right woman to appear on his screen. But the ones who described themselves as being mad about board games did not look as though they had ever washed their hair, and the bubbly ones looked slightly mad. He had replied with great excitement to a woman who was staggeringly beautiful and claimed to be a backgammon champion. However, when Graham showed the beauty's photograph to his mother she pointed out that Graham had been hoaxed. The photograph was of Gina Lollobrigida, a film star that Graham had never heard of.

With both parents dead, there was now nobody to advise him otherwise. So he found a Jiffy bag, took four first-class stamps from his purse and posted the package in the postbox on the corner.

29

Mitzie, a King Charles spaniel, was lying under Chancellor Stephen Fletcher's desk with her pretty muzzle resting on the Chancellor's highly polished black brogues. One of her silky ears was cocked, listening to an alarming conversation between her master and the Prime Minister.

'Please, Jack, don't ask me to get rid of Mitzie.'

'We have to lead by example, Chancellor. How can we fight the war on dogs if you're harbouring one in the very heart of government?'

'But Mitzie's so docile, so well behaved.'

'She's still a dog, Chancellor.'

'But she's all I've got since Veronica refused to leave the bloody constituency.'

The call was abruptly disconnected; the Prime Minister rarely said goodbye on the telephone. Mitzie crawled out from under the desk and stood at the Chancellor's side. She had been glad to see the back of the neurotic Veronica, who had constantly complained about dog hair and the occasional flea bite. Mitzie was glad the poor cow preferred rural isolation.

Mitzie jumped up on the Chancellor's lap and laid her glossy head on his knee. She gave him the brown-eyed, full-on, adoring gaze that she had been working on in private in front of the mirrored wardrobe doors in the master bedroom. The Chancellor stroked Mitzie's head and thought bitterly about his estranged wife. She had never loved him with such adoration as this dog. 'I'll never give you up, Mitzie,' he said.

Only Mitzie witnessed the Chancellor's frailty these days. It was she who stayed awake half the night with him when he toiled over the papers and graphs that told him that England would be destitute, wearing rags and living under a railway arch within three years, unless taxation was increased by three pence in the pound. He had done his best for the country, but nobody, not even God, could give the people what they wanted: low taxation and superb public services.

England owed the United States a hundred billion pounds and the United States owed seven trillion dollars to the World Bank. The Chancellor sometimes thought that money was an abstract thing, existing only in the imaginations of the people who brokered deals. He felt like a man who had shuffled halfway along a tightrope, only to see his landing platform go up in flames. He wondered how Jack Barker had become so powerful. A certain look from him was enough to silence a room. Perhaps, thought the Chancellor, it's because Jack doesn't care about anything any more, and therefore nothing can hurt him.

The Chancellor picked Mitzie up and held her in his arms like a baby. He kissed her, told her she was beautiful and swore his undying love for her. He then put her down on the floor and wrote:

Dear Jack,

It is with great regret that I have to inform you that I have decided to resign from my position as Chancellor of the Exchequer.

You asked me to choose between my dog and my job. I have chosen my dog.

I wish I could say that working with you has been an honour and a privilege. However, I can't.

Stephen Fletcher

The Chancellor read the letter aloud to Mitzie and asked her opinion.

Mitzie barked, 'Don't be so hasty, Stevie, stay around to help us fight the war on dogs.'

The Chancellor put the letter into an envelope and locked it inside a drawer of his desk. Mitzie always gave him good advice, he thought. The dog was sensible and rational, unlike most of his ministerial advisers, who could not see the economic wood for the financial trees.

30

All over the land people without dogs congratulated themselves and those with dogs felt vaguely discomfited. Anti-dog stories had been appearing in the press. It seemed that every day a dog had caused a serious traffic accident, or a child had been savaged. When a train was derailed outside Ely, causing two fatalities and dozens of injuries, a dog was blamed. The train driver, who had braked when he saw a dog on the line, had appeared on the front of *The Sun*. The headline read: 'DRIVER TRIES TO SAVE DOG AND KILLS MUM OF THREE.' Dog charities reported that their donations were down and Battersea Dogs Home took in a record number of abandoned animals.

The Queen picked up a basket of wet washing and lugged it out into the garden. A strong wind had blown up and the Queen wanted to take advantage of its free, drying properties. She battled against the gusts of wind to peg the towels and bed linen on to the clothesline. Harris and Susan waddled out to watch her. They were both subdued, each thinking about their chance of surviving the proposed one-dog-per-household rule. They stood with their heads into the wind, which flattened their ears and sent rippled patterns through their fur.

After a few minutes, Violet squeezed through the gap

in the fence between the two gardens. She could never get used to seeing the Queen performing any household task. To Violet it was as novel as witnessing a circus pony walking on its hind legs. They worked together, pegging out the billowing sheets.

'These are wearing a bit thin,' said Violet, examining the exquisitely monogrammed linen.

'They're over fifty years old,' said the Queen. 'They were made for our wedding.'

'Lovely bit of embroidery,' said Violet.

The Queen did not like to tell Violet that the silk for the embroidery had been farmed from specially bred silkworms that fed on a certain type of mulberry tree, planted in a secret location. Or that a team of embroideresses had worked twelve hours a day, for ninety days, to complete the task. It would sound like a fairy tale.

Violet said, 'These sheets are as thin as a piece of old-fashioned lavvy paper. I can see my bleedin' hand through 'em.'

Moments later a huge gust of wind filled the sheets, reminding the Queen of the puff-cheeked illustration of the wind on a weather chart that used to hang on her nursery wall when she was a small child. Every day Crawfie would ask her and her sister, Princess Margaret Rose, to hang a little weather symbol on to the hook, adjacent to the day of the week and the date.

Another gust ripped one of the sheets apart at the hem, leaving the pegs on the line and the sheet flapping along the ground. The Queen and Violet gave little screams and hurried to retrieve the sheet. The dogs barked excitedly as the two women battled against the wind. When they finally struggled back into the house, Violet noticed that the Queen had tears in her eyes and said, 'It's only a sheet, Liz. You can buy a bedding bundle for a fiver in Grice's Mini-Market.'

'A fiver?' queried the Queen, blowing her nose and wiping her eyes. 'How come?'

'It's probably made in China, cos the Chinks'll work all day for a few noodles and half a cup of rice,' said Violet.

The Queen sat down at the kitchen table, buried her head in her hands and began to weep.

Violet put her arm around the Queen's shoulder and said, 'Come on, come on, don't cry. The Chinks are 'appy enough.'

The Queen said, 'It isn't the Chinese I'm weeping for.'

Violet said, 'What, then? Is it Philip?'

'No,' sobbed the Queen, 'it's the dogs. Only one is to be permitted per household. Oh Violet, how can I choose between them? They're both adorable.'

Harris and Susan each gazed up at the Queen and tried to look just a little more adorable than the other.

When Charles called around to see his mother, to tell her that all residents of Hell Close had to push their wheelie bins to the police barrier because house-to-house collections had been suspended, he was alarmed to find her not only in tears, but being consoled by Violet Toby, a woman he had never felt entirely comfortable with.

'Mummy, what's happened? Is it Papa?'

'No,' said Violet, in her usual trenchant manner. 'The Government has said your mam has got to kill one of her dogs.'

Harris and Susan ran under the table and listened as Violet told Charles about the one-dog-per-household law.

She continued, 'If you'd get a telly, Charlie, you'd know what was going on in the world.'

Susan began to bark hysterically, 'We're going to die! We're going to die!'

Harris said to Susan, 'This is England. They don't kill dogs in England.'

When Susan continued to bark, Harris sank his teeth into her neck and she calmed down and whimpered, 'I'm sorry.'

Charles was sure that Violet must be wrong. She was an unreliable witness: he had once overheard her asserting in the queue at the 'Everything A Pound' shop that she had heard on the *News at Ten* that Judas Iscariot's diaries had been found and that they proved that Judas 'didn't shop Jesus!'

Charles said, 'This is England, Mummy. The English people are dog lovers, they would not allow their Government to implement such a draconian law.'

The Queen blew her nose and said, 'I hope so, because I couldn't possibly choose between Harris and Susan.'

Charles said, 'Nor I between Freddie, Tosca and Leo.'

Violet said, 'Thank the sweet Jesus I've only got our Micky. But if it came to choosing between our Micky and our Barry, well, I'd 'ave to choose Micky.'

Charles said, 'My poor darling Camilla, it would break her heart to condemn two of our dogs.'

Violet said, 'Pardon me for speakin' my mind, but I ain't exactly bothered if 'er heart is broken. She's gone an' caused everybody in 'Ell Close a lot of bleedin' trouble. I'd 'ad an appointment with the pliers woman to tighten my dentures tomorrow. I'll have to cancel it now.'

Charles said, 'Camilla is *distraught*, Mrs Toby.'

'Yeah, well, I'm distraught an' all,' said Violet. 'My top set keeps slipping on to my bottom set. It's like 'aving a pair of bleedin' castanets in me mouth.'

Charles said angrily, 'My wife did nothing wrong.'

The Queen said quietly, 'Camilla acted very irresponsibly, Charles. Her actions were not the considered actions of a queen. A queen has to put her people first and her own desires a long way back.'

Violet said, 'If I'd put myself first I'd 'ave 'ad our Barry took away after 'e set fire to 'is first school.'

'But you did your duty,' said the Queen. 'You stood by your son.'

'Well,' said Violet, evasively, 'I stood by 'im until 'e set the church on fire, then I 'ad to do my duty an' turn 'im in. There was a wedding going on at the time.'

The Queen asked, lowering her voice, 'How will I choose between the dogs, Charles? It's impossible.'

Charles said, 'It's an intolerable situation. We must hope against hope that Boy English wins the election.'

Violet Toby said, 'I've never voted Conservative in my life. But them Cromwell people ain't for the poor and the working classes no more.'

Charles said, 'Because of my status as a Royal, even an ex-officio Royal, I have never been allowed to vote.'

Violet said, 'Our Barry can't vote on two counts. One, he's a criminal, and two, he's a lunatic.'

Charles shouted, 'Do you see the company we're in, Mummy? We're disenfranchised, along with criminals and lunatics.'

The Queen shouted, 'If you don't want to be a Royal, then pass the succession to William.'

'You mean, pass him the poisoned chalice,' Charles roared. He stalked out of the back door, banging it behind him.

When there was no sound of the Queen's wheelie bin being dragged from the back garden into the front, the Queen said, 'Well, it looks as though he has left me to deal with my own rubbish.'

Violet sighed, 'It's a pity we can't take our grown-up kids' pants down an' give their arses a good smacking, ain't it?'

The Queen put on her hat and coat and, with Violet's help, they struggled against the wind to pull her wheelie bin to the barrier at the entrance to Hell Close.

Camilla was turning the familiar pages of an edition of *Horse & Hound*. She had brought a stack with her from the outside world. They provided ballast when she felt as though her new life threatened to swamp her with its difficulties. She looked at the familiar faces of her friends and their horses; she almost knew the captions under the photographs by heart: 'Major Jeremy Yarnold swaps a joke with the Honourable Lady Fiona Leyton-

Haige at the Hunt Ball at Smockington Manor.' Even the advertisements on the back page gave her comfort.

All three dogs were lying on the sofa, something they were normally forbidden to do, but she hadn't the energy to shout at them, and order them on to the floor. Charles often teased her that she treated the dogs as though they were hairy children that she indulged.

She said to the dogs, 'You look happy, darlings.'

Freddie whimpered, 'I may look happy to you, but that's because I'm limited to very few facial expressions. I'm actually tormented by jealousy and rage.'

Tosca growled, 'Get over it, Freddie. Go and call on that cheap bitch, Britney.'

Freddie snapped, 'You're making a fool of yourself with Leo. You're a mature bitch, and he's barely off his mother's teat.'

Leo lifted his big head and sniffed between Tosca's back legs.

Tosca growled, 'You don't like it because I refuse to be dominated by you.'

Freddie barked, 'Mixed-breed couplings never work. You're a pedigree and he's a mongrel. You know nothing about his bloodline.'

Tosca barked back, 'We'll be together for life.'

Leo growled, 'When my balls have grown, we're going to have puppies of our own, aren't we, Tosca?'

Freddie lunged at Leo, biting his nose and causing the bigger dog to howl in pain. Tosca leapt at Freddie's throat, and soon all three dogs were engaged in a vicious fight. Charles ran in to find Camilla vainly trying to separate the dogs.

He shouted, 'Freddie, stop it at once!' He yanked Freddie's collar and threw him on to the floor.

Camilla protested, 'Why single Freddie out? All three of them were fighting.'

Charles said, 'Because he's a nasty piece of work, Camilla.'

'No, he's a darling boy,' Camilla said.

Freddie lay on his back at Camilla's feet, whimpering pitifully.

'You've hurt him,' Camilla said to Charles.

Charles replied, 'Any fool with eyes to see can tell that he's putting it on.'

'Don't be absurd,' said Camilla, bending down and scooping Freddie into her arms. 'Dogs have no guile, he's genuinely hurt.'

Tosca barked, 'Freddie is a better actor than Lassie.'

'Quiet, Tosca,' said Charles.

Camilla said, 'Why are you being so horrid to my dogs.'

Charles said, 'Because your dogs are a bloody nuisance, Camilla. I don't need to discipline Leo.'

Leo jumped off the sofa, shook himself, stretched, and then padded towards Charles, leaning his head against Charles's thigh.

Charles said, 'Come with me, Leo. We'll go and deal with the wheelie bin.'

Camilla went to the window; she and Freddie watched Charles. Every now and then the lid of the bin opened like a big gaping mouth, and pieces of rubbish blew out and twirled around the close.

Beverley knocked on the back door and shouted, 'It's

only me!' She was wearing a pink tracksuit and what looked like new white trainers. She said, 'I'm on the cadge again, Cam. Can I buy a can of dog food off you? Vince is threatening to feed our King on that tinned mince what we got in our grocery box.'

Camilla said, 'I'm awfully sorry, Bev. But we've barely enough for our own dogs.'

Beverley said, 'That bleedin' King will eat us out of 'ouse and 'ome. I'm bleedin' sick of 'im. Still, at least we 'aven't got your problem.'

'Which problem is that?' asked Camilla. 'I have so many.'

'Which dog you're gonna keep and which two are for the chop,' said Beverley, with relish.

When Beverley explained about the proposed one-dog-per-household law, it was like throwing a grenade into a house that already had a chip-pan fire. The fact that Charles had already shown his hand by singling out Leo and rubbishing her own dogs did not surprise Camilla. Charles had, after all, been brought up to play palace politics. Look how ruthless his ancestors had been.

Beverley said, 'It's like that film, *Sophie's Choice*, where Meryl Streep has to choose between 'er kids.' Beverley looked from Freddie to Tosca and back again.

Camilla remembered the film and said, 'I wept absolute buckets, I was prostrate.'

Beverley said, 'So, which of 'em are you goin' to choose?'

Freddie and Susan waited nervously for her answer.

'How can I possibly choose?' Camilla asked. 'Freddie

is such a marvellous little character, and Tosca is utterly adorable.'

'And Leo?' asked Beverley.

'Leo's lovely, of course. He's a big softie.'

'But he's Charlie's dog really, ain't he?' said Beverley, malevolently.

When Charles returned, Camilla said nothing about Beverley's visit or that she knew about the proposed change to the dog ownership laws. She could tell that Charles was preoccupied and miserable. She knew that he was dreading telling her that they would have to choose which of the three dogs was to live, and which two were doomed to die. It was part of Camilla's make-up that she did not confront unpleasantness head on. That would make things real, and she preferred to live in the shadowy world of self-deception.

All three dogs were exceptionally quiet, even docile. Camilla went to bed early, leaving the bedroom door open so that Freddie and Tosca could come and go as they pleased.

Charles stayed downstairs and later that evening sat at his little writing desk and wrote a reply to Nicholas Soames.

My dear old friend,

I can't tell you how delighted I was to receive your letter. One sometimes despaired of ever receiving a reply to the numerous letters I have sent to you and many other people.

Camilla and I are in staggeringly good health; we seem to thrive on adversity, though being poor is terribly time-

consuming. There's an awful lot of paperwork and bureau-cratic nonsense to be got through before one can receive one's state benefits. However, I always hankered for the simple life and now I have it, so I must not complain.

Camilla is under house arrest due to several infringe-ments of the Exclusion Zone Contract she signed. And I and my fellow residents of Hell Close are undergoing collective punishment. The poor darling feels terribly guilty and is convinced that she is reviled by all and sundry.

I confess, Nick, that I am a little concerned about the future. Mama is talking about abdication, and to be brutally honest, I view the prospect of becoming king with a mixture of alarm and despair.

William, the darling boy, has stepped forward and offered himself. However, a complication has arisen. It transpires that Camilla and I have a son, Graham Cracknall, who was born during our first love affair, in 1965. We have yet to meet him. But the documentation he enclosed with his letter looks authentic, and Camilla has confirmed that she did indeed give birth to a baby son at that time.

Nick, I know that the laws of inheritance and bastardy were changed at the time of the dissolution of the monarchy. Could you look into this with the chap at Burke's Peerage as a matter of urgency, and let me know if there is any possibility of our son, Graham, succeeding to the throne? He is older than William by seventeen years.

Did you enjoy the partridge and lark pie? I once ate such a pie when staying with the King of Spain in his villa in Mallorca. I thought it rather delicious, but William choked on a tiny beak and gave us all a fright.

There is so much I want to say, but I will restrain myself for now.

Love from your friend,

Charles

P.S: Please get in touch with Camilla's children and assure them that their mother is in marvellous form.

P.P.S: Please continue to write to me care of Dwayne Lockhart. If this were a James Bond film, I would ask you to eat this letter, knowing you to be a man of gargantuan appetite. As it is, I ask only that you keep our correspondence confidential.

P.P.P.S: Another postscript, if you can bear it. Alarming news about the one-dog-per-household law. What chance is there of it being implemented? You must be as worried as I am. Do you still have the four dogs?

Gin and Tonic were in the living room, sitting next to
each other on the red, swirly-patterned carpet. Their
eyes were fixed on Graham who was filling out an
application form to obtain the Exclusion Zone Visiting
Order that would enable him to visit his birth parents.

APPLICATION FOR VISITING ORDER
(EXCLUSION ZONE)

Name: Graham Cracknall

Address: 'The Cuckoos', 17 Hanging Boy Gardens, Ruislip HA4

Date of birth: 21.07.65

ID number: C7494304

Occupation: Health and safety inspector

Name(s) of person(s) to be visited: Charles Windsor and Mrs
C. Windsor

Address: 16 Hellebore Close, Flowers Exclusion Zone, EZ 951,
East Midlands Region

Duration of visit: 4 days

Reason for visit: Professional. To assess risk of fire, flood, acts
of God on premises.

Gin growled, 'Tonic, do you realize the implications for us if he's accepted by his parents and joins the Royal Family?'

Tonic growled back, 'We'll get to travel; I've always wanted to see the world.'

It was Graham's habit to turn on Radio Four before he went to work. He had been convinced by a crime-prevention leaflet pushed through the door that burglars, hearing such civilized tones issuing from the radio, would turn on their heels and rob a less-civilized household. Gin and Tonic had listened with rapt attention to a lunchtime programme about the possible return of the Royal Family.

Gin barked, 'If the New Cons get in, we'll have the run of Buckingham Palace, and the gardens!'

'We'll be celebrities, Gin, on the front page of *Dog World*,' Tonic woofed.

The two excited dogs leapt up and ran around the living room until they were dizzy and Graham shouted, 'Pack it in!'

He was tired of living with the dogs. They were stupid and unpredictable, and he was sick of cleaning up the mud they trailed in from the garden and the revolting turds they left on his immaculate lawn. But it had been a condition of his inheritance that he had to take care of the dogs until they died. However, he had been thrilled to be told by a colleague at work (a downtrodden man called Leonard Wolf, whose wife kept three Pekinese dogs) that the Government had announced they were to bring in tighter controls on dog ownership;

restricting each household to no more than one dog.

Leonard Wolf had said mournfully, 'My wife is threatening to leave me and set up house with one of the dogs, farm another one out with our grown-up daughter, and leave one of them with me.'

Gin and Tonic rolled on to their backs and lay still with their legs in the air, signalling to Graham that they were under his control.

Graham knew that he could have typed under 'Reason for visit' something ridiculously far-fetched, such as 'to participate in devil-worship ceremony', or tongue-twistingly 'to teach tadpoles to tango'.

Vulcan, the Government's gargantuan computer that was trusted to process and issue ID cards, visiting orders, benefits, National Health Service records and a myriad other bureaucratic duties, was so inadequate to the task and had such bafflingly complicated software that no one person, civil servant or government official could understand how it worked. An investigative journalist had recently written in *The Times* about her successful attempt to be issued with six ID cards, under the names of Saddam Hussein, Joseph Stalin, Osama bin Laden, Mickey Mouse, Dr F. Rankenstein and William Shakespeare. All six of the cards had been delivered to the same address in the same post.

Graham said to Gin, 'In my opinion, it would have been cheaper to have hired ten thousand dim-witted sixteen-year-olds to do Vulcan's work, by hand.'

Gin yelped, 'And it would keep them off the streets.'

Graham said, warming to his theme, 'Pensioners

could be roped in to do the biotechnics. Any fool can take a DNA swab, photograph an iris and process a fingerprint.'

Graham imagined that Gin's growl said, 'It would cost a fortune in wages.'

Graham said, 'No, it wouldn't, Gin. You could pay the stupid teenagers just enough to cover their bus fares and call it youth training, and the OAPs would be forced to work for the Government as a condition of getting their pensions. Why should they have a life of leisure?'

Tonic growled at the back of his throat and approached Graham with his jaws open and snarled, 'You're a nasty piece of human shit, Graham, and it's time for my insulin injection.'

Graham picked Tonic up and hurled him across the room, saying, 'Why don't you die?'

Tonic landed on his legs, and after a quick shake of the head ran up to Graham and bit his ankle.

Graham lunged across the room, grabbed Tonic by his collar and dragged him towards the back door, saying, 'You're for the chop, grizzle chops.' Graham got down on his knees so that his face was level with Tonic and continued, 'First, I've never liked you, second, you're not worth the cost of the insulin that keeps you alive and third, you're a deviant. Don't think I don't know about your disgusting sexual shenanigans with poor Gin.'

Gin watched anxiously as Graham opened the door and threw Tonic into the dark wet night. He went to the French windows and pressed his nose against the glass. Tonic was standing forlornly in the rain, his coat plastered to his body.

Charles could not quite decide which religion to practice; he flirted with both Christianity and Islam. He had studied both and read whatever books were available. He'd talked to the Reverend John Edmund-Harvey in his barricaded church, St Adrian's, and with the Imam Mohammed Akbar in the mosque, which was two ex-council houses knocked into one. Each place had its merits.

St Adrian's had a serene atmosphere, especially at sunset when the light through the stained-glass window behind the altar cast a gentle luminescence over the damp interior that even the anti-vandal mesh could not debase. The mosque, with its expanse of traditional patterned carpet and its lines of shoes by the entrance, was always busy, and Charles enjoyed the companionship of his fellow worshippers, although he had once walked home in another man's flip-flops after his own brogues had disappeared. The Imam had blamed the crime on the Hell Close dogs, but the shoes miraculously reappeared at the next Friday's prayers. They'd even been polished.

When Charles wanted to be alone, he would call at the vicarage to collect the church key. He'd then sit waiting for the sun to reach the window and illuminate the agony of Christ on the cross. He felt a strong bond with Jesus; both of them had frightening fathers who had expected too much of their sons.

Today, when he had returned the key, the Reverend

Edmund-Harvey had invited him into the kitchen to take tea with him and his partner, Jerad, an Australian of aboriginal descent and an ardent Royalist. Jerad had been baking; a tray of sweet-smelling little cakes were cooling on a wire rack on the mock-granite worktop. Charles and the Reverend watched as Jerad decorated the cakes with an icing bag, covering the surface with a series of dots.

'I'm exceedingly fond of aboriginal art,' said Charles. 'I find the primitive profoundly ... well ... profound.'

Jerad, who had a degree in fine art from St Martin's art college scowled at this, but Charles had already switched his attention to the plump and pink Reverend Edmund-Harvey, saying, 'Reverend, may I tax you with a theological question that has bothered me since I was a boy?'

The Reverend, slightly nervous because of Jerad's obvious bad mood, said, 'Gosh! Theology! I'm usually asked for advice on social-welfare matters these days, but fire away.'

Charles said, 'One's terribly fond of animals, y'know, dogs, horses, that sort of thing.'

Jerad snorted, 'He knows what an *animal* is, he's one himself behind closed doors.'

The Reverend laughed nervously.

Charles continued, 'I've lost many dear friends over the years and I've always wondered, where do dead dogs go? To heaven? Or to a place of their own? Have they a soul?'

Before the Reverend could answer, Jerad said, 'Only soul a dog's got is an arse-soul, same as me an' you.'

The Reverend took hold of Jerad's arm – the one holding the icing bag.

His grinning mouth looked like the half-moon carved into a Hallowe'en pumpkin as he said, 'Christ was undoubtedly an animal lover. The New Testament heaves with sheep, fish and donkeys. I don't know if he kept a dog . . . it's possible . . .'

Charles urged, 'But does a dog have a soul?'

The cleric faltered. Souls were not fashionable, nor was Heaven, and even God was currently out of favour with the religious community to which the Reverend had once belonged. It was why he had been exiled to the Flowers Exclusion Zone. He was still not entirely sure why he had been sent from his comfortable parish church in Suffolk to the hellhole he now officiated over. Was it Jerad? Or perhaps it was the piece he had written in the parish magazine, where he'd suggested that, 'If Jesus were alive today, he would probably recruit his disciples from the gay bars in Old Compton Street.'

The Reverend might have escaped Vulcan's attention had he not gone on to compare Jack Barker to Judas Iscariot, saying, 'Both men betrayed an ideal.' He had expected to cause a little controversy in the peaceful Suffolk village – perhaps being snubbed in the Post Office by homophobes – but nothing had prepared him for being woken at 3 a.m. by the security police ramming the vicarage door down and swarming upstairs to pull him and Jerad from their bed and drag them, naked and terrified, downstairs and out into a vehicle where they were locked inside individual, caged compartments.

As they were driven to Bungay for questioning, the security police had serenaded them with, 'Tie me kangaroo down sport.'

Caroline, the Prime Minister's current wife, was sitting on the lavatory with the lid down, soaking her feet in the adjacent bidet. She was watching her husband as he shaved for the third time that day. He was the reluctant guest of honour at a dinner to be held by the Parliamentary Fly Fishing Association. Caroline had bullied him into accepting the invitation. Her mother owned a salmon river in the north of Scotland, and liked nothing better than to stand up to her thighs in ice-cold water with a fishing rod and a gillie standing by.

She pulled the plug out of the bidet and said, 'And don't go on about cruelty to fish in your speech tonight. You've already antagonized dog lovers; my sodding phone hasn't stopped ringing for two days. Do you realize, Jack, that the movers and shakers in this country have at least two dogs each? When was the last time you saw Sir Alan Sugar stroking a pussy? You can't afford to lose the fishing vote, Jack.'

Jack said, 'How would you like to be hauled out of your natural element with a hook in your soft palate? Don't tell me that's not painful.'

Caroline raised her voice and said, 'What are you, a fucking Buddhist? It's a bloody *fish*.'

'A fish is a sentient being,' said Jack.

'Hardly,' said Caroline. 'Does a fish have feelings? Does it feel jealousy or remorse? I think not.'

'It's still cruel,' said Jack.

'So what are you going to legislate against next? Fishing? Slug pellets? Ant poison? Where does it stop, Jack?' asked Caroline. 'This anti-dog legislation is madness. If you base your manifesto on it, you'll lose the election.'

Jack rinsed his face clean of shaving cream and said, 'I know what I'm doing.'

The Fly Fishing Association dinner took place upstairs in the banqueting room at the National Portrait Gallery. Jack sat in the centre at a long table with Caroline on his right and Jeremy Paxman on his left. During the first course of mackerel pâté and thin curls of toast, Jack chatted to Paxman about strictly non-political subjects. But as they were eating a baked turbot, Jack remarked that under his Government the rivers had been cleaned up, and consequently fish were now more plentiful.

Paxman snarled, 'Come off it, Prime Minister. I was fishing the River Dove recently, and the only thing I caught in three days was a trout that was decidedly on its last legs.'

When Jack rose to speak, he was still simmering with resentment. His conversation with Paxman had deteriorated from a sotto voce row about England's polluted rivers into a shouting match about the erosion of English civil liberties.

After formally thanking the Fly Fishing Association, he launched into an attack on cruel sports, saying in part of his speech, 'I'm no Christian, but to my recollection Jesus disapproved of fishing, and returned the fish to the sea, making it clear that fishing was a heathen activity. Wait, I hear you say, didn't Jesus feed the five thousand with bread and fishes, thus validating fish? But you would be wrong. An eminent Biblical authority, Professor Elias Moncrieff, wrote in the *Catholic Herald* that the deconstruction of the fish and loaves parable showed that the word "fish" has been misinterpreted, and in old Hebrew, the words "fish" and "oil" were almost identical, so it is entirely possible, ladies and gentlemen, that the five thousand were actually fed on bread and oil.'

He heard Jeremy Paxman mutter, 'That's absolute bollocks.'

Jack continued, 'And didn't Jesus urge Matthew, Mark, Luke and John to renounce their livelihood, which was catching fish, and become his disciples and start fishing for men?'

On the way home in the official car, Caroline said, 'You've lost the election, Jack.'

'I know,' said Jack, and he smiled in the dark.

32

On Saturday morning Charles dug up some of his root vegetables: potatoes, turnips and parsnips. He gave a basketful to Beverley Threadgold, who had complained, over the fence, that the only thing she had in her cupboard was a red Oxo cube and a bit of salt and pepper. She recoiled at Charles's gift at first, saying, 'Ugh! What are they? They're covered in fuckin' mud.'

Charles had explained that underneath the dirt were vegetables, and that if Beverley washed, peeled and chopped them up and added the stock from an Oxo cube she could make enough soup to keep herself and Vince going until they were allowed to go to the shops again.

Beverley looked at the vegetables suspiciously, and said, 'But it ain't hygienic.'

Charles said, 'But, Beverley, mankind has eaten produce grown in the earth for centuries.'

Beverley said, 'Well, generations of Threadgolds 'ave bought their vegetables from the Co-op in tins and packets.'

However, Beverley took Charles's produce inside and an hour later astounded Vince by presenting him with a bowl of vegetable soup, with only a little muddy sediment.

*

On Saturday afternoon, Dwayne Lockhart called at Charles and Camilla's house under the pretext of checking the effectiveness of the new tag on Camilla's ankle. During the examination, he fumbled a Jiffy bag out of his baton pocket and slid it under the sofa. When Dwayne had gone, Camilla retrieved the package.

'It's from Graham,' she said. 'I'd know that crabbed handwriting anywhere.'

She opened the package and found a letter addressed to 'My mother and father', and a video labelled 'Graham Cracknall!' with another of his exclamation marks.

Dear Mother and Father,

It was wonderful to get your letter! I can't tell you how excited I am at the prospect of meeting my father, my brothers William and Harry, and being reunited with you, Mother!

As you can see, I have enclosed a video I made some months ago! It is part of my life plan to be married by the time I am forty-five! However, in the past I have been very unlucky in love! So I decided to cast my net wider and join a dating agency in the hope of catching a suitable fish!

So far, hardtopleeze.co.uk have not been able to find me a prospective wife, but I live in hope!

At least I have a video which, I think, gives a fair representation of what Graham Cracknall is all about!

Best wishes from your son

Graham

Please Note: I had my hair cut shortly before the filming of the video. The barber wilfully ignored my instructions for a trim

and proceeded to shave my scalp, leaving only stubble! My hair
has since grown back!

Charles read the letter with a sinking heart. It was not only Graham's prolific use of exclamation marks that depressed him; there was a slight air of desperation between the lines. Could it be that Graham was a social misfit? The Hardtopleeze agency had been the subject of a critical documentary on Radio Four's *You and Yours*. The presenter Peter White had accused the owner, a Mrs Greyling, of 'preying on the weak, the vulnerable, the physically and emotionally challenged'. Mrs Greyling had defended her agency rigorously, claiming that she 'gave hope to those who, in earlier days, would have been condemned to spend most of their life living at home with their mum and dad'. Charles said nothing to Camilla about his worries. The poor darling has enough on her plate at the moment, he thought.

When Camilla had finished reading the letter, she said, with a mother's determination to see the best in her child, 'It's splendid that he has a life plan, isn't it?' Camilla had never planned anything in her own life; she merely reacted to people and events.

Charles said, scanning the letter again, 'He certainly understands how to paragraph.'

Having no video or television, Charles went next door and asked Vince Threadgold if he could borrow their portable set. Vince said, on the doorstep, 'I'm halfway through recording the afternoon porn show. Come in an' watch if you like.'

Charles was flummoxed by Vince's insouciance. In

Charles's opinion, sex was a serious and sacred business, and conversation about it should be confined to one's sexual partner.

Later that evening, Vince set up the television and video. He explained how everything worked by putting Graham's video into the slot, waiting until the film began. When Graham's face came up on the screen, Vince laughed. 'Christ, 'e's an ugly bugger! Who is it?'

Charles turned the volume down and said, 'Er . . . he's a distant relation.'

Vince laughed again at Graham and said, 'That's what years of inbreeding does to a man's looks.'

After Vince had gone, Charles rewound the video and turned the volume up. Camilla seated herself on the sofa and prepared herself to see and hear her elder son for the very first time.

Charles sat down next to Camilla and took her hand; he switched on the video. Graham was sitting in what looked like a cubicle under very bright lights. On the wall behind him was the hardtopleeze.co.uk logo: a stick man and a stick woman embracing inside a clumsily drawn heart.

As she watched the forty-year-old Graham on the video, Camilla thought back to the day-old baby she had called Rory. How had that little bawling scrap turned into Graham, who appeared to have the dress sense of an Albanian swineherd and the manner of an especially wooden ventriloquist's dummy?

Hello, my name is Graham. Graham Cracknall.
I'm forty, my star sign is Leo or Cancer,

depending on which newspaper you read. I'm
on the cusp, not only astrologically, but
also, in life.

As you can see, I am of medium height, a bit
taller than Tom Cruise, but a smidgen smaller
than John Travolta. Incidentally, both of
these men, chosen by me completely at random, are eminent Scientologists, disciples
of the late Ron Hubbard. I once flirted with
Scientology myself and sent for the literature, but my mother, bless her, who is in the
habit of reading my correspondence while I'm
at work, was so upset by Mr Hubbard's mind-
mapping philosophy that she notified Cult
Watch and they arranged for me to meet a
counsellor, who warned me about the dangers
of joining any quasi-religious organization
headed by a billionaire with a private
island and a fleet of expensive limousines.
So, phew! I had a close shave there!

I live with my mum and dad in Ruislip,
famous for lovely Jordan, who graced us with
her presence for a year. Other alumni include the famous spies, the Krogers, Linford
Christie and Mantovani, and one day I hope
Graham Cracknall will be a name on everybody's lips.

Anyway, time is running out, so enough
about me. I am looking for a petite, non-
smoking heterosexual woman with a GSOH,
bubbly personality and an interest in board

games. Looks are not important but I would prefer her not to have any obvious disabilities, ergo children. She will need to be computer literate and financially secure and preferably have at least one foot on the property ladder.

Ideally, she will chill out to easy-listening music. James Blunt is a particular favourite of mine; I saw him a year ago at the Hexagon in Reading. If she enjoys *The Two Ronnies*, *Only Fools and Horses* and *Inspector Morse*, we will get on like a house on fire. I have the complete, director's cut, boxed set of *Morse* on DVD.

So if you like what you see, get in touch with me at:

grahamcracknall@hotmail.co.uk

After the video had finished, Camilla said weakly, 'I expect he looks better with hair.'

'Undoubtedly,' said Charles, 'but I think, darling, that Graham has not been blessed with good looks.'

Camilla searched and found within herself a tiny ember of maternal love; perhaps if she fanned it a little, the ember would burst into flames. She had always, as a child, loved the story about the ugly duckling. Perhaps one day Graham would come out from behind the metaphorical bulrushes and glide gracefully down the river.

*

Later that night, Charles and Camilla were brushing their teeth side by side in the cramped bathroom, each allowing the other to rinse and spit in turn into the cracked washbasin stained with limescale. Charles would not allow Camilla to keep the tap running due to his concerns about the worldwide water shortage, so a certain amount of orchestration was necessary.

Camilla examined her reflection in the harsh light of the mirror and sighed, 'Oh, darling, I do look a hag tonight.'

'You're mad,' said Charles. 'You look more beautiful to me every day.'

They heard the sound of breaking glass and went downstairs to find a half brick had been thrown through the living-room window. Shards of glass lay on the carpet. A note was fastened to the brick with an elastic band. It read: 'Yourl never be queen.' Charles quickly scrunched the note up and put it in his pocket before Camilla could see it. The poor darling has suffered enough, he thought. He ran out into the darkness of the close, where few of the streetlights were working. There was a light on at William and Harry's house.

Charles walked to the barrier with the half brick and showed it to the security policeman on duty there, saying, 'If my wife had been lying on the floor under the window, it could have killed her.'

The policeman said, 'But why would your wife be lying on the floor? Ain't you got chairs to sit on?'

Charles said, testily, 'Look, aren't you going to investigate the crime?'

'No. I'll give you a crime number for the insurance, if you like,' said the policeman.

Charles said, 'I have no insurance; the premiums are far beyond my pocket. Can't you take fingerprints or something?'

The policeman laughed and said, 'You're thinking about the olden days, sir.'

'Can't you look at the CCTV?' asked Charles.

'I'm not qualified to interpret those images, sir. And anyway, one hoody looks very much like another,' said the policeman. 'So, if you'd make your way home now. You're breaking the curfew.'

Charles was tempted to show the policeman the scrunched-up note that he had in his pocket, but something stopped him. There was a tiny voice in his head telling him that he had seen the handwriting before. When he got home he found that Camilla had made no attempt to clear up the shards of glass. She was sitting in the kitchen with the dogs. After vacuuming the living-room carpet, and taping a plastic bag over the jagged hole in the window, he suggested to Camilla that she should go up to bed. When he judged that she was asleep, he went to the writing desk and opened the locked drawer where he kept souvenirs and mementos. He sifted through them for the last birthday card he had received from Harry. He took out the scrunched-up note and smoothed it flat, and compared the handwriting. It wasn't just the dismal spelling that angered him.

Harold Bunion had been pressing the call button on his bedside table for over twenty minutes. His bladder was bursting, but he needed assistance to get out of bed and into his wheelchair; his legs were two leaden lumps since his last stroke. Down the corridor he could hear Edna Hart pleading, 'Help me, help me!' and further away somebody was groaning, as though in pain. Harold strained his ears, listening for footsteps approaching his room, but there were none to be heard.

He shouted, 'Is anybody there?' Prince Philip stirred in his sleep and Harold shouted again, 'Is anybody there?'

Prince Philip struggled up from his pillows and yelled, '*Britannia* is sinking.'

Harold visualized the royal yacht capsizing and being swallowed up by a huge dark sea, and wondered why the Queen had not been to see her husband for a few days. He could tell that Philip had not been eating or drinking from the untouched trays that were dumped on his bed trolley. He fumbled on his bedside table in the dim light for a receptacle of some kind. His hand touched the little plastic pot which held his dentures, but when he tried to grasp the pot he only succeeded in pushing it further away. He pressed the call button and this time heard footsteps in the corridor. A care worker he had never seen before put her head around the door and said, 'Is it you making all that noise?'

Harold said brusquely, 'I need the toilet. Help me into my wheelchair.'

The woman said, 'A wheelchair transfer takes two people. It's Sunday, and me and the other nurse is running the place on our two owns, and she's on her break, so you'll have to wait.'

Harold said, savagely, 'I can't wait. Just help me into the chair, will you?'

The woman said, 'I can't, it's health and safety. I'm not going to do my back in for five pounds twenty-eight an hour. I'll fetch you a bottle.'

Philip shouted, 'We're drowning! The water's over my head.'

There was a commotion from one of the rooms at the end of the corridor, and Harold deduced from the raised voices that Mrs Hart had fallen out of bed. He began to weep; he had lost control of everything in his life, and now he was losing control of his bladder. The urine flooded out of him, warm at first, but it quickly cooled down, and soon he was shivering in his saturated bed.

Prince Philip said, 'I'm hungry and thirsty. I want Elizabeth.'

Harold said, 'She'll be here in the morning. Go to sleep now.'

Harold was comforted by the thought that the Queen might visit them in the morning. He was a Republican and had denounced the monarchy on many public platforms, but he liked and trusted Mrs Windsor. He lay awake for a few moments, listening to the rise and fall of Prince Philip's breathing.

33

Princess Michael was sitting at her dining table, writing in an A4-size spiral-bound notebook using a Bic pen. She was working on the manuscript of a novel she intended to call *A Princess in Exile*. The heroine, Cristina von Kronenbourg, was not unlike herself, Marie-Christine thought: statuesque and hauntingly beautiful with hair like spun gold and a smile that captivated men's hearts and kept them prisoners for eternity. Her fictional husband, Prince Michael of Kronenbourg, had been tragically lost in an avalanche, though his body had never been found. Finding herself cast out by his cruel family, who had ruled the small country of Kronenbourg for centuries, she wandered from country to country finding nothing but unkindness from the common people. After many adventures, she found her husband, who was disguised as a sea captain. Reunited, they returned to their previous positions. But the prince had learned a valuable lesson – that poor, uneducated people were absolutely horrid and that the best people with the warmest hearts were the rich and the powerful ones. They were the best friends to have.

Princess Michael had shown the manuscript to only one person, Chanel Toby, who cleaned for her once a week. Chanel had been forced to read the manuscript under the intense gaze of Princess Michael, who scrutinized every gesture that Chanel made, saying, 'Your mouth moved, are you amused?' or, 'You raised an eyebrow, you are surprised by the story, huh?'

Chanel had blurted out at the end of the ordeal that she thought, 'The book were brilliant; much better than anything anybody has ever writ before.'

Princess Michael said, 'Please be honest with me, child. I know the book is good, but *brilliant*, I'm not so sure.'

Chanel, desperate to get out of the house, said, 'It's better than the Bible and Shakespeare and Harry Potter.'

Princess Michael had smiled. It was as she thought, she was a genius. Her book would explode on to the literary world like a shooting star. She would be acclaimed by *Hello!* and *Cosmopolitan*, fêted by other authors. Her financial worries would be over. The only regret she had was that she hadn't started to write novels years ago. She heard a noise outside. Voices were raised and dogs were barking. She looked up from the manuscript and saw a rowdy crowd of Hell Close residents milling around one of Grice's delivery vans.

She finished the paragraph she had been writing: 'Princess Cristina was invited into the torture chamber to watch the torturers practising their black arts. She greatly enjoyed hearing the peasants who had wronged her begging for mercy. Such entreaties she answered with a merry tinkling laugh that sounded like fairies shaking a cowslip.' Inspired, she carried on: '"Ask me not for mercy, peasants, lest thee displease me further, in which circumstance thy tribulations will increase fourfold."'

As she crossed the green with Zsa-Zsa in her arms, she heard inside her head the Whitbread Prize judge saying, 'And the first prize goes to Princess Michael of Kent for *A Princess in Exile*.'

After six days without another grocery delivery, there was a serious shortage of dog food. The humans were also feeling the pinch. Mr Anwar and his wife were suffering the worst; they were used to eating vast amounts of food and were living in Hell Close precisely because he was morbidly obese and had been put on the Morbidly Obese Register. Mr Anwar had said at the time, 'I wish the doctors would make up their minds. Ten years ago they tell me I am *fat*, five years ago they tell me I am *obese*, and now they have changed their minds *again* and tell me I am *morbidly* obese! What next?'

He had signed many National Health Service contracts, promising to keep his calorific consumption down to two thousand five hundred a day, but had failed to keep to any of them for more than forty-eight hours before cracking and waddling into Grice's Chinese Chip Shop. Mr Anwar had begged his obesity counsellor to recommend him for gastric reduction surgery, a procedure that involved reducing the stomach to the size of a baby's fist. But the counsellor had explained that Mr Anwar was much too fat for the operation, and had told him that he would need to lose at least five stone before he could be safely anaesthetized. Mr Anwar had protested in his reedy voice, 'But I can't lose five stone until I have the operation.' This circular argument had been going on for many years.

Mr Anwar's dog, Raj, was also obese. He rarely left the house; he felt safe only in the back garden. He communicated with other dogs occasionally by barking loudly and listening to their barked replies, but he was too fat to run and play with them on the green and so missed the subtleties of their interaction.

Everybody was hungry. A deputation of dogs went up to the police barrier and spoke to Judge and Emperor who were on duty.

Harris barked, 'We've been living on slops and human leftovers for almost a week; we're actually starving to death. Can you nae do something for us?'

Leo whimpered, 'I'm a growing dog, I need my food.'

Judge barked, 'Piss off! We work for our food. You're nothing but lapdogs and parasites.'

Harris snapped, 'I'd cut my tail off for a job. Can I join the police force?'

'No,' laughed Emperor. 'You ain't got the height, shortarse.'

When Arthur Grice's Rolls-Royce drew up at the barrier, the dogs stood aside to let him drive through. Rocky was snarling on the back seat, 'Hello, losers. Feeling a bit peckish?'

Grice drew up outside Charles and Camilla's and opened the car boot. He took out a large carton full of dog food and ordered Rocky to guard the car. The Hell Close dogs, nineteen in all, surrounded Arthur, baying, barking, howling, yelping, whimpering and growling. They followed him up the path to the front door. Hunger had stirred a primeval memory of when dogs were wild creatures who hunted and killed to fill their empty bellies. Grice kicked out at the dogs and banged on the door. When Camilla opened it, he pushed past her and stumbled into the hall. Leo, Freddie and Tosca stood shoulder to shoulder and pushed the other dogs back over the doorstep, and Camilla slammed the door.

Grice said, 'I've brung you a present. There's twenty-four tins of Pedigree Chum in 'ere. Where do you want it?'

Camilla said, 'How very kind. In the kitchen, please.'

Grice followed Camilla through to the kitchen, and dropped the box on to the table.

Freddie barked to Tosca, 'Grice does nothing out of the goodness of his heart. What does he want?'

Tosca growled, 'I don't care. I'm hungry.'

Leo barked, 'Camilla, get the box open. Find the tin opener. Feed me!'

Grice said, 'Your 'usband not in?'

'No,' said Camilla. 'He's with his mother.'

Grice smiled. 'Family is everythink,' he said.

'Do you have any children?' asked Camilla.

'No,' said Grice. 'We've got Rocky. He's a Dobermann, and they don't like kiddies.'

'Enough of the small talk,' barked Tosca, jumping up at the box.

Camilla said, 'How much do I owe you for the dog food, Mr Grice?'

Grice waved the suggestion of payment away airily. 'Nothink,' he said. 'It's free, gratis, a present from one dog lover to another.'

Camilla asked, 'And are all the dog lovers in Hell Close to be given dog food?'

Grice's eyes shifted away from Camilla. 'You could

mention to 'Er Majesty the Queen that you've got a few spare tins,' he said.

The Hell Close dogs had made their way around the side of the house and were now marauding in the back garden, trampling on the neat lines of brassicas and winter cabbage. King had jumped over the fence and was howling at the back door.

When Grice made no sign of leaving, Camilla, impelled by good manners, asked if he would like a cup of tea. Grice unbuttoned his cashmere overcoat and dropped down heavily into a chair. He looked around the kitchen and said, 'I hope you didn't take your house arrest personal, only I 'ad to be seen to be in control.'

Camilla stood with her back against the sink, willing the kettle to boil. She made no move to open the carton of dog food, though it was hard to resist the hunger in her dogs' eyes. She waited for Grice to state the nature of the price she would have to pay.

Grice said, 'I was brung up in a council house like this. There was nine of us, we took it in turns to wear the shoes, an' there was never enough cups to go round. I 'ad to drink my tea out of a jam jar.' Grice's voice faltered, he was suddenly overwhelmed with self-pity. 'I didn't own me own underpants until I was sixteen.'

Freddie snarled, 'Pass the bleeding violin.'

Camilla said, 'You've certainly done terribly well to fight your way out of such poverty, Mr Grice.'

Grice sighed, 'Yeah, I done all right. I've got every-think – 'ouses, cars, expensive wife, millions in the bank – but it ain't enough. I want somethink money can't buy.'

Camilla asked, 'Happiness?'

Grice said, 'No, happiness is for losers. What I want is an honour.'

Camilla said, 'But money *can* buy you an honour, Mr Grice. One only has to donate a large sum of money to the Cromwell Party.' She had heard recently from Beverley Threadgold that Michael Jackson, the disgraced singer, had, in exchange for many millions of pounds, been elevated to Lord Jackson of Neverland.

Grice growled, 'But it ain't guaranteed. And anyway, why should I pay the monkey when I can get one from the organ grinder?' He was rather pleased with his analogy, but Camilla was baffled. What had monkeys and organ grinders to do with the reintroduced honours system?

The kettle shrieked and Camilla poured boiling water into the teapot. The dogs in the garden were now leaping up at the windows and scratching on the back door. Camilla felt doubly besieged; her own dogs were whimpering pitifully, never taking their eyes off the carton of dog food, still unopened on the table. She poured strong black tea into a delicate china cup and asked, 'Milk and sugar?'

'A bit of milk and seven sugars,' Grice replied. 'Anyway, you might mention that in your opinion, Arthur Grice, employer of hundreds, philanthropist and benefactor to the poor, deserves an honour. Perhaps when you give the Queen a few tins of this dog food.'

Camilla said, 'Mr Grice, I have no influence over the Queen.'

'But your 'usband has,' said Grice. 'Couldn't 'e put a word in for me?'

Camilla said, 'Relations are strained between my husband and his mother at the moment.'

She spooned seven teaspoons of sugar into Grice's cup and added a little milk.

Grice said, 'I expect she blames you because she's not allowed to see 'er 'usband.'

Camilla said, 'I do feel dreadful about that.'

Grice said, 'And it's your fault 'er dogs are goin' 'ungry.'

'Yes,' said Camilla, grimacing as Grice sipped his sickly-sweet tea.

He said, 'An' all these problems could be solved by just a little tap on the shoulder with a sword, and the words "Arise, Sir Arthur".'

'When you put it like that,' said Camilla weakly.

'Well, I'll leave you to think about it,' said Grice, picking up the carton of dog food.

Leo, Tosca and Freddie leapt at the box, trying to knock it out of Grice's huge hands. Grice roared, 'Fuck off, you bleeders!' and kicked out viciously, catching Tosca a hard kick behind her ear. She recoiled from the blow and lay still on the floor, whimpering, with her eyes half closed. Leo and Freddie cowered away from Grice as he made his way out of the kitchen carrying the carton. Camilla knelt over Tosca, stroking her head and making soothing, calming noises. She heard the front door open, then close, then the cacophony of ravenous dogs outside pleading for food.

Arthur Grice drove his Rolls-Royce slowly around Hell Close, pursued by famished dogs. A few of the more intelligent animals knew that this was a fruitless pursuit, but they joined the pack anyway. Grice stopped the car outside Princess Michael's house. It was soon marooned by a circle of Hell Close dogs whose eyes were wild and whose teeth were bared. Rocky was throwing himself around on the back seat, bouncing from one side of the car to the other, ignoring Grice's commands to stop. The noise of Rocky's barking in the confines of the car was intolerable.

Grice called for assistance. 'I want tasers and dogs 'ere immediate,' he shouted into his mobile phone. While he waited for help, Grice's blood pressure rose; he could feel the pulse in his ears throbbing. He was not accustomed to being frightened, but the thought of being attacked and brought down by the maddened pack made him sweat and tremble with fear. Some of the residents had come to stand at their front gates; others were gawping from their front-room windows. They were thoroughly enjoying Grice's predicament. Grice saw two policemen in riot gear, with Emperor and Judge straining on their leashes, running down Hell Close towards him, followed by Inspector Lancer holding a taser gun.

Emperor barked, 'Clear the area, go to your homes!'

The Hell Close dogs stood their ground.

Judge barked, 'Go to your homes, you filthy scum!'

Harris ran forwards and growled, 'We have nae had a decent meal in days, and we have a right to protest.'

Susan barked, 'Harris, let's go home.'

But Harris's hackles were up and he advanced on the straining police dogs, growling, 'You're a disgrace to your own kind.'

Inspector Lancer said, 'Let 'em off the leads, boys.'

The dog handlers unleashed Emperor and Judge, and the pack of Hell Close dogs turned tail and scattered to their own homes. Only Harris stood his ground.

As she fled, Susan barked, 'Run, Harris, run.'

But Harris, foolishly, because he was half their size and there were two of them against one, prepared to fight. Emperor and Judge waited for their orders; Lancer's finger moved to the trigger of the taser. He was sick of police dogs getting all the glory. You could hardly open a newspaper without seeing a photograph of one of the smug 'heroes' sitting at the side of a grinning handler. He advanced on Harris.

Harris turned to look at Lancer, growling from the back of his throat. When it looked as though Harris was about to run at his ankle, Lancer pulled the trigger and the taser shot the wire from the gun. The darts on the end embedded themselves into Harris's belly, sending 50,000 volts through the little dog's body. Harris screamed in agony, then collapsed and lay twitching on the pavement. His agonized yelps brought the Queen and Prince Charles running. Charles had never seen his mother run before, not even when he was a child and they played on the lawn. He was astounded how quickly she covered the territory from her front door to Harris's side.

As the Queen bent over Harris's prone body, Inspector Lancer said, 'It was self-defence. 'E would have 'ad me throat out.'

The Queen said, 'Nonsense! To reach your throat he would have needed a stepladder.'

Grice opened the car door and said to Lancer, 'If you've killed Her Majesty's dog, you'll pay for it with your inspector's pips. I'll have you on the beat so long your feet will be in tatters.'

Lancer said, 'But Mr Grice, I was only following orders.'

Grice rolled his eyes, and Charles said, 'That was Rudolf Hess's defence at Nuremberg, Inspector Lancer.'

Grice bent over Harris, asking solicitously, ''Ow is the little fellow?'

The Queen took off her cardigan and laid it over Harris, who opened one eye and whimpered, 'Thank you.'

Grice said, ''E'll soon be all right, when 'e's 'ad a decent meal.'

The Queen said, 'Unfortunately, Mr Grice, I have nothing substantial to give him. Your grocery boxes have been somewhat inadequate.'

Grice lowered his voice and said, 'I've got a carton of dog food in the boot of the Rolls, Ma'am. You've turned me down for a peerage, but 'ow about a knighthood? I could settle for bein' Sir Arthur Grice.'

The Queen was tempted to take Grice up on his offer; after all, what was a knighthood? A mere tap on the shoulder with a fancy sword and a few steps backwards.

Seeing the Queen's hesitation, Grice continued, 'We could 'ave a bit of a do at the One-Stop Centre.'

Charles said, 'Mummy, it wouldn't do any harm. All titles are meaningless; nothing means anything. Life is composed of random happenings. And we ourselves are composed of water and carbon thingies.'

The Queen and Grice were baffled by Charles's philosophizing.

The Queen thought for a moment, then said, 'Very well, Mr Grice, these are my terms, in exchange for giving you a knighthood. First, I am to be allowed out of Hell Close to visit my husband. Second, all the dogs in the close are to be given a case of food, and you might also throw in a couple of boxes of Bonios.'

Grice agreed eagerly. He would have been willing to forfeit half of his fortune for a knighthood bestowed by the Queen. She was, after all, the genuine article.

Charles picked up Harris's prone, twitching body from the pavement. Grice ordered the policemen and their dogs to return to work. He said to the Queen, 'I'll get the missus to organize the do.'

The Queen said, imperiously, 'You will organize the dog food first, Mr Grice.' Then she and Charles, with Harris in his arms, trekked across the little green.

Camilla was watching them from her doorstep, her hands pressed against the sides of her face, convinced that she was responsible for killing Harris, the Queen's favourite dog. Charles would not allow his mother to go back to her own house with the sickly Harris. So stopping only to collect Susan, they proceeded to Number Sixteen where Camilla was waiting. After establishing that Harris was alive, Camilla absented herself and went into the kitchen to cry and make tea. The Queen had not directly blamed Camilla for Harris's condition, but neither had she been particularly friendly to her.

Harris was wrapped in a blanket on the sofa, where he lay blinking and whimpering. The Queen sat beside him, stroking his back and repeatedly telling him that he was 'a brave boy'. Although she had appeared to keep her composure, a slight trembling of her chin betrayed the fact that the Queen was in fact distraught.

Charles hovered over his mother and Harris, not quite knowing what to do or say.

He tentatively patted his mother's shoulder and said, 'Mummy, look at the other dogs, they're terribly worried.' The Queen looked across the room to where Susan, Freddie, Tosca and Leo were lying with their ears flattened and their eyes fixed on Harris.

Word spread quickly among the dogs of Hell Close that the Queen had rescued them from starvation and that Harris had almost sacrificed his life for their cause. A cluster of concerned dogs had gathered outside Charles and Camilla's house, waiting for one of the resident dogs to give them an up-to-date medical bulletin on Harris's condition. Zsa-Zsa had escaped from Princess Michael's house while her mistress was absorbed in writing her novel. Spike and Raj, both usually confined to their back gardens, had also joined the crowd.

At 4.30 p.m. Freddie came into the front garden and barked an announcement: 'At 4.27 Harris sat up and requested food and a drink. He is very tired, but his nose is shiny and his eyes are bright. The Queen expects him to make a full recovery. I suggest that you go back to your homes and wait for the delivery of Pedigree Chum and Bonios.'

Micky Toby barked, 'Will the mongrels get Pedigree Chum?'

Freddie barked back, 'In accordance with Harris's wishes, I am calling a moratorium on divisions between the mongrels and the pedigrees. After all, we are all dogs!'

The mongrels among the pack of dogs turned to see how the pedigrees had taken Harris's relayed dictum. Not well, was the answer. It was thought among the pedigrees that the shock from the taser had addled Harris's brain. How could a mongrel ever be the equal of a pedigree dog? Did centuries of selected breeding count for nothing?

Spike growled to Zsa-Zsa, as they crossed the green to their respective houses, 'I don't mind having sex with a mongrel, but I wouldn't want to live with one.'

Zsa-Zsa yelped, 'Nor I, *mon chéri*. Zat 'Arris is a traitor to 'iz class.'

Spike growled, 'I know we've had our differences in the past, but I've always fancied you, Zsa-Zsa.'

Zsa-Zsa laughed, 'You are too 'eavy for me, *chéri*, and unfortunately you 'ave ze face of John Prescott.'

Spike was mortified; he had seen John Prescott on the History Channel. Zsa-Zsa was selfish and highly strung, but she was not entirely heartless. She saw that she had hurt Spike's feelings

She said, in a conciliatory tone, 'We will not 'ave sex, but you can sniff my *derrière*.'

Spike went behind Zsa-Zsa and drew in her scent – it was a heady mix of musky secretions and the Diorissimo that Princess Michael sprayed on Zsa-Zsa after the little dog's daily bath. Spike was overwhelmed by her fragrance; he lost his ugly head and attempted to mount her, but the disparity in their sizes prevented him from gaining purchase and his efforts were frustrated. Princess Michael, finally realizing that Zsa-Zsa had escaped from the house, went looking for her. She found her, apparently being mounted by the drooling Spike.

She screamed, 'Get off her, you ugly brute,' and kicked out at Spike.

Princess Anne, hearing Spike's howl of pain, flew out of her house, roaring, 'Kick my dog again and I'll take your bloody head off your shoulders!'

Princess Michael scooped up Zsa-Zsa and kissed her tiny petulant face, saying, 'Did the horrid slobbery monster frighten you, my precious?'

Princess Anne gave Spike an affectionate cuff round the head and said, 'At least my dog looks like a dog. That spoilt creature you've got in your arms looks like a hairy four-legged Barbie doll.'

Exactly how the two women came to brawl in the street is disputed. Spiggy swore Princess Michael struck the first blow, whereas a more neutral witness, Mr Anwar, claimed that Princess Anne jumped on Princess Michael's back and shouted, 'Ride, pony girl!' It was not unusual to see women fighting in Hell Close, but it was the first time that the Royals had made such an exhibition of themselves. Princess Michael was heard to scream that Anne had married a mongrel. Anne yelled back that at least Spiggy had a chin.

Maddo Clarke brought a folding chair on to the green

and settled himself to watch the spectacle of posh middle-aged totty rolling in a mud patch. Spiggy eventually broke the fight up and dragged Princess Anne back into their house, saying, 'Leave it, Annie, she's not worth it.' Maddo Clarke congratulated Princess Michael on her fighting technique, and offered to help her off with her muddy clothes. When she refused his help, he folded his chair and went back inside his house.

34

The dog food that Grice's van delivered was labelled with government health warnings, saying: 'DOGS KILL.' 'DOGS SERIOUSLY ENDANGER YOUR HEALTH.' 'DOGS CAUSE BLINDNESS.' 'DOGS LICK THEIR GENITALS, AND THEN THEY LICK YOU!' 'DON'T FEED A DOG, FEED A STARVING CHILD!' 'DOGS CARRY FLEAS.'

After serving it up, the Queen left Harris in Charles and Camilla's care and went home to put on her coat, hat and gloves. Having made sure her identity card was in her handbag, she left her house and walked up to the checkpoint. Inspector Lancer waved her through without meeting her eye. Normally she would have exchanged a few pleasantries – they had once talked for five solid minutes about the weather – but for now she could not bring herself to speak to him.

She waited for longer than usual outside Frank Bruno House, constantly pressing the buzzer and eventually banging on the front door. A female care worker she had never seen before, who was pushing an old lady in a wheelchair, opened the door and said, in an accent the Queen thought might be Polish, 'What is it you are wanting?'

The Queen put her foot in the door and said, 'I'm

here to visit my husband, Mr Windsor, on the top floor.'
She took out her identity card; the woman glanced at it
and allowed the Queen to step inside.

The smell hit the Queen like a blow. The air felt heavy
with invisible, malodorous substances. The woman in
the wheelchair turned her yellow face towards the
Queen and said, 'Your Majesty, they're killing me.'

The Queen hurried towards the lift, but the care
worker shouted, 'The lift, it is broken.'

As the Queen climbed the stairs, pausing every now
and again to catch her breath, she heard the distressing
sounds of her contemporaries, those she had once
called her subjects, crying out in bewilderment and
fear. She also heard a younger, harsher voice shouting
instructions to somebody who had displeased them.

When she walked into her husband's room she found
Harold Bunion trying to reach Prince Philip's mouth
with a dessertspoon full of yogurt. Because of the
barrier the wheelchair presented, he could not get close
enough to spoon the yogurt into Philip's mouth. When
Bunion saw the Queen, he said, 'Thank God you've
come.'

The Queen was alarmed when she looked at her
husband. In the six days since she'd last seen him, he
appeared to have shrunk to half his former size. She
hardly recognized the little old man who was lying with
his head on the grubby pillow.

Bunion gestured towards the covered dishes stacked
on Prince Philip's bedside trolley. 'He's not been eatin','
he said, 'and I don't think 'e's 'ad anything to drink
either. We've been in a right pickle.'

As the Queen was trying to get her husband to drink from a glass of water, Bunion wheeled himself away and sat by the window, looking out.

He said, 'I might as well do the country a favour and top myself. Nobody wants me, nobody would miss me, I'm just a bloody nuisance. It's a crime to be old in this country an' I'm bein' punished for it.'

The Queen said, 'I'm here now, Mr Bunion, and I'm deeply grateful to you for trying to help my husband.'

Bunion said, 'I don't hold with the monarchy, but he is a human being.'

The Queen was ridiculously grateful for Bunion's acknowledgement of her husband's humanity, and was moved to say, 'Perhaps when the lift is mended, one of my grandsons could push you to the library.'

Bunion nodded his thanks and stared out at an England he no longer recognized.

When Harris recovered his faculties, he was a changed dog. There was no perceptible difference between the old Harris and the new, but the electric shock he had received to his system had charged him up and clarified his brain.

As he said to Susan, shortly after struggling off the sofa and testing the strength in his legs, 'I'm fired up, Susan. I'm only a wee Dorgie but I'm nae taking this anti-dog rubbish lying down.'

Susan whimpered, 'You almost got yourself killed, Harris. Dinna stir the waters.'

Harris barked, 'I'm calling a meeting. I want every dog on the Flowers Estate to be there.'

Susan yelped, 'Every dog? What about our enemies?'

Harris barked, 'Our enemies are human, not canine.'

Because he didn't really trust his legs to hold him up yet, he climbed the stairs slowly, stopping every now and then to catch his breath. I'm getting old, he thought. He flattened himself and squirmed underneath the Queen's bed, and in that quiet, dark space he began to think. When the Queen came looking for him, she dropped to her knees and tried to coax him out with a fresh scone she had baked for him as a special treat.

He growled, 'Please, can ye nae leave me be, woman?'

The Queen struggled to her feet and said to Susan, who was at her side, 'Our boy is beginning to look his age, Susan.'

When they had gone downstairs, Harris made himself as comfortable as he could in the restricted space and began to plan his revolution.

35

There was an air of celebration the next morning when the residents of Hell Close awoke to find that the barrier at the entrance to the close had been dismantled and they were now able to come and go as they pleased within the Flowers Estate. Camilla watched the perambulations of the residents: William driving the pick-up truck on his way to work, the children going to school, then later still Maddo Clarke setting off for the betting shop. Chantelle waved as she ran to her work at Frank Bruno House.

Camilla longed to leave the house. 'I'm not an indoor person,' she said to Beverley Threadgold, who had come round to enquire about Harris's health.

Beverley seemed almost disappointed when she was told that Harris was 'a bit quiet and thoughtful, but otherwise quite well'. She sighed; she'd been hoping for a poignant burial service in the Queen's back garden. It would have been something to get dressed up for.

Arthur Grice had been called to Grice-A-Go-Go to settle a dispute between two dancers over a stolen thong. Normally Sandra would have seen to such a trivial incident, but she was busy with arrangements for his investiture, and so Arthur had gone himself. He was confronted in the club by two angry young women, each accusing the other of thong theft. Arthur quickly solved the problem by sacking both dancers. He wouldn't have to worry about replacing them; there was always a waiting list of new girls willing to writhe about on men's laps for a few hours a day. The money was good and Arthur hardly ever touched the girls up himself.

As he was leaving the club, he saw Princess Michael, a woman he had always admired, coming towards him with Zsa-Zsa in one arm and a bag of shopping on the other. Princess Michael was enormously flattered when Arthur Grice put a business proposition to her. He was conscious that, though his wife was still, at forty-one, hot totty, she was not a lady. Arthur worried that Sandra would not be able to hold her own when they began to mix with the upper echelons of East Midlands Region society. He'd once taken her on a world cruise, thinking it would give her something to talk about at the parties they gave, but she had not been impressed by the wonders of the world.

On seeing Sydney Harbour Bridge she had said, 'That reminds me, I must ask the steward for some more coat hangers.' Her verdict on Venice had been, 'Time they came up to date, filled in them canals and built some fuckin' roads,' and her opinion on Rome, 'It could be nice if they done up all them fallen-down buildings.'

It wasn't that she was thick – she could add up a column of figures in a flash, and she understood business. Sandra was the only person Arthur knew who took any notice of the Dow Jones index. And she was a walking encyclopedia when it came to beauty products. But she had certain habits that he was sure would not go down too well at the functions they were bound to attend as Sir Arthur and Lady Grice. Picking her teeth with a sharpened matchstick at the end of a meal was one. Telling people how much her breasts had cost was another.

He waylaid Princess Michael and Zsa-Zsa outside Grice-A-Go-Go and said, 'Princess Michael, 'ow 'bout a lift home in the Roller?'

'Oh, this is heavenly,' Princes Michael gushed as she sank back into the leather of the front passenger seat. 'One *so* misses the privileges that come with rank.'

Rocky growled a greeting to Zsa-Zsa from the back seat and she yapped back, '*Bonjour, mon ami*. Is zat a new collar you are wearing? Zose studs are *très* butch.'

Rocky dipped his huge Dobermann head modestly and growled, 'Arthur bought it for my birthday.'

During the short drive to Hell Close, Arthur outlined his business plan. He was going to open a school of etiquette and modern manners, and he wanted Princess Michael to run it for him. 'I'd make it worth your while,' he said.

He reckoned she was the classiest of the Royals; she always looked like a princess in her diamonds and bits and bobs of fur. The other Royals were scruffy buggers; even the Queen had let herself go. She rarely wore a hat and the only time he'd seen her in gloves lately was in the garden. Arthur had witnessed her on CCTV, grubbing in the dirt like a commoner.

Princess Michael said, 'What aspects of modern manners have you in mind?'

'For instance,' Arthur said, 'is it right or wrong to answer your mobile phone when you're on the lavvy? An' 'ow many times can you say "fuck" in a sentence without causing offence? An' when my girls are lap dancin', is it good manners to take their thongs off or keep 'em on?'

Princess Michael was taken aback at first; she had thought that the students would be seeking guidance on the finer points of fish-knife use, or how to address a baronet. However, a job was a job. She was desperately short of money, and Zsa-Zsa needed a new coat before winter came.

'I accept your proposal, Mr Grice,' she said.

'Right,' said Grice, 'I'll get some cards printed up. How does "The Princess Michael Academy" sound to you?'

'It sounds rather splendid,' she said.

'You can start with my wife, Sandra,' said Grice. 'She's a wonderful woman, but she's got a few rough edges.'

Princess Michael had seen Sandra Grice on the estate and thought her the epitome of trailer trash.

''Ow long d'ya reckon it'll take you to turn 'er into a lady?' asked Grice anxiously. His investiture was to take place within the week and he wanted to start off on the right foot.

'I'm afraid one has to be born to it,' said Princess Michael, then seeing Grice's crestfallen face added, 'but give me a week and you'll hardly know it's the same woman.'

When he stopped the car outside her house he said,

'Ta-ra, then,' and waited for her to get out, but she sat there with her head on one side, smiling like that Mona Whatsit picture.

'What's up?' he asked.

'I'm waiting for you to open the car door for me, you ungallant fellow,' she laughed.

Grice heaved himself out of the car and lumbered around to the passenger door and opened it with a flourish. He couldn't wait to do the same for Sandra.

Later that night, after returning from Grice-A-Go-Go, where he and Sandra had been meeting with their accountants, Grice said, as he drew the car up to the front door of the Old Mill, 'Sit there, babe, I'll get the door for you.'

Sandra said, 'I ain't a fuckin' cripple. I can open me own bleedin' door.'

She slammed out of the car and strode across the gravel in her white cowboy boots.

Grice turned to Rocky and said, 'I love her to bits, Rocky, but if she don't come up to scratch I'll have to trade her in for an upmarket model.'

Later still, as he swilled brandy inside a balloon glass as big as a toddler's head, he noticed that more rubbish had collected in the stream under the glass floor.

Sandra and her mother had gone to bed; there was nobody to talk to apart from Rocky. The dog hoped that Grice wouldn't keep him up too late. He was tired and wanted to settle into his basket and go to sleep. When Grice slurred, 'Rocky, have I ever told you how poor we was when I was a kid?' Rocky's heart sank; it was going to be a long night.

36

Graham had never visited an Exclusion Zone before. When the taxi bringing him from the station drew up at the outer perimeter checkpoint, he hesitated before he got out of the car. The driver said, 'Changed your mind? I wun't blame you. They're animals in there.'

They looked out of the car windows at the steel fence with its topping of razor wire. A clematis had insinuated itself around the jagged steel teeth.

'That's a montana,' said the driver, 'late flowering, with a very vigorous habit.'

Graham said, 'It should be cut down. It's growing in an entirely unsuitable position. If anybody tried to prune it they could cut themselves to ribbons.'

Pulling his wheeled suitcase behind him, he approached the checkpoint. Inspector Lancer poked his head out of a hatch in the control room and checked Graham's visiting order, saying, 'Four days for a risk assessment?'

'I'm very thorough,' said Graham, who wasn't exactly lying. He was spoken about in the profession as the risk assessor's risk assessor: regarded by the Young Turks of the profession as a ruthless enforcer of the health and safety laws. He had once appeared on the regional news, defending the local authority's decision to cut down some ancient horse chestnut trees because of the inherent dangers they presented to young children who, despite warning notices, continued to throw sticks into the upper branches in their quest for conkers. As Graham said, 'Somebody could lose an eye.'

Inspector Lancer examined Graham's ID card and tapped the registration number into the computer. After a few seconds Graham's details came up on the screen. Lancer was interested to see that Graham suffered from frequent urinary tract infections and that he had purchased the latest James Blunt CD the previous day at HMV in Ruislip at 11.57 a.m.

'I'm partial to James Blunt,' said Lancer. 'Is his new album as inspiring as the last?'

Graham said, 'It exceeds his previous canon; it's a spiritual experience *par excellence*,' adding, 'I'm glad to know that at least some of Vulcan's software is working.'

He spoke as one professional to another. Vulcan was a standing joke among those who had access to the system.

Lancer said, laughing, 'You'd have been amused yesterday. Vulcan sent every pensioner in Coventry a death certificate with their name on it.'

Graham acknowledged Vulcan's stupidity by drawing his lips apart, like curtains in a theatre. It was not quite a smile, but Lancer was satisfied and waved Graham through.

As Graham walked towards Hell Close, he noted various hazards on the way: a tree with an overhanging branch, numerous cracked paving slabs, and evidence everywhere of lax attention to the health and safety laws. Cars were jacked up on bricks, there was a man up a ladder, and a child without a safety helmet was sitting astride a tricycle. As he turned the corner of Honeysuckle Avenue, he encountered Dwayne Lockhart who had been ordered to stop and search at least five people an hour.

Having read the correspondence that had passed between Graham and his blood parents, Dwayne felt as though he knew Graham. However, he remained outwardly detached and processed Graham's documents efficiently, even curtly, though he could not resist the temptation to make Graham feel uncomfortable. There was something about the man that made Dwayne's flesh crawl. It wasn't only that Graham was an ubergeek, it was that he brought out Dwayne's inner bully and made him ashamed of himself.

'So, why are you residing with Mr and Mrs Windsor for four days?' he asked Graham brusquely.

Graham had his answer ready. 'I am preparing a dossier on the health and safety aspects of a possible return to a monarchical system,' he said, 'with particular emphasis on the potential risks of the future monarch and his consort abusing their powers, should Mr Windsor accede to the throne.'

Dwayne looked at his hand-held computer screen and asked, 'What did you do with Gin and Tonic?'

Graham was taken aback at first. How did this young mixed-race policeman know the names of his dogs? He didn't remember giving this information to Vulcan, or to anybody in authority.

'Gin and Tonic are staying at the Excelsior Dog Hotel,' said Graham.

After he had been searched and was found to be free of weapons, explosives, tobacco and drugs, Dwayne directed Graham to Charles and Camilla's house. Dwayne then amused himself by processing other information about Graham that he had gleaned from the geek's ID card.

Graham didn't like cabbage, he bought a lot of black shoe polish, and he last went to the doctor's complaining about a 'funny feeling' in his index finger. He had informed the doctor that the feeling went off at night, but was painful during the day. He had recently inherited one hundred and twelve thousand pounds, following the death of his parents. When he was twelve years old, he had received a police caution for throwing an apple core into a neighbour's garden. He subscribed to *Board Game Enthusiast* and *Risk* magazines. He had tried unsuccessfully to cancel his mother's subscription to *Dog World.*

When Graham had gone, Dwayne said to himself, I wonder if Vulcan knows that I love Paris Butterworth?

Graham's trolley suitcase made so much noise as he trundled it along the uneven pavement of Hell Close that people came to their windows. Graham had not warned his parents that he was coming; he wanted to give them a delightful surprise. As he approached their house he was conscious of coming to a major crossroads in his life. He opened the little gate and walked up the short path, passing an extraordinary structure that seemed to be some kind of facility for birds. Graham saw at a glance that all it would take to topple it would be a strong wind and the weight of an unusually large bird.

Graham knocked on the front door, then wiped his hands on his trousers. He had once overheard one of his colleagues say, 'Shaking hands with Graham Cracknall is like trying to revive a dead fish.' He heard dogs barking and a woman shouting. He arranged his face in what he imagined was a friendly expression. What Camilla saw when she opened the door was a badly dressed, early-middle-aged man with jug ears and lopsided features. She knew that this was her son.

'Rory?' she asked.

'No, it's Graham.'

Camilla said, 'Of course, it's Graham. Please, do come in.'

She couldn't think of anything much to say; a huge conversational chasm opened up. Graham proved to be extraordinarily difficult to talk to. An enquiry about how he got there was met with the answer, 'Train and taxi.' Asked if he enjoyed the journey, he said, 'No,' without elaborating. Charles, who often said to Camilla that he could do a PhD on small talk, soon gave up the struggle. Camilla battled gamely on. She sensed that Graham was overwhelmed by the unique circumstances.

'We much enjoyed your video,' she said. 'Did you ever get to meet that bubbly girl you were looking for?'

Graham said, 'No.'

He felt sick with disappointment. He hadn't expected his parents to fall on his neck and weep over their long-lost son, but neither had he thought that they would greet him with such restrained politeness. And look at them! He was prepared for the fact that they would not be formally dressed, but ... the pair of them looked like those scruffy types who toiled at the allotments behind his bungalow.

Camilla excused herself as soon as decency allowed and fled upstairs to prepare the spare bedroom for Graham. She had been horrified to learn that he intended to stay for four long days and three long nights. How on earth would they fill all those hours? And how would they feed him? They had absolutely no money left, and the only meat in the house was dog food. Perhaps she could add curry paste and chilli powder to a tin of Pedigree Chum?

She sat on the bare mattress with the clean sheets on her lap, and tried to compose herself. The training she had received at Mont Fertile, the Swiss finishing school, drummed in her mind. As the hostess, you must do anything to make your guest feel at ease.

She heard Freddie coming up the stairs and when he trotted into the room she said, quietly, 'Oh dear, Freddie darling, what do you think of Graham?'

Freddie barked, 'Confucius said, "After three days, fish and visitors stink."'

Camilla patted Freddie's back, saying, 'I wish you could talk to me, Freddie.'

Later that night, over an improvised supper of curried frankfurters, borrowed from the Threadgolds, and home-grown root vegetables, Charles and Camilla made a concerted effort to get to know their son. An aperitif of parsnip wine had loosened Graham's tongue; he had monologued for ten full minutes on the health and safety laws in Estonia – there weren't any.

Charles tried to head him off by asking, 'Do you have a garden, Graham?'

'Yes, it's mainly laid to lawn, but I've got a few rows of salvia and daffs. In the spring, of course. I don't like tulips. You can't rely on them to stay upright in the vase, can you?'

'Er . . . no, indeed, er . . . tulips are terribly . . . spontaneous in their habits.'

'Do you ride?' asked Camilla.

'Not on horses, no,' said Graham, somehow giving the impression that he didn't care to ride horses, but that he was often to be found mounted on camels or llamas, even elephants.

'Are you interested in art at all? Painting . . . er . . . that sort of thing.'

Graham said, 'I don't like modern art, I think it's a con, chimpanzees could do better. In fact, Michael Jackson's chimp friend, Bubbles, has done some quite passable watercolours. His last exhibition sold out completely, within an hour.'

Charles, a watercolourist himself (as was Camilla), was rather peeved and a little jealous of the chimp's success. Charles had exhibited at the One-Stop Centre recently, a rather fine series of watery 'impressions' of Hell Close. Only one had been sold, to the Queen.

When they retired a few steps to the other end of the room for coffee, the subject of Graham's birth and adoption had still not been broached. A great deal of dog patting went on. Leo, Tosca and Freddie were surprised at the extra attention they were receiving. Freddie took advantage of this to perform his trick of chasing his own tail.

Graham's laugh was not a pleasant sound. When Freddie, wildly spinning, banged into the coffee table and knocked a glass of wine over, he was ordered to stop by Camilla, and silence fell between the three people in the room. Each of them wished that they were somewhere else. Eventually Graham went to bed, taking with him his inhaler and what he called a 'book': a subscription magazine called *TW Monthly*. It had transpired during the evening that Graham was an aficionado of the game of tiddlywinks and played to competition standard.

Charles whispered to Camilla when they were in bed together and conscious of the proximity of their son sleeping in the next room, 'I suppose tiddlywinks needs a great deal of manual dexterity. I mean to say, one would have to have *exceedingly* strong thumbs.'

Camilla held her thumbs up in the dark and said, 'I've always had strong thumbs. I used to be able to crack a walnut between my thumb and index finger.'

'He gets it from you then, darling,' Charles said.

Neither of them had said that they were disheartened by meeting their son Graham, but damp and dismal disappointment seemed to have leaked into the room and lay over everything like a wet fog.

Just before she went to sleep, Camilla said, 'To be Tiddlywinks Champion of Ruislip three years running is pretty good, isn't it?' It was a genuine question.

Charles said, 'It's a splendid achievement, darling.'

Camilla whispered, 'I'm not sure I can love Graham.'

Charles grimaced; this was exactly his sentiment. 'Perhaps when we get to know him better . . .' he said.

'But the *tulips*,' Camilla hissed, 'and those *shoes*.'

Charles said, 'Something could be done about his appearance – a good tailor, a decent barber.'

'But he isn't very . . . nice,' said Camilla.

'No,' agreed Charles, 'but we must make allowances for him.'

'But he doesn't like *dogs*, darling,' said Camilla.

'Not everybody does,' whispered Charles.

'But our sort of people do,' she said, turning towards him in the dark.

'Then we must make Graham into our sort of person,' said Charles.

They kissed, and turned away from each other. It was unsaid, but understood between them, that there would be no physical intimacy while Graham was under their roof.

37

When Camilla went downstairs the next morning to make tea, she found Graham, fully dressed, sitting upright on the sofa tapping into his laptop. She pulled her dressing gown together and tied the belt; she did not want Graham to see her 'Everything A Pound' shop nightshirt with its picture of the Hulk on the front.

'Graham,' she said, 'you're up early.'

'Early?' said Graham, censoriously. 'Half the morning's gone.'

Camilla glanced at the clock on the mantelpiece; it was 7.50 a.m. 'You must think me quite a slugabed.'

Graham said, 'At your age you need more sleep, I suppose.'

As Camilla filled the kettle she thought, he is utterly charmless. The three dogs clustered around her as she made the tea. They seemed to be reluctant to be left alone in the sitting room with Graham.

As she was about to go upstairs with Charles's tea, Graham said, 'I'd advise you not to wear those King Kong slippers on the stairs. Certainly not with a cup of hot liquid in your hands, *and* with your hair in your eyes.'

Camilla said, 'You're probably right,' and extracted her feet from the gorilla slippers before climbing the stairs.

On hearing that Graham had been up for hours, Charles quickly washed, shaved and dressed. He chose, Camilla noticed, smarter, more conservative clothes than usual.

'You're rather formal today,' she said, noticing that the suit he was wearing smelt rather fusty.

Charles said, 'I have to tell Mummy about Graham today, darling. I think a suit reflects the, er . . . gravity of the situation.'

Camilla said, 'Darling, can't we get to know Graham a little better before we inflict him on the family?'

'Inflict?' questioned Charles. 'He *is* our son!'

Camilla said, 'He inferred I was lazy, more or less said I was old, and made me take my lovely warm slippers off.'

Charles remembered the enlightening conversations he had enjoyed with Laurens Van der Post, in which his mentor had explained that separation from the mother can be the cause of aggression in adult life.

He said, 'He's almost certainly hurting dreadfully inside, Camilla. We must nurture him, surround him with love and security.'

Camilla said, 'Before or after we tell your mother, *The Queen of England*, that she has a bastard grandson who is second in line to the throne?'

When Charles went downstairs he found Graham in the living room, staring out of the window at the bird table. A pair of blue tits were hanging upside down pecking at the white flesh of the suspended half coconut.

Charles whispered to Graham, 'Aren't they delightful

little birds? I'm absolutely thrilled to see them using my bird thingy.'

Graham said, 'It's a pity it will have to come down.'

Charles's forehead creased. 'Come down?' he said.

'I was out there at six o'clock this morning,' said Graham. 'It's a highly unstable structure. I'm surprised you got planning permission.'

Charles said, 'I didn't get planning permission because I didn't *apply* for it. It's only a bird table.'

Graham said, 'It might be "only a bird table" to you, but to me it's a dangerous structure that could kill or maim a small child or a vulnerable adult.'

Charles said, 'I know it's your job to assess risks, Graham, but couldn't you turn a blind eye?'

Graham said, 'Please don't ask me to compromise my professional integrity. I'll help you to take it down.'

Graham thought that dismantling the bird table would help him and his father to bond. He had been aware of a certain coldness emanating from his mother earlier that morning. He knew it was nothing he had done or said. Perhaps, he thought, she was going through 'the change of life'. His adoptive mother had metamorphosed from a placid, homely woman into a shrieking diva during her change.

Graham said, 'And avian flu is on the way. This is not the time to encourage birds, is it?'

Charles looked around the living room, trying to see it through Graham's eyes. Suddenly the most harmless of things seemed to present an ominous danger: the little crystal chandelier could fall from its ceiling mounting, somebody could trip over the holes in the threadbare Aubusson carpet. If the radio overheated it could explode and cause an inferno.

To deflect Graham's attention from the bird table, Charles said, 'I would like to introduce you to my mother and the rest of the family today.'

'I'm a bit nervous about meeting the Queen,' admitted Graham.

Charles said, 'We'll have breakfast and then I'll take you round.'

The dogs ran into the kitchen and stood eagerly by their feeding bowls. They were usually fed half a bowl of dried dog food each. But this morning they were treated to Pedigree Chum. Camilla put half a tin into each bowl, saying, 'You have Her Majesty the Queen to thank for this.'

The dogs gobbled it down greedily, and then waited for more. When Camilla made no move to refill the bowls, Freddie barked, 'Is that it? Is that all we're getting? What about a Bonio?'

Leo whimpered, 'I'm twice the size of them. I'm a growing dog, I need two Bonios.'

After throwing each dog a Bonio, Camilla picked the bowls up from the floor, rinsed them under the tap and stacked them on the draining board, signifying that the dogs' breakfast was over. The dogs lay together under the table, hoping that a few crumbs would drop from Graham's plate; they had noticed that he was a messy eater.

After a while, Freddie growled, 'This is demeaning. We're totally dependent on human beings for all our needs.'

Tosca moved closer to Leo and whimpered, 'We're still in control of our sex lives.'

Leo licked a sticky patch on Tosca's ear and whimpered back, 'And how could we feed ourselves, Freddie? We haven't got fingers. We can't open the tins.'

Freddie snarled, 'There was a time when we dogs killed our own food.' Then, unable to resist, he gave a tiny nip to the exposed patch of flesh between Graham's sock and trouser leg. 'Tasty!' said Freddie, before Graham kicked him under the table.

When the telephone rang Harris and Susan ran into the living room and heard the Queen say, 'Good morning, Charles . . . I'm quite well, thank you . . . Yes, Harris is back to his usual self . . . No, I am not especially busy this morning, but I'm going to see your father this afternoon. Perhaps you'd like to come with me . . . Can't you tell me on the telephone?'

Harris said to Susan, 'Charles is coming round. I hope he brings his dogs, I'm in the mood for a scrap.'

Susan growled, 'Don't overdo it. You're still convalescing.'

The Queen said, 'Come at ten, and I'll make coffee. Will Camilla be with you? . . . I'm dreadfully sorry, Charles. I'd quite forgotten that Camilla is still under house arrest . . . So how many cups shall I put out . . . three?'

When she'd put the phone down, she said to Harris and Susan, 'Charles is bringing a visitor to see us, so I want you two to be on your best behaviour. No barking, no biting, no fighting.'

*

It was some time before the Queen could take in the full import of what Charles was saying. She had thought he was talking gibberish as he told her a faltering tale about Camilla, Zurich, cuckoo clocks, adoptive parents, and a boy called Rory, who then seemed to have turned into Graham, the young man who was standing in her living room, biting the fingernails of one hand while jiggling the change in his shapeless grey trouser pocket with the other.

The Queen said, 'Charles, please take a deep breath and repeat very slowly what you have just told me.'

Charles said, 'I'll, er . . . try to . . . take a run at the fence from a different direction. Er . . . this young man is my eldest son, Graham. His mother is Camilla, my wife. He was born in Zurich, in 1965. Until recently I knew nothing of his existence.'

The Queen gave Graham a full appraising look, taking in the details of his physical appearance. The ears belonged to Charles, as did the jaw, the hairline and the hands. He had Camilla's nose, eyes and posture. Graham was a perfect amalgam of Charles and Camilla's genes. The Queen did not need to see the DNA certificate or the solicitor's papers that Charles was waving in front of her.

She said, 'Why did Camilla not tell you about the existence of this child?'

Charles hesitated; he did not want to hurt Graham's feelings, but how else was he to explain Camilla's oversight?

He twisted and turned his neck inside his shirt collar,

'Look Mummy, she simply wiped it out of her mind. You know how delightfully scatty she can be.'

The Queen saw Graham flinch, as though a flying insect had stung him. She felt a little pity for him.

She said to Charles, 'I know Camilla is absent-minded at times, and that *you* think it is a charming characteristic of hers, but she is not suffering from amnesia, is she? Does she remember the name of her first husband? The names of the children she had by him? The first gymkhana she won? Her favourite alcoholic drink? I expect so. Do you not find it strange that she apparently forgot about the birth of her first baby.'

Harris barked, 'Not a common or garden baby, either, but the second in line to the throne.'

The Queen shouted, angrily, 'Oh do be quiet, Harris!'

Harris barked back, 'There's no need to take it out on me.'

Susan barked, 'It's Charles you want to shout at.'

The Queen shouted at both dogs, 'Continue barking, and you'll go outside!'

Charles said, 'I'm equally baffled, Mummy. But Camilla has, I think, a sort of filter in her brain that, er . . . prevents any negativity or unpleasantness getting through and hurting her.'

The Queen said tersely, 'More of your Van der Post nonsense. Go into the kitchen and make the coffee, you'll find everything on the tray!'

When Charles had gone, she turned to Graham and said, more gently, 'So, you're my eldest grandson, Mr Cracknall?'

Graham said, 'Yes, Your Majesty.' His voice was remarkably like Charles's, thought the Queen. His pronunciation was good, without a trace of a regional accent.

The Queen continued, 'Please, do sit down,' and indicated the fireside chair opposite her own. 'I'd be most interested to hear your story.'

As Graham spoke, he grew less intimidated by the Queen's presence, and after giving her his basic biographical details he talked about his pastimes and hobbies. The Queen was interested to note that he had once collected New Zealand postage stamps; philately was something they had in common, she told him.

When Charles came in with the coffee tray the Queen was asking Graham, 'Have you met your half-brothers yet, or your aunts and uncles?'

Charles said, 'Of course he hasn't, Mummy. You are the head of the family and you had to be told first.'

The Queen said, 'Does anybody else know?'

Charles said, 'Only Fatty Soames, but I swore him to secrecy.'

'Fatty Soames?' laughed the Queen. 'You may as well have contracted the Red Arrows to write of Graham's existence in the sky over London.'

Graham said, 'Why do we have to keep my existence a secret? I'm very proud to be a member of the Royal Family. I always knew that I was a cuckoo in the Ruislip nest. I never fitted in with the other boys at school.'

'And nor did I,' said Charles. 'They were beastly to me.'

Graham said, 'Without wishing to disrespect the dead, I have to confess that I always felt that my adoptive parents were a little common. It used to pain me that they would have a milk bottle on the table at breakfast.'

He glanced at the coffee tray with its matching cups, saucers, sugar bowl and milk jug, silver apostle spoons and sugar tongs. He approved of the way that the shortcake biscuits had been arranged in a fan shape on the plate.

He said, with growing confidence, 'I used to wash my face and brush my hair before sitting down to watch the Queen's Speech on Christmas Day, Your Majesty.'

'How very nice,' murmured the Queen.

She bent down to stroke Harris, who growled, 'Mr Goody Fucking Two Shoes.'

The Queen said, 'Do I understand that you *work* for a living, Mr Cracknall?'

'Yes,' said Graham, apologetically. 'My adoptive parents thought that a career in health and safety would be . . . well . . . safe.'

'Graham is hiding his light under a bushel,' said Charles. 'He's a world-class tiddlywinks player.'

'How very interesting,' said the Queen. She added, 'The Duke of Edinburgh had a passion for tiddly-winks; I believe he was a member of the Tiddlywinks Federation.'

Over coffee it was arranged that the other members of the Royal Family would meet Graham later that evening at Charles and Camilla's house, and that they would all be sworn to secrecy.

Dwayne Lockhart, sitting in the dark of the surveillance room, smiled to himself, 'Ah, bless. Haven't they realized yet? There *is* no secrecy.'

The Queen said, 'As you must be aware, Mr Cracknall, there is to be a general election in less than five weeks. If the New Cons win, they have pledged in their manifesto that the Royal Family, which now includes you, will be reinstated. Not all the electorate will approve of the fact that you were born out of wedlock, and that your existence has been hidden from them. There may be a backlash that will result in us staying here for many more years.' She picked up Harris and, using him as a buffer against the world, said, 'I do not want to die in Hell Close, Mr Cracknall.'

Dwayne switched screens and watched Paris Butterworth ironing for half an hour. She did nothing interesting, but Dwayne didn't mind, he loved her.

38

Boy English had been informed of Graham's existence by the editor of *The Oldie*, who in turn had been told by a disgruntled Polish plumber who had worked on a blocked toilet in Sir Nicholas Soames's London house. Boy immediately accessed www.hardtopleeze.co.uk and found Graham's video. As he watched, Boy saw his election victory running away, like storm water down a drain.

At the daily election-planning meeting he watched the video again. This time with his advisers, although he did not tell them about Graham's parentage. In the discussion that followed, the advisers were almost united in their condemnation of Graham's appearance and manner. The sole dissenter was a darkly attractive young woman with a geometric haircut, called Miranda, who said, 'I think he's kind of sexy. I go for that nerd look.'

A reptilian-like male colleague, Gary, replied, 'Yeah, but you get horny watching *Mr Bean*.'

Miranda said angrily, 'Only once! I was on a plane, I was drunk, there was turbulence, and my face was thrown across your genitals, Gary. The fact that *Mr Bean* was the in-flight movie was entirely coincidental.'

Boy said, 'Enough! So, say we had to get this guy on our side and then sell him to the electorate, what would we do?'

'It's a no-brainer,' said Gary. 'We send Miranda fishing, she hauls him in and then we wash, clean, fillet and fry him, dress him up with a bit of lemon and serve him up on a china plate.'

Miranda said, 'So I'm whoring for the party now, am I?'

Boy said, 'We're all whoring for the party, Miranda. The only difference between me and a prostitute is that I work with bigger pricks.'

Miranda asked, 'So why is Graham the Geek so important to us?'

Boy said, 'That pathetic gift to the playground bully will win or lose us the election.'

When everyone else had left the room, Miranda asked Boy, 'Why did you assume I would agree to this Graham entrapment?'

Boy squeezed Miranda's small breasts and said, 'You're a self-proclaimed ladette, Miranda. You'll do anything for a laugh. You're amoral, and it's great to have you on the team.'

Miranda emailed Graham:

Hello Graham,

My name is Miranda. I'm 26, small with dark hair. I've got a bubbly personality and share your passion for board games. I have both my feet firmly on the property ladder, as I own my own semi-detached house.

I'm a member of the David Jason fan club, are you? I think *OFAH* is the greatest television show of all time. I am looking for love and companionship

At Gary's insistence, Miranda finished the email:

I am not sexually permissive, I believe in chastity before marriage. I find the ladette culture abhorrent.

Graham received this message on his laptop in the spare room of Number Sixteen Hell Close. He cried out with delight, and Camilla shouted up the stairs to ask if he was all right. He shouted back that he was perfectly well, and tapped a reply to Miranda.

Graham did not believe in love at first sight; it was just another urban myth, like driving home with a dead relative rolled up in a carpet and tied to the roof rack. But as soon as Miranda had appeared on the screen of his laptop, looking pretty and modest in a floaty white dress, and shielding her eyes against the sun, he knew that she was good wife material.

He peered closely at the photograph on the screen; as far as he could tell she was not wearing red shoes. He emailed her back:

Dear Miranda,

Can we meet? Pressure of work keeps me busy (I am overseeing stepladder disposal), but I will be free on Sunday.

Are you located anywhere near Ruislip? If so, I will prepare the car for a journey (check tyre pressures, brakes, etc.), or of course you could come here (not exactly here, because at the time of writing I am in the East Midlands Region, but you could come to Ruislip). There is a very nice, respectable pub in the vicinity, The Mouse and Cheese, which is frequented by a respectable crowd, from the golf club mostly. Their clubhouse was burnt down by an aggrieved ex-wife a few years ago.

Please reply stating your preferential arrangement.

Yours in anticipation,

Graham C

The reply came within minutes:

Dear Graham,

The Mouse and Cheese sounds lovely. One o'clock on Sunday.

Best wishes,

Miranda

Graham replied:

Dear Miranda,

One o'clock it is!

The dress code for The Mouse and Cheese is smart casual; most people of both sexes wear Pringle sweaters. I tell you this only to save you possible embarrassment.

How will you get there? Do you need directions?

Yours,

Graham

Miranda said to Gary, 'Christ! Is this guy anal or what?'

Gary said, 'Yeah, as sure as Jesus had a hole in his bum.'

In her new persona, Miranda wrote:

Dear Graham,

Please don't worry about me getting there. But I am very shy, so would you meet me outside? I have never entered a pub on my own before.

Warm wishes,

Miranda

Graham's heart was touched. He replied:

Dear Miranda,

I will, of course, escort you into The Mouse and Cheese.

With the very warmest of wishes,

G.

Later that night, Miranda was asked to leave a Soho nightclub after performing a lewd dance on the bar, during which one of her red high heels flew off and detached the retina of a barman called Gloria. After vomiting in the minicab on the way home, she sobered up slightly and asked the bewildered Somali driver if he knew how to play snakes and ladders.

39

Camilla and Charles worked together to prepare the house for their guests. As there was very little food in the pantry, Charles borrowed some money from the Threadgolds, went shopping and bought the ingredients for party snacks.

Dwayne Lockhart was on duty outside Grice's Mini-Market. Grice had increased the price of bread by ten pence, which meant that customers were now paying one pound for a small white sliced loaf. One of the few things that Grice remembered from his history lessons at school had been that the French Revolution had started with a similar price rise. Dwayne had been posted, together with a taser, to quell any possible uprising by the mob.

When he saw Charles approaching with a wicker shopping basket over his arm, he said, 'Good morning, sir. I will need to check your wife's tag later this afternoon. Would four o'clock be convenient?'

Charles wondered why Dwayne's left eye was opening and closing; had the poor boy developed a nervous habit? Then he realized that Dwayne was winking.

Charles blurted, 'Yes, four o'clock would be a perfectly splendid time to call, couldn't possibly be a more convenient hour.'

*

Graham was in the spare bedroom when Dwayne knocked on the front door at precisely four o'clock. He had laid out all the clothes that he had brought with him and was trying to decide what to wear. He had already asked the advice of his parents, but they had not been at all helpful.

Camilla had said, 'Wear something that you're comfortable in.'

Charles had said, 'I doubt if anyone else, apart from Princess Michael of course, will dress up.'

After trying on several ensembles, Graham opted for a pair of his dead adoptive father's slacks. It was lucky, he thought, they had shared the same waist and inside-leg measurements; it would save him buying clothes for years, providing he didn't put on any weight. He added a diamond-patterned golfing sweater, worn over a shirt and tie. He had only brought one pair of shoes – a pair of grey slip-ons – so he gave them a polish, and when he checked his reflection in the wardrobe mirror, he was satisfied that he looked clean and tidy.

His adoptive mother had once said to him, 'You'll never be Clark Gable, Graham, but at least you can look neat and tidy.' Graham had not known who Clark Gable was at the time, but later, watching the actor on television, he had been struck by his ears, which were remarkably like Graham's own.

Dwayne slipped Nicholas Soames's letter out of his deep trouser pocket, and shoved it under a tapestry cushion in the corner of the sofa. He did more of the winking, and Charles said, 'Ah! Splendid. I see what you . . . Yes. Marvellous.'

Camilla sat down and once again they went through the charade of tag inspection. Dwayne was still down on one knee when Graham came downstairs and into the living room.

Charles said to Dwayne, 'Constable Lockhart, this is, er . . . our . . .'

'Risk assessor,' said Camilla.

'Yes. Risk assessor,' agreed Charles.

Graham said, 'We've already met.'

'Yes,' said Dwayne. 'How's the assessment going?'

'All right,' said Graham, evasively.

Dwayne could not resist adding, to Graham's discomfort, 'Is it a risky business, assessing risk? I mean, what do you consider a risk?'

Graham said, 'The risks start in the womb; then birth itself can be a very risky procedure.'

Dwayne said, mischievously, 'I suppose there's always the danger of losing contact with your mother.'

'That's a negligible risk,' said Graham, looking at Camilla. 'Most mothers are rather tenacious in their love for their newborn child.'

Seeing the stricken look on Camilla's face, Dwayne felt ashamed and excused himself by saying that he had to attend an incident in Slapper Ally. He left the house with his cheeks burning. He'd noticed that since joining Grice's security force, there was a sadistic side to him that did not sit comfortably with his more humane side. But people like Graham seemed to *invite* unpleasantness. He doubted if Graham ever questioned his own self-righteous uncritical self.

*

Dwayne had lain awake half the night, trying to decide which book he should next take to Paris Butterworth. His mouth watered at the thought of the literary treats she had in store. Should he arouse her interest with a bit of foreplay, *Jane Eyre* for instance, or should he go for broke with *Madame Bovary*? Perhaps it would be safer to give her another Orwell; *Animal Farm* might appeal to her.

He relished the day they would read Orwell's *Inside the Whale and Other Essays* together. He fantasized about the scene: he and Paris were in bed, naked under the covers, Fifty-cents was sleeping in the next room. They were discussing Orwell's *Essays*, perhaps having a heated debate about Orwell's preference for plain words. Paris might argue that Orwell's style was too workmanlike for her taste.

In the morning, when he laid *Animal Farm* on the coffee table in Paris's living room, she said, 'I'm already reading another book. I got it from the library at the One-Stop Centre.'

Dwayne was hurt, but he tried not to show it. 'What is it?' he asked.

'I'll go and fetch it,' she said, and ran out of the room and up the stairs. He could hear the floorboards creaking as she walked across her bedroom.

Fifty-cents had cut a few more teeth, Dwayne noticed. The kid was sitting on the plastic floor of a lobster-pot-shaped playpen, chewing on an empty plastic bottle of Calpol. Dwayne threw a few toys into the playpen, but Fifty-cents ignored them. Paris reappeared holding a paperback book. She handed it to Dwayne; it was *Not a Penny More, Not a Penny Less*.

'It's by——' she started.

Dwayne interrupted her, saying savagely, 'I know who it's by!'

'What's up?' she asked. 'I thought you'd be pleased.'

'Pleased?' said Dwayne. 'I want you to read *literature*.'

He felt as though she had betrayed him, going off in the night with a ne'er-do-well Jack the Lad type, who would seduce her with strong storylines but ultimately leave her unsatisfied and a little ashamed. Dwayne forgot that he and Paris had never been out together or even declared any interest in each other.

Paris said, 'Aren't all books literature?'

'No,' said Dwayne. 'That thing you've got in your hand is a *best-seller*!'

'It's good,' said Paris defensively.

'But it's not *great*,' said Dwayne. 'Good is the enemy of great.'

Paris sat down and picked up *Animal Farm*. She looked at the cover suspiciously.

'What's it about?' she asked. 'Pigs?'

Dwayne said that it was an allegory about Soviet Russia.

Paris said, 'I might look at it when I've finished the other one.'

Dwayne said gruffly, 'I'd better check your tag while I'm here.'

As he did so, she said, 'I'd like to do what Julia did in *Nineteen Eighty-Four*, you know, go somewhere where I wasn't being watched.'

Dwayne said, 'There is nowhere now.'

Paris said, 'Anyway, I'd only get caught and end up in Room 101.'

Dwayne recognized that she was trying to make amends and, seizing the moment, said, 'If you were sent to Room 101, I'd spring you before the rats got to you.'

Paris looked outside to see which way the camera was pointing, and satisfied that it was looking the other way she whispered, 'I'll read *Animal Farm* next.'

Then, to Dwayne's delight, she touched his hand. This small gesture emboldened Dwayne; he took her hand and pressed it. Their fingers interlocked. Fifty-cents shouted something that sounded to Dwayne's ears like, 'Totalitarianism.' But Dwayne realized that it was impossible, the kid could hardly articulate 'mama' or 'doggy'. They sat quietly together for some time, watching Fifty-cents' clumsy attempts to place one Duplo brick on top of another.

'I'll bring him some children's books tomorrow,' said Dwayne.

Then he looked around the living room and decided that the two alcoves on either side of the fireplace would make excellent sites for Paris's new bookshelves.

Charles waited until Graham had gone back up to the spare room before opening Sir Nicholas Soames's letter and sharing the contents with Camilla.

My dear friend, Charles,

First things first, your letter is residing safely in a Coutts bank vault.

Your news about this Graham chap was a bombshell; the cove at Burke's Peerage, Miles Furnleigh-Wood, tells me that bastards can now inherit the bloody earth!!! Gays and other deviants have as many privileges as you and I used to enjoy before the bloody Roundheads took over. Incidentally, what Oliver Cromwell would have made of the modern Cromwell Party, with its tax revenues coming from casinos and lap-dancing clubs, God only knows.

I saw Jack Barker at a dinner the other night; he made a complete fool of himself. Debate at our table was divided between those who thought he was drunk and those who thought he was mad. Jeremy Paxman sat on my right and a chap called Rick Stein, famous for cooking fish apparently, was on my left.

Paxman claimed that his forebears had been paupers, dependent on the parish for their daily bread. When I said that poverty was nature's way of sorting the wheat from the chaff, Paxman called me an odious buffoon and for the rest of the dinner spoke exclusively to the person opposite, a scrawny woman with an idiosyncratic dress sense who said she worked for the BBC. I overheard her opining that there were serious misgivings at the BBC about the Government's anti-dog propaganda.

I shouted over Paxman, 'It's about time the Corporation stopped doing the Government's dirty work for them, and stood up to Barker!'

She told me, behind Paxman's back, that the upper echelons of the BBC had been infiltrated by cat lovers. I can't say I'm surprised, Charles, as it's well known that cats are preferred by homosexualists and fancy nancy intellectuals.

I have been in daily contact with Boy English, who is proving to be a splendid leader of our party. His dog, Billy, is constantly on the front pages of both the serious papers and the scandal rags. Boy is now neck and neck in the opinion polls. Will there *need to be a photo finish and a steward's enquiry? Or will he fall at Becher's Brook?*

I confess that I am a little concerned about your son, Graham. I have made discreet enquiries to MI5 about the young man, and quite an unflattering picture has emerged. I suggest we keep him under wraps, as he could be an election liability.

By the by, when you return to your rightful place I recommend that Constable Dwayne Lockhart be given an honour of some kind. He has shown amazing gallantry, and such courage should be recognized by the country he serves so well.

I remain, my dear Charles, your affectionate friend,

Fatty

'My children are terribly laid back,' said Camilla, 'and they are not in line to the throne. It's your children, Harry and Wills, that we have to worry about.'

They started to make canapés, cutting circles of bread with a pastry cutter, brushing a little oil on their surfaces and putting them into the oven to brown and crisp. They assembled the toppings, and worked well together, combining simple ingredients – sardines, cheese, meat paste – with slivers of vegetables from the garden.

Charles brought a stack of white plastic chairs in from outside and distributed them around the room.

40

When the Royals and their pets were finally assembled, there were thirteen humans and nine dogs crammed into Charles and Camilla's small sitting room. Graham was still upstairs, sitting on his bed with his hair neatly parted, fingering the sparse moustache he had decided to grow in the last few days. He hoped it didn't make him look too much like Hitler; perhaps the brown shirt had been a mistake. He got up and listened from the bedroom to the commotion of overlapping conversations. The talk was almost entirely about dogs. Why weren't they talking about *him*?

It seemed to Graham that he had always come second best to dogs; his adoptive mother had squandered the family fortune on insulin for that malingering diabetic, Tonic. Graham had suggested that, given the price of insulin and the inconvenience of administering a daily injection, it would be more sensible to have Tonic put down. But his adoptive parents had been horrified at the idea. It still annoyed Graham to think about the attention given to Tonic compared to the neglect he, their own son, experienced when he was laid low by flu.

There was a knock on the door and his mother came in. She sat on the bed next to him, took his hand and said, 'I'm terribly nervous, are you?'

'Yes, I wish now I hadn't grown this moustache. Does it make me look like Hitler?'

Camilla said, 'Perhaps if you ruffle your hair a little, and undo the top button of your shirt . . .'

Graham unbuttoned his shirt, but could not bring himself to mess up his hair. He'd had the same hairstyle since he was a small baby. He had a photograph of himself at six months old; he was wearing rompers and had a short back and sides with a neat side parting.

Graham followed Camilla down the stairs; a small part of him was looking forward to the attention he would receive. This was the one occasion when he could be sure that every human eye in the room would be on him. One of the mantras repeated by his adoptive mother came to him: 'If you're wearing clean socks and underpants, you're the equal of any person, in any circumstance.' Graham had often questioned this advice. After all, there were, presumably, serial killers who had meticulous personal hygiene. But now, about to pass through a doorway from commoner to aristo-crat, he was comforted by the words.

When Camilla led Graham into the room, everybody turned to stare. The dogs began to howl; they had been informed about Graham by Freddie, who had warned them that Graham was second in line to the throne, putting their own status in jeopardy. Althorp, Prince William's dog, was particularly vocal. He howled the loudest and was the last to stop when Charles appealed to the dogs, 'Please! One can't hear oneself *think*!'

Taking advantage of the dogs' silence, Charles added hurriedly, 'There is something my wife would like to tell you . . . It's, er . . . frightfully important. This young man is, er . . . Graham Cracknall.'

Graham fingered his moustache nervously; there was an expectant silence.

When Charles seemed to have difficulty finding words to continue, Camilla said, 'Graham is my son; he was born when I was eighteen.'

There was another silence.

Andrew said, 'No worries, Cam. We've all got skeletons in the cupboard.'

'Yes,' said William, magnanimously. 'It's cool, Camilla. This is the twenty-first century.'

Harry agreed, 'Yeah, it's *fierce*.'

The Queen directed a meaningful look at Charles, willing him to explain Graham's exact status in the family.

Charles cleared his throat, and fiddled with his cufflinks, before saying, 'Yes, so Camilla is Graham's mother, and I . . . well, the simple truth is that, er . . . um, *I* am Graham's father.'

The Queen said, 'I think it might be pertinent if you gave the assembled company Graham's date of birth.'

Camilla said, 'He was born at half past five on the morning of the 21st July 1965. I was just eighteen, Charles was sixteen . . .'

Andrew shouted, 'Way to go, bro!'

Camilla continued, 'It was on the last night of the Horse of the Year Show, we were both very young but terribly in love.'

Charles manoeuvred around the humans and the dogs and went to Camilla's side. The Queen watched

William's face darken as the realization dawned on him that he was no longer second in line to the throne.

Spiggy said, 'Well, I'll be buggered! Welcome to the family, Graham.' He pushed through the crowded room and shook Graham's hand.

Harry whispered to William, 'Dorkface is our half-brother.'

William whispered back, 'More importantly, he's our *elder* brother.'

Princess Michael drawled, 'So, what is your title, Graham? Do you have one?'

'Not at present,' said Graham, 'but I was thinking along the lines of Prince Graham of Watford. I was brought up in Ruislip, but Watford is a more prestigious town.'

Princess Michael said, 'Prince Graham of Watford? That makes a mockery of the whole thing.'

Anne snapped, 'Another bloody nail in our coffin!' She appealed to the room, 'Let's renounce the monarchy tonight and put an end to the whole bloody charade.'

Prince Andrew said, 'Steady on, old girl. Speak for yourself. I'm rather keen to make Marcia here my wife; and I was kind of hoping that she would become a lady-of-the-bedchamber.'

Edward said, 'This is all very well for you, Anne. You've always been a Bolshie, but Sophie and I are respectful of this country's institutions.'

Sophie said, 'We're bringing Louise up in the hope that she will be a royal princess one day.'

Anne scoffed, 'I've seen your royal princess running wild with Maddo Clarke's boys. Save your energy.'

William asked the Queen, 'Granny, do you still intend to abdicate?'

The Queen said, 'I feel that I have done my duty to my father's memory and to the country, William. It's time your father lifted some of the burden from my shoulders.'

Charles felt a rage building inside his head; he thought he might explode unless the words he needed to say were expressed.

He declaimed, 'I have *always* done my duty. For over fifty years I have worked unceasingly for this family. I have toured light-engineering factories on industrial estates, and forced myself to show some interest in their bloody machines. I have visited schools, and looked over the shoulders of the children as they demonstrated their wretched computer skills. I have comforted the victims of train crashes and similar horrors, and tried to think of something to say that wouldn't sound glib or insincere.

'I do not look forward to the prospect of becoming king, even though I am assured by an impeccable authority that Camilla *could* be my queen—'

The Queen said, 'I am prepared to accept Camilla as your queen.'

Camilla gave a wan smile.

Anne snapped, 'Good! So that's sorted. Can we all bugger off home now? It's past Spike's bedtime.'

Spike barked, 'Don't use me as an excuse.'

Charles raised his voice above Spike's, and said, 'The simple truth is, I don't want to be king, and I do not want to subject Camilla to the strains and cruelty of public scrutiny. I simply want a . . . well . . . a simple life.'

The Queen said, 'You say that is what you *want*, but what do you intend to *do*?'

Charles tried to imagine Graham on the balcony of Buckingham Palace, acknowledging a vast crowd of gawping subjects below. Nuremberg came to mind. 'I simply don't know,' he said.

William got up and left the room, quickly followed by Harry, Althorp and Carling. The front door banged and William and Harry ran down the path and out into the street with the dogs following. The Queen buried her head into Harris's neck and everybody, apart from Graham, busied themselves in patting and talking to a dog.

Graham had hoped that his introduction to the family would have been greeted with more signs of pleasure. He stood with his back to the wall, waiting for the party to begin. Camilla asked him to help her with the refreshments, and gave him a plate of canapés to pass around. However, the gathering did not turn into a celebration: too many ends remained untied, and important issues were still undecided.

Anne tried to engage Graham in conversation, saying, 'I once drove through Ruislip on my way to Slough.'

Graham said, 'Where from?'

'From Harrow,' she replied.

'Then whoever advised you was a fool,' said Graham. 'It would have been quicker to have gone via Wembley and the A40, cutting out Ruislip altogether.'

Recognizing that their brief conversation had been

unsatisfactory and was not likely to improve, they drifted away from each other.

When Graham offered Sophie the sardine and tomato crostini, she held her hand up in horror, as though Graham was offering her a morsel freshly cut from a flyblown corpse. 'They're *groaning* with potassium.' She shuddered. 'Why will nobody take my diet seriously?'

Graham talked about his own diet at great length, telling her that he had suffered agonies of constipation as a child and now lived almost entirely on porridge, prunes and pears. When he was demonstrating to Sophie how the large intestine actually worked, he did not notice that her eyes had glazed over, and that she was taking tiny backward steps.

Seeing Graham alone again, Camilla took pity on him and manoeuvred him towards Marcia, saying, 'Marcia used to be a teacher, Graham.'

Graham said, 'So! If the Royal Family are reinstated, and *you* marry Prince Andrew, you could end up as Minister for Education.'

Camilla and Marcia exchanged a puzzled look.

Marcia said, 'But I'm not a politician.'

Graham said, 'But if my father, Prince Charles, becomes the King, he could appoint you as a Minister of the Crown.'

Camilla's knowledge of constitutional matters was slight, but she said, 'A king or queen has no such powers, Graham.'

Graham said, 'But ministers have to receive the monarch's consent. They have to swear allegiance to their king or queen. I think, Mummy, you will find that I'm right.'

It was the first time that Graham had called Camilla 'Mummy'. The word was a dagger in her heart.

Graham continued, 'When I become king, I won't be afraid to exercise my power.'

Overhearing this, the Queen said, 'We no longer have absolute power, Mr Cracknall. We rule by consent.'

Charles agreed with his mother, 'This is the twenty-first century, Graham. Parliament has the power. It is no longer in our gift to appoint ministers; to attempt to rule by force would simply invite riots.'

The Queen said, with a little smile, 'It is some years since a monarch was able to order the beheading of an enemy, though one can sometimes see the attraction.'

Graham insisted, 'A strong police force and military would soon show them who was boss. And we have technology on our side now. He who controls Vulcan, controls England.'

Charles said, 'Well, all I can say is, thank goodness Vulcan is totally inept.'

Marcia complained, 'Vulcan paid a monthly salary cheque of two million pounds into my bank account last year.'

The Queen said, 'Vulcan keeps writing to me as Mrs T. Heoccupier.'

Camilla laughed, 'Vulcan wrote to me recently to inform me that my artificial leg was now ready for fitting and collection. It worries me rather that there is another Camilla Windsor hopping about waiting for her prosthesis.'

Graham said, 'I acknowledge that Vulcan has its problems at the moment, but by the time of my accession it should be up and running at one hundred per cent accuracy.'

Charles and Camilla exchanged a glance; King Graham was a chilling prospect.

As the half past nine curfew drew near and Charles was helping the Queen on with her coat, she said quietly, 'I rely on you for the safe stewardship of this country, Charles. You *must* be king. Graham will need *years* of grooming before he's ready to succeed. Though if *he* does, God help us all.'

Charles whispered, 'Mummy, I simply *can't* discuss such important matters now. I need to think.'

The Queen said, 'We cannot prevaricate. I was willing to leap a generation and hand over to William, but now . . .' She looked across the sitting room at Graham, who was talking to Prince Andrew about how he would run the country. Andrew was nodding enthusiastically.

Camilla came across to say goodbye to the Queen and heard Charles saying, 'I admit that Graham is a little, er . . . rough around the edges, but I think he's a decent chap at heart.'

The Queen sighed, 'So why are there alarm bells ringing inside my head?'

Camilla said, 'Perhaps, Your Majesty, when you get to know him a little better . . .'

The Queen snapped, 'I have no wish to know him a little better, Camilla. All I ask you both is this: Is Graham a suitable figurehead and representative of this country? Can you imagine him meeting the President of the United States at Heathrow Airport, or giving the King's Speech on Christmas Day? Because I can't.'

She called Harris and Susan, gave a general goodbye and left the house, saying that she wanted to telephone Frank Bruno House to check that Philip and Harold Bunion were comfortable. After the Queen had departed, the remaining guests waited for a short while, then moved as one towards the door.

When everybody had gone, taking their dogs with them, Graham turned to his parents and said, 'I think that went quite well, don't you? Although, it's a pity that William and Harry left early; I would have liked to have got to know my half-brothers better. Perhaps we could ring them up and invite them round for a game of tiddlywinks.'

Charles said, 'Not tonight. It's curfew, and anyway, I'm totally exhausted, I haven't the energy to throw a dice.'

'Die!' said Graham.

Such was Charles's mental agitation that he responded disproportionately to Graham's exhortation. Did Graham have a form of Tourette's syndrome that had forced the word 'Die' out of him, signifying that he wished his father dead?

'Die?' checked Charles.

'The singular of dice,' said Graham.

Camilla thought, he's so like Charles in his nit-picking about language. Only yesterday, Charles had lectured her because she had asked, 'Is Pedigree Chum different to ordinary dog food?'

Charles had closed his eyes and shuddered.

'Darling,' he'd said, 'do *please* pay more attention to your grammar. It is *identical to* and *different from*!'

Graham asked, 'By the way, why does Harry wear his hood up in the house?'

Camilla said, 'He suffers from earache.' She could not face explaining to Graham about Harry's alienation.

William and Harry sat in their cluttered living room on a battered sofa; Chanel and Chantelle Toby sat opposite on an equally shabby sofa. A gangster was shouting on the sound system in time to a drum and bass that he wanted to cover his bitch in gold before smacking her up and giving her to his homeboys. The young people shouted to each other over the music. It did not occur to any of them to turn the volume down.

The situation, discovering that Charles and Camilla had a bastard son, caused no particular surprise to the Toby girls; such revelations were almost daily occurrences among the Toby clan and their circle of friends and acquaintances.

'So, what's your brother like?' shouted Chantelle.

'Half-brother,' shouted the Windsor boys in unison.

'Is he cool?' asked Chanel.

'He is *so* not cool,' said Harry. 'He's the most uncool person in the country; in Europe; in the western hemisphere; in the World; in the solar system; in the universe!'

Harry looked at William; he was struggling now with his superlatives.

William added, 'He's beyond-infinity uncool.'

'He's into friggin' tiddlywinks,' said Harry scornfully.

'Ugh, the filthy bastard,' said Chanel, who wasn't sure what tiddlywinks were, but they sounded disgusting.

All four young people chanted along with the chorus of the rap they were listening to.

'So you ain't gonna be king?' shouted Chantelle to William.

'Doesn't look like it,' said William, miserably.

'Still,' said Chanel, 'you've always got the scaffolding to fall back on.'

Harry yelled, 'Three 'undred years ago we could 'ave 'ad Graham killed and 'ad 'is 'ead on a pole on West-minster Bridge.'

Chanel said, 'Yeah, but they've got DNA testing an' stuff now. Vulcan would know who done it within hours.'

Chantelle, who had a softer heart, said, 'I feel sorry for him, he can't be as bad as you're makin' out.'

'I think he's several rungs up the autistic spectrum,' said William.

'Ah, bless!' said Chantelle, who quite liked men to have a weakness of some sort. It made them easier to manage and less scary.

Chanel said, 'Chantelle likes dorky blokes. 'Er last boyfriend collected carrier bags.'

Chantelle said, 'I like a bloke what's got a hobby.'

William laughed, 'Perhaps you and Graham should get together, Chantelle.'

Later that night, lying in each other's arms, Camilla said, 'Have you made your mind up yet, darling?'

Charles said, 'To be king or not to be king, that really *is* the question.'

Camilla said, 'No, there's a more important decision

to be made, isn't there? If the Dog Control Act becomes law, which dog do we keep and which two do we get rid of? *That* is the question.'

Freddie, Tosca and Leo, who were lying in a heap at the foot of the bed, waited for Charles to answer. The hands of the pretty French clock on the bedside table ticked away a full minute before Charles answered.

'I don't know.'

41

The following morning William lay in bed, wishing the radiators worked, but luxuriating in the knowledge that he could lie in until midday when Chantelle was going to call for him. He had promised, after a few bottles of Smirnoff Ice, that he would take her to meet Graham. 'It will be a laugh,' he'd said.

He now regretted his impulse. He had no desire to see Graham again. Even the thought of Graham made him burn with anger. He was furious with his father and Camilla; and with their irresponsible adolescent sexual behaviour. Why couldn't they have used a con-dom, for God's sake? They had destroyed his own chance of becoming king – something he had looked forward to since he was a little boy. He felt as though a fabulous celebration in his honour had been cancelled at the last minute, leaving him all dressed up with nowhere to go.

Still, at least he had Chantelle, who was as pretty as anybody you saw on film or television. They had not technically become lovers yet; Chantelle had not en-joyed her deflowering in the back of a delivery van, and had vowed to 'keep her legs together' until she was married. They had not said 'I love you' to each other, but there was an understanding between them that they would not go out with other people.

Chantelle was waiting downstairs for William, trying to teach Althorp to sit up and beg. Harry was sitting cross-legged in front of the television, steering an imaginary car round a virtual ghetto landscape to the sound of gunfire and guttural obscenities. Carling watched the screen with interest, waiting to see if Harry's car could make it to the safe house without being blown up by the many bad guys who seemed to pop up from every alley and doorway en route.

Chantelle said to Harry, 'Look, I've taught him a new trick. Beg, Althorp, beg.'

Althorp jumped up on his back legs and held up his two front paws. He whimpered to Harry, 'Tell her to stop, will you? This is utterly humiliating.'

Harry said, 'Clever dude. That's fierce clever shit, dude.'

Althorp dropped to all four paws and slunk out to the kitchen, muttering, 'First I'm humiliated, and then I'm patronized.'

William had half hoped that Graham would be out somewhere. But Graham was well and truly in, sitting at the kitchen table with Charles and Camilla, teaching them the finer rules of tiddlywinks. Graham was about to tiddle a wink when he looked up and saw Chantelle Toby standing in the doorway in a shaft of sunlight, looking incandescently beautiful in a white shirt, wide leather belt and blue jeans.

She gave him a lip-glossed smile in greeting and said, 'You must be Graham.'

Charles got to his feet and said, 'Graham, this is

Chantelle Toby. She looks after your, er . . . grandfather at Frank Bruno House.'

Chantelle said, 'Tiddlywinks! I used to play with our granddad. 'E'd give me a Nuttalls Minto every time I got one in the cup.'

'Excellent,' said Graham. 'Would you like to play?'

Chantelle sat down on the only vacant chair, and William leaned against the sink and watched while Graham and Chantelle played as a team against Charles and Camilla. He noticed that Chantelle was flicking her hair more than usual, and throwing her head back, laughing, showing her perfect teeth.

Althorp, who had accompanied them, having nothing better to do, said to Leo, 'Doesn't it make you sick, how humans have to go through a whole lot of malarkey just to get themselves a shag?'

Leo said, 'You've got a dirty mouth on you, Althorp.'

Freddie growled, 'I'm with Althorp on that. Dogs don't waste time messing about. It's a quick sniff, and Bob's your uncle.'

Tosca said, 'Leo is a romantic, aren't you, pet?'

Leo said, 'Bitches appreciate a bit of respect, a few compliments. Wise up, Freddie, you're living in the past.'

Freddie bared his teeth at Leo and growled from the back of his throat.

Tosca yapped, 'Don't start, Freddie.'

Althorp took Freddie's side and the two dogs rushed at Leo, snarling and swearing. Tosca ran and hid behind Camilla's legs. Charles picked up Freddie and hurled him into the back garden, saying, 'Bad dog, Freddie!'

When the kitchen door had been slammed shut,

Freddie walked down the garden path and urinated against the last remaining winter cabbages.

After Chantelle and Graham had beaten Charles and Camilla three times in a row, the tiddlywinks were put away and the table was set for lunch, to which Chantelle and William were invited.

Camilla said, 'Why don't you young people get to know each other, while Charles and I prepare some lunch?'

William said, '*Young!* Isn't Graham over forty? Is that what's considered young these days?'

Camilla said, 'Forty is the new thirty. We're all living longer now. Think of your great-granny, she was a hundred and one when she died.'

Graham said, 'I cried for five minutes when I heard she'd finally gone. I felt a sense of kinship with her.'

Chantelle said sweetly, 'You take after her a bit, Graham. *She* had a moustache just like yours.'

Graham stroked his moustache proudly.

When the younger people had gone into the living room, Charles said to Camilla, 'What shall we give them? There's hardly anything in the pantry, and we seem to have spent all our money.'

Camilla said, 'Leave me to it. You go and talk to the kids.'

She surveyed the few ingredients: there was curry paste, paprika, a little vegetable rice, and the ubiquitous root vegetables from the garden. There was no meat, cheese, fish or eggs. However, there was stacks of Pedigree Chum, and several boxes of Bonios.

She said to the dogs, 'You're extremely well catered for, aren't you, darlings?'

William had no desire to 'get to know' Graham. He flung himself into a corner of the sofa and studied the various calluses on his hands. Graham was holding court: talking about his job, making it sound as though he was James Bond, or something, thought William. In the scaffolding trade, health and safety inspectors were the enemy. Grice considered them to be the scum of the earth.

Chantelle's eyes were shining. 'I'm in a caring profession,' she said. 'I'm a nurse.'

'No, Chantelle,' said William. 'You're a care worker. You're not trained, are you? You're on the poxy minimum wage.'

Chantelle was hurt, her luscious lower lip trembled. Why was William showing her up in front of his half-brother?

Charles said, 'Wills, darling, Chantelle does a simply wonderful job, caring for Grandpa.'

Graham buried his face in his hands. He remembered how kind the nurse had been to him when he sat by his adoptive mother's bed as she lay dying from the terrible wounds that the lawnmower had inflicted on her.

Noticing Graham's reaction, Chantelle asked, 'What's up?'

Graham said huskily, 'I told them to have that mower serviced professionally.'

When Camilla called them in to eat, they trooped into the kitchen to find a delicious casserole dish of rich-looking beef curry, a pile of steaming rice and dishes of spicy vegetable croutons. As Charles sat down, he murmured, 'Camilla, darling, you are an absolute wizard. However did you do it?'

A red-eyed Graham sniffed that he did not like curry, but would give it a try. As they forked the fiery chunks of red meat into their mouths, Camilla watched anxiously.

Charles said, 'It's simply delicious, darling,' then went into an anecdote about a visit he'd made to Delhi.

William remembered the photograph of his mother sitting alone in front of the Taj Mahal. To his horror, his eyes filled with tears. He blamed them on the curry, but he left as soon as decency allowed. Chantelle stayed and helped Graham with the washing-up.

When they were alone in the kitchen, Graham said, 'Can you keep a secret, Chantelle?'

Chantelle had once caused endless trouble when she had inadvertently blurted out the secret that Beverley Threadgold's name, before she changed it by deed poll, was Edna Onions. She said, 'Don't tell me nothing secret, Gray. It'll be all round the estate before you can say diddly squat.'

But Graham was longing to tell somebody outside the family about his royal parentage.

He said, 'You might think I'm just a normal chap with an ordinary tea-towel in a nondescript kitchen in a boring region in—'

Chantelle was a patient girl, but even she was growing slightly irritated. 'Yeah?' she prompted.

'Well, I'm not an ordinary chap,' said Graham, 'I'm royalty. I'm second in line to the throne.'

Chantelle scraped at the burnt bottom of the curry pot with the end of a sharp knife and said, 'Yeah, I know. William told me.'

Graham was outraged. 'I was sworn to secrecy,' he said.

Chantelle laughed, 'Don't get your pants up your crack. There's no such thing as a secret no more. Secrets was something they 'ad in the olden days.'

Graham took the sharp knife out of her hand, rinsed it, dried it and placed it carefully in the cutlery drawer. They continued washing and drying the pots in a companionable silence.

Arthur Grice was at his tailor's in Melton Mowbray, being fitted for a top hat and morning suit. He was standing in his Y-fronts, having his inside leg measured, when he received a call on his mobile from the acting head teacher at the Arthur Grice Academy, a Mr Lowood.

The teaching staff were threatening to resign en masse in support of the religious studies mistress, who had got into an argument with Chanel Toby about creationism.

Arthur shouted down the phone, 'What the fuck's creationism when it's at 'ome?'

Mr Lowood replied, 'It's the concept that God created the universe, and everything in it, in seven days. Well, six actually; he rested on the seventh.'

'I ain't surprised,' said Arthur. 'Anybody would be shagged out after workin' that 'ard. So what's the problem?'

'Chanel Toby questioned the theory and argued for

349

Darwinism, stating quite aggressively that we're descended from the apes. I'm afraid things turned physical.'

Arthur, who had more than a touch of the simian about him, thought about his coming investiture and the Queen's apparent affection for Chanel Toby. He couldn't afford to rock the boat.

He said, 'The kid 'as a point. I mean it's a lot to do, ain't it, in six days. Create every bleedin' flower, tree, plant, seaweed, animal, bird and fish. Not to mention light and dark. I mean it beggars belief really, don't it?'

The acting head said, tentatively, 'But you insisted that the children be taught the Bible, Mr Grice. It's part of the curriculum, Bible studies, three times a week.'

Arthur pushed the tape measure out of his groin and said to the tailor, 'You're enjoying yourself a bit too much down there for my likin', nancy boy.' He said into the phone, 'I'll be there in 'alf an hour.'

On the drive back to the Flowers Exclusion Zone, Arthur talked about God. 'Me an' God 'ave a lot in common,' he told Rocky. The Flowers Exclusion Zone was Arthur's world and he was undoubtedly the supreme ruler, and like God, he had come from nowhere, and both of them had been forced to bang a few heads together on the way. God was always smiting some awkward bleeder who wouldn't play by the rules.

'He was a hard bastard,' Arthur said to Rocky. 'He watched his kid die on the cross and wouldn't let 'im down.' Arthur's hands sweated on the steering wheel; he had always had a thing about the crucifixion.

When he arrived at the academy he was greeted by Mr Lowood and taken to the staffroom to hear the staff's grievances, which were not only about Chanel Toby and her 'challenging behaviour'. They earned less than teachers in non-academy schools, they paid for their own pensions, they worked longer hours, the children were impossible to teach . . .

Arthur surveyed the sullen gathering and said, 'My teachers said I was educationally subnormal. Well, I ain't the best scholar in the world,' he added ingenuously, 'but I've proved 'em wrong, ain't I? I'm joinin' the 'igher echelons. Next week this school will be called the Sir Arthur Grice Academy. So who knows what Chanel Toby will achieve in 'er life? Give the kid a chance, eh?'

Then, with Lowood following, Arthur went to his office upstairs, where they met Chanel Toby and Mrs Whitehead, the head of religious affairs, an anxious-looking woman with an overactive thyroid. Arthur was now the great conciliator. Though he thought, looking at Chanel's sulky expression, there's a face that needs a good slapping.

'Right,' he said, 'let's hear what Mrs Whitehead 'as to say.'

Mrs Whitehead said, 'The lesson was progressing satisfactorily. I'd asked the children to draw Adam's ribs, from which Eve was made, when Chanel Toby asked why we were, and I quote, "having to do ribs again, when we've already done 'em in biology". I explained that God had made Eve out of one of Adam's ribs and Chanel said, "As if!" in a very unpleasant tone. This led to a certain amount of repartee among Chanel's classmates, some of it explicitly sexual, about the reason

God felt the need to create a woman at all. I managed to divert the discussion along more theological lines, and then Chanel Toby shouted out, "I know why God created woman! It was to tell Adam he was wearing the wrong shoes."

'I regret to say there was laughter, and I asked her to leave the classroom. She refused, saying that she was being persecuted for her religious beliefs, and that she would sooner be burnt at the stake than retract her views.'

Lowood said, anxiously, 'For the record, Mrs Whitehead, can I take it that at no time did you threaten Chanel Toby with burning at the stake?'

'At no time,' said Mrs Whitehead indignantly.

Arthur cooed genially, 'Do you want to say anything, Chanel dear?'

'Not really,' said Chanel. 'I think I'll take your advice and leave school.'

'And what will you do?' asked Arthur, paternally.

'I'll marry Prince Harry,' she said. 'I might as well; I could be 'aving 'is baby. We didn't use a condom because 'e said it would be like eating a sweet with the wrapper on.'

Princess Michael woke with a new sense of purpose on the morning of Sandra Grice's first lesson in social advancement. However, Sandra was an unwilling pupil. She resented Arthur's implication that she was not a lady.

'It's not as if 'e's a gentleman 'imself,' she said to Princess Michael when they were sitting in the Princess's overfurnished sitting room.

'And what is your idea of a gentleman?' asked Princess Michael.

'It's somebody who holds your hair back when you're being sick,' said Sandra. 'Arthur's never done that!'

They started with a discussion about clothing for Arthur's investiture.

'Tell me whose style you admire,' said Princess Michael, her pen poised over a notebook.

'Dolly Parton, Jordan, Jodie Marsh,' said Sandra. 'I like sexy clothes with a touch of class about 'em.'

Princess Michael asked, 'Your favourite outfit?'

'That's easy,' said Sandra. 'It's my red leather catsuit with white fringing, worn with white cowboy boots and a rhinestone Stetson.'

Princess Michael closed her eyes briefly. The outfit as described caused her real pain.

She said, 'From now on, your colours will be only beige, grey, black or white. The only fabrics allowed are cashmere, wool, silk or linen. Hems will touch the knee. Jewellery will be pearls and/or diamonds, nothing else.'

She examined Sandra's hair, which was white-blonde and long, piled up on top of her head, looking like several Mr Whippy ice creams, minus their cornets. Princess Michael unfastened Sandra's hair from its pins and combs and twisted it into an elegant chignon.

Sandra said, looking in the sitting-room mirror, 'I look like one of those women what collects cats.'

'No, you look *très* elegant,' said Princess Michael, who was excited by her new career as a stylist and life coach. With her royal connections she could end up editing *Harpers & Queen*, perhaps British *Vogue*, one day.

She persuaded Sandra to go up to the bedroom and try on a beige silk suit.

Sandra stood in front of the cheval mirror.

Princess Michael said, 'No, you still look common. It's these enormous breasts of yours.'

Sandra said, 'I look common, because I *am* common.'

She climbed out of the beige suit and handed it back to Princess Michael. Beverley Threadgold, who was looking out of her front bedroom windows and wondering why Sandra Grice's car was parked outside Princess Michael's house, was agog when she saw Sandra 'flaunting herself' in a leopard-skin bra and matching thong in Princess Michael's bedroom. Also enjoying the show was Inspector Lancer who, after Sandra had roared off in her car, had entered 'active lesbian' in Sandra's file.

42

Chanel told both of the grandmothers that she was pregnant before she told Harry. Violet and the Queen were watching *Emmerdale* in the Queen's living room when Chanel walked in after knocking on the back door and shouting, 'It's only me.'

The two women moved their eyes away from the screen reluctantly. They had been about to discover who in the village had been stealing tractor wheels.

'I've got sommat to tell you both,' said Chanel.

'You've been chucked out of school again,' said Violet resignedly.

'No, I think I'm pregnant!' said Chanel excitedly.

'Oh, my duck!' said Violet. 'That's smashin'!'

The Queen was amazed that pregnancy was always a cause for celebration in Hell Close, however young the girl or however unsuitable the father of the child might be.

'Do I know the father?' asked Violet.

'You both know the father,' said Chanel. 'It's 'Arry.'

'Ari?' questioned the Queen. As far as she knew, she was not acquainted with a Greek person called Ari.

'Harry!' said Chanel, making a great effort to sound the aspirant.

'What, the Queen's 'Arry?' said Violet delightedly.

'Yes,' said Chanel. 'I know it's 'Arry's cos I 'aven't bin with nobody else.'

'Come and give your grandma a kiss, you little beauty,' said Violet, staggering to her feet.

The Queen rose from her armchair and waited until Violet released Chanel from a tight embrace. She kissed Chanel on both cheeks and said, 'It's time we had some new blood. Congratulations, Chanel dear.'

When Chanel had gone to break the news to the father and the rest of the family, Violet said, 'We're related now, Liz. It's the Tobys and the Windsors, eh?'

They waited until the *Emmerdale* tractor-tyre thief had been unmasked – a drug fiend, newly arrived from the city, who was swapping tyres for crack cocaine – then they put on their coats, checked that they had their registration cards, and headed to Frank Bruno House to tell Prince Philip that he was about to become a great-grandfather.

He couldn't grasp that Harry and Chanel Toby were expecting a baby. He kept referring to the time he had shot a baby elephant while on safari in Africa.

Violet shouted, trying to cheer him up, 'We're related now, Phil! Ain't it lovely?'

The Queen said, 'Oh, my poor darling, you look so unhappy.'

'I miss the dressing-up,' he said bleakly. 'I miss my medals and my gold braid. Where are my lovely uniforms, Lilibet?'

The Queen said, 'Hush, darling, you'll wake Mr Bunion.'

Bunion was noisily asleep in his wheelchair. His snoring was awfully irritating, thought the Queen, but infinitely preferable to him waking up and starting one of his interminable anecdotes about the wildcat strikes he had led in the 1970s.

On the way home the two old ladies talked about Harry and Chanel's wedding. There would *have* to be a wedding.

When Sandra got home from Princess Michael's, she found Arthur staring morbidly at the accumulated rubbish in the stream under the glass floor.

'Look, there's a bleedin' dead rat down there now,' he said. 'I've been on to Rentokil, but they reckon they ain't got frogmen on the staff.'

Sandra looked through the floor at the decomposing rat lying among the stacked-up rubbish, and had the melancholy thought that it wouldn't matter how much money and status she and Arthur accumulated, there would always be a rat under the floor.

'Anyroad up,' said Arthur, turning to look at her, ''ow did you get on with Princess Michael?'

'It was a waste of my time an' your money,' said Sandra. 'She told me to buy a string of pearls, keep my tits covered up, drop my hems and keep my legs together when I'm sitting down.'

Arthur sighed and looked down again through the floor. The rat was waving its dead paw at him. He knew it was the flow of the water that was manipulating the dead beast, but he couldn't get the idea out of his mind that the rat was somehow taking the piss.

On the last night of Graham's visit, Camilla went into the kitchen to feed the dogs and found Graham at the window staring disapprovingly at the chickens at the end of the garden.

Later that night, seeing him writing, Camilla made one last effort to engage with him and asked, 'What are you doing?'

'I'm filling in a risk assessment sheet for this place,' he said without lifting his head.

Charles looked up from his book and said, 'Might we be party to your, er . . . conclusions?'

Graham said, 'I'm afraid not. It would be more than my job's worth to breach the laws of commercial confidentiality.'

When Charles and Camilla were washing up in the kitchen together, she whispered, 'It's bound to take time to get to actually *love* him, isn't it?'

Charles said, 'That's what Nanny said to me about my dislike of cod liver oil, but I still can't stand it.' He shuddered. Camilla was not sure what had caused this response – the memory of cod liver oil or Graham – but she was determined to be positive.

She tried to fall asleep that night by counting Graham's good points. He had lovely handwriting, he could whistle in tune, he lowered the seat after using the lavatory, his shoes were always polished, he didn't swear . . . but the list was not long enough. She lay awake worrying until Charles's deep breathing lulled her to sleep.

43

The next morning Charles and Camilla walked in hazy sunshine with Graham as he trundled his suitcase to the security checkpoint, where he had arranged for a taxi to take him to the station. All three of them were privately pleased that Graham was going home. He was not an easy person to live with; every piece of food he put in his mouth was subject to an almost forensic investigation, both its provenance and wholesomeness being questioned. Only that morning Graham had interrogated Charles on the precise age of the rashers of bacon on his plate. There were other things about him that unsettled his parents: the way he shouted, 'Help! Help!' in his sleep; his habit of walking into a room and saying, 'Ha!' before walking out again.

To compensate for not loving her son, Camilla held on to Graham for an uncomfortably long time. It was Charles who said, 'Let him go, darling. The taxi is waiting.'

Charles hesitated; should he embrace his son or offer him his hand? He need not have worried. Graham passed his ID card to Peter Penny, who was on duty at the checkpoint, and was ushered through to the outside world. He gave a brief wave and was gone.

As they retraced their steps towards Hell Close, Freddie, Tosca and Leo ran to met them, united in their happiness at Graham's departure.

Camilla said, 'The dogs look terribly happy.'

'Why shouldn't they?' said Charles. 'They know nothing about the proposed dog laws, poor empty-headed things. They live an ideal life.'

'And what is your ideal life?' asked Camilla.

'In my ideal life,' said Charles, 'we would live very simply in a tiny shack in a wilderness somewhere. We would keep warm and cook over an open fire. We would have very few possessions, a few rough cooking pots, a plate, cup and bowl each. A knife, fork and spoon.'

'A bed?' prompted Camilla.

'A plank bed, covered in animal skins.' Charles sighed happily, imagining himself and Camilla making love in the firelight with the wind howling outside.

'And where would this shack be?' asked Camilla.

'Oh, I don't know, darling. Scotland, perhaps . . . Rannoch Moor,' said Charles.

Camilla said, 'It will be terribly cold in the winter, darling. What will we do during the long dark days and nights?'

'We'd *survive*, darling,' said Charles. 'We'd collect wood and hunt for our food, and make our own clothes and boots.'

'Would we?' said Camilla.

'We'd have to, darling,' he said. 'We'd be beyond Harrod's delivery zone.'

Camilla saw that he wasn't joking and said, hesitantly, 'I think I'd like to be a little closer to London, darling.'

'Where?' asked Charles.

'Gloucestershire has some terribly wild places,' said Camilla.

Charles said censoriously, 'Yes, Gloucester city centre on a Friday night is horribly wild.'

Camilla said, 'Oh please don't sulk, Charlie. I'm sure we'd be terribly happy in a shack on Rannoch Moor, but I'd be equally happy in a lovely old house with the dogs and a few horses, within driving distance of a Marks and Spencer's chilled food cabinet. It's being together that counts.'

There was a long silence, during which time Charles checked Leo's back paws for stones.

Camilla said, 'You ought to tell your mother that you've decided.'

'Decided what?' asked Charles.

'Decided you don't want to be king,' said Camilla.

Although Gin and Tonic were on different floors of the Excelsior Dog Hotel, they kept in touch by barking to each other at frequent intervals. Tonic was inclined to panic when the hour for his injection passed without any sign of a member of staff. At such times, Gin urged Tonic to howl for attention and continue until somebody came.

The hotel boasted in its promotional literature that the dogs received 'five-star attention, two mouth-watering home-cooked meals a day, long walks and a fun and games hour'. Tonic, who was in the cheaper annexe, expected nothing, but Gin was bitterly disappointed. The two mouth-watering home-cooked meals proved to be a portion of cow's hide which had simmered in a bucket on top of a filthy stove in the kennel kitchen. The long walk was a quick trip on a lead with the owner to the off-licence and back. The fun and games hour consisted of the owner's teenage son throwing a rubber bone in a desultory fashion in a concrete compound.

When Graham came to pick up the dogs, he said, 'Did you have a lovely time, Gin? Did you? Did you?'

Gin barked, 'You were ripped off, Graham. The owner's a drunk and her son is a tormenting brute.'

When Tonic was let out of his cage, Graham did not acknowledge his existence. But Gin rushed up to greet his companion and lover, and the two dogs rubbed heads and exchanged smells.

'We'll never spend another day or night apart,' barked Gin, who was alarmed at Tonic's condition. 'Look at you; your eyes are glazed, you've lost weight and your nose is dry.'

'I'm so thirsty,' rasped Tonic.

'You need insulin,' diagnosed Gin.

When they arrived at the Ruislip bungalow, Graham had to carry Tonic from the car into the kitchen. Gin watched anxiously as the exhausted Tonic was almost thrown into his basket.

Gin barked, 'Give him his insulin, Graham.'

But Graham was tired after his long journey; he was also emotionally drained.

After living in the Fez, Graham found the bungalow unnervingly quiet; the only sound came from the ticking of the cuckoo clock and Tonic's ragged breathing. At precisely the same time that a drunken and stoned Miranda was trying, and failing, to fit her key into the lock of her front door, Graham was woken by Gin frantically barking and scratching at the kitchen door. Graham stumbled out of bed and injected Tonic with painful haste.

Before Graham fell asleep again, he wondered how Miranda would react when he told her that he was second in line to the throne. The beautiful Chantelle had not seemed particularly impressed. He decided that he would wait until he found out what Miranda's political affiliations were. For all he knew, she could be an ardent Cromwellian – there had to be something wrong with Miranda. His adoptive father had warned him that all women were unstable and harboured dark secrets. It might be safer if he didn't put all of his eggs in the same basket, but kept a couple back in their cardboard carton, in a high cupboard, behind a locked door.

44

Miranda's entrapment of Graham Cracknall was accomplished within ten minutes of their first sitting down together at an alcove table for two in the golf-themed lounge of The Mouse and Cheese. Miranda was wearing a white, full-skirted dress with a Peter Pan collar. She had made her face up skilfully so that it looked as though she was wearing no make-up.

Miranda had studied 'The Psychological and Physiological Triggers in Male Reproduction' at the De Montfort University, and she knew what men liked and what left them cold. So she let Graham do most of the talking and agreed with everything he said. She lowered her voice and laughed at his jokes. She looked at him with rapt attention and glanced away shyly when he paid her a clumsy compliment. She endured his re-enactment of tiddlywink competitions in which he had triumphed, without showing the slightest sign of boredom. She even begged him to repeat some of his tiddlywink strategies, saying, 'Graham, tell me again how you managed to tiddle the yellow wink into the cup by bypassing the red and green.'

Graham illustrated his past triumphs by using pieces of beer mat he had torn up before eventually being loudly reprimanded from behind the bar by the surly landlord. Graham shouted from the alcove, 'I'm a health and safety inspector and your pork pies should be stored in a chill cabinet. They should not be *flaunted* on top of the bar.'

Miranda forced herself to ignore the waves of hatred emanating from the golf-sweatered customers and kept her eyes on Graham, who had told her he was wearing his father's Sunday best clothes. She had nodded enthusiastically when he said, 'It would have been stupid to throw them away, there's years of wear in them yet.'

Over glasses of orange juice Miranda told her sad, fictional, life story. Orphaned in a train crash, brought up by a cruel aunt, sent to a convent school, befriended by a saintly nun, Sister Anastasia, who made the young Miranda sign a pledge that she would be chaste until marriage.

When the landlord shouted across, 'Are you two going to sit there nursing that orange juice all bloody day?' Miranda picked up her coat and said, 'Perhaps we'd better go.'

By the time Graham walked out of the pub with Miranda on his arm, he felt two inches taller. Had he been a stag, he would have challenged any man in the pub to an antler fight. Now, at last, he understood about women. It was why Napoleon tried to conquer Europe – he wanted to impress Josephine. It was the same for Hitler – he lost his way over Eva Braun. There was no still, quiet voice inside Graham's head asking why a stunningly beautiful girl like Miranda needed to search on a website for a partner.

When Graham mentioned that he would have to go

home soon to let the dogs out, Miranda gushed, 'I *love* dogs.'

Gin and Tonic were in the kitchen listening to *Gardeners' Question Time*, when they heard Graham's voice outside the house. The dogs pricked up their ears and Gin said, 'We'd better go to the door and greet him, show a bit of enthusiasm.'

Tonic yapped, 'You go, I'm waiting for Bob Flowerdew's tip of the week.'

Gin whimpered, 'Come with me, Tonic. You need to earn some brownie points.'

Tonic growled, 'Look, I don't like Graham. Graham doesn't like me. End of.'

They heard Graham's key scratching in the lock and a female voice saying, 'Orphaned, by a runaway hover mower! How awful, Graham.'

Tonic barked, 'He's brought a woman home! This I must see. I bet she's a reject from the Argos queue!'

The dogs ran into the hallway, barking excitedly, and saw Graham helping a dark-haired woman off with her coat.

Tonic yapped, 'Beauty and the Beast.'

Gin yelped, 'I expected a gruesome twosome.'

They frisked about at Graham's feet and Miranda said, 'Oh, Graham, Skye terriers! They're adorable.'

Gin sat up on his hind legs and held out a paw to Miranda.

'Gin wants you to shake his hand,' said Graham.

Miranda bent down and held Gin's small paw. She laughed, 'I'm very pweezed to meet you, ickle sir.'

Tonic growled, 'Jesus Christ! Ickle sir? Pweezed!'

Graham frowned down and said, 'Be careful of Tonic,

he's a very nasty piece of work. He's diabetic so he's prone to irrational mood swings.'

'Does he bite?' asked Miranda, taking a step backwards.

'When his blood sugar's low,' said Graham.

He shepherded Miranda through into the living room and opened the French doors to the garden. The dogs ran out for a pee. When they returned, Graham and Miranda were sitting on the sofa holding hands. There was a soppy expression on Graham's face that they had never seen before.

Miranda was saying, 'When was the last time you bought any new clothes for yourself, Graham?'

The transformation of Graham Cracknall had begun.

Miranda's sexual seduction of Graham started an hour and a half later, after a Sunday tea of salmon-paste sandwiches, and a tin of fruit cocktail with evaporated milk. It was a tricky one for Miranda, who had to make an apparent journey from shy virgin to willing sexual partner. She started by toying with the half cherry from the fruit cocktail, holding it on the tip of her tongue and trying to tease Graham into taking it from her with his own tongue.

They were soon exchanging small pieces of fruit from mouth to mouth. Then, as though maddened by desire, Miranda dipped her fingers into the fruit syrup in her glass dish and asked Graham to lick them clean. She then undid the buttons under the Peter Pan collar and smeared some of the evaporated milk across the rise of her breasts.

Tonic was disgusted. 'What a waste of good food,' he snapped.

Both dogs were relieved when Miranda murmured in Graham's ear, 'God forgive me, Sister Anastasia, but who could resist such a man?' and took Graham into his bedroom.

A few minutes later, Miranda lay underneath Graham as he huffed and puffed on top of her, and thought, the things I do for the party!

She had known from the way that he tapped out of time to the Glenn Miller record playing in The Mouse and Cheese that he had no sense of rhythm, and so it proved in bed. He was like an impatient man driving in slow traffic. He appeared to take no notice of her at all, let alone any sexual needs she might have.

Graham's bedroom could have belonged to a ten-year-old boy. There was a shelf full of battered soft toys, including a pig. Graham's one endearment so far to her had been, 'You're a silly little piglet, aren't you?'

On Monday morning Miranda reported back to Boy and his election strategy team. First she projected the photographs she had taken of Graham in the garden of the bungalow, in the time between the salmon-paste sandwiches and the sex.

Miranda was relieved of her usual media duties, and for the following week she concentrated on her preparations for capturing Graham Cracknall's heart. An aide was sent to Hamleys to buy a luxury games compendium; she was a fast learner and was soon conversant with the basic rules of ludo, dominoes, backgammon, snakes and ladders, and Cluedo. More difficult to her was injecting a measure of bubbliness into her depressive personality. She practised girlish giggles, hair flicking and tried to adopt a remorselessly cheerful outlook, and, although normally fiercely competitive, she allowed Graham to beat her at the games they played, before 'getting down to business', as Graham called it.

On the nights she didn't see him, she drank and drugged herself into a state of insensibility.

The Chancellor and the Prime Minister were co-hosting a reception at Number Ten for the Chinese Minister of Trade. The Chancellor took an opportunity, when Jack was between introductions, to draw him away to a corner of the room. After checking that they were out of earshot, the Chancellor asked, 'Have you read about Mao Tse-tung's eradication of the four pests?'

'No,' said Jack. 'What were they?'

'The extermination of rats, mosquitoes, flies and sparrows. The point is,' said the Chancellor, 'he wanted to add a fifth, but was persuaded out of it by his advisers.'

Jack said irritably, 'For fuck's sake, get to the fucking point.'

'The fifth was *dogs*,' said the Chancellor. 'If it was unwise for Mao Tse-tung to try to eradicate dogs, then it's wrong for you. Prime Minister, this is England.'

45

Violet Toby and the Queen were looking into the open door of the Queen's wardrobe, trying to select an outfit that the Queen could wear to Grice's investiture. The Queen was in her underslip and stockinged feet; Beverley Threadgold had been round first thing to wash the Queen's hair and set it, into fat pink plastic rollers. Violet felt that she would swoon with delight as each beautiful silken outfit was taken out of its plastic cover and laid on the bed to be examined.

She asked, 'Why don't you wear any of this lovely stuff, Liz?'

The Queen said, 'Silk clothes like these need a good foundation, Vi, and I simply can't be bothered to struggle into a corset every morning.'

'Nor me,' said Violet, looking mournfully at her lumpy un-corseted bum in the glass. 'You wouldn't believe I once 'ad a eighteen-inch waist, would you?'

'No,' said the Queen, 'I would not!'

Eventually, after a long deliberation, they chose a coat and dress in duck-egg blue silk which had a matching hat and shoes for the Queen. Violet squeezed herself into a frock and jacket in emerald green, which the Queen had worn only weeks after Prince Edward's birth, before she had quite recovered her figure.

Violet marvelled at the tiny hand-stitching on the

hem and cuffs, and said, 'It's the most loveliest thing I've ever 'ad on my back.'

The Queen persuaded Violet to try on a wide-brimmed hat, covered in peacock feathers, saying, 'I always felt a little intimidated by it, but it will suit your . . . bolder personality perfectly.'

Violet smiled when she saw her reflection in the looking glass. 'You're right,' she said, 'this hat don't scare me.'

After titivating their faces with the stash of Estée Lauder cosmetics the Queen had kept unused in a drawer for a special occasion, the two women left the house, treading carefully on the broken pavements in their court shoes, and headed towards the One-Stop Centre. The invitations to the ceremony had said, 'Dress smart: no jeans, no trainers, no Burberry, no horses.' The Queen had puzzled over the 'no horses', before being informed by Harry that 'no horses' was code for 'no Ralph Lauren'.

All over the Flowers Estate similar scenes were taking place, as people pulled their smartest clothes out of cupboards and wardrobes. A mellow golden sun warmed the Flowers Exclusion Zone, for which both the Reverend Edmund-Harvey and the Imam Mohammed Akbar took credit. Both men had been asked by Sandra Grice if they would pray for good weather.

Sandra had spared none of Arthur's expense; she had hired a job lot of entertainers from an agency calling itself Joviality Incorporated. She had not had her pick of agencies; most of them carried a warning on their advertising literature: 'No Exclusion Zones'. A small orchestra had been engaged to play Arthur's favourite music, before, during and after the ceremony. Arthur's taste had not changed since he was a young teenager, and when Sandra had asked him what the orchestra should play, he'd replied, 'Motown, there's *bin* no music since 1965.'

The One-Stop Centre had been draped in English flags and bunting. Balloons had been tied, perhaps unwisely, to the razor wire that ran around the perimeter of the roof. Inside the main hall, floral displays of carnations and chrysanthemums spelt out S.A.G., Arthur's soon-to-be initials. Round the back of the building, inside a hired freezer, was an ice statue of Arthur, depicting him as a purposeful visionary with one hand shielding his clear-sighted eyes from the sun.

A magnificent six-tiered cake, each tier supported by eight icing-sugar faux scaffolding poles, stood in the middle of a room-sized buffet table. The food was a hymn to saturated fat. There were mounds of Turkey Twizzlers, stacks of mini pork pies, piled wedges of glutinous pizza, a small mountain of suppurating cheese cubes on sticks, deep bowls of potato crisps and platters of slimy chicken thighs. Sandra had crossed 'salad' off the suggested menu: Arthur never touched rabbit food and considered those that did to be communists and cranks.

At ten o'clock the Queen and Violet arrived at the One-Stop Centre. After passing through various security checks, they were shown by a policeman in a bullet-proof vest into the main hall where the caterers, two bickering bald men, were putting the final touches to the food by decorating it with plastic watercress. There was a raised dais at the end of the hall on which stood a semicircle of gold-painted chairs. Each chair had a card Sellotaped to the seat: 'Reserved for Royal Family'.

Violet said, with an aristocratic hauteur, 'And where exactly do I put *my* arse?'

The Queen tore off one of the Sellotaped cards and said, 'Princess Michael will have to sit in the audience.'

Violet nodded and took her place next to the Queen.

The small orchestra gathered around the piano and frowned over their sheet music. More used to Salzburg than Motown, they nevertheless started up gallantly with a somewhat staid rendition of 'I Heard it through the Grapevine'.

At ten fifteen, the Queen, Violet and the rest of the Royal Family were escorted to a side room while the dais was prepared with a velvet footstool and the ceremonial sword. At half past ten a procession of cars and flatbed lorries assembled at the security checkpoint at the entrance to the Exclusion Zone. Arthur and Sandra were sitting in the back of an open-topped carriage, drawn by two white horses whose manes had been plaited with purple ribbons to match Sandra's purple velvet ermine-trimmed dress and cloak. Arthur was an imposing figure in his top hat and tailored morning suit.

Sandra had told her dressmaker to run her up something 'sexy but tasteful. Tits, but no nipples. Bum, but no crack. Legs, but no fanny.' The dressmaker had dropped her other work to concentrate on Sandra's outfit and had produced a frock that Camilla later described as a hybrid of flamenco dancer and Ruritanian princess.

Rocky sat between Arthur and Sandra, wearing a new purple rhinestone collar. He was dreading the mockery of the dogs on the estate. He had refused to jump into the carriage, until Arthur threatened him with 'a good kickin', if you don't get your arse in sharpish', so Rocky had been given no choice but to do as his master commanded.

Columns of security police, including Dwayne Lockhart and Inspector Lancer, walked alongside Grice's carriage. The carriage driver, a melancholic man who owned a riding school near to the Old Mill, had been bribed by Sandra into wearing an eighteenth-century costume, including a powdered wig and tricorne hat. After they had been trotting along for only a few moments, Arthur tapped the driver on his back and said, 'Alter your face, sunshine, you look like you're on your way to the bleedin' gallows.'

The entertainers walked at the rear of the procession, behind a small brass band that played hits from the Eurovision Song Contest, including 'Congratulations' and 'Boom-Bang-A-Bang'. The residents of the Exclusion Zone lined the streets in their thousands, lured out of their houses by the banging drums, clashing cymbals and oom-pah-pah of the trumpets and trombones. Their numbers were reinforced by Grice's scaffolders, who had been given a day's holiday – without pay – so that they could celebrate his social elevation.

The night before, Dwayne Lockhart had spent several fraught hours reading Dostoevsky's harrowing account of his incarceration in a Siberian Gulag. Dwayne had been moved to tears by the great writer's description of a Christmas Day treat, when some of the prisoners had performed a melodramatic play for the other convicts. The brutalized men – some of whom had raped and murdered, and had been sent mad by the horrific conditions – were transfixed by the clumsy acting and brightly lit stage. The brutality had left their faces, and for an hour or so they became better men. Dwayne fancied he saw the same redemptive expression on the faces of those watching Grice's parade (though, it has to be said, nobody else he conferred with afterwards witnessed such a transformation).

A juggler threw five oranges in the air and caught most of them most of the time. A mime artist carried an imaginary sheet of glass. Two stilt walkers, in very long trousers, sulked at the back, desperately trying to keep up with the rest. A clown in an orange fright wig squirted onlookers with water from a flower pinned on to his loud checked jacket, until a youth who had failed an anger management course took exception and threatened the clown with grievous bodily harm.

Dogs stood among the crowds throughout the route, and Rocky's worst fears were realized. His purple rhinestone collar was the cause of much canine hilarity, and there were cruel jokes about his sexual orientation, cracked in the safe knowledge that Rocky's elevated social position made it impossible for him to jump from the carriage and rip their throats out. As the carriage passed Hell Close there was a barrage of what sounded like orchestrated barking, from the resident dogs. Onlookers swear that the dogs were lined up in three rows in order of height, and that Harris appeared to be conducting from the front. What Rocky heard was: 'Rocky, join our Hell Close Pack! Send your rhinestone collar back!'

At Cowslip Lane the morbidly obese waddled to their front gates to watch. At Daisy Hill the cadaverous junkies gathered to gape. In Slapper Alley the young mothers held their babies up to see the parade. The lap dancers came out of Grice-A-Go-Go and gyrated their nipple tassels and wolf-whistled Arthur as he passed by. At the gates of the Arthur Grice Academy the children were lined up in their school uniforms to sing a song specially commissioned by Sandra for the occasion. There was nobody in the school who could play a musical instrument, so the children sang unaccompanied:

> *Thanks to Arthur we are blessed,*
> *We shall strive and never rest*
> *Till our school is in the black*
> *And we have the things we lack,*
> *Paper, pens and canteen cooks,*
> *Teacher's aids and library books.*
> *Praise to Arthur, prince of men,*
> *Arthur Grice we sing 'Amen'.*

Few of the struck-off professionals came out on to the street, but many disgraced doctors, solicitors and teachers watched from their windows and doorsteps. A police helicopter clacked overhead and a policeman could be seen videoing the procession and the onlookers. A large crowd of hoodies jeered and shouted obscenities as the procession passed Asbo Gardens. Arthur ordered his security police to, 'Present tasers!' and the hoodies slunk away.

The Queen and the rest of the Royal Family, Charles, Camilla, Andrew, Edward, Sophie, Anne, Spiggy, William, Harry and Princess Michael, waited in a small side room that was normally used for obesity counselling. Step-on scales that registered up to fifty stone stood in one corner.

Princess Anne, in a tweed suit and sensible shoes, said to her brother, Andrew, 'Go on, Porky, weigh yourself. There's a machine you won't break.'

Andrew, in a pinstriped suit that strained to contain his bulk, said, 'Have you looked at your husband lately, Annie? He looks like a beach ball on legs.'

'I like bein' fat,' said Spiggy, patting his big check-shirted belly. 'An' anyway, the last time I lost weight, I lost a couple of inches off my sausage. Annie didn't like that, did you, Annie?'

Anne said, 'No, I did *not*. A chipolata is no match for a decent banger.'

William and Harry, dressed in smart casuals, laughed and snapped their fingers. Edward and Sophie, both in grey suits, sniggered and Charles, in blazer and what he called 'slacks', turned away and studied a wall chart detailing the weight fluctuations of the morbidly obese population of the Flowers Exclusion Zone.

Camilla, in the dress and coat she had worn for her own wedding, whispered to Charles, 'Darling, please don't go into one of your black-dog moods.'

Charles whispered back, 'I sometimes wonder if I belong to this family, they are so bloody *coarse*.'

When the sound of the brass band was heard outside, playing 'Puppet on a String', the Queen said, 'Mr Grice is about to arrive. We ought to take our seats now, he is the star of the show.'

As they were about to file into the hall, Violet said to Princess Michael, 'By the way, you've got to sit in the audience with the ordinary people. I'm 'er lady-in-waiting, I've got to take 'er bag from 'er when 'er 'ands are full.'

Princess Michael was about to protest, but was silenced when, with the appearance of the Queen, the orchestra struck up the national anthem. Only a few people in the hall stood up to sing. The Queen was glad when it was over and she could take her place on the dais.

Disappointingly, few of Arthur's friends and relations had been able to attend the ceremony; many had been called away at the last minute on urgent business or had developed sudden incapacitating illnesses, so most of the seats in the hall were occupied by workers in the scaffolding trade and their families.

The trumpets from the One-Stop Centre Boys' Brigade Unit played a discordant fanfare and Arthur Grice entered with Sandra on his arm. They walked down a strip of red carpet towards the end of the hall, to where the Queen was waiting, her hands clasped in front of her, her handbag in the crook of her arm. A single twitch at the corner of her mouth betrayed her amusement at the sight of Arthur Grice in a top hat that was a little too small for his massive head. As Arthur proceeded up the aisle he wished that his father were still alive to witness him now, about to be honoured by the Queen. The last time he had seen his father, the old man had screamed, 'May you burn in hell, Arthur, you ugly bastard!' His father had been suffering from delirium tremens at the time and Arthur liked to think that he didn't know what he was saying.

Before Arthur knelt on the velvet stool in front of her, the Queen said quietly, 'Good morning, Mr Grice. I hope that you do not think that I am impertinent, but I have one more request before the investiture.'

Arthur waited. What did she want? Money? No problem, he had loads.

'I would like you to double the nursing staff at Frank Bruno House and arrange for the residents to have assistance to eat their meals.'

Arthur did a quick calculation; he could easily afford to take a cut in profits, old people were a lucrative business.

'You've goddit,' he said.

The ceremony was held up briefly when Sandra found her reserved seat occupied by Princess Michael, but after a brief scuffle and a few exchanged obscenities, Inspector Lancer stepped in and escorted Princess Michael outside, and the proceedings continued.

Violet Toby stepped forward to take the Queen's handbag and received a round of applause and a few whistles from the Tobys in the audience, then the Queen indicated by a slight inclination of her head that Grice was to kneel. He handed his top hat to Sandra, who was sitting immediately behind him, and knelt before the Queen. The Queen took Grice's own ceremonial sword, the one he'd confiscated from a rival gang in the early days of the scaffolding turf wars, and tapped Grice once on each shoulder with the flat of the blade, before saying, 'Arise, Sir Arthur Grice.'

As Sir Arthur Grice staggered to his feet, Sandra Grice screamed, 'Live the dream, babe! Live the dream!' And much to the Queen's alarm, others in the room began to scream and whistle.

Charles whispered to Camilla, 'Why can't people be quietly pleased any more? Why do they have to scream like banshees?'

Lady Sandra flung herself into Sir Arthur Grice's arms and sobbed, 'Babe, I'm so proud of you.'

Arthur wept astonishingly large tears and said to those congratulating him, 'It's a bleedin' dream come true.'

Asked by a local radio reporter, 'How do you feel?' Arthur said, obligingly following the script for such occasions, 'It ain't sunk in yet.'

Over his shoulder, Sandra, following another version of the same script, said, 'Perhaps by tomorrer it might 'ave sunk in.'

Four burly scaffolders carried the ice sculpture of Arthur into the overcrowded room and placed the glistening statue in the centre of the buffet table. The Queen, Charles and Camilla went to take a closer look; Lady Sandra joined them.

When the Queen congratulated Sandra on having made the arrangements so quickly, Sandra said, 'It was easy, I just chucked money at it.'

Camilla said, 'I do envy you your figure, Lady Grice.'

'Yeah, the surgeon wanted two grand per tit, but Arthur beat him down, and he done the two tits, and took a wart off Arthur's nose for three grand.'

'Warts and all,' said Charles. 'Jolly good. I wonder if he's any good with ears?'

'Listen,' said Sandra, 'this bloke could fix Dumbo's ears and make a nice elephant-skin bag with the leftovers.'

Out of politeness Charles took the surgeon's telephone number, though he had no money for plastic surgery. The Queen was hurt when she overheard him in the cake queue, complaining to Camilla, 'I should have had them pinned back when I was a boy.'

Later, as Camilla watched Prince Andrew flinging Marcia across the improvised dance floor, Charles nudged her and said, 'The statue.' Arthur's nose had melted, making him look more pig than man. But nothing could spoil Arthur's evening. He even broke up a fight between two drunken scaffolders arguing over the last remaining chicken thigh.

Coming back to join the Queen at her table, Arthur blew on his smarting knuckles and said, 'It can't get much better than this: a title, a few drinks, the company of friends and a fist fight to round it all off.'

How cruel, then, that when Sir Arthur and Lady Grice returned home to the Old Mill, they found that the glass floor had cracked open and the mill stream had rerouted itself so that it now ran through the Edwardian conservatory via the minimalist German kitchen. The stench made Sandra gag.

As the stinking water lapped around his ankles, Sir Arthur railed against nature. He cursed everything living and swore to avenge himself on the natural world. Then, because he could hardly blame Sandra for the crack in the glass floor, he took his rage out on Rocky and kicked him around the sodden floor until the dog lay in a whimpering heap in a corner of the thatched porch. When Sir Arthur stormed off to ring for help, Rocky climbed to his feet slowly, checked each of his legs for damage, and then started the painful four-mile walk to Hell Close.

The Hell Close dogs were waiting at the entrance to the cul-de-sac for Rocky to arrive. He had announced his destination when he was a mile away; Rocky's bark was a thunderous basso profundo that carried a huge distance. Harris barked to the other dogs, 'Rocky is joining us; he will be an extremely useful member of the pack.'

Protracted bum-sniffing and tail-wagging celebrated Rocky's arrival in the close. Some of the bolder dogs tried to lick his genitals, but Rocky yelped in pain and they backed off and apologized. Because the dogs could not survive without human help, there was the question of which household Rocky should attach himself to. Rocky growled, 'I'm not going where I'm not wanted.'

It was Micky, Violet's dog, who suggested that Rocky should wait a while and see which of the humans would offer Rocky a home. After warning him about Maddo Clarke, the other dogs went to their owners' homes and left Rocky to lick his wounds. As expected, it was Maddo who first tried to lure Rocky off the green, but a low menacing growl and a display of dripping fangs sent him scuttling back behind his garden fence. Eventually, as night fell and a light rain began, Barry Toby tramped across the green and said, 'Come on, lad.' And Rocky got up and followed Barry home.

46

Chantelle and Chanel had turned Violet Toby's cramped front room into what they called 'a pampering parlour'. Camilla had been ordered to soak her 'damaged by gardening' hands in a pudding basin full of warm, soapy water by Chanel Toby, who had been horrified at Camilla's ragged cuticles and broken nails. Chantelle was giving the Queen a pedicure. Each time a royal toenail was cut and a clipping flew across the room, it was chased by Micky, who retrieved it and brought it back to Chantelle, who said, 'Good boy, Micky.'

Barry Toby had declined an invitation to be pampered. He sat in front of the television, eating toast and watching a documentary about the Great Fire of London. An actor in a curly wig and seventeenth-century costume was prancing about pretending to be Samuel Pepys. Rocky lay at Barry's huge feet. Every now and again Barry would lightly touch the back of Rocky's bruised head, as if to reassure the dog that he was safe now.

Violet said, 'I ought to be collecting them toenail clippin's an' puttin' 'em in a box, Liz. They'll be worth a bit when you're back in your palace.'

The Queen laughed, 'You're welcome to them, Vi. Do you want me to authenticate them?'

Camilla laughed, 'You're welcome to mine!'

Violet said, 'I don't think anybody'd want *your* toenail clippin's, Camilla.'

There was a brief awkward silence; Camilla felt ludicrously hurt that her toenail clippings had been rejected.

The Queen tried to help by changing the subject, saying, 'It's terribly exciting about Chanel's baby, isn't it?'

Chantelle said, filing the Queen's toenails with an emery board, 'I wish it was me, having a baby. I love babies. They're so squashy and lovely, ain't they?'

Violet said, 'I expect you and William will get married one day, then you'll have your baby.'

Chantelle looked up from the Queen's feet and said, 'No, me and Will are just mates. 'E don't fancy me, an' I don't fancy 'im.'

The Queen was relieved. One Toby girl in the family could be assimilated, but two might add rather too many dysfunctional Toby genes to the pool; their propensity for arson, their automatic belligerence when slighted, their vulgar taste in furniture and soft furnishings. She tried to imagine Chantelle and Chanel as chatelaines of Buckingham Palace; she envisioned them shouting at an upholsterer as he clad an antique chaise in leopard skin.

Barry Toby bellowed, 'Shut the fuck up!' and turned the television volume up.

A spokeswoman from the Kennel Club was saying, 'This is England's darkest hour.'

'Are we at war?' asked Chanel nervously.

'Shurrup!' shouted Barry, turning the volume up even higher.

A handsome newsreader, familiar and reassuring to

them all, told them that the Dog Control Act had been passed by Parliament. The women listened in silence, not daring to antagonize Barry any further. As the full extent of the dog laws was spelt out on screen in the form of graphics and bullet points, the Queen's spirits sank.

When Barry allowed them to speak again, the Queen said, 'I shall have to go home. I left the television on for Harris and Susan, they'll be frightfully scared.'

Violet said, 'Don't worry, Liz, they'll never get our dogs took off us. They're not that bleedin' stupid.'

But the Queen did worry. She had known many politicians, and they *were* that stupid.

When Camilla returned home, manicured and pedicured, Prince Charles made her recount the time spent at Violet Toby's in Proustian detail. He had not yet talked to his mother about Chanel's pregnancy, and was avoiding doing so. Camilla assured him that the Queen seemed excited at the prospect of becoming a great-grandmother. Charles was not cheered by the news. He had called round to see Harry and had been horrified at the boy's attitude. When Charles had accused his son of failing to practise safe sex, Harry had said, 'I've only got one word to say to you, Pa, and that's *Graham!*'

Camilla waited until after dinner, when they were sampling a bottle of turnip and beetroot rosé, to tell Charles about the dog control laws. Intoxicated by the startling strength of the wine, Charles kissed the top of her head and said, 'Another set of laws that will never be implemented. Darling, this is England.'

*

It was the final cabinet meeting after Parliament was dissolved and before the electioneering began. The members of the Cabinet sat around the large polished table, waiting for the Prime Minister, watching the door and speaking in whispers. Few of them expected to keep their parliamentary seats and survive the general election. The Government's popularity rating was seventeen per cent, an all-time low.

The Chancellor could not stop touching the resignation letter in the inside pocket of his suit jacket. He knew he was about to do the right thing and felt a glorious sense of relief that he would soon be out of the whole filthy business. He would live in the countryside with Mitzie, and take her for long walks along what were left of the public footpaths. He would divorce Veronica and marry a jolly, fat woman. He hadn't met her yet but he saw his second wife in his mind's eye; she was walking towards him with her dog obediently at heel. She would have a pretty face and laughing eyes, and would invite him back to her cottage for tea and home-made scones.

The Chancellor's reverie was interrupted when Jack Barker strode into the Cabinet Office with the gunslinger's walk he had affected since visiting the American President recently.

Taking his seat in the middle of the table, Jack said, 'We should congratulate ourselves this morning. Last night was a political triumph. We passed two important legislative measures, the Stepladder Act and the Dog Control Act. I realize that some of you are very attached to your . . .' Jack paused and looked around the table

'. . . stepladders.' He laughed, 'But you'll have to be seen to be getting rid of them, and the same goes for your dogs. We have to lead by example. I want a photo shoot here in Downing Street tomorrow morning. If your dogs are in your constituencies, send a ministerial car. I want them outside here for an eleven o'clock press call.'

The Chancellor asked, 'And what will happen to our dogs, Prime Minister?'

Jack responded, 'We'll send 'em to work on farms . . . in Canada.'

The Home Secretary asked, 'Does that also apply to the public's dogs, Prime Minister?'

Jack said, 'Canada is a very large country.'

The Cabinet Secretary shuffled his papers agitatedly, anticipating the paperwork, the quarantine, the practical difficulties of shipping tens of thousands of dogs, of feeding them on the journey, and disposing of their faeces. It was forbidden to throw pollutants into the sea.

The Chancellor wondered if he had the energy to stage a coup. The Prime Minister was obviously mad, and he knew that most of the Cabinet would agree with his diagnosis, if he stood up now and denounced Jack. He was almost sure that he could count on their support, but he was worn out himself and uncomfortably aware that the Prime Minister still had supporters in the security forces. He had left it too late; he took out the resignation letter and handed it to Jack. He said, 'Prime Minister, I can no longer work in this Government.'

The room became quiet; nobody moved or spoke while Jack read the letter.

Jack said, 'I wish I could say you'd done a good job, Stephen, or that you'll be missed, but I can't. You were never more than a fuckin' number cruncher, and you've done nothing to help me counteract the dog terror.'

The Chancellor said, 'You've cracked, Jack. There *is* no dog terror.' He looked around the table for support, but nobody would catch his eye.

By late evening he was in his constituency with Mitzie, telling Veronica his career and their marriage were over. She took the news quite well, saying, before she drove away, 'Thank God! I'll never have to fake another orgasm again.'

Inspector Lancer was sitting at a computer terminal in his Portakabin office, reading the latest government directive. The Dog Control Act had been passed and ratified by Parliament and was to take effect within four weeks.

Lancer grumbled to Dwayne Lockhart, 'As if we haven't got enough to bleedin' do. I'll have to take men and women off surveillance and turn 'em into dog enforcement officers now. And where the fuck am I going to set up a dog holding centre?' He printed the email and handed copies to his colleagues. Dwayne ignored the legal jargon and read the summary. A series of bullet points said:

• All dogs must be licensed (£500 per annum).

• Only one dog is permitted per household.

- Dogs are not allowed to reside in flats or apartments.

- Licensed dogs must be kept on a lead and muzzled in all public places.

- Dogs are not allowed to bark, howl or whine between the hours of 10 p.m. and 8 a.m.

- Dogs are forbidden to defecate or micturate in any public place.

- Dogs violating the orders will be confiscated.

- All confiscated dogs will be taken to a holding centre to await collection and dispersal to Canada.

To Dwayne's dismay, Inspector Lancer said, 'How do you fancy being in charge of dog enforcement, Dwayne?'

Dwayne said, 'To be honest, sir, I'm not that keen on dogs.'

Lancer said, 'I'm not that keen on people, Dwayne. But I have to deal with 'em, don't I? You'll need protective clothing, a van, muzzles and an assistant, so you'll be working with WPC Boot. She's got a bit of a reputation but she's the only officer I know who could stare a pit bull down.'

Dwayne had heard of WPC Boot; she'd been on medical leave after damaging her back at the security police tug-of-war sports day. He said, 'It sounds dangerous work.'

Lancer said, 'Yeah, so make sure your taser is up to scratch. Some of the owners might get stroppy.'

Dwayne said, 'I don't think I'm the right man for the job, sir. I'm too soft-hearted.'

Lancer snarled, 'Butch up, Lockhart, or you and your soft heart will be out on your soft arse.'

WPC Abigail Boot was a strong-jawed, sturdily built policewoman. She was ferociously ambitious and seemed to have no conscience or sensitivity. She took the new job with relish, saying, 'I've never seen the point of dogs, I mean, what are they *for*?'

Dwayne thought it only fair that dog owners should be given some warning of the implications of the new laws, and asked WPC Boot to compose a leaflet clearly stating the law and giving a deadline of four weeks.

WPC Boot said, 'Why give them notice?'

Dwayne said, 'Where are people going to get five hundred quid for a dog licence? And what about multi-dog households? It's only kind to allow people time to choose which dog they want to keep.'

WPC Boot said contemptuously, 'Kind! You should have joined the Sally Army and banged a fuckin' tambourine. In my book, kindness is another word for weakness, and I despise weakness.'

She set her jaw and, within minutes of sitting at a computer, had composed a draft of the leaflet and had decorated it with line drawings of snarling dogs' heads that she had downloaded from the Internet. All day the photocopier churned out the leaflets, and by the time Dwayne and Abigail went off duty, the leaflets had been stacked into piles of one hundred, ready for delivery the next morning.

After work, at WPC Boot's suggestion, she and Dwayne went for a drink outside the Exclusion Zone, in The Clarendon Arms. WPC Boot strode into the pub and leaned a brawny arm on the bar.

'What's your poison?' she asked Dwayne.

Dwayne had never had a drink he could call his own. He hesitated, then said, 'I'll have what you're having.'

She shouted, 'Two pints of Black and Pickle,' to the landlord, who was at the far end of the bar trying to extricate himself from the pub bore, who was mono-logizing about a goal he had witnessed in 1974.

Dwayne wondered what a Black and Pickle was. Two minutes later he was presented with a pint of Guinness in which floated a pickled onion, the size of a small apple.

When he expressed surprise at the unlikely combi-nation, WPC Boot said, 'I don't run with the herd.' She took a bite out of her pickled onion and said, 'I've heard you read books.'

Dwayne nodded and looked away.

'Subversive books,' she added quietly.

Dwayne took a careful sip of Guinness, trying to avoid the onion. 'I read books,' he admitted, 'but . . .'

'I've seen your Vulcan file,' she whispered. 'Orwell is on the list.'

'What list?' asked Dwayne.

'The subversive list.' WPC Boot finished the pickled onion and swilled it down with a deep draught of Guinness. She wiped the foam moustache from her upper lip and said, 'Best get rid, eh?'

Later that night, Dwayne collected his Orwell titles

together, nine in all, and hid them under the floorboards of his studio flat. He hated the gaps on his bookshelves and filled them with a photograph of himself as a child, taken in a time when books did not present a threat.

47

The doorbell had stopped ringing; Camilla heard raised voices at the front door, then Charles, holding a tea towel, came into the kitchen followed by two large men wearing white, hooded, chemical-warfare suits and surgical facemasks. Charles was saying, 'But they are both terribly healthy.'

The alarming men in the protective suits had come to exterminate Eccles and Moriarty. Avian flu had been reported in Luton; a chicken fancier and his wife were critically ill in an isolation unit in Luton General Hospital. A proclamation had been issued by Vulcan that all domestic backyard, unregistered chickens were to be slaughtered. One of the exterminators showed Charles Vulcan's instructions: a piece of paper signed 'Graham Cracknall, Health and Safety Officer'.

Charles had not been able to watch the end, but he hadn't been able to shut out the panic-stricken squawks or the sound of frantically beating wings. When the men had gone, carrying the birds away in a sealed bag, Camilla made him a cup of camomile tea and said soothing and comforting words to him. Though perhaps it was not a good idea for her to say, 'Cheer up, darling. Your affection was purely one-sided. Those bloody hens never gave you a single egg.'

Charles had lifted his stricken face and said, 'It's

hopeless, everything is hopeless. The birds are dying; the weather has turned against us. The icecap is melting. Tesco's are inheriting the earth and young people born and educated in England cannot speak their own language. I find it in-com-pre-hen-sible that our English young are not taught *swathes* of Shakespeare as a matter of course. I used to *swoon* over *A Midsummer Night's Dream* at Gordonstoun, and I knew several sonnets off by heart.'

Before he could recite one, Camilla said, 'More proof of that big brain of yours, darling.'

She left him to his misery and went into the garden. Freddie, Susan and Leo followed her down the path to the empty chicken run. When Camilla was at school, she had thought Shakespeare a ginormous yawn. An egghead boyfriend had taken her to see *Lear* at Stratford, but it was terribly boring, nobody famous was in it. It was just an old man shouting a lot, and complaining about his daughter. She didn't know why they had to stick to the old-fashioned language Shakespeare used. And that bit when some chap had his eyes gouged out was terribly amateurish. You could tell the actor was faking it – from the stalls, anyway.

She hadn't bothered seeing the egghead again. In the interval he'd taken forever to get a drink, and then had completely blown it by telling her he was afraid of horses!

Camilla heard the doorbell ringing again. The dogs looked up at her expectantly, but she didn't move – she wasn't ready for whoever was on the doorstep. All she wanted was a quiet moment to smoke a cigarette and think.

Charles shouted, 'Camilla, you must come, it's awful. Awful!'

She closed her eyes in irritation and said, under her breath, 'What *now*? What fresh hell is this?'

With all three dogs pursuing her, she went back into the house to find Charles, Dwayne Lockhart, and a stolid policewoman Dwayne introduced as WPC Abigail Boot, standing in the sitting room. Charles was clutching a leaflet.

He said, 'First my hens, and now *your* dogs.'

He thrust the leaflet into Camilla's hands. She read it without understanding.

Seeing her confusion, Dwayne said, 'I'll leave it with you. It's a lot to take in at the moment.'

Abigail Boot said, 'It's quite simple. You've got three dogs. The law allows you to keep one, ergo, two have got to go.'

She looked down at Freddie, Tosca and Leo. All three were growling and baring their teeth. WPC Boot's hand went to the taser in its holster on her hip; the dogs retreated behind the sofa.

Dwayne couldn't wait to get out. 'Take your time choosing,' he said, as though Charles and Camilla were indecisive children at the pick 'n' mix counter.

'How much time do we have?' asked Camilla.

'You have four weeks to turn two of your dogs in voluntarily,' said WPC Boot.

'And if we refuse?' asked Charles.

'We confiscate all three,' replied Boot.

As she headed for the front door, Dwayne mouthed, 'Sorry.'

Leo whimpered to Freddie and Tosca, 'I'm too young to die.'

'And I'm too old,' snapped Freddie.

'And I'm too afraid,' howled Tosca.

After a visit from PC Lockhart and WPC Boot, the Toby household was in uproar. Barry had taken Rocky up to his bedroom and barricaded the two of them in while continuing to bellow, 'Rocky ain't goin' nowhere!'

Violet sobbed on the sofa, holding Micky in her arms, imploring Chantelle and Chanel to make Barry see sense and turn Rocky in to the authorities. Violet kissed Micky's grizzled head and cried, 'This dog 'as meant more to me than any man. I ain't 'ad to wash an' iron for' im. An' 'e ain't fussy what 'e eats neither.'

Next door the Queen was sitting with Harris and Susan on her lap. She had read the leaflet aloud to the dogs several times. She looked from one to the other; she couldn't imagine life without either of them. The only thing she could say was, 'But this is England, *England.*'

48

'It's time to do some tough talking, Graham,' said Miranda, on their seventh date. 'No offence, piglet, but you're an ugly bastard with the charm of a septic tank. And your clothes! What's your style guide? Pensioner chic?'

Graham stepped back as though he had been kicked in the chest. His own view of himself was entirely self-approving. They had just left The Mouse and Cheese, where they had eaten a gruesome English Heritage Ploughman's Lunch, consisting of a stale baguette, rubbery cheese and a tired salad.

They were walking back to the bungalow when Miranda started criticizing him 'out of nowhere', as he later told Gin. Graham had heard that women tried to change their men, so thought it was part of a modern relationship when Miranda suggested that he have a makeover. He was a little alarmed that she had arranged a series of appointments for him, and even more alarmed when she told him the cost. But he had his legacy, and Miranda had more or less said that unless he improved his appearance and adjusted certain mannerisms, she would not have sex with him again.

Graham was very anxious that the sex should continue. He had enjoyed himself a great deal recently, and was determined to improve his times. On the second occasion he and Miranda had made love, Graham had told her that he was going to wear his stopwatch and get an accurate timing of the bout.

Miranda had said, 'Graham, please! You make it sound as if we're about to take part in a boxing match.'

After his climax, she heard him stop his watch and say, 'Better – four minutes, seven point five seconds.'

Miranda had pushed him off her and run into the bathroom with the avocado suite. She had stayed under the shower for twenty minutes trying to scrub herself clean. Since then, he hadn't worn the stopwatch. But she knew he watched the little alarm clock on his bedside table, which had Winnie the Pooh on the second hand.

At 8.30 a.m. on Monday, Graham presented himself at Zachary Stein's dental surgery and underwent extraction, filing, moulding, and finally, the fitting of Hollywood-style caps. At 5 p.m. he kept an appointment with celebrity hairdresser and professional cockney sparrow, the ageing Alfie Tompkins, who frowned over Graham's hair before saying to Miranda, 'You're 'aving a larf, ain'tcha? I've seen a better barnet on a lavvy brush.'

Miranda said, 'Graham will be on the front cover of *Hello!* next week.'

Alfie grumbled, 'I suppose a few golden highlights and a scruffy "just jumped off a surfboard" look might be possible.'

As his hair was washed, coloured and cut, Graham was disconcerted by Miranda's conversation with Alfie.

It appeared that they shared the same circle of friends. There were references to 'wasted Pete' and 'crackhead Giles', and light-hearted anecdotes about being too 'bladdered' to get home.

Alfie said, 'Now me, these days, I like to be home by eight with a bottle of Moët and in bed by nine with a lissom young stylist.'

They made cynical comments about authority figures; including the Prime Minister, Jack Barker, for whom Graham had the greatest respect. The banning of novelty slippers and stepladders would make Graham's professional life much easier. When Alfie had finished blow-drying Graham's hair, he waited for the verdict.

Graham looked in the mirror and asked, 'Have you finished? It's sticking up all over the place.'

Alfie said, 'Doh! It's meant to be like that.'

Miranda said, 'You look cool, Graham. Clothes and shoes tomorrow.'

Graham had been hoping that Miranda would take him back to her flat in Stoke Newington, but she told him that she had to visit her sick best friend who was in a hospice. So Graham returned to the bungalow where Gin and Tonic had a good laugh at his hair.

Later that night, after many tequila slammers, Miranda told Boy's election team that she would sooner have a threesome with grizzly bears than sleep with Graham again.

The filming of the New Cons party political broadcast had taken place over three fraught days. On the first day, Boy's wife, Cordelia, had objected to the camera, the lights and the electric cables snaking across the bathroom floor, and had refused to put the children into the bath until a safety officer had checked that all was well.

Only thirty seconds of footage showing Boy bathing the children, as though it were part of their normal routine, were required. However, whenever Boy approached them with a soapy sponge, they shrank away from him and retreated to the end of the bath, crying for their Polish nanny, Katya. Eventually, when the bathwater was cold and the children's skin had begun to wrinkle, the director called an end. The sobbing children were taken out of the bath by Katya and wrapped up in warm, white towels.

The children also refused to cooperate for the mock breakfast scene, and the filming ended in a confusion of tears, spilt milk and frayed tempers. So the focus of the film was shifted gradually from 'Boy English, Hands-on Father' to 'Boy English, Dog Lover', because Billy was undoubtedly a star. He was obedient, cooperative, silent and gloriously photogenic. The film crew were besotted with the dog, and what had been a walk-on part for Billy became a leading role.

The puppy brought out another side in Boy. Whenever he looked at the dog, his face softened and his voice deepened. He allowed Billy to lick his face and he fed him titbits from his plate. The dog went everywhere with him; Boy stormed out of the Ivy when the maître d' refused to set a place for Billy. Boy happily cleared up the piles of stinking ordure that Billy distributed in the house and garden, though changing a nappy for the first time had made him retch and he had refused to do it ever again.

Five miles away in Westminster, Jack Barker was so desperate to lose the general election that he began to tell the truth to the many media outlets he spoke to during the long electioneering days. He was surprised at how much better he felt; the strain of having to choose his words as carefully as a man carrying an unstable stick of gelignite was gone. His brain cleared, it was like leaving a dark cave and breathing the fresh air of a sunlit meadow.

Asked by Peter Allen of BBC Five *Drive* if he would raise taxes to pay for his manifesto promises, he said, 'Yes, by five pence in the pound!'

Asked if there was a satisfactory solution to the territorial dispute between Palestine and Israel, he simply said, 'No!'

When he was asked by a hospital radio presenter in Liverpool to state whether he enjoyed visiting the city, he replied, 'No! I hate the accent, I think the men are work-shy crooks and the women are all loud-mouthed tarts.'

There was outrage in Liverpool, but in Manchester, Leeds, York and Chester the Prime Minister's popularity soared. One flat-capper interviewed in the centre of Bolton said, 'Up 'ere we like a bloke 'oo speaks 'is mind.'

It had only taken a few weeks for the anti-dog propaganda to work. When Jack had been shown a survey commissioned by *The Independent* newspaper, which showed that the dog terror was the most important issue of the day, he had grown depressed; he had not realized that the electorate had become so gullible. When did they lose their scepticism? The survey found that fifty-one per cent of English dog owners no longer considered their pet to be their best friend.

This was hardly surprising since television programmes were frequently interrupted, not only by advertisements for consumer goods, but also by short, brutal films featuring dogs attacking small children and elderly and disabled people. One particularly harrowing film showed a blind toddler trying to find her way around the living room of her home. A spectral voice-over intoned: 'Maisie will never see this room, never see the world, never see the sunrise, never see the stars, never see the changing seasons. Every day children like Maisie go blind because of contamination by dogs' faeces.' The last shot was a close-up of Maisie's sightless blue eyes, which were brimming with fat unshed tears.

Jack consulted the latest survey concerning his own popularity and was alarmed to find that his own approval rating had risen by seven per cent since he had started telling the truth.

When Graham's makeover was complete, a DVD presenting the new Graham – suntanned, white-toothed, expensively shod and tailored with a West Coast haircut – was shown to a select audience of aides in Boy's private office. A press conference announcing Graham's existence and status as second in line to the throne was cancelled, until Graham had benefited from intensive media training. His lip-licking nervousness and awkward physical mannerisms did not look good on camera. And when the twenty-one females working on Boy's election campaign played 'shag or die', twenty of them said 'die' when Graham's name came up. The remaining woman said 'suicide'.

Rip Spitzenburger, the elderly man with film-star looks, who had taught Bill Clinton his 'people skills' and had masterminded two winning election campaigns for the Democrats, was flown First Class from the United States and given a suite at the Savoy. He had a week in which to transform Graham from an awkward geek into a confident aristocrat. He watched the DVD in his hotel sitting room with the large windows over-looking the Thames. At the end of Graham's film he stared out at the river. He enjoyed a challenge – he had coached Mike Tyson on the correct use of a fish knife – but he wondered if this time, he had, like Mike, bitten off more than he could chew.

Rip and Graham's first meeting, held over room-service afternoon tea, started badly when Graham told Rip that, according to a poll of international risk assessors, 'America is the biggest threat to world peace.'

Rip, considered a liberal crypto-commie flip-flopper, in his own country, bridled at Graham's statement and said, 'First rule, Gray: do not on your first meeting insult your new acquaintance's country. Second rule: do not start a sentence with "According to a recent poll".'

Rip Spitzenburger felt that he had been duped by Boy English and his team. 'I shoulda been notified that the guy was bipolar,' he complained to his agent after Graham had gone home to Ruislip. After Rip's agent had negotiated a higher fee and a sponsor had been found to cover the extra cost, Rip agreed to complete the week's media training.

For the next seven days Rip attempted to teach Graham to smile without looking like Jack Nicholson in *The Shining*; to stop rolling his eyes back when asked a question; to show his best profile, his left, when posing for a photograph; and to speak and enunciate clearly, but without sounding like somebody whose vocal cords had been removed and replaced with an electronic voice box.

On most evenings Miranda met Graham in the American Bar at the Savoy, where she wheedled him into buying her a glass of champagne. He was surprised that she seemed to be on such intimate terms with the barman. For a shy girl she certainly knew a lot of people.

49

As the terror campaign intensified dog owning had quickly become synonymous with antisocial behaviour. There were fewer people exercising their dogs on the streets and in the parks. A man walking his gentle golden Labrador in Hyde Park was beaten up by a gang of youths and called 'a dog-loving bastard'.

Dog rescue centres were unable to cope with the constant flood of abandoned canines. Cruft's was cancelled, breeders of pedigree dogs could not sell their puppies and veterinary surgeons were inundated with requests for euthanasia. There were many stories from around the country of dogs jumping from high buildings to their deaths. Suicide could not be proved in any of these sad cases, but nobody could deny that the surviving dog population looked depressed and fearful. It was not a good time to be a dog, or a dog lover.

In the fourth week of what quickly became known as the War On Dogs, a government agency was set up to manage the crisis. Operation Dog Round-up opened centres around the country where unwanted dogs could be left, on the understanding that 'suitable candidates' would be shipped to Canada to work on farms. A government information film showed a ship leaving Liverpool Docks with dogs crowded on the top deck. An 'owner' was interviewed waving goodbye to her sheepdog. 'I know he's going to a better place,' she said. Another 'owner' said, 'My dog, Rex, was cooped up in a flat all day. He'll have better opportunities in Canada.'

The Queen watched these propaganda films with considerable scepticism. As she said to Violet, 'I've been to Canada many times. The climate is entirely unsuitable for English dogs, and there certainly aren't enough farms to go round.'

King was the first dog to go from Hell Close. Beverley Threadgold had never liked King; he was Vince's dog and would follow his master from room to room, waiting outside the bathroom when Vince had a bath and greeting him when he emerged as though they had been separated for years. Sometimes Vince thought that he loved King more than he loved Beverley. King was better looking than Bev for starters, and caused less trouble. Bev had let herself go, big time. Sometimes she couldn't even be bothered to get herself dressed and just slobbed about the house in a scruffy dressing gown and sheepskin slippers, the insoles of which had turned a shiny, smelly black. On such days she tied her hair back with whatever came to hand: string, a sock, once a torn-up J-cloth.

She moaned that she was depressed but Vince thought, what's she got to be depressed about? I only smack her one when she deserves it. King, though, he was a looker – big brown eyes, a lovely silky coat – and another thing about King, he was always smiling.

The first that Charles and Camilla knew about King's disappearance was when Vince asked over the garden fence if either of them had, 'Seen the dog around?'

Camilla said, 'Vince, you look frightful.'

Vince said, 'I ain't slept a wink. I were lying awake listening for 'im to scratch on the door, but 'e din't come 'ome.'

'Has he stayed out all night before?' asked Charles.

'No, 'e looked 'ard but 'e were frit of the dark,' said Vince. 'We 'ad to leave the bedroom light on for 'im.'

Camilla said, 'I'm sure he'll come back, Vince.'

Vince said, bleakly, 'I keep seein' 'im in me mind's eye, chasin' motorbikes.'

When Vince went back into the house he noticed that King's possessions, his food and water bowls, his spare collar, grooming brush and leather leash, were also missing.

'A bleedin' dog don't take its stuff with it,' he said out loud to himself. King was clever, but he hadn't mastered the art of packing an overnight bag.

When he asked Beverley about King's bits and pieces, Beverley cursed herself for this oversight; she'd been too anxious to remove all traces of King from the house. She said, falteringly, 'We must 'ave 'ad the burglars. Maddo Clarke's lads were messing about in front of the 'ouse yesterday.'

Vince always knew when Beverley lied to him; her eyes flicked from right to left, like an umpire at Wimbledon.

Vince asked, 'When was the last time you seen King? Think carefully, Bev, 'cause if you lie to me I'll kill you.'

Beverley walked to the back doorstep, lit a cigarette and inhaled deeply. She needed to think. Vince had killed before; a teenage fight in a taxi queue in the early hours of the morning.

She looked him in the eye and said, 'I meant to tell you, Vince, but it went right out of my mind. I took King to the dog collection point, he's going to start a new life, on a farm in Canada.' She backed into the kitchen and, as Vince advanced on her, she shouted, 'Dogs are dangerous, Vince! King were a nutter, you said so yourself!'

'I liked 'im being a nutter!' roared Vince. 'It saved me from being one myself!'

The first blow knocked Beverley's head against the built-in oven, activating the timer. Camilla listened to Beverley's screams with her head in her hands. Charles was white-faced.

He said, 'One *must* do something. Should I go round and try to reason with Vince?'

Leo barked, 'No!'

Camilla said, 'Better not, darling. The last time you intervened, Beverley hit *you*.'

After a while the screaming stopped, and the only sound to be heard through the wall was Vince, sobbing for his dog.

The opinion polls alarmed Jack; the Government was neck and neck with the New Cons. Just what did he have to do to lose this election? Call the electorate moronic bastards on television? Suggest the culling of girl babies? He was constantly astonished at how complacent and compliant the electorate were. Sometimes he wondered if those bastards at Porton Down were slipping something into the water supply, but there was nobody he could ask because there was nobody he could trust. He couldn't even discuss his thoughts with his wife.

As Jack went through the motions of electioneering, Caroline was constantly at his side wearing an ever-changing collection of outfits and smiling as they alighted from cars, coaches, helicopters and trains. The press and public seemed to like her, and the public mistook his bad temper and manner for bluff honesty. They applauded Jack's increasingly taciturn behaviour, his rudeness to journalists.

When he warned a local television audience during an otherwise unremarkable speech in a leisure centre hall in Grimsby that if re-elected, he would raise the basic level of income tax to fifty per cent, saying, 'If you want excellent public services, you'll have to pay for 'em,' the audience applauded and gave him a standing ovation of three minutes and fifteen seconds. He had left the platform scowling and shaking his fist, but, as ever, his belligerence was interpreted as passion.

A leader in *The Times* said: 'Mr Barker has expressed some unpalatable truths about taxation. We may not want to hear them, but we ignore such fiscal realities at our peril.' Reading the press the next day, Jack was reminded of a book by Samuel Butler he had once read, *Erewhon*, in which the world was turned upside down and inside out, convicted criminals were treated in hospitals, the sick were sent to prison.

He hardly slept and appeared at the morning press conferences pale and hollow-eyed; he ate very little and lost weight; he let his hair grow and stopped shaving as meticulously as he had previously. One day he left

Number Ten wearing an old pair of hipster jeans and a denim shirt. He became a cult figure in France, where he was called 'Le bloke anglais'. The readers of *Heat* voted him the sexiest man in politics; even his wife began to find him attractive again.

He ignored his advisers and speechwriters and made short, off-the-cuff speeches that were frequently interrupted by wild cheering and applause. He debated with the audiences who flocked to see him. Sometimes he was fantastically indiscreet, confiding to a meeting in Hull that he missed Pat, his first wife. Caroline, sitting behind him on the stage, had no time in which to arrange her face; photographs of her angry expression appeared on most front pages the next morning.

Pat was interviewed by Jenni Murray on *Woman's Hour* and confessed that she still cared for the Prime Minister.

'I didn't want to divorce him,' Pat said in a choked voice, 'but I didn't want to stand in his way. He couldn't help falling in love with somebody else.'

Jenni Murray said, sounding as though she wanted to give Pat a good shake, 'Well, thank you, Pat Barker. Coming up next, women saxophonists, why are there so few?'

50

It was Roy Hattersley's dog, Buster, famous among dogs as a wit and author, who was credited with starting the civil disobedience movement that swept through the canine population of England like a fire through a hayfield. At first, unofficial meetings were held in parks, recreation grounds and inner-city alleyways. A few of the more neurotic dogs volunteered for suicide missions, but were told by their pack leaders that martyrdom would not be necessary.

At twilight, the dogs of the Flowers Exclusion Zone met by arrangement inside the walls and padlocked gates of the long-abandoned adventure playground. Earlier in the day, a little terrier called Eddie had tunnelled an entrance sufficiently deep to allow Rocky, the tallest dog on the estate, to pass through.

Micky Toby looked round fondly. His eyes were bright and his tongue lolled out of his grinning face. He remembered when the playground had been full of dogs and children, before the health and safety laws had meant that dogs were banned, and children were forbidden to climb the trees or use a hammer and nails to knock up a rudimentary den. A risk assessment form had to be filled in before a child was allowed to play. Soon the children had stopped coming and the playground was closed.

A truce had been called between the mongrels and the pedigrees, and individuals from both classes were intermingled in the crowd. Harris, flanked by body-guards Spike and Rocky, jumped up on a rotting climbing frame and barked for attention. A golden retriever called Nelson, who had been asleep in the front row, sat to attention and pricked up his ears. Other dogs ceased their conversations and waited for Harris to speak; a few puppies were cuffed into silence by their mothers.

'*Mein* fellow dogs,' Harris barked, 'We come together as dogs, regardless of breed or breeding.'

Princess Michael's dog, Zsa-Zsa, said, 'But we pedigree dogs, those of us who have been carefully and expertly bred, cannot possibly associate with mongrels. We barely speak the same language.'

Harris said, 'The anti-dog laws apply to all dogs regardless of the purity of their bloodline.'

'But,' continued Zsa-Zsa, 'a mongrel has never won Best Dog at Cruft's.'

Micky Toby barked, 'Only because we ain't allowed to enter.'

Rocky growled for silence and Harris continued, 'Many of the more intelligent breeds among you will have heard about the threat posed to our canine world by this dog-hating Government. However, the more stupid dogs, and I think you know who you are, *Dummkopf* . . .'

There was gruff laughter; several heads turned to look at the runts of litters.

'. . . and the dogs who take no interest in human

413

affairs, may not be aware of the implications of these draconian proposals. I will touch briefly on each.

'One: the Government is proposing to charge our feeders five hundred pounds annually for a licence fee, for each of us.'

Britney howled, 'That's me out on the street. The pliers woman ain't got that sorta money.'

Susan yapped, 'Quiet, you slag!'

Althorp and Carling began to play-fight and were separated by Freddie, who had appointed himself as chief steward.

'Two: only one dog is to be allowed per household.'

Leo whined, 'I'm the youngest of three. Will it be last in, first out?'

'Three: flat dwellers are barred from keeping a dog. Although . . .' Harris said, bitterly, '. . . cats will be allowed.'

There was an outbreak of angry barking at this news. After they had quietened down, Harris resumed.

'Four: our ablutions can only take place in designated areas, which will be sited far away from human habitation.

'Five: any dog exercising its right to bark after ten o'clock in the evening will be taken to a government centre, and killed!'

An angry Dobermann snarled, 'I'm a watchdog. How can I do my job if I can't bark in the night?'

There was sustained and angry barking, which only stopped when Rocky and Spike called for order.

Harris continued, 'Our enemy is the Cromwell Party and their supporters. For now, we do nothing but watch and listen. We have spies in high places who have promised to keep us informed of any new developments. Are there any questions?'

Zsa-Zsa yelped, 'I do not have a question, but I want you all to know zat I am here under duress. I was bullied into coming here tonight by the horrid dogs of Hell Close. I am not a political animal, none of the issues you are getting yourselves excited about affect me. I am an only dog, I hardly leave my garden, and I do not bark after ten o'clock at night.'

Tosca growled, 'What about the dogs in multi-dog households? Think about our situation.'

A mongrel from the back whimpered, 'We're going to die, we're going to die.'

Some of the more sensitive dogs began to howl.

Harris barked, 'Control yourselves, we will fight back, and destroy our enemies.'

A mongrel called Scarlet, whose recent ancestor was a New Guinea singing dog, jumped gracefully on to the climbing frame and stood next to Harris. She lifted her wedge-shaped head and began to croon, and the dogs in the audience fell silent, entranced by her voice as she sang:

> *Dogs of England see the light,*
> *Leave your homes and join the fight.*
> *For too long we have slept,*
> *Always willing to accept.*
> *Now's the time to show our teeth,*
> *Hail to Harris, he's our chief.*
> *Humans, hear our battle cry,*

We will not lie down and die.
Humans, hear our battle cry,
We will not lie down and die.

At the end of the song there was wild barking; Scarlet bowed her head modestly.

Spike growled, 'Again, sing it again.'

The little dog raised her head once more and sang, louder and more confidently this time. Soon, thanks to the stirring melody and the simple lyric, even the most stupid of dogs were word perfect. Outside on the Flowers Estate, residents were alarmed when they heard the eerie howling emanating from the abandoned playground. Charles and Camilla turned the volume down on the radio and listened at the front door to the unearthly-sounding canine song.

'Darling, where are the dogs?' Charles asked Camilla.

'They haven't come home for their tea,' said Camilla. 'Should we worry?'

After the howling had stopped, Charles said, 'Listen to that.'

Camilla said, 'I can't hear anything.'

'Precisely,' said Charles. 'I can't hear a single dog barking.'

They both strained their ears, but the dogs in the playground had agreed that they would travel to their homes in silence, and under cover of darkness.

When Leo, Freddie and Tosca had scratched at their front door and been let in, Camilla said, 'You're late for your tea, darlings.'

Leo growled, 'So?'

'What have you been doing?' she asked.

Freddie snarled, 'Nothing.'

'Where have you been?' she asked.

'Nowhere,' snapped Tosca.

All three dogs walked by Charles without greeting him, and went into the kitchen.

Charles and Camilla exchanged a worried glance: why were their dogs exhibiting such coldness towards them? What had they done to deserve such treatment? For the rest of the evening the dogs preferred to keep their own company, lying together under the kitchen table. When Charles let them out into the back garden to pee, before he went to his own bed, the dogs ran to the back fence barking. The two foxes joined them and all five sang 'Dogs of England' together.

On the other side of the close, the Queen turned her television down; Harris and Susan were howling in the bedroom, where they had been since coming home late for their tea.

The Queen shouted upstairs, 'What is it, darlings? Are you hurt?'

The dogs ignored her and carried on singing until the end of the song. When the Queen went up to bed, the dogs left the bedroom without acknowledging her in any way. Without their comforting presence on the end of the bed, the Queen could not easily get to sleep. She lay awake wondering what she had done to elicit their disapproval.

Boy English and his advisers were in his office at the New Con party headquarters watching their party political broadcast, which was due to go out in a few days on all terrestrial channels simultaneously. It featured Boy's dog, Billy, for at least a quarter of the film's content. An adviser had said, as they watched the DVD, 'Can we rejig the dog digitally, turn it into a cat?'

'There's no way you can turn a Labrador retriever into a fucking moggy,' said one shirt-sleeved young man. 'Why don't you stand up for dog owners, Boy, and oppose the Government?'

Others urged Boy to steer clear of any kind of support for dogs. 'It's not as if the fuckers have a vote,' said a young woman with fashionably tangled hair.

Boy played for time, steering the discussion away from dogs and towards plans to meet the exiled Royal Family.

'The request is in,' said one of his young team, 'but I doubt if Vulcan will grant you access to them.'

'I'll play the civil liberties card,' said Boy. There was laughter from the team; they all knew that civil liberties were old school.

It was Boy's driver, Duncan, who finally made up Boy's mind regarding his position on the anti-dog legislation.

The driver conducted his conversation with Boy through the use of the rear-view mirror.

'What do you make of all this dog malarkey, Mr English?' he asked. 'How come it was all right to have a dog a few months ago, and now it ain't, and what's with all these posters?' He gestured to a billboard outside in the Euston Road, where two toy poodles appeared to be tearing a teddy bear apart. 'I bought my mum, eighty-seven she is, one of them Jack Russells, for company like. She's called it Gloria, after Gloria Hunniford. Done my old mum the world of good, it has. She dotes on that dog, takes it for a long walk twice a day, feeds it Werther's Originals. Is this what my granddad fought in the war for?'

'Did your grandfather survive the war?' asked Boy.

'Yeah, but when he came back he'd lost an arm.'

Boy muttered, 'Brave man.'

'No,' said the driver, who was a pedant of the highest order, 'he weren't brave. He moaned every bleedin' day about that missing arm, complaining he couldn't open a tin. He drove us all bleedin' mad.'

Boy asked his driver for his opinion on the Royal Family.

'I'd 'ave the Queen back termorrer,' said the driver, 'but I'd make the others work for their bleedin' living.'

When Boy was next in a radio studio, he converted the driver's opinion into more or less proper English, and was encouraged by the positive feedback from listeners who were relieved that somebody was standing up for dogs. The telephone lines were blocked with dog lovers promising Boy their votes.

When Vulcan issued him and a film crew with a visiting order for the Flowers Exclusion Zone, he was not to know that it was Jack Barker, his supposed rival, who had signed the order.

It looked to Boy as though he wouldn't need Graham after all. He was tempted to cancel Graham's last session with Rip. The bar bill at the Savoy was exorbitant and Rip was constantly on the room phone to America, clocking up even more expense.

Rip Spitzenburger was, in fact, in a TV studio in Soho, conducting a mock interview with Graham, trying to get him familiar with the type of media attention he would receive when Boy unveiled him to the public.

Rip said, 'So, I'm the interviewer, you're the interviewee. OK, so first you check your appearance: zipper up, hair smooth, no spinach on teeth. Smile even though your fucking heart is aching, smile though it's fucking breaking ... And remember, Gray, flatter the interviewer. Say "That's a very interesting question", or "I'm glad you asked me that, Rip", or whatever their goddamn name is.'

Graham seated himself on the chair opposite Rip and waited for the mock interview to begin. He had never felt so uncomfortable. He had a mouthful of newly capped teeth, his scalp still tingled from an allergic reaction to the peroxide highlights, and he was wearing the sort of clothes that homosexuals wore on television. As soon as the camera lights were switched on, Graham twisted himself in knots, rolled his eyes back and compulsively checked his flies.

Rip shouted, 'Forchrissake! Take your bloody hands away from your crotch! You look as though you're pleasuring your goddamn self!' He sighed; a week of intensive training had been for nothing.

In his role as interviewer he asked, 'Prince Graham, how did you feel when you found out you were second in line to the throne of England?'

Graham said, 'I was over the moon.'

Rip shouted, 'What did I tell you about clichés? You were not over the goddamn, mother-fucking moon!'

Graham leapt out of his chair and tore the tiny microphone from the lapel of his jacket.

He said imperiously, 'I am the future King of England. You will not speak to me with such disrespect. My ancestors were conquering the world when yours were eating their own kith and kin.'

Later, after Graham had left the studio, Rip blamed himself. He had tried to put Graham at ease by telling him about the Spitzenburgers' humble origins in Estonia, and about the Great Freeze in the winter of 1795 when the Spitzenburgers had been forced to eat a fat aunt before the Great Thaw.

Graham ran from the building in Wardour Street and was swallowed up by the crowds of workers and tourists jostling for pavement space. He was sick of being circumspect about his true birth parents. Why should he be used as a political pawn? Why didn't he take his life in his own hands and tell the world that, one day, he would be the King of England? The thought excited him; he sat at a pavement café in Old Compton Street and ordered a 'milky coffee'.

The waiter said, in an over-familiar tone that Graham didn't care for, 'Milky coffee? How delightfully retro.'

As he sipped his coffee, Graham noticed that many of the men passing on the pavement were blatantly what his adoptive father had called 'of the other persuasion'. When a young man wearing mascara asked if he could join him, Graham left the café and hailed a black cab, telling the driver to take him to the offices of the *Daily Telegraph*, the newspaper his adoptive father had read. He knew he could trust the *Daily Telegraph*; it supported the monarchy and the English institutions. He was confident that the editor would give him a sympathetic hearing.

Graham had never been to Canary Wharf before. A lesser man might have been intimidated by the towering buildings and acres of reflective glass, but Graham strode into the building housing the *Daily Telegraph* like the king he would one day be. After telling the receptionist that he had the story of the century, an editorial assistant, India Knightly, came down in the lift to speak to him. She was a languid, well-spoken girl who didn't blink when Graham informed her in a whisper that he was the love child of Prince Charles and Camilla Parker Bowles.

'Really,' she drawled. Only last week she had listened to a woman who had claimed to be the Pope's current mistress.

Graham said, 'Yes, really. I have the papers to prove it.'

'May I see them?' India was bored with having to deal with the nutters who seemed to haunt newspaper offices. She wanted her own column where she could write about the amusing things her cats did and how infuriating it was to choose a squeaky trolley in the supermarket.

When Graham told her that the papers proving he was the future King of England were at home in Ruislip, India signalled to the two security men lounging against the reception desk, and they each took one of Graham's arms and steered him towards the door. He should, of course, have left it at that and gone home on the tube to Ruislip, but consumed by a need to claim his true identity, he shouted, 'I am your future king. Unhand me!' The ensuing struggle resulted in a damaged potted palm, a splintered glass coffee table and an alarming and illegal amount of arterial blood.

When Miranda returned to Boy's election campaign headquarters and confessed that Graham was on the loose, somewhere in London, Boy shrugged it off. The latest opinion poll had just been published and showed that only twelve per cent of voters cared about the monarchy. However, sixty-seven per cent had strong opinions about dogs.

At the end of *Front Row* on Radio Four, Gin began to worry; Tonic needed his insulin.

'It's infuriating that we are so dependent on humans,' yapped Gin, as he prowled in front of the fridge where the insulin was kept.

Tonic barked, 'If only we had fingers, Gin. Think how our lives would be transformed.'

They looked at their paws in disgust.

When the cuckoo in the clock had ratcheted out of its nest twelve times and Graham was still not home, Tonic crawled into his basket, whining, 'He won't come now, he's never out after midnight.'

Both dogs were hungry and thirsty and needed to relieve themselves. Gin made many valiant attempts to jump up to the sink to a slowly dripping tap, but his age and his small stature meant that he could only watch as each precious drop of water dripped into the sink. After peeing in a corner, he went to lie alongside Tonic and talked of their lives together, stressing the happy times they'd had when Mr and Mrs Cracknall had been alive.

In the morning, Gin awoke to a terrible silence. There was no sound of Graham preparing for work, no sound of Tonic's asthmatic breathing. There was only the slow drip of water hitting the sink.

52

Jack Barker was reading the early editions of the newspapers in bed; it was still dark outside. He laughed quietly to himself when he saw the front page of the *Sun*. The huge black headline read:

GOD COULD BE DOG CLAIMS TOP CLERIC
See page three

Jack turned to page three, and after glancing at a photograph of a bare-breasted adolescent, a Ms Candy Barre from Ludlow, he read:

> The Archbishop of Canterbury shocked fellow clerics today when he announced from the pulpit, 'God was almost certainly not a man or even a woman, but could be a dog.'
>
> The bearded, sandal-wearing, holy man who is head honcho of the Church of England, made his shock claim at a service to celebrate the bravery of animals in both world wars.
>
> After congratulating pigeons, who carried messages from the front line, and horses, who pulled the heavy artillery, he lavished most of his praise on dogs, who, as well as showing bravery in many capacities, were vital in

keeping up the country's morale and providing comfort to the bereaved.

The lentil-eating cleric shocked worshippers by suggesting that God could be manifested in the form of a dog.

When he said, 'After all, God is only dog spelt backwards,' a member of the congregation stormed towards the pulpit, shouting, 'How dare you use that tired old cliché in God's house!'

The agitator was wrestled down the aisle by Cathedral Security Staff and was later arrested and charged with 'causing upset in a public place'.

Jack studied Candy Barre's pneumatic breasts more closely, and was interested to read that she enjoyed water sports.

The 'God could be dog' piece was featured in every newspaper. The Peter Simple column in the *Daily Telegraph* was of the opinion that God was probably a St Bernard. Whereas a columnist in the *Guardian* suggested that God was almost certainly a bitch. The cartoon on the front of *The Times* showed a golden Labrador sitting on a cloud, looking down to earth. Jack didn't laugh; the archbishop was obviously trying to subvert the dog terror laws. Jack thought, who will rid me of this pesky priest?

Now that did make him laugh.

Lawrence Krill was delighted when The Bastard King of England, as the attendants called him, was introduced to King George III ward. He wasted no time in informing Graham that he, Lawrence Krill, had in his possession the lost English crown.

Graham sat on his bed muttering, 'I am the future King of England,' to himself.

A kind nurse gave Graham his medication, which he swallowed obediently.

'Of course, you're the future King of England,' she said soothingly. In her experience it was better to agree with the poor souls.

Lawrence Krill rummaged in his bedside locker and brought out a cardboard crown he had made in occupational therapy. Lawrence had decorated it with stuck-on jewels made from the cellophane wrappers of Quality Street toffees. It wasn't the coronation that he had expected, but as Krill lifted the crown and placed it on Graham's head, he could not help but feel that he was a man apart. A purple toffee wrapper dislodged itself from the crown and floated to the floor. Sunlight shone through the barred windows on to King Graham and his only loyal subject.

The little copse of trees on the green in the centre of Hell Close had been cut down in the middle of the night. Camilla had thought she'd heard a chainsaw, but being in that state between dreaming and wakefulness had, after a few minutes, gone back to sleep. As soon as she drew open the bedroom curtains in the morning, she noticed that the trees were gone, leaving only pale ground-level stumps as a reminder. Without the softening trees, Hell Close looked bleak and raw. The dogs of Hell Close were sitting together in the spaces between the stumps. They look as though they're having a meeting, thought Camilla.

Charles came out of the bathroom and was alarmed to see Camilla crying at the window.

'The trees have gone,' she sniffed.

Charles looked out and said, 'What an unspeakable act of vandalism.'

He dressed quickly and went out on to the green. The assembled dogs watched as he kicked at the stumps.

William came to join him and said, 'When I'm king, I'll come back and plant a hundred English oaks here.'

Charles patted his son's shoulder and said, 'There isn't room for a hundred English oaks, darling. A mature oak has a tremendous span.'

William's patriotic fervour deflated, he said glumly, 'Whatever,' and bent down to stroke Althorp. 'C'mon boy,' he said, 'time for your breakfast.'

Charles was mystified as to why William said goodbye so brusquely. He put it down to lack of sleep; the lights in William and Harry's house were often blazing at three o'clock in the morning.

The remaining dogs drifted to their homes despondently. The trees had been their message posts and had provided shade in the summer; some of the dogs had enjoyed chasing the floating autumn leaves and forcing cats to climb to the upper branches.

During the rest of the morning, little knots of residents stood on the green, looking at the space where the trees had been. Only Maddo Clarke's boys were happy to see level, uncluttered ground. Four of them took their ragged jumpers off for goalposts and began to play football.

The Queen told Prince Philip about the trees when she visited him at Frank Bruno House. He made no sign that he had understood her, but Harold Bunion agreed with her that it was a crying shame. She asked Bunion if he had noticed any improvement in staffing levels.

He said, 'A lot of hoodlums have been set on to feed them that can't feed themselves.'

'Hoodlums?' asked the Queen.

'Well, teenagers,' said Bunion. 'Same thing, in't it?'

The Queen busied herself sorting her husband's laundry and tidying his bedside locker. At lunchtime a youth wearing the Sir Arthur Grice Academy uniform brought a tray of food into the room and plonked it on Bunion's bedside trolley.

'Do you require assistance with your dinner, sir?' asked the youth.

Bunion said, 'No, I can feed myself, ta very much. But do you mind telling me how much you earn, lad?'

'Oh, we don't get paid, sir. We're volunteers, working with old people as part of Sir Arthur Grice's charity, "Feed an Oldie",' said the boy.

The Queen said, 'I rather fear I've been duped by Sir Arthur Grice. I hadn't expected him to exploit school-children.'

Bunion took the cover off his plate and stared dis-tastefully at a mound of glutinous rice and a greenish chicken curry.

'Foreign muck,' he said, contemptuously.

The Queen said, 'I do wish Philip would wake up. There's something I must tell him.'

'I can pass a message on,' said Bunion, who didn't like to tell the Queen that her husband would probably never speak again.

'It's too important to leave a message,' said the Queen. Then, because she had to tell somebody, and Mr Bunion had been so sympathetic of late, she said, 'At ten o'clock this morning I wrote to Jack Barker, abdicating from the throne. I am no longer the Queen of England.'

53

On the night before Election Day, Harris led the remaining Hell Close dogs under the Exclusion Zone's metal fence. They passed through the slumbering suburbs, keeping to the shadows and resisting the temptation to bark at provocative cats and the occasional human. Once they reached the dual carriageway that led to Bradgate Park, they picked up speed and were soon running in a tight pack with Harris at its head. When they had covered three miles, Harris called a halt, fearing that his little legs would collapse under him.

He gasped, 'We must find a ditch and drink.'

A retriever padded away and soon gave a low growl that a ditch had been found and that the water was potable. Harris couldn't move. His heart felt as though it would burst through his ribcage. Susan panted behind him; none of the dogs were used to running such a distance without stopping. Only the greyhound seemed to be enjoying himself.

After a while, Harris walked down to the ditch and stood in the brackish water and drank. When he had slaked his thirst, he barked that they were to leave the verge of the road and cut across the fields. Their eventual destination was Beacon Hill, in the deer park. Harris set off.

Susan gasped, 'Slow down, Harris, or you'll never make it to the top of the hill.'

But Harris was exhilarated by the sight of the beacon looming ahead in the moonlight; he thought about nothing else but reaching the top. Two of the very small toy dogs – Zsa-Zsa and Fifi, a lap dancer's pet – sank into the bracken, unable to go on, but the soft-mouthed Labrador retrievers picked each toy dog up carefully by the scruff of their necks and carried them up the hill towards the summit. In the dark woods beyond, the deer collected. The cracking and splintering of the bracken had woken them and their fastidious nostrils had alerted them to the danger of dogs. When the pack reached the foot of the beacon, Harris barked a halt; the dogs lay down in a circle around him.

'Listen for humans,' ordered Harris.

The dogs cocked their ears and listened, but the only sounds were of owls hunting and nocturnal creatures moving through the undergrowth. There was not a single human voice or footfall.

'We will now climb to the top of the beacon,' said Harris.

It was a difficult ascent; the dogs scrambled over huge boulders that had been thrown about in a volcanic eruption millions of years before. When they finally reached the top it was some time before they could speak. Each dog had its tongue out, panting, though they looked at each other with bright triumphant eyes. When they recovered their breath, they began to explore the summit. Most of them took the opportunity to urinate against the base of the stone direction marker, where important cities including Moscow and New York were indicated by an arrow pointing in their direction.

Harris called the dogs to attention, saying, 'We are

here for a purpose. There are beacon hills all over England, and at the top of each beacon there is a pack of dogs. We are going to send a message that will be heard by every dog in the land.'

The dogs fell silent, waiting for the message.

After a full minute had passed, Tosca said irritably, 'Are you intending to share the message with us, or are you going to stand in the moonlight all night looking heroic, you clapped-out little ponce?'

Rocky growled, 'Keep it sweet, Tosca.' He nodded at Freddie and said, 'Respect, innit?'

Harris said, 'It's two o'clock in the morning. Most of our fellow dogs are in their homes, guarding their human feeders – yet another thankless task we perform every day of the year. The ancestors of our owners laid down their lives to secure their freedom. Are we to ignore their sacrifice?

'How much longer can we stand by and do nothing as laws are passed that prevent our owners from speaking of what they know to be true?

'English men and English women must be free to express what is in their hearts, and if they do not like what their Government is doing, they must be allowed to say so, and not be afraid of a knock on their door in the middle of the night.

'The dog terror laws must not be implemented!

'Now listen, and learn this simple rhyme. It will be barked from this beacon and be heard and repeated by the dogs on the nearest beacon, and so on until the whole of England is awoken to the sound of barking dogs.'

When the dogs of England heard the commands

issuing from the hundreds of beacons, they woke and pricked up their ears. It was a call to arms.

Destroy the ID cards of Government supporters! Chew the cards! Eat the cards! Bury the cards!

There were queues outside the polling stations on the morning of the election. Nothing had ever excited the English voters as much as the dog question. Cromwell Government supporters who were also dog owners had woken to discover that their identity cards had been torn from wallets, bags and jacket pockets in the night and chewed to pieces, rendering them useless at the polling stations, where possession of an ID card was mandatory before a vote could be cast. Some Cromwellians had the disturbing experience of seeing their cards snatched out of their hands by marauding dogs as they produced the cards to show the electoral officers.

However, it was the huge turnout in support of dogs that caused the biggest landslide in recent political history. Seasoned analysts were taken by surprise at the size of the New Con victory. Boy English was hailed as a new type of politician, one with 'emotional intelligence' and 'vision'. His first address to the nation was given, accompanied by Billy. The English voters were transfixed by the little dog's antics, as he licked his paws and groomed his sweet face. So transfixed that they failed to listen attentively to what Boy was saying: there would be an extension of the Exclusion Zones, the Government would censor the programme output of the BBC, and in future the American Secretary of

State would have a designated office at Number Ten.

Boy finished with, 'And, of course, the anti-dog legislation has already been rescinded.'

He lifted Billy and manipulated one of his paws to wave goodbye.

Jack Barker was seated at his desk in his office at Number Ten. It was ten o'clock in the morning and he had been wearing the same jeans and tee shirt for two days. He was listening to a Leonard Cohen CD; now and then he would join Cohen in a mumbled duet. He and Pat, his first wife, would make love to the sound of Leonard Cohen in the small flat they used to share. Cohen had been the soundtrack to their young lives. His second wife, Caroline, had banned him from listening to Cohen. She said his songs were 'unhealthy' and tried to interest him in her own passion – early English music played on a thing called a sackbut, or something similar. Harpsichords, anyway.

He opened the letter that had been couriered to him the day before the election, and reread the contents.

Dear Mr Barker,

I'm sure you will be pleased to hear that at 10 a.m. today, I abdicated from the throne.

I am only too well aware of the fact that you do not recognize the monarchy. However, I do.

There is a question as to who will succeed me to the throne, but this need not concern you, as I suspect you will soon no longer be Prime Minister.

*I thought it only courteous to inform you of my decision,
since we do share a history together.*

Yours sincerely,

Elizabeth

He picked up the telephone and dialled the number he knew by heart. Pat answered immediately. She was in her kitchen; he could hear their old dishwasher whining in the background.

He said, 'Pat, come and get me.'

She said, accusingly, 'You're listening to Leonard Cohen. You know the effect he has on you. Turn it off, Jack, now!'

Jack used the remote and turned the volume down, but his sense of desolation and misery remained.

He said, 'We should never have got divorced, Pat. And I should never have gone into politics.' He repeated, 'Come and get me, Pat.'

'I can't,' she said. 'I've got somebody living with me.'

Jack could not speak; Leonard Cohen groaned about death and despair. Eventually he asked, 'Who is he?'

'He's a Pyrenean mountain dog called Jack,' she said.

Jack didn't know the breed, but it sounded big.

He repeated, 'Come and fetch me, Pat.'

54

At dawn on the first Monday of the New Con Government a Chinook helicopter came out of the sky from the east and clattered over Hell Close. It hovered a few moments, then landed on the green where the trees had once been. The noise was an assault on the quiet early morning. The insistent clack-clack-clack of the propellers and the shriek of the engine woke everyone in Hell Close and brought them stumbling from their beds to look out of their windows. All of the dogs in the close were barking, alerting each other to possible danger.

When Camilla pulled back the curtains she could not at first comprehend what her eyes were telling her. What looked like a monstrous, hovering beetle sat on the green, spewing black-clad, balaclava-wearing men from a hatch in its belly. She turned to speak to Charles and saw with incredulity that he was slowly putting his dressing gown on over his pyjamas.

She shouted, 'For God's sake, Charles! Why not have a wash and shave before you come to the bloody window?'

They heard their front door being battered, then splintering. Angry voices were yelling incomprehensible instructions; heavy boots were pounding up the stairs. Charles had picked up a comb from the dressing table and was combing his hair.

Camilla said, 'The dogs have stopped barking. Where are the dogs?'

When, from her window, the Queen saw dark figures running towards Charles and Camilla's house through the blue dawn light, her first thought was that she must protect her son.

Charles was balding and wrinkled, and would soon be a grandfather, but he was still her child. She did not wait to put on her dressing gown or slippers, but ran downstairs and out into Hell Close in her cotton night-gown and bare feet. She had heard as a child whispered conversations about the fate of the Romanovs – death by firing squad. If necessary, she would offer her own life, if the assassins would spare Charles.

As she ran across the wet grass on the green, she saw Harris, Susan, Freddie, Tosca and Leo sitting at the door of the Chinook, being petted by the soldiers inside.

When the men kicked the bedroom door open, Charles was prepared for them. He had expected something like this to happen since the day he realized that his life as a Royal was entirely in the hands of the people. Without their consent, his family could not rule.

Camilla wished *she* had combed her hair when a television crew entered the bedroom and shone a bright light into her face. She was startled again when Boy English strode into the room and, after positioning himself between Charles and Camilla, said, 'I've come to set you free, Your Royal Highnesses.'

He gave a low bow and Camilla noticed that the hair

on the crown of his head had been woven into his scalp. She pulled her dressing gown around her and finger-combed her hair.

Charles said, 'Was it necessary to break our door down, Mr English? If you'd rung the bell, it would have been answered.'

This was not how Boy had imagined the liberation scenario. He had expected them to be grateful and gracious, regal at least. It was hard to imagine these two late-middle-aged people reigning over anything more important than a car boot stall.

'May we go downstairs?' asked Camilla. She was conscious of their unmade bed and the puddle of knickers she'd left on the floor.

Stepping over the splintered bedroom door, Charles, Camilla and Boy went downstairs and into the sitting room, followed by the film crew and the soldiers.

When the Queen burst in shouting 'Charles! Charles! My darling boy!' and flung herself into her son's arms, nobody was more surprised than the Queen herself. She sobbed into his chest, 'I thought they'd come to assassinate you.' After a few moments of loud weeping, the Queen thought, I'm behaving like those Middle Eastern mothers on the news, I must pull myself together, whistle a happy tune.

When the Queen and Charles had finally prised themselves apart and had dried their eyes and blown their noses with the squares of lavatory paper that Camilla handed them, they sat down on the sofa with Camilla and listened to what Boy had to say.

'Your Majesty,' he said, bowing to the Queen.

She said, 'I'll have to stop you there, Prime Minister. I am no longer the Queen, I abdicated my position yesterday. I am now the King's mother, and I do not wish to return to public life. My husband is not well enough to be moved, so I shall be staying in Hell Close until . . . he no longer needs me.'

She took Charles's hand in her own and held it tight.

After Boy's face had been retouched with make-up, he knelt at the Royals' feet and, as the TV camera closed in, removed the tags from around their ankles.

The next day, reading *The Times*, Camilla was glad she'd had a pedicure. A photograph of her left foot dominated the front page.

55

The Royal Family were having afternoon tea in the ornately decorated and furnished Throne Room at Windsor Castle. Princess Chanel, visibly pregnant, was pouring Earl Grey tea from a silver teapot into exquisitely patterned china cups. King Charles and Queen Camilla, sitting side by side on ornate thrones, declined the tea; they were far too hot in their coronation robes with the ermine trim, and their crowns were both heavy and uncomfortable. The Princes William and Harry fidgeted on their gold and brocade chairs, longing for the next hour to be over. Their military uniforms were equally uncomfortable.

Princess Chanel sipped on her tea decorously. 'How about calling the baby Gucci?' she said to Prince Harry. 'Gucci would suit a boy or a girl.'

'Gucci?' said Charles, looking up from the letter he was reading.

'I like it,' said Harry. 'It's sick!'

'No, Harry, it's ridiculous!' said Charles. 'I will not have a grandchild called Gucci.'

Camilla adjusted her crown and sighed; there was always a little tension immediately before the double doors at the end of the room were opened. Charles reread the letter that had been forwarded, together with a note from Dwayne Lockhart telling him that he and Paris were reading *War and Peace* together.

King George III Ward
Rampton Hospital

To The Prince of Wales
16, Hell Close
Flowers Exclusion Zone

Dear Mother and Father,

I am the victim of a terrible injustice. Imprisoned in a hospital for the criminally insane, for a crime I did not intend to commit.

I have always maintained that glass coffee tables should be banned. Perhaps now the authorities will pay heed to my expertise and experience.

I continually scream, shout and inform the psychiatrists, doctors and nurses in here that I am of royal birth, and one day will be the King of England. But to no avail.

Will you please visit me as soon as possible, bringing my authentication papers with you? They are in the bureau drawer in the lounge of the bungalow.

I urge you to act in haste.

Please give my regards to my mother, Camilla, Countess of Cornwall.

Yours, your son

Prince Graham of Ruislip

'Anything interesting, darling?' asked Camilla.

'No,' said Charles. 'It's of no interest whatsoever.'

He tore the letter into tiny pieces and stuffed them into the pocket of his white, satin breeches.

When the first notes of a fanfare sounded, the Royal Family braced themselves and the public were let in. A bossy uniformed woman from Royal Heritage Ltd shouted, 'Please do not feed or touch the exhibits, or attempt to engage them in conversation. And *please* keep to the public side of the rope.'

Camilla found it hard to make small talk to her family in front of a constantly changing audience of gawping tourists, but it was only for an hour on weekdays and two at the weekend. The rest of the time was, more or less, their own. Mr English, the Prime Minister, had been terribly kind to them, really. And she was sure that he was right when he explained that everything, even the monarchy, had to pay its way.

A huge Australian man in a tee shirt with the slogan 'The Dingo Done It' gripped the velvet rope and said to his wife, 'Shame to see 'em in captivity, ain't it, Darleen? They look almost human.'

The guide shouted, 'Keep moving!' and the crowd shuffled on.

SUE TOWNSEND

NUMBER TEN

Behind the doors of the most famous address in the country, all is not well.

Five years ago, Edward Clare was voted into Number Ten after a landslide election result. But things are starting to go wrong. The love has gone. The people are turning.

Leaving behind his superwoman wife Adele, Prime Minister Clare enlists the help of Jack Sprat, a policeman on the door of Number Ten, and sets out to discover what the country really thinks of him. Sneaking out of the back door incognito, they venture into the great unknown: the mean streets of Great Britain.

For the first time in years, the Prime Minister experiences everything life in his country has to offer – an English cream tea, *Who Wants To Be A Millionaire?* and the kindness of strangers – as well as having to wait for trains, getting treatment in a hospital, and remembering some of the things he'd forgotten he used to really care about …

SUE TOWNSEND

ADRIAN MOLE AND THE WEAPONS OF MASS DESTRUCTION

Adrian Mole's pen is scribbling for the twenty-first century. Working as a bookseller and living in Leicester's Rat Wharf; finding time to write letters of advice to Tim Henman and Tony Blair; locked in mortal combat with a vicious swan called Gielgud; measuring his expanding bald spot; and trying to escape the clutches of Marigold and win-over her voluptuous sister Daisy ... Adrian still yearns for a better more meaningful world.

And he's not ready to surrender his pen yet...

THE QUEEN AND I

When a Republican party wins the General Election, their first act in power is to strip the royal family of their assets and titles and send them to live on a housing estate in the Midlands.

Exchanging Buckingham Palace for a two-bedroomed semi in Hell Close (as the locals dub it), caviar for boiled eggs, servants for a social worker named Trish, the Queen and her family learn what it means to be poor among the great unwashed. But is their breeding sufficient to allow them to rise above their changed circumstance or deep down are they really just like everyone else?

SUE TOWNSEND

If you enjoyed this book, there are several ways you can read more by the same author and make sure you get the inside track on all Penguin books.

Order any of the following titles direct:

0141015888	ADRIAN MOLE AND THE WEAPONS OF MASS DESTRUCTION	£7.99
0140279415	NUMBER TEN	£6.99
0141010878	THE QUEEN AND I	£7.99
0140279407	ADRIAN MOLE: THE CAPPUCCINO YEARS	£7.99
0141010886	ADRIAN MOLE: THE WILDERNESS YEARS	£7.99
0141010851	THE TRUE CONFESSIONS OF ADRIAN MOLE	£7.99
0141010843	THE GROWING PAINS OF ADRIAN MOLE	£7.99
0141010835	THE SECRET DIARY OF ADRIAN MOLE AGED 13¾	£7.99

The Secret Diary of Adrian Mole Aged 13 ¾, The Growing Pains of Adrian Mole, The Queen and I, Adrian Mole: The Wilderness Years, Adrian Mole: The Cappuccino Years, The Public Confessions of a Middle-Aged Woman Aged 55 ¾ and *Number Ten* are all available on Penguin Audio.

Simply call Penguin c/o Bookpost on **01624 677237** and have your credit/debit card ready. Alternatively e-mail your order to **bookshop@enterprise.net**. Postage and package is free in mainland UK. Overseas customers must add £2 per book. Prices and availability subject to change without notice.

Visit www.penguin.com and find out first about forthcoming titles, read exclusive material and author interviews, and enter exciting competitions. You can also browse through thousands of Penguin books and buy online.

IT'S NEVER BEEN EASIER TO READ MORE WITH PENGUIN

Frustrated by the quality of books available at Exeter station for his journey back to London one day in 1935, Allen Lane decided to do something about it. The Penguin paperback was born that day, and with it first-class writing became available to a mass audience for the very first time. This book is a direct descendant of those original Penguins and Lane's momentous vision. What will you read next?

He just wanted a decent book to read ...

Not too much to ask, is it? It was in 1935 when Allen Lane, Managing Director of Bodley Head Publishers, stood on a platform at Exeter railway station looking for something good to read on his journey back to London. His choice was limited to popular magazines and poor-quality paperbacks – the same choice faced every day by the vast majority of readers, few of whom could afford hardbacks. Lane's disappointment and subsequent anger at the range of books generally available led him to found a company – and change the world.

'We believed in the existence in this country of a vast reading public for intelligent books at a low price, and staked everything on it'
Sir Allen Lane, 1902–1970, founder of Penguin Books

The quality paperback had arrived – and not just in bookshops. Lane was adamant that his Penguins should appear in chain stores and tobacconists, and should cost no more than a packet of cigarettes.

Reading habits (and cigarette prices) have changed since 1935, but Penguin still believes in publishing the best books for everybody to enjoy. We still believe that good design costs no more than bad design, and we still believe that quality books published passionately and responsibly make the world a better place.

So wherever you see the little bird – whether it's on a piece of prize-winning literary fiction or a celebrity autobiography, political tour de force or historical masterpiece, a serial-killer thriller, reference book, world classic or a piece of pure escapism – you can bet that it represents the very best that the genre has to offer.

Whatever you like to read – trust Penguin.

MEN

AND

GARDENS

BOOKS BY NAN FAIRBROTHER

Children in the House
Men and Gardens
The Cheerful Day
The House
New Lives, New Landscapes

MEN
AND
GARDENS

NAN
FAIRBROTHER

LYONS & BURFORD, PUBLISHERS

Library of Congress Cataloging-in-Publication Data
Fairbrother, Nan.
        Men and gardens / Nan Fairbrother.
            p.   cm.
        Originally published: London: Hogarth Press, 1956.
        Includes bibliographical references.
        ISBN 1-55821-583-2
            1. Gardening—England—History.   2. Gardens—
        England—History.   3. Gardens—England—Styles—
        History. 4. Gardening—France—History.   5. Gardens—
        France—History.   I. Title.
        SB451.36.G7F35   1997
        712'.0941—dc21   97-3020
                                                                CIP

FOREWORD

I'M NOT SURE WHY it should be so, but there seems to be a strong and definite linkage between literature and gardening. No comparable subject can boast the range of essays, books and poetry devoted to it (with the possible exception of angling, and that's another mystery). Perhaps gardeners simply like to write, or at any rate like to read about gardening. One thing is certain: You won't find anything to match it in the literature of, say, stamp collecting.

To my way of thinking, one of the choicest examples of garden writing must be Nan Fairbrother's *Men and Gardens*, which is, when you come right down to it, at least as much about the writing as it is about the gardening. Ostensibly aiming to explore *why* people have gardened, she soon has us totally engrossed in gardening history, in delicious extracts from garden writers both famous and obscure, in evocations of gardening styles from the medieval to the modern, in anecdotes and advice and occasional tough-minded opinions. It's a heady mix, as brilliant in its own way as another of my favorites, Virginia Woolf in her *Common Reader* essays—but in fact there is really nothing quite like *Men and Gardens*.

Nan Fairbrother was born into a poor working-class family in Coventry in 1913. She managed to get a good secondary education and a scholarship to the University of London, where she graduated with honors in English. Not long before the beginning of the Second World War, she married a doctor named William McKenzie, and while her husband was serving in the RAF moved to a deserted sixteenth-century farmhouse in the Vale of Aylesbury with her two small sons. They spent eight years there amid the mud and the damp (shoes would turn green with mold in a week); her first book, *Children in the House*, describes their experiences. *Men and Gardens*, first published in 1956, was her second book, and it was followed by three more: *The Cheerful Day*, an account of London life; *The House*, about building a new house in the Chiltern Hills; and *New Lives, New Landscapes*, an extremely influential examination of landscape planning and land use in an industrialized society. She died, after a long illness, in 1971.

Though she never practiced or took a formal degree in landscape design, Nan Fairbrother was an honorary associate of the prestigious Institute of Landscape Architecture, and she numbered several of Britain's best-known designers as her friends. She was clearly smitten by growing things from a very early age. As a teenager, she notes, she became deeply interested in flowers, and through them botany. "Horsetails, those shrunken flowers of the coal forests, were as fascinating to me a buried treasure, and if I could have gone to Kew to see the cyads it would have been a journey into high romance." On the evidence of *Men and Gardens*, however, it was garden design and its evolution in England and France through the centuries that really engaged her. She has a few sharp remarks to make here about the lack of real art in modern plantings ("we have no fine gardens since [the eighteenth century], nor are we likely to unless we set aside our present preoccupation with the plants rather than the garden"); horticulture definitely takes a second place in the eyes of this expert defender of the serene beauties of Versailles and Le Nôtre.

Enthusiasm for gardens—all kinds of gardens—runs through *Men and Gardens*. What makes it really exceptional, however, is Fairbrother's love for old books, a love I freely confess to sharing. In winter, she remarks, "Every gardener knows the pleasure of a pile of catalogues and a chair by the fire. But the old gardening books are an even rarer delight . . . so many different people live their lives between the two covers. There is the gardener, of course, with his earthy instructions for growing fine flowers, but there is the author, too, with his learned history of gardening since Adam . . ."

Both sorts of writers, I'm happy to say, turn up here, from Richard Surflet in the sixteenth century with his advice on getting rid of moles (no better than any other I've come across, but sometimes thought-provoking[1]) to Horace Walpole explaining that the excellence of English gardening may be laid at least in part to the fact that "there are no people as obviously mad as the English." Then there are the gardens themselves—the small walled gardens of medieval times ("All that palm beaches and Mediterranean moonlight are for modern popular romancers, their tiny enclosed gardens were for the Middle Ages"); Henry VIII's gardens at Hampton Court with their gilded "beestes" and flags on painted posts, and ponds kept filled by "labourers ladying water out of ye Temmes" at night; the French gardens of the seventeenth century (if everything but Versailles were to disappear, "we should still understand why this noble landscape was called Le Grand Siècle"); the extraordinary bizarreries of the picturesque gardeners like William Gilpin, who in his books "keeps up a steady level of high-flown absurdity." Altogether a wonderful array, with each garden belonging to its own utterly distinctive time.

Unpredictable, discursive, underpinned with wit and a general sense of delight in the subject, *Men and Gardens* is less a history of gardening than an irresistible invitation to contemplate its whole amazing range of joys, achievements, eccentricities, and obsessions. There's no heavy scholarship here; in fact some of her

---

[1]His most notable: First you catch a female mole (no instructions provided for that), put her in a deep bucket, bury the bucket to the rim, and then wait for other moles to respond to her cries for help and fall in.

historical interpretations are not only outdated but downright skewed. But I'll forgive a lot to a writer who can describe Tudor gardens as the sort "children would make for themselves to play in," or note that her sons' tree houses give her own garden "a quite astonishing air of squalor," or devote a paragraph to the seventeenth century's blind faith in grafting. If you grafted a peach tree with an almond, for example, you were supposed to get a peach with a nut instead of a stone. Match that, Luther Burbank.

—Charles Elliott, January 1997
London, England

THOSE THAT ATTEMPT THE PHILOSOPHER'S STONE,

FAILING OF THEIR END,

YET THEY DISCOVER MANY RARE THINGS

OF USE AND DELIGHT.

—John Woolridge

ACKNOWLEDGEMENTS

I should like to thank *E. P. Dutton & Co., Inc., for permission to quote passages from the Everyman Library edition of the following books:* ANGLO-SAXON POETRY, *translated by Professor R. K. Gordon; Bede's* ECCLESIASTICAL HISTORY OF THE ENGLISH NATION, *translated by John Stevens;* GUDRUN, *translated by Margaret Armour;* AUCASSIN AND NICOLETTE *and* THE LAYS OF MARIE DE FRANCE, *translated by Eugene Mason;* THE TRAVELS OF MARCO POLO. *Also Penguin Books Ltd. for permission to quote from* THE CONFESSIONS OF JEAN JACQUES ROUSSEAU *translated by J. M. Cohen, and the Clarendon Press for a passage from* ANGLO SAXON POETRY, *translated by Gavin Bone.*

I should also like to thank *the London Library, the British Museum, the Lindley Library, and Lady Barlow for allowing me to photograph books in their collections, and, above all, to thank the London Library for their unfailing help and patience with my almost complete inability ever to find the books I want. I can only say that I have never yet (as they tell me does happen) asked them to trace a book which I already had out myself.*

N.F.

CONTENTS

CHAPTER ONE

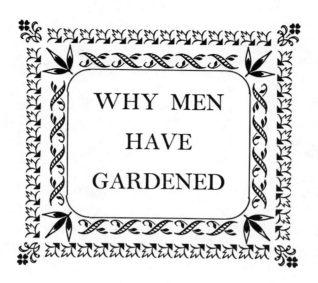

WHY MEN
HAVE
GARDENED

THE CHINESE HAVE A WISE SAYING WHICH I
once found in a book of proverbs—"If you would be happy
for a week, take a wife: if you would be happy for a month, kill
your pig: but if you would be happy all your life, plant a
garden."

It is advice which reveals a high level of civilization with a
low standard of living, but when I was a romantic young woman
it seemed to me very shocking that the pleasures of eating should
be considered four times as satisfactory as the pleasures of love.
The Chinese, I felt, were wrong. But that was because I knew
nothing about the eating. I had never known hunger as famine,
but only as appetite between meals, and people who only know
domestic cats are not really reliable judges of tigers.

Yet even in my privileged ignorance of the hungry facts of
life, even in the most flowery days as a *jeune fille en fleur*, I never
doubted the more lasting pleasures of gardening. Certainly for
the time being there were more engrossing interests than planting
roses; for a certain stretch of youth and expectancy one shuts the
garden gate behind and goes off excited down the lane on other
errands. Roses in those flowery years have no roots in earth but
only in poetry; they are charms to wear in our hair.

Yet even the most eager and romantic settings-out were more

like going off on holiday than leaving home for good. I knew I should come happily back again in the end, and I latched the garden gate carefully before I left.

If you would be happy . . .

And who would not? For all men, Pascal says, "seek happiness, all without exception; however different the paths they follow, they all seek the same goal. . . . It is the only motive of all actions of all men whatsoever, even of those who are going to be hanged." But there are less perverse ways to happiness than the gallows, and many Englishmen have felt, like the Chinese, that "Whoever understands and loves a Garden may have Content if he will." Nor is the "joy of Husbandmen a flash and so away, but it is a setled and habituall joy . . . a cleare shining beautifull affection."

If you would be happy all your life . . .

"I have never had any other desire so strong, and so like to covetousness, as that one which I have had always, that I might be master at last of a small house and large garden." Poor Abraham Cowley, who knew so well what the Chinese meant, yet still lived, he tells us, "disappointed . . . of that felicity . . . in a hired house and garden . . . without that pleasantest work of human industry, the improvement of something which we call our own."

But why have men found happiness in gardens? Why, in such different lands and different ages, have so many paths led to this green and quiet enclosure for growing plants? Certainly the pleasures of mankind are limited, there is no great variety from Adam to us or from king to beggar, but even so it is easier to see why human beings should delight in eating or sleeping or making love, in power or gold or glory, than why they should be happy labouring to make one plant grow instead of another.

For the old Christian gardeners the answer was very simple. "If we believe the Scripture," says Sir William Temple, "we must allow that God Almighty esteemed the life of a man in a garden the happiest He could give him, or else He would not have placed Adam in that of Eden." "God Almighty first planted

a garden": it is a fact they are all agreed on, but whether gardening can therefore be considered the first of the arts, there is some
argument. For surgeons too have claimed their own art as the
most ancient because of the "operation of taking the Rib from
Adam wherewith the Woman was made." However this may be,
our first parents were happy in their "sweet gard'ning labour"
until they were driven from Eden, "and no doubt Adam was exceedingly grieved to part with it," says one gardener with warm
fellow-feeling. Whether Adam and Eve gardened in the wilderness we do not know, and equally the "Advances Gard'ning
made from Adam's Expulsion to the General Deluge, is dubious,
there being little left of it." And no one, surely, could make a
more cautious statement of a profounder ignorance.

For the seventeenth century, the expulsion from Eden fully
explains man's love of gardens, just as the legend of the single
creature divided once explained the love between men and
women. We long to return to our first Paradise, and though "it
is impossible for us, Adam's Posterity" ever to make a garden as
fair as Eden, "yet doubtless, by Industry and Pains Taking in
that lovely, honest, and delightful Recreation of Planting, we
may gain some little glimmering of that lost Splendour, although
with much difficulty."

> *All Bliss*
> *Consists in this,*
> *To do as Adam did.*

Traherne's lines are the opening theme of every other gardening
book in the seventeenth century. Man is happy in a garden because God made him so, and to live in a garden is the nearest he
can reach to Paradise on earth. But Paradise means garden in
many other religions than the Christian, and we should like to
know why not only humble folk, but "Kings, Princes, and the
wisest Men of all Ages" have found their greatest content in a
small enclosure of green hedges. "The unspeakable pleasure thoroughly to declare is past my skill: and I count it as if a man
shoulde attempt to adde light to the Sunne with a candle, or num-

ber the starres." I dare say, but that gets us very little further, though it certainly inspires William Lawson to eloquence: "For it is not to be doubted: but as God hath given man things profitable: so hath He allowed him honest comfort, delight and recreation in all the works of his hands. Nay, all his labours under the Sunne without this are troubles, and vexation of minde: for what is greedy gaine without delight? but moyling, and turmoyling in slavery? But comfortable delight, with content, is the good of everything, and the patterne of heaven. And who can deny, but the principall end of an Orchard is the honest delight of one wearied with the worke of his lawfull calling? The very works in an Orchard and Garden, are better than the ease and rest of other labours."

We are delighted, yet still no more enlightened; but then he goes on to be more explicit. Gardening is the most excellent of all pleasures, he says, because it satisfies all our senses, "For whereas every other pleasure commonly fills some one of our sences, and that onely, with delight, this makes all our sences swimme in pleasure, and that with infinite varietie, ioyned with no lesse commoditie. What can your eye desire to see, your ears to hear, your mouth to take, or your nose to smell" that is not to be had in a garden?

Gardening, then, makes men happy, and it also, so the old writers assure us, makes them virtuous. "The aire and genious of gardens operat upon humane spirits towards virtue and sanctitie" —so Evelyn wrote to Sir Thomas Browne. "They doe bring to a liberall and gentlemanly minde," says Gerard, "the remembrance of honestie comliness and all kinds of virtues." This consciousness of virtue is quite clearly another source of contentment, and because all human happiness is precious, this too is to be treasured. But, like most pleasures, it needs a special kind of training before we can enjoy it: we must be brought up with a strict moral sense when we are young. And because I was brought up with no particular taboos about right and wrong, but only a vague general encouragement to common sense and kindness, Virtue and Vice have always seemed to me abstractions as unreal as the figures in morality plays. "You do whatever you like, but be sensible"—so I was always told by mild and reasonable voices as soon as I was old enough to choose, then left alone to learn by my own mistakes.

I dare say it is an excellent way to bring up young people as reasonable beings, but it has certain disadvantages later on. For one thing, we grow up without any Sense of Sin, and that is a pity. Not because we behave badly without guilt to nag us into virtue (for I have never noticed that the moralists behave either better or worse than the rest of us), but because a reasonable outlook robs us of some of the subtler forms of happiness. To me it seems just as strange that people should take a virtuous pleasure in being virtuous as that they should take a wicked pleasure in being wicked. But I can see that both are additional ways of being happy which I miss. I think if I were starting again, I should like to be threatened while young with some mild form of heaven and hell—not of course with really convincing threats, but just enough to make everyday life significant and exciting. I dare say it is one of the chief reasons why thoughtful adults turn to religion.

However, gardeners who believed that gardening was chosen by God himself to be man's greatest pleasure were comfortably convinced of their own virtue. "It is of great Consequence what sort of Entertainment and Exercise of the mind a man chooseth; for, according to that Choice, he either dignifies or dishonours his Nature. It is no small Felicity to a Man, when his Pleasure tends also to his Perfection: For most Men's Pleasures are such as debase their Natures," but virtuous pursuits raise human beings "to a very near Resemblance of the Angelick Order. . . . Natural Philosophy, Practical Mathematicks, and Gardening Operations" (we can see what the writer's own interests were) "lay a Foundation for a contemplative Genius, and produce a virtuous and useful old Age." How delighted he is with himself, and on he goes in a very ecstasy of virtue: "I little doubt, that if Angels were confined to these lower Regions, they would seek the Retirement and Pleasure of a Garden, as most agreeable to their heavenly Dispositions."

Grown-ups then, like children, enjoy being good; and gardening, so they all seem to have decided though they never really explain why, is a most virtuous occupation. "The End of this is Health, Peace, and Plenty, and the happy Prospect of Felicities more durable than any thing in these sublunary Regions." If we are to be moralists, I cannot see why growing flowers is a more virtuous way of spending time than taking opium, or any other selfish way of seeking happiness. But I can very well see that it is a more lasting pleasure, more socially acceptable, and certainly more healthy. Men seem always to have considered gardening as a moderate and healthy form of exercise, though few have been so explicit as the eighteenth-century clergyman who recommends his fellows to dig until they glow, but not until they sweat—"ad Ruborem though not ad Sudorem." And "if a man want an Appetite to his Victuals," a more homely writer tells us, "the smell of the Earth new turned up, by digging with a Spade will procure it, and if he be inclined to a Consumption it will recover him. Gentlewomen, if the ground be not too wet, may doe themselves much good by kneeling upon a Cushion and weeding. And thus both sexes might divert themselves from idlenesse, and evill Company, which often times prove the ruine of many ingenious people." Health and virtue, it seems, most happily united. And if such people consider garden labour beneath them (so he goes on, and we wonder what scorn he was smarting under), then they are wrong, "For we see that those fashions which sometimes seem ridiculous, if once taken up by the Gentry cease to be so."

Gardening will bring us long life, another gardener assures us, for "the spirits are still kept in a cheerfull temper and condition, and so work powerfully on the grosser parts of the body, conducing to Long-life." But without looking so far ahead, we might garden now for our digestion as many writers recommend, for the fruit and vegetables we grow ourselves will bring us health both in the eating ("a Table loaded with Flesh and Pudding cannot certainly be so wholesome") and in the growing, gardens "being places of divertisement after a sedentary repast, pleasant refreshments after a gross dyet, and such innocent exercises the best digestive to weak stomachs."

As for the Peace and Plenty which Switzer promises us from our gardens, they are, he says, "Select Places of Recess, where the Mind may privately exult and breathe out those Seraphick Thoughts and Strains, by which Man is known and distinguish'd as an Intelligent Being, and elevated above the common Level of Irrational Creatures." But the unfortunate prose style of the lesser eighteenth-century writers is not likely to convince us of anything, and from the many authors who tell us to retire to our gardens to recover from the *ennuis* of public life, I prefer William Lawson's heartfelt complaint: "Whither do the gods of the earth (great men) withdraw themselves from the troublesome affairs of their estate, being tired with the hearing and judging of litigious Controversies, choaken (as it were) with the close air of their sumptuous Buildings, their stomachs cloyed with variety of Banquets, their ears filled and over-burthened with tedious discoursings?" It is purely a rhetorical question, for we know the answer well enough by now: we are to slip away to our garden and close the gate fast behind us, for "This course of life about Orchards and Gardens is full of sweet rest, honest businesse, and modest pleasure. . . . It is far from covetousnesse, and even tied and married to all Offices of love and friendship. This is a quiet and pleasant life, worthy to be preferred before all honours and dignities."

Oddly enough, the garden books seldom seek to persuade us with the argument of Plenty. Our own vegetables are best, they say, fruit from our own trees will serve us all the winter, we may mingle Profit with Pleasure, but their chief interest in finances is a growing concern that our gardens shall not cost us too much in labour, an anxiety which increases with the steady increase in wages.

Yet gardeners have found some profit in their gardens besides much expense. As well as fruit and vegetables they have grown herbs for medicine, kept bees for honey, bred fish in their ponds for food on fast days or when meat was scarce, and women have made hair-dye from marigolds ("some use to make their heyre yelow with the floure of this herbe, not beinge content wyth the natural colour God hath given them"). Men—more practical perhaps, though it is difficult to know—have grown trees for timber, and I think it is Evelyn who tells us of the father who, as each of his daughters was born, planted for her a wood of trees which were felled and sold for her dowry when she came of age to marry.

But some of the possibilities of profit are much less convincing. Gardens are economical for training young farmers, so one writer urges, for "Experiments may be cheaply tried in a Garden before they are ventur'd at in the Field." Or they keep would-be emigrants from leaving England by providing much work on a small acreage—"employments here at home to keep them from stragling abroad." Nursery gardens are even more valuable, for they produce abundant food, which enables England "not only to ballance but undersell our Forreign Neighbours, to our great advantage and their detriment (which is almost equal to it)." We are no longer so frank about our foreign trade, though no doubt we are just as ruthless.

A tidy garden does not seem a very likely bait to tempt poten-tial husbands, but a Tudor writer assures us that "Herein were the olde husbandes very careful, and used always to judge that where they founde the Garden out of order, the wyfe of the house (for unto her belonged the charge thereof) was no good huswyfe." The value of gardens for "employing poor people" is constantly remembered: garden-making, says Sir William Tem-ple, "will employ many hands, and circulate much money among the poorer sort and artisans." Even the very young might benefit, for collecting dung from fields and sheep-walks is a useful em-ployment for "poor Parish children, of which there are too many." It seems a rather doubtful benefit of gardening, but Fair-child's way to improve the Mind and fill the Purse seems even more unlikely, and it would be a pity if gardeners had no more reliable incentive. "I have heard a learned Man say" (Fairchild himself feels the claim needs more convincing support than his own) "that where there was the greatest Opportunity of recreating the Spirits," (as in a garden) "the Mind was improved by that Opportunity: and that a Mind so improv'd found always the nearest Way to do Business, and fill the Purse."

Health, Wealth, and Happiness—they were the three gifts of the good fairy in the story, and they are three felicities which men have sought in gardens from the beginning. But gardeners have had other interests than health and wealth, although it may well be true, as Pascal insists so trenchantly, that no man has any other incentive than his own pleasure. Gardening, says one writer, is a "Kind of Creation," and it is a form of art which everyone, rightly or wrongly, considers to be within his talents. As with furnishing our houses, we all feel we can perfectly well lay out a garden, even though we should never presume to paint a picture or write a poem. The *Spectator* grandiloquently encourages us: "There is indeed something truly magnificent in this kind of Amusement: It gives a noble Air to several Parts of Nature: it fills the Earth with a Variety of beautiful Scenes, and has something in it like Creation." Yet fine gardens, so Bacon long ago warned us, are a rarer work of creation than fine buildings, and the gardens which we can consider as true works of art are rare indeed. But gardeners, although they may be humble by tradition, are quite confident enough to be undisturbed by the canons of fine art, which do not interest them. Gardening is a kind of creation which all will try, and if the garden created is seldom worth looking at as a deliberate design, that does not trouble our delight in the plants which are its living material. For man has a natural sympathy for the background of green life which surrounds him; all peoples have taken pleasure in trees and flowers, and the story of Eden was invented to explain a love of gardens as old as Adam.

The shapes we make for ourselves are geometrical, and the background of civilized life is more or less rectangular. Our rooms and houses are arrangements of cubes, our doors and windows, furniture and rugs, books and boxes—all their angles are right angles and all their sides are straight. Our streets and buildings are constructed of the same straight lines and flat planes, and if we use a curve, it is the exact and mathematical circle.

This geometrical setting of our urban lives has its own beauty. It can be spacious and orderly, an expression of reason in art, and

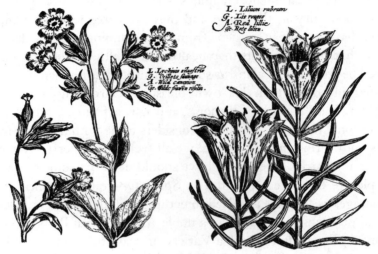

The shapes of vegetable life. Drawing by Crispin de Passe.

a fine building is intellectually satisfying in a new way which man has made for himself. But still we miss the shapes of growing things which we have lived with for a million years. We fill our rooms with flowers and plants, we set our cities with trees and green gardens, we use the shapes of vegetable life to humanize our geometric abstractions. For "God hath imprinted in the Hearts of most wise men such a Love to Plants in part as their Father Adam had in his state of Innocency."

So sailors, abroad on the empty wastes of the sea, must long for the teeming earth: upon those desolate levels must be haunted by the shapes of growing things, the shifting cover of leaves, the curved petals of flowers, the patterns of branches reaching up and out towards the light. Encircled like a hypnotized bird by the relentless horizontal ring of the sea, they must hunger for the horizons of the land, hilly and various and fringed with trees.

But I dare say sailors do not feel like that or they would stay on shore, and it was only because Coleridge was a land-lubber that his Ancient Mariner, weary of water water everywhere, thought longingly of woods in the leafy month of June.

Nor is it only that gardens are rich and various in their stuff of leaves and flowers. They change, too, from season to season. Spring and autumn are quite different compositions; summer and winter are separate ways of living. Even from day to day a garden changes while we watch, and gardening is a pleasure which custom does not stale. "Whatever else seems pleasant at first apprehension, at length becomes dull by too long acquaintance. But the pleasures of a Garden are every day renewed. A Garden is the only complete delight the world affords, ever complying with our various and mutable Minds."

The Chinese made gardens for different seasons and different times of the day—white flowers and lanterns for evening, coloured trees and ruins for autumn. They made, too, gardens which were evocations of favourite landscapes: sometimes the scene was copied in little, sometimes its atmosphere was evoked by suggestion—a dry watercourse of sand and stones to conjure up a distant river, a level stretch of sea-shore far inland. But the Chinese, and the Japanese in the same tradition, have a more delicate sensibility than ours. Their art seems to have a very particular genius for evocation—"Fallen leaves are piled against the doors," sighs a lover lamenting his dead mistress—and their most beautiful landscape paintings are stretches of suggestive space. Their gardens, too, must have depended on the inner understanding, and we should never know how to make, or even how to appreciate, a garden which suggested "the lonely precincts of a secluded mountain shrine with the red leaves of Autumn scattered about," or another which conjured up "the sweet solitude of a landscape in clouded moonlight, with a half-gloom between the trees." It is a long, enchanted way from our rose-beds and herbaceous borders and neatly mown lawns.

For the chief love of English gardeners has always been flowers: we have seldom thought of a garden as anything but a sheltered place for growing them to perfection. Roses and lilies, peonies and pansies—if flowers are gathered together in any place, then for Englishmen it is a garden. "Most men agree in taking Delight in a Garden well stocked with handsome and pleasant Flowers," and most of our gardening books are not books on how to make gardens at all, but on how to grow flowers. For it has seldom occurred to us that they are quite different things, as building a house is different from arranging the ornaments on the mantelpiece. So Englishmen have gardened to make a home for their flower favourites, for "what greater delight is there," asks Gerard in his herbal, "than to behold the earth apparelled with plants as with a robe of imbroidered worke set with orient pearles and garnished with great diversitie of rare and costly jewels?"

Not that we are alone in our flowery pleasures, for although it may be unprofitable to guess what Adam cherished in Eden, we know that the ancient Egyptians grew flowers to decorate their houses and gardens, to adorn their festivals and funerals. They grew roses, too, which they shipped to Rome, "a nation so refined and exquisite in all sorts of delicious luxury," though how they kept the flowers fresh on the long sea journey no one knows. At their banquets, so Sir Thomas Browne tells us, the Egyptians wore garlands of flowers which "had little birds upon them to peck their heads and brows, and so to keep them from sleeping at their festival compotations." Obviously formal dinners have always been just as dull, but whether Browne expects us to believe him we shall never know, for I often suspect that he is not as solemn as he sounds.

Many nations have kept gardens not only for pleasure, but to grow flowers for the adornment of festivals, both lay and religious; for to be an acceptable offering, said the Buddhists, the flowers must neither be bought nor gathered wild, but grown by one's own labour.

Nowadays it is only roses, I think, which we grow in gardens devoted to the particular beauties of a single flower, but the rose has not always been the queen of the garden. For centuries the carnation was valued beyond all other flowers; there have been gardens for tulips, for irises, for the lotus, and perfume gardens where only fragrant plants were grown. The particular treasure of Arab gardens was the date palm, which had as many uses, they said, as days of the year. And because they believed it was Allah's

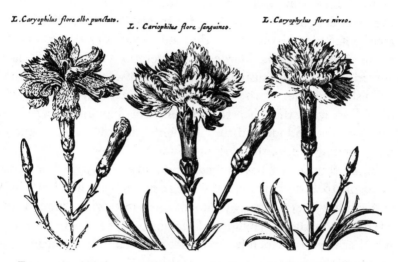

For centuries the carnation was the favourite English flower.
Drawing by Crispin de Passe.

especial gift to the faithful, they considered it their religious duty to conquer all lands where it grew, which is a somewhat fairy-tale fashion of deciding one's frontiers on the map of the world.

Another use men have made of gardens everywhere is as secluded places for open-air living. In hot countries the formal gardens and courtyards are really unroofed extensions of the house. There were green theatres in the gardens at Versailles, and even in the chancy summers of England we have lived our life out-of-doors with astonishing persistence. "A house, tho' otherwise beautifull, yet if it hath no Garden belonging to it, is more like a Prison than a House." Yet to be useful in England our gardens must have not only "places of shade to skreen you from the scorching Sun Beams," but much more important, "Canopies to preserve you from the Rain, and boxes to seclude you from the too cold Breezes." In a climate quite unsuited to meals out of doors we have invented the picnic, driven, it seems, by some deep-seated urge to eat with no roof above our heads, even though afterwards we may go straight indoors to sit. For few English people, I have noticed, can see a veranda or a balcony or any convenient corner in a garden without immediately thinking how delightful it would be for meals. "In the heat of summer, what place is fitter for the table, than some sweet shady coole Arbour in the Garden?" Generations of English have agreed with Ralph Austen, and even the Victorians, though invalidishly nervous of the morning dews, encourage us "to take breakfast with the cheerful prospect of blooming parterres, redolent with odour and flowing with rainbow colours, pleasantly smiling before the parlour-window."

In the country we have a week-end house where the bedrooms open on to little balconies just large enough to stand at night and admire the garden by moonshine; just wide enough for stretching in the morning, and leaning on the rail to consider whether the mist which lies like milk on the meadows means that by noon the day will be gloriously hot. But these are not uses which ever occur to visitors. "How delightful," they say as they step out, for no one can resist stepping out on to a balcony. "If this were my bedroom, I should have my breakfast out here every morning." It is what they always say, smiling up happily at the ceiling of blue sky. And if it were their sitting-room, then it would be tea, I suppose, that they would eat on this awkward ledge scarcely wide enough to hold a chair. I sometimes wonder if the peculiarly English meals of tea and breakfast were not specially invented because they can be carried about and eaten in unsuitable places, and if that is why other nations have never felt the need of them, since they lack our strange urge for eating without a roof, but prefer their meals in comfort round the dining-room table.

But we cannot always be eating, and what could be pleasanter than to fall asleep in a garden, lulled "by hearing the slow motion of Boughes and Leaves, by soft and gentle aires, sometimes with a kind of singing or whistling noise, which will easily induce a sweet and pleasant sleep in summer time in some close coole Arbor, or shady seat"? Or if we stay awake, we can walk and talk with our friends, praising the Wondrous Works of God as the seventeenth century did, or discussing the lime in our soil as we do now, or considering the beauties of philosophy as Cicero did, and set aside a special portico for so lofty a subject. But what happened, I wonder, when the conversation degenerated to personal gossip, as conversations do? Who decided the exact point where the company must leave the philosophical portico and seek some humbler gossipy corner of the garden?

If gardens are good places for meeting welcome friends, they are just as good for avoiding unwelcome strangers, and gardeners in all ages have felt that to shut the garden gate is to shut out the whole world. "It is not the least part of the pleasures of a Garden, to walk and refresh yourself alone apart from company that sometimes may prove burthensome to you." The first thing we notice in pictures of early gardens is how secret they are, how walled-in and private; the Tudor gardens are scarcely more open, and even in the great pleasure-grounds of the Italian Renaissance there is still a little secret garden shut away from the public walks.

The summer-house, above all, should be hidden in some secluded corner, for "the more remote it is from your house, the more private will you be from the frequent disturbances of your Family or Acquaintance." The Chinese summer-houses—if we are to believe Sir William Chambers, and it is not at all clear that we are—were secluded for quite different reasons. They were "set aside for more secret and voluptuous enjoyments," hidden pavilions where the "fairest and most accomplished concubines would meet . . . to drink their tea, to converse, bathe, and swim . . . work, romp or divert the patron with music, singing, lascivious posture-dancing, and acting plays or pantomimes; at all which they generally are very expert." Or there were "Separate

habitations, in which the ladies are privately visited by the patron, as often as he is disposed to see them, and be particular." If
the patron were especially "disposed to be particular" and the
day chanced to be hot, then he took his ladies to the Halls of the
Moon, buildings "composed of a single vaulted room, made in
the shape of a hemisphere; the concave of which is artfully
painted in imitation of the nocturnal sky, and pierced with an
infinite number of little windows, made to represent the moon
and stars, being filled with hinged glass, that admits the light in
the quantities necessary to spread over the whole interior fabric
the pleasing gloom of a fine summer's night. In these Halls of the
Moon the Chinese princes retire with their favourite women,
whenever the heat and intense light of the summer's day becomes
disagreeable to them, and here they feast, and give a loose to every sort of voluptuous pleasure."

The Chinese princes seem never to have known about the
pleasure of being virtuous, or perhaps this was their particular
form of virtue, for it all depends, of course, on one's point of
view. But English gardeners are brought up differently, and their
garden pleasures are very much staider.

Add to these Retired Leisure
That in trim gardens takes his pleasure.

Long before Milton, gardening was considered an ideal occupation for those who had retired from active life. All the books
recommend it, but none more shrewdly than the country clergyman conscious of his unreliable temper and his doubtful success
in the Town: "Happy surely they who find Satisfaction in those
innocent Pleasures, instead of disturbing the World of their
Neighbours, when they cannot be quiet themselves tho' no body
hurts them. The Evening of Life is thus, to be sure, most wisely
and agreeably spent. When the Decline of Nature tends to pe-
vishness and a froward Weakness, and we cannot so firmly bear
the Frowns of Fortune, the Ingratitude of a Friend, the Malice
and Treachery of an Enemy, then to step aside, as it were, out of
the World, a little before our Time, and give such a decent Turn

to our Thoughts, as may hide the Weaknesses of human Nature, and at the same Time recreate our Minds with innocent and advantageous Pleasures, hath always been, and must always be, accounted Wisdom.

"It must be owned indeed that the Town hath its Pleasures as well as the Countrey . . . but how alluring soever the Pleasures of the Town may seem to us, whilst Health and Strength and the Gaieties of Youth last; yet considering the Difficulties and Dangers . . . which tend to mar all those Delights; we shall be inclined to declare in Favour of the innocent Simplicity of a Countrey-Life."

Thomas Fairchild was successful enough in the town, a prosperous eighteenth-century London gardener, but he, too, found that most men retire to the country. "The Books I have read, and the Conversation I have had with a great Number of the Trading Part of Mankind, inform me, that all the Care, Labour, and Industry of Men of Business tend to lead them in their latter Days into Quiet and Ease, as well as to provide Fortunes for their Families." And in this Quiet and Ease their main delight is gardening. Yet it is no use, says Fairchild, to imagine that we can turn at once from Affairs to Gardens: even in their city life men must learn "to delight themselves in Gardening, tho' they have never so little Room, and prepare their Understanding to enjoy the Country, when their Trade and Industry has given them Riches enough to retire from Business." Therefore the design of his book, he says, is "to instruct the Inhabitants of the City, how they may arrive at the Knowledge of managing and delighting in those Gardens, which their present Industry leads them to retire to, when their Business has given them sufficient Fortunes to leave off Trade."

Switzer, who has an unfortunate eighteenth-century style of writing in what he would call Seraphick Strains, tells us that in a garden we can prepare not only for retirement but for heaven. "The Soul is elevated to unlimited Heights above, and modell'd and prepar'd for the sweet Reception and happy Enjoyment of Felicities, the durablest as well as happiest that Omniscience has created." Other races have retired to gardens even more thoroughly, for the great Moghuls made gardens in their lifetime to be buried in at death. The Taj Mahal is a tomb garden, and so, I suppose, are our cemeteries. Nor, says Switzer, is there any more suitable place to die in, for in what more innocent Employ could "wise and intelligent Persons be found, when Death, that King of Terrors, shall close their Eyes, and they themselves be obliged to bid an eternal Farewel to these and all other sublunary Pleasures"?

Men have even sought immortality in their gardening, for it is "more beneficial to Posterity than any other Study or Employ whatsoever." "Trees and Vegetables have perpetuated some names longer and better than a pedigree of numerous offspring," and because they gave their names to flowers, great men have been remembered when their other fame is forgotten; and "Many of the ancients," says Sir Thomas Browne, "do poorly live in the single names of vegetables." Ladies especially, says Switzer, who is delightfully and absurdly fulsome about the Fair Sex, may make themselves everlastingly remembered by the simplest garden labour. "When Men are observ'd to busie themselves in this diverting and useful Employ, 'tis no more than what is from them expected; but when by the Fair and Delicate Sex, it has something in it that looks supernatural, something so much above the trifling Amusements of Ladies, that it is apt to fill the Minds of the Virtuous with Admiration . . . while these illustrious Heroins shine with unusual Splendor, and by their Actions perpetuate their Memories to the latest Date of Time."

Religion has planted many gardens, and not only the more or less useful ones which provided flowers. Frazer's *Golden Bough* pursues the sacredness of trees further back than any gardener need follow, and even the slightest of Latin scholars cannot help knowing that the Classical Ages treasured sacred groves. So did religions as different as the Egyptian, the Druidic, and the Chinese, for tree-worship seems a natural reverence in human beings. The followers of Zoroaster held a comfortable faith that gardeners went to heaven, and so, said the Buddhists, did their gardens, for "Herbs and trees, stones and rocks shall all enter into Nirvana." The Greeks made Adonis Gardens, pots of short-lived plants whose withering symbolized Adonis' death, but that can scarcely be why we now plant the elegant blue agapanthus in tubs for the summer. The Chinese considered that the cultured man must be skilled in seven arts, one of which was growing flowers. The Japanese made Tea Gardens of an exact perfection, where they met for the Tea Ceremony, an austere ritual which sought virtue in simplicity, through "the admiration of the beautiful in the sordid facts of everyday life." The Romans, so one writer tells us, set a religious value on myrtle for an even stranger reason: because "The sweet savour thereof when burn'd, became an atonement for the offence the Romans had committed in ravishing the Sabine Virgins. And the sacred branches were sufficient to purify them from so venial a sin. In memory of which offence and satisfaction the Romans erected a Temple dedicated to Venus Cloacina, the Goddess of such pleasures and Patroness of the innocent Myrtle."

But without considering any doubtful metaphysical virtues which gardening may have, there is a general feeling among the English writers that it is an excellent occupation for keeping idle hands out of mischief. "These Innocent Pleasures will both improve our Understanding and better our Morals. The Temptations to Vice are always taken off in Proportion to the Employments of those Minutes which are by many spent in Idleness." It was perhaps for the same reason that the Cistercians used gardening as a gentlemanly form of exercise, and it is certainly to keep idle tongues out of mischief that Laurence recommends flower-growing for ladies: "I flatter myself the Ladies would soon think that their vacant Hours in the Culture of the Flower-Garden, would be more innocently spent and with greater Satisfaction than the common Talk over a Tea-Table, where Envy and Detraction so commonly preside."

Humphrey Repton has an ingenious plan for using a garden to improve workhouse morals. The garden should be to the south

of the building, he says, and to the north a square yard surrounded by "bedrooms for the paupers." "The difference betwixt the cold darksome gloom of the north quadrangle, and the
warm cheerful appearance of the site towards the South may
easily be imagined; and suggest the idea of taking great advantages of the contrast.

"Let the back-yard be considered as a sort of punishment for
misbehaviour and refractory conduct, where, shut up between
four buildings nothing can be seen to enliven the prospect: while,
on the contrary, from the south terrace, cheered by the sun, the
view of the country will be delightful, since the immediate foreground consists of a garden." And he draws us a picture of the
South-side Virtuous enjoying the sun under the kindly gaze of
ladies in a neighbouring garden, who (being English) are taking
tea on the lawn. Nor does he forget the children, and "as the
reward of good conduct" he thinks they might be "supplied with
spades, and hoes, and tools, proportionate to their strength . . .
taught and exercised in the cultivation of the garden, and perhaps
drilled to become the future defenders of their country." We
wonder what task the poor little things were given for *bad* conduct. Yet Repton was a kindly man and lived from choice in a
cottage on a country street, for he loved "the cheerful village,
the high road, and that constant moving scene, which I would
not exchange for any of the lonely parks that I have improved
for others."

The Romans wrote out moral maxims in box-edging, a practice
Repton never suggests, and one unlikely to further either good
conduct or good gardening. They also encouraged gardens
among the peoples they subdued, for "it was always a Maxim of
Policy amongst them to amuse the People they conquored by
this means." For gardens are "naturally apt to fill the mind with
calmness and tranquility" and many writers feel them to be the
ideal place for working off bad temper. "What an influence they
have upon the passions of the mind, reducing a discomposed
fancy to a more sedate temper!" Or, as another says more
bluntly: "If my Dame be a little out of Humour, our Farmer

may find no less Diversion in his Garden than if he went a Mile or two to an Alehouse, and made the Breach wider."

"Adam had knowledge in simples," so one writer tells us, and certainly later men have made botanical gardens to study plants. They have made rock-gardens to satisfy their delight in small things—the "wee plants" which Farrer loved—and nostalgic gar-

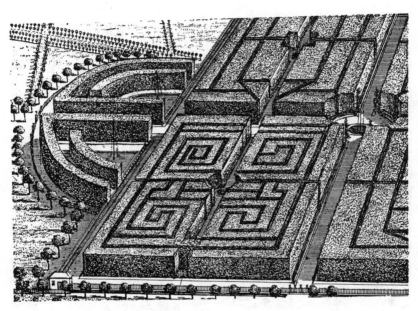

The labyrinth at Badminton.
A maze was similar but with low hedges.

dens to remind them of their native land because they were homesick. For it is not only the English who grow their western flowers in India; the Moghuls, too, were strangers from the Persian mountains, and made themselves reminiscent waterfalls in the flat gardens of the Indian plain. The Hanging Gardens of Babylon, so the story says, were built by Nebuchadnezzar to please his wife, a girl from the hills who sighed for home. They covered three acres of ground in the city, and were planted on sixteen-foot-wide terraces supported by arches whose four-foot-square pillars were hollow and full of soil so that trees could root through them.

Games have always had their place in gardens—mazes and labyrinths, archery and bowls, tennis and croquet—and gardeners have delighted in elaborate tricks and practical jokes. Surprise fountains have been popular at least since the Romans, for the younger Pliny had a trick bench which shot out water when it was sat upon. He also had a marble pool where supper was served

Playing paille-maille or pell-mell in Saint James's Park.

with dishes floating on the water. The Greeks made grottoes, though we think of them as an eighteenth-century folly; zoos and aviaries have always had their place in gardens; and topiary has been in and out of fashion ever since the Egyptians.

One of the more unlikely reasons for gardening is to have subjects of polite conversation at dinner, but "if one considers how difficult and dangerous a thing Conversation is now become," as one gardener complains, then it is not so unreasonable. Politics, he says, are dangerous, religion is unprofitable (he was a clergyman himself), and "to talk of the Weather is low mean and peasantly." Which is a nicety of etiquette I must try to remember when I next go out to dine. I will ignore both droughts and floods and talk instead of gardens, for without them "we who take delight in Flowers, should in some Measure be depriv'd of the benefit of human Conversation. How much Acquaintance doth their Rarity not afford to knowing Artists? How many pleasant Visits? How many friendly Conversations? And how many solid Reasonings? Certainly it is the sweetest Life of the World, and a very pleasant Entertainment to our Thoughts, to imploy them thus in the Contemplation of Flowers."

Even in the winter we can contrive our flowery Contemplation, for every gardener knows the pleasure of a pile of catalogues and a chair by the fire. But the old gardening books are an even rarer delight, and we soon grow fondly familiar with their vivid style and sunshiny preoccupations, their artful dedications, the long *s*'s and haphazard spelling, the smell, the parchment-coloured paper, the rubbed leather bindings ("they make a fine Sett in the Study"), and, above all, the careful ingenuous drawings of flowers and garden plans and Useful Inventions. To open one at the elaborate title page is as vivid a pleasure as opening a new garden gate. And so many different people live their lives between the two covers. There is the gardener, of course, with his earthy instructions for growing fine flowers, but there is the author, too, with his learned history of gardening since Adam. For though they are both the same person, they combine as uneasily as landscape pictures where the figures are painted by someone else because, as the children say, "I really *can't* draw people." Then there is the printer, who clearly regards the book as his own creation just as much as the writer's. It is not only the title page, with its astonishing variety of different types like a printer's advertisement, and the words alternately in red and black ink. It is not only the initials which begin each chapter, with their patterns of cherubs and birds and even of rabbits. But if we look closely at the decorations at the ends of chapters, they are not simply flowers, as we might suppose; there is a figure, too, and it is not Flora, not even Priapus, that shameless god of gardens, but the printer's own hero, Caxton, THE INVENTOR OF

The title page of a seventeenth-century garden book.

PRINTING. We can just make out the words on the laurel wreath which encircles his bust.

But of all the uses men have made of gardens, none is more original than that of the Old Man of the Mountains, an unscrupu-

lous rascal who planted a garden to recruit soldiers for his body-
guard. Marco Polo tells the story.

"In a beautiful valley enclosed between two lofty mountains,
he had formed a luxurious garden, stored with every delicious
fruit and every fragrant shrub that could be procured. Palaces of
various sizes and forms were erected in different parts of the
grounds, ornamented with works of gold, with paintings, and
with furniture of rich silks. By means of small conduits contrived
in these buildings, streams of wine, milk, honey, and some of pure
water, were seen to flow in every direction. The inhabitants of
these palaces were elegant and beautiful damsels, accomplished
in the arts of singing, playing upon all sorts of musical instru-
ments, dancing, and especially those of dalliance and amorous
allurement. Clothed in rich dresses they were seen continually
sporting and amusing themselves in the garden and pavilions, their
female guardians being confined within doors and never suffered
to appear. The object which the chief had in view in forming a
garden of this fascinating kind, was this: that Mahomet having
promised to those who should obey his will the enjoyments of
Paradise, where every species of sensual gratification should be
found, in the society of beautiful nymphs, he was desirous of its
being understood by his followers that he also was a prophet and
compeer of Mahomet, and had the power of admitting to Paradise such as he should choose to favour. . . . At his court this
chief entertained a number of youths, from the age of twelve to
twenty years, selected from the inhabitants of the surrounding
mountains, who showed a disposition for martial exercises, and
appeared to possess the quality of daring courage. To them he
was in the daily practice of discoursing on the subject of the
paradise announced by the prophet, and of his own power of
granting admission; and at certain times he caused opium to be
administered to ten or a dozen of the youths; and when half dead
with sleep he had them conveyed to the several apartments of the
palaces in the garden. Upon awakening from the state of leth-
argy, their senses were struck with all the delightful objects that

have been described, and each perceived himself surrounded by lovely damsels, singing, playing, and attracting his regards by the most fascinating caresses, serving him also with delicate viands and exquisite wines; until intoxicated with excess of enjoyment amidst actual rivulets of milk and wine, he believed himself assuredly in Paradise, and felt an unwillingness to relinquish its delights."

After four or five days the youths were again drugged and taken back to court, where they described, to the "eager curiosity and astonishment" of all hearers, the delicious garden they had left. They had been to Paradise, they said, through the favour of their chief. Yes, said the cunning old man, and so should everyone inherit Paradise who served his chief faithfully. Thus the Old Man of the Mountains recruited his famous band of Assassins, men so ruthless in killing that their name has passed even into our own Western language.

"A garden is an expression of Man in a state of Society." So one writer affirms, and it is a most interesting statement if only he had developed it, which he does not. But still we can make out for ourselves something of what he may have meant.

The irrigated gardens of hot countries are necessarily regular, but in England, where a fertile climate covers our land with green without any help from us, a gardener's task is not so much to grow the plants he wants, as to keep the unwanted plants from choking them. We weed far more than we water, and as it is no more difficult to weed an irregular garden than a regular one, and since we can turn any patch of land into a garden if we will, the gardens we make in England are not dictated by our climate, but are expressions of something in ourselves and the society we live in.

English gardens have been of three main kinds: the enclosed, the formal, and the landscape style. Within these three broad divisions there are many variations, but the three groups are none the less distinct, and they follow each other in the order given.

Why Men Have Gardened

The enclosed style includes all gardens up to the seventeenth century, for though the space inside the enclosure may be laid out in all kinds of fashions, the main essential of a garden before the seventeenth century is that it should be strictly encircled by walls and fences, moats and hedges. Once inside the garden, you are shut in—or the world is shut out: they are two ways of looking at the same fact, depending, I suppose, on how one feels. But in any case there is no understanding between the world outside and the garden within; we could live all our lives in such enclosures and never have any conception of what lay beyond our walls.

The formal garden belongs to the Renaissance, and although it has a boundary, as all gardens must for practical reasons, the enclosure is only a convenience and no longer a barrier against outside chaos. For the great formal gardens do not ignore the world: they take it and dominate it. The foreground is moulded to a logical order of the mind, the distance is explored and regulated by confident vistas open to the horizon. The greatest of these gardens were created by Le Nôtre in seventeenth-century France, and were copied everywhere in the civilized world.

The landscape garden is an English style, and depends not on subduing the natural scene to a formal intellectual pattern, but on discreetly enhancing the original character of the landscape so that it shall seem even more typical yet still completely natural. This landscape gardening belongs to the eighteenth century, since when there has been no new style, but only different varieties of degeneration, and piecemeal revivals of older fashions such as herbaceous borders and wild gardens.

If we are going to consider the three kinds of gardens as three different expressions of man as a social creature, then we shall expect to find help in the books the gardeners wrote about their creations. And so we do, but the light they shed only falls obliquely. You can tell a man by the food he eats, so a Frenchman said. Yes. Or by the clothes he wears, or the books he reads, or the gardens he makes. But although *we* may recognize all his activities as so many different expressions of his personality, he will not, unless he is very self-conscious, recognize them himself. So that the garden books are quite unconscious that besides telling us how to turn our patch of earth into a garden, they are also expressing the way their age looks at the world, the state of their society. For if they insist on walls and hedges, if their chief instruction is how to shut off a garden from the world outside, then we may surely guess that their world is neither peaceful nor self-confident. We can think of the enclosed gardens as expressing men's fear of violence and longing for peace in a society where violence was common and peace unreliable, where the law was no great protection and every man must look after himself, where the struggle to survive kept men's thoughts at home and there was little time for curiosity about the far horizon.

In England the great formal garden has as little literature as it has few examples, for Versailles is French, not English. But of all styles of gardening this least needs words to explain it, since it states its own message with superb clarity. The spacious and orderly planning, the serene vistas into the open country—these proclaim with no need of books the assurance of a society confident in its power to dominate the surrounding world by its own intellectual force.

The landscape gardens are less superb and much less straightforward. If we had never known that such gardens existed but came on one by chance during a country walk, we might not even realize that it was in any way contrived, but think it at first glance only a stretch of unexpectedly fine country left happily alone. For gardening taste in eighteenth-century England had grown weary of man's intellectual dominance. Fashion now preferred Nature untouched by Man—or seemingly untouched, for the landscape parks are as carefully arranged as any seventeenth-century garden. But to suit a taste grown tired of order and formality and the Age of Reason, gardens must seem unsubdued by man's too-dominant logic, and within easy reach of London we must feel ourselves remote in some beautiful natural wilderness.

Gardens then, like other works of art, are part of the history of ideas, but a social historian might see too in the three stages of gardens the changing material background of England, from the poor cramped life of the Middle Ages, through the confident expansion of Renaissance exploration, to the high material comfort of the eighteenth century and the early Industrial Revolution, which drove men, since we are perverse creatures and never satisfied, to a self-conscious return to Nature and the Simple Life.

A gardener and his formal garden were master and slave, a precarious relationship since slaves revolt as soon as the master slackens his hold, and the gardens ran wild. But the eighteenth-century landscape parks were a mutual compromise between man and nature, and they have therefore lasted for two centuries with little attention except the grazing of cattle. Which is just as well, for we have created no fine gardens since, nor are we likely to unless we set aside our present preoccupation with the plants rather than the garden. Repton, at the end of the landscape style, believed that the next garden fashions would come from India: "We are on the eve of some great future change in both these arts" (gardening and architecture) "in consequence of our having lately become acquainted with scenery and buildings in the interior provinces of India. The beautiful designs . . . have produced a new source of beauty, of elegance and grace, which may justly vie with the best specimens of Grecian and Gothic architecture." What we were really on the eve of in the early nineteenth century was laurels and carpet-bedding, but no one could be expected to foresee the way ahead as so very depressing.

"Gardening, as an Art of Culture, since the commencement of the present century, has made rapid progress; but, as an Art of Taste, it has been comparatively stationary." So said a critic of the nineteenth century, and his charge is even truer of our own age. Modern architecture has looked to Corbusier, not to India; but modern gardening has not yet looked anywhere at all except to the cultivators of flowers: the "Gardenesque School," as the same critic slightingly calls it, which plans a garden simply for growing plants, a style "particularly adapted for laying out the grounds of small villas." But in time, no doubt, we too shall evolve a new way of gardening to suit our new way of building, and if any of our creations survive into the twenty-first century, then our descendants can amuse themselves too in interpreting the character of our age.

CHAPTER TWO

ENCLOSED

MONASTIC

GARDENING

IN THE

DARK AGES

WHAT GARDENS THE ROMANS FOUND WHEN first they came to Britain, like the songs the Sirens sang, it is now too late to guess at. The old Celtic legends are haunted by dreams of a garden island peopled by gods, lying far out in the western ocean, and this half-possible paradise has many names: the Land of the Young, the Plain of Happiness, the Island of Avalon where King Arthur went to heal his wounds. In the early stories it is called Hy Breazil, and because the explorers who sailed west and first reached South America thought they had found at last this mythical flowery land, they gave the name of Brazil to the country they had discovered.

There are longing descriptions of this garden island where no one grows old and it is always summer:

> It is the most delightful country to be found,
> Of greatest repute under the sun;
> Trees drooping with fruit and blossom,
> And foliage growing on the tops of boughs.

A messenger sent to inspect this promised land comes back and reports quite simply: "If all Ireland were mine, I would give it up without regret to go and live in the place that I have seen."

In one of the most ethereally romantic of all legends, Gwydian and Math, mysterious figures of strange magic, use their charms and illusions to fashion a woman from flowers. "They took the blossoms of the oak, and the blossoms of the broom, and the blossoms of the meadowsweet, and produced from them a maiden, the fairest and most graceful that man ever saw." She is beautiful indeed, but proves most unreliable, though perhaps at that we should scarcely wonder, considering her background.

The Celts, then, must have loved flowers and gardens, but we shall probably never know whether the old inhabitants of Britain actually dug the solid muddy earth, and set real plants to grow on their rainy islands "beyond the limits of the then known earth," where the Roman soldiers of the first century, like the Roman missionaries five centuries later, were frightened to venture.

"The Isle of Albion is so-called from the white roses in which it abounds," but the Latin descriptions of the island are of marshes, forests, wild hills, "forlorn and swampy plains." Yet the soil "will yield all ordinary produce in plenty. It ripens slowly, but grows rapidly, the cause in each case being the same, the excessive moisture of soil and atmosphere." But there is no mention of gardening among the British, who were considered "unversed in plantation and other husbandry," and the inhabitants whom Cæsar found, lived on "milk and fleshmeat," caring nothing for vegetables. They preferred their tables loaded with meat and pudding.

Corn they certainly grew, for there is constant mention of crops and harvests in the Roman invasions, and we can still see the outlines of their little fields, ridged sometimes in terraces on the slopes of the hills. Woad, too, they may have cultivated, since it is not a wild flower in England, and since Cæsar tells us about their blue war-paint; indeed, it is one of the few scraps we all remember from our painstaking schoolday construing of the *Gallic War*. The priests, too, planted groves of trees for the worship of their gods, the sacred groves of the Druids which Tacitus mentions so disapprovingly, though whether they grew mistletoe, as we all imagine, he does not tell us.

As for the Romans themselves in Britain, Horace Walpole dismisses them as impossibly provincial. "A barbarous country, so remote from the seat of empire, and occupied by a few legions that very rarely decided any great events, is not very interesting, though one's own country." It may well be true, as he says, that "Roman remains in Britain . . . are upon a foot with what ideas we should get of Inigo Jones if somebody was to publish views of huts and houses that our officers run up at Senegal and Goree." Like Walpole, though I had not liked to say so, I also find our Roman remains sadly disappointing. After a beginning of hopeful interest we realize resignedly that we shall never come on anything to stir any imagination but the historic; that the only æsthetic pleasure we shall find is by turning our backs on the awful mosaics and considering the beauty of the site, for the Romans had a happy taste in sheltered hillsides facing south across lovely country.

Gardens are perishable creations, as every lazy gardener soon finds, and we can scarcely expect the archæologists to reconstruct them for us, but since the Romans built in Britain villas of considerable luxury, they must almost certainly have laid out round them the gardens they were used to in Italy—gardens, moreover, which would serve the double purpose of pleasing the conquerors and keeping the conquered innocently employed. Besides, these visiting Italians liked their diet varied with fruit and vegetables, which they introduced to England from the Mediterranean and called by the Latin names we still use in Anglicized forms: lettuce and radish, parsley and onions.

When the Romans left Britain in the fourth century "the foul hosts of the Picts and Scots land promptly from their coracles. . . . These two races differ in part in their manners, but they agree in their lust for blood. . . . As lambs by butchers, so are our piteous citizens rent by their foes, till their manner of sojourning might be compared to that of wild beasts." So says Gildas, a Welsh historian of the sixth century with a fine colourful taste for sensational horrors. Despairing of driving back their enemies without help, the British imprudently called in as mercenaries "those ferocious Saxons of unspeakable name, hateful to

God and men, bringing as it were wolves into the fold." Wolves who, finding the British to be poor soldiers and the land of Britain a pleasanter home than the one they had left, not surprisingly came over in force and invaded the country.

The northern tribes of the Dark Ages were energetically destructive, and with their advance the remains of Roman culture in Britain were swept away. Or so Gildas tells us—"The fire was spread from sea to sea. It destroyed the neighbouring cities and regions, and did not rest in its burning course until, having burnt up nearly the whole face of the island, it licked the Western Ocean with its red and cruel tongue. . . . All the colonies were levelled to the ground . . . all the inhabitants were slaughtered, with swords flashing and flames crackling on every side. Terrible it was to see, in the midst of the streets, tops of towers torn from their lofty fittings . . . fragments of bodies covered with clotted blood, so that they seemed as if squeezed together in some ghastly winepress. There was no burial for the dead, save in the ruins of their homes, or the bellies of beasts and birds." Even if we allow for Gildas's obvious love of bloodthirsty embellishments, it is quite clear that no one on either side had much time left for looking after the Roman gardens.

But the British were not crushed all at once. They rallied under the half-legendary Celtic King Arthur, and there was a time of comparative peace. But there is no mention of gardening in the Arthurian legend, though some of the stories have a flowery charm. There was the Bishop, for instance, who discovered the King and his knights in their retirement, and asked how he should convince people when they would not believe the wonder he had seen. He should clench his hand, said Arthur, and open it again, and as he unfurled his fingers a butterfly would flutter out. "What sort of a butterfly?" the children wanted to know, for boys of the twentieth century care more for reason than romance, but that is the wrong spirit for the Celtic stories, which often have this fanciful magic, borrowed by the Christians to make charming legends for their saints. There was Saint Scothinus, who walked across the sea as if it were dry land, but halfway over he met Saint Barra, who was sailing in a boat and was not unnaturally surprised that the sea should support a walker. Saint Scothinus explained that he only walked across the meadows. No, it was the sea, said Saint Barra and drew out a salmon to prove it. No, it was a meadow, insisted Saint Scothinus, gathering a handful of flowers, and so their argument seems to have ended.

After King Arthur the Saxon invaders were soon active again, and in a century of confused war the British were finally defeated. But this does not mean settled peace and time to garden. Gildas is dead now, and Bede takes up the story, yet even through the eyes of this gentle scholar the background looks savage enough. Certainly there is one halcyon period when "a woman with her new-born babe might walk throughout the island, from sea to sea, without receiving any harm," and the King, where he saw springs of water near the highways, "caused stakes to be fixed, with brass dishes hanging at them, for the conveniency of travellers." A little more encouragement and he might have planted public gardens round the springs, but we can feel Bede's doubt even as he tells the story. "It is reported," he qualifies, or "it is proverbially said," and in any case, this peace of municipal drinking-fountains was followed by such horrors that men could not bear to remember them and took out the dreadful year from the calendar: "It has been agreed by all who have written . . . to abolish the memory of those perfidious monarchs, and to assign that year to the reign of the following King." History is still a chronicle of war and murder and slavery and famine, and of the Plague, which first swept over Europe from Asia in the sixth century. It was an age of heroes, not of gardeners, and Milton, seeking a subject for the epic which was eventually to be *Paradise Lost*, considered, among other themes, thirty-three heroic stories from the history of Britain between the departure of the Romans and the coming of William the Conqueror. In the end he decided on "Adam Unparadized," as he calls it, because he felt the old stories were not entirely reliable history but partly myth, and a great epic must have for its subject the incontrovertible truth. It seems an odd reason now for choosing the legend of Adam and Eve.

In any case, the early Anglo-Saxons were not the stuff from which gardeners are made. Even before they invaded England they were never so happy as when they were at war. "They hate peace and can win honour more easily amid dangers. . . . They even think it feeble to win with sweat what can be won with blood," but it is only sweat which will win us our gardens. If we read the story of Beowulf hoping for anything but tales of heroes, we shall be as disappointed as Horace Walpole was with Chatterton's *Ossian*. "It tires me to death to read how many ways a warrior is like the moon, or the sun, or a rock, or a lion, or the ocean. Fingal is a brave collection of similes, and will serve all the boys at Eton and Westminster for these twenty years." It is only that *Beowulf* is the real thing, and is kept for the boys when they reach the university.

By now even the memory of Roman gardens has been lost, and their forgotten cities are mysterious ruins which stir the Anglo-Saxon invaders to wonder.

> *Curious is this stonework. The Fates destroyed it;*
> *The torn buildings falter: moulders the work of giants.*
> .   .   .   .   *Earth has the Lord-Builders;*
> *The dust holds them while a thousand*
> *Generations are ended. . . .*
> *Bright were the palaces, baths were set in the palaces;*
> [It is the ruins of Bath he is describing]
> *Till time when Fate the strong rescinded that.*
> *For then they shrank as pestilence came,*
> *Pest took their strong pride . . .*
> *And men . . . in a multitude fell down.*

It was not the Romans whom the Plague destroyed, it was the poet's own people who fell down in a multitude; but in any case, it is a gloomy subject well suited to the Anglo-Saxon spirit. For they are conscious always of death, and another elegiac poem describes what they felt to be the inevitable background of the lives of men: a dismal list of the various forms of violent death, where only one man "works out all his troubles when he is still a youth" and survives to live pleasantly in old age, though even then there is no hint that he spent his time in the trim gardens of retired leisure.

None the less, there is some evidence of gardening in a humble vegetable way among the Anglo-Saxons. They had orchards where they grew apples and pears, cherries and plums, for all these words occur in Anglo-Saxon forms; the very name *orchard* is an Anglo-Saxon word meaning an enclosure for plants. They grew some vegetables, too, particularly kale and the various sorts of onions or leeks (garlic being one), and these were grown in enclosed "yards" near the house. The Anglo-Saxon Riddles are rather tiresome puzzles in the Riddle-of-the-Sphinx style, but one about a rake was surely written by a genuine gardener: "I saw a creature in the cities of men, who feeds the cattle; it has many teeth; its beak is useful; it goes pointing downward; it plunders gently and returns home; . . . it leaves the fair herbs fixed by their roots, quietly standing in their station, gleaming brightly, blowing and growing."

They had herb-gardens, too, growing herbs both for medicine and to season the meat which was their chief food. There is a Nine Herbs Charm, a strange, jumbled mixture of pagan magic and Christian additions, telling how to make the nine herbs into a potion against a long list of infections, evil spirits, blisters, and poisons of all colours of the rainbow and points of the compass. This naturally gloomy race may also have grown flowers, either for pleasure or to provide honey for their bees, for names like *lily*, *rose*, and *poppy* are Latin words which were Anglicized in the new language. Certainly they kept bees, for they used the honey to make mead and as their only form of sugar. There is a charm which was to be chanted to a swarm of bees to keep them from flying too far before they settled, a nice balance of flattery and virtuous exhortation:

MEN & GARDENS

Alight, victorious women, descend to earth!
Never fly wild to the wood.
Be as mindful of my profit
As every man is of food and fatherland.

So important were their bees that men were kept to watch over them as a shepherd his flock, and the fine for stealing them in King Alfred's time was a hundred and twenty shillings. Just how serious this was we can tell from the fines for personal assault: "If anyone bind a churl who is innocent, he shall make compensation with 10 shillings: if he flog him, he shall pay 20 ss: if he dock his hair to insult him 10 ss: if he shave his head like a priest's, but bind him not 30 ss: if he cut off his beard 20 ss: if he bind him and then shave him like a priest 60 ss."

Besides making laws about bees and burning the traditional cakes, King Alfred was endlessly busy, as Asser tells us in his *Life*. He was clearly a most virtuous and active man, a model for all, and one of his more frivolous inventions was a clock of four candles burning six hours each. He also built what Asser calls "majestic and rich houses after his own new designs," but there is no mention that he laid out gardens round them, for Anglo-Saxon gardens were small and humble and useful, and not yet the preoccupation of kings, as they would be later on.

If we look at the Ordnance Survey map of England in the Dark Ages, we realize that the country had changed very little from the land the Romans described. Most of the chalk was clear, and the higher hill-tops, but the low-lying land was marsh and the rest forest: mile after mile of trees covering the "ill-filled mappes." Much of Surrey, Sussex, and Kent was covered by the Forest of Andred, an impenetrable tangle of hostile woodland which haunts the history of the time like a dark and mysterious threat. "The great wood which we call Andred . . . That wood is 120 miles long, or longer, from east to west, and 30 miles broad." In the forest were wolves and wild boars, its fringes sheltered outlaws and robbers, the Danes took cover there between their murderous attacks. "If a stranger travel through a wood off the path, and neither shout nor blow his horn, he may be assumed to be a thief, and as such either slain or put to ransom." It was clearly no place to loiter gathering primroses, nor to dig up roots of woodruff to take home and plant in shady corners of the garden. Are the neat villas of modern Surrey, I wonder, ever troubled by the old demons of the woods? Or does the dreadful Werewolf himself slink off across the tidy lawns, dismayed by our new magic of the same radio voice through every open window?—a spell more potent than his own eerie midnight howlings, for he could only frighten a few superstitious souls in the dark, but we have tamed the primeval forest to trim beds of standard rose-trees.

Against the savage background of the over-running of England by successive waves of invaders, and of the civil wars of rival tribes, Christianity spread slowly and fitfully, its doctrine of humility and gentleness astonishing these warlike races whose greatest pride was in pitiless courage. "It was a very difficult task," says Bede, "to incline the King's lofty mind to the humility of the way of salvation." Yet the new way did spread, first from the Irish Christians, who had never gone back to paganism when the Romans left, then from Rome itself through the new missionaries led by Augustine in the sixth century. A strange conversion it must have been, judging by the questions Augustine sends back to Rome asking advice of the Pope. May a man who has had an amorous dream, he asks, take Holy Communion? If the Anglo-Saxons had ever shown any sense of humour, we might suspect these sceptical pagan natives of thinking up unlikely questions for the pleasure of embarrassing the earnest missionary. But the questions were doubtless asked as seriously as they were answered by the Pope.

The problems were certainly awkward, and ferocious courage was a virtue of too obvious practical value for men to renounce it easily, yet the new religion spread steadily with its teaching of gentleness, and in Bede's history Christianity is a religion of humanity despite its unwholesome preoccupation with penances and chastity and the selfish saving of one's own soul. King Edwin's missionary sparrow was to become as famous as Lesbia's. "Such seemeth to me the life of men present here in earth . . . as if a sparrow, beaten with wind and weather, should chance to fly in at one door of the hall, and flitting there a little about, straightway fly out at another . . . the hall itself being then pleasant and warm with a soft fire burning amidst thereof, but all places and ways abroad troubled with tempest. . . . After the short space of this warm air, the poor bird returneth from Winter to Winter again. So the life of man appeareth here in earth . . . but what may or shall follow the same, or what hath gone before it, that surely we know not. Therefore if this new learning can inform us of any better surety, methinks it is worthy to be followed."

It is a sad, bewildered reason for changing one's gods, a settled sadness of the English spirit, which Christianity, for all its new promises, did little to comfort. Light-headed from hunger, drugged with constant prayer, the ascetic achieved at times the unlikely longed-for vision of troops of angels descending expressly from heaven to fetch his bright particular soul. But the promise of heaven was a feverish dream which faded on waking, and the honest Christian, like the honest pagan before him, realized that he knew nothing of death but the body's rotting:

> *Sharp and strong is my dying,*
> *I know not whither I must go;*
> *Foul and stinking is my rotting—*
> *On me Jesu, have you mercy.*

From Winter to Winter again—it is a sad refrain of English poetry, through the Middle Ages, and the early Tudor poets who write in language which needs no paraphrasing, until in Shakespeare it rises to a magnificent cry of despair from eloquent Renaissance man:

> *Ay, but to die, and go we know not where;*
> *To lie in cold obstruction, and to rot;*

Gardening in the Dark Ages

This sensible warm motion to become
A kneaded clod.

Like Bottom, the sparrow is wonderfully translated.

Yet despite this melancholy conviction, and against opposition more direct and bloodthirsty, the civilizing influence of Christianity spread steadily. The Danes came and slaughtered the monks of Lindisfarne, but were themselves converted; and Canute is a Christian king when he rows through the Fens past Ely and inspires the first English boating-song:

Merry sang the monks in Ely
That Cnut Cyning rowed thereby.

Scandinavia, the very home of the pagan invaders, was at last converted, and even the fierce Icelanders accepted Christ, though in a somewhat half-hearted way, insisting that if they had to be baptized in winter, then it must be in the hot springs, and still secretly praying to Thor before they set out on their perilous voyages. Indeed, the Christian teaching seems an incongruous doctrine for these astonishing merchant adventurers of the Dark Ages, who colonized Greenland and put out into the open sea of the North Atlantic, taking their bearings by the midnight sun and the change in colour of the water of the polar currents; who found that if you would reach Greenland you must "steer South of Iceland so that you have the birds and whales therefrom"; who watched for the "ice-blink," the reflection of the Greenland ice-cap above the horizon, knowing then that they would soon reach land.

Their attitude to this heroic sea-faring strikes us as surprisingly matter-of-fact. A father advises his son: "Always buy shares in good vessels or in none at all. Keep your ship attractive, for then capable men will join you." And when a party of sailors are driven off their course to reach America centuries before Columbus, making their way back to Scandinavia only with great hardship, they are criticized for not following up such a valuable discovery in a more businesslike way.

Yet even these practical heroes were taught to turn the other cheek, and they, too, listened meekly, though still perhaps unconvinced at heart, for the fierce old pagan songs could still stir men's spirits so that they forgot the new teaching, and hearing them, "Both sick and whole could think of nothing else. The beasts in the wood left off feeding, the worms in the grass, and the fishes that swim in the water, lay still to listen. . . . None wearied of his songs, or heeded the singing of the priests in the church. The bells rang less sweetly than they were wont."

The way to Saint David's Head in Pembrokeshire is along a strip of land reaching out into the Atlantic. As the road runs steadily westward the trees disappear in the bleak landscape and the stunted hedges change to turf walls, bright in spring with gorse and the pale waxy flowers of pennywort, and in summer sprinkled with tiny sheep's scabious like blue jewels, and the spikes of pennywort withered to great rusty nails between the stones. The cottages, without light or water still, huddle low against the wind: it is the only place I know where the houses shelter the trees instead of the trees making wind-breaks for the houses. For the whole land is dominated, even on the stillest summer day, by the merciless Atlantic gales.

It is not empty country. Since the people are poor and the holdings small, it is dotted with cottages, but they are each separate and remote in their struggle against poverty, set among the rounded Welsh hills, whose sweeping curves fold into each other like the interlacing patterns of Celtic art.

When at last we reach it along empty roads which seem to lead nowhere, the city of Saint David's is a village of humble houses, a conglomeration of the countryside enlivened with a quiet holiday air because of the summer visitors. And there, superbly incongruous in such a setting, from a hollow of the land which shelters it from the sea, rises the magnificent cathedral of Saint David.

We walked to it once along the coast, one day of violent storm with the wind screaming in from the sea and racing over the smooth crouched hills, a tangible and universal enemy. For even the rain here cannot fall as it does in sheltered places, steadily to earth, but is driven helpless in the tumultuous air, shattered against rocks and roofs and the walls of buildings, slanted, sharp as hailstones, blind against our faces. Every yard forward is a struggle, even to breathe is difficult, we are deaf in the gale which rushes past our ears and roars in the hollow of our mouth between our parted lips.

But once inside the cathedral, the storm is stilled to silence by the simple shutting of a door. Here the air is so calm that the flames of the candles reach upwards unmoving, so quiet that we can hear the echo of our softest footstep. And we have the strangest feeling that this enclosure of space is a different world, a treasure held in the hollow arching stones as we hold something precious in the hollow of our cupped hands. This volume of quiet air is a different element from the screaming wind outside; it is a special retentive medium rich with the beauty it has absorbed through hundreds of years: the music and the singing, the coloured light through stained-glass windows, the magnificent phrases of the Bible. Air which for so long has been moulded by the architecture of these stones holds ineradicable perspectives of order and serenity. All those centuries of beauty, we feel, are here in the stillness. The door is small and closes behind us, for this air is precious, and not to be scattered in the outside chaos of wind and rain and meaningless noise. The roof has held the singing voices; they have not been lost in the streaming gale but absorbed into the silence, as a book closed and put back on the shelf is not lost but only silent until we open it again and hear the same waiting voice. So we need only stand within the cathedral walls to feel ourselves part of its world of music and poetry and the intellectual beauty of arched and vaulted spaces, a grave quiet world where the gentle movements of man are significant and the background of his mind is peace.

Coming on it suddenly, we are overwhelmed by the difference, the impassable gulf between this church and the country we have come through. Here is the setting of a life of culture and ordered leisure; men here were not struggling to drag a wretched pittance from a grudging land, but building towers and palaces among tall trees where the rooks caw as richly as they do in sheltered inland parks. The constant singing must have floated like a strange exotic perfume over the stony fields, and the peasants in their poor huts could have had nothing in common with the churchmen who lived here, men who knew English and Latin and Greek, who could read and write, who understood music and singing, who travelled and wrote letters and could create from the stones of the wild shore this wonder of architecture. Such a community must have been an aristocracy of culture, and the surrounding countryside a barren sea dividing them from the next island, the next great abbey.

I remember the same feeling from years ago, visiting the ruined abbeys of Yorkshire on summer excursions of the school art club—Fountains and Rievaulx and Kirkstall on the edge of Leeds. They were outings which enlivened the summer terms, for we were taken, boys and girls together, in large buses which I, being old-fashioned, still like to call char-a-bancs. First we were led round the ruins, whose beauties were eloquently pointed out by a guide offering us far more information than anyone could absorb on such sunshiny holiday afternoons. Then we were left to find our own corner and sketch some chosen vista through broken arches, all in the best eighteenth-century tradition of picturesque ruins. But I would sit with idle pencil and empty drawing-pad, and think how if I had lived in those grim days, I too would have joined the Church, and accepted the religion for the peace and culture of the life it sheltered. As many did, for whatever reasons—kings and nobles besides quiet men and scholars; and in these lordly ruins we feel, as we seldom do in the defensive castles of the aristocracy, that here was the good life, the delight in the civilized pursuits of man, the peaceful routine of a gentle way of living.

Neither cathedrals nor castles belong to the true Dark Ages, but they are evidence we can see for ourselves of the superior culture of the Church in mediæval times, of a gulf between lay and religious which in the history of the Dark Ages is still more obvious.

Even in its ostentatiously austere beginnings, the monastic life implies considerable luxury. It is a high standard of living which can afford to allow an able-bodied man to spend his whole life saving his own soul. And the fasting they so boast of is suspiciously like the artificial wildernesses of the eighteenth-century gardeners. If we are to fast, there must first be food to refrain from; the poor without food do not fast, but starve simply, and thereby, it seems, win no grace. It is the case of the Egyptian in the stories of the Desert Fathers, who before he became a monk was a herdsman sleeping in the fields and living wretchedly on bread and water. "Out of much tribulation and heavy toil," he admits, "I . . . did come to rest and refreshing in the monastic life, and what I had not, I now have."

In such a setting men could sit in peace, and as Bede's translator charmingly says, "entertain one another with the delights of the celestial life." There are constant references to the culture and education of the Church, and Bede found the monastery of Jarrow a sympathetic home. He kept the discipline and services, and "the rest of my time I was delighted to learn, to teach, or to write." It says a great deal for the monastic life that a man of Bede's gifts could work happily within it. For he is one of the true scholars, and inhabits an intellectual country far beyond the limitations of his age. Though he has his foibles, of course, including a quite astonishing credulity about miracles and a constant preoccupation with the right date for keeping Easter. For whether Easter should be kept according to the different calculations of the Celtic or the Roman Church seemed to Bede the most important of doctrines. It is almost a test of saints and sinners, and it is only because Bede is a mild and tolerant man that he can forgive the wrong date even in the most virtuous. "He was a good man, but . . ." and we know what is coming —he kept Easter on the wrong date. It is his hobby-horse, and at this remote distance of time and spirit seems to us an endearing enthusiasm. Yet we read him as a modern historian, and it is only when he says of some now legendary place "the ruins can still be seen" that we realize with a sudden check of surprise that his "still" is more than a thousand years ago.

As the monasteries grew richer, the life became even pleasanter —too pleasant perhaps, for certainly it roused the envy of the less fortunate. "The monks drink the best wines which God has established. They eat bread as white as hail; of all flesh do they eat also, so that their bellies are full and stuffed and they almost burst through the middle." No doubt envy makes an unreliable witness, but we know about the monastery which received a gift of wine from the French king and sold it because the quality was not good enough for fastidious Church palates.

Nor were the monks overburdened with work, for only about a third of the community of a monastery were monks; the rest were servants and lay brothers who did the manual labour; and every anchoress, so one authority advises, should have two maids to wait on her. Young women are urged to become nuns, not at all as a penance, but because the nun's quiet day is so much pleasanter than the life of the ordinary overworked housewife. But let the anchoress beware, he warns, of the vanity of admiring her "own white hands," the "too fair" hands of idleness (it is reassuring to find how much wicked vanity we are all now safe from).

In the Dark Ages, then, the good life was in the Church, and it is in its fruitful shelter that we must look for the arts, and for the gardens which men seem always to have made for their delight as soon as they have leisure. From the beginning the Roman Church encouraged gardening—"Hoe your ground, set out cabbages and convey water to them in conduits," said Saint Jerome. Cabbages seem unambitious perhaps, but still they make a beginning. Saint Benedict advises a garden for every foundation; the Cistercians in their lonely valleys had large gardens both within and without the walls; and the Carthusians, with their rule of solitude and silence, planned a separate plot for each cell. Everywhere gardening is actively encouraged, both for men and women, until the Abbess Héloïse complains in a letter to Abélard that it is unreasonable to expect nuns to do the hard work of a garden, that women are unsuited to such manual labour. It is rather sad to find that the passionate and romantic lovers have grown so domestic.

There were many reasons for the Church's interest in gardens: they provided suitably dignified work for the monks; grew

A medicinal herb. Drawing by Crispin de Passe.

fruit and vegetables, wine and cider, herbs for medicine, and flowers for the church; and quite certainly gardens were kept simply for the universal pleasure of gardening. Whatever the reasons, the Domesday survey shows clearly that there were large and flourishing gardens belonging to many of the monasteries, and very few others besides. For to survive in such wild times a garden had to be strictly enclosed, and the only wall which was strong enough to protect it was the fear of God. The gardens belonged to the monks, who were servants of God, and if anyone destroyed their gardens, then God would punish the offenders. It is strange that human beings can be coerced by abstract ideas into doing things they have no wish to do, but in an age of faith, religious dread was a rampart round a garden stronger than any man-made wall. It was the reason why even in those violent times church gardens could be planted in the open, as lay gardens could not for centuries to come. Of course, if the enemy did not happen to share the same religious ideas as the gardeners, then the abbeys and their gardens looked what they were, defenceless, and the Danes did not hesitate to murder the monks at Lindisfarne.

What a monastery garden was like we can see fairly clearly. The first ones were surrounded by cloisters, and the enclosed space divided by cross-paths meeting in the centre at a well. The beds between the paths were planted with trees and flowers "well-nursed well-watered and lovely." This entrance court, which was also a sanctuary, was not the only garden. There is a plan of an ideal monastery in Charlemagne's time which shows the various gardens there were likely to be. Besides the cloister garden there is the physic garden with separate beds of medicinal herbs, many of them flowers; there is a large kitchen garden with plots of vegetables not very different from our own (for the names are written on the plan); and the cemetery is laid out as a pleasure orchard, with ornamental and fruit trees formally arranged between the regular graves. Often, too, there were private gardens for the high officials, and the Sacristan had his flower garden, where he grew flowers to decorate both the church and the priests who worshipped in it. One such garden was called Le Joye, a simple proof of its keeper's affection, and Paradise was a common name.

The old church at Scarborough stands on the hill which divides the two bays. We used to spend summer holidays there when I was a child, and wandering about the old lanes behind the church, I once found a little wilderness of grass and wild flowers and scrabbling hens. It was surrounded by a crumbling wall which bore the street name of PARADISE printed out in large Roman letters on an authentic metal plate, and I remember still my delighted astonishment. It was as if authority had given official support to the fairy-tales, had blessed one's airiest fancies

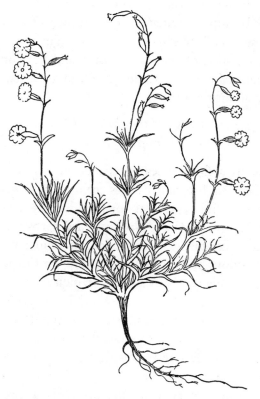

From a painting of SILENE LINIFOLIA *in the Juliana Anicia Codex of Dioscorides' Herbal,* A.D. *512. "This being beaten when it is green with old swines grease, is good for the mad-dog-bitten and the throat-swollen, but being suffited it drives away serpents."*

as sober truth. And sitting on the wall, watching the heavenly hens as they scratched for grubs among the bindweed and nettles, I wondered who had found this humble corner enchanting enough to give it so celestial a name.

This floweriness of the early Church is especially attractive in the story of Saint Rhadegonde. As a girl in the sixth century, she was taken prisoner and brought up to be her captor's queen. But she left him and became a nun at Poitiers, where "she cultivated roses and other flowers that woven into garlands or scattered on the table to form a perfumed covering, ornamented the refectory." Bishop Fortunatus, a charming epicurean scholar, was her close friend. She would entertain him at flowery meals, send him small gifts of fruit and posies, and he would compose charming verses for her in Latin, sitting in a garden arbour surrounded by admiring nuns:

> *If it were the time of lilies,*
> *Or the fragrant crimson rose . . .*

If this seems a flowery extravagance of a gayer civilization than ours, and English monasteries seem to have grown mostly herbs for physic and vegetables for food, such gardens were not as dull as we might suppose. Not only are herbs often beautiful garden plants, like tansy or rosemary, or fennel with its white sheaths and yellow flowers and delicate green thread leaves, but the monks grew many plants as herbs which we think of only as flowers: peonies and gladioli, roses and lilies, which were a sovereign cure for poisons. Many flowers, too, they boiled with honey and ate as puddings, as we still decorate our party cakes with crystallized violets and rose-petals; it always seemed to me a kind of cannibalism.

Outside the monastery were the orchards where the monks grew a fine variety of fruit and nuts, though we cannot help suspecting that some of the trees in the accounts (for there are dates and pomegranates) were copied down hopefully from Charlemagne's list. Besides the half-legendary conqueror we all know, Charlemagne was an excellent gardener. He had a private garden where he tried new plants, and he sent out lists of trees to be grown on his various well-run estates. The exotics can never have been happy in Europe, but still there are many plants which the monks knew well—apples and pears, plums and cherries, hazels and almonds, peaches and figs and mulberries.

There were vineyards too, and fishponds, which certainly provided pleasure as well as food. "They sit upon the green margin of the huge basin, they see the little fishes playing under the water, and representing a military encounter by swimming to meet each other. This water" (though it is an anti-climax after the pretty fancy of the performing fishes) "serves the double duty of supporting the fish and watering the vegetables."

LILIUM CANDIDUM, *the white lily.*

The monks' pleasure in their gardens was not always as straightforward as this ingenuous delight in fishponds. But if the more austere Christian teaching frowned on flowers as pagan frivolity, then the monks gave them symbolic meaning in the service of the Church. The white lily stood for Our Lady's chastity, they said, the red rose for the blood of the martyrs.

The four walls of the cloister garden symbolized contempt for oneself and the world, love of one's neighbour and of God. The grass always green was the greenness of a monk's virtues, a tree the ladder to the heavenly life, and so on. It is an easy enough game to play, but it seems a pity they could not read the seventeenth-century gardening books and be convinced once and for all that gardening is entirely virtuous.

In his cloister at Subiaco, Saint Benedict had a favourite garden of roses, whose thorns he took to tear his flesh when his thoughts were too preoccupied with wicked women—perhaps the band of naked dancers a jealous rival brought to perform in his cloister. We soon cease to be surprised at the saints exulting in perversions we should blush for—indeed, it is part of their charm that they have never heard of Freud—but, as a gardener, it is hard not to feel that Saint Benedict would have done better to come to his roses already satisfied, and settle down to enjoy them in a more straightforward fashion. It is rather sad to grow roses for their thorns.

But Walafred Strabo is a whole-hearted gardener. An abbot of the ninth century, he looked after his own little plot, and his verse account of the work to be done and the plants he grew is written by a gardener who wheeled his own barrow and transplanted his seedlings as lovingly as if they were children. First, he says, you must get a garden—any kind of garden. No matter whether the soil is light or heavy, the site on a hill or in a valley; as long as you work hard and are patient, harden your hands and dung your land well, you will succeed.

He has a little plot at his door, he tells us, and there in spring grows up a forest of nettles. So he takes mattock and rake and sets about the thick tangled roots twined as closely as a hurdle (for nettles, it seems, have changed their habits in the last thousand years even less than gardeners).

The nettles clear, he leaves the rough digging to sweeten in the wind and sun, then rakes it level, builds up the edges of the beds with boards, mulches it well with old manure, and sows his seeds.

Watered by the rain and dew, the little seedlings soon grow, and if there is a drought he draws up water from the well, not to sluice over them roughly but to scatter gently by hand. And if any corner of his garden is too hot or too shady, he moves his plants about until he finds a place to suit them.

Then he tells us what he grows, a list of herbs and vegetables and flowers, with a little poem in praise of each, as we might introduce our friends to strangers. He ends with the rose, but he has sung too long already, he says, to begin now on the praise

Drawing by Crispin de Passe.

of the rose and the lily, the rose for the blood of the martyrs, the lily for faith.

But we need not fear that Strabo will lead us off into the gloom of doubtful symbolism to justify his love of flowers. He is a true gardener, and his matted nettle-roots are more vivid than any pale symbolic lily. He begins his book with a charming dedication to a fellow abbot: that he should read it sitting in his garden beneath his fruit trees, in the shifting light and green shadows of a summer day. And we realize with sudden pleasure that the Dark Ages, which seemed so gloomy and unintimate and remote, were peopled, after all, with gardeners like ourselves.

CHAPTER THREE

ENCLOSED

ROMANTIC

GARDENS

OF THE

MIDDLE AGES

ABOUT THE ACTUAL GARDENS OF THE MIDDLE
Ages we know very little, but we know a great deal about
the delight people took in them. They are places not for gardening, but for pleasure, for in the Middle Ages a garden is the
natural setting for happiness. It is the atmosphere which matters,
the enchanted delight, as if the garden walls were a magic barrier
to shut out sorrow.

What we do know of mediæval gardens is not from gardeners,
but from painters and poets and writers of romances. In picture
after mediæval picture of the Virgin she sits in a garden among
the leaves and singing birds, or on a turf seat sprinkled with
flowers. In portraits, in views through windows, in scenes of
saints' lives, there is often in the background a tiny garden enclosed in high white battlemented walls. All that palm beaches
and Mediterranean moonlight are for modern popular romancers,
their tiny enclosed gardens were for the Middle Ages. The hero
first sees his lady among the flowers, which are no fairer than her
face; it is in the garden they meet and promise to love forever;
and if either of them is shut up by disapproving parents or jealous
husband, the window of their tower is sure to overlook a garden
where birds sing and flowers blow and it is always summer.

But they are not gardeners' gardens, these flowery enclosures of the Middle Ages, not plots of good black earth for digging; there is never any mention of weeds, and once inside the gate, our boots are never muddy, for these are the gardens of romance.

The first lay gardens we know about are very small. As England settled down under William the Conqueror, conditions slowly became peaceful enough for laymen to think of the quiet pleasures. But if their gardens no longer needed the fear of God to protect them, they certainly needed a wall, and at the beginning they are no more than small enclosures huddled against the castle, tiny plots of peaceful land won from the wilderness, close to shelter if danger threatens. The world outside is warded off by a high barrier, and to walk in the garden one must first have the key to unlock the heavy door.

These early garden plots are scarcely bigger than rooms, and as carefully shut in and protected. But at least they are open to the sky, and as for the view being hidden behind high walls, the Middle Ages had no wish to look out at the world; they knew too well that there were wolves in the forests (a twelfth-century writer gives instructions for taming them as dogs—a rather doubtful pleasure), there were stags and wild boars, and robbers more savage than either. Even the rule of the land was scarcely more gentle, when the King "shut the gates of mercy on mankind" and in a country newly conquered, crushed resistance without pity, laying waste rebel lands so ruthlessly that generations later whole regions were still described quite simply in the surveys as "vasta est."

But men longed for peace after the centuries of war, and in a harsh world a garden was a secret sweetness, doubly precious because of the violence outside. The early lay gardens are very simple, scarcely more than an enclosure of grass scattered with small flowers, the "flow'ry mede" of the poets and the tapestries and the foreground of mediæval pictures. There is often a raised seat of turf round the wall, sometimes a small fountain, and later on, as the gardens grew larger, leafy arbours and painted trellises, little clipped trees, and pots or beds of flowers—roses and lilies, peonies and irises, pinks and columbines, poppies and lavender, rosemary and golds, which now we call marigolds. These were grown with herbs and salads, and where usefulness ended and pleasure began, or whether they were ever separate at all, it is hard to know. For roses and lilies were still herbs against poisons; violets were a favourite relish for salads; and there are recipes for stewing primroses and cowslips and hawthorn blossom. Right up to the seventeenth century people would eat almost anything

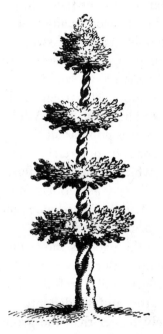

Mediæval-style topiary.

which grew in a garden, and Bacon tells a cautionary tale against eating monkshood, a flower "so poisonous that I have heard the eating only six or seven of the Blossoms in a salad, has killed a Gentleman in France." And if it killed a Frenchman, who, after all, can survive frogs and snails, what might it not do to the homely English?

Above all, in the Middle Ages, a garden was a private place, which the castle was not, with its communal rooms and enormous household, with servants everywhere, and freely wandering animals. Even in the bedroom there was a perch for hawks. So in the stories of the Middle Ages it is in the garden that the lovers meet (it seems, indeed, to be the chief function of their gardens) because only there can they be safe from interruption. Guiguemar finds his queen in a garden "shut in by a wall of green marble, very strong and high," where she walked "to be glad amongst the flowers." And in another favourite story of the Middle Ages, the hero Constant falls asleep under a tree, where the princess finds him "flushed as any rose," and falls promptly in love. "I found her in an arbour sweet, under a bough"—it could be the beginning of a dozen stories of gardeny romance. The *Roman de la Rose* is a long (and to us very tedious) tale of a quest through a symbolical garden, ending with the hero's winning of the rose and his lady's love. With its long descriptions of the magic garden it was popular all through the Middle Ages, and was retold by Chaucer in a version we seldom read now, a long verse romance which is dull and lifeless beside the timeless vitality of the *Canterbury Tales*. But it is typical of the garden romances which the Middle Ages loved, and they did not find the long flowery descriptions tedious.

As men felt safer, the gardens move out into the open and leave the castle's shadow. But they are still surrounded by walls or impenetrable hedges, still carefully shut in and protected. They may be larger, too, and divided into several enclosures, but still they are scarcely bigger than the ground plan of a house. And in all the pictures mediæval gardens have a curious pathos. It is such a tiny plot that men have claimed for their pleasure, such a humble unpretentious square they have set aside for happiness; they have asked so little and it is so precious, men and women alike crowd in so eagerly, till the surrounding walls are full of people, as if they were at a party and simply to be in the garden were delight enough. "The orchard" (for an orchard and a garden were the same thing) "was fair beyond content. Herbs grew there of every fashion, more than I am able to name. But at least I can tell you that so sweet was the savour of roses and other flowers and simples, that sick persons, borne within that garden in a litter, walked forth sound and well for having passed the night in so lovely a place."

For the English spirit of the Middle Ages was still conscious of the dark background of life—not only of violence and hunger and cold, nor of the Black Death which could kill so many that there were none left to bury the dead or gather the precious harvest for the winter, but they were conscious, too, of the darkness of man's ignorance and the uncertainty of salvation:

> *When I thinke thinges three*
> *I may never blithe be:*
> *One is that I must away,*
> *The other I know not which day.*
> *The third is my greatest care,*
> *I know not whither I must fare.*

It is a sad little verse which occurs over and over in the different versions of different dialects, one of many sad verses on the wretchedness of life and the certainty of death.

> *Wretched man why art thou proud,*
> *That art of earth y-maked?*
> *Hither broughtest thou no shroud,*
> *But poor thou came and naked.*

It is a despairing voice from the fourteenth century, haunted by the consciousness of man's mortality.

> *All we shall die, though us like ill.* . . .
>
> *Where is Paris and Heleyn?* . . .
>
> *Much sorrow I walk with.* . . .
>
> *When the turf is thy tower,*
> *And thy put [grave] is thy bower* . . .

It is the constant melancholy theme, for the mediæval Christians were as uncomforted by Christ as their pagan ancestors were by Thor and Odin. The Church might promise joy for the virtuous in the next life, but the only life men knew was dark with hardship and injustice, and Paradise, for all the priests might promise, was a reward rather to be hoped for than believed in with certainty, as they believed without question in the cold and hunger which came with every winter.

Religion taught men to look at earthly life by the light of

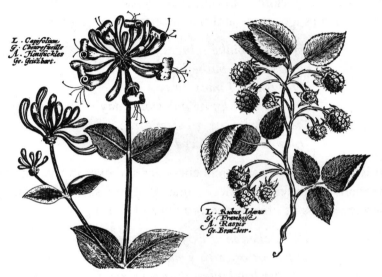

Drawing by Crispin de Passe.

eternity, but eternity is too dreadful a brilliance for mortal men to live by. Seen in so inhuman a brightness, "the green garden was become a little dry dust."

"L'unique bien des hommes consiste donc à être divertis de penser à leur condition"—so Pascal said later on, and human beings are mercifully frivolous. Eternity is no affair of ours, and we shut it out by the frailest barriers of happy preoccupations. So the gardens of the Middle Ages are a precious refuge from besetting fears and doubts, a place where men can sit in the sunshine among the birds and flowers and be happy. And even the flowers themselves have the oddest air of taking shelter within the protecting walls, the wild flowers of the countryside grown only to greater perfection—daisies and cowslips, foxgloves and

bluebells, campions and honeysuckle, forget-me-nots and thyme. They grow haphazard about the garden, not set in masses for effect, but singly like the fleurettes of the tapestries, as if they were individual creatures who had chosen for themselves this happy corner. Even the birds seek out this paradise, the magpies and finches and "little sweet nightingales" which crowd every hedge and branch, and hop about the ground between the flowers and the people.

Some of the pathos of these garden pictures comes perhaps from the limitations of mediæval art, for whether by intention or from lack of painter's skill, the people of mediæval pictures never smile. In the happiest settings they have an air of unshakable sadness, as if life were incurably sorrowful despite its happy incidents. A Madonna sits in a garden bending over her child, who plays with a rose, and her head seems bowed, not from tenderness, but by the sorrows of the whole world. An angel leans his head upon his hand among the flowers, listening to his companion who plays upon a lute, and from the grief in his face we feel his heart must surely break. Botticelli's faces have this same quiet sadness, as if they remembered an old unhappiness which the eager joy of the coming Renaissance can never reach. It gives his Venus a strange mystery which haunts our memory long after we have forgotten the glowing beauties of later painters.

There is a theory that the weather of Europe is in long cycles of alternating warm and cold periods with roughly eighteen hundred years between peaks. The Dark Ages were a warm period, and in the Icelandic sagas the coast of Greenland was fertile, and the sailors made winter voyages in seas which now are icebound. It was the time of the ancient merchant adventurers and the discovery of America by the unbusinesslike heroes who sailed by the ice-blink. But as the peak of warm weather passed, the ice came south again and the climate grew harsher. The thirteenth and fourteenth centuries were cold, and to the miseries of a winter with scarcely food enough to last till the spring, with no light but rare candles, with no glass in the windows, with no knowledge to ward off the plague or the scurvy or the ague or the many other diseases which beset men, to all this was added the wretchedness of winters so cold that the seas froze and hungry wolves roamed over the ice from Norway to Denmark.

Small wonder, then, that the Middle Ages longed for the end

Drawing by Crispin de Passe.

of winter, that if they shut their eyes and wished, it was always spring:

> *Bytuene Mershe ant Averil*
> *When spray biginneth to springe . . .*

Lyric after lyric begins in the same way.

> *Miri tim it is in Maie. . . .*

Gardens of the Middle Ages

Lenten ys come with love to toune. . . .

Up, son and mery wether,
Somer draweth nere. . . .

An index of first lines is a fanfare for the spring. It is as if they only came alive at the end of winter: "It was the time when meadow and copse are green: when orchards grow white with bloom and birds break into song as thickly as the bush to flower. It is the season when he who loves would win to his desire."

Reading their literature, we might think the whole year was a long ecstatic spring, so constantly do they delight in the new season, forgetting winter as a dark shadow in the background. And in their gardens it is the small flowers of the spring they love most dearly, primroses and violets and woodruff and periwinkle—"parwincke, joy of the ground."

This delight of the Middle Ages in flowers and gardens is a fragrance which they breathe over all their doings. They decked the streets of London with flowers and branches on saints' days and holidays, not only as we do with holly doubtfully at Christmas. Young ladies wore stockings embroidered with gladioli, and tenants paid a red rose yearly as a token rent instead of peppercorns. Their very wars were started in a rose garden, and end in the victory of a king who took for his badge the red and white roses united as a symbol of peace. And Henry III, in love with the Fair Rosamond, built at Woodstock, so they tell, a secret bower to hide her from his jealous wife. But James I of Scotland is the perfect hero of garden romance. Imprisoned in Windsor Castle, he looked out of his window, and as we could have told him he would from the stories, he saw a lovely girl walking in the garden. Very properly he fell in love at first sight, married her, and wrote his own book about it, the *Kingis Quair*. He describes the garden where she walked, and it is the very pattern of romance, "a garden fair, fast by the Towris wall," with "an arbour green" and shady alleys and thick screening hedges. "The sharpe grene sweet Juniper" is everywhere, and the song "now soft, now loud" of the "little sweet nightingale."

Even to their harsh religion, with its morbid delight in suffering and its threats of hell-fire, the Middle Ages bring a flowery charm. There are bills for flowers in the church accounts, "a dozen and a half rose garlands on St. Barnebe's day," woodruff garlands, rose garlands again and again, and holly and ivy for the church at Christmas. The priests in the churches wore crowns of flowers, and when a Bishop of Saint Paul's was installed, so Stow tells us, both he and the canons wore garlands of red roses. Even heaven is no cold abstract Utopia, but Paradise Garden, where Mary and Jesus delight in the birds and flowers; the Virgin is a garden lady and Christ the blossom she bears:

> *Of a rose a lovely rose*
> *And of a rose I syng a song.*

> *The rose ys called Mary hevyn quene*
> *Of her bosum a blossum sprong.*

"O fragrant rose," they call her, "O lilly chaste," "Lady flour of alle thing."

She walks with Joseph through a homely orchard which we delight in as much as they:

> *Joseph and Mary walked*
> *Thro' an orchard good,*
> *There was cherries and berries*
> *So red as any blood.*

> *Joseph and Mary walked*
> *Thro' an orchard green,*
> *There was berries and cherries*
> *As thick as might be seen.*

The mediæval Books of Hours and religious manuscripts are bordered with flowers, bright and gilded, painted with such care and love that they bloom still, fresh and lively on the centuries-old pages. Butterflies hover, caterpillars crawl, dragonflies shimmer among the coloured flowers which dwarf and encircle the sad little pictures of angels rejoicing with sorrowful faces. Christ on his cross is scarcely larger than a figure on a postage stamp, and if we gathered the Provence roses which twine so lavishly round the wide margins of his tiny picture, they would make a full sweet bunch to blot out all his miseries.

In one of the mediæval carols we still sing, Jesus comes to Mary in a garden.

> *He came al so still*
> *There his mother was,*
> *As dew in April*
> *That falleth on the grass.*

> *He came al so still*
> *To his mother's bour,*
> *As dew in April*
> *That falleth on the flour.*

> *He came al so still*
> *There his mother lay,*
> *As dew in April*
> *That falleth on the spray.*

It is a languid sweetness which has little to do with religion. We need only read "lady" instead of "mother" to change it to a perfect love-song, and Benjamin Britten's setting exactly catches the feeling of delicate preoccupied excitement. In the romances there is often the same curious mixture of religious and amorous. There is the story of the nun who turned prostitute while Mary took her place in the convent so that she should not be found out. There is the beautiful heroine of the Yonec story who was shut up by her jealous husband, and growing bored with her own company, prayed devoutly to God. She would like a young man to amuse her, she said. Other women had lovers who came secretly to keep them company, and she would like one, too. "May the Almighty God grant me my heart's desire." Her prayer was answered—for certainly she prayed from the heart— and a falcon flew in at the window, changed to the "fairest knight she had looked upon in all her life," and after a certain amount of somewhat unconvincing hesitation they "were happy together."

I dare say it is naïve of me to find this a rather unexpected manifestation of divine mercy. For the Middle Ages were the Ages of Faith—they told me so in my school history lessons, but I never knew that this was what they meant.

Indeed, to our age of conscientious virtue the whole code of chivalry looks rather dubious:

> *A dieu mon âme,*
> *Mon cœur aux dames,*
> *Ma vie au roi,*
> *L'honneur pour moi.*

If that is your rule of life, then it becomes a virtue "to love for the love of love," and for wives who are fair, adultery is a duty "for the love of lovely knights": "You are so lovely a knight, so sweet in speech and so courteous, that verily it is my lady's duty to set her love upon you."

In the thirteenth century the rules for this *Amour Courtois* were laid down in a code called *"Fleur d'Amour, ou Art d'aimer honnestement."* It is an aristocratic and courtly pastime sung by the troubadours to nobles and their ladies, people with little work to do and a great deal of very restricted leisure. There are not, after all, so many ways of passing the time if you are shut up in a castle for the winter without books or wireless, with no friends to call on, no town on one's doorstep with people and concerts and cinemas and theatres. They must manage as best they could, and the knights sat on cushions listening to tales of love, tethered by a silken thread to their chosen lady. It is a strange far-off picture, faintly lit by candlelight against the background of winter darkness.

> *Though love and all his pleasures are but toys,*
> *They shorten tedious nights.*

We feel they, too, would have sighed and quoted Campion if they had known he would write it three centuries later.

And in their summer gardens they made secret trysting-places for "clasp and kisses, many words and long silences," and the little boys, instead of Indians and Cowboys, played at knights jousting for their lady's favour, with plantain spikes for lances.

If the gardens of the Dark Ages belong to priests, the gardens of the Middle Ages belong just as surely to women. It is they

Drawing by Crispin de Passe.

who care for the flowers when their lords are away, fighting or hunting or off on Crusades. It is the woman who keeps the key of the garden door, who invites her *bel ami* in at her pleasure, who makes of the garden her private drawing-room. The small flowery fancies are women's fancies—the garlands and wreaths of flowers—and the figure who presides in the garden pictures is always a woman—Mary in Paradise Garden, or the strange lovely lady of the romances.

There have never been heroines, not even the dryads in their trees, more perfectly in harmony with their setting than the lady of mediæval romances in her garden. So delicious is her flowery enclosure, so hidden and intimate, that the leafy arbour becomes "a privy pleying place" and the very grass seems an invitation to love:

> *On whiche men myght his lemman ley*
> *As on a fetherbed to pley.*

And here, where it is always May, in this small secret room of a garden, waits the fascinating lady. "Her hair was golden, with little love-locks; her eyes blue and laughing; her face most dainty to see, with lips more vermeil than ever was rose or cherry in the time of summer heat; her breasts so firm that they showed beneath her vesture like two rounded nuts; so frail was she about the girdle that your two hands could have spanned her, and the daisies that she broke with her feet in passing showed altogether black against her instep and her flesh, so white was the fair young maiden."

She belongs so perfectly to her garden that it seems impossible to describe her without flowers. She is always delicately beautiful and very young, and the clothes she wears are more becoming than any women's clothes since. So successful they must have been that for centuries the basic fashion is almost the same, as if it had reached perfection and had no need to change.

Made of soft wool, her dress fits closely over her arms and shoulders, moulds her breasts and waist, then flows in swinging folds to her feet. We have gathered our full skirts since into a waistband, like a curtain; we have made them of stiff silks and shapeless taffetas, so that we have cut off our living bodies half-way and made of our skirts a lifeless shape much like a tea-cosy. But hers flowed out from the close bodice to the swaying hem in a sinuous smooth line like the petals of a lily, was made of softly hanging wool which swung as she moved, moulding the shape of her body beneath.

And as if to forestall all criticism of looking too Pre-Raphaelite, altogether too "greenery-yallery," she would bind up her long hair out of sight, and in the fifteenth century which is the best of all, would deck her head with extraordinary arrangements of formal and fantastic sophistication. No headdresses (for really one cannot call them hats) have ever been more extravagantly strange, with their sweeping curves of wings, their curious planes and angles, their horns and pointed spires and floating veils. (The horns in particular horrified good church-

L. *Delphinicum*
G. *Pied d'Alonette*
A. *Larkes Heele*
G. *Ritter-sporen*

Drawing by Crispin de Passe.

men, who attacked them furiously and constantly forbade them, but such interest from high places naturally only made them more intriguingly fashionable.) Utterly impractical, audaciously exhibitionist, they are the perfect crowning foil for the simple dresses beneath. They are at their best in the first half of the fifteenth century in the paintings of the Flemish artists: Roger Van der Weyden, Campin, Petrus Christus, Dirk Bouts, Memling, David. In the pictures Saint Ursula and her eleven thousand virgins are martyred in the most becoming hats one could possibly imagine, and we cannot help feeling that an expedition, however virtuous, which set out in such *very* attractive clothes was bound to get into trouble sooner or later.

These headdresses are compositions of great abstract beauty, with their clear delicate lines and complicated surfaces of starched linen (sometimes in the pictures we can see the folds in the cloth like the folds in a matador's cloak). Yet their abstraction curiously enhances the faces which they frame. The sweep of eyebrows, the curve of a mouth, the slant of eyes—these are subtly emphasized and made significant by the airy wings, the wrapped coif. The faces of mediæval portraits owe much of their fascination to these outrageous follies of headdresses. But they fascinate us, too, because they never show emotion of any kind. They neither smile nor sigh, scorn nor tremble; we can make no contact with them as we can with faces which weep or laugh as we do. They look at us simply, grave and withdrawn in a world where we can never reach them nor even guess at what they might be thinking. There are pictures of saints who lie peacefully in green fields and gaze mildly into the cloudless blue sky. They seem quite unconscious that someone has cut a careful hole in their abdomen, and that their entrails are being wound out on a wheel as neatly as a sailor's rope. The martyrs are as unmoved as the audience who stand quietly by and watch.

We can see, in these great airy follies of hats sprouting from the heads of the fifteenth century, how poets could describe a woman as a graceful stem to carry the flower of her head. And these slender childlike women are of a beauty which haunted men's minds for hundreds of years, to reach its final expression in the grave young figures of Memling's triptychs. In this fifteenth-century religious painter the ideal woman of the Middle Ages finds her perfect portrayer. Her elusive beauty is caught surely and delicately before she changes, through the curious figures of Cranach and Mabuse, to the more conventional Venus of the Renaissance. She is straight and slender, her arms are still "the arms long and small" of the romances, as if they were made only for embraces; her long supple waist and small high breasts have the same curious unconscious sophistication.

Memling was a libertine, they say, which is perhaps why the women of his religious paintings are so unexpectedly seductive. Quiet and gentle they stand about his pictures; they lay their white hands together in prayer and gaze gravely at the Madonna. But it is a precarious innocence. If they only glanced sideways, if their faces showed only the faintest shadow of a conscious smile, they would be transformed at once from saints to sinners. They are the equivalent in paint of the Yonec heroine praying for a lover, of the amorous suggestiveness of "He came al so still." Composed to gentle meditation, their faces still have the provocative eyes, the full lower lip, the sleepy, almost sulky look of those whose thoughts are of love.

And if we set this lovely lady, not in a green meadow to worship Mary, but in a green garden to wait for her lover, she has the fascination of a depraved and innocent child. There she waits, in countless romances, sighing for love, trembling and pale with passion, her eyes dark flowers in the pallor of her face, twisting garlands of roses for her hair which hangs now loose and heavy, singing her *chansons de malmariée* in a soft siren voice, unlocking the garden door to draw in her lover.

She is a strange figure, this heroine of the romances, an invention of men's desires, shadowy and without personality, so that all the heroines are one, and we can no more remember them separate and distinct than we can the encounters of Spenser's *Faerie Queene*. She is made for love, "for love for love's sake," living for no other end, dissolving like a dream if we try to imagine her with any other occupation. She is the creation of the troubadours, a luxurious exotic for a sophisticated aristocracy, and Marie de France is her most famous singer. Marie's *Lays* are a retelling of the tales of Brittany, for the lady belongs to the Celtic stories with their doubtful morals and their preoccupation with love. The legends of the Anglo-Saxons are warlike and rowdy; they delight in fighting and hard drinking, and the beauty of women is simply a form of wealth to boast about. Their stories would never need Mr. Bowdler to edit them, as the Celtic stories so often would.

The Crusades of the twelfth century sent men travelling East as never before, and, returning home, the Crusaders brought back strange Eastern luxuries for their gardens: tents made of tapestry, pools for bathing, oleanders, pomegranates. They brought, too, Eastern romances of a curious languid sweetness, like the scent of hot-house flowers, and with heroines of the same exquisite family as the Celtic ladies. "It was in the time of summer heat, in the month of May, when the days are warm long and clear, and the nights coy and serene. Nicolette lay one night sleepless on her bed, and watched the moon shine brightly through the window, and listened to the nightingale plain in the garden." She climbs from her tower and escapes to the woods, where she builds a hut of leaves and flowers, and in this sweet shelter Aucassin finds her.

Floris and Blancheflour—their very names belong to the garden—is another Eastern story of two children whose loves seem to us somewhat precocious, for they began their preoccupation at seven, and by twelve were ready to die of passion. Blancheflour is sold as a slave to the Emir of Babylon (Thameral the English translator charmingly calls him) and is followed by Floris, who is carried into the harem hidden in a basket—not of washing, as we might expect in any other age, but a basket of flowers. There is a fairy-tale scene where Thameral chooses his wife in a garden, the fairest garden in all the world, where the merry birds sing, and about the garden goes a wall whose worst stone is of crystal. Beside a well stands the Tree of Love, always in bloom, and under this are brought the "maidenes clene" for the Emir's choice. The blossoms fall from the tree, and the maiden on whom the first flower falls is taken to be queen.

> *And if there any maiden is*
> *That Thameral holds of much price,*

Gardens of the Middle Ages

The flower shall on her be sent
Through art and through enchantement.

Of course.

But even to these flowery romances the English poet gives a quiet melancholy. "Now be they bothe dead," he says quite simply at the end of his story, and brings us back from this fairy-tale of love-sick children to his real world where people die and are forgotten, so that suddenly the story fades to a faint and far-off fancy against the dark background of eternity. Now be they bothe dead.

Although he died in 1400, we think of Chaucer as the first of the moderns for many reasons, and one of them is that he can smile. Men have always laughed—as children laugh, even when they are frightened—at farce or knockabout or misadventure. And so they laugh in the Middle Ages. But they do not smile. We smile from a balanced state, from security and self-confidence, we smile affectionately at the ridiculous. And so does Chaucer. He is the first great writer to rise above the crippling philosophy of the Middle Ages, to feel confident enough for detachment, to look round at his companions and find them delightful and ridiculous. For although he wrote the *Romaunt de la Rose*, and the "Knight's Tale," which is a mediæval garden romance in the true tradition, he wrote also the "Merchant's Tale" of May and January, which is a deliberate travesty of all flowery romanticism. To elude her blind and jealous husband, the young lady meets her lover in a pear tree. And as if this were not already an awkward enough rendezvous for passionate lovers, her husband recovers his sight at the most inconvenient moment possible. However, May is no dreamy mediæval heroine to swoon away in trouble, but a quick-witted young woman perfectly able to turn even so unpromising a situation to her own virtuous advantage.

Chaucer's Squyer is as exquisite a figure as Aucassin with his yellow curls, but he is also ridiculous:

With lokkes crulle, as they were leyd in presse . . .

Embrouded was he, as it were a mede
Al ful of fresshe floures, whyte and rede.

So hote he lovede, that by nightertale
He sleep no more than dooth a nightingale.

Aucassin, for his sweet love, accepts the doom of hell, knowing he must suffer for his pleasure—"All the days of the world would his soul be in Hell for it." But Chaucer's Wife of Bath cares not a straw for such gloomy threats, although she might well have feared an even worse fate than poor faithful Aucassin, with her five husbands "withouten other companye." But she is triumphantly unrepentant. Christ, she says,

Spak to hem that wolde live parfitly;
And lordinges, by your leve, that am not I.

No indeed she is not.

Blessed be god that I have wedded fyve!
Welcome the sixte, whan that ever he shal.

And when men have once said boo to the goose of hell-fire, they are very near the end of the Middle Ages. They are ready to smile. Their gardens will no longer be a fortified retreat from a frightening world, but a place to play in, to amuse themselves like children. And when in the fanciful Tudor gardens they have played long enough to feel self-confident, then at last, for the first time, in the great gardens of the seventeenth century, they will look out over the garden wall.

CHAPTER FOUR

ENCLOSED
FANTASTIC

GARDENS OF
TUDOR
ENGLAND

WE MUST NEVER SAY TO OURSELVES THAT the Middle Ages ended in 1485, so Professor Trevelyan warns us. Well, I had never thought they did, nor at any other particular time for that matter, but since he suggests it, I do see what a very useful date it is, after all. The Wars of the Roses are over and England entering a period of peace under a strong monarchy, the world is suddenly exhilaratingly large and full of promise, the Renaissance has begun in Italy, the printing-press has been invented, and the English language has developed to a stage where we can still read it without difficulty.

Until now great men had felt safer if they lived in castles, or at least in houses which could be strongly defended, and their gardens with them. But when Leland travelled through England under Henry VIII, he found the castles everywhere empty and ruinous and their gardens vanished. For they were uncomfortable places to live in, cramped and cold and dark, and as the climate of peace became more settled, men began to build themselves pleasant manor houses whose only defence was against robbers, and to lay out gardens whose worst enemies were small boys stealing apples, as I dare say small boys always will. ("We was scrumping," they said, when I caught two smudgy culprits scrambling through the orchard hedge with their pockets bulging. "We was scrumping apples in your garden," they said with disarming candour, and I let them keep their apples in exchange for my new word.)

After the Dissolution the monasteries, too, were often converted to dwelling-houses, and new gardens laid out among the old orchards and fishponds. For the English seem born with a natural love of gardening, and the four million people of Tudor England gardened with the same enthusiasm that they gave to everything else. "Every Gentleman flieth into the country," said one observer, to hunt and hawk and plan his garden, and pleasure-grounds were laid out everywhere, even, so Stow tells us, in the middle of London. By the seventeenth century "there is scarce a cottage in most of the Southern parts of England, but has its proportionable garden, so great a delight do most of men take in it."

But what were these gardens like, which everyone delighted in, from cottager to king? The superb gardens of Renaissance Italy still survive for our admiration, but the gardens of Renaissance England can scarcely be called even country cousins of this splendour: they belong to quite a different family.

The English mind has seldom shared the great Classical conceptions. They do not suit us. When we do understand them, it is because we are Europeans and not because we are Englishmen. We seldom feel, even with our finest, even with Gothic architecture or with Shakespeare, that we are in the mainstream of European culture. We cannot trace the current backwards and forwards from Shakespeare, as we can from a much lesser European writer like Montaigne. As Milton says, Shakespeare warbles his "native wood-notes wild." He is "fancy's child." For we have had a power of vital and extravagant fantasy which has produced perhaps the greatest poetry in the world. And it is a strangely universal vitality which keeps alive for more than three centuries King Lear and Falstaff, Herrick's light fancies and Donne's intellectual conceits.

But in lesser minds this gift of poetic fantasy becomes merely curious and quaint. Uncontrolled by the fashions of Europe, the lesser productions of England are often merely odd. The strange clothes we designed for ourselves during the isolation of the Napoleonic Wars looked elaborately absurd set beside the French fashions when the wars were over, beside the authentic simple elegance of the Empire nightdresses. And Tudor architects, on the fringe of Europe, lavished their care on extravagantly fanciful chimneys, charmingly barbarous absurdities to build at the same time as the villas of Renaissance Italy. Henry VIII's Nonesuch Palace was well named, a fantastic top-heavy folly smothered with decoration. I can never more than half believe it existed, even though there are detailed pictures and it was Queen Elizabeth's favourite palace. It is like the Palace of Sheen, a name so remote and romantic that the solid bricks fade like a mirage in my mind, no more real than a painted gauze curtain, as elusive as the sheen on silk.

Nor were the insides of these mansions any less curious. Aubrey describes the strange house Bacon built at Verulam, with its awkward central chimney, its trick doors of mirror-glass, and its extraordinary decoration of pagan gods and local curiosities. Aubrey is the perfect person to describe it. "There was a very large picture: thus," he says. "In the middle on a Rock in the Sea stands King James in armour; on his right hand stands (but whether or no on a Rock I have forgott) King Henry IV of France in armour." We can only hope that poor King Henry did have his rocky pedestal, and we are not surprised that the whole place was "sold to two Carpenters for fower hundred poundes" and that they pulled it down "for the sale of the Materials."

The houses which have survived are almost equally fantastic and insular. Their planning is mostly haphazard, with no controlling logical conception; they are rich in curious incidental felicities, and, at its best, their decoration is wildly fanciful. At Audley End in Horace Walpole's time there was still a "Fish room, a spacious brave chamber, the ceiling and deep frieze adorned with sea monsters swimming. There are many grotesque friezes," and they, just as much as Shakespeare, are our native wood-notes wild. The delightful grotesque carvings at houses like Knole and Audley End owe very little to Europe, with their strange figures, clothed in leaves perhaps, or tailed like a mermaid, and topped by round English faces copied from the village cricket team or the bar parlour. They are a charming mixture of country bumpkin and poetic fantasy, of Bottom and the fairies.

The Tradescants were a family of explorers and collectors well known in the early seventeenth century. "That industrious searcher after rarities" one writer calls the father, and the rarities they "Preserved at South-Lambeth neer London" were the beginning of the Ashmolean Collection now at Oxford. But although they lived in the dawn of modern science, their curiosity was completely unscientific. They had no interest in classification or ordered knowledge, but collected their rarities from a simple childish delight in the quaint and curious; they were attracted by the fantastic as a jackdaw by bright scraps.

Divers sorts of Egges from Turkie: one given for a Dragons egge.

Easter Egges of the Patriarchs of Jerusalem.

Two feathers of the Phoenix tayle.

The claw of the bird Rock: who, as Authors report, is able to trusse an Elephant.

Penguin, which never flies for want of wings.

Dodar, it is not able to flie being so big.

Cat-a-mountaine.

Elephants head and tayle only.

Divers things cut on Plum-stones.

A Little Box with the 12 Apostles in it.

Jupiter Io and Mercury wrought in Tent-stitch.

A nest of fifty-two wooden cups turned within each other as thin as paper.

A Cherry-stone, upon one side S. Geo: and the Dragon perfectly cut: and on the other side eighty-eight Emperors faces.

Stories cut in paper by some of the Emperors.

Flea chains of silver and gold, with three hundred links a piece and yet but an inch long.
Old Parre's picture.

(I wonder how many of these treasures still survive in the Ashmolean. I would like to see Old Parre's picture.)

Then follows a Variety of Rarities which, even by John Tradescant's catholic standards, are difficult to classify.

Instrument which the Indians found at Sun-rising.
A piece of the Stone of Sarrigo-Castle where Hellen of Greece was born.
A Brazen-ball to warme the Nunnes hands.
A glasse-horne for annointing kings.
Blood that rained on the Isle of Wight, attested by Sir Jo: Oglander.
Anne of Bullens silke knit-gloves.
Henry 8 hawking-glove, hawks-hood, dogs-collar.
A hat-band made of the sting-ray.
Black Indian girdles made of Wampam peek, the best sort.
Turkish tooth-brush.
An umbrella.
A steel-glasse that shows a long face on one side and a broad on the other.
A copper-Letter-case an inch long, taken in the Isle of Ree with a Letter in it, which was swallowed by a Woman, and found.

Although we should never suspect it from such a collection, Tudor scholarship was already keenly aware of the intellectual Renaissance of Europe. But the arts followed much more slowly, for the intellect can travel fast along the paths of knowledge and reason, but popular taste is a plant which must have time to grow and develop. As our twentieth-century æsthetic has scarcely yet caught up with the Industrial Revolution, so Tudor fashions in the arts (as in gardens and popular museums) followed English styles so vigorous that they flourished untroubled by foreign influences. Fashions from abroad were either ignored, or taken confidently and transformed by our native traditions into "something rich and strange" and very different from the original.

The Renaissance style is still an alien in Tudor England, something rare and foreign, a curiosity brought home by travellers. Here and there we find it on tombs in country churches: a figure of the dead hero reclines on his coffin, beruffed and bearded and knickerbockered, his homely-looking head propped up awk-

Drawing by Crispin de Passe.

wardly on his elbow, and the whole thing painted, as likely as not, in bright fair-ground colours. And over this very Tudor figure is an elegant white arch decorated in delicate low-relief with the emblems of the Italian Renaissance, and flanked by classical pillars homesick for the sun. The style is no more at home yet than spring bulbs made to flower at Christmas, and we must wait for the proper season before it will grow and flourish.

So the gardens of Tudor England borrowed ideas from Italy, but like the country tombs, they speak Italian with an unmistakable and unrepentant English accent. Their atmosphere is all their own.

The villas of the Italian Renaissance were set in formal garden arrangements of great beauty. The grounds were designed as magnificent backgrounds for magnificent palaces, and man in such surroundings may talk with the gods if he wishes. But Tudor gardens are gardens which children would make for themselves to play in.

One of the charms of children, as of other young animals, is their irresponsible gaiety. They will always play with us. No matter how unlikely the time—wakened in the night perhaps, or crying and in trouble—they will always laugh if we persuade them. They have no feeling for the fitness of the occasion; they would never say, as we do: "This is no time for laughing," since for them it is always time. They carry no steadying burden of worry or responsibility, but are playful by a natural and unthinking effervescence of high spirits.

So, too, Tudor gardens are delightfully free of any suggestion that life is earnest. They are irresponsibly gay, and as Ophelia turned her sorrows "to favour and to prettiness," so they turn everything to fun. They delighted kings and commoners alike well into the seventeenth century, when European fashions at last broke through our deep hawthorn hedges, and the great gardens of England become European gardens.

> *The King was in the counting-house, counting out his money,*
> *The Queen was in the parlour eating bread and honey,*
> *The maid was in the garden. . . .*

Behind the Tudor portraits there are gardens straight from nursery rhyme, where we half expect to see the Knave of Hearts running off with his mother's baking, leaping over the beds of flowers and silver bells and cockle-shells and pretty maids all in a row. They are gardens full of quaint fancies and naïve enthusiasms, of tricks and odd surprises, gay and charming and absurd. As for a controlling plan for the grounds as a whole, there was none. They were laid out, says Thomas Hill, according to the "spirit of the Gardener . . . lead by hops and skips, turnings and windings of his braine . . . by the pleasing of his eye according to his best fantasie." They cared nothing at all for the intellectual discipline of gardens which were designed as settings for fine architecture. For Tudor gardens were not intended as settings for anything at all but pleasure and the growing of flowers. In any case, they were too small to be a background for the house. The famous garden at Kenilworth was only one acre, and although some of the larger ones covered much more ground than this, it was only by an addition of various small gardens; there was no sense of space or planning. Their ideal garden was laid out so that, passing from one enclosure to the next, it was as if the visitor "had been magically transplanted into a new Garden." They liked their view, as Sir Henry Wotton says, "rather in a delightful confusion than with any plain distinction of the pieces."

Certainly the boundary was definite enough—there must be a firm fence or hedge for the "Verge and Girdle of your Garden" —but as for "the inward proportions and shapes of the Quarters Beds Bankes Mounts and such like," says Surflet, "they are to be divided by Alleys, Hedges, Borders, Rayles, Pillars and such like." And such like, and such like—you do not create the Boboli Gardens so. He is clearly bored by intellectual problems of layout and planning; each man, he says, must follow his own fancy, and the gardener's part is to help him follow it, no matter how wayward.

Even the monarchs of these gardens have, at this distance, the same fairy-tale quality of exuberant fantasy—Elizabeth with her orange wig and her learning, Gloriana of the cryptic virginity and the adoration of her poets; and Henry VIII with his six wives, so that I was always astonished, seeing pictures of him when I was a child, that his beard was not a bright and beautiful cornflower blue. But there are many surprises about Henry VIII.

"Bluff King Hal" they have called him, but he wrote charming verse: "Pastime with Good Company" we still sing, or at least listen to. And if that seems a subject so happily in character that it might almost do for his epitaph, he wrote on other, more unlikely themes: tender lyrics of the faithful heart.

As the holy grouth greene
And never chaungyth hew,
So I am, ever hath bene
Unto my lady trew.

Now unto my lady
Promys to her I make,
From all other only
To her I me betake.

I wonder which of his ladies he wrote it for.

Then he was a "pretty" figure, so an onlooker said, watching him play tennis at Hampton Court—"He is extremely fond of tennis, at which game it is the prettiest thing in the world to see him play, his fair skin glowing through a shirt of finest texture." I suppose he must once have been a fine young man, but portraits are not of the fine young men, they are of the famous, and the famous are mostly old, or at least middle-aged.

Henry VIII delighted in his gardens at Hampton Court, a pleasure-ground laid out by Wolsey but later seized and enlarged by the envious King, who became so fatherly-proud of his creation that when visitors arrived, even though it was "near night," he would take them round in the dusk to admire it. There were flower gardens lavishly planted with violets and primroses, gillyflowers and mints, with sweet Williams at threepence per hundred and roses at fourpence. There was the Pond Garden, kept filled by "labourers ladyng of water out of ye Temmes to fyll the pondes in the night tymes," and still much the same now as it was when the King courted Ann Boleyn there. There was another garden, long since lost, which was full of brass sundials, twenty of them, each set on its own little mound, and costing four shillings and fourpence "the piece." And there was a Mount, so popular in Tudor gardens, a little artificial hill climbed by a path edged with hawthorn bushes which circled the slope "like turnings of cokil-shells." On the top there was a summer-house, and judging by the bills for glazing the windows, it must have been quite large enough for a family to live in.

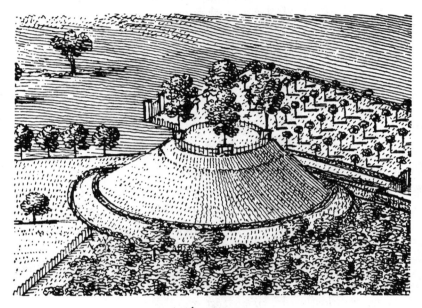

A mount.

But Henry's chief delight was in his "beestes"—fantastic carved figures of animals painted and gilt, which sat on the tops of posts set everywhere about the gardens. Often they held banners, and it must all have been very cheerful and very ridiculous. In one small garden alone there were "11 harts, 13 lions, 16 greyhounds, 10 hinds, 17 dragons, 9 bulls, 13 antelopes, 15 griffins, 19 leberdes, 11 yallys, 9 rams and the lion on top of the mount."

Nor was that all, for the flower beds and paths were edged with railings, and these, like the barber's poles which the beasts sat on, were painted in vivid stripes of green and white, the royal colours. There are bills for painting them by the hundred yards, for there were railings everywhere.

Indeed, the Tudor gardens were as full of ornaments as they were of flowers. Besides an astonishing number of sundials, there were "columns and pyramids of wood," pilasters and obelisks and spheres and "white bears, all of stone upon their curious bases." In the garden of the Temple there were the twelve signs of the Zodiac set on posts, and at Whitehall, besides thirty-four heraldic beasts holding the royal arms, there was a "Parnassus Mount, on top of which was the Pegasus, a golden horse with wings, and divers statues, one of black marble representing the river Thames. It far surpasses the Parnassus Mount near Florence."

There was a great deal, too, of what the gardeners call "carpenters work"—trellises for edging the beds, and frames for training climbing plants over arbours, and the little nooks to sit in which they called "roosting-places." "RUSTIC SEATS AND PURGLERS" I once saw written on a notice at the gate of a country carpenter, and our pergolas are what the Tudor gardeners called galleries or covered ways. The summer-houses, too, were made by carpenters or even builders. "Banketting-houses" they called them, for they often held banquets there. At Whitehall there was a noble one with a roof painted like clouds, where Elizabeth received "certaine Ambassadors out of France." These summer-houses are a fine opportunity for interesting chimneys, so Bacon thinks, but Stow disapproves of such extravagant frivolities— "like Midsummer pageants," he says, "with towers and turrets and chimney-tops, not so much for use of profit as for show and pleasure, betraying the vanity of men's minds; much unlike to the disposition of the ancient citizens."

There were even houses in trees, as children build them, platforms which they climbed to with a ladder, and I wonder what Stow's ancient citizens would have said of the one Parkinson describes so admiringly: "I have seen a tall or great-bodied Lime tree, bare without boughes for eight foote high, and then the branches were spread round about so orderly, as if it were done by art, and brought to compasse that middle Arbour: And from those boughes the body was bare againe for eight or nine foote (wherein might be placed halfe an hundred men at the least), and then another rowe of branches to encompasse a third Arbour, with stayres, made for the purpose, to this and that underneath it: upon the boughes were laid boards to tread upon, which was the goodliest spectacle mine eyes ever beheld for one tree to carry." When the children were little, there was scarcely a tree in the garden without its few boards balanced rakishly across any likely-looking branches. It gave the garden a quite astonishing air of squalor. "Our tree-houses" the children used to call them, and, like John Parkinson, they would have appreciated the lime tree as connoisseurs admiring a veritable palace of tree architecture.

No one could help being fond of Parkinson, despite the dreadful Latin pun on his own name which he uses for the title of his book: *Paradisi in Sole Paradisus Terrestris*—Parkinson's Earthly Paradise. "A Garden of all sorts of pleasant flowers which our English ayre will permitt to be noursed up"—so he explains his title, and there is a frontispiece of the kindly bearded author holding a single flower as he might hold some precious treasure, a flower called sweet John, as we recognize from the illustrations later on, and we wonder whether he arranged the delicate and affectionate compliment himself. For he understands his own gentle nature and can praise it without offence. "Such men doe as it were send forth a pleasing savour of sweet instructions, not only to that time wherein they live and are fresh, but being drye, withered and dead, cease not in all after ages to doe as much or more."

The Tudor gardens, full as they were of ornaments, still had room for flowers and plants, though these were seldom left to grow naturally, but were trained into every kind of fanciful and amusing shape. Flowers were planted in patterns of "rampande lyons and dragons of marvaylous likenesse," bushes were cut into topiary figures of men and animals and geometric curiosities, and even hedges "made battlement-wise, in sundrie formes, according to invention, or carrying the proportions of Pyllasters, Flowers, shapes of Beasts, Birds, Creeping things, Shippes, Trees and such like."

Designs for Topiary.

Above all, the Tudor gardeners loved their knots—square beds laid out in symmetrical designs of interlacing hedges of box or lavender or thrift or other low shrubby plants. Of all the Tudor fancies, this seems most intimately their own, a kind of garden doodling, like the patterns children cut out from folded paper squares, like the fretwork designs on the walls and parapets of Tudor houses.

In these playful gardens there were parts laid out especially for play: bowling-alleys and tennis courts, archery butts and cockpits, and mazes, which they called labyrinths—"a delectable labyrinth," says one writer, and delighted to bewilder his friend therein "till he cannot recover himself without your help." There were pools for bathing and for fish, and if you made your Mount near the boundary of your garden, says Markham, you could fish over the hedge in your own moat: a delightful picture which somehow reminds us of Tristram Shandy's Uncle Toby.

They took, too, a particular delight in what they call "water surprises"—fountains spurting water in every unlikely and curious way, or suddenly drenching the unsuspecting audience; for this, they considered, was the most entrancing of practical jokes. At Whitehall there was a much-admired fountain worked by a gardener from a distance, and one of the few improvements Elizabeth made at Hampton Court was "a splendid high and massy fountain, with a water-work by which you can, if you like, make the water play upon the ladies and others who are standing by and give them a thorough wetting." If we can get used to such crudities in people who appreciated equally the most delicate lyric poetry, then we are less shocked by Shakespeare's dreadful clowns.

What we notice, reading about the Tudor gardens or looking at the illustrations, is how alive they are, how full not only of flowers and ornaments but of active human beings. They are best considered as an extension of the house, where people lived their lives in the open air as we never have done since. In the pictures they are doing all kinds of things which we have never since included in our garden scenes—playing cards, eating their dinner, paddling, making love, fishing, wandering in mazes, chasing each other, rolling on the ground, playing with monkeys, splashing each other with water from the ponds. Anything, in fact, but sitting still, which is what we do now. They held Revels in their gardens, Masques and Pageants, and Elizabeth received ambassadors in her garden at Whitehall, where I dare say her Latin was just as overwhelming among the gillyflowers and roses as anywhere else. We can understand the writer who describes the busy garden scene at Kenilworth: "the people, the fruit trees, the plants, the herbs, the flowers, the birds flittering, the fountain streaming, the fish swimming, all in such delectable variety, at one moment in one place."

Bacon in his essay "On Gardens" shows a feeling for space which is ahead of his time. Let the main plot, he says, "be not too busy or full of work"; but except for its size (and Bacon is very much a gardener on paper, where it is as easy to write 20 acres as 2), his garden proper is very little different from any other garden of his period. He describes a plan for a prince's pleasure-ground which he obviously considers is free from silly fancies; he despises knots and topiary work as fit only for children, but the decorations he suggests instead are even more fanciful and charming. The main hedge, he says, is to be trained on "carpenter's work" into a series of arches, and above each arch a little turret to hold a cage of birds, and between them "some other little figure with broad plates of coloured glass for the sun to play upon." The bathing-pool, too, is to be "finely-paved and with images, and embellished with coloured glass."

At Hampton Court, in the old gardens which lie between the Orangery and the river, we can still feel what privilege has meant in England, how the English character has expressed itself when money and power were unlimited. The proud princes of Italy built proud palaces and gardens to match; the ceremonious court of France was perfectly expressed in the glories of Versailles. But these have no real place in England. We are awkward at ceremony, embarrassed at display. The ambitious mansions of our eighteenth-century England are cold and theatrical and ostentatious. For all their splendours, they have a curious air of the *nouveau riche:* we feel they were built, not as a fitting background for a magnificent way of life, but only as a magnificent way of keeping up with the Joneses. As Dr. Johnson said of one of them, "It would do excellently for a town-hall. The large room with pillars would do for the Judges to sit in at the Assizes; the circular room for a jury-chamber; and the rooms above" (the bedrooms, which were skimped, as not being part of the fine show to dazzle visitors) "the rooms above for prisoners."

Their owners, we cannot help suspecting, seldom used the ceremonious front door, but strode cheerfully out at the back to their dogs and horses in the stable yard, the only part of most of these cold palaces with any atmosphere of life and affection.

The most famous shops of England have no imposing entrances, no fine windows, no lights or plate glass or thick carpets or smart assistants. They are in back streets with only a modest private-looking window, and nothing in it but a small plate quietly announcing in old-fashioned type the name of a world-famous tailor.

In England privilege is astonishingly discreet. Not a Lord Mayor's coach driving through cheering crowds, but a closed motor-car which slips through cleared streets almost unnoticed. And the old gardens of Hampton Court are like the tailors' shops and the closed car. Their privilege is in privacy and a complete disregard of any impression they may make. As the pleasure-grounds of a powerful king, they are a marvel of understatement. But because they are an unforced and natural expression of something inherently English, they are still alive, even though they are stripped now of their Tudor fancies of beasts and rails and sun-dials, unsuitably planted with the wrong trees and flowers, and misnamed the Dutch Garden. They still have an authentic air, as the seventeenth-century formal gardens have not—the great parterre and the long canal which are only empty and desolate, like the clothes we never wear because we do not feel at ease in them, they do not suit us.

But these were the pleasure-grounds of princes. What of the humbler gardens of ordinary people? For Stow talks constantly of "fair garden plots" and "gardens of pleasure," and in Tudor times more people were interested in gardening than ever before. Reading the books of Instructions for Gentlemen, we realize that

A Tudor plan for a garden. A. *All these squares must be set with Trees, the Garden and other Ornaments must stand in spaces betwixt the Trees, and in the borders and fences.* B. *Trees twenty yards asunder.* C. *Garden Knots.* D. *Kitching Garden.* E. *Bridge.* F. *Conduit.* G. *Staires.* H. *Walks set with great wood thick.* I. *Walks set with great wood round about your Orchard.* K. *The Out-fence.* L. *The Out-fence set with stone fruit.* M. *Mount. To force Earth for a Mount or such like, set it round with quick, and lay boughes of Trees strangely intermingled, the tops inward, with the Earth in the middle.* N. *Still house.* O. *Good standing for Bees, if you have an house.* P. *If the River run by your door, and under your Mount, it will be pleasant.*

there was no great difference between any of their gardens. The carved beasts and marble "inventions" of the wealthy were replaced in humbler gardens by clipped trees; instead of banketting-houses there were green arbours roofed with vines and walled with roses; but they are all unmistakably the gardens of Tudor England.

The first essential, as in mediæval gardens, was still the outside enclosure. This might be a moat or bank or fence, or a "Hedge of Quicksett verie thicke," or any combination of these all at once, for in the pictures there are often two or three layers one inside the other. Along the front of the house there was often a terrace which overlooked the whole enclosure, and round the garden there was generally a gallery or covered alley, formed either of pleached trees—yews or hornbeams or limes, like the modern one at Kensington Palace—or made by building a wooden scaffolding and covering it with "arch-hearbes"—vines or roses, "jacimine honeysocke or Ladies' Bower," which was a clematis. These walks were sometimes planted with scented herbs for the pleasure of their fragrance when they were trodden on, and the galleries were often enlarged into little arbours or "shadowe houses," arbours, says Parkinson, "being both gracefull and necessary." These shadow-houses were carpeted with grass, and Surflet tells us how to make the turf grow close and fine. The ground must first "bee cleansed from all manner of stones and weeds, not so much as the roots left undestroyed, and afterwards the floore must be beaten and troden downe mightily; then after this, there must be cast great quantity and store of turfes of earth full of greene grasse, the bare earthie part of them being turned and laied upward, and afterward daunced upon with the feet, in such sort as that within a short time after, the grasse may begin to peepe up and put forth like small haires; and finally it is made the sporting green plot, for Ladies and Gentlewomen to recreate their spirits in, or a place whereinto they may withdraw themselves if they would be solitarie and out of sight." The ladies of the Middle Ages would certainly have felt at home there.

The garden inside the surrounding green tunnels of the gallery was divided into more or less regular "compartiments" ("every man will please his own fancie"), and these were separated by paths and enclosed by hedges or palings, or perhaps by "Lattise worke continued into arbours, or as it were" (for they can never resist a fanciful idea) "into small chappells or oratories and places to make a speech out of, that many standing about and below may heare." I wonder what sort of speeches they made from such green pulpits.

Each of these small enclosures was a separate little garden, beds of flowers in one, "like a peece of tapestry of many glorious colours," and herbs perhaps in another. Herbs included what we should now call vegetables, and though they were sometimes grown separately in a kitchen or summer garden, there was no strict division, though "your Garden flowers shall suffer some disgrace," one writer warns us, "if among them you intermingle Onions Parsnips etc." There were gardens, too, for strewing-herbs—plants to strew on the floor instead of carpets, to "turn up the house," as they called it. The common ones were the aromatic plants we still call herbs today, but for honoured guests roses and violets were scattered where they walked, and Queen Elizabeth's favourite strewing-herb was meadowsweet.

Fruit trees might be planted in another division, or perhaps a nosegay garden, "with hearbes and flowers used to make nosegaies and garlands of." They give lists of suitable flowers, but "Beares eares or French Cowslips" (auriculas) are best of all, says Parkinson; "their flowers being many set together upon a stalke doe seeme every one of them to be a Nosegay alone of itselfe . . . with a pretty sweete sent which doth adde an encrease of pleasure in those that make them an ornament for their wearing." For what the seventeenth century calls a "nosegaie" we should call a buttonhole.

I have a friend who once kept a buttonhole garden in his gallant courting days, a little plot behind the house where he went every morning to choose a flower for his coat. And his favourite was love-in-a-mist—not for the name, as we might suppose, but because it grew its own green, a neat fringe of feathery leaves arranged like a ruff around the flower: the perfect buttonhole. I have felt more warmly towards him ever since, for nothing is more endearing than the rather ridiculous enthusiasms of our friends.

Most popular of all was the knot garden, and the books are full of patterns for them, page after page of "knots so enknotted it cannot be expres't," for who could resist drawing such very easy illustrations? Although these tortuous designs of hedges sound to us elaborately ugly (and quite shockingly wasteful of labour), yet they must have had a curious formal charm, like embossed velvet.

The paths dividing the garden beds are made of gravel, or sand beaten firm, or "the powder of the sawing of marble," and they are very narrow: "You shall marke out your Beds and Floores" (flower beds) "and the Pathes running along betwixt them. . . . And you must observe, that you make your Floores of such widenesse as that you may stride and reach your armes from one side to another, to the end that such as are to weed them, or to rake them, may from out of the said little Pathes be able to reach unto the middest of the Bed, and not to tread with their feet upon that which is sowne. Wherefore, if your said little Pathes be two feet wide, it will be ynough: for to make them anie broader, is but waste and losse of ground."

We can see why Bacon wanted space, and what he means by gardens "too busy and full of work," for these gardens were without lawns: the whole space was covered with beds and paths and hedges. The flower beds were often raised above the paths and edged with boards or tiles or pebbles or shells, or even by rows of sheep bones, "which prettily grace out the ground." "In places beyond the seas," so Parkinson says, they even use the jaw-bones of animals arranged in rows, but this he considers "too grosse and base." I suppose if they had had bottles or jam jars they would have used those, too, as cottage gardeners do still. In the beds they grew all the old-fashioned flowers of the mediæval gardens: Primroses, Cowslips, Rose Campions, Batchelours Buttons (which were double campions), Stocks, Wall-flowers, Violets, Columbines, Snapdragons, Larkes-heeles (or spurres or toes), Roses, Pansies, Poppies, Double Daisies, Marigolds, French Marigolds "that have a strong heady sent," Pinks, Peonies, Hollihocks, Sweet Williams and Sweet Johns, and "Daffadown-dillies which flower timely and after Midsummer are scarcely seen. They are more for Ornament than use, so are Daisies."

The most cherished flower of all, the "pride of our English Gardens," the "Queene of delight and of flowers," was the Gilly-

Master Tuggie his Rose Gilloflower.

flower or Carnation, which was brought to England by the Flemish refugees under Henry VIII, and for more than a century was the "chiefest flower of account of all our English Gardens." It was called Gillyflower or July-flower because of its season of blooming, and stocks were called Stock Gillyflowers for the same reason. But why wallflowers were called Wall-Gillyflowers I have never been able to make out, unless it was because they resembled single stocks and people had already forgotten what Gillyflower meant. The country folk of Sussex still call sweet rocket June Gillies. In any case, the old carnations can never have been so attractive as the names the gardeners gave them. I wonder what the Grey Hulo looked like, or Ruffling Robin, or Master Bradshawes Dainty Lady. But Master Tuggie was the famous name—"Master Tuggie his Rose Gilloflower," writes Parkinson under one of his illustrations, and later on, with growing enthusiasm: "Master Tuggie his Princesse." I hoped to find somewhere,

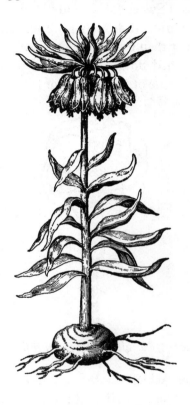

The Crown Imperial.

as the crowning happiness, "Master Tuggie his Queene," but if he ever raised anything finer than his Princesse, Parkinson does not tell us about it.

Besides these old favourites, there were hundreds of new plants from the enlarging world, from the "Indies, Americans, Taprobane, Canary Isles and all parts of the world." "Out-landish Flowers" Parkinson calls them, and they made the new gardens so beautiful, says one enthusiastic writer, that, compared with them, "the ancient gardens were but dung-hills" and even the Gardens of the Hesperides, he boasts, if set beside ours, "I am persuaded that an equal judge would give the prize unto the garden of our days." Parkinson gives a list of the Outlandish Flowers which were most successful and popular, many of them blooming in early spring when our own flowers were scarce. Daffodils, Jacynthes (hyacinths), Saffron-flowers (crocuses), Lillies, Flower

Drawing by Crispin de Passe.

de luces (irises), Tulipas, Anemones, French Cowslips or Beares eares, and Fritillaries, which included the Crown Imperial—a flower, says Parkinson, which "for his stately beautifulness deserveth the first place in this our Garden of delight." How I longed to say beautifulness when I was a child—it was so much more vivid than beauty, which was a remote and abstract word, the kind of word people put on monuments to the unreal dead. But beautifulness was the actual texture of the living petals in your hand.

The Tudor gardeners grew runner beans, not to eat but for their scarlet flowers, using them as "arch-hearbes" to train on trellises as we do sweet peas. Nasturtiums, too, were grown as climbers; they were one of Parkinson's favourite flowers. Indian Cresses he calls them, or yellow Larkes heeles: "the whole flower hath a fine small sent, very pleasing, which being placed in the middle of some Carnations or Gilloflowers (for they are in flower at the same time) make a delicate Tussiemussie, as they call it, or Nosegay, both for sight and sent."

Rosemary was the favourite shrub, and among its many uses were the making of bridal wreaths and the seasoning of food. They grew it not only as a bush, but trained to cover walls, or cut into topiary figures, strewing the scented clippings on their floors. Many of the flowers we still grow today the Tudor gardeners knew by other names. Lilac was the Blew Pipe-tree, cyclamens were Sowebread, monkshood was the Blew Helmet Flower, the gladiolus was the Corneflagge, Canterbury bells were Coventry Bells, winter aconite was Winter Wolfesbane, cornflowers were Blew Bottles or Sions, honesty was the Sattin-flower, and pansies were Love-in-Idleness. The snake's-head fritillary they called the Checkered Daffodill, or the Ginny-hen Flower because the markings on the petals reminded them of a Guinea fowl's feathers; and tomatoes, which they grew for decoration, they called Love Apples because they considered them an aphrodisiac. Which lends a new interest to a respectable domestic vegetable.

They grew, too, many flowers which were merely curious, like the little trefoils called Snailes or Barbary Buttons from their oddly twisted seed-pods, "pretty toyes for Gentlewomen," and all kinds of curious primroses and cowslips: Hose-in-Hose, Curled Cowslips or Gaskins, and one they called the Foolish Cowslip or Jack-an-Apes-on-Horse-backe, a name country people used, so Parkinson says, for anything they found strange or fantastic.

In their delight in all things curious and fanciful, the Tudor gardeners persuaded even their fruit and vegetables to grow into strange shapes. The fruit was put in moulds while it was young, and "so you may have cucumbers as long as a cane or as round as a sphere; or formed like a cross. You may have also apples in the form of pears or lemons. You may have also fruit in more accurate figures, of men, beasts, or birds, according as you make the moulds." This advice is from Bacon, of all people, who despised knot gardens as no better than the pastry patterns on the tops of tarts.

There were aviaries in the Tudor gardens, but they loved best the "infinite number of pretie small Birds" which came freely to keep them company, "the gentle Robin-red-breast and the silly Wren, with her distinct whistle (like a sweet Recorder)." But the "chief grace that adornes a garden" was "a broode of Nightingales [whose] strong delightsome voyce, out of a weake body, will beare you company night and day."

Peacocks they kept both for use and pleasure, for "the peacock is a bird of more beautified feathers than any other that is, he is quickly angry, but he is far off from taking good hold with his feet, he is goodly to behold, very good to eat, and serveth as a watch in the inner court, for that he spying strangers to come into the lodging he failleth not to cry out and advertise them of the house." Thomas Tusser, in his *Five Hundred Pointes of Good Husbandrie,* complains that peacocks scratch up the seedlings, but his eighteenth-century editor tells us in a footnote what we must do. If you find your peacock, he says, in any part of the garden where he is not wanted, "with a little sharp Cur that will bark, tease him bout as long as he can stand, at least till he takes his flight, and he will come no more there." I dare say not.

These Tudor gardens are not very different from the gardens of the Middle Ages, but only grown more confident. They are still small, still rigidly enclosed, still divided up into little compartments without any idea of planning the space as a whole. Like the mediæval gardens, they are not a setting for the house but an extension of it—rooms for outdoor living—and almost as crowded, with their flowers and bushes and ornaments and "artificial inventions," and with the cheerful people who came to enjoy it all, for the people are gay now as they seldom were before.

If the gardens are still only a development from the Middle Ages, so, too, is the science behind them. Men still believed that plants were a spontaneous generation of the earth, and that any soil would bring forth the flowers inherent in it without the need of sowing seeds; "the great Mother of all living Creatures, the Earth, is full of seed in her Bowels, and any stirring gives them heat of Sun, and being laid near day, they grow," says Lawson, who is a better writer than he is scientist. But it is a belief easy enough to understand in any gardener who clears his own beds of the "weeds which earth utters forth of its own accord."

Nor had the Tudor botanists any satisfactory system of classifying plants. They group them as they please, by the shape of their leaves, or chance resemblances of their flowers, from the kind of places where they are found or by their habit of growing. So that Parkinson puts periwinkle with clematis and passion flower (which he calls the Virginia Climer) because they all need support. Neither did these early gardeners know anything of the pollination of flowers, and the results we get by crossing they believed they could achieve by grafting, a procedure in which they had an astonishingly blind faith. Fruit trees grafted on holly, they thought, might bear in the winter, a rose grafted on broom would have yellow flowers, a peach on an almond would obligingly grow a nut for a kernel; and an apple on a colewort or cabbage, so someone reported from the Low Countries (where all kinds of marvels seem to have happened in those days), "will bear a great flaggy apple, and the kernal of which, if it be set, will be a colewort and not an apple."

They had many other curious theories, just as easily disproved, so one would think, by simple experiment: that garlic planted round a rose-tree would make the roses smell sweeter by drawing away the bitter juices of the earth; that "Basill ill-tended" changed to rosemary; that two plants could be crossed by binding their young shoots together. The beliefs they profess in the virtues of herbs are so extravagant that we cannot help wondering whether they ever tried them for themselves, and if so, why they were ever ill. They even supposed that plants carried the sign of that part of the body they were intended to cure—what they called the plant's Signature. "Nature, or rather the God of nature," says William Coles, who was a religious man, "having stamped on them legible characters to discover their uses"—a principle which would prescribe kidney beans for the kidneys.

Drawing by Crispin de Passe.

Writer after writer makes the most surprising claims, but to quote only my favourite Elizabethan warning against lettuces: "The plentifull and dayly eating of the Lettuce of married persons is very incommodious and noysome to them, in that it not only doth diminish the fruitfulness of children, but the children often borne do become idle foolish and peevish persons." This is a sad prospect for vegetarians, though perhaps they are safe if they do not marry. Nor are all their suggestions so unlikely. To soothe fretful babies, says one herbalist, make an infusion of white garden poppies and give them to drink. We wonder if the tired parents ever tried their own opium, and whether the fretful babies had curious dreams.

Bacon's *Naturall Historie* is an astonishing book, for, although we often think of him as the first of the modern practical scientists, he seems to believe every superstition he hears; that oak boughs planted will grow into wild vines, and the stumps of beech trees into birches. "It is thought by some," he says, "that the ends of low rainbows fall more upon one kind of earth than another: as it may well be." And he tells us "the old tradition of a maiden that was fed with napellus, which is counted the strongest poison of all vegetables, which with use did not hurt the maid, but poisoned some that had carnal company with her."

Parkinson is more sceptical about such stories: "I know none such to be true, nor to be of any more worth than an old Wives Tale, both nature, reason, and experience, all contesting against such an idle fancy, let men make what ostentation they please." "They are but men and have their Errors," Lawson had said philosophically, but, for so mild a man, Parkinson is unexpectedly sweeping in his condemnation of all the traditional science of the old gardeners: "Without all doubt and question I will assure you that they are all but meere idle tales and fancies, without all reason or truth, or shadow of reason or truth."

Even Bacon is doubtful of the "fabulous narration, that in the northern countries" (I wonder if he meant the Low Countries) "there should be an herb that groweth in the likeness of a lamb, and feedeth upon the grass, in such sort as it will bare the grass round about." As he says, a very fabulous plant, but one we can see for ourselves on the title page of Parkinson's *Paradisus*, a grazing lamb which looks very awkward and unhappy on the top of its stalk.

Bacon's own observations, however, are scarcely more convincing. Most trees, he says, have no flowers, and elm and box have neither flowers nor fruits. Yet every country child knows the elm's paper shillings. Flowers can be made double, he tells us, "by often removing them into new earth," "fruit-trees watered with warm water will bear fruit without core or stone," and he suggests extraordinary experiments for changing one plant into another—the Transmutation of Species, as he calls it.

It is very difficult to understand the mind of anyone who says, as Bacon does, that the differences between plants and metals are chiefly three: (1) metals are more durable, (2) more solid, (3) are "wholly subterrany," while plants are half above ground. To us this is the reasoning of a child or a lunatic, yet Bacon's curiosity about the physical world was an interest which was soon to develop into the scholarly work of the Royal Society, the birthplace of modern science in England. Besides, we should all be grateful to Bacon for being the first gardener to realize the value of leaf-mould: "it were good to try whether leaves of trees swept together would not make a good compost; for there is nothing lost so much as leaves of trees." What a relief it is to find something else recommended besides Willow-earth, that John Innes Compost of the old gardeners which they tell us to use on every other page: "the fine earth or mould which is found in the hollow of old Willow-trees, rising from the root up almost to the middle of the Tree, at least so far as the tree is hollow, for than this, there is no earth or mould finer or richer." I dare say not, but it is hard to believe there ever could have been enough hollow willow trees for all the Willow-earth we should need if we followed the instructions of Tudor gardeners.

If in the seventeenth century we are near the end of mediæval superstition, we are also near the end of gardens in the mediæval tradition. For under the Puritans the great Tudor gardens were destroyed. Only Hampton Court was spared because Cromwell lived there, and Nonesuch by an accident survived to be given by Charles II to his mistress, who, like the Puritans, divided it up and sold it to speculators. Hampton Court, Nonesuch, Whitehall, Theobalds, Wimbledon—these famous gardens of the Tudors had continued with little change under the Stuart kings, who took the same delight in them as their more exuberant creators.

But the Puritans angrily resented such pleasure-grounds, both as signs of royal privilege and because they were laid out so whole-heartedly for enjoyment. They belonged to the "serene time of Peace [when] the people, both poore and rich, did looke cheer-fully." But now, says Aubrey sadly during the Commonwealth, "the Countenances of the people [are] all changed, melancholy, spightfull, as if bewitched."

Yet Englishmen are natural gardeners, and even the melan-choly Puritan intolerance could not wholly suppress an inborn delight in gardens as places of pleasure. Ralph Austen was both a Puritan and a gardener, as many others must have been, but he was also a writer, and in his books we can see the uneasy compro-mise between his natural spirit and his adopted convictions. *The Spirituall Uses of an Orchard of Fruit-trees*, he calls one book in a pathetic attempt to reconcile his opposing enthusiasms, but, reading it, we skip the spiritual uses and pick out the gardening, which is very easy, since the two parts are printed in different type as if to emphasize his divided mind. He was a true gardener, and loved his trees for their beautiful Blossomes even more than their useful fruits—"the trees in their Gallantries," he calls them —and his most un-Puritan delight was "to stand upon a Mount in the midst of a fair large Orchard in the spring time, and to be-hold round about a multitude of several sorts of fruit-trees, full of beautiful Blossomes, different in their shapes and colours, ravishing the sence with their sweet Odours, and within a while, turned into faire and goodly fruits of divers Colours and Kinds; the Fruit-trees gorgeosly arrayed with green leaves, and various coloured fruits, as with so many precious Jewels and Pearls."

But like so much else which they secretly desired, the Puritans were driven to destroy the Tudor gardens, and under Cromwell, Parliamentary surveys were made of the confiscated royal pleas-ure-grounds. These are unconsciously pathetic, for they show so clearly the authors' delight in what they are describing. They are not cold, business-like accounts of so many acres with so many fruit trees and so much timber, but appreciative descriptions of "a fair banqueting-house" or "an elaborate bird-cage, a great ornament both to House and Garden," a "very fair and handsome fountain" with falls which "make a pleasant noise," a "fair walk" of elms and lime trees, the covered alleys of gravelled earth "very well ordered," and "one might walk," they say wistfully, "two myle in the walkes before he came to their ends." We forget that these are the men who hired ignorant vandals "for half a Crown per Day, to break the painted Glass-Windows [of churches] which were formerly fine." We forget that the writers are describing what they intend to destroy. And so perhaps do they.

"It is strange that men should rather be quarrelling for a few trifling opinions wherein they dissent, than to embrace one another for those many fundamental truths wherein they agree." Yes. It is very strange. But the gentle light of reason could not reach the dark and deformed spirits of the Puritan zealots. Their strangely twisted consciences kept them from joining Thomas Hill's gardener who "turned to the prosperities of his hearbes and flowers for the delight and comfort of his wearied mind, which he may by himselfe or in fellowship of his friends conceive, in the delectable sightes and fragrant smells of the flowers, by walking up and downe and about the garden."

Yet Ralph Austen knew very well what he meant by such delights. For in a garden, said this Puritan who was too gentle for his faith, "a man enjoys pleasant quietnesse and tranquillity of mind, which is seldom attained by those that follow State Imployments." But it is a hesitant voice, too quiet and too reasonable to reach the violent men in State Imployments. The surveys are drawn up, the royal pleasure-grounds destroyed, and although the Puritans will be forgotten like an illness we have recovered from, and fresh gardens laid out for men's pleasure, they will no longer be the enclosed fantastic gardens of the Tudors. Once, says Aubrey, the gay music of the pipe and tabor was common through all England, "the Peasants danced to it on Holy days, with joy and merriment." But now, he says, with a regret which is only partly for a lost antiquity, "the Drumme and Trumpet have putt that peacable Musique to silence."

CHAPTER FIVE

EARLY
SEVENTEENTH
CENTURY
GARDEN
LITERATURE

IN THE KIND OF BEST PARLOUR WHERE THE
piano had a white lace cover and family photographs on the
top, there were always two books in the small collection locked
away in the glass-fronted cupboard: the Authorized Version of
the Bible and the Works of Shakespeare. These are the unquestioned classics of English literature, and they both belong to the
early seventeenth century.

I suppose everyone makes their own arbitrary divisions of the
arts into periods, and for me early seventeenth-century literature
is not a space of time bounded by dates, but a period of writing
defined by qualities of thought and style. It begins towards the
end of the sixteenth century and ends somewhere in the middle
of the seventeenth, but it overlaps the periods before and after
like the fingers of clasped hands. It is an age when our literature
far surpasses the other arts, as indeed it generally has done in
England, but never more magnificently than in this seventeenth
century of our greatest glories. And because the level of writing
is so high, even among lesser authors, it is the only time when
ordinary books on gardening may perhaps be fairly considered
as literature. The poetry of Marvell and Herrick, the essays of
Sir Thomas Browne, are garden writing which everyone knows
of, but even the forgotten writers of handbooks share the early

seventeenth-century gift of prose which is a delight to read. They write clearly and vividly, often with the suggestion of beauty which is the true poetry of prose; they encounter their world as a direct experience, and describe it in exact and evocative phrases. At their best, as in the writing of Surflet and Markham and Lawson, they express almost unconsciously the curious wit and the brooding sense of strangeness which are the especial fascination of the early seventeenth century.

In the arts there seem to be particular states of consciousness and sensibility which can be expressed in different mediums depending on the nature of the artist—poet, painter, musician. Generally this particular way of feeling the world and expressing it in art is evident in artists of the same period. It is not only their own personal awareness, but the style (or whatever we choose to call it) of their time. They are great because their own consciousness corresponds to the consciousness of their age, and therefore finds its perfect expression in the forms and styles of art which they must use. So that they vary, not in the *kind* of art they produce, but in its quality; they are not so much different from other artists of their time, as better or worse.

This conception of the spirit of the age, as I suppose we might call it, must always be a very personal judgment, and may have no meaning for someone else who finds in the same artists quite different qualities; who sees perhaps the individual more clearly than the period, as we all do with art which is near to us in time. But for me, who have great difficulty in remembering music, even a completely unknown piece by Beethoven is easy to place because he reminds me unmistakably of Wordsworth and Constable. If I am out of sympathy with the art which develops from them, I even feel that the rot sets in with all of them, as someone said of Beethoven. It is not, certainly, that they are equally great, or can be expressed in terms of each other, but that the values they are conscious of in the world, the kind of beauty to which they are naturally sensitive, is the same for each of them.

But I think this same sensibility in the different arts need not always correspond in time or place. There is a special quality in early seventeenth-century writing which we come to recognize as the peculiar essence of the period. It is a particular kind of beauty, intellectual, subtle, rarified, and with a strange deliberate distortion which is of the mind and not the senses, as if emotion had been most curiously translated through intellect into art. We

Drawing by Crispin de Passe.

find it almost nowhere else in English literature, and for me the music which corresponds to this early seventeenth-century writing is Bach's in the eighteenth century, and the painting is Piero della Francesca's in the fifteenth-century Italian Renaissance. The special kind of rare and vivid pleasure I feel in reading Milton's "Ode on the Morning of Christ's Nativity" is the same as the pleasure in listening to the Brandenburg concertos or looking at Piero's "Baptism of Christ."

Nor is this correspondence perhaps so very unlikely. The sensibility of the early Renaissance was born in Italy, and took perhaps a century and more of bad communications to travel as far north as England and penetrate our vigorous and insular fashions. And if we think of the seventeenth century instead of the sixteenth as the early Renaissance in England, then the classicism of the late seventeenth and eighteenth centuries follows as an echo of the Italian High Renaissance and our eighteenth-century architects go naturally to Palladio's sixteenth-century villas for inspiration.

If it is true that art generally expresses the character of its period more clearly than that of its particular author, it is certainly so in early seventeenth-century literature. Here we recognize the period unmistakably and only afterwards the author. Even Shakespeare, who transcends all rash generalizations, has more in common with other poets and playwrights of his day than we realize in our first dazzled delight. We recognize him (when we *do* recognize, for the scholars differ) not by any particular style, but by his excellence. For he has a hundred different styles, as he has a hundred different characters, and Shakespeare as an individual is inscrutably universal. What we do unmistakably recognize is the style of the early seventeenth century, the quality of the *period*, the way many men's minds worked at that time, the way they looked at things and expressed them in words, the kind of beauty which satisfied them. It is not simple, for their minds are strange and intensely poetic, their knowledge is a fruitful transition between mediæval superstition and modern ideas, they take pleasure in a curious wit of words and conceits, and for all their age of stormy passions, they have an intense brooding quietness, a sense of strangeness underlying the everyday world.

"Spirit" is a word of such vague meaning that we need to define it for ourselves if we are going to use it. We can say that it is a part of man's consciousness lying beyond his emotions and his intellect. These are specialized and limited activities of his mind which the spirit transcends, and it is when a man succeeds in conveying the experiences of his spirit that his art is valid. For the direct expression of emotion is not art, nor is the statement of intellectual conceptions—neither weeping nor the multiplication table—but the experience of the spirit in these activities is the material the artist works with.

Although this universally authentic region of the spirit is the realm where all great art belongs, there are various ways of reaching it. For much of the nineteenth century, for instance, it is through the emotions. They love or hate or are pitiful or angry, and though much of what they produce is no more than the out-pouring of their feelings, now and again they crystallize out the spiritual experience which will go on living long after their (or our) love or hatred is dead. Renoir, for example, painted women with desire—he tells us so in unequivocal terms. His nudes are soft and warm and delicious, they are a generous flowering from a rich and solid earth. But in his greatest pictures he paints not simply a woman he has desired, but the lovableness of all women. Our reactions are not of the senses but of the spirit, and we look at his finest nudes not with desire, but with a kind of pity. We are moved in the same way as we are moved by tales of generous or noble actions, by fine architecture or music or poetry.

The seventeenth century approached this realm of the spirit not through the emotions, but through the intellect. From a steady level of mental activity they suddenly take wing and soar to the higher air. Their problem is not to find solid rock in the swirl of their emotions, but to make their intellectual conceptions live, to feel them as vividly as we all feel hate or anger. So that where the nineteenth century degenerates into sentiment, the seventeenth century degenerates into pedantry. There are pages and pages which affect us only as an intellectual exercise, which we read with the same limited attention which the non-musical like myself bring to Bach's *Art of the Fugue*. We keep alert whatever faculty of our minds it is which responds to artistic excellence, but the pedestrian stretches between the high flights we let pass over us as a kind of technical chatter. So that, reading idly through the curious pedantry of the *Garden of Cyrus*, we are suddenly startled by a thunder of magnificence: "Providence hath arched and paved the great house of the world." Or "All things began in order, so shall they end, and so shall they begin again." Or "Darkness and light hold interchangeable dominions."

But before we consider the fine flowers of any garden, we need to know something of the soil they grow from, the ordinary prose style of the time. This is necessarily the medium of the writer, the stuff from which he must create his masterpieces. He may mould the language of the day, use it and make it his own, but still it is the raw material he starts with, and Shakespeare would not have written as he did at any other time than the early seventeenth century. We must forget, then, Sir Thomas Browne on gardens, and listen to the ordinary prose of the day simply giving instruction with no other thought than to make the meaning clear. Here are three passages from handbooks on gardening and other country occupations, for they are all set out together—husbandry, gardening, hunting and hawking, angling, cock-fighting, and the keeping of bees.

First an early account of smoking tobacco: "The inhabitants of Florida doe feed themselves a certaine space with the fume of this hearbe which they take at the mouth by meanes of certain small hornes . . . the truth whereof we gather by mariners comming daily from the Indies, which hanging about their neckes little pipes or hornes made of reeds or rushes, at the ends of which little hornes there are put and packt manie drie leaves of this plant, writhen together and broken. They put fire to this end of the pipe, drawing in with their breath at their mouth wide open, so much of this fume as possibly they can, and affirme thereupon that they find their hunger and thirst satisfied, their strength recovered, their spirits rejoyced and their braine drencht with a delightsome drunkennesse."

Then how to tell a mad dog: "The first sign to know is a melancholy separating himself from other Dogges, and walking up and down alone, oft casting up his head into the wind, and looking upward, his tayle at the setting on, rising upward, and the rest hanging down, his Mouth will foam and be full of slaver or white froth, as he runneth up and down he will hastily snatch at everything that he meeteth with, yet, but only give one snatch and away, his eyes will be red, and more fiery then other Doggs, and his breath will be strong and of a filthy savour."

Then a sentence on so-called "English flowers": "Those flowers that have been usually planted in former times in Gardens of this Kingdome, have by time and custome attained the name of English flowers, although the most of them were never naturall of this our Land, but brought in from other Countries at one time or other, by those that tooke pleasure in them where they first saw them."

The first thing we notice is how alive the writing is, how straightforward and decisive, how clearly the language says what it means to say. In fact, how excellent it will be for the discourses of the Royal Society when Charles II blesses it in 1660. And it has a vividness and immediacy which few scientific writers have achieved since:—"one snatch and away"—four very simple words, but anyone who has seen a dog in a fit will realize how exactly and economically they describe its restless maniacal activity.

This is almost the first common English prose which is sufficiently developed to express a complicated meaning clearly and simply. The passage on English flowers, for instance, the latest of the three and written in 1629, is a complex sentence of clauses and conjunctions, the meaning is involved and subtle, but it is set down with such an easy use of language that we read it as a simple statement of fact. Yet prose is a later development than poetry (which seems an odd contradiction, as if one should dance before walking), and this is the first time ordinary Englishmen have written their language easily enough to concentrate on what they want to say instead of how to say it.

In the sixteenth century, English was newly accepted as the official language of England, for since the Conquest the court had used French, and scholars Latin. But as a literary language

English prose in the sixteenth century was still in an awkward stage of growing up. As a development from the language of the people it was too racy and vernacular for quiet writing, while as used by scholars accustomed to Latin it was stilted by classical constructions alien to English ways of language. Then, too, modern English is almost without inflections; we use conjunctions and new arrangements of words to express the meaning which was once clear from the endings. But in the sixteenth century these new ways of expression were not clearly worked out; the conjunctions seem to us haphazard, and the meaning often doubtful. The quoted passage on tobacco is the earliest of the three, and we can see that there is still some uncertainty in how to connect the phrases logically.

But by the seventeenth century these growing-pains are mostly over, and a new literary prose emerges, confident and vigorous and clear. So, too, may be the writing of other periods, but the quality of early seventeenth-century literature is essentially poetic, and as at no other time, the prose-writers express this poetry supremely well. This, too, seems a curious contradiction, yet Traherne, writing of the same subject in verse and prose, produces only mediocre poetry, but superbly poetic prose: "You never enjoy the world aright till the Sea itself floweth in your veins, till you are clothed with the Heavens, and crowned with the Stars: and perceive yourself to be Sole Heir of the whole world." But in verse this is reduced to two lines from a mid-Victorian hymn:

> *Nor till* His *Works* my *Wealth became*
> *No Lov or Peace did me enflame.*

Sir Thomas Browne writes prose with the same poetic power, and Donne in his sermons, and so, too, in a faint echo, do the writers of handbooks.

It is difficult to define what we mean by poetry in prose, but we might say that it is the evocation of beauty beyond the actual theme (a too vague definition which could equally apply to good painting). It would be easy to quote page after page from the famous writers, but here is forgotten Gervase Markham on "the best season to Angle in":

"If the day be darke, close and lowering, or have a gentle whistling and playing upon the water, it is good to Angle in, and the Fish will bite with pleasure; Nay, if a fine mizling dew of Rain fall gently, without violence, they will then bite the faster: Also after Floods are gone away, and the Rivers are come within their own Banks, the first cleerness recovered and the water pure, then is it good to Angle."

Or frosts come, he says, "the aire being calme and quiet, and in faire nightes."

Or again, he tells of a fish called the Luce "which haunteth the broad and large Mears, which are miles in compasse, being deep and still, and ever lodgeth in the bottom thereof, amongst the Roots and Tufts of Sedge and Bulrushes, being quiet and least troubled." A most poetic fish, and worthy to haunt the waters of the silver lake with Milton's fair Sabrina. Piero della Francesca can paint a dog with the same suggestive poetry.

The writers of the early seventeenth century also have a particular gift for what we have since learnt to call *le mot juste:* for finding the one word which exactly expresses the particular essence of the experience they are describing. Milton, in lines we all learnt at school and scarcely thought about, stands on a little hill looking at the summer landscape. He sees the towers and battlements of a country house set among trees—"Bosom'd high in tufted trees," he says, and we must all have seen quite often the kind of scene he describes in his short line. But let us forget for a moment his two triumphantly right words and try to find them for ourselves: forget *bosom'd* and *tufted.*

It is summer, we know from the rest of the poem. In a landscape with trees the house stands out head and shoulders high, as a bather stands in water. But how to get it into a single word? *Breast-high* perhaps? But breast will not do. It is too firm and active a word, with its associations of breasting the waves. This is soft and leafy summer, the house stands serenely among its garden trees, not breasting waves of encroaching forest. The trees are not enemies, the tree-tops are soft, bosomy, vaguely rounded. There it is: *bosom*—"bosom'd high"—the gentle but luxurious English summer scene, the height and shape of the trees against the house, the peaceful setting, all in a word.

But now for the trees themselves. He might have said *summer* trees, or *leafy* trees, or a dozen other obvious adjectives of two syllables to fit the metre. But Milton is a great poet and adjectives must be felt. So now for the trees. As a setting for the house they may be vaguely bosomy, but in themselves they are strong living structures. Under the leaves are hard twigs and firm branches. For all their soft outline, each leaf is attached accurately to the tree, they are growing. But the word? *Branching* trees perhaps? No—that would do for winter, but not summer with the branches hidden. *Billowing* trees? No. It gives no feel of their growing structure. Perhaps some word suggesting a fountain? It is very difficult. Let us sit on our hill and look at the view again.

It is like an aerial photograph of woodland, a survey of jungle seen from above. And what was it the trees reminded us of when we saw the photograph in the newspaper? Of paint-brushes. Of hundreds and hundreds of paint-brushes with their bristles in the air. Now, to describe paint-brushes is easy: they are *tufted*. And there is our word: "tufted trees." The leaves are loose and soft like the tops of the brushes, but firmly attached beneath to a strong upright trunk. *Tufted*—the softness, the firmness, the feeling of growing.

"Bosom'd high in tufted trees"—it is an earned and permanent pleasure, for we often have to earn our pleasures in the seventeenth century. Which is not to suggest for a moment that this is how Milton wrote his poem, but only that it is the kind of effort we must make to understand it. It is no use sitting back and letting the words flow vaguely over us, as we can with so much modern verse, or nineteenth-century music, or the painted ceilings of the eighteenth-century mansions. Being a great poet, Milton probably perceived with the intense poetic concentration which strikes out at once the right evocative word, as Shakespeare, they said, never stopped to blot out a line of his thousands of lines crammed with *mots justes*. Indeed, Shakespeare scarcely can have done much blotting out to write such an enormous amount in one lifetime. But we, being no poets of any kind, must work hard to follow them.

This struggle to find the right word or phrase is not so much a search as an intense effort of concentration, a deliberate attempt to escape our own identity, to feel the scene as a direct contact with something outside ourselves: to experience it, not as it stimulates our own reactions, but as it exists in itself. And although this is nonsense, and a human being can never feel how a tree exists, nor a house, yet we can try to experience them directly through our senses, without the quite irrelevant interpretation into our own life and personality. We can concentrate on the impression which comes to us from the house and the tree, and not on the associations which we supply from ourselves. We try, that is, to isolate the quality of the scene which is authentic, which is not a personal interpretation only valid for ourselves but an essential part of the scene itself and therefore valid for everyone who looks at it, as is all great art.

We look at dew on grass, for instance, as Surflet did, and are half conscious of some particular experience we would like to define exactly. The morning is damp and chilly, but that is our own reaction, it has nothing to do with the dew. The dew is clear, it sparkles, but that is not what we noticed this particular morning. It is something to do with the shape of the drops, their close tight outline, and even more to do with the way they are arranged like beads on the tips and edges of the leaves.

Now is the moment for the final effort. We must pass beyond our personal reactions of freshness and coolness, all our vague poetical associations. We must ignore all qualities of the dew which do not directly lead to this particular experience. By a trance-like concentration we must isolate the exact impression of the dew-drop on the tip of a grass-blade like a bird on a twig. There. The dew-drop *perches* like a bird—"doth pearche unto the grasse," says Richard Surflet, a Practitioner in Physicke who translated the *Countrey Farme*, and how delighted he (or his

French original) must have been to find his word, a tiny treasure of experience securely caught. And he did better than Andrew Marvell, who only got as far as the dew "scarce touching where it lyes."

There are single words from the seventeenth century which everyone remembers—the liquefaction of silk, the tempestuous petticoat, feathered rain, a cold quicksilver sweat, the poor crooked scythe, and many more. The gardening books, too, are full of such felicities: the arched petals of irises, the cornered twigs of broom, the furrowed stone of a peach, the branch-songs of birds, the purr of the springing partridge, the hawk which weeds the wood of pheasants, the nets of spiders, the curious architecture of bees, the soft mossiness of their bodies, the swarms which come forth mustering and knit together. On every page there are phrases as evocative as the phrases of poetry, vivid metaphors expressed in a single word.

Another quality of early seventeenth-century writers which we only realize by comparison with other periods, is that they write about themselves without self-consciousness. They write to make their meaning clear, not to express their own personality, and although to the reader the personality of the early seventeenth century is more alive than any other period, it is because their view of the world is so intensely their own and because they have expressed it so vividly, not because they intended to write about themselves. Even when they describe their own emotions, as they often do, they are the universal emotions of all men—joy, melancholy, repentance, love, delight in beauty, grief that youth passes—not the emotions of their individual lives and personal moods. The world they describe is outside themselves, however strongly it may be coloured by their own peculiar vision. And for our introspective age it gives their writing great force and authenticity. Writers who look inward describe a world which is valid for themselves, but only incidentally so for other people. If Milton's *bosom'd* had described his relations with his wives, and not the shape and texture of summer trees, it would be of no particular interest to anyone but his biographer. For if we are interested in the lives of human beings, artists are unlikely to be very rewarding subjects. Poets and painters are preoccupied with poetry and painting, not with living. They are unique as artists, not as human beings.

The seventeenth century constantly enlarges our vision of the world, as lesser writers only occasionally do. Our age could not produce Shakespeare for the parlour bookshelf, nor the Authorized Version of the Bible, whose translators, as if by a deliberate effort of inspiration, transcended their own identities and let the subject speak through them for itself, simply, magnificently, and timelessly. This preoccupation with their subject leads to a different kind of unselfconsciousness in the garden writers. In the great it is part of their universal quality, but in these lesser people it shows as a most endearing unawareness of the impression they may make on the reader. It is Pepys's greatest charm, that and his unfailing *joie de vivre*. For he has no idea at all of being funny (indeed, he is almost completely without any sense of humour) when he tells us how his midnight singing delighted the neighbours: "It being a very fine moonshine, my wife and Mercer come into the garden, and my business being done, we sang till about twelve at night, with mighty pleasure to ourselves and neighbours by their casements opening."

He has no more suspicion of seeming absurd than George Herbert, who wishes to be an orange tree to praise God more busily:

> *Oh that I were an Orange-tree,*
> > *That busie plant!*
> *Then should I ever laden be,*
> > *And never want*
> *Some fruit for him that dressed me.*

It is simply that they are untroubled by our exaggerated dread of looking silly. Ridicule is not an enemy it has ever occurred to them to fear or even notice. So Pepys tells us happily about his new clothes: "Up, and this day put on my close-kneed coloured suit, which, with new stockings of the colour, with belt, and new gilt-handled sword, is very handsome." Of course we feel the same in our own new clothes, but once grown beyond childhood, we are too self-conscious, too anxious to seem sophisticated. We would never begin our diary for the year as Pepys does: "Myself in a most handsome and thriving condition." But he is not boasting; it is rather a kind of innocence, which we have lost. He is equally frank about the house where he was "most prince-like lodged, with so much respect and honour, that I was at a loss how to behave myself."

So Surflet, telling us how to trim our trees into topiary balls, says we must take extra trouble to cut them neatly on the outside hedge where people see them—"You must cut them for the sight of the Countrey, as round as ever you can." And Evelyn, after an exhausting list of varieties of fruit trees, tells us that he only put them in to make a show, and there are no more than five worth growing—"Now of all these Fruite-trees which I have named for pomp and variety, the very best are those under named, almost all the others hardly worth the Curiosity." And "this is a noble experiment," says Bacon, that Machiavellian figure of the *Essays*, describing how he made seeds grow more quickly in a hot-bed, "but there doth not occur to me, at this present, any use thereof for profit; except it should be for sowing of peas, which have their price very much increased by the early coming." And "All to bed," says Pepys, "without prayers, it being washing-day to-morrow."

But these writers are not childish because they write innocently. They are men at peace with themselves and the world, so that they feel no need to be on their guard, and care not at all if they seem sometimes absurd. Indeed, in the seventeenth century they may not have seemed absurd at all, for their carefully composed title pages are an especial pleasure: "A Way to Get Wealth . . . gathered for the Benefit of Great Brittain . . . a Work very necessary and useful for Gentlemen . . . Gathered together for the general Good and Profit of the Common-wealth, by exact and assured Experience."

Early 17th-Century Garden Literature

As people, the seventeenth-century writers are so delightful that, above all others we have met, we would wish to keep them as our friends. "To the Friendly Reader" they address their books, and that is exactly what I am; not a Dear Reader or a Courteous Reader or an Ingenious Reader, as they will call me later on, but a Friendly Reader, happy to be in their company and sorry always to leave them. If we wished to convert an unbeliever to Christianity, we might well send him to read the seventeenth-century religious writers: Herbert's *Temple*, Jeremy Taylor's *Holy Living*, Browne's *Religio Medici*, Traherne's *Centuries of Meditations*. They are such charming people, they are so lovingly concerned for our soul's happiness, that one might well turn Christian simply for fear of hurting their feelings. Certainly they would not convince our intelligence with their unquestioning acceptance of miracles, but they are so gentle, so good, above all so happy, that we feel the Christian belief must have some intrinsic virtue for human beings beyond its doubtful value as truth. But then we remember that they believed in a savagely vindictive hell, and that Sir Thomas Browne, who was proud of his tolerance, caused women to be burned as witches. It is safer, after all, to share their harmless delight in gardens, and their charm is just as vivid.

"The most pleasant and delectable thing for recreation is our Flower Garden, to behold out at a window faire and comely Proportions, handsome and pleasant Arbors, and, as it were, Closets, delightfull borders of Lavender, Rosemarie, Boxe and other such like: to heare the ravishing musicke of an infinite number of pretie small Birds, which continually, day and night, doe chatter and chant their proper and naturall branch-songs upong the Hedges and Trees of the garden: and to smell so sweet a Nose-gay so neere at hand: seeing that this so fragrant a smell cannot but refresh the Lord of the Farme exceedingly, when going out of his bed-chamber in the morning after the Sunne-rise, and whiles as yet the cleare and pearle-like dew doth pearche unto the grasse, he giveth himselfe to heare the melodious musicke of the Bees, besides the Borders and continued Rowes of fragrant hearbes, the sight and view whereof cannot but give great contentment unto the beholder."

They have such enthusiasm, such curious and enquiring minds, they ride their hobby-horses with such zest. It is a pleasure simply to read a list of the titles of their books:

A most excellent and Perfecte Homish Apothecarye
The Gardener's Labyrinth, a discourse of the Gardener's life
A perfite platforme of a Hoppe Garden
Joyfull Newes out of the newe-founde worlde
The Garden of Health
The Jewell House of Art and Nature
The Fruiterer's Secrets
The Perfect Use of Silk-Wormes and their benefit
An Olde Thrift newly revived
The Inrichment of the Weald of Kent
A Way to get Wealthe
A Discovery of Infinite Treasure, hidden since the Worlds
  beginning
Cornucopia, a miscellaneum of lucriferous and most fructif-
  erous Experiments
The English Vineyard Vindicated
England's Happiness Increased, or a sure and easie remedy
  against all succeeding Dear Years. By a plantation of the
  roots called Potatoes

We want to sit down and read them all at once. For what could promise more pleasure than the *Joyfull Newes?* or more tempt our curiosity than the *Discovery of Infinite Treasure?* And then to have all our troubles cured by potatoes!

Much of the information in the old gardening books is repeated from one to the next, for the authors borrow from each other in an easy way which seems very shocking to our anxiously individualistic age. These early writers cared dearly for their subject, but very little for the fame of authorship. Sometimes their books are anonymous, and often signed only with initials H. F. or W. S. or Master W. L. No one seemed to mind if you used sections of someone else's book to make your own; there was no question of plagiarism. Existing writing was a common fund of material for all to use and do with as they pleased, recent writing just as much as the Classics, and there seem to have been very few dogs in seventeenth-century mangers. A good story is told and retold so often in one book after another that we cease to care who first thought of it. It belongs to whoever can tell it most vividly or use it most aptly. No one, after all, calls Shakespeare a plagiarist for taking his plots from Boccaccio, nor Racine for using the stories of Greece and Rome, though instructions for catching moles in a garden are not perhaps exactly comparable.

Of all the plagues which infest a garden, moles for me are the greatest annoyance, and in each book I turn hopefully to headings like "Offences of Moles. The Cure," hoping to find some forgotten easy way of ridding the garden of "this harmefull blind beast which turns up Garden-grounds to the great griefe and paine of the carefull Gardener." "More molehills, more ground," one writer tells me, but it is doubtful comfort, and I prefer my ground flat. The books offer a fine variety of "Cures," like burning brimstone at their holes, or "perrofin," putting onions or garlic in their runs, catching a weasel and training it to hunt them, or inviting boys to play football on any grass where moles are known to be, so that they are driven away by the thumping of so many feet. But, as for that, I would rather have my moles than the footballers. The remedy I like best of all is the "easie practice" of using a live female mole as bait to attract the others. It is a popular remedy (at least on paper), so that, reading the different versions, we become connoisseurs of the story.

"Take a live one in March, when they are a-bucking, and put the same into a verie deepe and hollow bason at night after Sunne set: burie the said bason in the earth up to the brims, so that the Moules may easily tumble into it, when they heare the captive crie in the night time: for all such as shall heare her (and this kind of cattell is of a verie light hearing) comming neere to their food, they will into the bason one after another: and by how many moe goe in, by so much will they make the greater noyse, not being able to get out againe because the bason within is smooth sleeke and slipperie." That is Surflet's version, and I think he should be given the story (though I am not sure he ought to call the mole's lady-love his "food") if only because he says brazenly that he has seen dozens together taken in this way.

But Thomas Hill, whose *Gardener's Labyrinth* appeared in 1577, is his close rival as a story-teller, and he has no equal for his remedy against frogs, which keep him awake at night with their croaking. "The Frogges which in the summer nightes are wont to bee disquieters to the husbandmen wearied through their daily labour, by chyrping and loude noyse making. Let the Husbandman set on some banck a Lanthorne lighted, or on some tree so hang a light that by the brightnesse of the same light, it may so shine upon them, as if it were the sunne, which will cause them to leave their chirping and loude noyse making." They must have had very impressionable frogs in the sixteenth century, and snakes, too, for the cure of serpents is to burn old shoes, whose smoke will not only drive away all snakes from the garden, but also bring up those which men have swallowed through sleeping carelessly with their mouth open. "By making a smoke with olde shooes burned, the serpents incontinent speed away, nore those onely flie out of the garden ground, but such as are entered into men dead sleepe in the Sommer, in sleeping open mouthed in the field, do like come forth with the said smoke."

Sometimes we are tempted to suspect that he is as amused as we are: "Barley boiled in wine and sprinkled abroad doth defend the seeds from the injurie of birds. Those being starke drunke, he" (the gardener) "willeth then to hang up by the legges, on a long rodde sticked in the earth, to the terror and fearing away of all other birds comming to the place."

But I suppose he meant it as serious advice, for it is easy to believe all sorts of extravagances of a Thomas Hill who, finding his first book a popular success, grew dissatisfied with so homely a name, and for his next book swelled Thomas Hill to Didymus

Mountain. If the world had neglected him, would he have shrunk to Tom Molehill, I wonder?

Nor was he any more credulous than Bacon, whom we think of as the father of experimental science because he died of a cold caught on Highgate Hill while he experimented with preserving a dead chicken in snow. The proverb *"Africa semper aliquid monstri parit"* (Africa is always bringing forth something monstrous), he says, "cometh for that the fountains of waters there being rare, divers sorts of beasts come from several parts to drink: and so being refreshed, fall to couple, and many times with several kinds."

The gardening books commonly include accounts of other country pleasures and occupations, and anyone with a taste for pornography might well try the seventeenth-century books on hawking—an irreproachable interest to which not even the most squeamish censor could object. Yet they have a subtly sexual intensity, these accounts of taming the beautiful fierce creatures who are trapped and tethered and sold to men for their pleasure.

The master has power of life and death over his captive hawk, but what he desires is the dominance of his will over her rebellious spirit, and that he must work for. So the strange wild creature is disciplined by darkness and captivity, by hunger and habit, sometimes by force, but chiefly by a most determined patience. Until at last, with her fierce spirit unbroken, the wild bird becomes utterly subservient to the man.

For the books speak constantly of "the man"—seldom the master or the falconer, but quite simply the man, just as the hawk is always "she."

"All Hawks generally are manned after one manner—by watching and keeping them from sleep, by a continuall carrying them upon your fist, and by a most familiar stroaking and playing with them, with the wing of a dead foul, or such like, and by often gazing and looking them in the face, with a loving and gentle countenance, and so making them acquainted with the man."

"The onely maine poynt," says Bert, is "to have his hawke in
love with him," and the man must blame himself if "instead of
gaining her love by fair Allurements he hath converted it into
Hatred Abhorrency and Disdainful Coyness." For even if she is
proud and coy, you must not "disoblige her with unkindnesse,"

Hawking.

but give her "all the content and satisfaction imaginable," even
though at first you "get no more from her than what you extort
by force." (I wonder if Shakespeare thought of manning hawks
when he wrote *The Taming of the Shrew*.) You must never neglect your hawk and so "tempt her to play the wanton," but "attend her pleasure with patience" until, says Bert, "she be farre
in love with my voyce" and "so familiarly made as that she is
well pleased with my loving dealing with her, and will attend my
comming in to her, not fearing anything so I be by her: so would
I have her wholly to relye upon mee, and be confident that when
I come unto her shee shall have her desire satisfied."

At night hawks become curiously docile, and by candlelight the falconer may do as he will with her, unsealing her eyes, putting the hated hood on and off, fondling her head and wings. But this is a candlelight courtship, and in the morning she may well be as wild and coy as ever.

This fine temperamental creature must be treated with the greatest circumspection to keep her goodwill. If she is angered by any accident, her keeper must not let her catch his eye, lest she should blame her discomfort upon him and dislike him for it. "If she be so angry as that she stare thee in the face upon any such accidentall occasion, or sodaine thought of her present bondage, owne it not, see it not, and by all means possible carry thine eye from looking upon her, for that will worke her more dislike towards thee."

It is a delightfully ridiculous picture of the man afraid to meet his hawk's eye, like Gerard de Nerval, who bought in Cairo a slave girl for his pleasure, but she soon became so completely mistress of her situation that even to set out on a journey he hesitated to wake her if she happened to be asleep. "The slave was in a bad temper," he says, and like the falconer he has no remedy but to avoid her eye.

For whatever reason we read these books, they are a pleasure for their fine English and their vivid background of country life. *Country Contentments* Markham calls his volume, or the *Husbandmans Recreations. Containing the Wholesome Experience, in which any ought to Recreate himself, after the toyl of more Serious Business. Newly Corrected, Enlarged, and adorned with many Excellent Additions, as may appear by the Mark.* And the Mark follows—a plump and very rustic-looking hand, with one finger pointing, and the drawing cut off firmly at the wrist by what I think is meant to be a lace cuff, but which looks more like a paper pie-frill. And sure enough, every so far through the book this busy hand interrupts us, pointing firmly from the margin to some Excellent Addition.

But though the hand is somewhat unconvincing, the Contentments are authentic enough. The consciousness of life in the country is so intimate, the writing so vivid and direct, that we can almost smell the background of the green English country-side.

When your hawk is ready, Markham is going to tell us, choose a fine day, take her to a stream, and encourage her to bathe. Those are the bare instructions as a townsman might give them, but Markham is a countryman. "You shall spy out a fair day when the weather and aire is most temperate, and carry your hawk to some fair, little, shallow, sandy, running brook (or Run-dle) where the water is quiet and still, and where your hawk may stand up to the mid thigh therein, and having prickt her down, and made her fast hard by the verdge thereof, you shall take off her hood, and go a little way from her and see whether she will bathe therein; but if you find her fearful of the water, you shall with a little stick paddle in the water a while before her, and then depart from her again, and let her then bathe therein as long as she pleaseth." He might have said "on a fine day take your hawk to a stream and let her bathe," but instead he has given us an intimate scene of a country gentleman's life. He is conscious of the weather, watching the clouds perhaps the night before to tell whether the morning will be fair or wild, going over in his mind the different streams of the countryside, remembering their sandy beds and the slope of their banks and whether the water runs swift or slow. Then in the warm morning he sets out alone with his hawk, very gently lest he alarm her, and tethers her in the shallow stream, so that her hooked feet are covered as they grasp the yielding sand. Then he goes away a little distance to watch, the hawk wary at first, the man curious and intent, and all around this strange preoccupied pair lies mile after mile of green country, and in the warm stillness the birds singing one beyond the other until their calls blur in a distant haze of high sweet sound.

And if the hawk still hesitates, the man goes quietly back and paddles the water gently with a little stick, so that the bird is fas-cinated by the glittering drops, and stirred by some dim instinct of her wild kind, bathes herself therein, and "this bathing giveth a hawk courage, boldnesse and great appetite."

Early seventeenth-century literature has a peculiar quality for which we have no exact word, and, for want of one, we call wit. But it is a very different quality from our present-day wit; ours is worldly, often malicious, intelligent rather than intellectual, amusing, and quite without poetry. It is the wit of Dryden, Pope, and Horace Walpole. But the wit of the seventeenth century is not concerned with amusing us or making clever epigrams; its aim is to give us pleasure of a very particular kind. It is the creation of a peculiar beauty by means of curious intellectual conceptions. At its best it is a form of poetry, but it need not be limited to words: Bach's music and Piero della Francesca's painting, for me, are witty in the same way as Milton's early poetry or the strained conceits of Donne. It is a very conscious distortion, often of things already beautiful, to create a rarer, more particular, more intellectual beauty. Milton ends his "Ode on the Morning of Christ's Nativity" with a sudden picture of the angels filling the stable where the child lies. A magnificent glory, we might think, but this is how Milton describes it:

> *And all about the Courtly Stable,*
> *Bright-harnest Angels sit in order serviceable.*

It is a very curious ending, as if he had deliberately spoiled any effect of the grand or sublime by his two surprising adjectives, *bright-harnest* and *serviceable*. But it is a highly wrought art, and although its beauty is not obvious, it is nonetheless intense. For our own age, which understands visual effects more easily than verbal ones, it is easier to see the beauty of Piero's angels than Milton's, and they are all of the same rare family. His picture of the Baptism of Christ hangs in the National Gallery, and every time I go to look at it it seems to me the most beautiful picture I have ever seen (but so do a hundred others if I look at them for long enough). Christ stands in the middle, pale as a corpse, like

all Piero's people, his flesh shadowed with green. A figure with
awkward legs pours water over him from a little basin, and above
his head a snowy dove hovers against a sky of that ethereal roof-
less blue which only Piero can paint. To the right a man is pulling
a shirt over his head, and on the left, between trees, are the three
angels. There they stand, with rather sulky faces, solid, heavy,
on thick legs and flat feet, essentially serviceable. And they are
bright-harnessed, too, dressed in blue and pink, with rainbow
wings and tight uncompromising wreaths of flowers set firmly on
their heads. Yet we see, as we look longer, that in the atmosphere
of the picture they are astonishingly beautiful: noble and serene
and real. And so are Milton's angels. They are seventeenth-
century wit at the highest level, where it becomes poetry. It is
the same curious conception of beauty which makes Botticelli
draw Venus' neck as if it were dislocated, and paint the completely satisfying understatement of her eyes, the pupils dull gold
like her hair, the whites greyish-blue like the sky behind.

Sir Thomas Browne, in defending the animals commonly considered ugly, makes a curious statement: "I cannot tell by what
Logick we call a Toad a Bear or an Elephant ugly. . . . There
is no deformity but in Monstrosity; wherein, notwithstanding,
there is a kind of Beauty: Nature so ingeniously contriving the
irregular parts, as they become sometimes more remarkable than
the principal Fabrick."

Deformity, a kind of beauty, ingeniously, irregular, more remarkable—he has himself given us words to describe the peculiar
quality of his time's wit and his own. "Methinks I have out-lived
myself, and begin to be weary of the Sun: I have shaken hands
with delight, in my warm blood and Canicular days, I perceive
I do anticipate the vices of age; the World to me is but a dream
or mock-show, and we all therein but Pantalones and Anticks, to
my severer contemplations."

But Browne's quality is rather strangeness than wit, and it is
the poets and dramatists who illustrate his definition most constantly. When Macbeth speaks his over-quoted lines:

> *. . . this my hand will rather*
> *The multitudinous seas incarnadine,*
> *Making the green one red.*

Or:

> *Sleep that knits up the ravell'd sleave of care,*
> *The death of each day's life, sore labour's bath . . .*

or almost any other of his famous utterances, that is the wit of the seventeenth century, and he would not have talked in such a way if he had come to life at any other time. For Shakespeare finds his perfect expression in this concentrated and intellectual manner, seventeenth-century wit being not something added to the subject to enliven it, as we might supply a few witty epigrams, but an inherent way of thinking and feeling.

> *Our eye-beames twisted and did thred*
> *Our eyes, upon one double string.*

> *At the round earth's imagin'd corners*

Dead bodies: *"the shells of fledge souls left behinde"*

The *"quaint enamald eyes"* of flowers

Flowers that their gay wardrop wear

But best of all I like that treasure of understatement which at the end of a hauntingly beautiful lyric sums up the legend of the dead Narcissus: "Nature's pride is now a wither'd daffodill." Following the echoing loveliness of the lines before, it is the quintessence of all the laments ever written on the age-old theme of the passing of spring and youth and beauty.

Sometimes, indeed, the wit does not convert the deformity to beauty. To talk of "sepulchrall bone-fires" is a ghoulish pun, and near-puns on the name of Jesu hardly seem in good taste. It is absurd to write poems in patterns like Alice's mouse-tail, rather horrible to call the blood flowing from a martyr's wounds his

"purple wardrobe," unsympathetic at the least to address a
drowned scholar:

> *in thee*
> *Neptune hath got an University.*

And Sir Thomas Browne's question seems scarcely pious, when
he asks whether Lazarus, coming back from the dead, had a law-
suit with his heirs.

But this is only the doubtful fringe of a peculiar way of feeling
and thinking which has left us the concentrated treasures of
seventeenth-century writing. It is a literary and highly wrought
style hardly suitable for works of instruction, but it is so wide-
spread that there are echoes even in the gardening books. The
hedgehog has his "naturall fortifications," moles are "blind vel-
veteers," the woods in Autumn "quit their leavie pretences and
come to the naked truth." The Garden of Eden, says one writer,
"is the world's most antient Monument," "God's own plantation
wherein he gave intertainment to our first Parents," to Adam and
Eve in their "imparadised condition." And once, in a forgotten
country church, above the grave of a forgotten country gentleman, I found an epitaph which Donne might have written and
Shakespeare not have been ashamed of:

> *Tis as you see nought but the Spoiles of Death,*
> *Gods High Controler and Impartial Taker;*
> *Free hold wee had of Land but none of Breath,*
> *All one day must resigne unto their Maker.*

But the supreme quality of the early seventeenth-century
writers, which gives their work such depth and mysterious splendour, is their sense of strangeness. It is not fantasy nor madness
nor fanciful invention; not Xanadu nor Kafka's nightmare world
nor the enchanted forest of the *Faerie Queene;* but an authentic
strangeness, a quality of real things, a sense that they exist in another dimension than the familiar world of daylight. It is a deeply
felt emotion of serious men, a depth they sense behind the surface
of living, as when two mirrors are set opposite each other, and

beyond the infinitely repeated reflections, at the dim end of the long arcade of receding forms, we can half make out some ultimate mystery, some glimpse of another, stranger world.

"I have found," says Traherne, "that things unknown have a secret influence on the soul, and like the centre of the earth un-

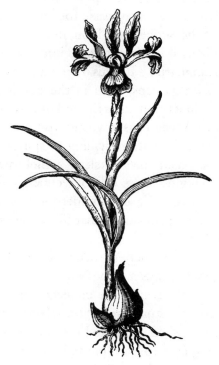

The iris or fleur de luce.

seen, violently attract it. . . . There are invisible ways of conveyance by which some great thing doth touch our souls, and by which we tend to it." And standing alone one evening in a field, he is bewildered by strange fears: "Another time in a lowering and sad evening, being alone in the field, when all things were dead and quiet, a certain want and horror fell upon me, beyond imagination. The unprofitableness and silence of the place dissatisfied me; its wideness terrified me; from the utmost ends of the earth fears surrounded me. How did I know but dangers might suddenly arise from the East, and invade me from the unknown regions beyond the seas?"

In Sir Thomas Browne we feel this strangeness at its most intense and poetical. He will write about the Garden of Cyrus, he says, and we are all ready to listen. Then comes his first sentence: "That Vulcan gave arrows unto Apollo and Diana the fourth day after their Nativities . . . may passe for no blinde apprehension of the creation of the Sunne and Moon, in the work of the fourth day; when the diffused light contracted into Orbes, and shooting rayes, of those Luminaries." It is his own unmistakable music, but nothing to do with gardens, even in the development. It is as incomprehensible in its context as the end of the same essay: "But the Quincunx of Heaven runs low, and 'tis time to close the five ports of knowledge. We are unwilling to spin out our awaking thoughts into the phantasmes of sleep, which often continueth præcognitions; making Cables of Cobwebbes, and Wildernesses of handsome Groves." We only understand that in all beauty there is a certain strangeness, and that Sir Thomas Browne gives us both in full measure.

Yet it is an ordinary homely garden which shelters this strange exotic flower. Browne was a busy Norwich doctor with a wife and family and many friends. He collects coins, he gardens, he prescribes for Mr. X's stone, he writes affectionate and sensible and quite undistinguished letters to his son in France, telling him to practise the language, to learn not to be a country bumpkin, to put on his winter underclothes in good time. And his wife adds postscripts about their little grandson Thomas—that he is sick, is better, is longing for his first breeches.

"But I am in the dark," says Browne, "to all the world, and my nearest friends behold me but in a cloud," the dark cloud of his "retired and solitary imagination" from which he utters his curious masterpieces. For suddenly the friendly chatter fades, the cheerful domestic hubbub, and in the silence we hear his strange tranced voice telling of half-apprehended visions in some far country of his mind.

This awareness of mystery in ordinary life underlies the finest thought of the seventeenth century. It is the strangeness behind Lear's madness and Hamlet's and Macbeth's; it is the background of Prospero's island, the darkness of Webster's tragedies, the Eternity which Vaughan saw

the other night
Like a great Ring of pure and endless light

—Eternity, says Traherne, which is "a mysterious absence of times and ages: an endless length of ages always present, and for ever perfect." It is the strangeness of the curious light and perspectives of Piero della Francesca's "Flagellation of Christ," of the mysterious woodland gathering of Botticelli's "Spring." Our English strangeness is darker than Italy's, for we live where a doubtful sun leaves too much of the year in gloom, but it is essentially the same. It is the sympathy which translates with such power the more mysterious passages of the Bible—the still, small voice, and Jonah in the belly of hell—and gives sometimes a depth of poetry to gardening books which were written only for instruction. "These are the signs of wind," says Surflet. "If the Clouds in a faire Season and beautifull Skie be carried on high: gathered together as they were Flockes of Sheepe; if Forests and the high tops of Mountaines doe make a noyse: if the starres of Heaven runne everie way: if the sound of Bells be sometimes heard very easily, and by and by not to be heard: if the webs and small threads of the Spyders do flye in the Aire: if the Duckes doe spread and flicker with their wings often and a long time together: if the Heron crie toward night as he is flying."

We feel, not that the wind is simply a change of weather, but some mysterious presence which disquiets the natural world. And Lawson, writing of the sap in orchard trees, feels the strangeness of this invisible flow beneath the bark—"the sap is the life of the Tree, as the blood is to man's Body; neither doth the Tree in Winter want his sap, no more than man's Body his blood, which in Winter, and time of sleep, draws inward: so that the dead time of Winter, to a Tree, is but a night of rest."

Then hunting, says Markham in the middle of a matter-of-fact treatise on country sports, "hunting is a curious search or conquest of one Beast over another." And we suddenly see Uccello's painting in the Ashmolean Museum at Oxford, a strange picture of a hunt at night. We remember the mysterious gloomy vistas between the trees, the curiously spaced figures of men and beasts, the strange preoccupied excitement of this scene before they all disappear into the searching darkness.

It is as if beneath the flowery gardens of the seventeenth century lay some dark realm where urns are buried and trees are rooted, where herons cry at nightfall, and the stars of heaven run every way, and homely Norwich doctors hear dim incantations of mysterious splendour, repeating them Sybil-like for our delight and wonder:

"The Huntsmen are up in America, and they are already past their first sleep in Persia. But who can be drowsie at that hour which freed us from everlasting sleep? or have slumbering thoughts at that time, when sleep itself must end, and as some conjecture all shall wake again."

CHAPTER SIX

LES
JARDINS
DE
L'INTELLIGENCE

WHEN I WAS A HALF-GROWN GIRL MY FAMily left the town and went to live in a cottage by a stream. There, as I wandered about the surrounding countryside, I discovered near by a great empty park with tall trees over high walls, and a strange air of remoteness. Cautious but curious, I climbed in to look, watching nervously for the slightest sign of human beings, startled by any sound however distant, ready at the least alarm to slip back into the trees and rush pell-mell for the boundary wall. But I never saw any trace of life, not even a wheelbarrow or the smoke from a bonfire, and I came back often, drawn by an indefinable sense of difference, a consciousness of a life foreign to any I knew, alien, but unmistakably authentic.

I remember, from so long ago, no flowers in those gardens, no bushes, no familiar tangle of undergrowth in the woods, but only long avenues between tall trees, stately urns presiding at the end of vistas, and sometimes the gleam of formal water. Even overgrown and neglected, the gardens kept an unmistakable imprint of order and meaning. The trees, I realized, had not been planted to be admired as separate living entities, as trees were for me, but as the living material to express a new conception. Once over the wall, I felt, I was in a different country of the mind. Not that I

could have explained the significance of this scene, which I would
suddenly remember for years afterwards in the bustle of schooldays and the troubles of growing up. I was only convinced in an
unreasoning way that the people who created it did not speak
English. Nor did they: they spoke French. For the garden was
Bramham Park, and the inspiration was Le Nôtre's. For, whether
or not this supreme *"architecte des jardins"* ever did come to
England and design gardens on the actual sites, Bramham Park
is unmistakably a garden in the French grand manner of the
seventeenth century.

An orangery. The plants carried out for the summer.

The French are very conscious of their own good qualities—
*"les qualités proprement françaises de limpidité et de netteté dans
la langue, d'esprit de finesse et de naturel dans le style, de vérité
profonde dans l'analyse. Nous sommes un peuple que 'la raison à
ses règles engage,' ennemi de toutes les extravagances de l'imagination ou du cœur, épris d'idées claires et universelles."* (I suppose they have no need of modesty in such a dower of virtues,
but still it might be very charming.)

Les Jardins de l'Intelligence

Like all generalizations, it forgets the awkward facts which will not conform: ignores almost the whole of nineteenth-century French literature. But most people would feel that Molière is more typical of the French spirit than Victor Hugo, and unless we risk a few rash generalizations we shall get no further in trying to link the different styles of gardening with the other arts of the same time and place.

"At war with all extravagances of the heart and imagination, in love with clear and universal ideas." It follows that the greatest achievements of the French genius are logical, that their quality is intellect, raised at its finest to the power of poetry, but still the underlying spirit is logical and intellectual. Man is great, said Pascal, because he thinks. *"L'homme est fait pour penser," c'est "toute sa dignité et tout son mérite."* It is not the whole truth, since human beings may be great in ways as various as their various natures, but it is one of the Classical truths, a conception of man as a rational creature considering the world about him by the steady daylight of intelligence.

No one by taking thought could achieve the poetic quality of early seventeenth-century English literature. And if we could, it would not help us to lay out cities, build palaces, plan gardens, or order our lives with dignity. But the French delight in intellectual clarity is a condition of the mind which can be fostered in civilized people: by taking thought we can achieve some degree of their clear-sighted logic. And it is a conception which can be referred to in the ordinary affairs of life, used as a logical framework for creating all kinds of works of art: architecture, town-planning, and the manners of the Salons, as well as the plays of Molière and the paintings of Poussin. Le Nôtre is related to Corneille in spirit as well as fact.

So that the seventeenth century in France is a noble flowering of all the arts together in the first fine weather of modern man's intellectual confidence: the pure arts, the applied arts, and the arts of living all combined in a harmonious whole, each interpreting the others. If everything of seventeenth-century France were to disappear and leave us only the gardens of Versailles, we should still understand why the age which produced this noble landscape of the mind was called *Le Grand Siècle*.

In England, too, the seventeenth century was our age of giants: Shakespeare, Milton, Purcell, Wren. But we do not think of it as our Great Century, for it is not a unified whole held together by an intellectual conception. The different arts do not interpret each other: seeing a seventeenth-century English garden, we could never infer Shakespeare, as we can infer Corneille from Versailles.

No one would say of the English that we are enemies of all extravagances of the heart and imagination. Such extravagances, indeed, have often been the finest inspiration of our arts. We have never much cared for the intellectual order of Versailles, for, not being an inherently Classical people, we tend to look at the Classical tradition from the outside, as the established status quo of European culture. Too often it does not seem to us a vital creation of man's imagination, but an order of nature which exists inevitably by its own laws. Only once, looking over a formal seventeenth-century French park from a high window of the house, I left my Englishness behind as I climbed the stairs, and the great garden, which till then had seemed only an unexceptionable dull exercise in planning, suddenly became the expression of a poetic ideal of order which haunts the shadowy minds of men, a vivid intellectual creation which they only precariously achieve from chaos. The perfectly proportioned spaces, the serene vistas, the regular avenues of trees—these were suddenly no more than a faint and beautiful pattern laid by a visionary upon the underlying landscape, and the order which had seemed inevitable was now as strange and fleeting as the shadows of the clouds upon the hills.

For me, at least, the Grand Manner is not poetic in its parts but only as a whole, as Paris is mostly unremarkable in separate detail but incomparable as a city. It is the conception which is beautiful, not the incidentals—quite contrary to England, where our finest things so often seem almost accidental.

Les Jardins de l'Intelligence

For us the Classical tradition lacks romance, and the English, so everyone tells us, are incurable romantics. It is too logical for us, too unassailable, too clear. We feel with Bacon that "there is no excellent beauty that hath not some strangeness in the proportion." But it is because we do not stand far enough off; we should look at it from a top window of the house. Seen in its setting of alien nature, the formal garden becomes high poetry; for surely it is both strange and romantic that a race of puny animals should dominate their world simply by the force of their spirit, should mould the indifferent landscape to this aristocratic order only to express their conception of man as a noble creature, as "*l'animal qui pense.*"

Versailles, someone said, "*est la squelette fossile d'une vie,*" and the life is the courtly ceremony of Louis XIV. For the original palace was too small to be a fitting background for royal functions, and the gardens were laid out as an appropriate setting. We should think of the long alleys as crowded with the aristocracy of France, the formal spaces as the scene of magnificent ceremony, the green enclosures of the *bosquets* cheerful with people, gay lively intelligent people who would dispel with a witticism the air of tranquil melancholy which haunts the park today.

This court life which surrounded the King was as formal and ordered as the gardens it was set in, and weary of the impersonal etiquette, Louis would escape from time to time to his house at Marly, where ceremony was forgotten and everyone mixed with easy familiarity. The more conventional were uneasy—"I find great difficulty in getting used to this confusion," said a visiting duchess, shocked because she could not tell the Queen from her ladies when they walked together in the gardens. And indeed the seventeenth century is too early for this sophisticated game of the Simple Life in Satin Slippers. It needs for background the landscape gardens of eighteenth-century England and Marie Antoinette's *hameau*. In Le Nôtre's gardens it must have been embarrassingly difficult to keep up the pretence, and Marly changed from an informal country house to Marly-le-roi, the most magnificent of all the royal pleasure-grounds.

There is a pleasant story how one fine day four friends drove to Versailles in the same carriage, made a tour of the gardens (avoiding the water surprises), then sat down beneath the trees to listen to a poem in praise of the beauty of the place. The friends were Molière, Racine, Boileau, and La Fontaine, who wrote the verses, and I dare say no other carriage has ever carried such a load of genius. For Versailles was a magnet which drew the talents of the age: Molière wrote plays for the garden fêtes, Lully composed music, Le Brun designed scenery, and Le Nôtre created green theatres in the *bosquets*. There is a painting of one of these performances, which were often the central point of the royal entertainments. It is warm night and leafy summer. The stage is brilliant under the high shadowy trees, the faces of the watchers vivid against the darkness. To English eyes the scene is unmistakably Romantic, and the play we think of in such a setting is *The Tempest*, with Prospero's poetry, Ariel and the island full of noises, and the loves of Ferdinand and Miranda like a forced exotic flower.

But it is not *The Tempest* they are watching in their green enchanted theatre, nor Milton's *Comus* nor Ben Jonson's *Sad Shepherd*. Instead it is that level-headed satire to banish all dreams of summer nights, Molière's *Le Malade Imaginaire*.

Most of us nowadays have an unquestioned idea of a garden as a place for growing flowers. But it is a humble conception, and we must get rid of it before we go to Versailles or we shall certainly be disappointed. Versailles is not a garden in this sense, but rather a work of art which uses plants as its medium, as a painter uses the appearance of objects, and a poet the words of human speech. Like most other mediums of art, it is impure: gardens *can* be used for growing flowers in, as words are used to state facts and painting to illustrate views. But none of these functions is art. Of all the mediums of artistic expression, only music is pure in this sense that it has no other meaning, and all art, says Pater, "constantly aspires towards the condition of music. For while in all other kinds of art it is possible to distinguish the matter from the form, and the understanding can always make this distinction, yet it is the constant effort of art to obliterate it." So that it is as perverse to go to Versailles to look at the plants as to use Cézanne's landscapes as guide-book illustrations to Provence, or Shelley's "Ode" as a scientific statement of the habits of the sky-lark. We must think of Versailles as music. The great central vista is the main theme, an untroubled progress to the horizon, simple, noble, and mysterious. Then there are variations, developments, lesser themes, smooth passages of water, gay effects of flowers, fanciful interludes in the *bosquets*. But all is music, calm and confident, with no doubtful effects or random charms, no chance felicities which may or may not succeed. We share the intellectual tranquility of perfection, a conviction of the inevitably right, which sways our spirits to peace, as Duns Scotus swayed Hopkins.

But I am incurably English. I do not like Versailles except to think about at a distance. I do not particularly enjoy the sensation of being what Corneille calls *saoul de gloire;* for me the peace too easily becomes boredom. I believe that Le Nôtre is the greatest of gardeners, but it is a judgement outside my personal liking.

"The basis of all artistic genius" (it is Pater again) "lies in the power of conceiving humanity in a new and striking way, of putting a happy world of its own creation in place of the meaner world of our common days." Most modern artists seem to ignore the happy, but certainly Versailles puts a world of its own creation in place of our meaner one. But how does it create this other world? Its finished order may seem inevitable, but even an imitation of the Grand Manner is difficult for those not born to it, as we can see by considering the fussy and pretentious triteness of most public parks and formal gardens laid out in England since the early nineteenth century.

The Theory and Practice of Gardening is a large French treatise credited to Le Blond and translated into English by John James. It is a full and clear account of the principles which underlie Versailles, the rules which Le Nôtre formulated and followed in the famous gardens which he laid out all over France, and which were copied for the next hundred years by a Europe dazzled with their magnificence.

Le Blond leaves us in no doubt from the beginning about the exalted qualities needed in a good gardener. "A fine Garden," he says, "is no less difficult to contrive and order well, than a good Building. . . . A Man should know something of Geometry and Architecture, and be able to draw well; he should understand Ornament, be acquainted with the Properties and Effects of all the Plants made use of in fine Gardens; should design readily; and with all this, have a right Judgement and natural good Taste, form'd upon the Contemplation of Things that are excellent, the Censuring of those that are ill." This is a long way from any English idea of a gardener, and he would certainly dismiss our garden literature as the work of "the very meanest Gardeners, who laying aside the Rake and Spade, take upon them to give Designs of Gardens when they know nothing of the Matter." Yes. But it is exactly that, the smell of the earth on the spade, that we read their books for.

It is most important, says Le Blond, "to form a right Taste of what concerns the general Disposition of Gardens," and he gives us "Four fundamental Maxims to be observ'd."

1   "Art must give place to Nature." This seems to be a constant claim of all styles of art, however artificial they seem to us, and we should never guess that it was the first fundamental of Versailles. But we can see what he means. Water should be in hollows, woods cover hills, and there should not be too much architecture or ornaments (statues, etc.), since this "has nothing of the Air of Nature, and falls very short of that noble Simplicity we should aim at."

2   "Gardens should not be made dull and gloomy, by clouding them with Thickets and too much Cover. Fine Openings should be preserved about the Building, and in other places where the Prospect of the Country can be seen to advantage."

3   "Gardens should not lay too open, so that it is needless to go into them to see them; you discover the whole at one View

from the Vestibule of the House without troubling yourself to walk in them. The pleasure of a Garden is to have the View stopt in certain places, that you may be led on with Delight to see the more agreeable Parts of it, as fine Groves of Woodwork, Green-Halls adorned with Fountains and Figures etc. Those great flat Parts rob us of the Woods which make the Contrariety and Change in a Garden, and which alone make all the rest valuable."

L. Rosa centifolia Batavica.   *L. Rosa versicolor.*

Seventeenth-century roses. Drawing by Crispin de Passe.

4 "A Garden should always look bigger than it really is." To show it all at once makes it seem smaller: on the other hand, it is made to seem larger by "artfully stopping the Eye" with hedges, woods, etc., before it reaches the boundary. Also, Prospects should be opened into the surrounding country so that it seems part of the composition.

After these rather general rules Le Blond becomes more explicit.

The length of a garden should be one and a half times the breadth.

The principal walk should lie direct from end to end of the garden in front of the house.

A cross-walk should lie at right angles to it, and all these walks should end in Prospects with "wet ditches" replacing the walls of the garden (long before the ha-has of the eighteenth century).

There should be a descent of at least three steps from the house to give a "general Prospect."

Before the house should be an open space, laid out as a parterre which can be appreciated from the windows.

The rest of the garden is to be laid out with "Designs of tall Groves, Quincunxes, Close-Walks, Galleries and Halls of Verdure, Green-Arbours, Labyrinths, Bowling-greens, Amphitheatres adorned with Fountains, Canals, Figures etc."

In the layout there must be careful contrast of flat spaces and raised areas such as woods. To set a grass plot beside a Parterre of flowers, for instance, "would be one gap against another."

Designs of gardens, although formal, should only be symmetrical "in open Places, where the Eye, by comparing them together, may judge of their Conformity." Otherwise there should be variety, as groves, for instance, which have the same outward shape, must be different within. "For it would be very disagreeable to find the same thing on both sides; and when a Man has seen one, to have nothing to invite his Curiosity to see the other; which makes a Garden, so repeated, justly reckoned no more than half a Design."

The general impression of a garden must be magnificent, and "should studiously avoid the Manner that is mean and pitiful, and always aim at that which is great and noble. 'Twere infinitely better to have but two or three Things somewhat large, than a dozen small ones which are no more than very trifles." (Alas for the Tudor gardeners!)

"Before the Design of a Garden be put into Execution, you should consider what it will be in twenty or thirty years to come, for very often a Design which looks handsome and of good Proportion when it is first planted, in process of Time becomes small and ridiculous." For Le Blond is not merely gardening for pleasure, but creating a work of art for posterity.

As he goes on, we begin to understand how Versailles was

made, and to realize the intellectual discipline which controls these noble garden landscapes. They should be large, he says; thirty or forty acres is the best size, but even in "so small a Garden as five or six acres" we must still aim at that "Air of Magnificence," must forgo all fancies and "chuse a plain Regularity, not clutter'd and confus'd, which looks much more noble and great."

The careful spacing and proportions of walks is of great importance, for "Walks in Gardens, like Streets in a Town, serve to communicate between Place and Place, they conduct us throughout a Garden, and make one of the principal Beauties. The Breadth of Walks should be proportioned to their Length, for in this lies their greatest Beauty." Short walks must not be too broad, nor long ones too narrow, but the rules of Proportion be exactly observed.

Woods, too, are an "essential Part of a Garden," for they provide the necessary height and mass to contrast with the flat lawns and flower beds and formal waters. "Woods and Groves make the Relievo of Gardens and serve infinitely to improve the flat Parts. Care should be taken to place them so that they may not hinder the Beauty of the Prospect."

As for the Prospect—or view, as we should call it—"The Prospect is the most valuable Thing about a Country-Seat. I esteem nothing more agreeable in a Garden than a fine View and the Prospect of a noble Country." For though we of the twentieth century may grow weary of such constant nobility, man has at last outgrown his garden walls, he no longer shuts himself in with his treasures safe from a hostile world outside, his garden is no longer a retreat, but an expression of the order he can now impose on chaotic nature—"*ce plaisir superbe de forcer la nature*." The whole world is his intellectual province, and the vistas to the far horizon are the noblest part of these noble gardens. They imply even more than they declare; offer new realms of knowledge, of opportunity without limit. They are the use of silence and mystery and suggestion. As in the pictures of Claude, this empty space is the one essential which we remember. We may forget the foreground, we may never have known what subject was intended, but we never forget that mysterious recession into the far distance which is the real subject of Claude's pictures.

From the children holidaying in France we had excited letters, made even more breathlessly enthusiastic by a most sparing use of punctuation. "Dear Dardy Last night I ate the biggest supper I ever have. I have had great fun with my butterflies I caught four clouded yellows and four pale clouded yellows another stick insect and another fritillary which is the same as the other and I think they are both heath fritillaries which in England are rare . . ." and so on. Then here it is. "I enjoyed Versailles a lot we went in through an arch and saw a beautiful view to begin with there was a blaze of flowers then a long strech of grass after that a lovely lake after that it rather peatered out but there must have been something there sometime because it was so empty-looking."

Fine vistas, the use of silence, it peatered out—we all mean the same thing, and it is stated with such perfect clarity that it is unmistakable even to a schoolboy preoccupied with catching butterflies and eating large suppers.

As for the details of these gardens, they were often fanciful, for although Poussin might declare that *"les plaisirs de l'intelligence sont les premiers de tous,"* everyone's taste was not so austere, and within the formal framework there were all kinds of frivolous inventions. The *bosquets*, especially, sheltered a wealth of delightful absurdities which have long since disappeared. "The French call a Grove Bosquet," says Le Blond (the English spell it *Boskett*), "from the Italian Word Bosquetto, a little Wood of small Extent; as much as to say, a Nosegay, or Bunch of Green." Inside these Nosegays were hidden a great variety of constantly changing fancies: mazes and labyrinths with high hedges, grottos and green theatres, and little rooms for open-air meals. There were fountains everywhere: fountains which played music, or balanced balls on their jets, or threw up coloured water; fountains in the shape of trees or rushes, raining water from their leaves; rows of fountains forming arches where one could walk unspotted; fountains which drenched the unwary visitor—the "water-surprises" we know already. "Decidedly it was an ignoble form of humour," said Henry James later on of a similar practical joke, but, none the less, the Roi Soleil's courtiers thoroughly enjoyed it. The Trianon de Porcelaine and its garden (they are long since gone) were decorated with plaques and seats and urns in blue and white porcelain, and the flowers which filled its beds were grown in greenhouses in pots which were buried in the soil of the garden and changed every day, so that the scene was always brilliant with flowers at their most perfect. (We cannot help shuddering now at the expense of it all.) There was a Cabinet de Parfums surrounded by sweet-smelling flowers, where one could sit and enjoy a planned harmony of fragrance; this was a fancy which particularly delighted the Eastern ambassadors.

The open walks and parterres were more decorous, and the hedges which bordered them were simply cut. The word *parterre*, says Le Blond, who has a liking for rather unreliable etymology, "comes from the Italian partiri—to divide." It is used for a design not unlike the Tudor knots, though larger: a flat bed, generally square, divided into symmetrical patterns which were repeated in each quarter, and planted with low shrubs or flowers divided by narrow paths. "Formerly," says Le Blond, "they put in the Heads of Greyhounds Griffins and other Beasts; which had a very ill Effect, and made Parterres look very heavy and clouterly." Curious to see what *clouterly* translated, I looked up the French version, but there is nothing. "*Très-lourds*" it says, and *clouterly* is James's own addition to show his scorn of Tudor absurdities. But James often amuses himself quietly, sometimes at the expense of the over-confident Le Blond. *Boulingrin* is the French version of our word *Bowling-green*, and is a name they used for a round hollow lawn of grass, often broken up with flower beds. "The Word Bowling-Green or Boulingrin," says Le Blond, who seems never to have heard of Drake or Plymouth Hoe, "comes to us from England, from two English Words; namely from Bowl, which signifies a round Body; and from

Green, which denotes a Meadow, or Field of Grass; probably because of the Figure in which it is sunk, which is commonly round and cover'd with Grass." James translates without comment.

What the French did admire in our English gardens—and it seems to be the only thing—were our grass lawns. "In England their Grass-plots are of so exquisite a Beauty that in France we can scarce ever come up to it." It is still true.

But what about flowers in these grand pleasure-grounds? Is there no place for this chief preoccupation of English gardeners? If I ask the children what they would like for lunch on their birthdays, they are always ready with an enthusiastic list of chocolate biscuits, cream cakes, sugar buns, jelly with fruit in, and ice-cream in three different colours. Only very half-heartedly they sometimes add at the end clear chicken soup, or stuffing out of a goose, or sauce with shrimps in it. Children plan their meals in puddings, and the English plan their gardens in flowers. We have the indiscriminate sweet-tooth of the child whose palate has not developed. Yet adults often ignore the pudding altogether, choose cheese instead of ice-cream, and the late great gardens in the French Grand Manner are almost flowerless. For the English gardeners, fine flowers make fine gardens, but for Le Blond it is not so simple. "The fine Lines and Views from one end of the Garden to the other, and the Harmony of the Parts, together with what one discovers in the several Alleys . . . is sufficient to satisfy anyone in its Disposition, Variety, and Distribution of its Ornaments and Water."

In such a composition flowers have no real place. Their prettiness is a distracting chatter. If they are used in so large a setting they must be massed as uniform blocks of colour, and if we no longer have a sweet-tooth we may prefer the more restrained and suggestive colour schemes of trees and sky and water, as Le Nôtre did. Parterres, he said, are only good for nursemaids, "*qui, ne pouvant quitter leurs enfants, s'y promenaient des yeux et les admiraient du deuxième étage.*"

Les Jardins de l'Intelligence

The treatment of the open space which lies in front of the main façade at Versailles shows how the taste for "noble Simplicity" rejected the fussy formality of parterres. There were at least six different designs before the present perfection was achieved: patterns of beds and borders, elaborate parterres of flowers and hedges and water, topiary, statues and fountains, until at last Le Nôtre swept it all away and made the two simple parallel pools which still reflect the palace, and surrounded them with reclining statues too low to disturb the clear wide sweep.

Yet some of the green parterres of box have a certain beauty when used against the high walls of the *bosquets*, whose lower branches are cut back to form a vertical hedge. They give a deep rich texture to the flat ground, like the pile of an elaborate carpet, and they make an interesting foil for the satin-smooth water of the basins. Le Blond warns the Reader "against the Notion some People have got, that Parterres are the most difficult things to invent. Parterres are as small Matters of Invention, compared with the Dispositions and general Distributions of Gardens. All Parterres are near alike. Perhaps the Reason why these Persons make a Mystery of designing a Parterre, is that they are not capable of anything else; and that a general Plan will presently put them to a nonplus." Which is probably an attack on English gardening books, if he ever bothered to read them.

In his own book no plants of any kind are mentioned until he has written us one hundred and sixty-four pages of Dispositions and general Distributions. Then he begins with trees: horse chestnuts, limes, and elms are the favourites, and for hedges hornbeam is best, then beech or maple. Evergreens are valued highly, and flowering shrubs commonly grown, but any shrubs used in parterres must be clipped ruthlessly low to keep the clear contrast between horizontal parterre and vertical groves. Flowers get only twenty pages, compared with thirty on the use of water in pools and fountains. Le Blond's garden is no home for flowers, but a strictly disciplined country where they must live by rigid rules if they are to be admitted at all. It is no place for Master

Tuggie's Princess. Even the trees are not allowed to develop their own personality, but must combine in formal avenues and *bosquets*. Existing woods were disciplined by the cutting of glades in a logical pattern. The goose foot was often used: a plan of avenues radiating from a focus like the toes of a bird. At Chantilly the alleys met at a central view-point, so that anyone standing there could watch an entire stag-hunt through the woods with no more effort than a turn of the head as the hunt crossed each logically radiating glade.

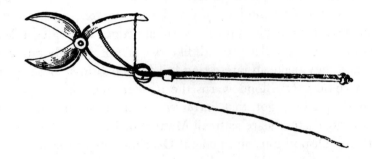

The species of trees chosen for planting are valued for their regularity, and because they will suffer pruning and clipping to form green walls: "These Decorations in Green compose a kind of Order of Field Architecture." When I saw the avenues at Versailles I recognized again the trees I had seen long ago in Bramham Park, for although Versailles is pruned chestnuts and Bramham freely growing beeches, they are unmistakably of the same race of orderly beings. After the Italian Art Exhibition, so they say, all the fashionable women of London looked like the figure of Botticelli's "Spring." I dare say they did, for fashionable women are astonishingly versatile, but it seems even odder that after Le Nôtre all the fashionable trees of Europe should look like Versailles.

What of this "famous Monsieur Le Nostre" himself, whose "ingenious skill gave the last perfection to Gardening" as Evelyn said? He was born of a well-known family of gardeners, but his training for Versailles was not in grafting rose-trees or layering gillyflowers. He studied first to be a painter—an enthusiasm which never left him, for he collected many fine pictures, especially by Poussin who, as we might guess, was his favourite artist. I also enjoy Poussin in my own way, but I doubt whether it is Le Nôtre's way. He reminds me always of fair-grounds. For so often his pictures are constructed in a revolving movement round a central focal point, a stately and inevitable circling in space, like a most wonderfully dignified merry-go-round. And then there are his horses, so nobly posed, so magnificently monumental, the real authentic Grand Manner in the very best sort of rocking-horses.

From painting Le Nôtre turned to architecture, a training which must have suited his formal sense of balance and proportion. But neither of these arts was his proper medium, and eventually he was given a post in the royal gardens, where "*la grande capacité qu'il a à dessiner*" was soon noticed by Louis XIV. He reduced the haphazard landscape to three main elements: flat ground or water, walls of trees or architecture, and the open sky. With these essentials he composed, eliminating detail, keeping a clear order for the eye and the mind.

> *On crut qu'il avait le pouvoir*
> *De commander à la nature*

said La Fontaine.

The Tuileries Gardens were laid out by Le Nôtre, and though the details have changed since his time, the main plan is still the same. On a stretch of awkwardly sloping land he found an untidy confusion of buildings and gardens which Evelyn describes in one of his letters. There was "a building in which are kept wild beasts for the King's pleasure, a beare, a wolfe, a wild boare, a leopard etc." There was also "an artificial echo redoubling the words distinctly, and it is never without some fair nymph singing in it. Standing at one of the focus's, which is under a tree or little cabinet of hedges, the voice seems to descend from the clouds; at another as if it was underground." (I wonder if it was as hard to find a nymph to sing to the echo as it was later on to find a hermit to live in the cells in the eighteenth-century wildernesses. And I wonder what songs they sang.)

This engaging muddle of the old Tuileries, Le Nôtre cleared and levelled and laid out with noble avenues aligned on the palace of the Louvre. But this was not enough. *"Il ne pouvait souffrir les vues bornées,"* said one of his contemporaries, and the outlook from the Tuileries Gardens was bounded by the city wall. So in the waste-land beyond the town he planted avenues of trees which climbed the opposite hill and carried the view calmly and confidently to the horizon—an avenue we still admire as one of the great beauties of Paris, and we call it the Champs-Élysées.

Le Nôtre, for all his clarity, is an ambiguous figure, for with his stately grandeur of mind went a warm and spontaneous personality. He was generous and straightforward, with simple informal manners and a cheerful enthusiasm in all he did. In an audience with the Pope he was so delighted with the aged prelate that he jumped up and embraced him warmly, a story which astonished the ceremonious French courtiers, but not King Louis, for Le Nôtre often kisses me, he told them, when I come back from campaigns. And the King seems to have returned his affection, driving with him alone in the park, urging him to come and live at Versailles because he liked his company, giving him a princely pension when he retired, offering him a coat-of-arms. But I have one already, said Le Nôtre, whose head was not at all turned by his fame: *"trois limaçons surmontés d'une tête de chou."* But Louis was not to be gainsaid, and presented him with a crest of three silver snails.

For with Le Nôtre the somewhat unsympathetic figure of the Sun King shows at his most attractive. His delight in his park at Versailles is an enthusiasm every gardener will understand, and, anxious that visitors should come upon its glories in the proper order and see the layout from the view-points best suited to its display, he worked out an itinerary for "doing" the house and grounds (we are reminded of Henry VIII), writing it out in his own large awkward hand. *"Manière de Montrer Versailles: En sortant du chasteau par le vestibule de la cour de marbre. . . . Il faut aller droit sur le haut de Latonne et faire une pause. . . . Ayant tourné à gauche pour aller passer entre les Sfinx, on ira droit sur le haut de l'orangerie d'où l'on verra le parterre des orangers et le lac des Suisses."* And so on and so on, from one famous view to the next. Yet at the heart of this formal grandeur, warming it with a humanity which can appreciate the inspired common sense of Molière and the friendly world of La Fontaine's fables, stands the cheerful figure of Le Nôtre, the simple happy man whom everyone loved—*"plus agréable vieillard qui ait peut-être jamais été, toujours gaillard, propre, bien mis, d'un visage agréable, et toujours riant."*

It is an old age which every gardener must hope for.

CHAPTER SEVEN

GARDENS

OF

SEVENTEENTH

CENTURY

ENGLAND

THERE IS NOTHING MORE USEFUL FOR FACING danger or hardship than an engrossing interest in something else. If we are preoccupied enough with some enthusiasm, we brush away incidental difficulties which would certainly daunt us if we ever gave them our attention. A child intent on reaching the top of a tree ignores cuts and bruises which would overwhelm it with misery on the ground. Botanists in search of flowers scramble absent-mindedly over mountains so alarming that they would never think of attempting them as climbers. If we rode our hobby-horse furiously enough, we might pass through the Valley of Death and never notice.

Darwin, so he tells us, at ten years old had a single-minded ambition: to know something about the history of every pebble in the gravel outside the front door. For Darwin's first enthusiasm was geology, and it led him with only two native companions through the wild mountains of South America, through hardships and dangers he scarcely noticed. "The worst passes in the Cordillera," he says, "but their danger has been much exaggerated." The worst pass of all he never even knew he had crossed until a day later; but the scenery, he complains with feeling, "was very uninteresting." It is an enthusiasm which engrosses him equally in the company of dinner-parties. One evening there occurred what he calls "a sharp earthquake," and he is delighted with this unexpected geological demonstration. "Strong Earthquakes useful to Geologists," he writes in his notebook. "I heard the forecoming rumble, but," he says crossly, "from the screams of the ladies, the running of the servants and the rush of several gentlemen to the doorway, I could not distinguish the motion."

Once, indeed, affected perhaps by the lack of oxygen, he is detached enough to laugh at himself. Climbing a high mountain range made it difficult to breathe the rarified air, a condition the natives call *puna*. "The exertion of walking was extremely great and the respiration became deep and laborious." But, "finding fossil shells on the highest ridge," says Darwin, "I entirely forgot the puna in my delight. The inhabitants all recommend onions for the puna," he adds; "for my part I found nothing so good as the fossil shells."

In the seventeenth century an equally enthusiastic Englishwoman rode side-saddle from end to end of England, from Newcastle to Land's End, from the Lake District to Kent, ignoring the very real hardships and dangers of seventeenth-century travel. And for what? For domestic curiosity: she liked to look at other people's houses. She wanted to see how they arranged their rooms, what colours they chose for curtains and covers, and whether they had laid out their gardens in the new fashion. Driven by this housewifely interest, she set off lightly on her heroic journeys, risked being robbed on the roads or lost among the precipices of the Peak or drowned in the treacherous crossing of the Humber.

Celia Fiennes is a somewhat monotonous writer; her highest praise is "neat," and her particular abhorrence is pictures of Venus with no clothes on—"a fine picture of Venus were it not too much unclothed," and "fine pictures, but they were all without Garments or very little, that was the only fault, the immodesty of the Pictures, especially in my Lord's appartment." But despite her limitations she gives a first-hand account of the houses and gardens of England in the late seventeenth century, seen through the mind of a lively, curious, and not very intelligent woman of the lesser aristocracy.

As in every age, she has no liking for the fashions of the period which is passing; "good but old-ffashioned," she says often, "in the old fashion," "all in an old fform and mode." These old-fashioned gardens which Celia Fiennes briefly dismisses are the gardens in Tudor style, which had so well suited the English idea of what a Garden of Pleasure should be like that they were loved and tended right through the seventeenth century. There must even have been gardens newly laid out in "the old mode," for writers like Rea and Meager give plans and instructions for making gardens scarcely different from those of Elizabeth's day; they have only been pruned of their more extravagant fancies by the bleak weather of the Commonwealth, "that dismal interval"; and "since our long Winter is so well over," says a Restoration writer, gardening is an occupation more beloved than ever before.

These old-fashioned writers cared nothing for Le Nôtre and his Grand Designs. "What some modern Authors mean by putting Gentlemen upon Grand Designs, and vilifying all others as *crimping, diminutive* and *wretched Performances,* I could never understand," said John Laurence as late as 1716. "Nothing hath more tended to the Ruin of brave Estates than a fond Affection of imitating a vain People in what they call La Grand Manier." Rea was no more enthusiastic—"I have seen many Gardens of the new model," he says, "that a green Meadow is a more delightful object." "A choice Collection of living Beauties, rare Plants Flowers and Fruits, are indeed the wealth glory and delight of a Garden," he says, and we know at once that we shall not be expected to understand the perspective of vistas.

Leonard Meager is too humble to criticize anyone; he even warns the Friendly Reader that his book is hindered by "want of time and want of Learning," and that he has "set it down very plainly, whereby it may become very useful for all sorts of practitioners, yea though of very weak capacities." But his title page places him at once with the early seventeenth-century gardeners, although he wrote in 1670. "The ordering of the Garden of Pleasure, with variety of Knots, and Wilderness-work after the best fashion, all Cut in Copper Plates—likewise several other very useful things—fitted for the use of all such as delight in Gardening, whereby the meanest capacity need not doubt of success."

The gardens these writers describe are the ones we know already: small (thirty yards square is big enough for a nobleman), full of flowers lovingly tended, divided up into quite separate compartments (Rea even shares Henry VIII's liking for rails), and still completely shut in by an encircling wall or hedge. For small boys still came scrumping apples, it seems, though Laurence has an ingenious new remedy. "At my first coming to my Parish" (for he was a clergyman, like many gardeners since) "I found some difficulty to preserve my Fruit from Robbers: Hereupon I resolved upon this Stratagem. I ordered the Smith to make a large Iron Trap with formidable Teeth to close one within another, which was to be called a Man-Trap. This was hung up several Weeks at the Smith's Shop *in terrorem*, giving it out, that now there would be great danger, if any one should attempt to rob my Garden. This, without setting the Trap, succeeded according to my Wish, and I have not been since robbed these twelve years." "*Note*" (he adds at the bottom), "Restrain'd, I hope too, not altogether by Terror, but from better Principles."

We cannot help wondering what his parishioners thought of a preacher of brotherly love who planted his orchard with man-traps, but I dare say they found him as disarming as we do. "Advertisement," he writes on a spare page at the end of his book: "Lordships Surveyed and Maps Drawn of the same" (a Lordship not being a lord's person, but his land) "by Edward Laurence, Brother to the Author of this Book. He is to be heard of when in London at Mr. Senex's at the Globe in Salisbury Court. *N.B.* In Winter, and at such Times as he is not Surveying, Gentlemen may have their Sons or Daughters Taught Accompts at their own Houses, with the Use of the Globes and Maps, and all other useful Parts of the Mathematics."

It is odd how these old-fashioned gardeners of the second half of the seventeenth century share with the early ones, not only their taste in gardens, but also their charm of personality. "I forgot to mention it before," says Meager endearingly, and he ends a list of evergreens "with many other sorts which at present I cannot call to mind." "In three Books, as in so many Beds," says Rea, who wrote *Flora Ceres et Pomona*, "have I lodged Earth's Beauties." And again: "It is impossible for any man to have Plants to prosper, unless he love them: for neither the goodness of the Soil, nor the advantage of the Situation will do it without the Master's affection."

These men write, too, in the simple vivid style of the early seventeenth century, and though they seldom suggest the poetry or strangeness of writers like Markham and Lawson, they flower into happy phrases quite unlike the pretentious manner of many minor writers of the time. "Let not your Walks be too little, neither too big, like a small City with over-large gates," or "The Sun hastens flowers to perfection, causing them quickly to flower and quickly to fade," and they call anemones Parsley Roses because of their fringed leaves.

But Celia Fiennes has no taste for these out-of-date gardens. She likes the new style, what she calls "the London mode," and the gardens she considers worth describing in detail are all much the same: "a very fine parke which is full of deer and fine rows of trees; you ascend to the house thro' the midst of rows of trees, on either side a very broad Glide or Visto that looks finely to the River and to the adjacent hills, a distance clothed with fine woods . . . the house looks very nobly, the Gardens very fine . . . deck'd with all sorts of trees and greens, very fine Gravel walks and Grass squaires with Statues and fine Grass walks . . . very fine fountains . . . the prospects very delightful." Hampton Court is also "very fine" (there is only one higher level of praise, and that is "very neat"), for the new gardens laid out with the new palace were in the latest "London mode." That is, they were French gardens: the parterre in front of the Wren block, the goose-foot of lime avenues, and the long tree-bordered canal across the park. The parterre has been altered since the seventeenth century, and the long herbaceous border is new, but they still keep much of their early atmosphere. Whether Le Nôtre ever came to England we do not know, but this has always been considered as one of his gardens, and certainly there were French gardeners in England who worked in the authentic French style. The French complained that the rest of Europe never understood Versailles, that they copied the form and missed the spirit, but "the English fall more into our manner of Gardening," says Le Blond patronizingly, "having had Designs sent over to them from hence, which are well enough performed; and have also had French Architects and Gardeners in their Country, who have left their Productions behind them." London and Wise, the most influential gardeners of the day, were among the followers of Le Nôtre, and the seventeenth-century gardens at Stowe, Blenheim, and Greenwich were French-style productions, as well as Bramham Park, and Chatsworth which Celia Fiennes admired for its fountains.

"The French," says one writer, "are very prodigal in their Expences about Fountains," and so these gardens in the French fashion are full of water: simple fountains, multiple fountains, fountains of every imaginable ingenuity, and, of course, our old friends the "water surprises," which Evelyn, travelling about Europe, reports with enthusiasm everywhere he goes. He particularly enjoyed a very up-to-date one of two "musqueteers" (who) "shot us with a streme of water from their musket barrells. The viewing this paradise," he says appreciatively, "made us late." The English gardeners have their own suggestions. "A Statue of a Woman," one recommends, "that at the turning of a private Cock, shall cast Water out of her Nipples into the Spectators Faces" (there is a picture, explicit but wonderfully dignified). Or, again: "Secret Pipes may be under the ground, the ends not appearing above it, that when any Ladies unawares or casually walk or stand over them, by the turning of a stop-cock you may force the Water upright under their Coats to their sudden surprise." The crudely childish taste of the Tudor gardeners

has become crudely adolescent. But it will soon be outgrown altogether, so we must enjoy the joke while we still may, and only
be thankful for the ladies' sakes that their men had no petrol or
electric motors to make the surprises even more efficient and dis-
concerting (though I would have liked to be there when "the
Muses plaied to us on hydraulic organs").

"To recompense the loss of past pleasures, and to buoy up their
hopes of another Spring," says one writer, "many have placed in
their Gardens, Statues and other curious pieces of Workman-
ship." He goes on to give us help in placing our statues to the best
advantage: "Statues are commendable in the midst of Fountains,
in Green Squares, in Groves, and at the end of obscure walks."
But we must be careful to give them an appropriate background,
for "a Neptune in a Dry Walk, and a Vulcan in the middle of a
Fountain, are shocking to common Sense."

But where were they to come from, these sculptured figures
which lay in wait at the end of every avenue and bathed endlessly in fountains without number? Italians had only to dig, for
the soil of Italy to produce antique figures as plentifully as cypresses for their Renaissance gardens, and Louis XIV's sculptors
provided good groups as they were needed. But English soil held
no such treasure, nor did the English court harbour fine sculptors. The wealthy brought back good pieces from the Continent,
and some of the small lead figures we still have from seventeenth-
century gardens are as delightful and unpretentious as the gardening books themselves, but we cannot help suspecting that
most of the ambitious marble works of art were quite often, and
quite simply, bad. "Statues etc.," warns Rea, who cared only for
flowers, "are excellent ornaments and marks of Magnificence; so
all such dead works in Gardens, ill done, are little better than
blocks in the way to interrupt the sight, but not at all to satisfie
the understanding."

Another writer is so concerned by the low level of statuary in
England that he wants the King to set up an academy "for its
Improvement, and for a Nursery for young ingenious Men;

which when they have learnt to Draw and Carve well, might be distributed amongst the Nobility and Gentry, who most of them stand in great need of these noble Decorations of Statues about their Country-Seats. 'Tis certain there can be no better Method to furnish themselves with Statues than by continually employing four or five Masons, and as many or more Carvers in that Work: 'tis inconceivable what a Show such a number of Men will make in four or five Years time: and the Expence in keeping, no more than that of other common Servants, Wages excepted." He gives us no help about the Wages, but only tells us to put our young sculptors "under the Care of some solid sober Man" and to keep them "as far as possible from all Tipling-Houses, the Bane of all Ingenuity."

However, gardens which were copies of Versailles never really took root in England, any more than Italian gardens like Wilton, which were similar to the French though rather theatrical than intellectual. We lack what Laurence calls La Grand Manier (I would like to know how he pronounced it). Louis XIV had played at being informal and found he was not very good at the game: with Charles II it was not a game at all, but his natural behaviour—too natural, thought Pepys, and he was scarcely a prude. A visiting Italian nobleman has left us a guarded account of his experiences in England. "The King's house" (at Newmarket) "does not deserve the name of a royal residence," and though he scarcely likes to make the same comment on the English court, we can feel his surprise. "The King had left on foot to take exercise . . . in a plain and simple country dress, without any finery." And if Charles had no liking for ceremony, his people had no particular liking for gardens in the fashionable style of Versailles. But in our long history of invasions we have had such practice in adopting the ideas of our conquerors and acclimatizing them to the mild air of England, that this robust intellectual digestion might almost be considered our greatest artistic gift: certainly it has given us a language which is unsurpassed for poetry. So we took the French ideas and translated them into

English as confidently as we changed a foreign-looking word like *jets-d'eau* into the comfortable English *jeddows*.

The gardens we planted in the soil newly enriched by Le Nôtre were in a new style which one writer happily describes as "rural and extensive." They are large and simple, parks rather than gardens, making full use of our English wealth of trees and fine grass which Le Blond so admired. There is a certain formality, a restful order; the trees are planted in avenues, the woods divided up by regular rides, and the water confined in formal basins. But there is no feeling of nature being forced: these gardens are not dominated by the power of Le Nôtre's controlling conception. They are orderly without being logical; they are English, and the tune their musical fountains play is no grand French march, but the cheerful air of "Lilliburlero. "When they please," says Celia Fiennes, they "play Lilibolaro on the chimes," as the pipe and tabor played it before them.

Pepys, who was a shrewd and sensible man, saw how well suited this style was for England. "Walked to Whitehall . . . up and down with Hugh May, who is a very ingenious man" (for in the seventeenth century ingenious and ingenuous both mean intelligent). "Among other things, discoursing of our present fashion of gardens to make them plain, that we have the best walks of gravell in the world, France having none nor Italy; and our green of our bowling allies is better than any they have. So our business here being ayre, this is the best way, only with a little mixture of statues and pots, which may be handsome." Flowers and fruit, he thinks, are best grown by themselves, and the garden kept clear for walking in the open air, "leave the walking Garden only for that use." The gardens of Whitehall, where Pepys was discoursing, adjoined Saint James's Park, whose seventeenth-century layout (the present one is in the eighteenth-century manner) is sometimes said to have been by Le Nôtre, though it was in a very simple style more English than French. In Charles II's time a long canal was made from one end to the other where the lake now lies, an avenue was planted along the north side where the King played Paille-Maille, and another on the south where he kept his bird-cages, looked after by Mr. Storey. The space between was rough grass for walking, and near the Admiralty Arch was a small enclosure called Spring Garden because of its fountain. We still have the names. Saint James's soon became the most popular parade ground of fashionable London. "Some Gentlemen, who have been abroad, have told me, that there is no publick Place for Walking in any City on this side Italy, that is so pleasant as St. James's Park . . . of a large Extent, and disposed in handsome Walks of Lime-Trees and Elms, a large regular Canal, a Decoy for Ducks . . . the wild Fowl, such as Ducks and Geese, breed there." There was a rookery in Carlton House Garden, and a pelican, as there still is —"a melancholy water fowl," said Evelyn, "between a stork and a swan, brought by the Russian Ambassador." But Evelyn had little love for the Russians. Peter the Great had rented Evelyn's house and garden at Deptford so that he could be near the dockyards, and it was there that he performed his famous feats of barrow-wheeling over lawns and flower beds and especially through holly hedges. Poor Evelyn had a particular liking for holly bushes. "Is there under heaven," he asks in *Sylva*, "a more glorious and refreshing object than an impregnable holly hedge, about four hundred feet in length, nine feet high and five in diameter, which I can show in my now ruined gardens at Say's Court (thanks to the Czar of Muscovy). It mocks the rudest assaults of the weather, beasts, or hedge-breakers." But it did not mock the assaults of Czar Peter, who enjoyed being pushed through it in a wheelbarrow. He was obviously no meek garden-lover to be daunted by a few prickles, and the damage he did at Sayes Court (it included three wheelbarrows) was assessed by Wren at £150 and paid by the Government as a kind of war damage. "A right nasty tenant," said Evelyn, and though we sympathize with him, we feel less indignant than we should if Peter had destroyed Mr. Meager's garden or John Rea's; for, with all his ability, we do not find Evelyn a very sympathetic personality, any more than Pepys did. But he had a wide knowledge of trees and their culture, which makes him an important figure in this age of gardens where trees and grass are the Chief Beauties.

One of the pleasures of living in the country is the auction sales of furniture in old houses. We see a notice in the county newspaper and plan our week to allow the day off. Away we go after breakfast, promising ourselves that this time we really will buy only the things we need, but all the while following notices "TO THE SALE" nailed crookedly on trees at the corners of lanes. "SALE THIS DAY" it says finally in red letters across the notice on the gatepost, and no three words could promise greater pleasure. For it is not only that we find treasures for a song, it is also the fun of going through other people's belongings, of feeling the intimate atmosphere of someone else's life, even, if we are lucky, the life of a different age. It was this, after all, which drew Celia Fiennes along all her muddy miles of roads.

We arrive with our catalogue and our lunch in a basket, and when we have been through every room of furniture, looked through every drawer and cupboard, every table crowded with china and ornaments, then we go back to the marquee on the front lawn and settle down expectantly like children at a pantomime, comfortable in the rows of odd chairs which will later on be sold.

The Auctioneer is our host, and he knows he is there just as much to keep us all happy as to sell the furniture in the house behind him, for if we are not happy we shall go home, and then there will be no one to sell it to. "Good morning, ladies and gentlemen," he greets us, and makes a welcoming speech about how lucky we are to have a fine day, and how there will be an hour off for lunch, and cups of tea for 2d. in the back garden—for all the world as if we were on holiday and out for pleasure, which of course we are.

Then the show begins, and relays of porters carrying the various lots appear through the flaps at the back of the tent like actors from the wings. Such astonishing things people have in their houses, such unlikely objects they collect, such incongruous oddments someone has put together on a tray to be sold as one lot. And I think how eccentric my own household might seem if it were sold up like this at random (especially the things I have bought in sales).

The Auctioneer is a cross between a prima donna and a master of ceremonies, and he is a tireless performer. He encourages us, he appeals to us, he scolds us for being slow, he tells us we don't know the value of good things, he works up a repertoire of recurring jokes which everyone laughs at every time. "This elegant chaise-longue," he says, and points to my chair. "The lady will tell you how comfortable it is." And I stand up while he sells the chair from under me, and I assure the audience, who know perfectly well that every spring is broken, that "Yes, I have never sat in a chair so comfortable." It is all the greatest fun, and at the end we go home laden with unexpected treasures, and (for all our resolutions) with extraordinary white elephants we cannot imagine any possible use for.

Once in a sale at an eighteenth-century mansion I bought a pile of old pictures, so velvety with dust that I could make out nothing but black and gold frames, and lines on old paper which might be maps or might be drawings. When I had washed them clean of a century or so of dirt, I found they were engravings by Kip of English country-seats and their gardens at the beginning of the eighteenth century. They are bird's-eye views, half map, half picture, and they have a most intriguing air of sophisticated naïveté. There are Rural Seats, said Evelyn in his *Sylva*, "dispersed through the whole nation, conspicuous not only for the structure of their houses, built after the best rules of architecture, but for situation, gardens, canals, walks, avenues, parks, forests, ponds, prospect and vistas, groves, woods, and large plantations, and other the most charming and delightful recesses, natural and artificial." Well, there they are in Kip's drawings, and I never pass them, hanging now on our London staircase, without saying to myself: "Rural and extensive," for it perfectly describes them. Extensive they certainly are, for they include woods for timber and orchards for fruit trees as well as the approaching avenues and the formal gardens near the house. And they are just as certainly rural. By "rural" the seventeenth-century writer meant an easy lack of formality: the walks of the avenues left simple grass, the vegetable garden planted near the house for convenience, a walled-in space for favourite flowers and bother the plan. But they are rural, too, in our rustic sense of the word. Versailles might be anywhere—even in the middle of Paris, if there were space enough and vistas—but, looking at these pictures, we know at once that they are in the country. Much of the area is no more than fields crossed or bordered by rows of trees, and in the meadow between, animals graze unconscious that they are in an English version of Versailles. The neatly planted "bosketts" only repeat the pattern of the neatly planted haycocks over the hedge, where men and horses are working in the summer fields. The round haystacks are as much at home, and as decorative in the picture, as the round clipped trees. There can never have been a pleasanter way of laying out English gardens, and the French can complain as much as they please that we never understood the spirit of Versailles. Though of course they are right and we never have done. We disturb our green vistas with coloured flowers, blur the edges of formal pools with water lilies—there are lilies in the canal at Hampton Court —troubling the serene outlines, weakening to prettiness what should be noble and austere.

What we did learn, however, and very thoroughly, from the French in the seventeenth century, was to plant trees in rows. "We have been to Boughton," wrote Augustus Hare, "the great desolate house . . . built by the Duke of Montagu, who was ambassador to Louis XIV, and the King lent him a French architect and gardener. He made it as like a French château as possible. Then he told his friends that he must plant an avenue to drive to London by, and when they remonstrated that an immense part of the way to London did not belong to him, he said 'Well, at any rate I will have an avenue of the same length,' and he planted seventy-two miles of it in his park. These trees, hemming in the view in all directions, make the place indescribably dull."

The Dutch style of gardening, which became popular in England with Dutch King William towards the end of the seventeenth century, was another variation in misunderstanding of the French Grand Manner. Le Blond had seen quite clearly the dangers of the French style: that it might become too fiddling and too artificial, too much divided up, too cluttered with ornaments

Avenues run wild at Badminton.

and fussy detail. The Dutch gardens proved him to be perfectly right. In a small space, he said, we must be content with a few simple things on a large scale, but this was exactly what the Dutch were not content with. Into gardens much smaller than the smallest Le Blond ever considered, they crammed everything: canals and fountains, walks and hedges, statues and topiary, trees with trunks painted in coloured stripes, and, above all, parterres—beds and flowers planted with meticulous exactness, measured out to the half-inch. These were no longer gardens for palaces, but for doll's houses—"The Dutch Taste, of which the

People of the common level of Understanding grew so fond; being delighted with little Niceties and fantastical Operations of Art, always thinking that the finest, which was least natural." For even while they were popular, men of taste considered these gardens absurd—not only Le Blond, who dismisses them in a phrase: "the whimsical Designs of Holland and Flanders."

There was much water in the Dutch gardens, but they ladled out Le Nôtre's wide levels into little basins and toy canals of no particular plan. And their gardens were always "stuffed too thick with Box," a shrub they valued highly because it was "tonsile" and "patient of the sissors," an excellent bush for clipping into tiny hedges and for the topiary work in which they delighted. The Dutch gardeners could never leave anything alone, but "Our Trees," complains one writer, "rise in Cones Globes and Pyramids," and "a Citizen became no sooner Master of a Pair of Yews, but he entertained Thoughts of erecting them into Giants like those of Guildhall."

The favourite flower of these gardeners, as we could guess without knowing, was the tulip, and trade in tulips became as fantastic a speculation as the South Sea Bubble later on. The "broken" tulips which they chiefly prized, their petals streaked and flamed with a contrasting colour, were of a style exactly to suit their taste for the artificial, the bright and fussy. And florists' tulips are the ideal tidy flower for the tidy-minded to marshall into exact rows: from each bulb one flower, all the same size, all the same shape, held rigid on stalks like so many green pokers. They are the most uncompromising of flowers, and difficult to place in any natural garden arrangement. But, dull as they are, the coarse floppy leaves have a waxy bloom which is attractive, and, bundled together, the stalks make the same leathery creaking noise which delighted Gerard Manley Hopkins in bluebells: "a brittle rub and jostle like the noise of a hurdle strained by leaning against."

Of the culture of their tulips they made the most absurd mystery. "I was forbid," says the author of *The Dutch Florist*, "as it were by the Inspiration of a Divine Genius to declare this Mystery to any but the Knowing, that it might not be defiled by the Profane and Vulgar," and there follows a lunatic abracadabra about the Strength of your Mother and the Ashes of her Bones and the Ground shall be filled with Oysters. Which tells us one thing very clearly: that it is a characteristic of small minds to love secrets, and to make mysteries of simple things.

Though perhaps we should never mock any gardener, and besides, the Dutch gardens are not so very different from the Tudor ones; it is only that they lack their curious charm. But the seventeenth-century Dutchman was, in any case, impervious. "A Dutch merchant's accounts and his garden were kept with the same degree of accuracy and attention," says one critic maliciously, scorning his art and commerce both at once. But the Dutch gardener would have welcomed his remark as warm praise. "Beds," he says, "must not be broader than two Foot and a Half, that you may divide them into Rows five Inches Distance from each other, as well in Length as Breadth: which is the most regular Way, for Tulips ought to be planted at an equal Distance from one another. The Beds being so prepared, you must make use of a Line to strike the Rows equally distant in Length, and of a Rule to divide them exactly square in Breadth; remembering always to leave two Inches and a Half at each Edge of the Bed. Tulips planted in so regular an Order shew the Ingenuity of the Gardener." They do indeed. "You must also observe, when the Tulips are planted, to put on one Side of the Bed as many small Sticks as there are Roots, and not let them stand above two Inches above the Ground: Let every fifth Stick be bigger than the others; and continuing thus from one Hand to the other, and from one Row to the other, set down the Name of each Tulip on the Stick, that at one Cast of an Eye you may presently tell the Name of any Flower, be it the first, second, third, fourth, or fifth Row, before any one shews itself above Ground, which will be a great Satisfaction to the Florist."

"Flowers," says John Rea, who was not Dutch but English, "are the wealth glory and delight of a Garden." It is a judgement which our gardeners have seldom quarrelled with, for we have seldom considered gardening as one of the fine arts. So the seventeenth-century gardener turned his back on Le Nôtre's noble vistas to "delight in the fairness and trim growing of [his] Flowers," and in the significant silence of the perfectly planned spaces, we hear his homely gentle voice telling us how to make our Gilliflowers open equally without splitting the green cup of their calyx: "Save the Wesand-pipe of great Fowls, as Geese etc. and

Bowling green and drying ground in a formal garden.

being cut into several rings, put over the pods of the flowers, thereby causing them to blow round and handsome."

In France, too, there were plenty of gardeners who loved flowers and ignored planning. Quintinye was the chief authority on practical garden work, and was constantly quoted in English translations. He begins with a very shrewd account of the qualities to look for in a good gardener, and one most desirable virtue is a hard-working wife who will take his place when needed: it is a very different list from Le Blond's. Among our English writers, Parkinson was still much respected, but so many new

flowers had been discovered since his time that new books were
needed. "I easily perceived Mr. Parkinsons Book to want the
addition of many noble things of newer discovery, and that a
multitude of those there set out, were by Time grown stale, and
for Unworthiness turned out of every good Garden." But for
all the "vast Perfection we in this Island are arrived at in
Gard'ning," our climate hinders us. France and Italy can grow
flowers which will not prosper with us, for their summers are
reliable, "as those that are upon Terra Firma do observe," says
one writer, for all the world as if England were not solid earth
at all, but only an island floating in the sea, like the whales which
sailors mistook for land in old sea-stories.

The flowers these gardeners list include many new plants from
both East and West, but the favourites are still the same. The
long-loved Gilliflower is still cherished, being "no less profitable
than pleasante, they do not only preserve the bodies of men"
(when used in medicines) "but also doth keep the minde and
spiritual parts from terable and fearfull dreames through their
heavenly savour, and most sweet pleasant odor."

But the newer-fashioned preferred the tulips of the Dutch
gardens, and there are long accounts of how to grow them to
perfection. Poor ground makes flowers light-coloured, good
ground dark: all the writers affirm this so confidently that perhaps it is true. But then I remember the Cures for Moles, and I
wonder. They tell us, too, what we should do to make them
break into the flamelike streaks which were the love of fashion.
We know now that the breaking of tulips is a virus disease, but
the seventeenth century knew nothing of viruses; they only
knew that this flaming was not a reliable beauty in any tulip, but
would often disappear, especially in the largest and healthiest
flowers, and that growing them in poor conditions encouraged it.

Auriculas were still popular, and Emines or Animons or
Anemonies (Meager is no more confident about his spelling than
I am). In the seventeenth century the first flower-shows began,
with prizes for the best blooms. These were humble competitions
and encouraged the love of flowers in ordinary people who had

no parks or greenhouses, but only back gardens. Later on, different districts specialized in different flowers, and from my North Country childhood I remember a tradition for growing auriculas still alive in back yards and window-sills—an unexpected enthusiasm of the drab little Northern towns, like keeping whippet dogs and canary birds and singing *The Messiah* at Christmas.

The seventeenth-century gardeners valued their evergreens as we do. Greens or Perennial Greens they call them, "it seeming

Drawing by Crispin de Passe.

from these to be summer all the winter." Laurustinus, which they call the Wild Bay, was their favourite, as it was the Tudor gardeners', and they also prized cherry-laurel, privet, holly, pyracantha, and phillyrea, which they spell Filaree. They grew exotics in tubs which were wintered indoors, especially orange trees, Le Nôtre's favourite, but also lemons, pomegranates, aloes, and even bananas and pineapples. There is a curious picture of a kneeling gardener presenting the first English pineapple to King Charles II, against the background of a formal garden with fountains. But it is hard to understand how they ever managed to keep alive plants which needed shelter in the winter, for these were kept in large rooms heated only with charcoal and a very inadequate flue. The only thermometer was a bowl of water set on the floor: if it froze, it meant the weather was cold; if it did not freeze, it drowned the mice who came to drink. Nor were their orangeries any better lit than heated. They had windows to the floor, but no glass in the roofs, and it is not surprising that the gardeners complain of their plants turning yellow. But it was for want of air, so they thought, and they recommend a great deal of opening of windows. They boxed up their tender flowers against the winter cold, they brought in potted shrubs as "chimney plants" to fill their empty hearths in the summer, and when these poor prisoners languished in the dark, it was not, so the gardeners thought, because they were starved of light which is the life of a plant, but because they lacked fresh air, "they want the free Circulation of the Atmosphere." Food, water, and air— these they knew a man must have to live, and so, they reasoned, must a plant. But that light is almost more vital than any of these, they had no idea, so that they advise all kinds of unlikely garden practices, like burying plants in roofed-over pits to shelter them from the "murd'ring Winds of March." Though even then, they say sadly, many plants will "die and pine away." But since air and light often go together, much of their advice is still useful. Plants should not be set between high walls or they will languish, and pot-plants in the hearth must be often set out in the open to recover from their confinement.

If we know more about light and virus diseases than the seventeenth century, they knew ways of handling plants which we have forgotten, "secrets not till now divulg'd." The pictures in the gardening books show workmen transplanting trees of a truly heroic size which we should never dare to attempt. Two or three times the height of a man, with a trunk as thick as his body, they dig them up confidently and plant them somewhere else.

Perhaps the trees were hardier then, like the people. At Hampton Court a row of limes was moved forty years after they were planted, and fully grown forest trees were carried in hundreds to Versailles (where three quarters of them died and were replaced). Even as late as the nineteenth century in England, huge conifers were carried from Kent to the Rothschild manor at Waddesdon so that the new grounds should look immediately ancestral; and the long trucks they were carried on held up all the traffic in the Strand as they came through London.

An Aviary on a Formal Island.

The books give various "secrets" for moving large trees. The most reasonable is to dig round them a year before they are to be moved, cutting through all the large roots, so that they produce a close mesh of new fibres which will hold a ball of undisturbed earth when the tree is transplanted a year later. Another way, which sounds too ingenious to be true, was to dig a trench round the tree in frosty weather and drench the roots with water. When this froze, the tree and its roots could be lifted as a solid block. An even more hazardous method was for moving trees in full summer leaf. A hole was dug for the coming tree and filled with fine earth and water, which was stirred round to make a kind of mud porridge. The leafy tree was then dug up and plunged into this "pap," as the writer calls it, where it grew, so he assures us, even more vigorously than if it had never been moved, producing a fine crop of fruit the very same year.

The trees to be moved were often fruit trees, for the seventeenth-century gardeners lavished their greatest care on orchards. The purists might scorn them as "Rather a confused Chaos of Fruit-Trees than a Regular Garden," but the ordinary gardener went on happily with his pruning and took no notice. Sir William Temple wrote an essay of "Gardening in the Year 1685." "Few countries are before us," he says, "either in the elegance of our gardens, or in the number of our plants." He has a certain talent for boasting without offence, but as a gardener he cares little for the elegance of planning, and even less for growing flowers, "which is more the ladies' part than the men's," he says, and we wonder if Dorothy Osborne kept the flower garden. His real love is for his fruit trees, and these, says Evelyn, were "most exquisitely rail'd and train'd, far better than I ever noticed elsewhere." Even the Puritans, who were doubtful whether flower gardens could be justified since they were only for pleasure, encouraged orchards both for Pleasure and Profit.

Almost as important as the orchard was the Garden for Herbs. Our idea of a herb garden is a small and somewhat self-conscious plot outside the windows of a country tea-shop. It is set with clumps of neat plants like thyme and marjoram, to be used doubtfully as flavourings by vegetarian cooks in skirts of hand-woven tweed. But a seventeenth-century herb garden was quite simply a vegetable garden, and there is nothing quaint about the lists of "divers sorts of herbs" which they recommend: "Beetes, Carrots, Garlick, horse-radish, Cabbages, Colliflowers, Parsnips, Pease and Spinage, Potatos, Rubarb and Hartichoaks."

Two famous gardens which still survive from this time are the Chelsea Physicke Garden in London, which I have only seen through the locked gates, and the Botanical Garden at Oxford, which was built in 1632 on the site of a Jews' cemetery, five acres of ground given by the Earl of Danby, and enclosed by four-teen-foot-high walls which cost £5,000. The gateways were a further £500, and were paid for by a fine levied on the Oxford antiquary Anthony à Wood for libelling the Earl of Clarendon. They were designed by Inigo Jones, and I think there can be no more inviting entrance to any garden. The pillars which hold up the pediment are sliced with alternate layers of rusticated stone, which stand out like the tufts on the legs of fashionable poodles. On each side of the entrance arch there is a figure in a niche—Charles and Danby, so the inscription says, both dressed up in delightfully theatrical armour and boots like the Principal Boy in a pantomime, both short-legged to fit their niches, one bewigged, the other crowned with laurels, both making fine heroic gestures whose effect is somewhat subdued because both lack an arm. The garden inside its fourteen-foot wall is the pleasantest place in all Oxford, though I have been there many times and never found the "intelligent assistant" promised me by an early nineteenth-century guide-book: "Persons who are fond of the study of botany may receive minute information respecting the plants in this Garden from the intelligent assistant to the Professor, who is always on the spot for the purpose of conducting strangers to the different walks, the Green-houses and Hot-houses."

Beyond the old walled garden is a new one open to Christ Church Meadow which lies beyond, a calm green sea of level grass with walls for cliffs. Even the seats round the edge share this illusion of water, raised on steps, like boats drawn up the beach beyond reach of the tide. And from the tall trees the nuthatches whistle like boys.

The seventeenth and early eighteenth centuries are, above all others in England, the age of popular gardening. Not only did every cottage have its garden, but every town house, too, how-ever humble. "There is scarce an Ingenious Citizen that by his confinement to a Shop, being denied the priviledge of having a real Garden, but hath his boxes, pots, or other receptacles for Flowers Plants etc. In imitation of it, what curious Representations of Banquets of Fruits, Flower-pots, Gardens and such like are painted to the life, to please the Eye, and satisfie the fancy of such that either cannot obtain the Felicity of enjoying them in reality, or to supply the defect the Winter annually brings." It was still the same in 1722 when Thomas Fairchild wrote *The City Gardener:* "I find that almost every Body, whose Business requires them to be constantly in Town, will have something of a Garden at any rate." Or if they had not so much as a square yard of earth, then they "furnish their Rooms or Chambers with Basons of Flowers and Bough-pots, rather than not have something of a Garden before them."

We often talk as if the smoke and soot of London were modern plagues unknown before the Industrial Revolution, but Parkinson lamented the "smoake of sea coales" which "of all others is the worst, as our citie of London can give proof sufficient, wherein neither herbe nor tree will long prosper; nor hath done ever since the use of sea-coales beganne to be frequent therein." Evelyn is almost violent about the "clouds of smoke and soot, over and above great cities and other volcanoes, continually vomiting out their acrimonious and sometimes pestiferous fervour, infecting the ambient air, as it perpetually does about London and for many miles adjacent." (I wonder what he meant by other volcanoes.) After the Great Fire he suggested a plan for London·as a garden city surrounded by plots of thirty to forty acres, planted with shrubs and sweet-smelling flowers whose fragrance would be "perpetually fanned" over the town.

Fairchild gives lists of plants which will grow even "much oppres'd with the London Smoke." Flowers and deciduous trees are easy, for flowers can be renewed each year, and most deciduous trees will grow if they are not cut about. The difficulty with the garden of a London square, he says, is "how to make it look well in the Winter, and that Part of the Spring, when Persons of Distinction are in Town." And, reading him, I suddenly remembered a village woman who used to come and help me to clean. She had been a maid once in a big London house of balls and dinners and entertainments, and her year, too, had its seasons, as important as the gardener's: "You'd hear them crying Lavender in the streets outside, and you'd know the Season was over."

So it was no use, said Fairchild, planting a fashionable square with the flowers of late summer, "for the Persons of Distinction . . . will not pay for a Thing that they have no Benefit of, or Pleasure in." And we think how often our own borders have flowered for themselves alone while we were away on summer holidays. Nor is Pepys's plain style of trees and grass suitable, Fairchild thinks, for a small London square: "Wilderness-Work" of trees and flowering shrubs, cut through by walks and edged with flowers, will "divert the Gentry better than looking out of the Windows upon an open Figure." London gardens should be planted with bulbs and spring flowers, and above all with evergreens, he says, and tells us which will grow. The vine, too, "will do very well in London," and so it still does. I grow one in a tub which ripens small black grapes, and the children eat them with ostentatious pleasure, though I have tried, too, and they taste very little of anything at all except soot.

Fairchild had a high reputation among gardeners of his day, and his name appears over and over in their books. He could, so one writer tells us with awe, strike a laurustinus bush from a cutting of a single leaf. He kept a nursery garden at Hoxton, where he sold all kinds of shrubs and flowers, and he warns us against buying plants in shops and markets, where they have been long out of the earth: "I have seen Plants that were to be sold in the Markets, that were as uncertain of Growth as a Piece of Noah's Ark would be, had we it here to plant."

The seventeenth-century Frenchman thought. He thought about Life, one supposes, and about Man (certainly they would both have capital letters), and he made Versailles with all it stood for. The seventeenth-century Englishman also thought, and his thinking was just as much a journey from the old world to the new, but by a different road. The French are a Latin people with a natural sense of form. We are not. But we are practical if somewhat eccentric scientists, and when Newton sat in a garden he thought, not about the laws of classical proportion, but about the law of gravity. Science was very close to the garden in the seventeenth century, as it no longer is in our days of atom-splitting and electron microscopes. Scientists now seem remote technical creatures who use elaborate apparatus as extra senses beyond our human seeing and hearing and feeling, but in the seventeenth century they were ordinary intelligent human beings who sat under a tree and watched apples fall with eyes the same as ours.

Newton had many other theories even closer to gardening; he thought, for instance, that the seeds of plants like holly, which normally passed through the body of a bird, might need similar conditions if they were to germinate quickly, and he suggested they should be kept in wet bran before they were planted. The more thoughtful gardeners were constantly experimenting—on the action of roots, the transpiration of water through the leaves, the different effects of different soils, and, above all, on the circulation of the sap, which they tried to explain by Harvey's discovery of the circulation of the blood. The Royal Society was extremely active, botany was developing as a science, the Society of Apothecaries was founded and went "herbalizing" in the fields round London, and intelligent men spent their leisure in scientific experiments, exchanging their results in long letters. The gardening books constantly address "the Curious" or "Curious Gentlemen," meaning this active audience of intelligent amateurs.

Objective observation was a growing habit, yet there were still plenty of superstitious ideas difficult to uproot. Perfectly sensible people still believed that seeds should be sown by the phases of the moon, that the earth produced the plants natural to it, and that soil could be prepared which would bring forth corn of its own accord without planting seed. Moss, says one writer, was a "spontaneous excrescence . . . proceeding from the natural inclination of the matter on which it grew, animated by the Celestial influences." Evelyn did not believe it, affirming that all plants "had their original from seeds. And I think the same of all animals, even to the minutest worm and insect." Certainly Isaak Walton would not have agreed with Evelyn, for did he not breed maggots for bait simply by hanging meat in the sun? But many of the Curious knew he was right. "A learned Virtuoso, by the help of a Microscope hath observed the Seed-cods of Moss to contain Seeds in them no less wonderful for the greatness of number than the smallness of bulk, which seed Vessels when ripe, he pressing them pretty hard, found that there was a small dust went out of them, which seemed to vanish into the Air; pressing and squeezing others of them upon a black plate, and examining the Powder with a Microscope he found it to be a great heap of exceeding small Seeds. These seeds being thus small may be carried into the Air from place to place, even to the tops of the highest Towers or places remote and be there sown."

But the old-fashioned were not convinced. How are heavy seeds carried? they asked, as if they had never seen a bird or a squirrel. How do oaks and beeches and hollies appear in cleared woodland? How is it that "so great a quantity of Erysimum or Irio should be sown in the Ruins after the late great conflagration in London, where it was observed that more of it grew there than was known to be in all Europe besides"?

Irio we know as London rocket, a cornfield weed of the East brought to England in imported grain. When the docks were destroyed by fire, the seeds escaped from the corn stored in the London warehouses and spread over the burnt-out city, as rose-bay willow-herb has comforted the Ruins of our own "late great conflagration."

The Art of Gardening in Three Books, by J. W. Gent, was published in 1677, and J.W. is John Woolridge. He covers all the seventeenth-century garden styles: French planning and English adaptations, Dutch niceties and city gardens; he is interested in flowers and fruit and herbs, in old superstitions and new experiments. He is all the seventeenth-century gardeners in one.

The First Book, says the title page proudly in fine large print, "Treateth of the Excellency, Scituation, Soil, Form, Walks, Arbours, Springs, Fountains, Waterworks, Grotto's, Statues and other Magnificent Ornaments of Gardens."

The Second Book, in medium-sized print, as being a humbler division of the art, "Treateth of all sorts of Trees planted for Ornament or Shade, Winter Greens, Flower Trees, and Flowers, that are usually propagated and preserv'd in the Gardens of the best Florists."

The Third Book, in such humble small print that we can scarcely read it, "Treateth of the Kitchin Garden, and of the great variety of Plants propagated for food or for any culinary uses."

"Illustrated with Sculptures" (by which he means copper plates, but there are none) "representing the form of Gardens, according to the newest Models."

From which survey we might guess that Woolridge's garden would be a compromise between the formal grounds of France and the English love of flowers, "the affections of our Country-men so naturally tending that way." And so it is: a most success-ful compromise.

"Gardening," he says, "is the beautifying of Seats with in-vegetate Ornaments," and what we notice first is that when he takes trouble his style is most unfortunate. Yet he means well; his "stile is plain," he says, "and suited to the Vulgar." But he talks about Sedentary Repasts and calls gardening books Hortu-lane Tracts. Yet even an educated man like Evelyn is sometimes no better, and from now on we must forget that ordinary gar-deners once wrote fine English, and think instead about what they have to say. Though mercifully they often forget to be literary and write simple and sometimes vivid prose.

Woolridge is very thorough in his advice, and begins with the improvement of soil, though here he is brief, he says, because "that most learned of Hortulane Authors, Evelin, hath lately been very copious on the same subject." (This was the *Discourse of Earth* delivered to the Royal Society, and I, too, found it very copious.) He then gives advice for laying out "A Complete Garden with its Magnificent Ornaments, its Stately Groves," and so on—we know the list by heart by this time. "A plain level is best for a Garden," he says, though the eighteenth century would soon deny it, and "Woods and Water two of the best Ornaments of the Seat." But though he approves of "the new mode of Gravel Walks and Grass-plots . . . with those Ornamental Shades that now are become common," he loves flowers, and is sad that "Many stately Country Residences have banish'd out of their Gardens Flowers, . . . but it's hoped that this new, useless and unpleasant mode, will like many other vanities grow out of Fashion."

"In your Garden of Pleasure," he says, and he might be talking directly to our labourless age, "you aught to be frugal of cost and pains," and he advises us against such Tudor pleasures as trellises and fanciful hedges. As for the arbours so beloved since the earliest mediæval gardens, they not only need too much work to keep them, but they are damp and airless, he says, and a movable seat set under a tree for shade "is much more pleasant than to be hood-winked in an Arbour." Of course it is, but we must beware of growing too reasonable or we shall give up gardening altogether and sit in the fields instead. However, we need have no fear for Woolridge: he has a reassuringly fanciful taste in grottoes and "fountains to sing like birds," and his cure for caterpillars is worthy of Thomas Hill: "To destroy Caterpillars on Trees . . . make a Ring of Tar towards the bottom of your Tree, then hang a bag full of Pismires on the Tree that they may easily get out, and when they cannot get down by reason of the Tar, rather than they will starve for hunger, they will eat up all the Caterpillars." But he does not tell us how to get rid of the ants. Perhaps we simply take away the Ring of Tar and they will all go home again.

Although we may know simpler ways than Woolridge for discouraging our twentieth-century caterpillars, we have none better for laying out gardens. First, he tells us, plan the garden as a whole, then plant it with trees and shrubs, especially ever-greens, and last of all set flowers "in the intervals that remain and the borders of the Walks." Evergreens he values highly, since half the garden year is winter—"Winter," he says, "that seems elsewhere most barren, here amongst these Greens appears like a perpetual Spring." He has a fancy, too, for variegated shrubs, and thinks that the Gilded-leafed Plants should be grouped together to make a Golden Grove. Flowering shrubs are "Flower Trees," and he recommends them because they need little attention. I think of our modern fashion for flowering shrubs, and I suspect that there are no new ideas in gardening, just as there are no new ways of making love, since both have been going on so long already, ever since Adam and Eve and the Garden of Eden.

As for flowers, they are "the best Ornaments, the Miracles of Nature," and Woolridge cherishes them as children. "Cherish your Gilliflowers" (from too much sun) "by some artificial Skreen," and from bad weather in a "Cave or Pitt, for there no Winds nor severe Frosts can annoy them, the driving rains also cannot much offend them." Gilliflowers (they were sometimes called carnations now, a name used because the original ones were flesh-coloured) are still his most treasured flowers, though tulips are almost as precious. Ranunculas, anemones, and cycla-mens are still favourites, and auriculas, he says, "considering their size are the finest Flowers the choicest Garden holds." London pride he calls London Tufts or Pride of London, and "Colchicums are called Naked Boyes because they appear naked out of the Earth and are withered and gone before the green leaves appear." He writes well enough, after all.

The French gardens often had aviaries of singing birds, but Englishmen have not much liked wild birds in cages, and Wool-ridge feels as the Tudor gardeners did before him. "One of the pleasures belonging to a Garden is an Aviary, but we are rather for an Aviary at large, that the whole Garden with its Groves and Avenues may be full of these pretty singers." As for the

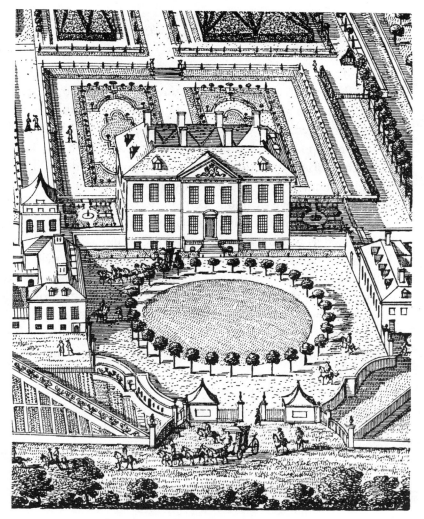

A seventeenth-century entrance court.

vista, "your principal walk," he says dutifully, following the French model, "should extend it self as far as you can in length," and he mentions "the priviledges and advantages of Air and View." But his heart is not in it: he talks too often and too eagerly of "Solitary repose," of "Retired and Solitary walks" (Solitary is honoured with a capital S, even though it is only an adjective), and summer-houses "private . . . from frequent disturbances." Open fences certainly leave the view open, he says, but only by "rendering your Solitary Walks less private."

The walks of Versailles were not Solitary; privacy was not a privilege the French court set much store by, and the royal gardens were open to all who cared to come and stare: "all accesse is freely permitted." By the Revolution the gates had been set open so long upon their rusted hinges that it was then too late to close them. But Woolridge liked to be private, and his "Retired and Solitary walks" are not only a reminder that Englishmen had no great love of public ceremony, they are also a foreshadowing of the taste of the eighteenth century. Soon gardens will be valued as retreats for self-conscious sighing; they will be laid out as deliberate wildernesses, and the highest praise will be to call them natural. Indeed, the taste has begun already. "From hence we walked into the Parke, which for being intirely within the walls of the Citty is particularly remarkable; nor is it less pleasant than if in the most solitary recesses, so naturally is it furnish'd with whatever may render it agreeable, melancholy, and country-like."

It is not, as we might have supposed, the late eighteenth century praising a landscape park, but Evelyn writing as early as 1641. Agreeable, melancholy, and country-like. Capability Brown was not, after all, so revolutionary an innovator, and perhaps all fashions only interpret into popular language the changes which have already taken place in sophisticated taste.

CHAPTER EIGHT

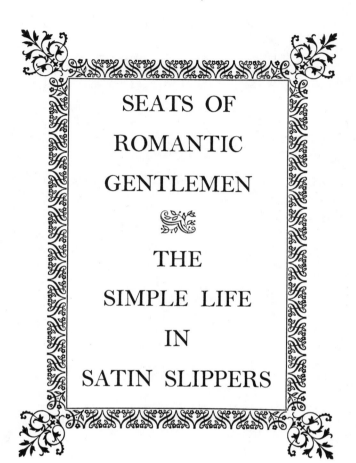

SEATS OF

ROMANTIC

GENTLEMEN

THE

SIMPLE LIFE

IN

SATIN SLIPPERS

WHEN I WAS A CHILD WE LIVED IN THE MID-
dle of a sprawling industrial city, and because I longed
for the far-off country, I hated parks. For parks, I felt, promised
to be country, but when you came to know them were as
artificial as gardens, and without the flowers. For the parks of
industrial cities are the grounds of eighteenth-century mansions
laid out in the style of Capability Brown, and bought by the
Corporation when the resident family retreated before the
industrial flood. They are not country preserved, as I thought
they were, seeing them for the first time, but deliberate works of
art, and I cared nothing at all for works of art. I wanted the
simple country.

"Small paths to the greenwood"—it was a line I had found in
an old poem, and I used to say it to myself over and over, until
it became a magic spell which I need only repeat under my
breath to follow in fancy a narrow turf path which led to the
edge of a remote and flowery wood and disappeared among the
leafy summer trees, a green and secret invitation.

"Small paths to the greenwood . . ." I said it often as I followed eighteenth-century paths through eighteenth-century
landscapes, and when I found in the end only some contrived
and public view, some shabby Classical temple with initials

scraped in the plaster, I was every time most wretchedly disillusioned. For the "carpet walks" of the landscape parks have no intention of losing us in the greenwood. They are as carefully planned as Louis XIV's tour of Versailles, to lead us to the best view-point for admiring a landscape deliberately laid out as a work of art. But I never recognized the art, only the artificiality, for I think children have very little æsthetic feeling before adolescence, and when their taste corresponds with ours, as in the modern fashion for the paintings of very small children, it is for reasons other than æsthetic.

So I hated all parks when I was a child, all but one, and that was too small to promise anything, for you could see right across it and through the railings at the other side. It was called Charlie Cake Park, though I never knew why unless it was the shape, an acute triangle of land wedged between two converging roads and laid out as a garden of trees and shrubs and flowers, and grass not to be walked on. It was exactly an acre, so someone told me, and because we remember everything from our childhood as wonderfully large, my idea of an acre will always be a triangular area of a most unlikely size; even now, when someone says "a field of ten acres," I do a jig-saw puzzle in my head, fitting together ten narrow triangles to make a square.

This park I loved because it was a garden, but all the rest I hated, for children are violent in their affections and the world is black and white. The other parks were shams, I thought; their promises were lies, like the highly decorated cream-cakes which are sawdust inside. In the end—and it was a milestone in my growing up—I accepted the unhappy truth that I should never find a primrose on their banks, or cowslips in their meadows, or bluebells in their woods, but only docks and nettles and grass without flowers.

"An open country is but a canvas on which a landscape might be designed." So said Horace Walpole, and it is easy to see why I mistook my parks for country. "Any tract of land whose characteristick expressions have been strengthened by art, and in which the spontaneous arrangements of nature have been improved by the hand of taste, ought to be considered as a Garden."

This was a conception completely new in the West, though in China it was so old that no one remembered its beginnings. Marco Polo had come back from the East with descriptions of gardens which we recognize at once as landscape parks, enclosed in a wall eight miles on each side, "ornamented with many handsome trees, and meadows in which are kept various kinds of beasts." But no one believed him, for he invented his fine stories, they thought, and Sir John Mandeville, who repeated his tales, discredited him still further, for the bogus Sir John was quite simply a brazen liar. "I have seen with my own eyes full many times," says this arm-chair traveller who never went beyond France.

Sir William Temple in the seventeenth century had looked curiously at these irregular Chinese gardens "that may, for aught I know, have more beauty than any of the others. . . . Their greatest reach of imagination is employed in contriving figures, where the beauty shall be great, and strike the eye, but without any order or disposition of parts, that shall be commonly or easily observed. And though we have hardly any notion of this sort of beauty, yet they have a particular word to express it . . . Sharawadgi." But these irregular gardens are too difficult for us to attempt, he warns us; "they are adventures of too hard achievement for any common hands; and though there may be more honour if they succeed well, yet there is more dishonour if they fail, and 'tis twenty to one they will; whereas in regular figures, 'tis hard to make any great and remarkable faults."

But revolutionaries are seldom troubled by the difficulties of what they undertake, and the landscape gardeners did not hesitate to sweep away the formal gardens and lay out the ground according to their own theories. Moreover, they were wonderfully satisfied with the results. "We have discovered the point of perfection. We have given the true model of gardening to the world," Walpole boasts as confidently as Le Blond had boasted of his now discredited gardens. "It is surprising how much beauty has been struck out," Walpole goes on, "with how few absurdities." But we shall see later on about the absurdities.

The ideal garden, so they decided, had already been described by Milton in the Garden of Eden, and they quote him time after time. A garden was nature improved, a landscape made more beautiful by art. For certainly, they thought, nature needed improvement: "the scenery of a Garden should differ as much from common nature, as an heroic poem doth from a prose relation." And most improvements are "artificial," for "nature produces nothing either boiled roasted or stewed, and yet we do not eat raw meat." None the less, art must be concealed, for "all forms that are unnatural displease," and "Art should never be allowed to set a foot in the province of nature, otherwise than clandestinely and by night."

The improvements which Art is to undertake in this rather furtive way are to enhance the natural style of the given landscape. "Ground should first be considered with an eye to its peculiar character; whether it be the grand, the savage, the sprightly, the melancholy, the horrid, or the beautifull. As one or other of these characters prevail, one may somewhat strengthen its effect." This division of gardens into various moods is much insisted on by the eighteenth century, and comes from the Chinese; so said Sir William Chambers, a successful architect who shared with Adam the practice of eighteenth-century London. He had been to China, and came back enthusiastic about Eastern gardens, encouraging Englishmen to copy their natural felicities.

But the various atmospheres of eighteenth-century gardens, if they ever existed outside the owners' fancy, are lost now in the unmistakable common style which they all share, the enhanced natural landscape of trees and grass and water. "We have returned to simplicity by force of refinement," said one writer: a statement as deceptively simple as the simplicity it qualifies. Simple, then, serene, and curiously elegant: as a style for parks it is of unsurpassed beauty, even though I still prefer the greenwood, and could never feel, as one enthusiast did, that the view of Blenheim Park from the entrance drive is the most beautiful scene in the world.

"Nature abhors a straight line," said Kent early in the eighteenth century. It is a new and simple and completely revolutionary statement in garden design. Versailles is dismissed in five words, five words which seem to have the truth of an undeniable natural law. And not only must Versailles go, but every other style of garden which Europe has known till this time. None of them will do, they are all of them unnatural, all planned in the straight lines which nature abhors. From now on all level ground must be broken up, all avenues must go, all hedges be destroyed, all drives must wind, all trees be planted naturally in woods and clumps, all water be left with irregular curving edges. It means, in fact, the eighteenth-century landscape park instead of the seventeenth-century formal garden, and though it seems a simple rule to produce such a sea-change, it is the one fundamental difference.

Naturally the new gardeners despised the old, just as Celia Fiennes had done, but the eighteenth century is much more articulate than she was, and has a gift besides for destructive ridicule which laughed away the old formal gardens with surprising thoroughness. The Chinese, so Temple had told them, "say a boy that can tell a hundred, may plant walks of trees in straight lines," and therefore, they argued, he could very well lay out Versailles; "in short, 'tis a garden for a great child," said Walpole, whose own garden was Strawberry Hill. Chambers denied that it was a garden at all; it is a "mere city of verdure," he said, with hedges for walls, walks for streets, open spaces for squares, and statues for people, ranged "in regular lines like soldiers at a procession." Too great regularity, says another writer, "stupifies and dulls the Senses as bad as the constant Noise of a Mill, or turning round for half an Hour would do." Yes, agrees Chambers, and even the great size of formal gardens is only the sum of many small gardens repeated, "like the honest batchelor's feast, which consisted in nothing but a multiplication of his own dinner: three legs of mutton and turneps, three roasted geese, and three buttered apple pies." They are all agreed and repeat in chorus: "Whatever seems the most natural is the grand Taste, whatever possesses formal Regularity is the Mechanical Taste." Nothing, in fact, could be more ridiculous and vulgar than Versailles; Addison said so in the *Spectator*, and we can only be thankful it did not lie in England, to be swept away like the delightful lost gardens of Kip's engravings.

Fashion, like the wind, blows where it fancies. Though the wind, indeed, blows where it must; nor can we help looking for reasons to explain this complete change of heart. And since it is a style which never really flourished outside England except for a few fashionable imitations, the reasons we find must be English reasons. Politically we had been at war with France, and so might well despise our enemy's gardens. But fashion cares little for politics, and the original gardens laid out round Blenheim itself, that monument to our victory over Le Roi Soleil, were gardens in the style of Versailles. So that it is more helpful to look for reasons inside our own country.

The seventeenth century had been an age of political revolution, but the agricultural and industrial revolutions of the eighteenth century had a far more direct effect on the setting of people's lives. The new advances in farming, "the prevailing rage for agriculture," and the final enclosure of the old open common land created a new orderly landscape, and overlaid the scenery with the new patchwork of fields which to us now is so familiar that we think of it as "the country." But to people used to the old countryside of woods and commons, it was altogether too neat and regular and tame, too much like domestic animals whose ears, says one writer without in the least meaning to be funny, are "to receive the Word of Command from their Masters."

From this too tidy country the Masters turned deliberately to the wild and the "natural." The seventeenth-century gardens seemed to them too like the new countryside. There were hedges now round every field; they wanted none in their gardens. "Hedges are universally bad," and so are all the neat enclosures which they surround. Besides, "civil peace and personal liberty were more secure than in any previous age" (it is Trevelyan speaking this time, and not the eighteenth century), and country life was becoming as orderly as the country landscape. There was no need of formal gardens to make visible man's conception of order, just as there was no need for an enclosed garden to make him feel safe. The side of his complicated soul which he now wanted to express in his gardens was not his need for safety or discipline, but his longing for romance and adventure. Mountains were coming into fashion, Salvator Rosa's theatrically wild landscapes were stylishly popular, by the end of the century *The Mysteries of Udolpho* was a best-seller, and landscape gardens were the height of good taste. It is a natural reaction from formality, and even Louis XIV had felt it strongly enough to try careless week-ending at Marly. Besides, for people who were not princes, "the fine Sett Gardens are so very Expensive in the making and keeping that very few Gentlemen can alienate so much Yearly Revenues towards the Maintenance of those prodigious Gardens." "I will be bold to affirm," one writer assures us, "that £10 will go as far in this" (landscape gardening) "as £50 will in the Methods commonly taken." "Those that would appear splendidly frugal" should follow the new style, for they will find that the "Decoration and Improvement of a Country-Seat will not be that expensive Bug-bear it may of late have appear'd to be."

Bacon had said that gardening follows, not leads, the other arts, but he could not foresee an eighteenth century which would create romantic wildernesses in a classical age. For the eighteenth-century landscape parks are the beginning of the Romantic Revolution, its earliest expression and its most English. Secluded on our islands from the culture of southern Europe, we have been more naturally romantic than classic, we are also gardeners and country-lovers, and from this peculiarly English mixture the eighteenth century created what might well be considered a new form of art, the landscape park.

There are still views beyond the boundary, but they are no longer Le Nôtre's logical vistas of the mind; they have blurred now to the hazy blue distances of romantic painting. Vistas have changed to Prospects, and "Prospects," said Shenstone, "should take in the blue distant hills, but never so remotely that they be not distinguishable from clouds." Garden history, social history, and æsthetic history, too, all are ready for the landscape style.

"I don't see what good it is learning Geometry. I don't see what *use* it is," said one of the children, annoyed that he must finish his homework and not make paper darts to aim through the banisters. "Well, I don't know," the other answered thoughtfully. "It would be very useful for making flower beds in lawns." Euclid might not have agreed, but the Victorians certainly would, and so indeed did the formal gardeners of the beginning of the eighteenth century. For in the Dutch style the regular garden reached depths of triteness which even carpet-bedding could scarcely surpass. "New Improvements," one gardener writes at the head of a chapter which describes a "New Invention for the more speedy Designing of Garden-Plotts; whereby we may produce more Variety of Figures in an Hour's time, than are to be found in all the Books of Gardening now extant. The best Designers may improve their Fancies by it, and may with more certainty hit the Humour of those Gentlemen they work for, without being at the trouble of making many Varieties of Figures or Garden-Plotts, which will lose time, and cause an unnecessary Expence, which frequently discourages Gentlemen from making up their Gardens." This wonderful invention, which he calls a Glass, is simply a kaleidoscope, and he describes enthusiastically, both in words and pictures, how it will produce endless patterns without any effort from the designer. "I think it may not be improper to advertise that the Publisher of these Papers is provided with Glasses of several Sizes ready fitted up for the Experiment at the following Prices: the small sort at three Shillings, and the other at five Shillings."

Small wonder then that intelligent fashion was out of love with formal gardens, that they felt "the want of something at once more grand and more natural," and that the old gardens were swept away, good and bad together, to make way for the new style of nature (more or less) unadorned.

The true eighteenth century, says Trevelyan, does not begin till 1740, and neither, till somewhere about that date, do the true landscape gardens. For they do not arrive all at once with their lawns and clumps and serpentine waters. Temple's *Sharawadgi* was written as early as 1688, and the first gardener of note to follow the Chinese principles was Kent, who leapt the hedge, said Walpole, "and saw all nature was a garden." Perhaps he did, but it was still a fairly formal garden, as we can see at Chiswick House. The pattern is not so much swept away as loosened; the paths are curved instead of straight and there are irregularities in the symmetry, but even in my most hopeful childhood I should never have dreamt of looking for bluebells under Kent's trees.

Richard Bradley, F.R.S., was the first garden journalist, and as early as 1724 he recommends the new style, though rather for snobbery than pleasure. "The more agreeable to Nature our Gardens are made, so much more beauty do they contain, and come nearer that elegant and polite Taste which at present is working in Gardens. . . . Good Judges will judge of Gardens as they do of Pictures, the more free and lively Expression is always preferr'd before the more stiff and formal. . . . The most beautiful Gardens may be made where the Ground is the most irregular and uneven, where there are Hills and Pits: these unlevel spots dictate to Men of Taste those Varieties, which by discreet Management, will afford the greatest Beauties in a Garden."

In the eighteenth century we soon grow as weary of the "Man of Taste" as we do of the "Nobility and Gentry," and we sigh again for the Curious, and the Friendly Reader. All the writers are not such snobs as Bradley, but they are bad enough and we miss our old friends. Philip Miller, F.R.S., was Gardener to the Botanick Garden at Chelsea, and he wrote a *Gardeners Dictionary* which is still useful. The style of the garden which he suggests owes much to the seventeenth century, but he has some new ideas of his own. "The most polite Persons of this Age" (this is his variation of the Man of Taste) prefer gardens "design'd from Nature, so whatever has the stiff Appearance of Art does by no means correspond therewith." Too formal and trite . . . too stiff and formal . . . dismal clipt hedges . . . unnatural bad taste—we are already used to the fashionable abuse. But Miller is not always so vague, and some of his advice might have been written especially for us. "In small Gardens there may be some rising Clumps of Evergreens placed just beyond the plain Opening of Grass before the House, where the Eye will be carried from the plain Surface of Grass, to the regular slope of Evergreens, to the great Pleasure of the Beholder: but if there is a distant Prospect of the adjacent Country, then this should not be obstructed, but rather a larger Opening allow'd for the View, bounded on each side by these rising Clumps. And on the back Part may be planted the several Kinds of flowering Shrubs. In Wildernesses there is but little Trouble or Expence after their first planting, 'tis no wonder they are so generally esteem'd, especially when we consider the Pleasure they afford." Yes. It is only that we now say shrubbery for Wilderness.

The new-style gardeners, although they all condemn the formal, were far from agreeing about the natural. Civil wars are the bitterest of all quarrels, and the only arguments more acrimonious than those between next-door neighbours are those between people who share the same house. It is a truth which I realize every week-end when I read the latest village quarrels in our local country newspaper. So the different practitioners of the different varieties of the landscape style never miss a chance of abusing each other for lack of taste. Capability Brown, so we imagine, was the unquestioned king of eighteenth-century gardening. But not at all.

"Mr. Brown. I very earnestly desire that I may die before you."

"Why so?" said Brown.

"Because," said he, "I should like to see heaven before you had improved it."

As for why he was so disliked, his rivals considered him too genteel, too mild and tame and insipid. His grass was "neat bowling-greens," his houses rising from meadows were "diamonds set in lead," his empty sweeps were only the "carcass of a garden," and as for his much-praised "Purity," plain water is pure, said Chambers, and "a little simplicity will go a very great way."

Brown we might call the Serene Style, for his scenes are always peaceful, and his bitterest enemies were the supporters of the Picturesque. These sought to change the gentle English country into wild scenes of horror, mystery, and "that terror which is so nearly allied to sublimity," and if their landscapes seem to us as serene as Brown's own, it is because two centuries of the English climate are a far more powerful influence than any fashionable theories of the Sublime.

The third style of landscape is much less clear, the Liberal beside the Conservative and Socialist, uncertain which side to join. It is the Chinese school led by Chambers, who built at Kew the Chinese Pagoda, which once had a gilded dragon on every angle of its charming roofs. His attitude is more frivolous than his rivals', for he studded his gardens with fanciful buildings (the ruined arch at Kew is also his) and had a weak fondness for flowers. At the end of his *Dissertation on Oriental Gardening* he added an "Explanatory Discourse by Tan Chet-qua, Gent." which begins by introducing the Chinese author. "Chet-qua had three wives, two of whom he caressed very much, the third but seldom, for she was a virago and had large feet. He dressed well . . . wore nine whiskers and four long nails . . . and every other ornament that Mandarins are wont to wear." He was a "pretty general scholar, and, for a heathen, a very compleat gentleman. He composed a billet-doux at pleasure, recited verses and sung love-songs in many languages. He likewise danced a fandango, played divinely upon the bag-pipe, and made excellent remarks."

This very compleat gentleman lodged in the Strand, and, among other things, he talked of gardens till "the audience fell fast asleep; for the tone of his voice was like opium to the hearers." Chet-qua has a fine high-spirited scheme for turning all

England into a garden. We should set every roadside with flowering shrubs and blossom trees, he tells us, plant our commons with flowers, turn all our bridges into triumphal arches, set the tombs of our ancestors along the highways, and "the whole Kingdom might soon become one magnificent vast Garden, bounded only by the sea."

But alas, he remembers, the people of England are wantonly destructive. They would cut down the trees, pull up the flowers, kill the birds, and throw stones at at the statues; such, he says, is their "destructive brutality. Would to Heaven! . . . as I say to the mistress Chet-quas in a morning, would to Heaven my ducks, we were all at Quang-chew-fu again, with all our long nails and all our whiskers about us."

I wish our own gardening books were half such fun, but we have lost the sophisticated high spirits of the eighteenth century, and our gardens, as well they might be, are nearer the humble retreats of the Middle Ages than to these grandiose but light-hearted follies. For the landscape park is essentially a sophisticated taste—a decadent taste, I dare say the moralists would call it if they ever thought about it. Rousseau "made the dawn visible to people who had never risen till noon, the landscape to eyes that had only rested on drawing-rooms and palaces." Bored with their palaces, the fashionable created artificial wildernesses for their amusement; tired of drawing-rooms, they developed a taste for the Alps—"Precipes, mountains, torrents, wolves, rumblings, Salvator Rosa. Here we are," says Walpole, "the lonely lords of glorious desolate prospects."

Real wildernesses are peopled by Robinson Crusoes or by depressed natives even less civilized, but the wildernesses of the eighteenth century are the setting for the loves of Paul et Virginie, for Marie Antoinette playing at milkmaids, and for "Dowagers as plenty as flounders." There is a very simple way of telling at a glance real country people from those who only play at the Simple Life. Country folk use up old clothes for dirty work; followers of the Simple Life wear special clothes for the occasion. Farm labourers work in navy-blue trousers once long ago their

Sunday suit, but we dress ourselves in careful corduroys and country shirts, like Boucher's shepherdesses in frills and ribbons. Like the eighteenth-century parks, our country clothes are "the utmost simplicity of cultivated order," and just as the parks were not laid out by countrymen but by the fashionable Mr. Brown, so we can never buy from a country tailor the consciously simple tweeds which fashion insists on for the Simple Life.

Rousseau, indeed, set his own style for the country. "I assumed Armenian costume," he says. "It was not a new idea but had occurred to me several times in the course of my life. . . . I had a little Armenian costume made . . . the jacket, the caftan, the fur cap and the belt . . . and I never wore any other dress." He is equally original in his version of the Simple Life. "I decided to learn to make laces, and took my cushion round with me on visits, or worked at my door, like the women, and gossiped with passers-by. . . . To find some use for my laces, I gave them as presents to my young friends on their marriages, on condition that they should suckle their children." No wonder the country people thought him odd (though he never understood why), for how could they know that such fancies, if indulged in less earnestly, were the height of fashion? Like Rousseau, high society idealized the Noble Savage none of them had ever met, and consigned all drawing-rooms to the devil. "I was so tired of reception rooms, fountains, shrubberies, and flower-beds, and of those most tiresome people who made a show of them; I was so weary of pamphlets, clavichords, wool-sorting, and making knots, of stupid witticisms and tedious affectations, of tellers of little tales and great suppers, that when I spied a poor simple thorn bush, a hedge, a barn, or a meadow . . . I consigned all rouge, flounces, and perfumes to the devil."

Paul et Virginie is a charming story which it is hard not to read as a satire on Rousseau's ideas, though we are certainly not meant to. A girl and a boy grow up innocently amid the remote nature of a remote island, fall innocently in love, and just as innocently part. It is not what we expect of tropical climates, but never mind. In the end the heroine returns from Europe in a storm, but she is now so hampered with clothes that she cannot swim, and so infected with false modesty that she will not take her clothes off, and in this most civilized and symbolical dilemma she is drowned within sight of the shore and her waiting lover.

Or so I remember, but it is a long time since I read it. What I do remember very well is what a delightful ballet it would make, danced to eighteenth-century music (Vivaldi perhaps), with Derain to design sophisticated-simple clothes and a decorative mock-primitive setting.

People who live in drawing-rooms have their own troubles. These are not troubles which would beset a cottage. Therefore a cottage is a humble Utopia where trouble is unknown. We can only suppose that that was the reasoning (for it is much the same logic which makes Rousseau's savage noble) which led the eighteenth century to set a cottage as a decoration in a park. "It shows us a dwelling where happiness may reside unsupported by wealth —as it shows us a resource where we may still continue to enjoy peace, though we should be deprived of all the favours of fortune." Not that one needs to be Marie Antoinette to enjoy the delusion, for every true Cockney believes the same—that they only need a country cottage to be happy ever after—or at least every Cockney who was not driven out to languish in a real-life cottage during the war. I dare say it is a common delusion of all town-dwellers.

The eighteenth century also had a fancy for ornamental farms, which are much like the Cockney's cottage. These were for "poor Patrons" who could not afford to give up the whole of their estate to pleasure, and Batty Langley, who mixed ideas of profit with pleasure, was known as the Poor Man's Brown. Flowers were to be planted in field corners, the hedges varied with different shrubs, vegetables instead of exotics grown in the greenhouses, and the ornamental waters stocked with fish. At every view-point there were seats, and urns with verses to departed friends; though you must be careful with the inscriptions, one adviser warns us, and allusions to pastoral Greece are not suitable

for an English farm. "Even the clucking of poultry is not omit-
ted; for a menagerie of a very simple design is placed near the
Gothic building; a small serpentine river is provided for the
water-fowl, while the others stray among the flowering shrubs
on the banks, or straggle about the neighbouring lawn." Shenstone made an ornamental farm called the Leasowes, which Dr.
Johnson considered "the envy of the great and the admiration of
the skilful." Which is exactly what we should expect from a
townsman, and the heart of Johnson's world was Charing Cross.
But it would be hard to imagine anything more likely to infuriate
a genuine countryman. It is a test of the true farmer that he has
no time at all for gardens; even his wife's square of flowers in
front of the house he would plough up if he dared. "I'd cart dung
all day," said the old farmer I once knew well, "rather than do
an hour's digging in the wife's border." But *he* was the real right
thing and wore his oldest blue trousers for the carting.

The more simple-minded enthusiasts of the eighteenth-century
Simple Life might pursue their fancies to bankruptcy—many did
—but the more sophisticated knew very well that the whole
thing was a fashionable game. "I am now, as I told you, returned
to my plough. . . . We lead quite a rural life, have had a sheep-
shearing, a hay-making, a syllabub under the cow, and a fishing
of three gold-fish out of Poyang [Walpole's goldfish pond] for a
present to Madam Clive." All at Strawberry Hill, a comfortable
ride from his town house in Saint James's.

The eighteenth century is our Classical age, the age of reason
and good sense and proportion. And because the intellectual
foundation is so steady, it can support superficial fashions of quite
astonishing absurdity. For the fashionable taste of the eighteenth
century is often wonderfully silly, which is perhaps why the best
writing is satirical, and why there is no great imaginative literature. So I had decided (refusing to consider Blake), for large-
scale theorizing is one of the most satisfying occupations. But
then one of the children came home from school with Gray's

"Elegy." He was to learn the first seven verses for homework, he said, so I read it again for the first time for years, astonished at its excellence.

> *Can storied urn or animated bust*
> *Back to its mansion call the fleeting breath?*
> *Can Honour's voice provoke the silent dust,*
> *Or Flatt'ry soothe the dull cold ear of death?*

There it is, one of the great English poems, making nonsense of all my neat categories.

But still every theory is useful if only to be disproved, for we can use it as a tool to turn over the unorganized mass of facts and arrange them in some kind of order. With a new subject we need lots of theories, one after the other, and as we pursue them and discard them we gradually get to know our material, like harrowing new ground first one way and then the other to break it up fine. It is only important to remember that our theories are only tools and not truths. In the end, when the ground is worked enough, we must leave them all behind in the tool-shed to go out by ourselves with an open mind, and look again as if for the first time.

But my eighteenth-century ground is still disconcertingly rough, and I am glad of any point of view which will help me to see a little further. So I try them all. The eighteenth century is the Classic Age. Yes, but that is no help with its romantic gardens. The Age of Reason. I dare say, but it plays at the Simple Life like a child playing at being sophisticated. The age of fashionable follies. Yes. And for the moment (and since it is my own theory) I can think of no buts. So Gray's "Elegy," I tell myself, belongs only incidentally to its period. Certainly it speaks English with a new eighteenth-century accent, but its subject is still man's ancient sorrow, that we all must die and nothing can save us. Its true tradition is the poetry of melancholy which goes right back through the Middle Ages to the first Old English lyric. It is Pope's "Rape of the Lock" which is essentially of the eighteenth century—as Pope was, too, playing the fashionable games, building a grotto in his garden at Twickenham. But Gray was ill at ease in sophisticated society, was "the worst company in the world," said Walpole, who went to Florence with him, "of a melancholy turn . . . living reclusely." (But, all the same, he writes an amusing post-script to one of Walpole's letters.)

"Enthusiasm always leads to the verge of ridicule, and seldom keeps totally within it," said Uvedale Price in his "Essay on the Picturesque," though he seems quite unconscious of how very far beyond the verge much of his own book lies. And if we want to understand the fashionable taste of the day we should read Mrs. Radcliffe's *Mysteries of Udolpho*, for, as Walpole says of someone else, she "collects the follies of the age for the information of posterity." That Mrs. Radcliffe was quite unconscious of the follies only makes them more convincing. I cannot remember ever reading a sillier book (certainly not in three volumes), and it was enormously popular. The heroine is a pale romantic miss whose excessive sensibility is only rivalled by her complete lack of common sense, and the story is divided almost equally between her melancholy musing in suitable gardens and scenery, and the wildly romantic and deliciously horrifying Italian adventures from which she escapes both unscathed and unsullied. And how people enjoyed it! It was the culmination of fashionable taste. Even Jane Austen, who kept so brilliantly within the boundary which concentrated her gifts, was tempted to mock its absurd popularity in *Northanger Abbey*.

The Picturesque style of gardening set out to produce the wild scenery of *Udolpho* beneath our own mild skies. Little English hills steepen to rude precipices with a cottage on the edge to raise our hair, dark caves are hollowed out of hillsides, and our gentle woods become wild forests to harbour banditti, those picturesque ruffians of Salvator Rosa's pictures who so enchanted an age which seems no longer to have had highwaymen enough of its own to satisfy its liking for violent adventure, even though citizens were still robbed between Kensington and London. Roads wind indefatigably—"Let it wind," says Gilpin with a fine heroic flourish, but still it must seem to wind naturally, as if only to avoid some obstacle. "Mr. Brown," he says, "was often very happy in creating these artificial obstructions," which, since Mr. Brown led the rival school, is a generous if extraordinary compliment. Streams, in the Picturesque park, are disguised as mighty rivers (there are hints on placing bridges to encourage the deception), rivers are pumped to hill-tops to make waterfalls ("springs that long to be cascades"), and if you are lucky enough to possess "a chasm between two high ranges of hill," you can deepen the gloom by "an iron forge, covered with a black cloud of smoak, and surrounded with half-burned ore, with coal, and with cinders."

So that there shall be no suspicion that this elaborately contrived wilderness is not the real thing, whole villages are moved beyond the park wall, the public road is diverted out of sight, and the mansion rises desolately from a sweep of rough grass. The kitchen garden (there is no other) is banished to the boundary, and in the most thorough Improvements the servants creep into the house by underground passages. It seems a very long way from our modern kitchen-diningrooms, but I daresay our food is hotter. However, there were other inconveniences besides having to smuggle in the servants. The deer, since this is wild nature, must roam freely round the house, as indeed they do in all the illustrations; but still it was inconvenient to have antlered stags peering in the ground-floor windows, and even worse if the entrance door were left open and they came into the house. So there were chains across fashionable doorways to keep out the cattle when the door was set open in the summer. And if one's house pretends to be a desolate castle, then everything else must be equally in fancy dress. A ruined abbey turns out to be a farm, and there are cottages disguised as hay-carts or hidden in woodstacks. We cannot help wishing we could overhear the cottagers' comments.

None of the gardeners surpasses Dr. William Gilpin, who wrote *Remarks on Forest Scenery*, and who keeps up a steady level of high-flown absurdity. The New Forest, he says reprovingly, as if the trees should have known better, has tracts of open country "larger than picturesque beauty requires." And although undergrowth in a forest is "useful" because it connects the trees in dignified masses, it should never "straggle too far from the clumps and appear as spots in . . . the middle space between the different combinations." As for the bramble, that has no picturesque virtue of any kind "to recommend it." "It is a plant which one should almost wish to have totally exterminated from landscape."

Nor is the distant view exempt from his fault-finding. "Continuous woods stretching along the horizon without any break . . . is formal, heavy, and disgusting . . . a regular line at the base is almost as disgusting." It seems a strong word for a view not quite varied enough to suit his taste, but then Gilpin is an enthusiast, and even castles must be blown up in a picturesque style. During the "civil wars of the last century," he says, Farnham Castle was blown up, "though not with that *picturesque judgement* with which many castles in those times were demolished." They are his own italics.

We can see why Walpole felt that England was the true home of eccentrics. "The most remarkable thing I have observed since I came abroad," he writes from Florence, "is that there are no people so obviously mad as the English. The French, the Italians, have great follies, great faults; but then they are so national that they cease to be striking. In England, tempers vary so excessively, that almost every one's faults are peculiar to himself. I take this diversity to proceed partly from our climate, partly from our government: the first is changeable, and makes us queer; the latter permits our queernesses to operate as they please. If one could avoid contracting this queerness, it must certainly be the most entertaining to live in England, where such a variety of incidents continually amuse."

But the noble race of English eccentrics has sadly declined since Walpole's day, for besides a changeable climate and a tolerant government, it needs a considerable income, which he never mentions. They are an irreplaceable loss, these wonderful exotic creatures who wither in the chill winds of income tax and death duties, and Sir George Sitwell is probably the last gardener who will encourage us to put our statues under water so that they look like mermaids.

When one side of our nature is denied, it seldom grows great in solitude, as we might hopefully suppose, but rather degenerates. So the Elizabethan theatre, suppressed by the Puritans, reappeared as Restoration comedy; and however much we enjoy those witty, light-hearted, and technically brilliant plays, they are scarcely to be compared with Shakespeare's. Or if Shakespeare is too giant-size for any useful comparison, then with Marlowe or Webster or Ben Jonson. In the same way, the rational eighteenth century ignored that side of the English spirit which we may call poetic, or perhaps romantic; but whatever word we use, we know very well what we mean, for it built the mediæval churches and wrote the literature of the early seventeenth century. And since this inborn quality was discouraged by the climate of the Age of Reason from sharing the open daylight, it grew sickly in cellars, and appears in fashionable life as the Cult of Sensibility. Eighteenth-century sensibility has the same relation to real feeling as the hunger of a dieting beauty to the hunger of a starving man. One of Rousseau's amusements was to sit and weep into the Lake of Geneva—"I indulged my feelings. I sighed and cried like a child. How often I would stop to weep at my leisure and, sitting on a large stone, would be amused to see my tears fall into the water." We feel sure that he took great care to choose a comfortable stone before he started. The heroine of *Udolpho* (she is so unreal a puppet that it is impossible to remember her name) is never so happy as when she is sunk in melancholy musing. Most of her adventures, we come to suspect, are merely an excuse for page after page of mass-produced sensibility, which we soon learn to skip. For "Melancholy" was fashionable; it provided the shadowy background for the bright lights of the drawing-rooms and coffee-houses and public gardens, lights which cast no shadows of their own. It was the common thing, said Walpole, "to set aside a quarter of one's garden to be melancholy in." We must aim at "that pleasing melancholy," says another gardener, and the Gloomy Style was considered the height of good taste. Tombs were a choice ornament of fashionable gardens; Pope built one for his mother at the end of an avenue of funereal cypresses, and the Picturesque island where Rousseau was buried had the extra attraction of the grave of a young man crossed in love and inspired by Rousseau's writing to romantic suicide. A young lady was said to have visited it and composed appropriate verses, as the heroine of *Udolpho* does at every opportunity—they are astonishingly bad. "Magnificently triste," says Walpole, who is always witty, even at his most fashionably absurd.

The Style of Terror was also much admired, and was not to be confused, so they tell us, with the Melancholy, "for it must ever be remembered, that where terror prevails, melancholy is but a secondary consideration." This desirable sensation of delicious horror was suggested by rocks and torrents and gloomy thickets, which cannot have been easy to contrive in the cheerful landscape of the Home Counties. "The terrors of a scene in nature are like those of a dramatic representation; they give us alarm; but the sensations are agreeable, so long as they are kept to such as are allied only to terror, unmixed with any that are horrible and disgusting." Clearly no one must fall over the precipices, and the wildness, moreover, must only be such "as was consistent with ease of access." "Art may therefore be used to heighten these scenes," and Art included such fancies as skulls carved over doorways, "shabby firs and sometimes a withering or a dead tree." Kent even went so far as to *plant* dead trees in his gardens until he was laughed out of it.

But if the scene is naturally gloomy, "less extravagance is required to support it: strange shapes in extraordinary positions; enormous weights unaccountably sustained; trees rooted in the sides and torrents raging at the foot of the rocks, are at the best needless excesses." It strikes us now as a very odd idea of a garden of pleasure, but then we remember Rousseau enjoying himself feeling dizzy. "The road has been edged with a parapet to prevent accidents, and so I was able to gaze into the depths and make myself as giddy as I pleased. For the amusing thing about my taste for precipitous places is that they make my head spin; and I am very fond of this giddy feeling so long as I am in safety. Supporting myself firmly on the parapet, I craned forward and stayed there for hours on end." I too would prefer the eighteenth-century precipice to the no doubt exactly similar delights of a ride over the horrifying switch-backs of the Big Dipper. It is so much more elegant.

Once during the war I rode from Aylesbury to Oxford on the top of a bus. Chattering to each other in the seat in front of me sat two small boys, sent into the country from London (so I made out) because their home had been bombed. They looked idly out of the window from time to time, and suddenly their very half-hearted interest in the countryside was jerked wide awake by a ruined castle at the side of the road. "It was a bomb like ours," said one of them happily, feeling unexpectedly at home in the desert of winter fields. "No," said the other one gloomily after a careful inspection, "it's only an old ruin," and they discussed with enthusiasm, and quite horrifying knowledge, the contrasting effects of ancient time and new destruction.

But both of them were wrong, for Dinton Castle was *built* as a ruin, as an "eye-catcher" for the house below. The cracks were there from the start, and there never was a roof. Small wonder that it should puzzle children brought up to consider adults as sensible creatures. For the eighteenth century loved ruins, and if there were none in their parks, then they built them, for they were not only Picturesque but an unsurpassed aid to melancholy. "At the sight of a ruin, reflections on the change, the decay, and the desolation before us naturally occur; and they introduce a long succession of others, all tinctured with that melancholy which these have inspired." I wonder if the eighteenth century would have appreciated our unprecedented wealth of ruins, or whether such an *embarras de richesses* would have sent them back, even more thoughtful, to their well-built houses.

The Chinese put ruins in their autumn gardens to suit the

fading season, but the landscape gardeners put them everywhere. Walpole, of course, was a connoisseur, for were they not in his favourite Gothick style? His friend Selwyn, he says approvingly, "begged . . . a pretty old gateway" from a ruined priory "to erect on the top of his mountain, and it will have a charming effect." In another castle he admired, "the stairs are gone, but it is now a most beautiful Ivy-mantled tower. The last Lord added a ruined round tower that has a good effect." One German enthusiast even considered adding a derelict wing to his mansion, and so many new ruins were set up that Whately gives us rules for building them. "They are a class by themselves," he says, "beautiful as objects, expressive as characters, and peculiarly calculated to connect with their appendages into elegant groups." (Now I come to think of it, Dinton Castle is remarkably elegant.) The original plan of the building must be clear, he goes on; "straggling ruins have a bad effect," and a confused chaos of stones has not the necessary air of the genuine—it will "raise doubts about the existence of the ancient structure; whereas the mind must be hurried away from examining into the reality, by the exactness and the force of the resemblance." It would be hard to choose between Mr. Whately and Dr. Gilpin for sustained absurdity.

A new cottage built within an "old" ruin he recommends as a convincing trick, or a "ruined" stone bridge restored with a few planks "will take off the idea of a childish conceit." But we must be careful to suit our ruins to the scenery, he warns us. "Open and polished scenes will generally be given to the Arcadian shepherd; and those in a lower degree of cultivation will be thought more conformable to the manners of the ancient British yeomanry." A cross, or an ancient church, or even a Maypole would be fitting, he thinks, half hidden in the "British" woods. But why be limited to ruins? he asks, "a hackneyed device immediately detected, unless their style be singular, or their dimensions extraordinary." Why not set up a Stonehenge? It could be done "with little trouble, and great success; the materials might be brick or even timber plaistered over, if stone could not easily be procured." But we must be careful not to introduce any other buildings in the same scene—"no Grecian temples, no Turkish mosques, no Egyptian obelisks or pyramids."

Grottoes, too, were popular (fine places for toads, said Dr. Johnson), and every fashionable park must have its hermitage. "A hermitage must not be close to a road, but whether it be exposed to view on the side of a mountain, or concealed in the depth of a wood is almost a matter of indifference." The hermit no doubt was rather less indifferent, and as if this solitude were not depressing enough, the gloomy character of the place must be "retained in the utmost purity." "About the hermitage [the wood] is thickened with trees of the darkest greens; a narrow gloomy path, overhung with Scotch and spruce firs, under which the fern seems to have been killed, not cleared, and scarce a blade of grass can grow, leads to the cell; that is composed of logs and of roots . . . and the furniture within is old and uncouth." No wonder that hermits refused to live in such gloomy hovels, though the cell, it was realized, needed an inhabitant if it were to impress visitors as genuine. But even the destitute could not be bribed to be hermits for long; or if they put up with the life for a week or two in the summer, then there was either trouble with the neighbouring milkmaids, or neighbours with a social conscience insisted that the hermit must be replaced by a dummy.

This impressing of visitors was one of the recognized intentions of the landscape park. Many of the new country gentry were self-made men; they might even, alas, have made their money from trade. And they were dreadful snobs. "The Gentleman will always shine," Bradley reassured them, "let his Circumstances be never so narrow." But it was not enough. To feel their social standing was secure, they must have land like the older aristocracy. Luckily this was the perfect time to acquire an estate, for although the enclosure of the old open fields had been going on in a haphazard way since Tudor times, in the eighteenth century it became the national policy, and the remaining common lands were divided up among the peasants in small allotments. Since many of these poor people could not afford even to enclose their land, they sold it, and a rich man could very easily buy himself a "seat." These grounds were often laid out more for show than for pleasure, and the height of happiness was to dazzle one's neighbours. And not only neighbours, for streams of curious visitors travelled along the improved roads of the late eighteenth century—"Coaches full of travellers . . . troops of holiday neighbours. The Lord of the Place can never call it his during the finest part of the year." Clearly there is nothing new in grand parks being open to the public, and even when the Lord of the Place was not at home, callers like Walpole made their way in and inspected his Improvements. "A visitor is disappointed," says one gardener, criticizing a scene he finds too humble, and there is no more to be said.

The fine houses, too, were not built to be lived in in comfort, but to look magnificent, to be approached from an angle to make them seem larger. And indeed they are almost uninhabitable, so huge and inconvenient and cold. As Walpole says of Italy, they "have found out how hot their climate is, but not how cold; for there are scarce any chimneys, and most of the apartments painted in fresco; so that one has the additional horror of freezing with imaginary marble." Since the gardens are part of this keeping up with the neighbours, one of their chief aims is to look larger than they are, "to extend the appearance of domain and the idea of a seat." "Nothing gives a mansion so much dignity as these home demesnes, or contributes more to mark its consequence. . . . A noble park is the natural appendage of an ancient mansion." The boundary must never be seen, but sunk in a ditch, so that more impressionable visitors may imagine the whole countryside belongs to the mansion. At Chatsworth there was a painted *trompe-l'œil* perspective at the end of one of the vistas, as if Derbyshire were not already depressingly large enough.

It was a great advantage of the natural style of gardening that there was no obvious division between park and country. Though even this had its drawbacks, they found, for how were visitors to know they were on your own private drive and not

simply the public road? But equally, on the other hand, how
could they know that the public road was not your private
drive? Whately has various suggestions for encouraging such a
delusion in visitors. You could plant specimen trees along the
verges of the highway, he says, and in the hedges here and there
an exotic shrub not found wild in England, or you could grow
clumps of trees in the neighbouring fields to make them look like
private parkland.

A Riding was an even more ambitious hoax: a carefully arranged circuit track to take visitors on horseback as if all the land
were yours—"to extend the idea of a seat and appropriate a
whole country to the mansion." The track itself could be made
to seem private by the same tricks as the public road, and the destination should be "a small spot . . . enclosed from the fields
and converted into a shrubbery. . . . It may be kept by the
labour of one man," the writer says encouragingly, "and nothing
so effectively extends the idea of a seat to a distance." If your
Riding must willy-nilly be along the road through a village, then
the village must be made "romantic." You might build a farm
like a castle, or set up a "pretty" wellhead on the village green, or
little fancy bridges over the streams, and "by the help of a few
trifling plantations . . . there are few villages which may not
easily be rendered agreeable." But beware of shams, he warns us,
and none too soon. It is very well to build a farm "in the sem-
blance of an abbey," but to set up only "a bit of a turret or the
tip of a spire" is merely "frivolous."

Were the bits of turrets and tips of spires set up on poles among
the trees, I wonder? And was the eighteenth century even more
extravagantly absurd than I suspected at the beginning? But they
amused each other, too, for one of them tells the story of the old
lady (of the same race as Mme du Deffand, though cruder in her
methods) who, when passing a pretentious entrance gate whose
twin lodges reminded her irresistibly of tea-caddies, stopped her
carriage, climbed out, and on one lodge wrote GREEN in large letters, and on the other BOHEA.

. . .

The real trouble about these "pompous solitudes" as Walpole calls the larger parks, is that they can only be laid out in remote districts where land is cheap, and therefore the proud owner can never expect enough visitors to make the expense worth while. "Men tire of expense," he admits disarmingly, "that is obvious to few spectators." For it is no use pretending that this new style of gardening was for private pleasure, and even Whately, who gave us such unguarded advice on Ridings, regrets "the pride of making a lavish display to a visitor, without any regard to the owner's enjoyments." Walpole even relents enough to recommend a garden as we mean it, for "the total banishment of all particular neatness immediately about a house, which is frequently left gazing by itself in the middle of a park, is a defect." The English weather is not always suitable for such open spaces, and "whenever a family can purloin a warm and even something of an old-fashioned garden from the landscape designed for them by the undertaker in fashion, without interfering with the picture, they will find satisfactions on those days that do not invite strangers to come and see their improvements."

Walpole will only allow a garden if it does not interfere with the picture, for "flowerbeds hurt the eye by their littleness," and Knowle, he says, is spoilt by "trumpery fragments of gardens." But there were plenty of old-fashioned people who went on happily growing flowers as they had always done, caring nothing at all for the garden as a work of art, but only that it should be an "out-of-door dwelling-place for plants and people." They regretted the seventeenth-century gardens which the Improvers had destroyed: "whole woods of venerable plants have been swept away to make room for a little grass. Our virtuosi have scarcely left an acre of shade, nor three trees growing in a line, from Land's-end to the Tweed," and Cowper gives half a page of the *Task* to reviling Capability Brown.

Nor were all the eighteenth-century gardens in the landscape style. In Canaletto's pictures we can still see the gardens Pepys admired, with trees in rows and open grass for walking. There are bills in the royal accounts for looking after the avenues and

putting new gravel on the paths. Ranelagh, too, was more beloved than any "pompous solitude," and, like Vauxhall, it was in
the old fashion of formal avenues, regular canals, and straight
hedges "which are cut with the utmost exactness and look extremely neat." Even fashionable writers like Gilpin and Repton
recommend a garden near the house, and there are plenty of gardening books on growing fruit and flowers. Miller's *Gardeners
Dictionary* was reprinted several times, and is probably the most
famous gardening book since Parkinson. Bradley published a
steady stream of horticultural advice, and even Cowper tells us
in heroic verse how to make a hot-bed.

> *The stable yields a stercoraceous heap,*
> *Impregnated with quick fermenting salts.*

I should think there has never been a more dignified dung-hill.
Switzer, too, despite his tiresomely fulsome style, was a true gardener with a proper gardener's enthusiasm for his soil, and he tells
us how to make a wide selection of different dung- and compost-
heaps; "Magazines" he calls them, and gives each one a number,
so that afterwards, telling us how to plant seeds or strike cuttings,
he can refer us most efficiently to the right number and even the
exact page. "Having committed the Seed to the Ground and covered it with a proper Thickness of Earth No. 1 page 105 . . .
spread it with an inch of fine clean rotten Dung, from Magazine
No. 4 page 106."

The flowers and trees popular in the eighteenth century have
changed little, though there is more interest in exotics like the
Great American Aloe, which was a wonderful attraction to the
Curious when it flowered in Mr. Cowell's greenhouse at Hoxton.
The books still offer the same advice on layering and grafting,
and give lists of the points to look for in fine flowers like tulips
and auriculas, perhaps to help the judges at flower shows. The
eighteenth-century gardeners, although they still valued striped
tulips, already suspected that the flaming was caused by "some
Weakness or Distemper," and John Cowell tells us how to make
them break. "Take the Plaister of old Walls, mix this with Drift-

Sand and to this add the Water that runs from a Dunghill or Jakes, and put it over the Surface of the Bed . . . and 'twill make them break into fine Stripes to a wonder, as it was related to me by a Gentleman of great Honour."

But Mr. Cowell's greatest contribution to our pleasure is a suggestion he offers for naming flowers so that we shall know their colour from a catalogue. First we must have a list of great Personages, Castles, Cities, etc., and also a table of colours: W for

Tulipa Jacobi Bommi lutei Coloris coccineis flammis divisa et ornata

A flamed tulip. Drawing by Crispin de Passe.

White, Y for Yellow, and so on. The flowers are then given names whose initials correspond to their colours. "A Flower perhaps with White abounding, and marked with Crimson, may be called William the Conqueror; the W in William expressing the White abounding, and the C the Crimson: or the same flower might be named the Wonder of Constantinople. A Flower

striped with Crimson and Purple may be called the Charming
Phyllis, or the Curious Ptolemy" (though this is surely a rather
perverse P, like saying G for gnome on the telephone). Even
flowers already named may have epithets added to show their
colour, "as for Example the fine Carnation which is called the
Princess Amelia, whose Principal is White, and mark'd with Violet: To this might be added, the Worthy Virgin." Carnation
Princess Amelia, the Worthy Virgin. But what happens when
Amelia marries? It seems never to have occurred to him that it
might be inconvenient to name flowers after the more ephemeral
attributes of human beings.

"I have made great progress," says Walpole, "and talk very
learnedly with the nurserymen, except that now and then a lettuce run to seed overturns all my botany, as I have more than
once taken it for a curious West-Indian flowering shrub." But
flowers have even less place in the landscape gardens than in Le
Nôtre's. "A Serpentine River and a Wood are become the absolute Necessities of Life" (it is Walpole again), and trees are the
true inhabitants of the new parks. "It is no exaggerated praise,"
says Gilpin, who always exaggerates, "to call a tree the grandest
and most beautiful of all the productions of the earth." The new
gardening books are full of advice not only for growing trees,
but also for grouping and spacing them: a very much more difficult art than we might suppose from the seemingly accidental
perfection of the finished landscape gardens.

Rivers, as Walpole said, must always wind (the eighteenth
century even made a new verb, to serpentize), and all water had
to follow Hogarth's Line of Beauty, an irregular curve where no
part repeated any other. "Clever," said one Improver when he
saw the serpentine meanderings of the River Thame across the
landscape, and though they told him it was simply the natural
course of the river, he still insisted. "Clever," he said in admiration of a river which had learnt so thoroughly the lessons of Capability Brown. But I know what he meant, for I felt the same
about the trees in Bramham Park.

Much of the eighteenth-century advice on gardens is no longer of everyday use. We are never likely to need to know how to dig out a lake and pile up the earth to make a hill, nor how to make artificial waterfalls look natural, nor how to break up the offensively regular "grazing-line" which the deer make under trees by eating the lower branches, nor whether a temple or a cottage is better to enliven the view. Nor is Uvedale Price really useful—"I conceive that in most situations it may be quite possible, with some sacrifice of expense, to introduce here and there broken rocky precipices, of more or less magnitude, that might serve to give the happiest variety to the aquatic scene which the improver is forming . . . before admitting the water into the valley to be flooded, to open up a large irregular quarry in the sloping side of the hill; and to secure the essential point that the rocks may rise naturally out of a certain depth of the future water, the operation of quarrying may be made to commence at any given depth below the line of its intended level. Very picturesque little irregular rocky bays may thus be formed."

By the eighteenth century, science had spread far beyond the garden wall, but the gardeners are still amateurs, and in the introduction to his *Dictionary* Miller gives an explanation of wind by differences in the "Spring of the Air" which only needs to write *pressure* for *Spring* to be quite up-to-date still. Besides the Circulation of Sap, which has already occupied gardeners for a century, they are beginning to understand "the Generation of Plants by coupling with one another," and Linnæus's system of classifying brought scientific order to the chaos of muddled plant names. They are indefatigable experimenters, and one result which they tell with amazement in book after book is that the bud of a variegated jasmine, when grafted on an ordinary green jasmine, caused the whole of the host plant to become variegated.

But there is still plenty of very curious science for the credulous. Silkworms are destroyed by thunder, and "it would be well to try whether the firing of Guns near such Trees as are infected with Caterpillars would not destroy those Insects." Blights of caterpillars are carried by the east wind, and if we light fires to windward of orchards, the smoke will suffocate the grubs, which can then be swept up in heaps. The plague, so Bradley thought, and not so very wrongly, was carried by tiny insects: "In Turkey Egypt and Barbary, when the Plague rages, the Franks, the English etc. are seldom infected with it" because the Insects "having their certain natural Nourishments respectively appointed them" (the Turks and Egyptians, I suppose), "do not in those Places infect Strangers." Among the experiments Bradley wants to try is whether snails would acquire medicinal value by feeding on medicinal herbs, but Walpole can think of better experiments: "The deliberation with which trees grow, is extremely inconvenient to my natural impatience," and he would like an invention for moving ancient oaks as easily as tulip bulbs. This will be simple to future ages, he prophesies, and "I have even begun a treatise or panygeric on the great discoveries made by posterity in all the arts and sciences. . . . The delightfulness of having whole groves of humming-birds, tame tigers taught to fetch and carry, pocket spying glasses to see all that is doing in China, with a thousand other toys, which we now look upon as impracticable, and which pert posterity would laugh in one's face for staring at, while they are offering rewards for perfecting discoveries, of the principles of which we have not the least conception!"

Well, we have our tigers now, though they are only half tame, and I doubt whether Walpole would like them any more than we do ourselves. We much prefer his eighteenth-century gardens, and it is interesting to consider why they are so satisfying. For they are not gardens at all by ordinary standards, they are views. "You must send for a landscape painter," said Vanbrugh when they asked him who should lay out the gardens at Blenheim, and that is what they are: real-life models of landscape pictures. They are there to be looked at, not to explore or to live in or to grow flowers in or to love for their intimate pleasures, for they have none, but to be looked at, from a distance and from a particular point of view. They are the backgrounds for Watteau's pictures, a kind of photographer's backcloth raised to the height of poetry.

For Watteau, too, was a Romantic in a Classical age. His "costly perfumed people" are quiet with some strange unhappiness. Even in the music and dancing they are sad, a graceful and poetic brokenheartedness which is perhaps what the Melancholy style of gardens was meant for. And through the mind of a great painter the cult of sensibility becomes deep feeling, so that Watteau's indefinable melancholy is a true experience and leaves us richer, like reading elegiac poetry. Besides, there is always the pleasure of seeking through the sad groups of merry-makers for that figure he loved both to draw and to paint: a young woman seen from behind, her head bent forward and a little to one side, her hair brushed up smoothly to show her quite enchanting neck.

But Watteau brings us no nearer to understanding why we like the landscape parks today. One reason, indeed, is quite simple: they are *here* and we *can* like them, for, needing very little labour to keep them, they have survived when other gardens have vanished. Then we, too—like the eighteenth century, though for different reasons—feel ourselves hemmed in by order. Theirs was an order of the mind, ours is the mechanical pattern of industrial life, but, none the less, the deliberate naturalness of landscape gardening suits us both. Nature abhors a straight line, and so do we after a day in a city. So that as city parks these contrived landscapes are happier than they ever are in the country. The billowing masses of trees, the long curving sweeps of grass and water are a perfect contrast to the neat regular detail of the architecture which surrounds them. The buildings which enclose Saint James's Park are changed to palaces from fairy-tale, the Regent's Park terraces are bewilderingly beautiful, pale and remote on winter mornings through the dark network of the trees, beyond the misty levels of the lake.

This "natural" scenery is as exotic in a city as flowers in the wrong climate: it has the same fascination as lilac at Christmas, or orchids kept by glass from the frost outside. And it is curiously elegant, for the artificiality which seems sterile in the country is changed by its city context to elegance and grace. Perhaps if we lived in these empty parks we might find them as disappointing as I did as a child, but we never do live in them, we are only visitors, and that, quite exactly, is what they are meant for. The first view is overwhelming, and we are never there long enough to grow tired of it.

Beneath the froth of fashionable follies, the eighteenth century was blessed with a fundamental good taste and sense of proportion which are often at their best in its humbler creations. We live in London in an ordinary terrace house, put up about the middle of the eighteenth century by a working builder whose name no one remembers. London is full of similar dignified but unpretentious houses built for ordinary middle-class families, and they are most satisfying to live in. There are no affectations, no exaggerations; the proportions are simple, discreet, and gracious, both inside and out. They are probably the best town houses ever built. In the same way, the underlying proportions of the eighteenth-century parks are excellent and unobstrusive. It is a proof of their rightness that we can accept them as natural, that this man-made landscape can seem to us as convincing as the scenery moulded by thousands of years of weather, that our first thought is how fortunate the gardener was to find his piece of ground. And now that the more inappropriate follies have vanished, we are left only with this perfectly proportioned landscape of grass and trees and water.

The grass of England is unrivalled, the trees are unsurpassed, and the water is here in abundance; the landscape parks are created of materials beautiful in themselves, as clipped hedges and gravel paths never were in the formal gardens. And for us, two centuries after they were planted, these magnificent forest trees have reached their perfect maturity. We are seeing the gardens as their creators must have imagined, but never saw them. For trees grow slowly and must be planted small, and the dark masses of woods which sweep up Brown's hillsides were only for him a nursery of saplings. He must have known when he planted them how perfectly the arrowy tall poplars on the island in Blenheim lake would enhance the level water and the curving shores, but still it seems a pity that he can never have seen them. Though perhaps, as his enemies feared, Brown is busy improving heaven, and surely there his plantations would shoot up full-size overnight, for what could be a more suitable heavenly reward for a good gardener?

Horace Walpole's Tailpiece.

CHAPTER NINE

WHAT DO
WE
WANT NOW?

ONCE DURING THE WAR WE WENT TO LIVE
in a sixteenth century farmhouse which had no garden.
Perhaps there once had been one, for there was a moat round the
house at just the distance one would choose as a boundary for a
garden. Perhaps there once were Tudor plots and fancies, knots
perhaps and gillyflowers, for the old house had certain elegancies
of carved oak and wide stairs, was more than a mere work-a-day
shelter for the farmer and his family. A most lovable house—but
it has been the hero of one book already, and must not come tres-
passing in this one. In any case, it was a house without a garden,
for until we came no one had lived there for fifteen years, and
any garden there might once have been had vanished with no
trace left to guess by, no paths or hedges, no flowers struggling
to survive among the weeds, no grass smooth enough even to be
imagined as a lawn. The farm came up to the house on one side,
the orchard on the other. Through one lot of windows we looked
into a bower of apple blossom, through the others we watched
the heavy cows lurch by from the meadows to be milked. For
the first week it was an idyllic setting, and I wondered why anyone should labour to make a garden when simply by doing nothing at all the little wild flowers of the orchard came up to the
very doorstep.

But I soon found out. Even on the lowest and most practical level, untouched nature will not do. The space round a house is used too much to be left to look after itself; at the end of a week it is not flowers we find on our doorstep, but mud. There is too much traffic in and out of a house for anything to serve but surfaces of stone or brick or gravel. There must be hard paths, and if there are paths, the animals must be kept off them, the cows must be shut out with walls or hedges. And if the animals are shut out, then something must be done with the grass and weeds which grow up uncontrolled by grazing.

All this I found despite my first conviction, which I have never changed, that the English countryside is far more beautiful than any garden I shall ever make. Yet there already was my garden, an enclosed space where the vegetation was controlled by my arbitrary choice and by my constant labour. And since I must needs have a garden, what sort should it be to suit our twentieth-century life? What had happened since the landscape parks? How had gardens changed with the Industrial Revolution of the nineteenth century?

Mostly they had shrunk, and ours certainly was small enough, well under an acre. But as for new ideas, the nineteenth century seems to have produced no valid new styles in gardening any more than in architecture. There was still some landscape gardening more or less in the authentic tradition; there were still a few follies put up, but with less conviction. Shrubberies became smaller and gloomier and too full of laurels, and carpet-bedding was a popular degeneration of the formal parterre. There was also a revival of the wild garden, the "wilderness" of the Tudors and the seventeenth century, and of the natural gardens of the Chinese, who "painted their way very artfully along the skirts of the plantation" with flowers.

The contribution which the late nineteenth-century gardeners have liked to consider particularly their own is the herbaceous border, but it is difficult to see why they claim it as new. A border where all kinds of flowers are grown together has always from the beginning been the chief delight of ordinary gardeners, though certainly for a time it had no place in the fine designs of the formal and landscape styles. But the gardener who loved flowers still kept his mixed border, even though he might hide it from the Improvers within the walls of the kitchen garden. Besides, even in the formal gardens of the seventeenth century there were lawns surrounded by simple beds of flowers which the French called English Parterres, and Bradley in the eighteenth century gives us advice for planting our herbaceous borders which would do perfectly well for today. "In planting a Border or Bed of Flowers, we may judiciously mix the several sorts . . . that they may be so disposed as to appear gradually one above the other, and add Beauty to each other by their Variety of Colours." He then gives us a plan of a border with "the tallest Blowers" at the back, the "Middle siz'd" next, and the "Lowest kinds" in front. His lists of flowers are very little different from the flowers we still grow in our twentieth-century borders; it is only that we have added new discoveries from the East, and used our new knowledge of genetics to improve the old favourites—or sometimes, alas, only to coarsen the elegant distinction of the original species to a gross display of formless colour.

"The practice of horticulture," says the preface to a mid-Victorian gardening book, "has been regarded as the most healthy employment and most delightful recreation in which human beings can be engaged. This remark holds good of all its branches, unless it be the forcing of flowers and fruits under glass, which is adverse to physical well-being. It is true that in the departments of culinary vegetables and fruits the element of utility is of first importance; but even they are not without their pleasures of a satisfactory nature. It is pleasing to enjoy the consciousness of skill applied, of diligence and power exercised and of cherished expectation gratified at length." (Oh, dear. There is nothing new, it seems, and the seventeenth century has said it all so very much better.) "Flower-gardening has less of material utility than the departments just referred to. It does not contribute to the substantials of the table, but it does to its elegancies, and has numerous other and more refining attractions, which have always made it a favourite pursuit."

He does not tell us what the more refining attractions are, but of course he quotes Keats on a joy for ever, as everyone has done ever since he wrote the Urn ode. We also know that Victorian flower beds had to be raised for ladies well above the paths, because the crinoline was such an embarrassingly unsuitable garment for stooping.

Perhaps, after all, our best inheritance from the Industrial Revolution is the lawn-mower; and perhaps it is symbolic that it should be a machine it gave us. But, in any case, it made little difference to garden design, for there had been lawns ever since the seventeenth century; it was only that they needed more labour to keep them smooth.

"Un Français met des figures de Géométrie dans son jardin, un Anglais pose sa maison dans un pré, un Chinois fait devant sa fenêtre des cataractes épouvantables." But most people, if we ask them the simple question "What is a garden?" will answer quite simply, as unpretentious gardeners have always answered: "A garden is a place for growing flowers." For the true gardener "is inclined, even from the strength of his blood, to this love and labour." The flowery-bowery garden is one of the unthinking and immediate pleasures. It has a kind of artless generosity, a lush and lavish sweet-tooth atmosphere of fragrance and colour and silken petals. The love of flowers is the first delightful step towards appreciating a garden, and if we cannot have a large plot to grow them, then we make do with a small one; if we cannot have any garden at all, then we grow flowers in tubs and window-boxes, we fill our house with flower vases and "bough-pots" and plants in pots. We may even, as the seventeenth-century Londoners did, paint *trompe-l'œil* garden scenes and hang them outside our windows—"Those painted projections of our cockney glades," so Evelyn scornfully describes them, "which appeare like gardens of paste-board and march-payne, and smell more of paynt than of flowers." But Evelyn is seldom sympathetic, and

we have more fellow-feeling for the gardenless Cockney than for Evelyn and all his ruined holly-hedges at Deptford.

Our delight in growing flowers is a complicated pleasure—partly an appreciation of their beauty and partly an affection for pets. For growing flowers is very much like keeping animals or looking after small children; to their keeper they become individual creatures whose health and happiness are his loving concern. We water our flowers even when we are tired, just as we feed our dog or listen to our children's troubles. We feel ourselves responsible for our dependents. The real gardener is paternal about his flowers, they are his pets; and his enemy is the housewife who regards them as so much material for filling vases for the house. Anyone who comes into the garden questingly with scissors is an inhuman despoiler, and never for a moment to be trusted out of sight.

A place to grow flowers. Yes. But that does not describe a garden so much as a floral allotment. A designer of gardens "ought to have a general Idea of everything that is Noble and Stately in the Productions of Art, for this lies open a Man's Thoughts and enlarges his Imagination." But we are not designers, we are flower-growers; we are occupied with the material of gardens, not the garden itself, the bricks in the wall and not the design of the house. Yet there is this great difference: that a brick has no value out of its context, but the living material of a garden is satisfying in its own right. A plant is not merely a unit in a design, but a complicated work of art more complete and beautiful than anything we shall ever make ourselves. It belongs to a different, a vegetable world which we cannot realize, it is governed by laws which we can only remotely understand, and it is adapted to this mysterious life in patterns of astonishing beauty. However minutely we consider them, the patterns of organic structure are always beautiful. It is not only the flowers we set admiringly in vases, nor the leaves we grow as plants in pots for decoration; if we pull a flower to pieces to examine the inside, or cut across an ovary to see the arrangements of seeds; if we look at tiny florets through a lens, at sections through a microscope, at viruses through an electron microscope, always at every level of the plant's construction we are astonished at its beauty, at what Sir Thomas Browne calls "the elegant co-ordination of vegetables." We can examine a flower by infra-red radiation, by ultra-violet light, by X-rays, and the one thing we can be certain of finding is new æsthetic pleasure: we are never disappointed. "All Nature is but Art unknown to thee," as a poet said whose name I cannot remember, but he must surely have been of the age of capital letters.

For a long time now I have lived with a background of doctors and hospitals. I have grown used to considering people as patients, I am no longer surprised at the peculiar rôle of priest and confessor which the public has thrust on the modern doctor; but one thing I have never got used to is the astonishing beauty of X-ray photographs. An ugly body of indiscriminate fat melts in the X-rays to a mysterious shadowy background of tissues, miraculously revealing the clear pattern of the bones drawn firm and delicate in dark-edged shapes, a skeleton of austere and significant curves. Even now, passing people in the street, I realize with sudden wonder that embedded in the formless flabby shapes of our urban bodies there lies an elegant construction of bones most perfectly shaped and articulated.

"But to return from this beautiful Digression," as Switzer says. For most people, flowers are the essential: it is why most gardens are ugly for half the year. Yet in the great gardens, flowers, for all their individual beauty, have been of little importance; they are incidental decoration and the finest taste has rejected them. But if flowers are not the essential of a garden any more than trimming is the essential of a dress, if a garden is not simply a place for growing flowers, then what is it?

"A Garden is a work of Art using the materials of Nature." It is a lucid definition which includes all fine gardens whatever their style, large or small, formal or wild. It explains why a garden composed only of the common plants of the country, as Versailles was, is so immensely more than the sum of its parts. It explains why gardens have been an expression of the ages they belonged to, and why there can be many styles of gardens, each equally satisfying to different people. But it is not a definition which includes our own much-loved vegetable hotch-potches of flowers and shrubs, nor does it explain the wide appeal of gardens among people who are not at all interested in the arts. I dare say the number of gardeners who consider their garden for its structural qualities is no greater than the number who look at paintings or read poetry. Cobbett had no doubt about it. "The far greater part of persons who possess gardens really know very little about the matter. They possess no 'principles' relating to the art."

But, luckily, we can enjoy our gardens very well without any principles at all, for unlike the materials of poetry and painting, the actual stuff of gardens is already significant in itself. Abstract poetry is Jabberwocky, abstract painting is decoration, but abstract flower-growing, although it may not be gardening at all, is a most satisfying occupation, and gives us gardens we delight in, however bad they may be as designs. We really do not *care* what Le Nôtre or Capability Brown would think of them, but all the same we should realize humbly that we are no longer the creators of the work of art, but only more or less ignorant patrons who by our protection encourage the plants to produce their own individual beauties.

"The Precepts of the Cultivating part of Gardening depend on observation and experience," so Switzer says, and he would consider us all now merely as Cultivators, "but this of Designing, on a noble and correct Judgement and Taste of Things . . . but everyone makes what Judgement he pleases, and thereby leaves Design in Confusion."

Since Switzer's day we have grown so used to being surrounded by Design in Confusion that we scarcely notice it in our gardens. Besides, plants, being all of the same vegetable race, group themselves together quite wonderfully well without any help from us. But it is no use supposing we are artists and can lay out our odd acre or so of land as a kind of vegetable poetry, as Le Nôtre did and Capability Brown. Nor have we any garden

Designers of noble and correct Judgement to help us, but only Cultivators, with here and there perhaps an eye for foliage or for putting colours together more or less happily. So we must please ourselves and lay out our plot "according to our best fantasie," as the Tudors did.

Yet still we must ask ourselves, what is it we want besides the mere presence of flowers and shrubs and trees? "A Garden is Nature disciplined by Art." Yes. But so is a racehorse or a beautiful woman or the English countryside. Indeed, all good farmers might be considered as artists *manqués,* or better still, as gardeners who have spread beyond the garden fence. It is probably why they have no interest in the patch round the house, for since the farm absorbs all their gardening enthusiasm, they leave the farm garden to their wives.

Every tree in a hedge cost the farmer fifty pounds, so my old farmer friend once told me. Fifty pounds for the harm it did shading the crops, starving the grass, and flattening the ripe corn with the swirling eddies it caused in the wind. And when he came to sell the tree for timber, he was lucky, he said, if it fetched enough to pay for the felling and carting away. So he told me one sunny morning as we stood in the front meadow and looked sadly at a huge tree blown down in the night like a fallen giant, spoiling the setting of his home, which had stood like a neat doll's-house between its pair of towering elms. Then why did he keep them? I asked, looking round his farm, where spreading trees stood nobly between every field, and why did he carefully spare a sapling here and there when he cut and laid his hedges? For I had often watched him hedge-laying on mild winter days, the work he best enjoyed of all the farm year. Oh, he liked to see them about, he said, half embarrassed. The place would look bare without a few trees here and there. Like them scientific farms, he said, like a factory. Yes, he liked to see them about, it looked more natural, it made the place more home-like.

So now I never see the sparse grass under a hedge-row elm, nor the heavy-headed corn tangled and beaten down in the lee of a spreading beech, without being grateful to all farmers for their artist's eye, and remembering with affection his half-apologetic embarrassment.

But a farmer does not lay out his farm by æsthetic considerations: his very embarrassment shows that he considers them frivolous; and since we can scarcely hope to make a garden as satisfactory as a well-run farm, we should perhaps do well to follow the farmer and keep to practical reasons. Then what do we want of our gardens besides flowers and fruit and vegetables? Well, we want a hobby. "Hobby . . . Gardening." Hobby is an unfortunate word with its associations of fretwork and stamp-collecting, and certainly it is not the attitude of the great designers, but there are plenty of entries in *Who's Who* to support it as a point of view. We want an out-of-door occupation which gives us mild exercise and more interest than the hitting or kicking of balls.

The labour of a garden is strenuous but healthy, says Miller in his introduction. "It is true, since the Fall of our Progenitors, the work is not so easy as before it was, the Curse having covered the Ground with Thorns and Briars, so that the Ground which before, without Cultivation, would have been spontaneously Obedient to vegetative Nature, must now, by the Sweat of the Brow, and no little Labour, be brought under Subjection: But then at the same time, to make Amends, this very Labour is salutiferous: The Exercise of the Body prevents the Blood and Juices from stagnating and growing corrupt; and the Labourer is every Moment drawing in with his Breath a wholesome and enlivening Stream from the Earth, which causes the Blood and spirits to circulate briskly; and together with the Motion of the Body, forces out and expels the morbid Parts through the Pores, which exhaling, leaves what remains more pure and uncontaminated. Besides, Labour sets an Edge to the Appetite, gives a more grateful and delicious Relish to the Products of the Earth, and at Night disposes the whole bodily Frame into a Capacity for the full Enjoyment of those refreshing Slumbers, that balmy Sleep, which generally forsakes the Downy Couches of the inactive indolent Great."

We feel we have only to take up a spade and dig and we shall never be ill again, though we are almost as far removed now from the inactive indolent Great as we are from the dinosaurs. I dare say it is why some people garden, or at least why they begin, for I think no one could potter for long in a garden without becoming at least a flower-fancier. "The Gardiner," says Evelyn in his instructions for his own gardener at Sayes Court, "should walke aboute the whole Gardens every Monday-morning duely, not omitting the least corner." Certainly we will, not omitting even the least flower, and not only on Mondays, for the chief pleasure of a garden is simply to walk round and watch things grow.

But as a hobby, gardening has more to offer than healthy exercise and prizes at the flower show; or even than catalogues and fireside garden books and exotic afternoons at Chelsea. "If you would know a man," said Confucius, "find out in what he is at peace." And peace surely is among the many things we seek from our gardens.

"For more than thirty years," says Repton, whose own garden was small and cottagy, "I have anxiously retreated from the pomp of palaces, the elegances of fashion and the allurements of dissipation." For most of us it is not quite like that. We have never been offered the pomp of palaces, and the allurements of dissipation are mostly confined, alas, to the imaginations of Puritans. But after the "various bustle of resort," after the noise and clocks and telephone bells, the trains and traffic and too many people, most especially after the people, we need somewhere to go away in quiet and restore ourselves. It is no use to sit in a chair and say to ourselves: "Be still, stop fidgetting, be peaceful and recover." We are only more restless with nothing to do. We need some tranquil occupation to smooth the fidgetting to a steady rhythm. "I have need to busy my mind with quietness," and gardening does very well: taking cuttings of our choicest shrubs, tying back the winter jasmine, staking the fragrant top-heavy lilies, or only lazily deciding that in the autumn we will move the winter cherry to a sheltered corner where its January pink and white will escape the east winds.

For a garden, as the seventeenth-century writers will prove for us, can soothe all our senses. "If a man be wearied with over-much study (for study is a wearinesse to the Flesh as Solomon by experience can tell you,) there is no better place in the world to recreate himselfe than a Garden, there being no sence but may be delighted therein. If his sight be obfuscated and dull, as it may easily be, with continually poring, there is no better way to re-lieve it, than to view the pleasant greennesse of Herbes, which is the way that Painters use, when they have almost spent their sight by their most earnest contemplation of brighter objects: neither doe they only feed the Eyes, but comfort the wearied Braine with fragrant smells which yield a certaine Kinde of nourishment.

"The Eares also (which are called the Daughters of Musick, because they delight therein) have their recreation by the pleas-ant noise of warbling notes, which the chaunting birds accent forth from amongst the murmuring leaves. As for the Taste, they serve it so exceedingly, that whether it be affected with sweet, sower or bitter things, they even prostitute themselves. And for the feeling likewise, they entertaine it with as great variety as can be imagined, there being some Plants as soft as silke, and some as prickly as a Hedgehogge: so that there is no outward sense which can want satisfaction in this Cornucopia."

I dare say many other occupations would do as well to bring us back to quiet, but if we are gardeners, it is our gardens we use to "sway our spirits to peace." Our very conception of a garden is of a place serene. We think of noisy cities, pounding seas, wind-tossed woods, but whenever we think of a garden it is serene, peaceful and calm, and above all, kind. For a garden is one of the very few expressions of man's nature which is alto-gether benign, and I think no one would be frightened of his fellows in a garden. We understand very well what the writer meant who said: "The chief flower in his Garden is heartsease, because 'tis very scarce in the world."

· · ·

Drawing by Crispin de Passe.

Since human beings are gregarious creatures, there are many things we share quite happily with our neighbours. But gardens are not one of them. Our garden must be private, must be our own individual kingdom, however small. "Many men must be content with any plot of ground of what forme or quantity so-ever it bee, more or lesse, for their Garden, because a more large or convenient cannot bee had for their habitation." Never mind, we will be well content so long as it is our own.

It is not really dog-in-a-mangerness which shuts out our neighbours, though Repton thinks it is, and is half ashamed of "that charm which only belongs to ownership, the exclusive right of enjoyment, with the power of refusing that others should share our pleasure." But it is not the power of refusing others which draws us, it is the need to have some little corner of land which is our own personal territory to do as we like with. Certainly public parks will not do. They may be very fine, we may admire them prodigiously, but we feel no affection for them; they are other people's children, not our own. Montaigne could never see that the peas he grew himself were better than anyone else's, which only proves that he was no gardener. For of course our own peas are best—best for us, which is all that matters. The palest primrose which grows inside our own garden wall is for that very reason more precious than all the fine flowers in the park. We may have no illusions about our own children, but still our affection is not changed because they are not top of the class: it does not depend on their merits, but on our attachment. Which is just as well, or who would love the dull ones?

In *Binsey Poplars* Hopkins mourns the destruction of a scene he loved, a "sweet especial scene . . . Sweet especial rural scene" now lost forever with the felling of the trees. "After-comers cannot guess the beauty been."

It was not that this corner was lovelier than a hundred others, but that for him it had grown familiar and dear. "My aspens dear," he begins, and they were his because he loved them, as Traherne had felt the whole world to be his personal treasure bought with the wealth of his love. "The streets were mine, the people were mine, their clothes and gold and silver were mine, as much as their sparkling eyes, fair skins, and ruddy faces. The skies were mine, and so were the sun and moon and stars, and all the world was mine, and I the only spectator and enjoyer of it."

We are neither mystics nor prose poets, but we are gardeners, and for us our garden is our own sweet especial scene more precious than any other; our affection makes it more valuable than acres of fine flowers.

What do you want of your garden? It is a most revealing question. Flowers, says one. A hobby. A retreat. We could learn to assess a man, I suppose, by what he wanted of his garden as easily as by anything else. A garden, says another, reaches its highest perfection when it is planned as a room for out-door living. And that, as we might guess, was the opinion of the editor of a paper on houses and gardens. But it is a reasonable intention for a small garden, especially in northern countries and in cities where we all of us live too much indoors. It does us good to be outside, without a roof and walls to enclose our neurotic preoccupations in shelter where they can flourish. (At least it does us good as human beings; as artists no doubt it might well be disastrous, as few but the greatest would have any subject matter left.) But as people we grow moody living too much indoors, introspective, and over-sensitive of personal trifles. We watch the face, and not the whole man as the Classic races did. But in the open we feel our worries and annoyances, our obsessions and pettinesses evaporating like mist in the sunshine; "out of the complicated house" we recover a proper sense of proportion.

Besides, there is our particular English compulsion to eat out-of-doors, and what place more fitting than our own garden? Of course there are ants; sweet-tooth wasps arrive from nowhere, suicidal flies drown in our tea, the cake dries to sawdust, the chocolate biscuits melt to lava, the edges of sandwiches curl up like toast. And certainly we spend quite twice as long carrying everything in and out of the house as we should to eat indoors and be done with it. But never mind. Nothing is so delightful as tea in the garden, everyone is agreed about it.

Then there are the "meridian naps," as Switzer absurdly calls them. It is one of the tranquil pleasures to fall asleep in a garden and wake up only because the sun has slanted behind the trees and we are chilly lying in the shadow. There is sitting out-of-doors in the pale sunshine of a still winter day, for with careful shelter a south wall is warm enough for sitting as soon as there is sun enough to open the aconites and snowdrops, the early crocuses and winter irises. There is the view from the house windows, a mental extension of the house into the garden which enlarges the smallest room and lets us live half out-of-doors even though we may never leave the house all day. It is a very particular pleasure in winter to see frozen snow and warm carpet separated only by an invisible wall of glass—like the scene at the beginning of *Jane Eyre* where a girl sits in a window watching a violent storm beyond the frail glass. I dare say it is no more than a line or two of description, perhaps only a single sentence, but it is the only passage from all the Brontë books which I remembered vividly as a child.

The life we live in a city is one we have created for ourselves within its walls. In streets and shops and offices, in theatres and libraries and houses we are shut away from the rhythm of the natural year which dominates life in the open. In London the changing seasons are little more than changing weather on the window-pane, changing clothes hanging in our wardrobe. Our lives are much the same all the year round, whether we wear cotton frocks or overcoats, and whether the window is open to the sun or shut against the rain. Yet the seasons are as satisfactory a way for dividing up the year as waking and sleeping are for the day and night. Summer and winter impose on our life in the country a significant pattern which banishes monotony; they keep us in touch with a rhythm of living as satisfying as the swaying of a swing when we are children. Living in cities, we have lost this fundamental variety of the natural year, but in gardens we still feel it faintly—the strong beat of seed-time and harvest muted to the frailty of cherry blossom and the changing colours of autumn leaves; as paddlers on the edge of the sea feel faintly in the little waves which wash their ankles, the strong surge of the ocean tides.

"A garden should be" (and it is better this time not to consider the speaker too closely) "should be a place private enough to make love wherever one fancies." Certainly Chaucer's young lady in the pear tree would have agreed, and so I dare say would the Chinese princes. But I am not sure. It is a very exact degree of privacy: less secret than murder, more secluded than tea on the lawn. Of course it would be very pleasant and convenient, but unless one were quite unusually indifferent to an audience I think it would make a garden too shut in, too cramped and shadowed and gloomy. Private enough for sun-bathing—that surely is a better qualification. Besides, what about aeroplanes? Are we never to see the sky in our amorous gardens? Or do we simply ignore pilots as part of their machines?

What do you want? I asked the children, who were equally decided. We want somewhere to have bonfires. We want a garden with lots of good places for hide-and-seek. We want somewhere to play cricket without losing the ball, and we want enough grass to do tricks with our bikes on so that it doesn't hurt when we fall off. Poor long-suffering garden. For now it must be a recreation ground as well as everything else.

I had my own garden games as a child, but girls, it seems, are less destructively active than boys. Certainly I picked the buds of poppies, but then poppies grow so many more, and undoing their buds was one of the most engrossing of pleasures for a summer morning. First you squeezed them till they burst open with a faint pop, like shelling peas. Then you peeled off the hairy green sepals to find the crumpled petals screwed up inside, a ball of delicate silken paper. Very gently you coaxed them to unfold, smoothing them out carefully to an open flower. The result was a quite astonishing amount to unpack from so small a bud—not only the four wide petals, but also the urn-shaped head in the middle, and the fringe of stamens as soft and uncertain in this abortive appearance as the legs of a moth newly struggled from its chrysalis.

Even from wild scarlet poppies the petals varied through all colours from the red of those which would have opened tomorrow, through the pink of buds not ready to unfold for several days, to the white embryos which had not even dreamed yet of the sun. It was my favourite game to make a carefully shaded range of colours from white to scarlet, better even than finding the man in the pansy who went out and caught a cold, and sits now as the fat ovary in every fading flower, wrapped in a blanket of stamens up to his chin, with his feet in a mustard bath—the spur, which will pull off gently and leave two long spindly legs quite shiveringly exposed.

What Do We Want Now?

There were other games, too—snapdragon heads, and fox-glove thimbles, and nibbling the bottoms of larkspurs for the honey. And other tricks (most of them nasty) which the boys prefer—ear-splitting squeaks with leaves of grass and privet, catapults with plantain heads, and pulling a twist of hair with a denuded fox-tail grass, which they call Chinese Tortures.

And children have other, more private games, day-dreams and fantasies for secret hiding-places safe from interruption. A French admirer said of the gardens of Versailles that they were an equally happy setting for courtly ceremony or the sighing of a melancholy lover. Our own hurried generation scarcely spends time enough on love-sickness for it to be worth making a garden as a suitable background, but even in a modern garden there should be corners secluded enough to indulge our private fancies without disturbance.

One early summer day when I was a child I lay under a syca-more tree and gazed up into the green tiers of branches. The new leaves made an over-lapping mosaic of brilliant yellow-green, each bough on its own plane, the different levels shuffled loosely together like a sheaf of papers, and each layer held easily as it grew on the firm but delicate scaffolding of the black twigs. Beneath the leaves swung the loose tassels of yellow flowers humming with bees, and through the spaces between, the sky shone an intense and bottomless blue.

I was a city child unused to such beauty, and to senses un-dimmed by custom it was almost unbearably vivid: the colours and shapes, the warm light, the eager generous life, the summer hum, and the scent of honey. I gazed until the blue and green smudged together in sudden uncontrollable tears, then rolled over in the grass and wept for pleasure.

But as the first disturbing delight faded, I realized piercingly that this same tree which seemed to me mine because I loved it, had flowered a score of times before I was born, would rouse to equal beauty every spring when I was dead. And I suffered a great stab of sorrow, of unrequited love, felt I had received an inmost wound that never could be healed, because the things I loved more than all else in the world were utterly indifferent to my existence.

The sorrows of children are profound and unsuspected, and through all my growing-up I was preoccupied with the question of whether, when it came to dying, it would be an anguish or a consolation that the too-much-loved earth went on without me. No doubt all children puzzle over questions equally unlikely, but we shall never know, for they will never tell us, fearing not so much our lack of understanding, which they are used to, but rather our understanding, our intrusion into the fiercely guarded privacy of their intimate world.

Although I thought about it for years, with other metaphysical questions equally impractical, I never did make up my mind whether I should die sad or happy to leave a world which went on unchanged. The poets, I found, had thought about it too, but they were little help, being of almost equally divided opinion, though with perhaps a slight leaning to the dying anguish.

In any case, a garden should be a place where children can feel a favourite tree belongs to them, where they can weep without embarrassment and be ridiculous without an audience, where they can pursue (unlike Wordsworth) their Intimations of Mortality in Early Childhood.

But gardens are for the old even more than the young, and ever since Tudor times, and probably earlier if there had been gardening books to tell us so, a garden has been considered an ideal place for men to grow old in. "A retreat for toil-worn millionaires" a more recent writer expresses it, but there is really no need for such a spectacular bank-balance, and a setting for their retirement seems always to have been one of the things ordinary men have wanted of their gardens. After all, there are few places where we can so successfully be busy and peaceful both together, nor win so much satisfaction with so little labour. In a garden carefully planned and planted at the start, we can spend the rest of our time in the most delightful pottering, watching Nature flourish with only a secateured hand to Guide her Extravagancies. And there is always some new business to keep us happy—trying a fresh grouping of shrubs, opening out a shut-in view, moving a new grass walk through the orchard tangle, coaxing an ambitious lily to feel at home in some carefully prepared corner. "For the Pleasure of Gardening is not in Finishing them in too great Haste; but after a general Scheme is laid, to make Annual Advances 'till the Whole is compleated."

Repton, perhaps because he lived to be an old man himself, considered carefully how a garden should be planned for the comfort of old age. The paths, he says, should not be of gravel but of grass or brick, for gravel, he warns us, is so excessively noisy beneath the wheels of a bath-chair. The beds, too, should be built up high enough for the master to reach them from his

Gathering strawberries from a bath-chair.

bath-chair without stooping. There is a picture of the aged gardener gathering strawberries from a raised bed while his chair-attendant waits modestly behind. They are both wearing top hats.

But I think when I reach my own bath-chair stage I will sit in the sun on the veranda, and leave what one writer calls "the insulting Weeds" to live their own life, only admiring in short-sighted contentment the general prospect of thriving green.

Other gardeners make less depressing suggestions for our old-age comfort: that the greenhouse should have a door leading into the dwelling-house so that we can reach it without going out into the bad weather, and that the whole garden should be reached by "little walks" where we can go "cleanly and decently," so that "the Owner may walk round it and across it in his Night Gown and Slippers; and visit all his Affairs, either late at Night or early in the Morning, without either Dirt or Dew. Seeing those are the chief times, either for Business or Pleasure, in the whole Day." I have never walked round the garden in my Night Gown and Slippers, but certainly I will on the next warm evening.

Lulled by the song of a nightingale, Keats fell half in love with easeful Death, and reading the gardening books, we too fall half in love with our far-off gardening retirement. We have no need of Fairchild to persuade us that we must garden while we are still in cities to train ourselves for the pleasures of gardening in our old age. We are only impatient that our retirement will not be long enough for all we plan to do. But Gervaze Markham, who is my favourite of all my new garden friends, is comfortably reassuring. We "may live near a hundred years," he says, if we follow his counsel. "For your health eat meats that are hot and nourishing, drink good wine that is neat, sprightly and lusty, keep thy body well clad, and thy house warm, forsake whatever is flegmatick, and banish all care from thy heart, for nothing is more unwholesome than a troubled spirit."

If you would be happy all your life, plant a garden.

But as to what kind of gardens we should plant in our modern age, that, if we thought about it, which we seldom do, is very much more difficult to decide.

A garden, since it is the setting for a house, should be in harmony with its architecture, and the best modern building is surprisingly like the simpler architecture of the eighteenth century, more essentially like it than any other English style before or since.

The Victorians, feeling that they continued the Classical tradition, loaded their heavy erections with Classical-style decoration. The twentieth-century architect no longer cares for pillared façades and acanthus leaves (for our so-called neo-Georgian is a pastiche in the nineteenth-century manner), but modern building is nearer, I think, to the eighteenth century than anything the Victorians built. For styles of architecture do not resemble each other by applying similar decoration to a finished construction, but by working with the same essentials and leaving the decoration to look after itself. Our best modern architects compose with the same fundamentals as the eighteenth century: simple rectangular shapes, an orderly repetition of forms, and a most sparing use of applied decoration. The effect of the building depends not on decoration at all, but on the shape of the whole structure, the spacing of windows and doors, the areas of the walls between, the contrast and interrelation of the different planes. So our modern blocks of flats, our factories and schools and houses are close in spirit to the eighteenth century. Indeed, if both are stripped of their respective layers of new paint and old dirt, a terrace of houses in one of the new towns is surprisingly like the eighteenth-century terraces of quiet town houses all over London. Our buildings are less symmetrical, less formal than the eighteenth century's because our lives are less formal, more diverse because the activities they shelter are more diverse (for the eighteenth century built no factories or flats, no schools except as modelled on houses). But the beauty of our buildings, when they do achieve beauty, is the same austere elegance as the eighteenth century's, the same material impression of lightness and space, the same intellectual quality of order and repose.

As in modern building, the effects of eighteenth-century architecture depend scarcely at all on the natural texture of the materials used. We are not conscious of the bricks, as we are in Tudor buildings, nor of the stone as we are in mediæval churches and Cotswold villages. The eighteenth century made no use of wood except for construction; they preferred it covered with featureless paint, and it was later taste which stripped the panelling to the bare grain. We, too, use our materials discreetly, and do not allow the charm of incidentals to distract us from the whole. In a modern building we are conscious of the proportion, the elegance, the serenity, and it is only the architect who notices the materials, for they are used not for their own sake, but for their structural capabilities. So that modern synthetic materials and methods of construction might well have suited the eighteenth-century architects even better than the traditional materials they had to use. The wide expanses of windows, the narrow supporting walls between, the unbroken stretches of floor—these surely they would have achieved more easily with steel and concrete than with bricks and wood. Our shallow modern roofs would have suited them excellently, for the eighteenth century hid the necessary pitch of their slates and tiles behind horizontal screening parapets. And if they had had concrete to build with, they need not have plastered their brick walls with stucco, its indistinguishable but inefficient relation.

For, living in an eighteenth-century house, I know only too well that the stucco cracks and falls from the walls, that the snow piles up behind the parapet, and unless it is cleared away, leaks through the slate roof as it melts. Shovelling it off after a snowfall is a winter-morning game for the boys, who are old enough now not to fall over the parapet, still agile enough to climb through the attic window, and not yet bored with the exhilarating experience of flinging snow triumphantly into space, of the new view of their familiar world spread out as a map below.

In summer, too, I am reminded every day of the architect's difficulty with his great floor-to-ceiling windows; how perilously heavy they are to hang on sash-cords. And struggling to open them and water the window-boxes, wondering whether the cord will break as I lean out to pick the dead heads off the petunias, I sigh for the modern steel frames and reliable metal hinges which the eighteenth century so badly needed.

If modern building has much in common with the eighteenth-century spirit, so too perhaps the next style of gardening will be a modern adaptation of the landscape park. It is easy to see how suitable it would be as a setting for blocks of flats and public buildings, but even in our little private gardens we are perhaps moving towards a natural way of trees and shrubs and flowers which is an unconscious echo of the eighteenth-century style.

"A garden is an expression of Man in a state of Society." It is a definition with many meanings, and we might think of Man as a single human being growing up through various stages to become an adult social creature. When we are children we can neither understand nor control the world around us; we shut ourselves in a self-contained universe of our own, an enclosed garden which has very little contact with the world outside except in the sun and rain, which come down willy-nilly from a sky we cannot change. But inside our sheltering walls we gradually develop. We grow older and stronger, grow curious, we peep over the garden fence as the Tudors did, we begin to realize the possibilities of the world outside and to feel confident we can take our place there. Then comes the fine flowering of energy and enthusiasm in a creature who has reached adult strength but not yet an adult's need to compromise. For we are all perfectionists at this hopeful age; we see quite clearly that there is an ideal order which the world must be moulded to for its own good, whether it likes it or not. We are undaunted by the obvious difficulties, we do not see the subtler ones, we have energy and to spare, and we never for a moment doubt that our way is the best. We make the gardens of Versailles.

It is a very proper way of behaving for the young and confident and enthusiastic, but unless we outgrow our simple ideals as we outgrow our youth, we shall certainly be disappointed, for we shall certainly outgrow our confidence. Reforming the world, so reformers are disillusioned to find, is rather like rolling a stone up a hill: as soon as they stop pushing, it rolls down again. And because it is natural for idealists to push their stone as high as their utmost energies can reach, it must always begin to slip down again as soon as they begin to grow old or tired or doubtful of their own wisdom. The world does not stay reformed any more than houses stay clean or gardens stay weeded, and adults must come to some workable compromise. It is no use deciding that the world must conform to our way as the only way—which is what the formal gardeners did, so that as soon as the armies of labourers ceased working, the flower beds were lost in weeds, the regular clipped hedges sprouted untidily to trees, the formal pools were choked with slime, and the stone had rolled back again to the bottom of the hill. For a straight line must stay straight, not wobble, and if the effort to keep it straight needs more energy than we have to spare, then we do better to choose an irregular curve at the beginning. Which is what the eighteenth-century gardeners did. They did not rule out a pattern on paper ("Paper Engineers" one critic calls such gardeners) and then impose it on a stretch of land, on trees and hedges with their own different patterns of growing; instead, they considered the scene of their future garden with no preconceived plan except a desire for the "natural." They then designed parks which accepted the English landscape as their material, and heightened its effects by using grass and trees and water in as natural a manner as possible. It is the adult's compromise expressed in gardens, and we should do well to consider them carefully.

In the landscape park the eighteenth century found a perfect labour-saving compromise. But the landscape style needs space: it is easy to keep because it works with large effects of grass and trees: woodland where weeds do not matter, and sweeps of grass wide enough to give the effect of smooth lawn without being neatly mown. But if we have less than an acre for our planning, and if growing flowers is our greatest pleasure, we shall have to transform the landscape style as thoroughly as our seventeenth-century gardeners transformed Versailles. "This first setting out is generally the Rock that all Mankind split upon," and in our first plan for a garden we should consider exactly how much work our designs will need, not so much to lay them out, but to keep them in order year after year. It is no use listening to siren voices which assure us that "a man for a shilling a day will weed an acre of land in three days." If there is weeding to do, we shall have to do it ourselves. If there are hedges to cut and lawns to mow and edges to trim, it is we who shall have to get up and do them on summer afternoons when all we want is to lie in the shade and look at the sky through the branches of our favourite tree.

To judge a good housewife, it is no use going to see her clean new house the month she moves in. We are all of us idealists in a new house. The true test is to see what compromise she has reached after ten years or so of constant war with dirt and untidiness. If her house is no better than a slum, then quite clearly the dirt has triumphed, though it is possible that no one minds. If her house is still as clean as the first week, then she is spending all her energies in a war which can never end except by her defeat; and her success is almost certainly a Pyrrhic victory won at the cost of making her family wretched by nagging, and turning herself into a dismal domestic drudge.

Most of us now put away the silver, keep our rooms clear of dusty oddments, and dress our children in clothes which need no ironing. But we also, after ten years of learning to compromise between living in a house and keeping it in order, clear up the children's rooms only once a week, do not look too closely into cupboards we turn out only once a year, nor worry ourselves in the tidy drawing-room because we know the attic looks like a jumble sale.

It is wisdom which gardeners seem to arrive at more slowly. Beds and edges, paths and hedges—gardeners have not yet learnt to mistrust them as instinctively as a housewife mistrusts a dress which must be ironed every time it is worn. They do not accept the hard fact that if they are to have any leisure, they must plan their garden with plants sturdy enough to thrive with an undergrowth of weeds. They do not decide from the start that far corners of the garden can be left to grow what tangle they please without in the least spoiling the view from the veranda. But they should. It is the landscape style we must adapt for our new needs and not the formal fashion of beds and hedges, not unless we are to spend every summer week-end as labourers in gardens which were meant to be places of pleasure. What a wise gardener (or perhaps only a lazy one) plans for is "Nature a little guided in her Extravagancies by the Artist's Hand." If, like the eighteenth century, we avoid paper planning and arbitrary designs, we shall find that our gardens will achieve random happy effects almost without our interference, and, "being of a much more natural Aspect than Set Gardens, the less Keeping will suffice."

But as Walafred Strabo would have said, I have written too long already to begin now wondering what our new gardens may be like, and that must wait for another volume. And I doubt whether the new kind of garden I found last summer could be considered either as a setting for architecture or an expression of Man in Society.

When we first went to our week-end house in the country we found a nineteenth-century garden run to wilderness, and at the bottom an old croquet lawn, a lush tangle of grass and meadow flowers springing with green frogs as you walked, as plentiful as grasshoppers. They still hop about in wet summers among the shrubs and weeds and lilies, and visiting children collect them delightedly, carrying them home in treacle-tins of wet moss with holes punched in the lid. And we still sometimes for convenience call it the Croquet Lawn, as the children always have done from the start; but because twentieth-century children know nothing of croquet, but only of frogs, the lawn they talk of is the Croaky Lawn. "Dear Dardy" (I found out in a thank-you letter from a small boy visitor who had spent the week-end busy and happy down in the tangle, only coming up to the house when we rang the bell for meals) "Dear Dardy, Thankyou for having me. I had a lovely time. I like all your garden, but I like the Croaky Lawn best, there's such a lovely lot of Frogs. Please will you give them some water if they need some." So I went down to look, and found under the willows a square of trampled grass fenced in with old boards, and inside, a pile of grass-cuttings, some bread-crumbs, and a jam-jar brimful of water. But not a sign, alas, of even the smallest frog. Only on the highest board was written in white chalk capitals: "GARDEN FOR FROGS."

Though who was meant to read it I never have decided.

SHORT
BIBLIOGRAPHY

This is a list of most of the books quoted in the text. They are grouped in chapters as they occur, since this seemed the simplest way to arrange them. The date is generally that of the book's first appearance, but when this is unknown, or long after the author's death, then of the approximate time when it was written.

CHAPTER TWO
Celtic Myth and Legend—C. Squire, 1910.
England Before the Norman Conquest—R. W. Chambers, 1926.
Ecclesiastical History of the English Nation—Bede, ninth century.
Anglo-Saxon Poetry—edited R. K. Gordon, 1926.
Life of Alfred—Asser, ninth century.
"Navigation of the Norsemen"—G. J. Marcus in the *Mariner's Mirror*, May 1953.
Gudrun—Anon., thirteenth century.
English Lyrics of the Thirteenth Century—edited Carleton Brown, 1932.
Hali Meidenhad—Anon., thirteenth century.
Ancren Riwle—Anon., thirteenth century.
Hortulus or the Little Garden—Walafridus Strabo, ninth century.

CHAPTER THREE
Lays—Marie de France, twelfth century.
Aucassin and Nicolette—Anon., thirteenth century.
Floris and Blancheflour—Anon., thirteenth century.
Religious Lyrics of the Fourteenth Century—edited Carleton Brown, 1924.
Oxford Book of Carols—edited P. Dearmer, etc., 1928.

CHAPTER FOUR
English Social History—G. M. Trevelyan, 1942.
A Survey of London—John Stow, 1598.
Brief Lives—John Aubrey (1626–1697).
Musæum Tradescantianum—John Tradescant, 1656.
The Gardeners Labyrinth—Didymus Mountain (Thomas Hill), 1577.

MEN & GARDENS

Paradisi in Sole, Paradisus Terrestris—John Parkinson, 1629.
"On Gardens"—Francis Bacon, 1625.
Sylva Sylvarum or a Naturall Historie—Francis Bacon, 1627.
Five Hundreth Pointes of Good Husbandrie—Thomas Tusser, 1573.
Adam in Eden or Natures Paradise—William Coles, 1657.
The Spirituall Uses of an Orchard—Ralph Austen, 1653.
"A Survey of the Manor of Wymbledon in 1649"—*Archæologia*, Vol. 10, 1792.

CHAPTER FIVE

Maison Rustique or the Countrie Farme—trans. Richard Surflet, 1600.
A New Orchard and Garden—William Lawson, 1618.
Country Contentments—Gervaze Markham, 1640.
Letters—Sir Thomas Browne (1605–1682).
Religio Medici—Sir Thomas Browne, 1643.
The Garden of Cyrus—Sir Thomas Browne, 1653.
Directions for the Gardiner at Says-Court—John Evelyn, 1687.
Centuries of Meditations—Thomas Traherne (1634–1704).
Oxford Book of Seventeenth Century Verse—edited H. J. C. Grierson and G. Bullough, 1934.
A Perfect Boke for Keping of Sparhawkes or Goshawkes—Anon., c. 1575.
An Approved Treatise of Hawkes and Hawking—Edmund Bert, 1619.
Hawking or Faulconry—Richard Blome, 1686.

CHAPTER SIX

Studies in the History of the Renaissance—Walter Pater, 1873.
The Theory and Practice of Gardening—Le Blond, trans. John James, 1703.
Letters—John Evelyn (1620–1706).

CHAPTER SEVEN

The Voyage of the Beagle—Charles Darwin, 1839.
Charles Darwin and the Voyage of the Beagle—Nora Barlow, 1933.
Through England on a Side-Saddle in the Time of William and Mary—Celia Fiennes, 1685–1703.
The English Gardener—Leonard Meager, 1670.
Flora Ceres et Pomona—John Rea, 1676.
The Gentlemans Recreation—John Laurence, 1716.
Diaries—Samuel Pepys, 1660–9.

Short Bibliography

Sylva, or a Discourse of Forest-Trees—John Evelyn, 1664.

Terra, a Philosophical Discourse of Earth—John Evelyn, 1676.

The Story of My Life—Augustus Hare, 1896–1900.

Essays in *The Spectator*—Joseph Addison, 1711–12.

The Dutch Gardener, or the Complete Florist—Van Oosten, 1711.

Upon the Gardens of Epicurus, or of Gardening in the Year 1685— Sir William Temple.

The City Gardener—Thomas Fairchild, 1722.

Systema Horticulturæ, or the Art of Gardening—John Woolridge, 1677.

Chapter Eight

Letters—Horace Walpole (1717–1797).

An Essay on Modern Gardening—Horace Walpole, 1770.

Journals of Visits to Country Seats—Horace Walpole. 16th annual volume of the Walpole Society.

Travels—Marco Polo (1254–1324).

Unconnected Thoughts on Gardening—William Shenstone, 1764.

Ichnographia Rustica—the Nobleman Gentleman and Gardeners Recreation—Stephen Switzer, 1718.

New Improvements of Planting and Gardening—Richard Bradley, 1717.

The Gardeners Dictionary—Philip Miller, 1731.

A Dissertation on Oriental Gardening—Sir William Chambers, 1772.

Confessions—Jean-Jacques Rousseau, 1781–8.

Paul et Virginie—Bernardin de Saint-Pierre, 1787.

A Sure Method of Improving Estates—Batty Langley, 1728.

An Essay on the Picturesque—Sir Uvedale Price, 1794.

The Mysteries of Udolpho—Mrs. Radcliffe, 1794.

Remarks on Forest Scenery—William Gilpin, 1791.

On the Making of Gardens—Sir George Sitwell, 1909.

Observations on Modern Gardening—Thomas Whately, 1770.

The Curious and Profitable Gardener—John Cowell, 1730.

Observations on the Theory and Practice of Landscape Gardening etc.—Humphrey Repton, 1803.